QUANTITATIVE
STRATEGIES
—— FOR ——
ACHIEVING
ALPHA

QUANTITATIVE
STRATEGIES
—— FOR ——
ACHIEVING
ALPHA

RICHARD TORTORIELLO

New York   Chicago   San Francisco   Lisbon   London
Madrid   Mexico City   Milan   New Delhi
San Juan   Seoul   Singapore   Sydney   Toronto

1 2 3 4 5 6 7 8 9 0   DOC/DOC   0 1 4 3 2 1 0 9 8

ISBN   978–0–07–154984–4
MHID   0–07–154984–6

McGraw-Hill books are available at special quantity discounts to use as premiums and sales promotions, or for use in corporate training programs. To contact a representative please visit the Contact Us pages at www.mhprofessional.com.

This book is printed on acid-free paper.

To Theresa M. N., who always thought her son would become an author, but never imagined a book like this.

CONTENTS

Chapter 13

ACKNOWLEDGMENTS

I am deeply indebted to a number of people for their help on this project. Foremost among these is Jung-Hoon (Joshua) Kang. For nearly a year, Joshua worked as my intern in the Standard & Poor's equity research department and as computer technician extraordinaire on the quantitative project that led to this book. He is responsible for running nearly all of the quantitative tests presented in this book, and also helped to generate a few of the investment ideas. I consider myself lucky to have crossed paths with someone possessing such an unusual combination of technical skill, intelligence, diligence, good nature, and good humor as does Joshua.

I'd like to thank Sam Stovall, S&P Equity Research's Chief Investment Strategist, for his help and encouragement on this project, along with Steve Biggar, Equity Research Managing Director, for making this project possible. Thanks also to James Branscome, former Managing Director of Standard & Poor's Equity Research, who took time out of a very busy "retirement" schedule to not only read and comment on the manuscript, but aslo to provide a number of very useful suggestions along the way. Thanks to Chris Burba, a very talented technical analyst here at S&P, for his substantial help with the Price Momentum chapter. Thanks to H. Russell Fogler, PhD, of Fogler Research and Management, for his thorough read of the manuscript, insightful comments, and overall encouragement. Russ's comments were doubly encouraging, coming as they did from someone with years of experience in the quantitative analysis field. Also thanks to Ralph Acampora, of the New York Institute of Finance and formerly Director of Technical Analysis at Prudential Equity Groups, for reading the Price Momentum chapter and for his encouragement. A special thank you is also due to Mitch Abeyta, Managing Director of S&P Compustat, who provided us with the Point in Time Database with which all the research in this book was conducted.

Last but far from least, my sincere thanks to Marcus C. Bogue III, Wendy A. Weber, and Joe Jelenovic of Charter Oak Investment Systems. Marc and Wendy's many trips to New York, their frequent guidance on the backtests, and their overall enthusiasm helped make this project possible. Joe's well-informed answers to my many questions also aided the project greatly. Finally, thanks to Marc for his thorough read of the manuscript and for his creative work on both the software and the database that together formed the heart of this project.

LIST OF ABBREVIATIONS

CAGR	compound annual growth rate
capex	capital expenditures
CAPM	capital asset pricing model
EBIT	earnings before interest and taxes
EBITDA	earnings before interest, taxes, depreciation, and amortization
EPS	earnings per share
EV	enterprise value
EVA	Economic Value Added
FCF	free cash flow
FY	fiscal year
GAAP	generally accepted accounting principles
GARP	growth at a reasonable price
GICS	Global Industry Classification Standard
LTCM	Long-Term Capital Management
NOPAT	net operating profit after tax
P/E	price/earnings
PP&E	property, plant, and equipment
P/S	price/sales
R&D	research and development
ROA	return on assets
ROCE	return on capital employed
ROE	return on equity
ROIC	return on invested capital
RSI	Relative Strength Index
SEC	Securities and Exchange Commission
S&P 500	Standard & Poor's 500 Index

CHAPTER 1

Introduction: In Search of Alpha

I do not know what I may appear to the world; but to myself I seem to have been like a boy playing on the sea-shore, and diverting myself now and then finding a smoother pebble or a prettier shell than ordinary, whilst the great ocean of truth lay all undiscovered before me.

Sir Isaac Newton

Don Quixote: Dost thou see? A monstrous giant of infamous repute whom I intend to encounter.
Sancho Panza: It's a windmill.
Don Quixote: A giant! Canst thou not see the four great arms whirling at his back?
Sancho Panza: A giant?
Don Quixote: Exactly!

From Man of La Mancha, Dale Wasserman, Miguel de Cervantes

I've read with interest the journals of Meriwether Lewis and William Clark as they undertook, at the request of Thomas Jefferson, to explore the unknown western frontier and to find a route to the Pacific. These journeys contained as many dangers as they held wonders (and were financed by Congress for $2,500—the dollar went further back then). Their expedition, which did much to open the West to further exploration and settlement, became known as the Corps of Discovery. Although the greatest dangers faced by the author of this work were perhaps fatigue and eye strain—a far cry from grizzly bear, white-water rapids, and belligerent natives—the same spirit of discovery motivated the undertaking of the tests and explorations that form the basis of this book.

Unlike the western United States in the early 1800s, the frontiers of finance have been well charted. Many of the investment field's greatest minds have put their ideas and methods, earned through years of hard work and experience, down on paper for anyone with a few dollars or a library card to explore. The student of common stock investing can find hundreds of books covering almost every imaginable topic, from valuation analysis, to risk arbitrage, to day trading. With such a vast literature, developed by thousands of market participants over many decades, one might ask What is there left to discover?

One answer, I believe, is that, while investment theory has been mapped out well qualitatively—based on the experiences and insights of market participants—it has yet to be mapped out comprehensively from an *empirical* point of view. The reason for the wealth of qualitative literature and dearth of quantitative (outside of the university) is quite simply that investing is more art than science. Some of the best investment strategies are too dependent on the capabilities of the human mind to be reduced to a few lines of computer code. However, the advent of the personal computer and the database has provided a wonderful tool with which many investment strategies can be effectively modeled and tested. Numerous individual quantitative studies have been published, particularly in academia. Most, however, have been specialized, and some have been of questionable practical value. Quantitative professionals, on the other hand, have primarily written technical volumes (how-to guides for quantitative analysis), when they have written anything at all.

My quest began with two primary goals: to create a series of quantitative stock selection models for the Standard & Poor's Equity Research department and to provide myself and others with a "map" of the market from a quantitative point of view. This book presents investors with this map, as far as I have been able to draw it. Specifically, the work seeks to determine *empirically* the major fundamental and market-based drivers of future stock market returns. To arrive at this empirically drawn investment map, we tested well over 1,200 investment strategies: some worked well, and others didn't. Some of the strategies presented here are well known and widely employed; others are less well known and much less used outside of the world of professional money management. However, all of the factors presented in this book *work,* from a quantitative standpoint.

A true quantitative investor uses sophisticated mathematical models to gain an edge, sometimes ever so slight, over the market. This edge is then magnified with lots of money and lots of leverage (borrowed money). This book is not written for the "quant." Indeed, I am not qualified to write such a book. Readers need neither a Ph.D. in math nor an advanced knowledge of statistics to understand any of the tests contained herein. What readers *do* need is some interest in quantitative analysis and a desire to understand the basic drivers of stock market returns. This book was written with *qualitative* investors in mind, particularly those who wish to "understand" the stock market from a quantitative (empirical) point of view and who desire to integrate quantitative screens, tests, or models into their investment process—or simply into their thinking. Such integration is where art meets science. My personal belief is that the quantitative approaches outlined in this book can provide a proven way to generate investment ideas for the qualitative investor as well as a discipline that can help improve investment results.

QUANTITATIVE VERSUS QUALITATIVE ANALYSIS

Perhaps a couple definitions are in order here. Quantitative analysis differs from qualitative analysis in a variety of ways. In qualitative analysis, the investor typically focuses on a small number of individual companies and conducts research on each to determine its business strengths and weaknesses, its market opportunities and competitive position, the capabilities of management, and the comparative value offered by its stock relative to other stocks available for purchase.[1] Qualitative investors often use a company's historical record (income statement, balance sheet, cash flow statement, etc.) as a jumping off point to project future trends in earnings and cash flows. The focus in qualitative analysis, as in the stock market itself, is on the future. Analytical techniques are tailored to the company and industry in question, and the investor seeks to make large gains in individual stocks. In short, qualitative analysis favors depth over breadth and the art of investment over a more "scientific" approach.

Quantitative analysis, on the other hand, seeks to discover overall tendencies or trends in the investment markets, particularly those that are predictive of future "excess" returns.[2] To identify these trends, the quantitative analyst examines large numbers of companies over long periods of time. Analysis is by necessity standardized and depends entirely on the historical record: income statement, balance sheet, cash flow statement, and market-based data.[3] That is, unlike most qualitative research, quantitative tests primarily *look backward*. Quantitative analysis emphasizes breadth over depth and science (testing and observation) over art. The quantitative analyst may apply the art of investment analysis in devising investment models and backtests, but once the models are determined, they're often purely mechanical in their operation. In sum, quantitative analysis relies primarily on computer-assisted inquiry, while qualitative analysis relies primarily on the workings of the human mind.

Although there are many similarities between the computer and the human mind, there are also vast differences. Of the two, only the human being can stake any real claim

---

[1] Or the value currently offered by its stock relative to its "intrinsic value," an investor's subjective estimate of the business value of a firm's assets at a given point in time.

[2] Quantitative analysts sometimes refer to such predictive factors as "market inefficiencies."

[3] Although these four data types are the only ones used in this book, quantitative analysis is not limited to these. A quantitative test might include, for example, macroeconomic data, industry statistics, or demographic data.

to intelligence. The mind has the ability to digest and synthesize a diversity of information (e.g., investors must consider everything from the industry, economic, and political climate to the individual products of a company and the demand for its shares in the stock market), an ability that even the most advanced computer can't come close to matching. By carefully weighing a variety of factors, the human being can make projections about events that have some probability of occurring in the future.

Computers, on the other hand, are in essence sophisticated adding machines: they "act" only according to instructions given them from the outside. It's taken decades to develop a computer capable of beating a champion at a chess game, and here the variables are limited to the moves available to 32 pieces on a 64-square board. So, in a field such as investing, where returns may be affected by almost any type of activity, human or natural, the computer seems to be disadvantaged.

However, the computer has two distinct advantages that the human being does not. It can process large amounts of data very quickly (e.g., the way that IBM's "Deep Blue" supercomputer beat chess champion Garry Kasparov), and it lacks emotion. Both points are important, but the second especially so. Consider the following scenario (one that occurs frequently in real life):[4] You've bought $10,000 worth of Apple Computer common stock, which has advanced 20% since your purchase. Sales of iPods are going strong, and positive stories on Apple are in the press almost every day. You're feeling exuberant and thinking of purchasing more, despite a rather high market valuation for the shares. Before you do so, however, Apple announces that it has seen a "mix shift," in which unit volumes of iPods have decreased (i.e., it has shipped fewer iPods), but revenues and earnings growth have remained about the same because it is now shipping more high-end units than low-end ones. Over a period of a couple months following this news, the stock drops 22%, and your original shares are now selling well below their purchase price—you are now losing money, and euphoria (most likely) has given way to anxiety.

However, Apple's stock market valuation now looks much more reasonable, its business is doing well, and the untapped market for iPods seems large. Do you (1) sell your original shares, (2) hold your shares but buy no more, or (3) hold your original shares *and* buy more? On paper, this may all seem simple. If the business is doing well and its valuation looks attractive, *buy more*. But try to imagine yourself in this situation: You are now sitting on a $640 paper loss that used to be a $2,000 profit. News articles are appearing frequently, speculating on *why* Apple shares have declined, and you're wondering if there is some bad news on the horizon that hasn't yet been released.

---

[4] Although the example is hypothetical, the experienced investor will recognize the scenario of a good company that has reported temporarily "bad" news as one that occurs over and over again.

Under these circumstances many investors would *sell*. They sell not because there is a good reason, but because they are losing money, and emotions have the upper hand. Multiply the one investor in our example by thousands, and you'll understand why the psychological factor has such a strong influence on stock prices. In fact, the psychological factor in the stock market often creates opportunity, and it is here that our computer might come in handy.

The academic finance profession has struggled for decades to develop an "efficient market hypothesis" that works in practice. The EMH holds that financial markets quickly discount all available information, and thus that outperforming "the market" over any stretch of time simply isn't possible (or that such a stretch is just plain luck). Many professional investors, with long track records of consistently generating above-market returns, have proven that the EMH doesn't reflect the whole financial truth. The stock market is often efficient in rationally evaluating available information, but at other times its "judgment" becomes impaired by the psychological factors mentioned above. In other words, the market is also often inefficient. A quantitative example might illustrate the point. Over the 20 years from 1987 through 2006 (the period over which most of the backtests in this book were conducted), the average annual difference between the 52-week highs and 52-week lows of stocks in our Backtest Universe (about 2,000 of the largest publicly traded stocks) was 32%. Over the same period this same group of companies recorded compound annual growth in net income of just 9%. With income growing at an average rate of 9%, there is no reason that stock prices should jump up and down by 32% each year, yet they do.[5] Where money is concerned, emotion regularly overcomes rationality, and stocks go up and down for no other reasons than fear, greed, hope, or despair.

The quantitative tests presented in this book seek to uncover investment strategies that consistently outperform the market, based only on historical data. The strategies assume neither an efficient market nor an inefficient market. Rather, they exploit the two previously mentioned advantages of the computer—its lack of emotion and its ability to process large amounts of data—to determine which investment strategies hold the most promise for the investor. With a single inexpensive computer, an investor can now examine thousands of companies and hundreds of data items over several years in a matter of minutes or hours. In addition, the investor can model with the computer a strategy that applies perfect discipline. The model determines the strategy, and the computer follows the discipline of that strategy until instructed to do otherwise.

---

[5] A colleague suggested that temporary imbalances in supply and demand could cause this price volatility. However, this begs the question of what caused the supply/demand imbalances. In an efficient market, a sudden (non-news-related) decline in a stock price would attract buyers, and a sudden rise in a stock price would attract sellers.

The strategies presented in this book are deliberately tested in a crude fashion. We do not divide our backtests into deciles, or take only the top so many and bottom so many companies, because we simply want to know if the strategy works. (Our criteria for a strategy that works are (1) the top quintile[6] outperforms the market by a *significant* margin; (2) the bottom quintile significantly underperforms; (3) outperformance and/or underperformance have been consistent over the years; and (4) there is some linearity in the performance of the quintiles, indicating a strong relationship between the strategy and excess returns.) I call this a shotgun or buckshot approach to investment-strategy testing. If a strategy passes the shotgun test—if it hits the target more than it misses—we say that it works. It won't work for every stock selected by the strategy, and it won't work every year, but overall, the strategy can be said to have investment value.

I call strategies that have investment value *building blocks.* All of the strategies presented in this book have investment value for a particular reason; that is, we can explain why it is that stocks in the top quintile outperform and stocks in the bottom quintile underperform. When we understand why a strategy works, it becomes a building block that can be combined with other strategies to form an even stronger investment model. Some strategies work for similar reasons (e.g., they each have to do with profitability or with valuation). Others are complementary (one has to do with growth, and the other has to do with value). Thus, knowing why a strategy works helps one to combine it effectively with other strategies. Building blocks are determined only through testing (*empiricism*), and are verified through a sort of *triangulation*—the strategy must work in a variety of ways under a variety of circumstances.

Another concept key to the understanding of this book is the idea of a *mosaic*. A mosaic is a picture or pattern made by putting together many small colored tiles. In a real mosaic, each tile is meaningless when viewed alone, but when put together by an artist, a beautiful pattern emerges. In our mosaic, each tile is an investment strategy that has investment value (consistently outperforms or underperforms the market) and is understood by the reader (we know *why* it works). By understanding the drivers behind these strategies, we begin to comprehend certain characteristics of companies and stocks that aid investment returns. When all the investment strategies presented in this book are put together, a mosaic emerges that shows us quite clearly "what drives the market" from a quantitative point of view, and what characteristics to look for or to avoid in the companies and stocks in which we plan to invest.

The quantitative strategies presented here can certainly be improved upon and refined. However, one should always bear in mind that quantitative analysis by itself is

---

[6] All of our quantitative tests divide the companies in our Backtest Universe into five separate groups, or quintiles, based on the investment criteria being tested (see Chapter 2).

a mechanical approach to investing. It is not a science, in the strict sense of the word, but it is also not the more pure art practiced by great investors like Warren Buffett, John Templeton, Julian Robertson, Jim Rogers, John Neff, Ken Heebner, and a host of others. After reading that John Neff's favored approach to valuation was the "total return ratio," which he defines as projected earnings per share (EPS) growth plus dividend yield divided by the price/earnings (P/E) ratio, I was slightly surprised to find that the strategy did not test well quantitatively.[7] The reason, I realized, is that Neff brought a high degree of art to his investment process. Joe Smith, off the street, using the same simple approach would probably record lackluster results at best.

TOWARD AN INTEGRATED MODEL OF INVESTMENT ANALYSIS

Although qualitative and quantitative analyses form separate disciplines, they also complement and reinforce each other. My hope is that this book will help bridge the divide that exists among fundamental (qualitative) analysts, market technicians,[8] and quantitative analysts alike. During my career as an equity analyst, it has become obvious to me that investors involved in different investing disciplines often segregate themselves accordingly. Fundamental analysts often affect disdain for "chartists" (although I've never known a fundamental analyst who when analyzing a stock didn't first look at its chart, and in times of trouble many can be seen quietly consulting the neighborhood technician). Technical analysts, on the other hand, sometimes make it a point of pride to know nothing about a stock other than its ticker symbol and price action. (Attending a conference for technical analysts, I was once asked what I did for a living. My response, "I'm a fundamental equity analyst"; the parry, "I'm sorry to hear that.") And quantitative analysts are literally segregated from their qualitative and technical peers, often working with little contact with either. (I am encouraged by the fact that there seems to be a movement to more closely integrate qualitative and quantitative analysts—a recent conference in New York on this subject was well attended by major investment houses, even if the motive of the attendees might have been simply to use quantitative analysis to improve risk management.)

I have always believed, and experience has borne out my belief, that qualitative analysis, quantitative analysis, and technical analysis are mutually complementary disciplines (see Figure 1.1). In a research publication written for Standard & Poor's some years ago, a colleague of mine and I laid out the case for integration as follows:

---

[7] John Neff managed the Vanguard Windsor Fund for over 30 years, significantly outperforming most other mutual funds during that period.

[8] Market technicians use price and volume data to forecast stock price movements. Quantitative tests based on price momentum, a major category of technical analysis, are covered in Chapter 9.

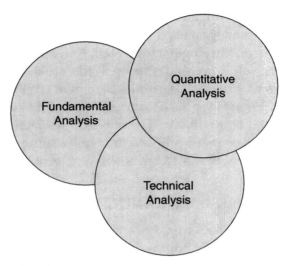

Figure 1.1 Fundamental, Quantitative, and Technical Analysis

We believe that, given the complexity of the financial markets, an analytical approach that integrates the three disciplines may yield superior insights and investment decisions:

- Fundamental analysis provides the important hypotheses about economic, industry, and company-specific trends, upon which good investment decisions are made.
- Quantitative analysis allows the investor to take a wide-angle view of a variety of fundamental trends that might otherwise be difficult to encompass.
- Technical analysis provides a summary analysis of investor expectations for a wide variety of assets, and offers clues as to timing for investment ideas.

Although I have gained a lot in experience since those words were written, I would not now add or subtract a single phrase.

THE CONCEPTS USED IN THIS BOOK

Investment value (Alpha[9]): An investment strategy that consistently outperforms and/or underperforms the market, thus allowing the investor to achieve greater than market returns. (Underperforming strategies show the investor what to avoid, or they can be used as part of a short sale or long/short strategy.) Since any investor today can achieve

---

[9] Strictly speaking, Alpha is a measure of the risk-adjusted "active return" (the return in excess of a market benchmark) produced by an investment. Alpha is more fully defined in Chapter 2. Here, I simply use it to mean "investment value-added" (i.e., above-market investment returns).

returns similar to those of the overall market simply by buying an index fund, with very low associated fees and little or no investment research, a strategy that meets or only slightly exceeds the market return has no investment value. In addition, since statistical tests vary greatly according to the time period over which testing has taken place and often have a significant margin of error, a test that shows only slight outperformance and/or underperformance or works less than 60% of the time is highly suspect. Therefore, only tests that work consistently and outperform or underperform significantly (by a couple percentage points annually and preferably more) are considered to have investment value.

Basics: A basic is a class of investment strategies that generally work. There are certainly more basics than are covered in this book, but the seven categories tested here— profitability, valuation, cash flow, growth, capital allocation, price momentum, and red flags (risk)—span a very wide spectrum of investment analysis. In Chapter 3, I cover the basics that drive stock performance from day to day (i.e., retrospectively). The remaining chapters cover basics that work prospectively, that is, basic investment strategies that can be used in quantitative tests with historical data to predict future stock market returns.

Building blocks: A building block is a specific strategy that has investment value and works for a clearly understandable, nonstatistical reason. We tested over 1,200 individual and combined strategies in preparation for this book. Seven broad categories of tests that drive investment results—the basics—and a larger number of individual building blocks based on these categories emerged from this testing. We've found that some building blocks are so similar that combining them creates little additional value (or, in some cases, actually reduces value), while combining others results in greatly enhanced returns. Knowing why building blocks work will aid one in constructing sophisticated investment models that consistently outperform.

Mosaics: A mosaic is a picture or pattern formed by inlaying many colored tiles; the picture "emerges" as more and more pieces are put in place. By testing a large number of individual investment strategies, one can little by little build a mental model—a mosaic—of those factors that are most significant in driving stock market returns.

Empiricism: Empiricism means that seeing is believing—it is the pursuit of knowledge through experimentation and observation. While much of investment is an art, and an art can be "proven" only through the work of a great artist, the basic principles underlying stock performance can be proven empirically. Our approach to testing has been to formulate a theory, conduct a test, then follow the results of that test in whichever direction they lead—whether contrary to conventional wisdom or contrary to our expectations or not. Too much in the field of investment, as in other fields, is based on so-called conventional wisdom, which often comes down to something written down in a book that is then copied by many other writers-of-books. To the extent that investment principles can be discovered scientifically, this book seeks to identify, explain, and evaluate these principles using the light of empirical tests.

Triangulation: A good scientist tests a theory in various ways to see if he or she can disprove it, or if it can be proven true by withstanding all scrutiny. In this work, the technique of triangulation—looking at an investment theory in a variety of ways to see if it proves true—has been used extensively. Triangulation allows us to speculate with some assurance on the reasons why an investment test works the way it does.

One final thought: like Don Quixote, my hope is that, after having jousted with windmills for a while, it may turn out that one or two have been actual giants, and that this work will thus make some small contribution to the great literature of this field.

CHAPTER 2

Methodology

Not everything that can be counted counts, and not everything that counts can be counted.

Albert Einstein

In this thought-provoking work, [the author] tests more than 6,400 technical analysis rules and finds that none of them offer statistically significant returns when applied to trading the S&P 500.

From a customer review of a book advertised on Amazon.com

In 1994 John Meriwether, a former head of the fixed-income arbitrage group at Salomon Brothers, founded a hedge fund called Long-Term Capital Management. LTCM, which boasted two economists who were later to win the Nobel Prize on its board of directors, developed quantitative strategies that were essentially based on bets that the price difference, or spread, between different classes of bonds would converge. The company used large amounts of leverage to amplify the small spread it planned to make on each trade and was wildly successful. It branched out from fixed-income arbitrage into other kinds of trades. Then the bottom fell out. In 1998 a currency crisis that began in Asia spread to Russia and caused turmoil in the global bond markets. Many of LTCM's trades failed, and the huge amount of leverage it had taken on came crashing down on it. The Federal Reserve Bank of New York organized a $3.6 billion bailout to prevent a string of defaults that it worried would cripple financial markets. The problem that caused this downfall: despite the presence of Nobel Prize–winning economists, LTCM didn't fully understand the quantitative strategies it employed. It engaged in data mining to analyze historical spreads between bonds and as a result didn't realize the underlying risks it was taking (risks that might have suggested a more conservative use of leverage).

Data mining involves using computers to look for correlations between items in a database (e.g., the historical spread between different classes of bonds), without necessarily seeking to understand the underlying factors that cause and can alter those correlations (e.g., a repricing of risk). An additional risk of data mining is that the analyst can develop strategies that simply "fit" the database: they work with one set of data but are unlikely to work well with another set (i.e., in the future). The strategies presented in this book were *not* discovered through data mining. Almost all of the tests we undertook are based on existing financial and investment theory. Some of this theory worked from a quantitative point of view, and some didn't. The tests that worked proved the underlying investment theory, by showing the results that accrue—in terms of excess returns—when that theory is applied to stock selection.

One principle I've followed consistently throughout this book is not to present any test I don't understand well. A quantitative test that is thoroughly understood forms part of one's investment toolkit: since one understands both *why* it works and *how* it works, it becomes a building block that can be profitably exploited and effectively combined with other strategies. In addition, a thoroughly understood quantitative test that is based on sound investment theory becomes part of the investor's mental model of how the stock market works. The tests presented in this book should enable the investor to better understand important investment strategies based on profitability, valuation, cash generation, growth, sound capital allocation, the importance of timing, and how the market assesses risk.

Basing quantitative tests on sound financial theory is not enough, however. Quantitative tests are necessarily based on statistical samples, and as a friend once reminded me, statistics is (or can be) the art of proving anything you'd like with numbers. The tests in this book were carefully designed to avoid statistical bias, including look-ahead bias, survivorship bias, restatement bias, and bias that occurs from using too short of a test period or too small of a test sample. This chapter describes our test methodology, including our research database, how we structured the tests, and how we evaluate test results, as well as how to read the backtest summaries, which will appear frequently in subsequent chapters. A careful reading of this chapter should provide a good foundation for understanding the chapters that follow.

Finally, as hinted at in the quote from Albert Einstein above and discussed in Chapter 1, not all investment strategies that count can be counted. Quantitative analysis, as practiced in this book, allows the investor to see broad trends or tendencies in the investment markets. However, there is much in the art of investment practice that is difficult if not impossible to encapsulate in a quantitative test. Therefore, we'll use the tests presented here to capture the primary drivers of investment returns and leave the finer aspects of the art of investment to the artists.

THE DATABASE

Our research starts with the Standard & Poor's Compustat Point in Time database. Point in Time, in my opinion, is the premier database currently available for back-testing fundamental data with U.S. and Canadian companies. It was created by Marcus Bogue III, founder of Charter Oak Investment Systems, Inc., for Standard & Poor's Compustat, based on as-first-reported data originally collected by Compustat. It contains about 25,000 individual companies over time and has about 150 fundamental data items for these companies beginning from 1987. In 1987 the database contains data for almost 7,000 active companies; this number climbs to about 10,000 by 1997 and remains at just above 10,000 for the rest of the period we studied. With a few exceptions, our backtests cover a 20-year period, based on data from 1987 through 2006.

The Point in Time database has three key features that are essential to researchers in constructing unbiased statistical tests. First, it contains not only companies that are currently in business but also companies that have gone out of business, been acquired, gone private, and so on. (Compustat distinguishes these companies by calling them "research" versus "active" companies.) By including all companies in a backtest, whether they are active today or not, researchers avoid *survivorship bias,* which results when poorly performing companies are dropped from the database, while better performing peers remain.

Second, each data item in the Point in Time database is identified with the historical date ("point in time") at which it was first available in the actual database. This critical feature avoids *look-ahead bias*—the use of backtest data that were not actually available to investors at the time specified by the test. For example, if a company reports earnings for the fourth calendar quarter of 2007 in March 2008, but a backtest uses these results as of December 2007, a substantial performance boost can occur that the investor could not have predicted based on the historical data, particularly if the company reports better than expected results. As S&P Compustat succinctly puts it, the Point in Time database answers not only the question What did investors know? but also, and more importantly, When did they know it?

When using databases other than the Point in Time database, researchers commonly lag fundamental data by three or four months to prevent look-ahead bias. However, this technique has its problems, as certain companies do not file quarterly and/or annual results on time, due to accounting difficulties, with filings in some cases delayed by over a year. In addition, the Securities and Exchange Commission (SEC) filing requirements for public companies have become more stringent over the years, so lags used with recent data may not be sufficient when used to lag older data. We believe that this "stamped with the date available"[1] feature of the Point in Time database makes it well suited to providing valid backtest results.

Third, the Point in Time database contains unrestated, or as first reported, data. Unrestated data are data as they were originally reported by the company, prior to any subsequent changes to the historical data. When a public company sells or discontinues a business, makes a large business acquisition, changes accounting policies, or corrects a prior period accounting error (misstatement), accounting rules allow it to restate its past results, so that prior periods can be more easily compared to current periods by users of financial statements. When such restatements are made to a research database, they distort the data that were originally reported and make them unreliable for use in a backtest. For example, in 2006 defense contractor Raytheon discontinued its business jet division to focus on military equipment. As a result, it restated its 2005 earnings per share (EPS) down to $1.80, from $2.08, and its 2004 EPS to $0.85, from $0.99 (see Table 2.1). In 2007 Raytheon also discontinued its Flight Options private jet fractional ownership business, resulting in upward restatements in 2005 and 2006 EPS. Restatements such as these happen often as

TABLE 2.1

Raytheon as First Reported and Restated Earnings

| | Raytheon Co. | | |
| | Diluted EPS from Continuing Operations | | |
	As First Reported	Restated 2006	Restated 2007
2004	$0.99	$0.85	
2005	$2.08	$1.80	$1.98
2006	$2.46		$2.63
2007	$3.80		

Source: Company Reports

---

[1] The data availability date represents the month in which the data in each company's historical record became available to users of the then-current Compustat database.

companies make large acquisitions or shed money-losing businesses and can significantly bias test results (since the restated data was not available during the period being tested).

All tests were run with the Charter Oak Investment Systems' *Venues* data engine, which is specifically designed for sophisticated financial analysis of data. This flexible software program provides the analyst with the ability to establish relationships between data items (e.g., industry to company to security issue), and to simultaneously conduct cross-sectional (using one or more sets of companies) and time-series (across different time periods) analysis. With the Venues data engine, the Compustat Point in Time database essentially became our playground.

THE BACKTEST UNIVERSE

All of the tests in this book begin with our Backtest Universe. This is a subset of the companies in the Compustat Point in Time database, containing an average of about 2,200 U.S. companies. The smallest market cap in 2006 was about $500 million, while the largest (Exxon) was $447 billion. We chose this universe of small-, mid-, and large-cap companies, because the market capitalizations of these firms are large enough to be invested in by both individuals and institutions. They are also large enough to avoid some of the volatility and erratic results found among micro-cap stocks. In order to construct our Universe, we first exclude foreign companies, certain holding companies and investment funds, and other unusual entities (the list of exclusions includes Canadian companies, American Depository Receipts/Shares, limited partnerships, real estate investment trusts, closed-end funds, and indexes). We then include all remaining companies with a current (non-split-adjusted) price greater than $2 and a stock market capitalization greater than 1/50th of the *average* market capitalization of the S&P 500, at that historical point in time. The requirement that the current price be greater than $2 screens out certain volatile, low-priced stocks. The market capitalization constraint ensures that we choose companies in a similar market capitalization class despite the ups and downs of the market.

As Table 2.2 shows, the size of our Universe ranges from 1,800 companies in 1990 to 2,700 in 1996, but it averages out to about 2,200. In addition, Figure 2.1 shows the distribution of companies in the database by market capitalization, as of the end of 2006. Note that over 1,100 companies in the Universe have a market cap between $1 billion and $5 billion. I consider this market cap class, somewhere between small-cap and mid-cap, to hold a lot of potential investment ideas for the enterprising investor.

TABLE 2.2

Backtest Universe: Number of Companies, Market Capitalization, and Price Per Share

Date	Number of Active Companies in Database	Number of Companies— Backtest Universe	Average Market Cap— Universe (Mil.)	Minimum Market Cap— Universe (Mil.)	Average Market Cap— S&P 500 (Mil.)	Average Price Per Share— Universe	Minimum Price Per Share— Universe
Dec-87	6,949	2,095	$1,129	$69	$3,441	$79.91	$2.02
Dec-88	7,010	2,105	$1,234	$76	$3,790	$50.56	$2.01
Dec-89	6,912	1,987	$1,600	$95	$4,732	$27.44	$2.05
Dec-90	6,839	1,799	$1,603	$88	$4,401	$29.14	$2.03
Dec-91	6,826	2,083	$1,864	$114	$5,693	$43.55	$2.02
Dec-92	7,078	2,308	$1,854	$121	$6,064	$43.21	$2.03
Dec-93	8,064	2,612	$1,869	$133	$6,644	$49.38	$2.03
Dec-94	9,027	2,591	$1,843	$134	$6,697	$79.29	$2.11
Dec-95	9,483	2,671	$2,424	$184	$9,210	$61.14	$2.07
Dec-96	9,957	2,730	$2,898	$226	$11,273	$54.44	$2.08
Dec-97	10,422	2,636	$3,907	$303	$15,095	$66.80	$2.09
Dec-98	10,366	2,031	$5,945	$399	$19,948	$76.81	$2.57
Dec-99	10,259	2,067	$7,600	$497	$24,831	$143.27	$2.10
Dec-00	10,198	1,853	$7,787	$474	$23,605	$86.32	$2.38
Dec-01	10,317	1,968	$6,531	$423	$21,130	$70.06	$2.35
Dec-02	10,642	1,959	$5,142	$325	$16,251	$61.54	$2.18
Dec-03	10,789	2,191	$6,067	$412	$20,572	$68.94	$2.55
Dec-04	10,198	2,317	$6,449	$452	$22,597	$75.59	$2.02
Dec-05	10,208	2,328	$6,765	$466	$23,219	$83.23	$2.08
Dec-06	10,119	2,352	$7,503	$524	$26,203	$87.95	$2.01
Average	**9,083**	**2,234**	**$4,101**	**$276**	**$13,770**	**$66.93**	**$2.14**

Source: Standard & Poor's Compustat, Charter Oak Investment Systems, Inc.

PORTFOLIO RETURNS AND HOLDING PERIODS

Annual returns for our backtest portfolios are calculated as the average annual price change for the portfolio plus dividends and cash-equivalent distributions of value over the 12 months following portfolio formation (e.g., if we form a portfolio of companies in December 1988, we calculate returns for those companies from January 1989 to

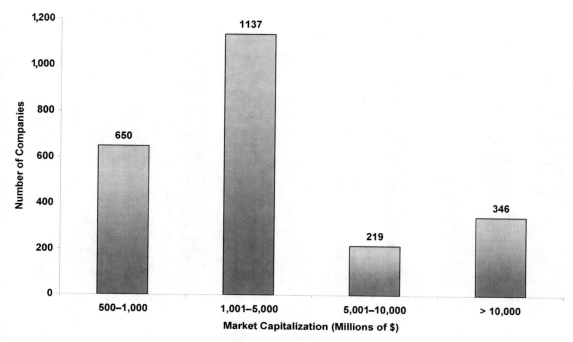

Figure 2.1 Market Capitalization Distribution of Backtest Universe (2006)

December 1989). Distributions of value consist of items such as spin-offs.[2] Returns are compounded only on an annual basis. Some quantitative studies assume quarterly or even monthly compounding of price and dividends. We took what I believe is a more conservative approach, assuming that theoretical investors in each strategy would hold each portfolio for a year and not immediately reinvest any dividends received. However, we assumed that all monies received in one year, including dividends and distributions of value, would be reinvested in the strategy the following year. The measures of return you will see throughout this book (compound annual growth rates and average excess returns) represent this method applied to strategy portfolios, the Backtest Universe, and the S&P 500 constituents, all on an *equal-weighted* basis. We chose to use equal-weighted (versus market-cap weighted) returns because we assume that

---

[2] In a spin-off, a subsidiary or division of a company is divested from the parent company, and shares in the new company are distributed to existing shareholders. The result is usually that the price of the parent company declines, as a piece of it now trades as a separate entity. If spin-offs and other distributions of value were not accounted for, shareholders of the "parent" stock would appear to have lost significant value, when in fact that value has just been redistributed.

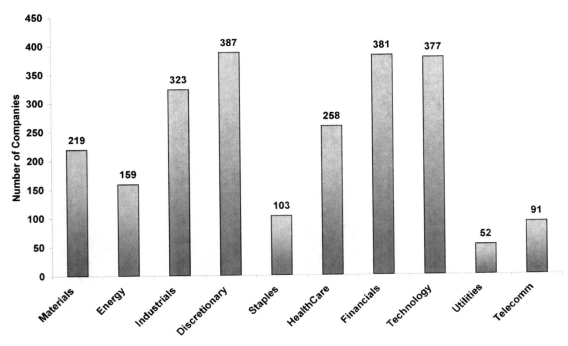

Figure 2.2 Sector Distribution of Backtest Universe (2006)

investors may buy *any* selection of stocks within the portfolios, regardless of size, and put an equivalent amount of money into each stock. Since the minimum market cap in our Backtest Universe in 2006 was over $500 million, only large institutions would be prevented from purchasing even the smallest stocks in the portfolio.

All portfolio holding periods throughout this book are 12-month holding periods. I chose 12-month holding periods, rather than monthly or quarterly periods or periods longer than a year, because a 12-month period avoids problems associated with excessive trading, while still being a "reasonable" time period for most investors to see their stock purchases work out or not work out. For example, at Standard & Poor's Equity Research, we primarily follow a "growth at a reasonable price" investment philosophy, in which the analyst seeks to recommend stocks of growing companies selling below their "fair" market values. We use a 12-month target price with an average holding period of six months to one and one-half years, and S&P's actual investment record over the years has worked out well. Quarterly or monthly holding periods are suitable primarily for high net worth investors or quantitatively oriented institutions that can mitigate the transaction fees involved in such a high-turnover strategy by committing large amounts of money to each position. One-year holding periods also have the benefit of tax efficiency, since long-term capital gains tax rates currently take effect after one year.

HOW THE TESTS ARE STRUCTURED

All tests in this book are structured as *quintile* tests, meaning that our Backtest Universe is divided into five equal groups, according to the values for each company for the factor(s) we are testing. For example, if we test a strategy of buying companies with high operating profit margins and selling those with low operating profit margins, the software first ranks all of the companies in our Backtest Universe by operating margin, from highest to lowest. Companies that do not have a value for operating margin are eliminated. Then the top 20% of companies by operating margin are put in the top quintile, the next 20% in the second quintile, and so on, with the bottom 20% of companies by profit margin put in the bottom quintile. We could have divided our tests into deciles (10 portfolio groups), quartiles, thirds, or even halves. However, the primary goal of our testing was to determine which investment strategies work from a quantitative point of view. Quintiles provide a clear answer to that question: if a strategy works, the top quintile should outperform, the bottom quintile should underperform, and there should be some linearity of returns among the quintiles in between (i.e., the top quintile should have the highest excess returns, followed by the second quintile, the third, etc.).

We run most tests over a 20-year period, from 1987 through 2006, with the exception of tests involving data from the cash flow statement[3] (which goes back to 1989 and gives us 18 years of data) and some technical, or market price–based, tests in which we use daily pricing (which goes back to 1991 and gives us 16 years). In backtesting investment strategies, it is very important that a test be conducted over as long a period of time as possible. The shorter the test period, the more likely a strategy that worked over the test period may not work in the future. Reliable backtests work through a variety of economic and market conditions, a characteristic that can only be discovered by testing the strategy over a sufficient number of years. The 20-year time span over which we test the majority of our strategies includes three major bull markets (1988–1990, 1991–2000, 2003–2007[4]), three bear markets (1990, 1998,[5] 2000–2002), a few extended periods of sideways market movement (1992, 1994, much of 2004), a stock market bubble (1999), and two official economic recessions (1990–1991, 2001).

---

[3] In 1987, the Financial Accounting Standards Board mandated that companies provide a cash flow statement that divided cash flows (incoming and outgoing funds) into operating, investing, and financing categories. However, this statement wasn't widely adopted until 1989.

[4] Although we run the tests from 1987 through 2006 (form the portfolios in each of these periods), returns are calculated 12 months forward, from 1988 through 2007.

[5] The 1998 market decline can be thought of as a "mini-bear"; the Dow Jones Industrial Average fell 19.3%, from 9,338 in July 1998 to 7,539 at the end of August 1998. The ostensible cause for the decline was a global currency panic (plunge in currency prices) that began in Asia and spread to Russia.

Each quintile for each year tested should be thought of as a *portfolio*, which represents the group of stocks that, based on their values for the strategy being tested, fall into a given quintile in a given year. Each year we calculate the average total return for each portfolio. Then we link the returns for each portfolio together by quintile, to determine the total return and *compound annual growth rate* (CAGR) of returns for each quintile. If a test works, the CAGR for the top quintile should be higher than the CAGR for the entire Backtest Universe, and the CAGR for the bottom quintile should be lower than the CAGR for the Universe.

A simple test should give you an idea of how this works. Let's say we'd like to test a strategy of buying stocks with low price-to-sales ratios and selling stocks with high price-to-sales ratios. For simplicity, we'll only test this strategy over three years, 2003 to 2005. We'll form our portfolios in December 2003, December 2004, and December 2005.[6] Companies with the lowest price-to-sales ratios will be assigned to the top quintile, and companies with the highest price-to-sales ratios will be assigned to the bottom. Since we're forming our first set of quintiles at the end of 2003, our first year of portfolio returns will be calculated from January to December 2004. Then we'll calculate quintile (portfolio) returns for 2005 and 2006. The results are shown in Table 2.3 (note that the returns shown below are *indexed*, meaning that 1 has been added to them so that they can be multiplied together to form compound returns—so the actual returns for quintile 1 are 26% in 2004, 11% in 2005, and 21% in 2006).[7]

TABLE 2.3

Sample Price-to-Sales Strategy: Indexed Returns by Quintile

	Quintile 1	Quintile 2	Quintile 3	Quintile 4	Quintile 5	Universe
Dec-04	1.26	1.23	1.20	1.13	1.08	1.18
Dec-05	1.11	1.07	1.11	1.09	1.03	1.08
Dec-06	1.21	1.18	1.16	1.12	1.09	1.15

[6] These three years were deliberately chosen because they generate strong results for this test, so don't be overly impressed by the numbers.

[7] The actual computer code used to generate these returns will vary according to the software package used. For the test shown above, companies were ranked by total full-year sales divided by total end-of-year market value. Companies that were missing values for either sales or market value were excluded. A "fractile" function was used to do the ranking and divide the companies into quintiles. Returns were calculated as year-to-year change in price plus dividends plus cash-equivalent distributions of value.

T A B L E   2.4

Sample Price-to-Sales Strategy: Linked Returns, Total Return, and CAGR

	Quintile 1	Quintile 2	Quintile 3	Quintile 4	Quintile 5	Universe
Dec-04	1.26	1.23	1.20	1.13	1.08	1.18
Dec-05	1.40	1.32	1.32	1.23	1.11	1.27
Dec-06	1.69	1.55	1.54	1.38	1.21	1.47
Total Return	69%	55%	54%	38%	21%	47%
CAGR	19%	16%	16%	11%	7%	14%

Table 2.4 shows *linked returns*—returns that have been multiplied by each other to create a compound return. The linked return for quintile 1 for 2004 is simply the original return of 1.26 (the actual return for 2004 from Table 2.3 multiplied by 1).[8] The 2005 linked return of 1.40 is 1.26 multiplied by 1.11 (the actual return for 2005 from Table 2.3), and the 2006 linked return of 1.69 is 1.40 multiplied by 1.21 (the actual return for 2006). The total return is calculated by simply taking the last linked return and subtracting 1. The compound annual growth rate of returns is calculated by taking the final linked return, raising it to the power of $1/3$, where 3 represents the number of years of compound returns, and subtracting 1. For example,

$$1.69^{1/3} - 1 = 19\%$$

Portfolio sizes for single factor tests tend to be large, since we begin with a Universe that has an average size of 2,200 companies and exclude only those companies that don't have data for the factor(s) being tested. Portfolio sizes for the test above were about 450. Remember that the idea behind the backtests presented in this book is to show that an investment strategy works. I wouldn't necessarily recommend buying a portfolio of 450 stocks. Once we know that a strategy works, the strategy can be applied in different ways. For example, depending on the software you use, it is usually easy to form a portfolio of the top 30 or 50 companies for a given strategy (e.g., the 30 stocks with the lowest price-to-sales ratios). Our experience in testing a variety of strategies is that concentrated portfolios perform better than widely diversified portfolios—as long as the strategies used work. Chapter 13, Integrating the Factors into Your Investment Approach, goes into depth on how to apply the strategies.

---

[8] We multiply the first return of each quintile by 1 because 1 represents the indexed starting point of each quintile (a 0% initial return).

Two-Factor Tests

In a single-factor backtest, we sort our Backtest Universe into quintiles based on one investment criterion (e.g., price to sales, return on equity, or EPS growth). However, a significant part of this book is devoted to showing investors how to effectively combine strategies. For the most part, our combined tests will consist of two investment criteria, for example, price to sales and price to book value; return on equity and relative price strength. The same basic method shown above for forming quintiles and calculating returns is used for two-factor tests. However, in forming the portfolios for the two-factor test, we do not weight both factors equally. Instead, we first form a set based on the initial factor, and *from that set* we select the second factor.

An example should help to make this clear. Let's say we'd like to test a combination of price-to-sales and price-to-book value ratios. For our top quintile (quintile 1), we want those companies that have *both* the lowest price-to-sales ratios and the lowest price-to-book value ratios. To form the top quintile, our software program performs the following steps:

1. It ranks all companies in our Backtest Universe by price to sales. In this case, it ranks price-to-sales values *from lowest to highest*, since we want the lowest values in the top quintile.
2. It selects the top 20% of this ranked list—the 20% of companies with the *lowest* price-to-sales values. If we start with 2,000 companies, this step should select about 400 companies.
3. It then ranks the 400 companies that passed the price-to-sales test by price-to-book value, again from lowest to highest.
4. It selects the top 20% of this ranked list—those with the *lowest* price-to-book valuations. If we started with 400 companies in step 2, we should end up with about 80 companies at the end of step 4.
5. Steps 1 to 4 are repeated until we have formed portfolios for the top quintile for *each year* to be tested.

The analytical software repeats the process above for each of our five quintiles. The only difference from quintile to quintile is which 20% slice of ranked companies the program selects: the second quintile selects companies that rank between 20% and 40%, the third between 40% and 60%, and the fourth between 60% and 80%, with the bottom quintile selecting those with ranks below 80% (the bottom 20%). Otherwise, the ranking process shown above is the same for each.

By testing two-factor strategies in this manner, we are intentionally emphasizing the first factor. The reason for this is twofold. Some strategies are stronger than others, and therefore one wants to emphasize the stronger factor and deemphasize the weaker.

Also, by selecting portfolios this way, rather than using the intersection of two factors, we end up with consistent and relatively large portfolio sizes (versus the variable sizes we would get by using the intersection of the two factors). Having relatively large and consistent portfolio sizes helps ensure that the tests are reliable.

THE EXCESS RETURNS[9] TESTS

Each single-factor and two-factor strategy presented in this book is run once annually, over an 18- to 20-year period, to calculate the compound annual growth rate of the strategy versus the Universe and equal-weighted S&P 500 over this period of time. In addition to running the returns annually, however, we run each test quarterly over our 18- to 20-year test period. Although we are running the test quarterly, *the holding period remains 12 months*. That is, quarterly portfolios are held for overlapping 12-month periods. By running quarterly tests, we end up with 72 to 80 sets of annual portfolio returns instead of just 18 to 20. This larger number of portfolios, taken at four different points during the calendar year, helps ensure that the test isn't being unduly affected by statistical or seasonal effects. In short, the quarterly tests provide increased reliability. We use the results of the quarterly tests to calculate the average excess returns for the quintiles, shown in each Backtest Summary (see Figure 2.3).

THE BACKTEST SUMMARY TABLE AND GRAPHS

Both the annual and quarterly test results are presented in our Backtest Summary results table and accompanying graphs (Figure 2.3). It would be worthwhile to familiarize yourself with this template, which is used to present nearly all statistical test results throughout this book.

1. The years over which the test returns were calculated. Most tests are run for 20 years (tests involving cash flow are run for 18). It also shows the column headings for each quintile, our Backtest Universe, and the equal-weighted S&P 500. S&P 500 returns were included because the investor can easily get returns that are similar to the 500 by buying an index fund.
2. Compound annual growth rates by quintile, based on the annually run portfolio returns.
3. Average excess returns versus our Backtest Universe. These returns represent the average of the excess returns (i.e., returns above or below the return for

---

[9] Throughout this book, I'll use the term *excess returns* to mean returns above (for the top quintile) or below (for the bottom quintile) the returns for the Backtest Universe.

	1988 ~ 2007	1st Quintile	2nd Quintile	3rd Quintile	4th Quintile	5th Quintile	Universe	S&P 500*
1								
2	CAGR – Annual Rebalance	16.6%	14.2%	15.3%	9.2%	−3.8%	11.2%	12.9%
3	Average Excess Return vs. Universe**	5.9%	2.4%	1.8%	−1.8%	−8.2%	NA	1.6%
4	Value of $10,000 Invested (20 Years)	$204,908	$132,426	$163,311	$48,050	($5,428)	$73,161	$102,895
5	% of 1-Year Periods Strategy Outperforms the Universe	70.1%	61.0%	55.8%	39.0%	27.3%	NA	59.7%
6	% Rolling 3-Year Periods Strategy Outperforms	82.6%	66.7%	62.3%	30.4%	8.7%	NA	71.0%
7	Maximum Gain	72.1%	59.4%	41.8%	50.4%	147.9%	59.2%	54.1%
8	Maximum Loss	−26.1%	−19.2%	−21.4%	−27.7%	−78.6%	−24.9%	−25.9%
9	Sharpe Ratio	0.78	0.68	0.74	0.39	0.00	0.49	0.69
10	Standard Deviation of Returns	0.18	0.15	0.13	0.16	0.41	0.16	0.14
11	Beta (vs. Universe)	0.83	0.75	0.61	0.88	1.79	NA	0.78
12	Alpha (vs. Universe)	0.08	0.05	0.07	0.00	−0.18	NA	0.04
13	Average Portfolio Size	76	76	76	76	76	NA	NA
14	Average Number of Companies *Outperforming*	37	37	37	32	22	NA	NA
15	Average Number of Companies *Underperforming*	36	37	35	40	50	NA	NA
16	Median Portfolio Value – Return on Invested Capital	27.7%	13.7%	10.0%	6.5%	−30.5%	9.4%	11.4%
17	Median Portfolio Value – Price-to-Sales	0.5	0.9	1.1	1.9	24.1	0.9	0.8
18	Average Market Capitalization	$3,209	$3,580	$3,975	$5,371	$1,418	NA	NA

* Equal-weighted average of S&P 500 returns.** Annual holding period run quarterly for a larger sample size; arithmetic average excess returns.
Source: Standard & Poor's Compustat Point in Time Database, Charter Oak Investment Systems

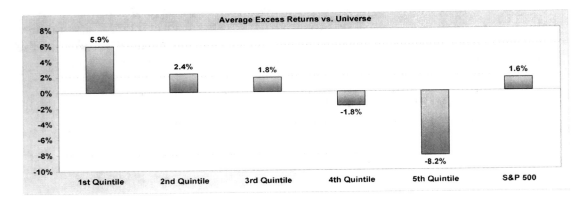

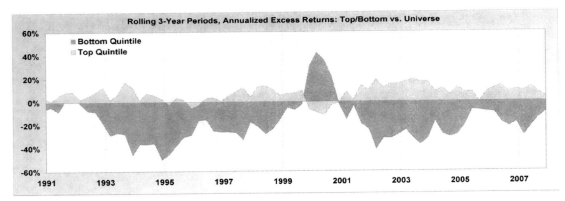

Figure 2.3 Sample Backtest Summary: Return on Invested Capital and Price to Sales

the Universe) based on the quarterly run portfolio tests (see explanation under Excess Returns Tests, above). N.B.: Because these returns are run quarterly, versus the annually run returns used to calculate the compound annual growth rate, above, *average excess returns should be viewed as more reliable than the compound annual returns.*

4. Value of $10,000 invested X years ago, where X indicates the number of years included in the backtest. Based on the annually run portfolio returns.

5. The percentage of one-year periods that the strategy outperforms the Universe. Based on quarterly run returns.

6. The percentage of rolling three-year periods that the strategy outperforms the Universe. That is, if an investor followed the strategy for three consecutive years, what percentage of times would the investor outperform the Universe? Based on quarterly run returns.

7. The maximum gain realized over any one-year period (quarterly run).

8. The maximum loss sustained over any one-year period (quarterly run).

9. Sharpe ratio of quintile returns. The Sharpe ratio is a widely used measure of a strategy's risk-adjusted return. Here, risk is defined as volatility, specifically, the standard deviation of a strategy's excess return over a risk-free rate of return.[10] The Sharpe ratio is calculated by subtracting the return for Treasury bills (the "risk-free" rate) from a quintile's average return, then dividing the result by the standard deviation of quintile returns. The higher the Sharpe ratio, the more excess returns the strategy generates per unit of risk (standard deviation).

10. The standard deviation of quintile returns. This is a measure of the volatility of returns for each quintile for the strategy. Higher numbers indicate a more volatile strategy, lower numbers a less volatile one.

11. Beta of quintile returns versus the Backtest Universe. This represents a measure of how volatile a strategy is relative to the overall Universe. A number greater than 1 indicates a strategy that is more volatile than the Universe, while a number less than 1 indicates a strategy that is less volatile.

---

[10] I define risk as the potential for real (versus "paper") loss of capital. Another, more precise, definition is the probability of permanent loss of purchasing power, a definition that also takes into account the steady erosion in capital that occurs due to inflation. If you plan on holding stocks for a year or less (we assume one-year holding periods in this book), volatility could certainly be a risk. For longer term holding periods, investment risk (the potential for an impairment of the business itself) becomes a much more important factor. Valuation (the risk of overpaying for an investment) is another important risk factor.

12. **Alpha of quintile returns versus the Backtest Universe.** Alpha represents a strategy's risk-adjusted excess return.[11] Alpha differs from the Sharpe ratio in a couple of ways, but primarily in its use of Beta to represent risk rather than a strategy's standard deviation of returns, which is used to calculate the Sharpe ratio.

13. **Average portfolio size.** The average size of the quintile portfolios over the testing period.

14. **Average number of companies outperforming.** This indicates how many companies within the quintile portfolios outperformed the Universe on average.

15. **Average number of companies underperforming.** This indicates how many companies underperformed the Universe on average.

16. **The median portfolio value of the first factor used in the strategy.** In this example, the values shown are the median values for each quintile for return on invested capital. We use median instead of average, so the values won't be skewed by the effects of outliers (e.g., a stock having a P/E ratio of 500).

17. **The median portfolio value of the second factor used in the strategy.** If the strategy is a single-factor strategy, this row will not exist. In this example, values shown are the median portfolio values for price to sales.

18. **The average market capitalization of the portfolios by quintile over the testing period.**

The Graphs

An example of the two graphs that accompany each strategy is shown in Figure 2.3. The first graph shows the average excess returns versus the Backtest Universe by quintile (including the equal-weighted S&P 500). The excess returns are based on the quarterly run returns test. The second graph, also based on the quarterly run test, shows the annualized excess returns of the top and bottom quintiles over rolling three-year periods. To calculate these returns, we subtract the three-year compound rate of return for the quintile from the three-year compound rate of return for the Backtest Universe, then annualize this value. This graph shows you what kind of returns you can expect if you employ the strategy (long or short) for three consecutive

---

[11] In technical terms, Alpha measures the difference between an investment's *actual* return and its *expected* return, given the level of risk carried by the strategy (its volatility versus a market benchmark) as measured by Beta. Put another way, Alpha is that portion of a strategy's above-market return that cannot be explained by Beta.

years. It also provides a good overview of how the strategy performed historically. (Note that the three-year compound annual rates of returns shown in the second graph show returns for the *preceding* three years. I.e., the dates shown on the graph indicate the end of each three-year period.)

HOW TO IDENTIFY A STRONG QUANTITATIVE STRATEGY

A quantitative strategy that works should have all or most of the following characteristics. With a few exceptions, the strategies presented in this book meet these benchmarks:

- *Significant outperformance for the top quintile.* For single-factor strategies, which have large average portfolio sizes (usually over 300 companies), I like to see at least a 2% average excess return for the top quintile versus the Universe. For more focused, two-factor strategies, excess returns of 4% or more are preferable.
- *Significant underperformance of the bottom quintile.* For single-factor strategies, the bottom quintile should underperform the benchmark by 2% or more on average (i.e., excess returns should be −2%—negative 2%—or lower); for two-factor strategies, 4% underperformance or more. If a strategy is to be used for short sales, underperformance of 8% to 10% or more is preferable.
- *Good linearity of excess returns among the quintiles.* This means that the top quintile should outperform the second quintile, which should outperform the third quintile, and so on. The smoother, or more linear, the trend of excess returns, the higher my assurance that the strategy really works (i.e., that it is a general, well-founded strategy that works for many stocks and not a statistical anomaly).[12]
- *Strong consistency of returns over time.* The top quintile of a strategy should outperform the Universe for 60% or more of the annual periods tested. Strategies that outperform 70% or more are preferable.[13] The bottom quintile should underperform the Universe by 60% or more. Again, 70% underperformance or higher is preferable. Along with this, I'd much prefer a strategy that provided consistent but moderate excess returns over the years to

---

[12] Excess returns that are linear indicate that there is a strong correlation over time between the investment factor being tested and the excess returns.

[13] In his book, *The Warren Buffett Portfolio: Mastering the Power of the Focus Investment Strategy,* author Robert G. Hagstrom shows that even the best investors outperform the market only 60% to 70% of the time. (The notable exception was the Buffett Partnership, which outperformed every year from 1957 through 1969.)

one that had very large excess returns that occurred over a short period and very low excess returns over the remaining periods.

- *Low volatility and low maximum loss for the top quintile/high volatility and high maximum loss for the bottom quintile.* The importance of these factors depends on your risk tolerance and your time horizon. Investors who plan to stick with a particular discipline for a number of years need worry little about volatility. Investors seeking to "try" a strategy for a single year should consider trying low volatility strategies that have low maximum losses.[14] Both the Sharpe ratio and Alpha can be used to provide an idea of a strategy's risk-adjusted returns, where risk is represented by volatility. (See notes on Alpha and the Sharpe ratio in the preceding section.)

HOW TO USE THE BACKTEST SUMMARY AND GRAPHS

When assessing a quantitative test, I begin by examining the CAGR and the excess returns versus the Universe (lines 2 and 3 of the Backtest Summary, Figure 2.3). The criteria here, as mentioned above, are outperformance of the top quintile, underperformance of the bottom quintile, and overall linearity of the results for the quintiles in between. The average excess returns vs. Universe graph (Figure 2.3) provides a quick view of quintile excess returns. Note that there will be some difference between the CAGR of the portfolios minus the CAGR of the universe and the excess returns listed below. There are two reasons for this difference: (1) the CAGR reports compounded returns, while excess returns are simply averaged; and (2) the CAGR is based on a test that is run annually, while the excess returns are based on a test that is run quarterly (the holding period—12 months—is the same for both tests). The quarterly run test provides a much larger sample size and therefore should provide more statistically reliable results. However, in most cases the difference between the excess returns based on the annual CAGR rates and the quarterly average excess returns is relatively small. Note that for some strategies the second and not the first quintile has the strongest outperformance. As long as this outperformance is significant and consistent, the strategy could be useful.

The next point of comparison is always the consistency of the strategy. If a strategy worked well only 40% or 50% of the time, it's not worth looking at. I start by looking at the percent of one-year periods the strategy outperforms the Universe and the percent of rolling three-year periods (lines 5 and 6 of Figure 2.3). I also like to look at the rolling three-year periods, annualized excess returns graph (also shown in Figure 2.3). This

---

[14] I would also favor strategies in which the maximum loss is linear (it is lowest for the top quintile and progressively higher for each succeeding quintile) and has a high maximum gain for the top quintile.

graph gives you an idea of what kind of annual excess returns you could expect if you stuck with a strategy for any three-year period over the last 20 years. Generally speaking, this graph should show few periods where the top quintile underperforms and/or the bottom quintile outperforms.

Also, although risk tolerance is relative, the maximum loss (line 8) for a quintile is not. I particularly favor strategies in which the maximum loss for the first quintile is equal to or lower than the maximum loss for the Universe, and where the maximum loss is more or less linear as one moves down the quintiles (the maximum loss on the fifth quintile is the highest, the fourth quintile is the next to highest, etc.). A strategy in which the top quintile has high excess returns, strong consistency over the years, and a maximum loss of 15% or less is my idea of an excellent strategy.[15]

For those concerned with the volatility of strategy returns, the standard deviation of returns (line 10) and the Beta of the strategy versus the Universe (line 11) offer insight. I prefer the maximum loss, because it tells me what I can expect in terms of downside by the end of each holding period.

Alpha (line 12) is the first cousin of Beta. Specifically, Alpha is the difference between the actual return of an investment strategy and the expected return calculated using the strategy's Beta versus the market. As such, Alpha can be considered a "risk-adjusted" measure of above-market returns.[16] In interpreting Alpha, a higher number is better. Alpha can be read as a percentage. Thus, a strategy with an Alpha of 0.05 for the top portfolio can be viewed as a strategy in which the risk-adjusted above-market returns for the top portfolio are 5%. We'll show you lots of consistent strategies in which Alpha for the top quintile is 0.05 or higher (and also in which Alpha for the bottom quintile is −0.10—negative 10%—or lower). As an alternative, one might use the Sharpe ratio (line 9). Here, a Sharpe ratio for the strategy above the Sharpe ratio for the S&P 500 might indicate a strategy worth investigating.

Other factors one might consider are the average portfolio size (line 13), the number of companies outperforming and underperforming (lines 14 and 15), the median portfolio values of the ratios used in the test (line 16 and line 17, if the test uses two factors), and the average market capitalization (line 18). The average portfolio size provides an idea of how focused a strategy is. The more focused the strategy, the more outperformance you should expect from the top quintile and underperformance from the bottom. The number of companies outperforming gives you an idea of how broadly the strategy works for the top quintile, while the number of companies underperforming gives you an idea of how broadly the bottom quintile works (e.g., for a short sale strategy). You'll note that, all other

---

[15] As mentioned previously, not all tests in this book have low maximum losses. The reader must decide how much volatility to accept in a strategy.

[16] That is, if one accepts Beta as a measure of risk.

things being equal, the ratio of winners (outperformers) to losers (underperformers) for the top quintile goes up as a strategy becomes more focused (the portfolio size is smaller). The median portfolio values of the ratios used in the test provide the investor with a benchmark for sizing up potential investments or creating stock screens.

THE SECTOR TESTS

For each single-factor strategy presented in this book, we also provide a test that shows how that factor works by economic sector. Sectors represent broad swaths of related industries within the global economy and are defined according to the Global Industry Classification Standard (GICS), jointly developed by Standard & Poor's and MSCI Barra. Companies in the same economic sector often have common fundamental characteristics. There are 10 GICS economic sectors. The list below shows these sectors along with the major industries (called "industry groups") included in each:

Energy
Materials
Industrials
    Capital goods
    Commercial services & supplies
    Transportation
Consumer discretionary
    Automobiles & components
    Consumer durables & apparel
    Consumer services
    Media
    Retailing
Consumer staples
    Food & staples retailing
    Food, beverage, & tobacco
    Household & personal products
Health care
    Health care equipment & services
    Pharmaceuticals, biotechnology, & life sciences
Financials
    Banks
    Diversified financials

Insurance

Real estate

Information technology

   Software & services

   Technology hardware & equipment

   Semiconductors & semiconductor equipment

Telecommunications services

Utilities

We run sector tests for the top (first) and bottom (fifth) quintiles of single-factor strategies only. The idea of the sector test is to determine if a strategy works better for some economic sectors than for others. Since the returns for the individual economic sectors of our Backtest Universe varied over our test period (e.g., financial stocks outperformed the Universe, and consumer discretionary underperformed), and we don't know how each sector will perform in the future, we calculate excess returns for the top and bottom quintiles of our sector tests by comparing the quintile returns to the appropriate sector returns, not by comparing them to the Universe. For example, if we take our sample price-to-sales strategy, we'd calculate the energy sector returns for 2003–2004 as shown in Table 2.5.[17] Excess returns are calculated simply by subtracting the compound annual growth rate for each quintile from the CAGR for the energy sector.

TABLE 2.5

Sample Sector Test: Price-to-Sales Strategy for the Energy Sector, Linked Returns

	Quintile 1	Quintile 5	Energy Sector
Dec-04	1.50	1.01	1.28
Dec-05	1.44	1.21	1.36
Dec-06	1.93	1.59	1.79
Total Return	92.7%	58.5%	79.2%
CAGR	24.4%	16.6%	21.5%
Excess Returns	3.0%	−4.9%	

Source: Company Reports

---

[17] Note that Table 2.5 shows linked returns; that is, the actual annual returns (not shown) have been multiplied by each other to create a compound total return.

Note that for the sector tests we only calculate returns annually; that is, unlike the basic, nonsector test for the strategy, we do not calculate excess returns by running the strategy on a quarterly basis. This may make the results a little less reliable, but the annually run tests should be good enough to give you a basic idea of how a strategy works for each sector.

THE SECTOR SUMMARY TABLES AND GRAPH

The elements of the sector tables are essentially the same as those for the basic, nonsector Backtest Summary, except that the sector tests are presented using *two* tables instead of one and a few elements that are in the nonsector table are left out of the sector tables. Each set of sector tables also includes a graph that shows the average excess returns (top and bottom quintiles) for each sector. Figure 2.4 shows an example of a sector test for the return on invested capital strategy. The top table presents the results for each sector for the top (first) quintile, while the bottom presents the results for the bottom (fifth) quintile.

1. The years over which test returns were calculated (and column headings).
2. The compound annual growth rate for the top quintile (top table) or bottom quintile (bottom table) for the strategy, by sector.
3. The same compound annual growth rate for the entire economic sector (sectors are subsets of our Backtest Universe formed using the GICS codes, described above).
4. The excess return for the quintile (top or bottom), by sector, calculated as the CAGR for the quintile (line 2) minus the CAGR for the overall sector (line 3).
5. Value of $10,000 invested X years ago, where X indicates the number of years included in the backtest.
6. The percentage of one-year periods that the return for the strategy outperforms the return for the corresponding sector.
7. The percentage of rolling three-year periods that the return for the strategy outperforms the return for the corresponding sector.
8. The maximum gain realized over any one-year period.
9. The maximum loss realized over any one year period.
10. Standard deviation of quintile returns.
11. Beta of quintile returns versus the corresponding sector.
12. Alpha of quintile returns versus the corresponding sector.
13. Average size of the sector portfolios (top or bottom quintile) over the testing period.

Top Quintile

1 1988 ~ 2007	Energy	Materials	Industrials	Consumer Discretionary	Consumer Staples	Health Care	Financials	Information Technology	Telecom Services	Utilities	Universe	S&P 500*
2 CAGR – Quintile	16.0%	11.3%	12.9%	10.8%	14.2%	17.6%	17.6%	11.5%	9.4%	13.7%	11.2%	12.9%
3 CAGR – Sector	13.5%	10.2%	11.2%	8.8%	12.6%	12.3%	14.5%	7.6%	9.2%	13.0%	NA	NA
4 Excess Return vs. Sector	2.5%	1.1%	1.6%	2.1%	1.6%	5.3%	3.1%	4.0%	0.2%	0.7%	NA	NA
5 Value of $10,000	$184,653	$74,434	$102,256	$68,406	$133,205	$247,720	$244,523	$78,896	$50,702	$120,417	$73,161	$102,895
6 % 1-Year Outperformance	65.0%	50.0%	75.0%	55.0%	50.0%	70.0%	65.0%	75.0%	60.0%	60.0%	NA	NA
7 % 3-Year Outperformance	66.7%	66.7%	83.3%	72.2%	55.6%	77.8%	66.7%	77.8%	61.1%	72.2%	NA	NA
8 Maximum Gain	64.1%	40.6%	45.0%	55.7%	72.7%	70.0%	83.8%	85.7%	42.0%	53.6%	44.0%	41.4%
9 Maximum Loss	−54.6%	−13.3%	−11.5%	−15.5%	−15.2%	−12.0%	−16.8%	−34.1%	−39.6%	−13.0%	−19.1%	−18.1%
10 Standard Deviation	0.27	0.14	0.14	0.17	0.21	0.23	0.24	0.28	0.23	0.17	0.16	0.14
11 Beta (vs. Sector)	0.97	0.79	0.93	0.86	1.24	0.83	1.03	0.69	0.38	1.02	NA	NA
12 Alpha (vs. Sector)	0.04	0.03	0.02	0.03	−0.01	0.07	0.03	0.06	0.06	0.01	NA	NA
13 Portfolio Size	24	31	57	69	20	40	40	58	9	25	NA	NA

Bottom Quintile

1 1988 ~ 2007	Energy	Materials	Industrials	Consumer Discretionary	Consumer Staples	Health Care	Financials	Information Technology	Telecom Services	Utilities	Universe	S&P 500*
2 CAGR – Quintile	9.8%	4.5%	9.5%	7.0%	10.0%	7.9%	10.5%	7.3%	8.6%	13.3%	11.2%	12.9%
3 CAGR – Sector	13.5%	10.2%	11.2%	8.8%	12.6%	12.3%	14.5%	7.6%	9.2%	13.0%	NA	NA
4 Excess Return vs. Sector	−3.7%	−5.7%	−1.7%	−1.7%	−2.6%	−4.4%	−3.9%	−0.3%	−0.6%	0.3%	NA	NA
5 Value of $10,000	$54,907	$14,288	$51,731	$28,988	$57,163	$35,688	$64,031	$30,631	$42,223	$111,485	$73,161	$102,895
6 % 1-Year Outperformance	30.0%	30.0%	30.0%	50.0%	35.0%	30.0%	35.0%	60.0%	55.0%	55.0%	NA	NA
7 % 3-Year Outperformance	16.7%	27.8%	27.8%	33.3%	50.0%	11.1%	22.2%	55.6%	50.0%	38.9%	NA	NA
8 Maximum Gain	71.5%	56.6%	56.7%	50.1%	42.1%	85.6%	47.3%	190.3%	191.6%	70.2%	44.0%	41.4%
9 Maximum Loss	−51.7%	−39.3%	−22.1%	−36.3%	−30.1%	−31.7%	−35.4%	−64.1%	−69.3%	−28.5%	−19.1%	−18.1%
10 Standard Deviation	0.31	0.24	0.18	0.25	0.15	0.33	0.21	0.54	0.54	0.22	0.16	0.14
11 Beta (vs. Sector)	1.21	1.45	1.18	1.26	0.91	1.24	0.90	1.42	1.36	1.24	NA	NA
12 Alpha (vs. Sector)	−0.06	−0.02	−0.02	−0.06	0.05	−0.04	0.00	−0.09	−0.05	0.06	NA	NA
13 Portfolio Size	25	31	59	73	22	41	43	58	9	25	NA	NA

* Equal-weighted average of S&P 500 returns.
Source: Standard & Poor's Compustat Point in Time Database, Charter Oak Investment Systems

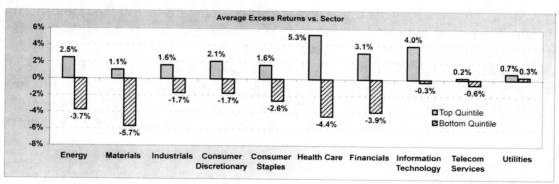

Figure 2.4 Sample Sector Strategy Results Tables and Graph: Return on Invested Capital

The graph in Figure 2.4 simply shows the excess returns, from line 4, for the top and bottom quintiles of each sector. The graph is an easy way to see the overall sector performance of the strategy at a glance.

One note on the sector return calculations: because sector results may be biased due to the varied nature of the industry groups within a sector, we calculate the quintile returns on an "industry group neutral" basis. The individual industry groups are shown above, in the list of sector groups following my discussion of the GICS standard. An industry group neutral test means that we select the companies that form the top and bottom quintiles by industry group and then combine the results from the industry groups to form the sector portfolios. For example, in the GICS health care sector, there are two industry groups: (1) health care equipment & services and (2) pharmaceuticals, biotechnology, and life sciences. Since biotechnology companies have historically had high price-to-sales ratios (the average for our test period was 10× sales), a simple health care sector test for price to sales would likely load the bottom quintile with biotechnology companies. To avoid this bias toward one particular industry group, we use the industry group neutral test.

EPILOGUE: WHY AREN'T WE ALL RICH?

Many of the strategies you will see tested in this book provide excess returns versus our Backtest Universe of over 6%, for top quintiles, and less than –8%, for bottom quintiles. Over the twenty years from January 1988 to December 2007—the test period used in this book—the average annual return for our Backtest Universe was about 14%. If you could earn an average of 20% annually on your stock portfolio (the 14% Universe return plus a 6% excess return from the top quintile of one of the investment strategies presented here), you'd be on your way to retirement and a large yacht in no time. Unfortunately, 20% average annual returns are very hard to achieve over an extended time period.[18]

Although the strategies presented in this book *are* predictive and do offer the investor the potential to achieve above-market returns, there are a couple obstacles to realizing the full excess returns you'll see in the Backtest Summaries. The first and primary obstacle is transaction costs. The costs of buying and selling 30, 50, or more stocks each year can be substantial. These costs include not only brokerage commissions, which the individual can minimize by trading through an Internet-based broker, but also the small "spread" an investor pays when buying or

---

[18] Even the Universe component of this return is high. Stock market studies have shown that, over the long-term, stock investors can expect total returns (price plus dividend) in the range of 11% to 12%.

selling shares.[19] For example, if a stock is listed with a bid of $25 and an asked of $25.25, then the buyer, who must pay the asked price, is paying 12.5 cents above the stock's equilibrium price (which is assumed to be the middle of the spread). This means that the investor loses 0.5% on the purchase, and may also lose another 0.5% on the sale. Although spreads will vary, primarily according to the liquidity of the stock being traded, the transaction costs involved can be significant.

For institutional and other large investors, market price impact, or *slippage,* is often the largest component of transaction costs. Slippage occurs when a money manager seeks to make a large purchase or sale, thereby bumping up the purchase price or pushing down the sale price. Market impact depends a lot on the liquidity of the stock in question and the size of the trade. Professional money managers know the ins and outs of market impact much better than I, and individuals need worry little about market impact for most actively traded securities.

For bottom-quintile strategies, excess returns are also reduced by costs specific to short-selling, including dividend costs (dividends on borrowed shares must be paid to the owner) and margin loan interest charges, if applicable. For institutional portfolios short sales may involve even more substantial costs, and sometimes shares cannot be borrowed at all (this is true also for the individual investor).

Another potential obstacle is the fact that a strategy that worked well in the past may not work as well in the future. In this book, we seek to uncover what I call the *basics,* investment approaches that work year after year, under various economic and market conditions. Basics such as profitability, valuation, and cash flow generation will never go out of style precisely because they *are* basic to what makes a worthwhile investment. However, specific investment strategies can and do go out of style for extended periods or can become over-exploited by market participants. For example, in 1998 through 2000, investors who followed a strategy of buying low P/E stocks—a strategy that has worked well historically—underperformed miserably. From March 1999 through March 2000, this strategy underperformed by a whopping 31%, returning only 3% to the investor (including dividends) during a roaring bull market. Although I fully expect that many of the strategies presented in this book will provides strong excess returns in the future, past results are no *guarantee* of future success (I can see my "compliance officer" smiling with satisfaction at this point).

---

[19] When you buy shares you pay the *asked* price, the lowest price at which a dealer is willing to sell, and when you sell shares you sell at the *bid* price, the highest price at which a dealer or other buyer is willing to buy the shares. The *spread* between the bid and asked price is an important component of transaction costs, and is worse for some stocks than for others. For example, illiquid over the counter stocks usually have a much higher spread than more liquid listed stocks.

Finally, it's worth keeping in mind that the excess returns shown in the tests that follow are averaged over a period of 18 to 20 years. This means that excess returns in any given year may be far from the average. Although the strategies in this book were chosen for their consistency over time, the longer you maintain your discipline and follow a strategy that has proven successful in the past, the greater your chances of achieving strong excess returns in the future.

CHAPTER 3

The Day-to-Day Drivers of Stock Market Returns

In the short term the market is a voting machine, but in the long run it is a weighing machine.

Benjamin Graham, *The Intelligent Investor*

One nonacademic observer noted that Compaq Computer fell 65% between 1991 and 1993, with its price declining from $9 to $3, before soaring to $79 in late 1997. Fundamentals varied little during this time. "When was the market efficient?" he asked. "When it took Compaq down to $3 or drove it up to $79?"

David Dreman, *Contrarian Investment Strategies: The Next Generation*

Most investors would agree that a few basic factors cause stocks to rise, fall, or simply move within a trading range. Earnings growth is foremost among these, as perhaps is cash flow. Profitability would fall within this same category, as would efficient capital utilization. We call these factors *fundamentals* precisely because they are the basic elements that drive stock returns. But equally important over the short run are investors' emotions, perceptions, and beliefs. I'll call these factors—collectively, the social or psychological element within the stock market—*investor sentiment*. Investor sentiment defines how market participants see the prospects for a company or stock, an industry, or the economy: it reflects their *expectations*. However, there is one final link in this investment chain: *valuation*, or the price investors are willing to pay for an asset. In the long run, as Benjamin Graham observed, company fundamentals drive stock market valuations. For example, the long-term earnings growth rate of a company should ultimately determine its price; that is, market price and intrinsic value[1] should be more or less equal. Over the short run, however, which may mean anything from a couple months to several years, valuation is the result of the interplay between fundamentals and investor sentiment; that is, *investors are the arbiters of stock market valuations based on their views of company and industry fundamentals.*[2]

This chapter looks at one set of what I call the basics, the essential factors that drive stock market returns. While the remainder of this book focuses on the basics that *predict* future returns, this chapter focuses on the basics that drive returns in the market from day to day—the news events and changes in investor attitudes that move stock prices. Specifically, it poses this question: if at the beginning of the year, Investor A had perfect knowledge of how each publicly traded company would do fundamentally over the next 12 months, in addition to knowledge of current expectations by other investors[3] (who lack that perfect fundamental knowledge), which investment factors would enable Investor A to pick the best performing stocks for that year? In other words, this chapter takes a *retrospective* look at company and stock market performance to discover the basic elements that drive day-to-day returns. It may not surprise you to learn that these basics fall squarely within the three categories defined above: fundamentals, investor sentiment, and valuation. Just for fun, we'll also take each of the basics and look ahead to the stocks' performance over the following 12 months, to see how they work *prospectively.* We'll see that the answer for some of these factors is that while they work exceedingly well from day to day, they work quite poorly when used to predict the future.

If a factor, such as earnings growth, is not predictive, you might ask, why bother presenting it at all? There are a few reasons. One is that elements such as earnings growth can be very important qualitative factors. Past earnings growth may not predict future returns; therefore, earnings growth may not be a useful factor in quantitative models. However, an investor who reads annual reports, follows industry trends, and evaluates the quality of management can gain a very important edge if he or she can do a better job than other investors at gauging the earnings prospects of a company. On the other hand, it's important for quantitative investors to know that a key stock market driver like earnings growth doesn't work as a predictive factor. And for investors in general, it's important to understand how fundamentals such as earnings growth, investor sentiment,

---

[1] Intrinsic value is often defined as the value of a company's future cash flows, discounted at an appropriate rate to take into account the time value of money and the riskiness of those flows. It can also be defined more simply as the price a well-informed private investor would be willing to pay to buy the company.

[2] Note that while fundamentals act on investor sentiment and investor sentiment determines valuations, valuation can also act on fundamentals, for example, by restricting a company's access to capital.

[3] As reflected in earnings estimates and stock market valuations.

and valuation interact to create the dramatic movements seen in stocks such as Compaq Computer in the 1990s, and almost any other stock on any exchange at any time.

Sometimes, as in the case of Compaq, investor sentiment is the dominant force in driving stock performance; sometimes fundamentals dominate; and at all times valuations reflect the interplay between the reality of a business (its current fundamentals, management, business environment, etc.) and what market participants understand, believe, hope, and fear.

THE METHODOLOGY USED IN THIS CHAPTER

The tests shown in this chapter differ in format from the tests shown in the rest of this book. First, many of the tests shown here calculate portfolio returns over the past 12 months.[4] In the rest of the book, we are only interested in, and only show, returns calculated over the 12 months following portfolio formation, since we are looking for factors that are predictive of future returns.

Second, in this chapter we use a matrix format to present the tests. A sample matrix test for earnings growth by market capitalization is shown in Table 3.1 (for simplicity, the sample matrix divides each of the two factors into thirds—resulting in 9 cells; the

T A B L E   3.1

Sample Matrix: Earnings Per Share Growth by Market Value: EPS Growth Values

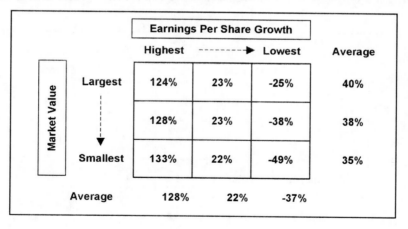

| | Earnings Per Share Growth | | | |
	Highest ------> Lowest			Average
Largest	124%	23%	-25%	40%
	128%	23%	-38%	38%
Smallest	133%	22%	-49%	35%
Average	128%	22%	-37%	

(Market Value, from Largest to Smallest)

---

[4] In other words, we calculate returns for these tests for the 12 months *preceding* the formation of each portfolio. For example, if we calculate earnings growth for a portfolio as of December 2004, we calculate portfolio returns from January to December 2004.

actual matrices you'll see later divide each of the two factors into quintiles—resulting in 25 cells). In our sample matrix, the rows represent different market capitalization groups, from largest to smallest, so market capitalization categories are read from top to bottom. The columns represent different EPS growth groups, from highest to lowest, so EPS growth categories are read from left to right. Finally, the values in each cell represent the average EPS growth for the companies represented by that cell. For example, the top left cell tells us that companies with the highest EPS growth and the largest market capitalizations had EPS growth over the test period of 124%.[5] The bottom left cell tells us that companies with the highest EPS growth and the smallest market capitalization had average EPS growth of 133%. The top right cell shows the value for the largest cap companies with the lowest earnings growth (−25%), and the bottom right cell shows the value for the smallest cap companies with the lowest earnings growth (−49%), and so on. We also provide averages for each row and each column to aid in comparisons.

Table 3.2 also shows the EPS growth by market capitalization matrix. However, here the cells of the matrix show excess stock market returns, instead of actual EPS growth. Specifically, each cell shows the average excess return (versus our Universe) for the stocks of the companies contained in that cell, as determined by the EPS growth and market capitalization categories represented by that cell. For example, the top left cell

T A B L E   3.2

Sample Matrix: Earnings Per Share Growth by Market Value: Excess Returns over the Past 12 Months

Market Value		Earnings Per Share Growth			Average
		Highest ------►		Lowest	
Largest		10%	-8%	-13%	-4%
		15%	-4%	-9%	0%
Smallest		23%	-3%	-10%	3%
Average		16%	-5%	-11%	

---

[5] The test period used for this example is 2003 to 2005. We run each of the actual tests in this chapter quarterly from 1990 to 2007, then average the results.

of the matrix represents those companies with the highest EPS growth and the largest market capitalizations. The value in this cell shows that the stocks of these companies had an average excess return of 10% versus the Universe. Similarly, the bottom left cell shows that the stocks of companies with the highest earnings growth and the smallest market capitalizations had an average excess return of 23%. Before you get too excited about these returns, remember that this matrix is taking a look back in time. In other words, returns are being calculated over the same period in which the actual earnings growth is taking place. In order to get the excess returns shown in Table 3.2, you'd have to be able to predict the future. However, these returns do show clearly that high earnings growth is one major driver of excess stock market returns. The goal of this chapter is to identify these major day-to-day drivers of stock performance.

Table 3.3 shows the third kind of matrix test given in this chapter. This sample shows companies arranged by EPS growth and market capitalization categories. Also, like Table 3.2, this table shows excess returns. However, the excess returns in Table 3.3 look forward over the 12 months following the EPS growth being measured. Like the tests you will see in the rest of this book, this one seeks to determine whether the strategy being tested is predictive. Table 3.3 shows that the largest companies that have experienced the highest EPS growth over the past 12 months (the top left cell) have slightly positive excess returns (2%) over the 12 months following portfolio formation. Likewise, the smallest companies that have had the lowest earnings growth over the past 12 months have slightly negative excess returns (e.g., the –1% value for the bottom right cell). Don't read too much into this test, as it is a sample calculated over only three different periods. However, you'll see

T A B L E   3.3

Sample Matrix: Earnings Per Share Growth by Market Value: Excess Returns 12 Months Forward

Market Value	Earnings Per Share Growth			
	Highest --------▶ Lowest			Average
Largest	2%	0%	0%	1%
	1%	-1%	-1%	-1%
Smallest	0%	1%	-1%	0%
Average	1%	0%	-1%	

later in this chapter that factors that drive the stock market from day to day, such as EPS growth, don't necessarily predict future stock market returns.

EARNINGS GROWTH DRIVES STOCK MARKET RETURNS

Entrepreneurs and investors put their time and money into businesses with the idea of making profits, so it should not be surprising that earnings growth drives stock market returns. Table 3.4 shows the actual EPS growth of companies in our Backtest Universe, arranged according to EPS growth and market capitalization categories. Note that the average range between the highest growers and the lowest growers is over 200%. Also note that small caps have much more variable earnings growth than large caps, with the highest growth small caps averaging 142% EPS growth and the lowest growing small caps averaging 119% EPS declines. We'll see that this volatility in earnings growth results in a similar volatility of excess returns for small caps.

Table 3.5 shows the average annual excess returns (i.e., returns above or below the average return for the Universe) for the same companies presented in Table 3.4. The returns shown in Table 3.5 look backward in time; that is, we look at excess returns for the stocks over the same period that earnings growth is taking place. This table shows that growth in earnings has a strong correlation with excess returns. For example, the companies in the highest earnings growth quintile (column 1) have average excess

TABLE 3.4

Earnings Per Share Growth by Market Capitalization: EPS Growth

Market Value	Earnings Per Share Growth					Average	Range
	Highest --------------------------------▶ Lowest						
Largest	111%	8%	-10%	-26%	-86%	-1%	197%
	126%	13%	-9%	-28%	-97%	1%	223%
	127%	16%	-9%	-29%	-101%	1%	228%
	134%	18%	-9%	-32%	-108%	1%	242%
Smallest	142%	19%	-10%	-36%	-119%	-1%	260%
Average	128%	15%	-10%	-30%	-102%		

Cells contain average EPS growth rates.

Source: Standard & Poor's Compustat Point in Time Database; Charter Oak Investment Systems, Inc., Venues® Data Engine

TABLE 3.5

Earnings Per Share Growth by Market Capitalization: Excess Returns over the Past 12 Months

Market Value		Earnings Per Share Growth					Average	Range
		Highest ----------------------------► Lowest						
	Largest	12%	3%	-6%	-12%	-10%	-3%	23%
		18%	6%	-6%	-10%	-9%	0%	27%
		22%	9%	-3%	-10%	-11%	2%	33%
		23%	11%	-2%	-11%	-10%	2%	33%
	Smallest	20%	10%	-5%	-14%	-14%	-1%	34%
	Average	19%	8%	-4%	-11%	-11%		

Cells contain excess returns for the 12 months PRECEDING portfolio formation.

Source: Standard & Poor's Compustat Point in Time Database; Charter Oak Investment Systems, Inc., Venues® Data Engine

returns of 19%. By contrast, companies in the lowest earnings growth quintiles (columns 4 and 5) have average excess returns of –11%. In addition, note that the magnitude of excess returns, positive or negative, generally increases as we move down the market capitalization scale. For example, while the highest growing, largest cap companies (top left cell) had excess returns of 12%, the highest growing, smallest cap companies (bottom left cell) had excess returns of 20%. Similarly, while the lowest growing, largest cap companies had −10% excess returns, the lowest growing, smallest cap companies had −14% excess returns. We can thus deduce that excess return varies with the level of earnings growth: earnings growth was more variable for small caps, and the excess returns were also more variable. So, what happens if we look at the effect of this year's earnings growth on next year's stock prices?

Table 3.6 shows the average annual excess returns by EPS growth and market capitalization quintiles over the 12 months following the formation of each earnings growth/market cap portfolio. This table shows that past earnings growth is a poor predictor of future returns. Companies with the highest earnings growth show a tendency toward outperformance, and companies with the lowest growth show a tendency toward underperformance, but this tendency is neither large nor consistent. The average excess returns for companies with the highest earnings growth is 1%, while the average excess returns for those with the lowest earnings growth is −1%. This lack of

TABLE 3.6

Earnings Per Share Growth by Market Capitalization: Excess Returns 12 Months Forward

Earnings Per Share Growth						
Highest ---------------------------->				**Lowest**	**Average**	**Range**
Largest 1%	1%	0%	-1%	-2%	0%	3%
4%	1%	0%	0%	0%	1%	5%
3%	0%	0%	-2%	0%	0%	3%
-1%	-1%	0%	0%	-1%	-1%	1%
Smallest -1%	-2%	0%	-1%	1%	0%	-2%
Average 1%	0%	0%	0%	-1%		

Market Value (vertical axis, Largest to Smallest)

Cells contain excess returns for the 12 months FOLLOWING portfolio formation.

Source: Standard & Poor's Compustat Point in Time Database; Charter Oak Investment Systems, Inc., Venues® Data Engine

predictiveness of past earnings growth is likely due to two factors: (1) it is very difficult to sustain a rapid rate of growth for an extended period of time; and (2) stocks with the highest level of historical growth tend to be accorded the highest valuations, so it often takes even higher growth to push the stock price higher. (The same applies in reverse for stocks of companies with the lowest earnings growth.)

SALES GROWTH ALSO DRIVES RETURNS

Earnings growth arises from sales growth. While it is possible to increase earnings by trimming expenses and increasing employee productivity (many of the best managed U.S. corporations seek to continually improve cost efficiency), efficiency improvements alone can only go so far. Thus, the highest quality earnings growth—earnings growth that can be counted on to continue—is linked to sales growth. Table 3.7 shows the actual sales per share growth of companies in our Backtest Universe, arranged according to sales per share growth and market capitalization categories. We'll refer to this table later. For now, just note that sales growth is far less volatile than earnings growth.

Table 3.8 shows the average excess annual returns by sales growth and market capitalization category, calculated over the 12 months prior to portfolio formation. Note that sales growth is a far weaker driver of excess returns than was earnings growth.

TABLE 3.7

Sales Per Share Growth by Market Capitalization: Sales Per Share Growth

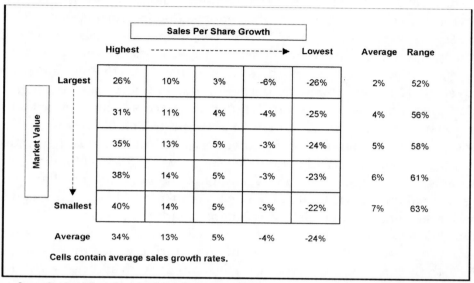

		Sales Per Share Growth					
	Highest	----------------------➤			Lowest	Average	Range
Largest	26%	10%	3%	-6%	-26%	2%	52%
	31%	11%	4%	-4%	-25%	4%	56%
	35%	13%	5%	-3%	-24%	5%	58%
	38%	14%	5%	-3%	-23%	6%	61%
Smallest	40%	14%	5%	-3%	-22%	7%	63%
Average	34%	13%	5%	-4%	-24%		

(Market Value on vertical axis)

Cells contain average sales growth rates.

Source: Standard & Poor's Compustat Point in Time Database; Charter Oak Investment Systems, Inc., Venues® Data Engine

TABLE 3.8

Sales Per Share Growth by Market Capitalization: Excess Returns over the Past 12 Months

		Sales Per Share Growth					
	Highest	----------------------➤			Lowest	Average	Range
Largest	7%	-6%	-7%	-3%	0%	-2%	7%
	12%	-2%	-6%	-4%	0%	0%	12%
	18%	0%	-5%	-4%	-2%	1%	20%
	17%	1%	-2%	-4%	-4%	1%	21%
Smallest	13%	2%	-7%	-6%	-5%	-1%	18%
Average	13%	-1%	-5%	-4%	-2%		

(Market Value on vertical axis)

Cells contain excess returns for the 12 months PRECEDING portfolio formation.

Source: Standard & Poor's Compustat Point in Time Database; Charter Oak Investment Systems, Inc., Venues® Data Engine

For example, while the top sales growth category (column 1) recorded average excess returns of 13%, the top earnings growth category (Table 3.5, column 1) showed average excess returns of 19%. Similarly, while the bottom sales growth category (column 5) shows average excess returns of −2%, the bottom earnings growth category (Table 3.5, column 5) shows excess returns of −11%. The conclusion: while sales growth is important, earnings growth is what counts in driving excess stock market returns.

Table 3.9 shows excess returns by sales per share growth and market cap categories over the 12 months following portfolio formation. Like past earnings growth, past sales growth does a poor job predicting future excess returns. Note that smaller companies with the highest sales growth over the past 12 months (shaded cells) actually underperform the market slightly going forward. This is probably because these smaller companies have very high rates of sales growth (38% to 40%; see Table 3.7)—growth rates that are very difficult to maintain—and because smaller companies have less overall business stability than larger companies. Also note the tendency for negative excess returns to persist for companies with the lowest sales growth rates (column 5). These are companies with average sales declines of 24% (Table 3.7, column 5). The result is that over the 12 months during which those sales declines take place, these companies underperform the market by an average of 2% (Table 3.8,

TABLE 3.9

Sales Per Share Growth by Market Capitalization: Excess Returns 12 Months Forward

	Highest				Lowest	Average	Range
Largest	1%	0%	0%	-2%	-3%	-1%	4%
	2%	2%	1%	1%	-2%	1%	4%
	1%	2%	1%	1%	-2%	0%	3%
	-1%	2%	1%	0%	-3%	0%	2%
Smallest	-3%	1%	1%	1%	-2%	0%	-1%
Average	0%	1%	1%	0%	-3%		

Cells contain excess returns for the 12 months FOLLOWING portfolio formation.

Source: Standard & Poor's Compustat Point in Time Database; Charter Oak Investment Systems, Inc., Venues® Data Engine

column 5), and during the following 12 months these companies underperform by 3% (Table 3.9, column 5). Overall, however, past sales growth is not predictive of future returns.

EARNINGS GROWTH IS THE STRONGER FACTOR

Table 3.10 presents excess returns for the 12 months prior to portfolio formation by sales per share growth and EPS growth categories. It shows that both sales and earnings growth matter, but earnings growth is key. Companies with the highest level of EPS growth but the lowest level of sales growth (three shaded cells in the top right corner) still show positive excess returns, despite the low level of sales growth. Conversely, companies with the highest level of sales growth but the lowest level of earnings growth (three shaded cells in the bottom left corner) showed negative excess returns, despite the high level of sales growth. Also note that the average excess returns for earnings growth quintiles (the table rows) ranged from 15% to –14%, while the average returns for sales growth quintiles (the table columns) ranged only from 5% to –7% (the middle quintile for sales growth actually performed the worst). Clearly, earnings growth is the more significant of the two factors in driving excess returns.

T A B L E   3.10

Sales Per Share Growth by Earnings Per Share Growth: Excess Returns over the Past 12 Months

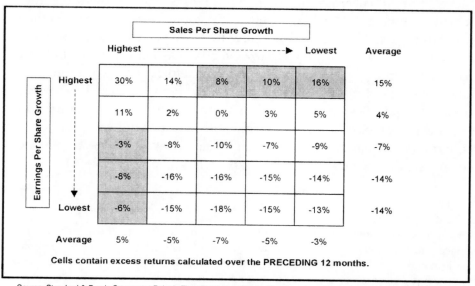

	Highest				Lowest	Average
Highest	30%	14%	8%	10%	16%	15%
	11%	2%	0%	3%	5%	4%
	-3%	-8%	-10%	-7%	-9%	-7%
	-8%	-16%	-16%	-15%	-14%	-14%
Lowest	-6%	-15%	-18%	-15%	-13%	-14%
Average	5%	-5%	-7%	-5%	-3%	

Cells contain excess returns calculated over the PRECEDING 12 months.

Source: Standard & Poor's Compustat Point in Time Database; Charter Oak Investment Systems, Inc., Venues® Data Engine

FREE CASH FLOW GROWTH: THE FIRST PREDICTIVE BASIC

Generally accepted accounting principles in the United States require that the recognition of expenses be matched to the period in which the associated revenues are recognized, whenever it is practical to do so. For example, a company may pay for nails, wood, glue, and labor to make furniture now but not recognize those expenses on the income statement until the furniture has actually been sold. This is called *accrual accounting*, because expenses are accrued on the balance sheet but not charged to income until the related revenues are recognized.[6] Because of the inherent timing difference between *cash basis* accounting and accrual basis accounting, and because of the greater potential for accounting sleight of hand with accrual basis accounting, investors also look at a company's cash flow to determine its profitability. Operating cash flow for a period shows the actual cash inflows and outflows that occurred during the period and were related to operating activities. Although operating cash flow is more volatile than accounting earnings, it is also harder to fake.

Cash flow from operating activities less cash needed to maintain and expand plant and equipment (capital expenditures) is referred to as *free cash flow*, since this amount represents cash available to pay dividends, expand the business, repurchase shares, and so on. Growth in free cash flow is a key indicator looked at by many investors to gauge the underlying profitability of a corporation.

Table 3.11 presents excess returns by free cash flow per share growth and EPS growth categories over the 12 months prior to portfolio formation. It shows that free cash flow growth also exerts a significant influence over stock market returns. Companies with the highest levels of both earnings and free cash flow per share growth recorded average excess returns as high as 30% (shaded cells in the top left corner), while companies with the lowest earnings and free cash flow growth recorded excess returns as low as –17% (shaded cells in the lower right corner). However, free cash flow growth, like sales growth, is subordinate to earnings growth in driving excess returns. While average excess returns for earnings growth quintiles (the table rows) range from 18% to –10%, average returns for free cash flow quintiles (the table columns) range only from 6% to –6%. On the other hand, the linearity of excess returns for the table columns indicates that free cash flow growth is a more independent variable than is sales growth when compared to earnings growth (compare the column averages of Table 3.11 to those of Table 3.10).

---

[6] Accrual accounting also affects revenue recognition. Revenues are generally recognized when earned—when services are rendered or goods are sold and delivered—and not necessarily when cash is received. For example, companies that receive upfront payments for long-term subscriptions often book part of the subscription payments received on the balance sheet as deferred revenue, which is not recognized on the income statement until the period when delivery is deemed to have taken place.

TABLE 3.11

Free Cash Flow Per Share Growth by Earnings Per Share Growth: Excess Returns over the Past 12 Months

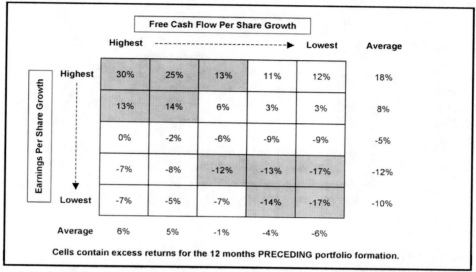

| | Free Cash Flow Per Share Growth | | | | | |
	Highest ----------------------------► Lowest					Average
Highest	30%	25%	13%	11%	12%	18%
	13%	14%	6%	3%	3%	8%
	0%	-2%	-6%	-9%	-9%	-5%
	-7%	-8%	-12%	-13%	-17%	-12%
Lowest	-7%	-5%	-7%	-14%	-17%	-10%
Average	6%	5%	-1%	-4%	-6%	

(Earnings Per Share Growth, vertical axis)

Cells contain excess returns for the 12 months PRECEDING portfolio formation.

Source: Standard & Poor's Compustat Point in Time Database; Charter Oak Investment Systems, Inc., Venues® Data Engine

However, free cash flow growth has one quality that earnings growth and sales growth do not: it is predictive of future returns. Table 3.12 shows excess returns by free cash flow per share and EPS growth categories, calculated over the 12 months following portfolio formation. Companies that had the highest free cash flow growth over the past 12 months (column 1) consistently outperform over the next 12 months, by an average of 2%. On the other hand, companies that had the lowest free cash flow growth over the past 12 months (column 5) underperform over the next 12 months, by an average of 3%. Why should free cash flow growth predict future stock market returns, while EPS growth alone does not? Most likely because free cash flow is less of a "marquee" number than earnings, and therefore less likely to be discounted immediately in the stock price. In other words, the stock market is less efficient when it comes to discounting free cash flow growth than it is with regard to earnings or sales growth. Investors—qualitative and quantitative alike—can use this fact to their advantage, as we'll see in Chapter 6.

EARNINGS SURPRISES SIGNAL CHANGES IN INVESTOR SENTIMENT

When a company's earnings come in above or below the average earnings estimate of Wall Street brokerage firm analysts, we say that the company has recorded a positive or negative "earnings surprise." A positive surprise means the company has performed

T A B L E   3.12

Free Cash Flow Per Share Growth by Earnings Per Share Growth: Excess Returns 12 Months Forward

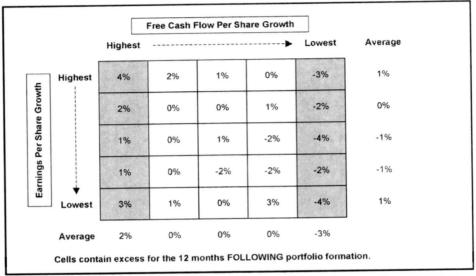

	Free Cash Flow Per Share Growth					
	Highest	--------------------------→			Lowest	Average
Highest	4%	2%	1%	0%	-3%	1%
	2%	0%	0%	1%	-2%	0%
	1%	0%	1%	-2%	-4%	-1%
	1%	0%	-2%	-2%	-2%	-1%
Lowest	3%	1%	0%	3%	-4%	1%
Average	2%	0%	0%	0%	-3%	

(Left axis label: Earnings Per Share Growth)

Cells contain excess for the 12 months FOLLOWING portfolio formation.

Source: Standard & Poor's Compustat Point in Time Database; Charter Oak Investment Systems, Inc., Venues® Data Engine

better than the average analyst estimate, while a negative surprise means it has fallen short. Because earnings estimates, which are widely followed, indicate how Wall Street professionals expect a company to perform, these estimates serve as a gauge of *investor sentiment*. As we'll see, changes in investor sentiment are another important driver of stock market performance.

Table 3.13 shows average annual earnings surprise values sorted by the level of the earnings surprise and by market capitalization. To calculate the earnings surprise, we took the average of Wall Street analysts' estimates at the beginning of the year and compared that to the actual earnings recorded by the company at the end of the year. Surprises of greater than 200% and less than −200% have been excluded (often these consist of, for example, a company that had an average earnings estimate of a penny and proceeded to earn three or four cents or to lose two or three cents—a surprise that is perhaps not as significant as a company with an average estimate of $2.00 that actually earns $2.50).

Note that, like earnings growth, earnings surprises are much more volatile for smaller cap companies than for larger caps. The earnings surprise range for the largest cap companies (row 1) is only 66%, while the earnings surprise range for the smallest companies (row 5) is 116%. Note that smaller cap stocks tend to have much higher negative than positive surprises, resulting in high negative average figures for rows

TABLE 3.13

Annual Earnings Surprise by Market Value: Earnings Surprise Values

		Annual EPS Surprise					
	Highest	- -▶			**Lowest**	**Average**	**Range**
Largest	31%	6%	0%	-6%	-35%	-1%	66%
	39%	7%	0%	-10%	-48%	-3%	87%
	41%	8%	0%	-11%	-53%	-3%	93%
	44%	8%	-2%	-15%	-61%	-5%	104%
Smallest	45%	7%	-4%	-20%	-71%	-9%	116%
Average	40%	7%	-1%	-12%	-54%		

(Market Value — vertical axis label, Largest to Smallest)

Cells contain average earnings surprise percentages.

Source: Thomson Reuters I/B/E/S Estimates; Standard & Poor's Compustat Point in Time Database; Charter Oak Investment Systems, Inc., Venues® Data Engine

4 (−5%) and 5 (−9%). A few factors may come into play here. First, smaller companies have much more volatile earnings than larger peers. Second, smaller companies tend to have less analyst coverage than larger companies; hence the average earnings estimate may be less accurate. Finally, a bump in the road, whether a production line hiccup, increased competition, or an industry slump, will usually hurt a smaller company much worse than a larger and more diversified one.

Table 3.14 shows the average excess returns by earnings surprise for the 12 months prior to portfolio formation, for different market cap groups. This table shows that earnings surprises are an important driver of day to day stock market returns. Companies in the top quintile by earnings surprise (column 1) generated average excess returns of 15%, while those in the bottom quintile (column 5) generated excess returns of −3%. Note that companies in the third quintile had excess returns of −7%. These are the same companies in Table 3.13 that had average earnings surprises of just −1%. The conclusion that can be drawn here is that merely meeting analyst estimates, or missing them slightly, is a disappointment—investors expect companies to beat analyst estimates, and when companies do not, their stocks underperform.

It might seem inconsistent that companies in the bottom quintile by earnings surprise (column 5) underperform less (by 3%) than the companies in quintiles 3 and 4

TABLE 3.14

Annual Earnings Surprise by Market Value: Excess Returns over the Past 12 Months

		Annual EPS Surprise					Average	Range
	Highest	-----	-----	-----▶	Lowest			
Largest	16%	-1%	-8%	-8%	-4%		-1%	21%
	18%	0%	-5%	-7%	-2%		1%	21%
	16%	1%	-6%	-8%	1%		1%	16%
	16%	2%	-6%	-8%	0%		1%	15%
Smallest	10%	-2%	-10%	-13%	-9%		-5%	20%
Average	15%	0%	-7%	-9%	-3%			

Market Value (vertical axis label, Largest → Smallest)

Cells contain excess returns for the 12 months PRECEEDING portfolio formation.

Source: Thomson Reuters I/B/E/S Estimates; Standard & Poor's Compustat Point in Time Database; Charter Oak Investment Systems, Inc., Venues® Data Engine

(columns 3 and 4, which underperform by 7% and 9%, respectively). After all, the companies in column 5 had average earnings surprises of −54% (Table 3.13), while those in columns 3 and 4 had average surprises of −1% and −12%, respectively. Upon examining the data, however, the reason becomes clear. The companies with the highest negative earnings surprises (those in column 5) significantly outperform the market during three periods: 1991, 1999, and 2003. During these three periods excess returns are very high. Two of these periods—1991 and 2003—represent the early stages of bull markets. When a bear market bottoms and a new bull market begins, stocks of low-profitability companies that have missed earnings expectations and have been unduly depressed in price are quickly bid up, in anticipation of an economic recovery. These same low-quality stocks are bid up during speculative tops in bull markets, such as in 1999. Throughout this book, you'll note that a number of strategies do not work during these three periods.

Table 3.15 shows excess returns by annual earnings surprise and market capitalization categories for the 12 months following portfolio formation. This table was calculated by subtracting end-of-fiscal-year earnings estimates from companies' actual end-of-fiscal-year results. Thus, the earnings surprise groupings in this table are based on fourth-quarter surprises, not the annual earnings surprises used in the prior two tables (we do this because we are looking forward, and three quarters of the previous

T A B L E   3.15

Earnings Surprise by Market Value: Excess Returns 12 Months Forward

		Earnings Surprise						
	Highest	---------------------------->			Lowest	Average	Range
Largest	0%	-1%	-2%	0%	-2%	-1%	2%
	1%	1%	0%	2%	-1%	1%	2%
	1%	-1%	-1%	1%	0%	0%	1%
	0%	-1%	-1%	-1%	0%	-1%	1%
Smallest	1%	-1%	1%	0%	0%	0%	1%
Average	1%	0%	0%	0%	-1%		

(left axis label: Market Value)

Cells contain excess returns for the 12 months FOLLOWING portfolio formation.

Source: Thomson Reuters I/B/E/S Estimates; Standard & Poor's Compustat Point in Time Database; Charter Oak Investment Systems, Inc., Venues® Data Engine

year have already been reported and can no longer be considered "surprises"). Unfortunately, the table shows that earnings surprises do not significantly or consistently predict future returns. Our research shows that, although earnings surprises have been predictive in the past, their predictive power has gradually eroded in recent years.

EARNINGS GROWTH AND INVESTOR SENTIMENT

Table 3.16 shows excess returns for earnings growth by earnings surprise quintiles over the 12 months preceding portfolio formation. The table shows that, although earnings surprises matter, earnings growth is the stronger driver of excess returns. The three shaded cells in the top left corner show that companies that have both high EPS growth and high annual EPS surprises outperform strongly. The five shaded cells at the bottom right show that companies that have both low EPS growth and low earnings surprises underperform significantly. However, the column and row averages show that earnings growth is the stronger factor. While the highest EPS growth quintile (column 1) outperforms by an average of 13%, the highest EPS surprise quintile (row 1) outperforms by 8%. Also, while the lowest EPS growth quintile (column 5) underperforms by 9%, the lowest EPS surprise quintile (row 5) actually outperforms.

TABLE 3.16

EPS Growth by Annual Earnings Surprise: Excess Returns over the Past 12 Months

| | EPS Growth | | | | | | |
	Highest	------------------------------►		Lowest	Average	Range
Highest	27%	13%	2%	-2%	2%	8%	25%
	10%	6%	-2%	-8%	-7%	0%	17%
Annual EPS Surprise	8%	1%	-5%	-12%	-14%	-4%	22%
	5%	2%	-6%	-12%	-15%	-5%	20%
Lowest	14%	8%	6%	-6%	-12%	2%	26%
Average	13%	6%	-1%	-8%	-9%		

Cells contian excess returns for the 12 months PRECEEDING portfolio formation.

Source: Thomson Reuters I/B/E/S Estimates; Standard & Poor's Compustat Point in Time Database; Charter Oak Investment Systems, Inc., Venues® Data Engine

This brings us to the shaded cell in the bottom left-hand corner. This cell contains those companies that have the lowest EPS surprises and the highest EPS growth. The companies represented here generally have high earnings growth from a low or negative base but have recently missed expectations. These are the same low-quality companies that outperformed in the early stages of bull markets (1991 and 2003) and at speculative market tops (1999).

Valuation Is the Strongest Measure of Investor Sentiment

Table 3.17 shows excess returns for EPS growth and forward price-to-earnings (P/E) ratio[7] categories for the 12 months preceding portfolio formation. P/E ratios are taken at the beginning of the year, while earnings growth is calculated at the end of the year. Returns are calculated over the course of the year. There is a lot to be learned from this table.

This table shows the highest levels of excess returns, both positive and negative, we've seen yet. The six shaded cells at the top right show excess returns that range from

---

[7] Forward P/E ratio is calculated as current price divided by the average analysts' earnings estimate for the current year.

TABLE 3.17

Forward P/E Ratio by Earnings Per Share Growth: Excess Returns over the Past 12 Months

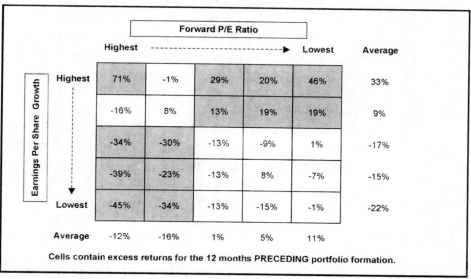

Source: Standard & Poor's Compustat Point in Time Database; Charter Oak Investment Systems, Inc., Venues® Data Engine

13% to 46%. These six cells contain companies with the lowest forward P/E ratios at the beginning of the year that went on to record the highest levels of earnings growth during the year. These companies not only recorded strong earnings growth, they also beat investor expectations. Companies with the lowest expectations, as measured by their forward P/E ratios, and the highest earnings growth at the end of the year record huge (46%) excess returns (top right cell).

Note that because the P/E ratio used here is based on analyst earnings estimates for the year, this test also incorporates earnings surprises, since companies with the lowest valuations at the beginning of the year and the highest earnings growth during the year are likely to have beat earnings estimates, while companies with the highest valuations at the beginning of the year and the lowest levels of earnings growth are likely to have missed earnings estimates. However, valuation and not earnings surprise is the stronger measure of investor sentiment.

The six shaded cells at the bottom left contain companies with the highest P/E ratios at the beginning of the year that went on to record the lowest levels of earnings growth during the year. The companies represented by these cells underperform by an average of 23% to 45%. These companies not only recorded low growth, they also significantly missed investor expectations. Companies with the highest forward P/E ratios at the beginning of the year that subsequently go on to record the lowest levels of earnings growth (bottom left cell) underperform by an average of 45%—the highest underperformance we've seen so far.

Another important takeaway from this table is that while earnings growth is the stronger factor in driving outperformance of a stock, valuation is the stronger factor in driving underperformance. This is shown by the shaded cells: the six shaded cells with the highest positive returns are all located in the top two earnings growth quintiles (rows 1 and 2), while the six cells with the highest negative returns are located in the top two valuation quintiles (columns 1 and 2). This means that if earnings growth is high, a moderately high P/E ratio can be overcome (resulting in outperformance), but if valuations are too high, moderate EPS growth is not enough to prevent underperformance.

Notice that although the excess returns shown in this matrix are not perfectly symmetrical, they form a very clear pattern. This pattern is a sign that the factors being measured here have a high correlation with stock market returns.

The results of this test show that valuation provides the best gauge of investor sentiment (not earnings surprises), and earnings growth provides the best measure of fundamentals in driving day-to-day stock market performance.

Finally, the top left cell in Table 3.17 (shaded) appears to be an anomaly. It represents companies with the highest earnings growth during the year and the highest forward P/E ratios at the beginning of the year. You might think that the stocks of these companies would be fully valued, so that excess returns would be modest, at best. This point of view would be a mistake. The group of stocks in this portfolio reads like a list of great growth stories: Nike in 1990–1991, Western Digital (hard disk drives) in 1993–1994, Allstate in 1995–1996, Valero Energy (numerous years), Hovnanian Enterprises during the housing boom of 2003–2004, and AK Steel during the commodities boom in 2006–2007. Although these companies were expensive, they delivered great earnings growth, and valuations increased even further in many cases.[8] Although the returns generated by these high-octane growth companies may seem enticing, identifying them is likely to be very difficult. All of the portfolios for this cell put together (from 1990 through 2007) contain only 70 individual companies, a very small fraction of the companies in our Universe over the same span.

---

[8] Note that the 71% average excess return is influenced by Emulex, which had extraordinary returns in the late 1990s. However, even after subtracting Emulex, average returns for the group remain very high. (Emulex adds about 13% to the average, so the excess return without Emulex would be 58%, still the highest excess return in this table.)

SUMMARY

- Earnings growth is the primary driver of day-to-day stock market returns. Companies that generate high earnings growth outperform, while companies that record low levels of growth underperform. Sales growth is a secondary factor.

- Earnings growth is *not* predictive of future stock market returns. That is, the market is very efficient in pricing in changes in earnings growth as they are reported.

- Free cash flow growth is also a significant factor in driving stock market returns. Free cash flow growth is not nearly as strong a factor as earnings growth, but it appears to be somewhat independent from earnings in driving returns.

- Unlike earnings growth, free cash flow growth *is* predictive. That is, the market appears less efficient in discounting changes in free cash flow growth than it is in discounting earnings growth. (Therefore, free cash flow growth is the first *basic* that could be used to form a forward-looking quantitative test.)

- The stock market isn't driven wholly by fundamentals, however. The thoughts, hopes, beliefs, and fears of investors—what we call *investor sentiment*—also drive market returns. The interaction between fundamentals and investor sentiment determines a stock's price.

- Wall Street analysts' earnings estimates reflect investor expectations. Positive earnings surprises (earnings reports that beat average analyst estimates) cause stocks to outperform, on a day-to-day basis, while negative earnings surprises (earnings that come in below estimates) cause stocks to underperform.

- In terms of predictive power, however, our research shows that earnings surprises were predictive of excess returns in the past but seem to have lost that predictive power in recent years.

- A stock's valuation, in terms of its P/E ratio, reflects investor sentiment and is a strong factor in driving day-to-day stock market returns. Low valuation stocks of companies that perform better than expected, in terms of earnings growth, outperform significantly, and high valuation stocks of companies that perform worse than expected underperform significantly. (We will see later that valuation is a predictive factor.)

- While earnings growth is the strongest fundamental driver of returns, valuation (as measured here by the price-to-forward earnings estimate ratio) is the strongest investor sentiment–related driver of returns.

CHAPTER 4

Profitability

The quality and quantity of resources existing in a business and the long-term wealth-creation potentials of a business are each consequential factors in value investing, and each factor is related integrally to the other. If future wealth creation, in the form of increased operating profits, increased cash flows, or enhanced underlying takeover values, cannot be created out of the present existence of high-quality assets and high-quantity assets, then either those assets never existed in the first place or what assets did exist were mismanaged.

Martin Whitman, *Value Investing: A Balanced Approach*

Benjamin Graham's investment credo was to buy assets at a discount. [George] Michaelis suggests a variation: *Earning power is as valuable as assets, therefore try to buy earning power at a discount.* If appropriate, Michaelis is prepared to pay up for the assets in a business if the earning power is exceptional.

John Train, *The New Money Masters*

A note before we begin. Chapter 3 looked at the primary day-to-day drivers of stock market performance. That is, it looked backward, and in so doing showed the excess returns available to the investor who has some ability to predict the future. The tests you will see in this chapter—and in all subsequent chapters in this book—look forward. They show the returns that can be achieved by an investor who relies solely on historical data to form portfolios and then holds those portfolios for 12 months into the future. In other words, the strategies presented in this and succeeding chapters are all predictive *of future excess returns.*

A common format will be used throughout each of the next seven chapters, which cover the seven basics presented in this book: profitability, valuation, cash flow, growth, capital allocation, price momentum, and red flags. In each chapter, you will see a number of single factor tests—I call these building blocks. *Each single-factor test will be followed by a sector test that shows how that particular building block works across different industries. Finally, each single-factor test will be followed by one or more two-factor tests. These two-factor tests will often include second factors that aren't introduced as single-factor tests until later chapters. The purpose of the two-factor tests is to show how a given building block combines with other investment strategies. Also, note that the tests presented in the next seven chapters all work well—that is, only the most predictive tests have been presented to the reader. With very few exceptions, tests that don't work well or show only mediocre returns have been omitted.*

Although profitability is a basic requirement of any business venture—businesses, after all, are started by entrepreneurs with the goal of making money—most business ventures are not immediately profitable. Entrepreneurs are often willing to sacrifice current income to realize future gains, particularly if such gains promise to be substantial and to compensate owners for the risk entailed in contributing capital to a currently unprofitable business. However, if profitability is not ultimately reached, or if profits do not sufficiently compensate investors for risk-capital invested, the business venture has failed. For this reason, I chose to focus on profitability first out of the seven key factors that our testing has shown drive future stock market returns.

Profitability can be measured in a variety of ways, from profit margins to return on equity and assets, to broader measures that include not only the expenses of the business but also the opportunity cost and risk of the contributed capital (if a relatively risk-free investment can return 5%, why put your money in a risky venture at 6%?). In this chapter, we'll look at a variety of profitability measures, to determine which work best from a quantitative standpoint. The good news is that profitability tests work. Although past performance is no guarantee of future results, as legal compliance personnel in any respectable Wall Street firm would have you understand, *past profitability does serve as a barometer reading of a company's potential for future success.* One reason for this is that profitability serves as an indicator of the results that can be expected if current and future profits are reinvested in the business (i.e., current profitability is a predictor of the potential for future profit growth).

Profitability measures we tested include return on invested capital (ROIC), return on capital employed (a different ratio than ROIC), return on equity, return on assets, profit margins, income per employee, economic profits, incremental return on capital, and a few other specialized ratios. From a quantitative standpoint, some of these measures provided strong results, and some didn't.[1] As a group, however, profitability strategies work well quantitatively, with significant outperformance for the top quintile (the most profitable companies), significant underperformance for the bottom (the least profitable), good linearity of returns among quintiles (meaning quintile returns occurred in descending order with the highest return in the first quintile, the next highest in the second, etc.), and strong consistency of outperformance/underperformance over time for the top and bottom quintiles. In a word, profitability should be viewed as an important combining factor in constructing a quantitative test or stock screen. As you will see in this chapter, combining profitability and valuation is an especially strong strategy; it reflects a basic principle of sound investment that has been true for centuries—investors should seek to own business ventures that generate ample profits, purchased at a discount to their intrinsic, or "fair," value.

RETURN ON INVESTED CAPITAL

A favorite profitability measure within Standard & Poor's Equity Research, as well as many other financial firms, is return on invested capital. The formula used by the equity analysts at S&P is shown in Figure 4.1. The analyst first calculates net operating profit after tax (NOPAT). This consists of operating profit minus special items and cash operating taxes (see the definition for cash operating taxes below—their purpose is to approximate the tax that would be due on operating income only). Next, the analyst calculates invested capital, which is equal to the book value of common equity plus long-term debt, plus preferred stock and minority interest. ROIC is simply NOPAT divided by invested capital.

Return on invested capital can be defined in a number of ways, and, as you will see later in this chapter, most of them work. The main advantage of ROIC as a measure of profitability is that it compares income to the total investment in a firm—investments made both by owners (equity investments) and creditors (debt investments). Thus, ROIC provides a good overall picture of a company's level of profitability.

ROIC works well as a single-factor strategy. The top quintile outperforms by 2.3%, on average, and does so for 69% of one-year and 78% of rolling three-year periods (see Figure 4.2). The maximum loss is a low 19%, and the maximum loss is linear,

---

[1] Profitability measures that didn't provide strong quantitative results included return on capital employed (ROCE), profit margins, return on assets, and income per employee. This is not to say that these measures are not valid or are not useful to the analyst/investor, just that they are not predictive from a quantitative point of view.

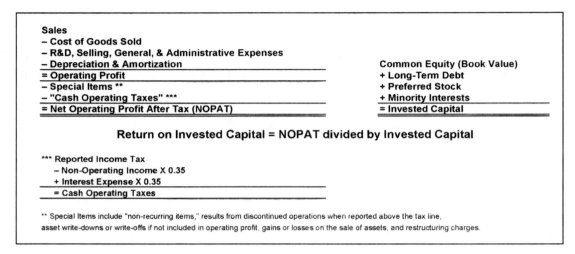

Figure 4.1 Return on Invested Capital Calculation

meaning that the loss increases as one moves down the quintiles. Average portfolio values for ROIC for the top quintile range from 25% to over 50%, indicating that companies in this quintile are highly profitable. The top quintile works very well in bear markets: in 1990 the top quintile outperformed by 10% (with 181 out of 300 companies outperforming the Universe), and in 2000 through 2002 it outperformed by an average of 8% (with winners significantly outnumbering losers). Note that companies in the top quintile tend to be large caps, with an average market capitalization of $7 billion.[2]

The bottom quintile underperforms by a strong 4.3%, on average, and does so for 74% of one-year and 90% of rolling three-year periods. Average portfolio values for ROIC range from −2% to less than −30%, indicating that these companies had significant operating losses after tax.

Return on Invested Capital by Economic Sector

The ROIC strategy is very consistent among economic sectors, as well (see Figure 4.3), with significant outperformance of the top quintile and underperformance of the bottom quintile in all sectors except telecom services and utilities. It is particularly strong for health care, energy, industrials, and financials. (For banks and other financials,

---

[2] Keep in mind throughout this book that the average market cap figure does not take into account the effects of inflation. For example, although the average overall market cap for the top quintile of ROIC is $7 billion, average market caps in 2005 through 2007 were $10 billion to $11 billion.

1988 ~ 2007	1st Quintile	2nd Quintile	3rd Quintile	4th Quintile	5th Quintile	Universe	S&P 500*
CAGR – Annual Rebalance	13.7%	12.7%	12.5%	10.9%	5.0%	11.2%	12.9%
Average Excess Return vs. Universe**	2.3%	1.5%	0.6%	0.1%	-4.3%	NA	1.6%
Value of $10,000 Invested (20 Years)	$130,702	$109,898	$106,248	$79,057	$26,442	$83,161	$112,895
% of 1-Year Periods Strategy Outperforms the Universe	68.8%	51.9%	57.1%	53.2%	26.0%	NA	59.7%
% Rolling 3-Year Periods Strategy Outperforms	78.3%	66.7%	65.2%	44.9%	10.1%	NA	71.0%
Maximum Gain	51.6%	54.2%	50.5%	56.2%	87.2%	59.2%	54.1%
Maximum Loss	-18.9%	-20.3%	-23.2%	-29.7%	-67.0%	-24.9%	-25.9%
Sharpe Ratio	0.69	0.67	0.63	0.54	0.13	0.49	0.69
Standard Deviation of Returns	0.15	0.14	0.14	0.15	0.29	0.16	0.14
Beta (vs. Universe)	0.87	0.82	0.77	0.86	1.54	NA	0.78
Alpha (vs. Universe)	0.04	0.04	0.04	0.02	-0.11	NA	0.04
Average Portfolio Size	376	376	376	376	377	NA	NA
Average Number of Companies *Outperforming*	171	172	168	164	137	NA	NA
Average Number of Companies *Underperforming*	191	188	190	191	216	NA	NA
Median Portfolio Value – Return on Invested Capital	27.9%	13.8%	9.9%	6.3%	-13.3%	9.4%	11.4%
Average Market Capitalization	$6,939	$4,773	$4,555	$3,474	$2,076	NA	NA

* Equal-weighted average of S&P 500 returns. ** Annual holding period run quarterly for a larger sample size; arithmetic average excess returns.
Source: Standard & Poor's Compustat Point in Time Database, Charter Oak Investment Systems, Inc., Venues® Data Engine

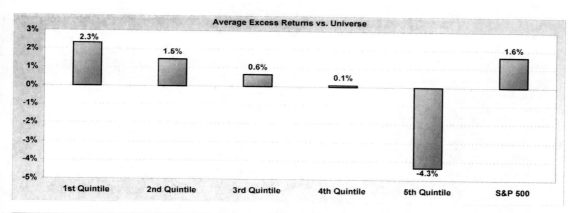

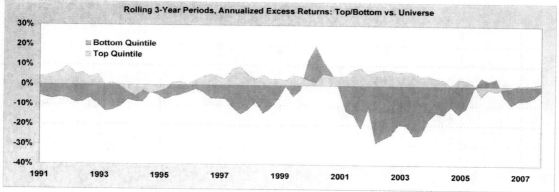

Figure 4.2 Return on Invested Capital

Top Quintile

1988 ~ 2007	Energy	Materials	Industrials	Consumer Discretionary	Consumer Staples	Health Care	Financials	Information Technology	Telecom Services	Utilities	Universe	S&P 500*
CAGR – Quintile	16.0%	11.3%	12.9%	10.8%	14.2%	17.6%	17.6%	11.5%	9.4%	13.7%	11.2%	12.9%
CAGR – Sector	13.5%	10.2%	11.2%	8.8%	12.6%	12.3%	14.5%	7.6%	9.2%	13.0%	NA	NA
Excess Return vs. Sector	2.5%	1.1%	1.6%	2.1%	1.6%	5.3%	3.1%	4.0%	0.2%	0.7%	NA	NA
Value of $10,000	$194,653	$84,434	$112,256	$78,406	$143,205	$257,720	$254,523	$88,896	$60,702	$130,417	$83,161	$112,895
% 1-Year Outperformance	65.0%	50.0%	75.0%	55.0%	50.0%	70.0%	65.0%	75.0%	60.0%	60.0%	NA	NA
% 3-Year Outperformance	66.7%	66.7%	83.3%	72.2%	55.6%	77.8%	66.7%	77.8%	61.1%	72.2%	NA	NA
Maximum Gain	64.1%	40.6%	45.0%	55.7%	72.7%	70.0%	83.8%	85.7%	42.0%	53.6%	44.0%	41.4%
Maximum Loss	−54.6%	−13.3%	−11.5%	−15.5%	−15.2%	−12.0%	−16.8%	−34.1%	−39.6%	−13.0%	−19.1%	−18.1%
Standard Deviation	0.27	0.14	0.14	0.17	0.21	0.23	0.24	0.28	0.23	0.17	0.16	0.14
Beta (vs. Sector)	0.97	0.79	0.93	0.86	1.24	0.83	˙.03	0.69	0.38	1.02	NA	NA
Alpha (vs. Sector)	0.04	0.03	0.02	0.03	−0.01	0.07	0.03	0.06	0.06	0.01	NA	NA
Portfolio Size	24	31	57	69	20	40	40	58	9	25	NA	NA

Bottom Quintile

1988 ~ 2007	Energy	Materials	Industrials	Consumer Discretionary	Consumer Staples	Health Care	Financials	Information Technology	Telecom Services	Utilities	Universe	S&P 500*
CAGR – Quintile	9.8%	4.5%	9.5%	7.0%	10.0%	7.9%	10.5%	7.3%	8.6%	13.3%	11.2%	12.9%
CAGR – Sector	13.5%	10.2%	11.2%	8.8%	12.6%	12.3%	14.5%	7.6%	9.2%	13.0%	NA	NA
Excess Return vs. Sector	−3.7%	−5.7%	−1.7%	−1.7%	−2.6%	−4.4%	−3.9%	−0.3%	−0.6%	0.3%	NA	NA
Value of $10,000	$64,907	$24,288	$61,731	$38,988	$67,163	$45,688	$74,031	$40,631	$52,223	$121,485	$83,161	$112,895
% 1-Year Outperformance	30.0%	30.0%	30.0%	50.0%	35.0%	30.0%	35.0%	60.0%	55.0%	55.0%	NA	NA
% 3-Year Outperformance	16.7%	27.8%	27.8%	33.3%	50.0%	11.1%	22.2%	55.6%	50.0%	38.9%	NA	NA
Maximum Gain	71.5%	56.6%	56.7%	50.1%	42.1%	85.6%	47.3%	190.3%	191.6%	70.2%	44.0%	41.4%
Maximum Loss	−51.7%	−39.3%	−22.1%	−36.3%	−30.1%	−31.7%	−35.4%	−64.1%	−69.3%	−28.5%	−19.1%	−18.1%
Standard Deviation	0.31	0.24	0.18	0.25	0.15	0.33	0.21	0.54	0.54	0.22	0.16	0.14
Beta (vs. Sector)	1.21	1.45	1.18	1.26	0.91	1.24	0.90	1.42	1.36	1.24	NA	NA
Alpha (vs. Sector)	−0.06	−0.02	−0.02	−0.06	0.05	−0.04	0.00	−0.09	−0.05	0.06	NA	NA
Portfolio Size	25	31	59	73	22	41	43	58	9	25	NA	NA

* Equal-weighted average of S&P 500 returns.
Source: Standard & Poor's Compustat Point in Time Database, Charter Oak Investment Systems

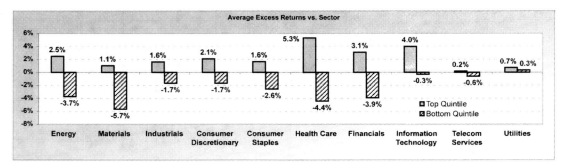

Figure 4.3 Return on Invested Capital by Economic Sector

operating income consists of net interest income minus provision for loan losses, plus noninterest income minus noninterest expenses.)[3]

Return on Invested Capital and Price to Sales

This test combines valuation with profitability, a strong combination. The top quintile of this strategy produces a portfolio of highly profitable companies whose stocks are available at low prices relative to sales levels. (Recall that in two-factor tests, we first choose the top quintile—the top 20%—by the first factor. From this group, we then choose the top quintile, in this case the lowest valuation, for the next factor. So, we choose the top quintile in this strategy by ROIC, then from this group we select the lowest 20% by price to sales. In other words, the test emphasizes ROIC.)

The top quintile outperforms by 5.9%, on average, and does so for 70% of one-year and 83% of rolling three-year periods (see Figure 4.4). The Sharpe ratio improves significantly from 0.69 for the ROIC single-factor strategy to 0.78 for this test. The strategy failed completely in 1999, with the top quintile underperforming by 16% and the bottom portfolio outperforming by 122%;[4] although this is undesirable, it doesn't at all invalidate the strategy. Average portfolio values range from 24% to over 30% for ROIC and from 0.3× to 0.6× for price to sales.

The bottom quintile underperforms by 8.2%, on average, and does so for 73% of one-year and 91% of rolling three-year periods. The bottom quintile is extremely volatile, however, with a standard deviation of returns of 0.41 versus 0.16 for the Universe, and a Beta of 1.8. The bottom quintile has underperformed consistently in recent years, with the exception of 2003 (coming out of the prior bear market, where high-valuation "junk" stocks that had been oversold rallied strongly). Average portfolio values range from −14% to less than −60% for ROIC and from 7× to well over 40× for price to sales.

Return on Invested Capital and Cash Return on Invested Capital

We'll look at cash return on invested capital in greater depth in Chapter 6. However, the basic difference between ROIC and cash ROIC is that the cash version is based on a company's statement of cash flows, which shows cash receipts and disbursements, while the

---

[3] Noninterest expenses include salaries, occupancy, equipment expense, depreciation, and other. Special items are also subtracted.

[4] The average price-to-sales (P/S) ratio of the bottom quintile in 1999 was 220×, while the average return on invested capital ratio was −67%, the lowest ever seen for this quintile. Meanwhile, the top quintile had an average P/S ratio in 1999 of 0.6× and average ROIC of 25%. The long-short spread between these two quintiles was −138%, meaning returns for the top quintile lagged the bottom by this amount. This provides some idea of how topsy-turvy the stock market was in 1999.

1988 ~ 2007	1st Quintile	2nd Quintile	3rd Quintile	4th Quintile	5th Quintile	Universe	S&P 500*
CAGR – Annual Rebalance	16.6%	14.2%	15.3%	9.2%	−3.8%	11.2%	12.9%
Average Excess Return vs. Universe**	5.9%	2.4%	1.8%	−1.8%	−8.2%	NA	1.6%
Value of $10,000 Invested (20 Years)	$214,908	$142,426	$173,311	$58,050	$4,572	$83,161	$112,895
% of 1-Year Periods Strategy Outperforms the Universe	70.1%	61.0%	55.8%	39.0%	27.3%	NA	59.7%
% Rolling 3-Year Periods Strategy Outperforms	82.6%	66.7%	62.3%	30.4%	8.7%	NA	71.0%
Maximum Gain	72.1%	59.4%	41.8%	50.4%	147.9%	59.2%	54.1%
Maximum Loss	−26.1%	−19.2%	−21.4%	−27.7%	−78.6%	−24.9%	−25.9%
Sharpe Ratio	0.78	0.68	0.74	0.39	0.00	0.49	0.69
Standard Deviation of Returns	0.18	0.15	0.13	0.16	0.41	0.16	0.14
Beta (vs. Universe)	0.83	0.75	0.61	0.88	1.79	NA	0.78
Alpha (vs. Universe)	0.08	0.05	0.07	0.00	−0.18	NA	0.04
Average Portfolio Size	76	76	76	76	76	NA	NA
Average Number of Companies *Outperforming*	37	37	37	32	22	NA	NA
Average Number of Companies *Underperforming*	36	37	35	40	50	NA	NA
Median Portfolio Value – Return on Invested Capital	27.7%	13.7%	10.0%	6.5%	−30.5%	9.4%	11.4%
Median Portfolio Value – Price-to-Sales	0.5	0.9	1.1	1.9	24.1	0.9	0.8
Average Market Capitalization	$3,209	$3,580	$3,975	$5,371	$1,418	NA	NA

* Equal-weighted average of S&P 500 returns. ** Annual holding period run quarterly for a larger sample size; arithmetic average excess returns.
Source: Standard & Poor's Compustat Point in Time Database, Charter Oak Investment Systems, Inc., Venues® Data Engine

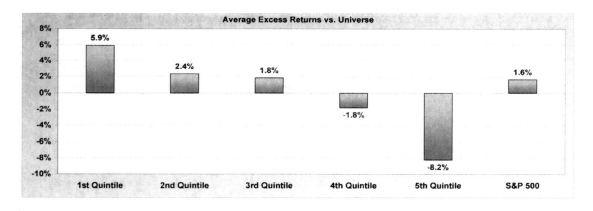

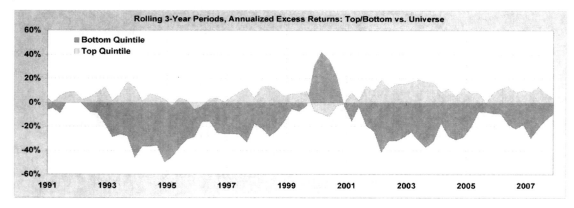

Figure 4.4 Return on Invested Capital and Price to Sales

noncash version is based on the income statement. The denominator (invested capital) is the same for both ratios. Because income statement values are based on *accrual accounting*, an accounting method in which expenses are matched to the revenues they generate, income statement results often differ significantly from actual cash inflows or outflows. The idea of this test is to find, in the top quintile, companies that have the highest profitability when measured on both an accrual accounting and a cash accounting basis.

The top quintile of this strategy worked extremely well from 1990 through 2002, but it appears to have lost some of its predictive power since then (see Figure 4.5). Our research shows that the statement of cash flows contained a lot of predictive power from when it was first put into use, in 1989, until the late 1990s. Although cash flow–based factors remain predictive, particularly when combined with valuation measures, the consistency and degree of their predictiveness have declined. The top quintile outperforms by 8.4%, on average, and does so for 78% of one-year and 89% of rolling three-year periods. The Sharpe ratio is a very high 0.92, versus 0.64 for the S&P 500. Average portfolio values range from 31% to over 80% for ROIC and from 40% to over 60% for cash ROIC, so the companies in this portfolio tend to be very profitable on both an income and cash flow statement basis. They also tend to be large caps, with an average market cap of $8.2 billion.

The bottom quintile underperforms by nearly 11% on average, and does so for 79% of one-year and 95% of rolling three-year periods, making it a good short-sale strategy. It is volatile, however, with a standard deviation of returns of 0.36 and a Beta of 1.7. The strategy fails to work well in the early stages of bull markets (1991, 2003) and at speculative tops in bull markets (1999). Average portfolio values are in the high negatives for both ROIC and cash ROIC, indicating that these companies are recording significant losses on both on an accrual accounting and cash flow basis. Companies in the bottom quintile tend to be small caps, with an average market capitalization of $1 billion.

Return on Invested Capital and One-Year Reduction in Shares Outstanding

As you will see in later chapters, a company's ability to efficiently allocate its excess capital (profits) is as important to stock market performance as how much profit it makes. The top quintile of this simple test contains highly profitable companies that are buying back shares. The top quintile provides modest outperformance but isn't as consistent as we'd like. However, this test shows the investor what to avoid: unprofitable companies that are diluting the ownership stakes of current shareholders by issuing large numbers of shares (the bottom quintile). Companies that issue large numbers of shares often do so to make stock-based business acquisitions. As we'll see later in this book, a simple strategy of avoiding companies that make large acquisitions works very well, so in general, business acquisitions represent a negative for future stock performance.

Companies in the top quintile outperform by 4.6%, on average, and do so for 62% of one-year and 67% of rolling three-year periods (see Figure 4.6). The Sharpe ratio is a

1990 ~ 2007	1st Quintile	2nd Quintile	3rd Quintile	4th Quintile	5th Quintile	Universe	S&P 500*
CAGR – Annual Rebalance	17.9%	13.4%	11.1%	9.8%	−5.3%	10.3%	12.0%
Average Excess Return vs. Universe**	8.4%	3.2%	0.8%	0.2%	−10.9%	NA	1.5%
Value of $10,000 Invested (18 Years)	$194,797	$95,755	$67,013	$54,238	$3,745	$58,670	$76,297
% of 1-Year Periods Strategy Outperforms the Universe	77.8%	55.6%	55.6%	52.8%	20.8%	NA	56.9%
% Rolling 3-Year Periods Strategy Outperforms	89.1%	73.4%	59.4%	50.0%	4.7%	NA	68.8%
Maximum Gain	67.0%	55.0%	48.0%	68.3%	104.9%	59.2%	54.1%
Maximum Loss	−20.4%	−34.5%	−24.7%	−32.7%	−73.8%	−24.9%	−25.9%
Sharpe Ratio	0.92	0.70	0.61	0.43	−0.09	0.46	0.64
Standard Deviation of Returns	0.18	0.16	0.14	0.18	0.36	0.17	0.14
Beta (vs. Universe)	0.91	0.77	0.72	0.96	1.67	NA	0.78
Alpha (vs. Universe)	0.10	0.06	0.04	0.01	−0.19	NA	0.04
Average Portfolio Size	63	63	63	63	64	NA	NA
Average Number of Companies *Outperforming*	31	30	28	27	18	NA	NA
Average Number of Companies *Underperforming*	30	31	32	33	42	NA	NA
Median Portfolio Value – Return on Invested Capital	38.7%	14.6%	10.2%	6.1%	−40.6%	8.9%	11.4%
Median Portfolio Value – Cash ROIC	47.2%	13.5%	4.9%	−2.0%	−43.3%	3.8%	7.7%
Average Market Capitalization	$8,205	$5,254	$5,043	$3,466	$1,086	NA	NA

* Equal-weighted average of S&P 500 returns. ** Annual holding period run quarterly for a larger sample size; arithmetic average excess returns.
Source: Standard & Poor's Compustat Point in Time Database, Charter Oak Investment Systems, Inc., Venues® Data Engine

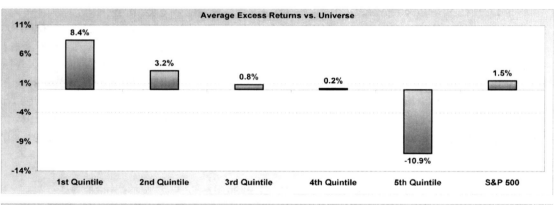

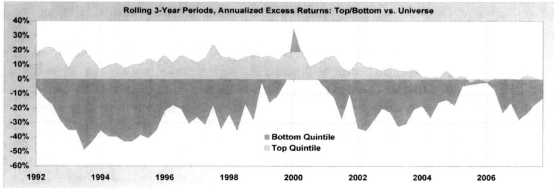

Figure 4.5 Return on Invested Capital and Cash Return on Invested Capital

1988 ~ 2007	1st Quintile	2nd Quintile	3rd Quintile	4th Quintile	5th Quintile	Universe	S&P 500*
CAGR – Annual Rebalance	17.2%	13.4%	12.6%	10.7%	−6.9%	11.2%	12.9%
Average Excess Return vs. Universe**	4.6%	1.2%	2.6%	−0.6%	−12.8%	NA	1.7%
Value of $10,000 Invested (20 Years)	$239,859	$124,352	$108,213	$76,972	$2,399	$83,161	$112,895
% of 1-Year Periods Strategy Outperforms the Universe	62.3%	54.5%	64.9%	44.2%	22.1%	NA	61.0%
% Rolling 3-Year Periods Strategy Outperforms	66.7%	59.4%	73.9%	36.2%	2.9%	NA	71.0%
Maximum Gain	55.3%	50.6%	49.0%	61.8%	90.7%	59.2%	54.1%
Maximum Loss	−14.4%	−22.3%	−18.5%	−32.4%	−82.7%	−24.9%	−25.9%
Sharpe Ratio	0.86	0.72	0.81	0.43	−0.15	0.49	0.69
Standard Deviation of Returns	0.15	0.13	0.13	0.17	0.32	0.16	0.14
Beta (vs. Universe)	0.66	0.66	0.70	0.98	1.70	NA	0.78
Alpha (vs. Universe)	0.09	0.05	0.06	0.00	−0.21	NA	0.04
Average Portfolio Size	72	72	72	73	72	NA	NA
Average Number of Companies *Outperforming*	35	33	32	31	21	NA	NA
Average Number of Companies *Underperforming*	35	36	36	37	46	NA	NA
Median Portfolio Value – Return on Invested Capital	28.0%	14.1%	10.0%	6.5%	−22.2%	9.4%	11.4%
Median Portfolio Value – Change in Shares O/S	5.5%	−0.1%	−1.0%	−4.0%	−81.6%	−18.1%	−15.6%
Average Market Capitalization	$8,845	$6,045	$3,667	$2,891	$2,794	NA	NA

* Equal-weighted average of S&P 500 returns.** Annual holding period run quarterly for a larger sample size; arithmetic average excess returns.
Source: Standard & Poor's Compustat Point in Time Database, Charter Oak Investment Systems, Inc., Venues® Data Engine

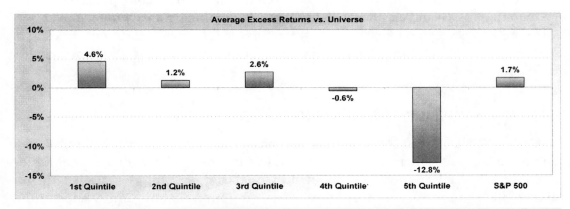

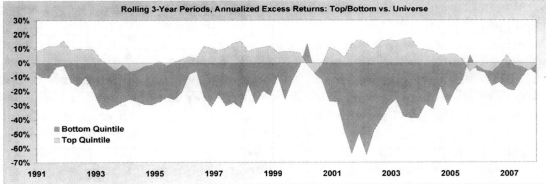

Figure 4.6 Return on Invested Capital and One-Year Reduction in Shares Outstanding

high 0.86. However, the strategy is inconsistent, underperforming in 1988, 1992–1993, 1999, 2003, 2005, and 2007. Average portfolio values range from 23% to over 50% for ROIC and from 3% to 9% for one-year share reduction, so companies in this quintile are highly profitable and are using excess cash to significantly reduce shares outstanding.

The results of the bottom quintile are intuitive: if a company is earning a terrible return on capital—such as the companies in the bottom quintile, which have a median ROIC value of −22%—it should not seek to dilute current owners and expand an unprofitable business by issuing shares. This is a strategy known as "making a bad situation worse." The bottom quintile underperforms by nearly 13%, on average, and does so for 78% of one-year and 97% of rolling three-year periods. It is quite volatile, with a standard deviation of returns of 0.32, a Beta of 1.7, and a maximum gain of 91%. The maximum gain occurred from March 2003 through March 2004, so short sellers should beware of the early stages of bull markets. The strategy also recorded strong gains in 1999. Average portfolio values range from −4% to −40% for ROIC and from −45% to less than −80% for one-year share reduction, so these companies have after-tax operating losses and are increasing shares outstanding by an average of over 50%. Note that, in 1998, companies in the bottom quintile increased shares outstanding by an average of 182% and in 1999 by 275%—one of many signs that 1999 represented a market mania.

EBITDA MINUS CAPITAL EXPENDITURES TO INVESTED CAPITAL

To calculate ROIC as it is used above takes a bit of work and is perhaps more suited to qualitative analysis, where an analyst can adjust income and invested capital figures according to special circumstances at an individual company. It turns out that, quantitatively, this extra work isn't worth the effort. We found that by simply substituting operating income for NOPAT in the ROIC equation shown in Figure 4.1, we get results that are just as strong as ROIC from a quantitative standpoint. My preferred approach is to use EBITDA (earnings before interest, taxes, depreciation, and amortization) minus capital expenditures as the numerator of the ROIC equation.

EBITDA is a widely used metric, a creation, as Warren Buffett points out, of overzealous investment bankers who wanted to put corporate profitability in the best possible light. The problem with EBITDA is that, used alone as a yardstick of profitability, it leaves out *depreciation expense,* the accounting estimate of the productive cost of plant and equipment during the period. (It's hard to argue that plant and equipment aren't a real and necessary expense for any company.) This problem can be solved in one of two ways: by using EBIT, or earnings before interest and taxes (EBIT includes depreciation); or by using EBITDA and subtracting capital expenditures. I prefer the latter method, since capital expenditures are actual cash outlays for plant and equipment, whereas depreciation is a noncash accounting estimate. However, from a quantitative standpoint, the choice is academic. EBIT works, EBITDA minus capital expenditures works, and even EBITDA alone works, with very little difference between the three.[5] Each of these three numerators would be expressed as a percentage of invested capital, the denominator shown in the ROIC equation in Figure 4.1.

One note about financial companies: we include financials in all of our tests, because we found that excluding them made little or no difference (and in some cases weakened the tests). One major difference between financial companies and other companies is that for financials, debt doesn't just represent invested capital; it represents the vital funding financial companies need to make loans, provide leasing arrangements, make investments, and so on. Thus, even long-term financing might be considered "working capital" rather than invested capital for finance companies. Also, the definitions of revenues and income differ significantly for financial companies (where revenue may consist primarily of interest income, investment income, etc., and expenses consist of interest expense and other costs of funding) versus industrial-type companies. Nevertheless, our sector tests show that return on investment metrics work for financial companies nearly as well as for industrial-type companies.

The performance figures for EBITDA minus capital expenditures to invested capital are very similar to those for ROIC, so I won't go over them in detail. Average portfolio values for the top quintile of EBITDA minus capex to invested capital range from 35% to over 45%. Also, the strategy is slightly more consistent than the top quintile of the ROIC strategy, outperforming for 71% of one-year and 84% of rolling three-year periods (see Figure 4.7).

EBIT to Invested Capital

The EBIT[6] to invested capital strategy produces somewhat weaker returns in the top quintile than EBITDA minus capex, and the consistency of outperformance is slightly weaker. Otherwise the two strategies are very similar. Average portfolio values for the top quintile for EBIT to invested capital range from 39% to over 50%, while average portfolio values for the bottom quintile range from 0% to −31% (see Figure 4.8).

---

[5] The investor seeking the simplest calculation can use EBIT as a percentage of invested capital, since operating profit (EBIT) is a number most companies report in financial statements.

[6] EBIT stands for earnings before interest and taxes. In this book, we use operating income in place of EBIT. Although technically nonoperating income should also be included in EBIT, the distinction makes little difference for a quantitative test.

1988 ~ 2007	1st Quintile	2nd Quintile	3rd Quintile	4th Quintile	5th Quintile	Universe	S&P 500*
CAGR – Annual Rebalance	13.6%	12.4%	12.0%	11.9%	4.7%	11.2%	12.9%
Average Excess Return vs. Universe**	2.6%	0.9%	0.6%	0.2%	−4.5%	NA	1.6%
Value of $10,000 Invested (20 Years)	$127,754	$103,858	$96,101	$93,933	$25,135	$83,161	$112,895
% of 1-Year Periods Strategy Outperforms the Universe	71.4%	57.1%	50.6%	51.9%	24.7%	NA	59.7%
% Rolling 3-Year Periods Strategy Outperforms	84.1%	63.8%	56.5%	42.0%	14.5%	NA	71.0%
Maximum Gain	50.9%	55.1%	60.3%	60.3%	78.7%	59.2%	54.1%
Maximum Loss	−18.7%	−23.1%	−26.8%	−29.4%	−60.6%	−24.9%	−25.9%
Sharpe Ratio	0.76	0.63	0.58	0.50	0.13	0.49	0.69
Standard Deviation of Returns	0.14	0.14	0.15	0.17	0.27	0.16	0.14
Beta (vs. Universe)	0.82	0.83	0.85	0.99	1.46	NA	0.78
Alpha (vs. Universe)	0.05	0.03	0.03	0.00	−0.10	NA	0.04
Average Portfolio Size	319	320	320	320	320	NA	NA
Average Number of Companies *Outperforming*	147	144	142	136	114	NA	NA
Average Number of Companies *Underperforming*	160	161	160	167	188	NA	NA
Median Portfolio Value – EBITDA-Capx to Inv. Cap.	37.3%	19.2%	12.8%	6.3%	−14.2%	12.1%	16.8%
Average Market Capitalization	$7,236	$4,428	$4,765	$3,916	$1,923	NA	NA

* Equal-weighted average of S&P 500 returns. ** Annual holding period run quarterly for a larger sample size; arithmetic average excess returns.
Source: Standard & Poor's Compustat Point in Time Database, Charter Oak Investment Systems, Inc., Venues® Data Engine

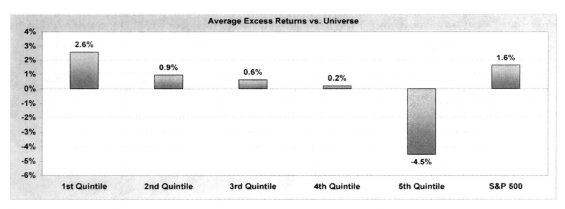

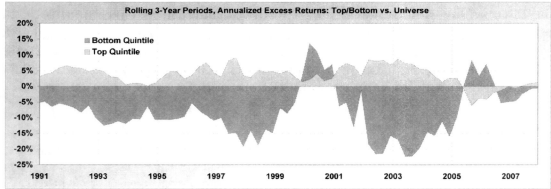

Figure 4.7 EBITDA Minus Capital Expenditures to Invested Capital

1988 ~ 2007	1st Quintile	2nd Quintile	3rd Quintile	4th Quintile	5th Quintile	Universe	S&P 500*
CAGR – Annual Rebalance	13.2%	13.0%	12.9%	11.5%	4.2%	11.2%	12.9%
Average Excess Return vs. Universe**	2.2%	1.2%	1.3%	0.2%	−4.7%	NA	1.6%
Value of $10,000 Invested (20 Years)	$118,514	$115,670	$113,997	$88,643	$22,966	$83,161	$112,895
% of 1-Year Periods Strategy Outperforms the Universe	67.5%	54.5%	63.6%	49.4%	23.4%	NA	59.7%
% Rolling 3-Year Periods Strategy Outperforms	75.4%	65.2%	68.1%	46.4%	13.0%	NA	71.0%
Maximum Gain	51.4%	54.0%	53.9%	56.4%	84.6%	59.2%	54.1%
Maximum Loss	−18.7%	−22.7%	−23.1%	−27.8%	−68.1%	−24.9%	−25.9%
Sharpe Ratio	0.71	0.64	0.68	0.55	0.12	0.49	0.69
Standard Deviation of Returns	0.15	0.15	0.14	0.15	0.29	0.16	0.14
Beta (vs. Universe)	0.84	0.84	0.78	0.88	1.54	NA	0.78
Alpha (vs. Universe)	0.04	0.03	0.04	0.02	−0.11	NA	0.04
Average Portfolio Size	376	376	376	376	377	NA	NA
Average Number of Companies *Outperforming*	170	172	169	167	134	NA	NA
Average Number of Companies *Underperforming*	191	188	188	189	219	NA	NA
Median Portfolio Value – EBIT-to-Invested Capital	42.1%	21.6%	15.4%	10.5%	−7.3%	17.0%	19.0%
Average Market Capitalization	$7,090	$4,807	$4,282	$3,681	$1,957	NA	NA

* Equal-weighted average of S&P 500 returns. ** Annual holding period run quarterly for a larger sample size; arithmetic average excess returns.
Source: Standard & Poor's Compustat Point in Time Database, Charter Oak Investment Systems, Inc., Venues® Data Engine

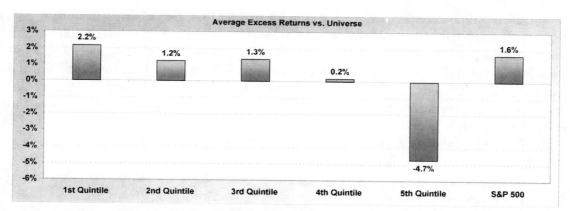

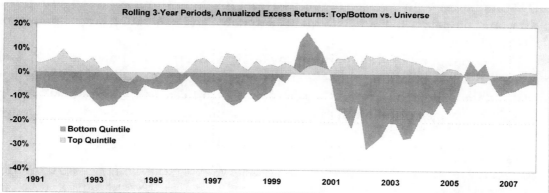

Figure 4.8 EBIT to Invested Capital

EBITDA Minus Capital Expenditures to Invested Capital by Economic Sector

Results by sector for EBITDA minus capex to invested capital are similar to those for ROIC, but not the same. Although energy, materials, and industrials outperform in both tests, outperformance is much stronger using EBITDA minus capex. In particular, industrials results are much stronger for both top and bottom quintiles using the EBITDA minus capex test. Also, the EBITDA minus capex test works much better for the consumer staples and information technology sectors. In health care, ROIC works better for the top quintile, and EBITDA minus capex works better for the bottom (see Figure 4.9).

EBITDA Minus Capital Expenditures to Invested Capital and Free Cash Flow to Price

Like the ROIC and price-to-sales test, this test combines two very strong strategies: profitability and valuation. Profitability determines the quality of the assets being purchased, and valuation determines the price paid for those assets. In addition, this test combines an accrual accounting–based (income statement) profitability measure with a cash flow–based valuation measure. This test helps ensure that a company's cash flow—its real return to shareholders—is doing as well as its reported earnings. To calculate valuation, we use free cash flow, which is equal to 12-month cash flow from operating activities minus capital expenditures, as a percent of total market capitalization.[7] Capital expenditures represent expenses that a company must incur in order to maintain plant and equipment and remain competitive. Note that free cash flow to price, covered in depth in Chapter 5, is one of the strongest valuation measures that we tested.

The top quintile outperforms by 7.8%, on average, and does so for 74% of one-year and 94% of rolling three-year periods (see Figure 4.10). The top quintile significantly underperforms only in 1999–2000 and, briefly, in 2003–2004. Its Sharpe ratio is a strong 0.89, versus 0.64 for the S&P 500. Average portfolio values range from 33% to 47% for EBITDA minus capex to invested capital and from 10% to 40% for free cash flow to price, so these are companies that are both highly profitable and generating large amounts of excess cash flow.

The bottom quintile underperforms by 5.3%, on average, and does so for 75% of one-year and 86% of rolling three-year periods. The bottom quintile is somewhat volatile, with a Beta of 1.5, and outperforms significantly in 1999–2000 and in 2003–2004.[8] Average portfolio values for EBITDA minus capex to invested capital range

---

[7] Price per share multiplied by shares outstanding.

[8] Throughout this book, you'll see consistently that beaten-down stocks of low quality companies tend to outperform in the early stages of bull markets (e.g., 1991 and 2003). These stocks tend to show up in value tests as having high valuations because earnings and cash flows have reached very low levels as business activity has waned.

Top Quintile

1988 ~ 2007	Energy	Materials	Industrials	Consumer Discretionary	Consumer Staples	Health Care	Financials	Information Technology	Telecom Services	Utilities	Universe	S&P 500*
CAGR – Quintile	18.6%	13.0%	14.8%	10.1%	15.9%	15.3%	16.8%	12.4%	9.4%	12.8%	11.2%	12.9%
CAGR – Sector	13.5%	10.2%	11.2%	8.8%	12.6%	12.3%	14.5%	7.6%	9.2%	13.0%	NA	NA
Excess Return vs. Sector	5.0%	2.8%	3.5%	1.3%	3.4%	2.9%	2.4%	4.9%	0.2%	−0.1%	NA	NA
Value of $10,000	$302,154	$114,511	$157,418	$68,481	$192,569	$171,269	$225,193	$104,111	$60,489	$111,496	$83,161	$112,895
% 1-Year Outperformance	70.0%	55.0%	75.0%	60.0%	55.0%	55.0%	65.0%	70.0%	55.0%	55.0%	NA	NA
% 3-Year Outperformance	88.9%	72.2%	94.4%	61.1%	72.2%	66.7%	66.7%	83.3%	61.1%	44.4%	NA	NA
Maximum Gain	56.8%	39.8%	37.9%	53.0%	75.6%	71.0%	79.1%	63.8%	63.8%	47.7%	44.0%	41.4%
Maximum Loss	−40.8%	−18.4%	−8.1%	−18.9%	−20.0%	−16.1%	−25.3%	−30.2%	−29.4%	−16.4%	−19.1%	−18.1%
Standard Deviation	0.23	0.15	0.12	0.17	0.21	0.22	0.24	0.23	0.24	0.17	0.16	0.14
Beta (vs. Sector)	0.82	0.84	0.81	0.85	1.24	0.82	1.04	0.57	0.45	1.02	NA	NA
Alpha (vs. Sector)	0.07	0.05	0.06	0.03	0.01	0.05	0.02	0.07	0.05	0.00	NA	NA
Portfolio Size	21	29	53	64	19	36	40	50	8	25	NA	NA

Bottom Quintile

1988 ~ 2007	Energy	Materials	Industrials	Consumer Discretionary	Consumer Staples	Health Care	Financials	Information Technology	Telecom Services	Utilities	Universe	S&P 500*
CAGR – Quintile	9.6%	5.0%	7.3%	6.5%	9.9%	4.1%	11.0%	5.8%	7.8%	14.1%	11.2%	12.9%
CAGR – Sector	13.5%	10.2%	11.2%	8.8%	12.6%	12.3%	14.5%	7.6%	9.2%	13.0%	NA	NA
Excess Return vs. Sector	−3.9%	−5.2%	−3.9%	−2.2%	−2.7%	−8.2%	−3.5%	−1.7%	−1.5%	1.2%	NA	NA
Value of $10,000	$62,579	$26,299	$40,819	$35,538	$65,862	$22,360	$80,218	$31,019	$44,578	$140,412	$83,161	$112,895
% 1-Year Outperformance	30.0%	35.0%	25.0%	35.0%	30.0%	20.0%	35.0%	45.0%	50.0%	40.0%	NA	NA
% 3-Year Outperformance	22.2%	27.8%	11.1%	22.2%	27.8%	5.6%	27.8%	33.3%	38.9%	50.0%	NA	NA
Maximum Gain	70.9%	67.4%	51.3%	50.9%	36.8%	73.5%	45.3%	211.3%	247.9%	77.4%	44.0%	41.4%
Maximum Loss	−49.1%	−33.3%	−28.0%	−28.1%	−12.9%	−35.8%	−30.7%	−60.7%	−70.2%	−33.1%	−19.1%	−18.1%
Standard Deviation	0.32	0.23	0.17	0.22	0.14	0.29	0.21	0.55	0.64	0.24	0.16	0.14
Beta (vs. Sector)	1.21	1.41	1.13	1.13	0.80	1.10	0.90	1.44	1.56	1.32	NA	NA
Alpha (vs. Sector)	−0.06	−0.02	−0.04	−0.06	0.04	−0.09	0.01	−0.09	−0.04	0.06	NA	NA
Portfolio Size	21	30	56	68	21	38	43	52	9	25	NA	NA

* Equal-weighted average of S&P 500 returns.
Source: Standard & Poor's Compustat Point in Time Database, Charter Oak Investment Systems, Inc., Venues® Data Engine

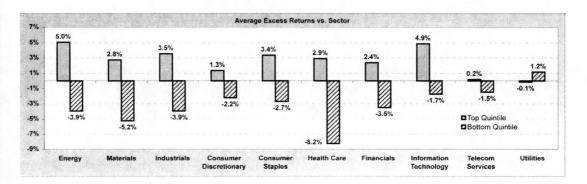

Figure 4.9 EBITDA Minus Capital Expenditures to Invested Capital by Economic Sector

1990 ~ 2007	1st Quintile	2nd Quintile	3rd Quintile	4th Quintile	5th Quintile	Universe	S&P 500*
CAGR – Annual Rebalance	18.3%	12.9%	10.4%	7.1%	4.4%	10.3%	12.0%
Average Excess Return vs. Universe**	7.8%	2.4%	0.3%	−1.7%	−5.3%	NA	1.5%
Value of $10,000 Invested (18 Years)	$206,273	$88,191	$59,591	$34,371	$21,641	$58,669	$76,297
% of 1-Year Periods Strategy Outperforms the Universe	73.6%	58.3%	50.0%	33.3%	25.0%	NA	56.9%
% Rolling 3-Year Periods Strategy Outperforms	93.8%	64.1%	54.7%	23.4%	14.1%	NA	68.8%
Maximum Gain	65.3%	50.6%	45.6%	95.3%	93.7%	59.2%	54.1%
Maximum Loss	−19.0%	−22.6%	−29.4%	−40.5%	−53.1%	−24.9%	−25.9%
Sharpe Ratio	0.89	0.69	0.56	0.27	0.09	0.46	0.64
Standard Deviation of Returns	0.17	0.15	0.14	0.22	0.29	0.17	0.14
Beta (vs. Universe)	0.80	0.65	0.74	1.14	1.48	NA	0.78
Alpha (vs. Universe)	0.10	0.07	0.03	−0.03	−0.11	NA	0.04
Average Portfolio Size	63	63	63	63	64	NA	NA
Average Number of Companies *Outperforming*	32	31	28	25	24	NA	NA
Average Number of Companies *Underperforming*	28	30	32	35	37	NA	NA
Median Portfolio Value – EBITDA-Capx to Inv. Cap.	36.9%	19.7%	13.3%	6.2%	−23.1%	13.1%	17.3%
Median Portfolio Value – FCF-to-Price	15.9%	6.9%	3.9%	−0.5%	−29.1%	2.1%	3.3%
Average Market Capitalization	$3,838	$3,763	$6,242	$4,317	$1,402	NA	NA

* Equal-weighted average of S&P 500 returns. ** Annual holding period run quarterly for a larger sample size; arithmetic average excess returns.
Source: Standard & Poor's Compustat Point in Time Database, Charter Oak Investment Systems, Inc., Venues® Data Engine

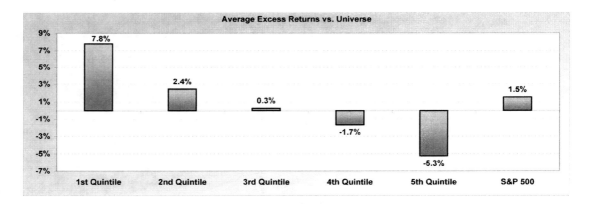

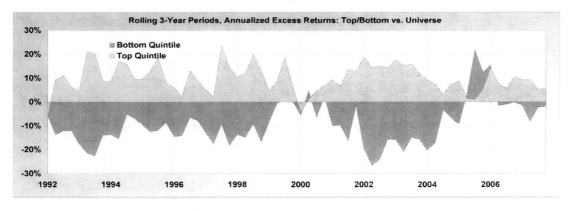

Figure 4.10 EBITDA Minus Capital Expenditures to Invested Capital and Free Cash Flow to Price

from -14% to less than -30%, meaning that EBITDA minus capital expenditures represents a significant loss. Average portfolio values also have high negative values for free cash flow to price, indicating cash outflows after accounting for capex.

EBITDA Minus Capital Expenditures to Invested Capital and Operating Cash Flow to Capital Expenditures

This strategy shows the importance to a business of being able to fund its capital expenditures. Capital expenditures record cash paid for *capital assets,* which are long-life assets such as land, buildings, office equipment, machinery, and exploration costs (in the case of oil and gas companies). Corporations that do not maintain, replace, or expand facilities and equipment used to make products or provide services cannot remain competitive. However, maintaining and expanding capital expenditures require cash. The top quintile of this strategy contains companies that generate high returns on capital invested and have more than ample cash to fund capital expenditures. The bottom quintile, on the other hand, contains companies that have poor profitability and lack the cash necessary to maintain and expand plant and equipment. Like the strategy shown in Fig. 4.10, this strategy combines both a measure of accounting profitability and a measure of cash flows.

The top quintile outperforms by 6.2%, on average, and does so for 76% of one-year and 89% of rolling three-year periods (see Figure 4.11). It significantly underperforms only in a couple of periods; unfortunately, they are recent periods: 2003–2004 and 2007. The Sharpe ratio is a moderate 0.79. Average portfolio values range from 38% to 98% for EBITDA minus capex to invested capital and from 8× to over 20× for operating cash flow to capex, so these are highly profitable companies, on an income statement basis, that are also generating a lot of free cash flow.

The bottom quintile underperforms by 9.6%, on average, and does so for 75% of one-year and 91% of rolling three-year periods. The bottom quintile is very volatile and significantly outperforms in 1991, 1995–1996, 1999–2000, and 2003–2004, either at the beginning of bull markets or at speculative market tops.[9] Average portfolio values range from -16% to -40% for EBTIDA minus capex to invested capital and from $-1\times$ to $-10\times$ for operating cash flow to capital expenditures. With an average of 42 of the 64 stocks in the bottom quintile underperforming each year, this quintile provides a good list of stocks to avoid.

---

[9] Although technically not the beginning of a bull market, 1995 was a very strong year that followed a mini-bear market in 1994.

1990 ~ 2007	1st Quintile	2nd Quintile	3rd Quintile	4th Quintile	5th Quintile	Universe	S&P 500*
CAGR – Annual Rebalance	15.9%	12.9%	12.5%	12.1%	−4.2%	10.3%	12.0%
Average Excess Return vs. Universe**	6.2%	2.6%	0.8%	2.2%	−9.6%	NA	1.5%
Value of $10,000 Invested (18 Years)	$141,901	$89,474	$83,039	$77,769	$4,658	$58,670	$76,297
% of 1-Year Periods Strategy Outperforms the Universe	76.4%	61.1%	45.8%	61.1%	25.0%	NA	56.9%
% Rolling 3-Year Periods Strategy Outperforms	89.1%	67.2%	54.7%	56.3%	9.4%	NA	68.8%
Maximum Gain	58.9%	51.1%	58.3%	63.0%	122.2%	59.2%	54.1%
Maximum Loss	−18.6%	−22.0%	−27.2%	−23.3%	−67.3%	−24.9%	−25.9%
Sharpe Ratio	0.79	0.72	0.59	0.60	−0.05	0.46	0.64
Standard Deviation of Returns	0.18	0.14	0.14	0.17	0.39	0.17	0.14
Beta (vs. Universe)	0.95	0.75	0.74	0.86	1.66	NA	0.78
Alpha (vs. Universe)	0.07	0.06	0.04	0.04	−0.18	NA	0.04
Average Portfolio Size	63	63	63	63	64	NA	NA
Average Number of Companies *Outperforming*	30	30	29	28	18	NA	NA
Average Number of Companies *Underperforming*	30	30	32	33	42	NA	NA
Median Portfolio Value – EBITDA-Capex to Inv. Cap.	47.3%	20.1%	13.2%	6.2%	−34.6%	12.2%	17.0%
Median Portfolio Value – CF from Opers. to Capex	12.5	3.5	1.7	0.9	−4.2	1.4	1.5
Average Market Capitalization	$7,010	$4,189	$6,652	$4,159	$912	NA	NA

* Equal-weighted average of S&P 500 returns. ** Annual holding period run quarterly for a larger sample size; arithmetic average excess returns.
Source: Standard & Poor's Compustat Point in Time Database, Charter Oak Investment Systems, Inc., Venues® Data Engine

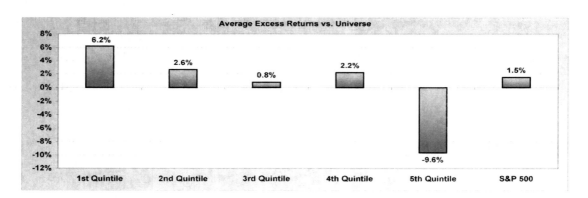

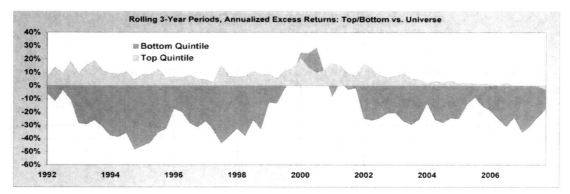

Figure 4.11 EBITDA Minus Capital Expenditures to Invested Capital and Operating Cash Flow to Capital Expenditures

RETURN ON EQUITY AND RETURN ON ASSETS

Return on equity (ROE) is another simple profitability strategy that works. We calculate ROE as income before extraordinary items minus preferred stock dividends as a percent of average common stockholders' equity for the past 12 months. Preferred dividends are subtracted because we want to calculate income available to common shareholders[10] (and preferred shareholders are usually paid dividends before any money is made available to common shareholders). We also require that stockholders' equity be positive. Return on assets (ROA), on the other hand, which is calculated as income before extraordinary items as a percent of average total assets, doesn't work as a stand-alone ratio. I believe the reason for this is that a quantitative test based on total assets alone does not take into account the quality of those assets. A company can have large assets on its balance sheet, such as goodwill, that have fair values well below their book values, or vice versa. In other words, total assets are too broad a base for a profitability test. Stockholders' equity, in contrast, represents funds actually invested or reinvested in the company. One drawback of ROE is that it does not consider investments in the company by creditors. Combining ROE and ROA makes a slightly better two-factor strategy that looks at profitability from both a narrow (equity) and a broad (total assets) perspective. However, as we will see later, other two-factor ROE strategies are even stronger.

The top quintile outperforms by 2.2%, on average, and does so for 68% of one-year and 81% of rolling three-year periods (see Figure 4.12). The top quintile significantly underperforms only in 1988, 1992–1993, and 2003. Average portfolio values for return on equity range from 32% to over 70%, so either profitability is high at these companies or shareholders equity is low (the latter case can occur, for example, if a company takes a large asset write-off). Like other profitability strategies, this strategy selects large cap stocks. Larger companies are often better able to generate higher profitability due to strong competitive positions in their markets and economies of scale.

The bottom quintile underperforms by 3.6%, on average, and does so for 73% of one-year and 85% of rolling three-year periods. Average portfolio values for ROE in the bottom quintile range from −9% to less than −50%, indicating large net losses.

Return on Assets

Although ROA (see Figure 4.13) does not work nearly as well as ROE for the top quintile, the bottom quintile—those companies with the lowest return on assets (an average

---

[10] However, running the ROE test without subtracting preferred dividends makes very little difference in terms of excess returns or consistency of returns.

1988 ~ 2007	1st Quintile	2nd Quintile	3rd Quintile	4th Quintile	5th Quintile	Universe	S&P 500*
CAGR – Annual Rebalance	13.6%	12.5%	12.3%	11.3%	6.0%	11.2%	12.9%
Average Excess Return vs. Universe**	2.2%	1.4%	0.8%	−0.1%	−3.6%	NA	1.6%
Value of $10,000 Invested (20 Years)	$129,210	$105,923	$102,012	$85,589	$31,863	$83,161	$112,895
% of 1-Year Periods Strategy Outperforms the Universe	67.5%	54.5%	54.5%	50.6%	27.3%	NA	59.7%
% Rolling 3-Year Periods Strategy Outperforms	81.2%	63.8%	66.7%	50.7%	14.5%	NA	71.0%
Maximum Gain	52.3%	48.6%	50.6%	57.1%	84.3%	59.2%	54.1%
Maximum Loss	−20.5%	−23.1%	−22.0%	−28.0%	−61.1%	−24.9%	−25.9%
Sharpe Ratio	0.67	0.68	0.64	0.53	0.17	0.49	0.69
Standard Deviation of Returns	0.15	0.14	0.14	0.15	0.27	0.16	0.14
Beta (vs. Universe)	0.90	0.79	0.77	0.89	1.51	NA	0.78
Alpha (vs. Universe)	0.03	0.04	0.04	0.01	−0.10	NA	0.04
Average Portfolio Size	407	407	407	407	407	NA	NA
Average Number of Companies *Outperforming*	184	186	182	176	152	NA	NA
Average Number of Companies *Underperforming*	206	203	205	206	229	NA	NA
Median Portfolio Value – Return on Equity	42.7%	17.5%	13.1%	8.4%	−33.9%	11.7%	14.7%
Average Market Capitalization	$7,989	$5,000	$3,493	$2,853	$2,059	NA	NA

* Equal-weighted average of S&P 500 returns. ** Annual holding period run quarterly for a larger sample size; arithmetic average excess returns.
Source: Standard & Poor's Compustat Point in Time Database, Charter Oak Investment Systems, Inc., Venues® Data Engine

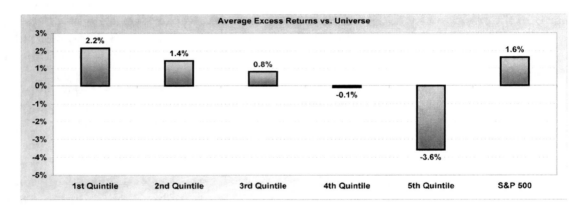

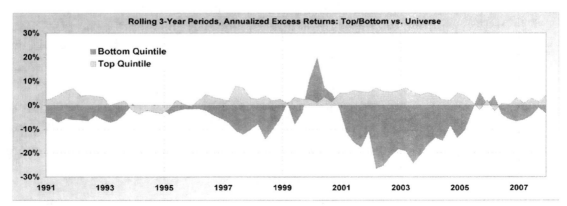

Figure 4.12 Return on Equity

1988 ~ 2007	1st Quintile	2nd Quintile	3rd Quintile	4th Quintile	5th Quintile	Universe	S&P 500*
CAGR – Annual Rebalance	12.2%	11.8%	12.0%	13.4%	5.8%	11.2%	12.9%
Average Excess Return vs. Universe**	1.4%	0.4%	0.4%	1.9%	−3.0%	NA	1.6%
Value of $10,000 Invested (20 Years)	$100,499	$92,966	$96,851	$123,538	$30,855	$83,161	$112,895
% of 1-Year Periods Strategy Outperforms the Universe	51.9%	45.5%	53.2%	57.1%	36.4%	NA	59.7%
% Rolling 3-Year Periods Strategy Outperforms	56.5%	44.9%	50.7%	68.1%	27.5%	NA	71.0%
Maximum Gain	59.9%	50.9%	55.0%	53.4%	86.2%	59.2%	54.1%
Maximum Loss	−25.1%	−22.0%	−23.4%	−20.9%	−67.0%	−24.9%	−25.9%
Sharpe Ratio	0.56	0.60	0.62	0.67	0.18	0.49	0.69
Standard Deviation of Returns	0.17	0.14	0.14	0.15	0.29	0.16	0.14
Beta (vs. Universe)	0.95	0.83	0.75	0.76	1.61	NA	0.78
Alpha (vs. Universe)	0.02	0.02	0.03	0.05	−0.11	NA	0.04
Average Portfolio Size	419	420	420	420	420	NA	NA
Average Number of Companies *Outperforming*	181	184	186	194	162	NA	NA
Average Number of Companies *Underperforming*	222	218	212	200	230	NA	NA
Median Portfolio Value – Return on Assets	16.6%	7.9%	4.7%	2.0%	−10.2%	4.1%	5.4%
Average Market Capitalization	$5,925	$4,596	$3,596	$4,518	$2,417	NA	NA

* Equal-weighted average of S&P 500 returns. ** Annual holding period run quarterly for a larger sample size; arithmetic average excess returns.
Source: Standard & Poor's Compustat Point in Time Database; Charter Oak Investment Systems, Inc., Venues® Data Engine

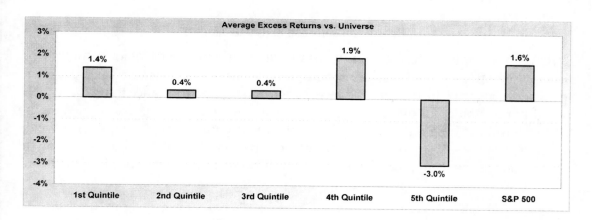

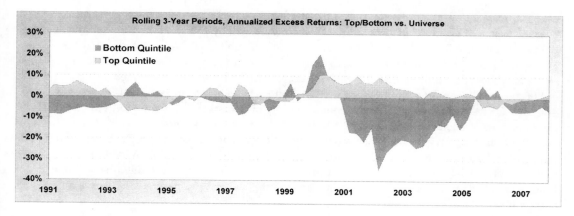

Figure 4.13 Return on Assets

of -10%)—underperforms quite nicely. We'll see that a combined ROE and ROA strategy makes a strong negative test, by pointing out stocks to avoid or sell short.[11]

Return on Equity by Economic Sector

Sector performance for the ROE strategy is quite different than for ROIC or EBITDA minus capex to invested capital. The ROE strategy works poorly for the top quintiles of materials and industrials (although the bottom quintiles of these sectors work well). ROE works very well with the consumer discretionary sector, a very diverse group of industries, including retail. Surprisingly, ROE does not work well for financial companies or utilities, two sectors in which this ratio is commonly employed. However, it does work well for information technology and telecommunications services, sectors that did not work as well for ROIC or EBITDA minus capex to invested capital (see Figure 4.14).

Return on Equity and Return on Assets

Although this strategy has a weak top quintile in terms of consistency of outperformance, the bottom quintile is very strong in terms of both consistency and degree of underperformance. The top quintile owes much of its outperformance to 1998 and 1999, as highly profitable but overpriced stocks became even more overpriced (see Figure 4.15). I consider strong outperformance for the top quintile during this period a weakness in a strategy—1998 and 1999 represented a period of extremes that is unlikely to recur as long as the memory of the losses that followed is alive in the minds of investors.

---

[11] Although some of the strategies presented in this book would make strong short-sale strategies, I don't recommend selling short during a bull market for most investors. The greatest underperformance of the fifth quintiles of the strategies presented in this book occurs during bear markets. For example, in 1990 our Backtest Universe fell by 15%, and the fifth quintile of the ROA strategy fell by 30%; in 2000 the Universe fell 3%, and Q5 ROA fell 35%; in 2001 the Universe fell 3%, and Q5 ROA fell 26%, and so on. Note that many short-sale strategies outperform strongly when a new bull market begins. For example, in 1991 the Universe rallied 39% coming out of the 1990 bear market, and Q5 of the ROA strategy rallied 52%; in 2003 the Universe rose 44%, and Q5 ROA climbed 66%. At the end of a strong bear market, companies with the weakest fundamentals often become extremely underpriced, as investors fear they may go out of business and abandon stocks in general. When it becomes apparent that the economy will recover and that the outlook for these weak businesses is improving (the beginning of a new bull market), they are rapidly repriced and often see much larger price gains than more conservatively financed and fundamentally sounder peers. This is a phenomenon that has happened over and over again in stock market history.

Top Quintile

1988 ~ 2007	Energy	Materials	Industrials	Consumer Discretionary	Consumer Staples	Health Care	Financials	Information Technology	Telecom Services	Utilities	Universe	S&P 500*
CAGR – Quintile	16.4%	7.9%	11.9%	11.5%	15.2%	16.9%	14.1%	10.7%	13.0%	12.9%	11.2%	12.9%
CAGR – Sector	13.5%	10.2%	11.2%	8.8%	12.6%	12.3%	14.5%	7.6%	9.2%	13.0%	NA	NA
Excess Return vs. Sector	2.9%	−2.3%	0.7%	2.8%	2.6%	4.6%	−0.4%	3.2%	3.7%	0.0%	NA	NA
Value of $10,000	$209,791	$45,931	$94,500	$88,659	$169,576	$226,794	$139,316	$76,723	$114,543	$113,639	$83,161	$112,895
% 1-Year Outperformance	45.0%	25.0%	55.0%	75.0%	50.0%	70.0%	45.0%	65.0%	65.0%	50.0%	NA	NA
% 3-Year Outperformance	66.7%	33.3%	66.7%	88.9%	61.1%	88.9%	33.3%	61.1%	66.7%	61.1%	NA	NA
Maximum Gain	52.6%	36.3%	46.9%	59.5%	68.4%	77.7%	58.0%	106.6%	60.8%	64.3%	44.0%	41.4%
Maximum Loss	−45.3%	−19.3%	−18.1%	−19.5%	−20.5%	−15.7%	−24.7%	−32.2%	−38.5%	−27.9%	−19.1%	−18.1%
Standard Deviation	0.24	0.14	0.15	0.18	0.22	0.24	0.22	0.30	0.26	0.19	0.16	0.14
Beta (vs. Sector)	0.90	0.86	1.00	0.96	1.39	0.89	0.97	0.77	0.40	1.16	NA	NA
Alpha (vs. Sector)	0.04	−0.01	0.01	0.03	−0.01	0.06	0.00	0.04	0.10	−0.02	NA	NA
Portfolio Size	24	31	58	68	20	41	62	59	8	25	NA	NA

Bottom Quintile

1988 ~ 2007	Energy	Materials	Industrials	Consumer Discretionary	Consumer Staples	Health Care	Financials	Information Technology	Telecom Services	Utilities	Universe	S&P 500*
CAGR – Quintile	9.9%	6.5%	8.7%	4.3%	10.1%	5.8%	15.9%	5.0%	6.5%	13.4%	11.2%	12.9%
CAGR – Sector	13.5%	10.2%	11.2%	8.8%	12.6%	12.3%	14.5%	7.6%	9.2%	13.0%	NA	NA
Excess Return vs. Sector	−3.6%	−3.7%	−2.5%	−4.4%	−2.5%	−6.6%	1.4%	−2.6%	−2.8%	0.4%	NA	NA
Value of $10,000	$66,637	$35,067	$53,372	$23,412	$67,899	$30,617	$191,319	$26,549	$34,956	$122,617	$83,161	$112,895
% 1-Year Outperformance	30.0%	40.0%	40.0%	50.0%	45.0%	30.0%	65.0%	40.0%	50.0%	50.0%	NA	NA
% 3-Year Outperformance	22.2%	22.2%	16.7%	16.7%	33.3%	11.1%	66.7%	44.4%	33.3%	72.2%	NA	NA
Maximum Gain	76.4%	51.6%	55.2%	51.1%	33.8%	84.2%	63.7%	215.0%	182.2%	56.2%	44.0%	41.4%
Maximum Loss	−50.1%	−35.1%	−24.5%	−43.5%	−25.0%	−32.8%	−35.4%	−61.3%	−77.8%	−24.4%	−19.1%	−18.1%
Standard Deviation	0.35	0.22	0.18	0.24	0.16	0.31	0.25	0.58	0.51	0.19	0.16	0.14
Beta (vs. Sector)	1.31	1.36	1.18	1.24	1.03	1.18	1.09	1.52	1.28	1.09	NA	NA
Alpha (vs. Sector)	−0.06	0.01	−0.03	−0.07	0.05	−0.06	0.05	−0.11	−0.03	0.05	NA	NA
Portfolio Size	25	31	61	72	23	42	65	61	9	26	NA	NA

* Equal-weighted average of S&P 500 returns.
Source: Standard & Poor's Compustat Point in Time Database; Charter Oak Investment Systems, Inc., Venues® Data Engine

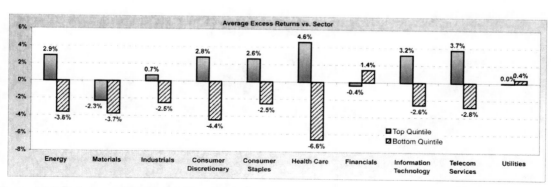

Figure 4.14 Return on Equity by Economic Sector

1988 ~ 2007	1st Quintile	2nd Quintile	3rd Quintile	4th Quintile	5th Quintile	Universe	S&P 500*
CAGR – Annual Rebalance	14.0%	9.6%	11.9%	13.5%	−4.9%	11.2%	12.9%
Average Excess Return vs. Universe**	3.4%	0.1%	0.9%	0.9%	−8.3%	NA	1.6%
Value of $10,000 Invested (20 Years)	$136,759	$62,425	$94,364	$126,252	$3,651	$83,161	$112,895
% of 1-Year Periods Strategy Outperforms the Universe	53.2%	48.1%	57.1%	51.9%	24.7%	NA	59.7%
% Rolling 3-Year Periods Strategy Outperforms	68.1%	47.8%	60.9%	56.5%	10.1%	NA	71.0%
Maximum Gain	80.3%	51.4%	47.8%	58.8%	148.5%	59.2%	54.1%
Maximum Loss	−38.9%	−20.3%	−25.4%	−30.2%	−77.3%	−24.9%	−25.9%
Sharpe Ratio	0.52	0.57	0.65	0.57	−0.01	0.49	0.69
Standard Deviation of Returns	0.22	0.14	0.14	0.16	0.41	0.16	0.14
Beta (vs. Universe)	1.12	0.76	0.67	0.78	1.88	NA	0.78
Alpha (vs. Universe)	0.02	0.03	0.05	0.04	−0.19	NA	0.04
Average Portfolio Size	81	81	81	81	82	NA	NA
Average Number of Companies *Outperforming*	37	35	38	39	23	NA	NA
Average Number of Companies *Underperforming*	42	44	40	38	54	NA	NA
Median Portfolio Value – Return on Equity	55.0%	17.7%	12.9%	7.6%	−98.7%	11.7%	14.7%
Median Portfolio Value – Return on Assets	30.2%	10.0%	5.2%	2.6%	−34.0%	4.1%	5.4%
Average Market Capitalization	$6,294	$3,589	$3,474	$3,051	$1,152	NA	NA

* Equal-weighted average of S&P 500 returns. ** Annual holding period run quarterly for a larger sample size; arithmetic average excess returns.
Source: Standard & Poor's Compustat Point in Time Database; Charter Oak Investment Systems, Inc., Venues® Data Engine

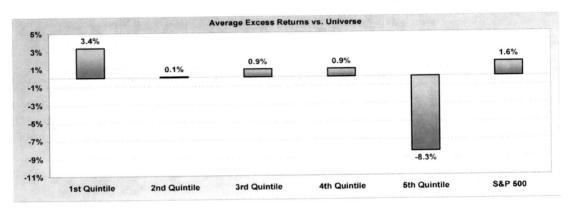

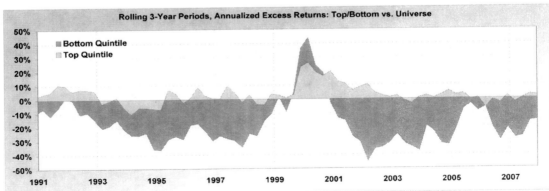

Figure 4.15 Return on Equity and Return on Assets

However, the bottom quintile would make an excellent short-sale strategy. It underperforms by an average of 8.3%, and does so for 75% of one-year and 90% of rolling three-year periods. It underperformed the market by significant percentages in all years except 1991, 2003, and 1998–1999. In other words, it doesn't work at the beginning of bull markets (1991 and 2003) and at speculative market tops (1998–1999). During the most recent bull market, from 2004 to 2007, the fifth quintile of the ROE and ROA strategy underperformed the market by a minimum of 10% per year. Therefore, the stocks in the bottom quintile would make a good list to be avoided. The bottom quintile contains companies with high negative values for both ROE and ROA.

Return on Equity and Price to Book Value

This strategy combines two investment factors that share a common denominator. Return on equity looks at profit generated on common equity, while price to book value looks at the price that must be paid for shareholders' equity.[12] Like other profitability and valuation strategies, the ROE and price-to-book value strategy considers both the quality of company resources (their ability to generate strong returns on capital) and the price the investor must pay for these resources. The top quintile selects companies with high-quality resources that are attractively valued, while the bottom selects companies that are generating losses and appear overvalued. The strength of this strategy is shown by what it did after the stock market bubble of 1998–1999: the top quintile outperformed by 25% in 2000, 16% in 2001, and over 10% in each year from 2002 through 2005 (see Figure 4.16).

The top quintile of this strategy outperforms by an average of 4.6%, and does so for 65% of one-year and 83% of rolling three-year periods. Its one flaw is that it has a relatively high maximum loss of 30% and a high standard deviation of returns (0.19), resulting in an unimpressive Sharpe ratio of 0.66. Average portfolio values range from 26% to 34% for return on equity and 1.2× to 2.3× for price to book value, so companies in the top quintile are both very profitable and relatively inexpensive.

The bottom quintile underperforms by 7.4%, on average, and does so for 73% of one-year and 90% of rolling three-year periods. The bottom quintile is very volatile, outperforming significantly in 1991, 1998–2000, and 2003–2004. Average portfolio values are in the high negative numbers for ROE, indicating large net losses, and range from 4× to over 20× for price to book value.

---

[12] Although shareholders' equity is not the same as common equity (shareholders' equity, or total equity, also includes preferred equity), the two are very similar from a quantitative point of view.

1988 ~ 2007	1st Quintile	2nd Quintile	3rd Quintile	4th Quintile	5th Quintile	Universe	S&P 500*
CAGR – Annual Rebalance	16.5%	13.5%	11.6%	11.6%	−1.6%	11.2%	12.9%
Average Excess Return vs. Universe**	4.6%	2.3%	0.5%	−1.4%	−7.4%	NA	1.6%
Value of $10,000 Invested (20 Years)	$213,446	$124,991	$89,059	$89,424	$7,268	$83,161	$112,895
% of 1-Year Periods Strategy Outperforms the Universe	64.9%	53.2%	53.2%	42.9%	27.3%	NA	59.7%
% Rolling 3-Year Periods Strategy Outperforms	82.6%	63.8%	62.3%	37.7%	10.1%	NA	71.0%
Maximum Gain	71.8%	50.7%	45.6%	51.4%	174.4%	59.2%	54.1%
Maximum Loss	−30.1%	−24.5%	−21.2%	−32.6%	−80.2%	−24.9%	−25.9%
Sharpe Ratio	0.66	0.68	0.62	0.39	0.02	0.49	0.69
Standard Deviation of Returns	0.19	0.15	0.14	0.17	0.40	0.16	0.14
Beta (vs. Universe)	0.95	0.66	0.64	0.95	1.65	NA	0.78
Alpha (vs. Universe)	0.05	0.07	0.05	−0.01	−0.16	NA	0.04
Average Portfolio Size	81	81	81	81	82	NA	NA
Average Number of Companies *Outperforming*	39	38	36	34	25	NA	NA
Average Number of Companies *Underperforming*	37	39	41	42	52	NA	NA
Median Portfolio Value – Return on Equity	28.6%	17.3%	13.2%	8.5%	−99.3%	11.7%	14.7%
Median Portfolio Value – Price to Book Value	2.0	2.3	2.1	2.5	9.3	2.3	2.3
Average Market Capitalization	$3,906	$4,374	$3,115	$3,442	$1,910	NA	NA

* Equal-weighted average of S&P 500 returns. ** Annual holding period run quarterly for a larger sample size; arithmetic average excess returns.
Source: Standard & Poor's Compustat Point in Time Database, Charter Oak Investment Systems Venues® Data Engine

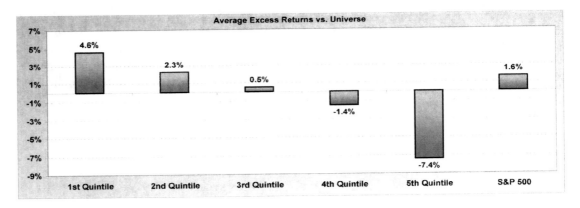

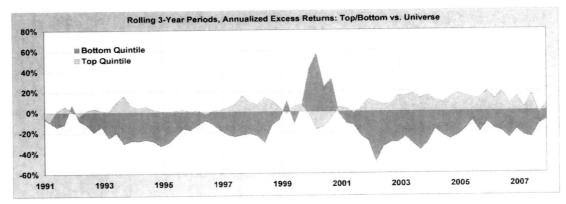

Figure 4.16 Return on Equity and Price to Book Value

ECONOMIC PROFITS

Economic Value Added (EVA) is a concept developed by management consulting firm Stern Stewart & Co. In general terms, EVA seeks to calculate the difference between the income generated by a firm and the real or implied cost of the capital that has been invested in the firm. If the difference between income and the cost of capital is positive, the firm is said to have created value for shareholders, or to have made "economic profits." If the difference is negative, the firm is said to have destroyed shareholder value. The precise calculation of EVA involves a number of accounting adjustments to arrive at net operating profit after taxes (NOPAT—the income part of the equation) and invested capital (the denominator of the profitability calculation).

We use an admittedly crude approximation of EVA, primarily because it is impossible to perform custom adjustments of accounting figures within a large quantitative test. To distinguish our tests from a true EVA test, which should be done in accordance with Stern Stewart's methodology, we'll call ours "economic profits." Our concept starts with NOPAT, calculated as shown in Figure 4.1 under return on invested capital: sales less costs of goods sold, less other operating expenses and depreciation, less adjusted taxes. Invested capital also follows the definition given in Figure 4.1: the book value of common equity plus long-term debt, plus preferred stock and minority interest. The result of NOPAT divided by invested capital is ROIC.

To arrive at economic profits or losses for a company, we begin with ROIC—the company's level of profitability—and subtract from this the cost of the capital that has been contributed to (or reinvested in) the business. The cost of contributed capital is sometimes called the *weighted average cost of capital*. The calculation is shown in Figure 4.17.

Weighted Average Cost of Capital

= cost of debt (after tax) X% total debt to total capital
+ cost of common equity X% common equity to total capital
+ cost of preferred equity X% preferred equity to total capital

where:

cost of debt (after tax) = interest expense / total debt X (1 - tax rate)
cost of common equity = Risk Free Interest Rate + (Beta X Equity Risk Premium)
cost of preferred equity = total preferred dividends / preferred equity

Notes:

We use the average yield of 10-Year Treasury notes from 1980-2006 as the Risk Free Rate (7.5%).
We use the difference between the average annual return for our Universe & the RFR from 1980-2006
  as the Equity Risk Premium (9%).
Beta is a measure of the volatility of an individual stock versus the volatility of the overall market.
We test economic profits without Beta; we also test economic profits using price-to-sales in place of Beta.
When price-to-sales is used, it is limited to no higher than 2.0 and no lower than 0.2.

Figure 4.17 The Weighted Average Cost of Capital

Our first version of "economic profits," which uses Beta times the equity risk premium (9%) plus the average 10-year U.S. Treasury note yield (7.5%) to calculate the cost of common equity for a company, works slightly better than ROIC alone as a quantitative test. The top quintile outperforms by an average of 2.7% versus 2.3% for ROIC alone, and does so for 65% of one-year and 78% of rolling three-year periods (versus 69% and 78% for ROIC). In addition, the Sharpe ratio for the top quintile is 0.78, significantly higher than the 0.69 value for ROIC. Average portfolio values for the top quintile of economic profits range from 8% to over 13% (see Figure 4.18).

However, the bottom quintile underperforms by an average of just 0.9%, versus −4.3% for ROIC. Consistency of returns is also lower, with the bottom quintile of the economic profits test underperforming for 65% of one-year and 74% of rolling three-year periods, versus 74% and 90% for ROIC.

Economic Profits: No Beta

Results for the bottom quintile of the economic profits strategy can be improved simply by removing Beta. When Beta is removed from the cost of capital calculation, results for the top quintile of the economic profits strategy stay about the same as when Beta is included. However, excess returns for the bottom quintile improve slightly, with the bottom quintile for economic profits excluding Beta underperforming by an average of 1.4% versus underperformance of 0.9% with Beta (see Figure 4.19). I question the value of Beta as a measure of risk, which is the function it is intended to serve in the capital asset pricing model (CAPM), the model used to calculate the cost of common equity in our economic profits test (see Figure 4.17). In the capital asset pricing model,[13] the equity risk premium, which is defined as the excess return of stocks over the return of a "risk-free" security, such as U.S. Treasury bills, is multiplied by Beta to arrive at a "risk-adjusted" equity premium for a particular stock. The fact that taking Beta out actually improves quintile returns suggests it serves no useful purpose, particularly since Beta is intended as a quantitative and not a qualitative measure of risk.

Economic Profits: Price to Sales in Place of Beta

If Beta is not a good measure of risk, perhaps valuation is. Few investors would disagree that, other things being equal, purchasing a stock that carries a high valuation multiple is riskier than purchasing a low valuation stock. Shares of MEMC Electronic

---

[13] The capital asset pricing model (CAPM) is a formula that is used to describe the relationship between risk and expected return when pricing risky securities, such as stocks. The Sharpe ratio was invented by William Sharpe, who received a Nobel Prize in 1990 for his work on developing the CAPM.

1988 ~ 2007	1st Quintile	2nd Quintile	3rd Quintile	4th Quintile	5th Quintile	Universe	S&P 500*
CAGR – Annual Rebalance	14.9%	13.1%	13.5%	11.3%	9.5%	11.2%	12.9%
Average Excess Return vs. Universe**	2.7%	1.3%	1.4%	0.3%	−0.9%	NA	1.6%
Value of $10,000 Invested (20 Years)	$159,753	$116,752	$125,847	$85,604	$61,956	$83,161	$112,895
% of 1-Year Periods Strategy Outperforms the Universe	64.9%	50.6%	54.5%	55.8%	35.1%	NA	59.7%
% Rolling 3-Year Periods Strategy Outperforms	78.3%	63.8%	65.2%	55.1%	26.1%	NA	71.0%
Maximum Gain	51.5%	50.2%	55.1%	56.8%	80.6%	59.2%	54.1%
Maximum Loss	−21.2%	−19.2%	−22.9%	−28.1%	−36.6%	−24.9%	−25.9%
Sharpe Ratio	0.78	0.70	0.69	0.57	0.32	0.49	0.69
Standard Deviation of Returns	0.14	0.13	0.14	0.15	0.23	0.16	0.14
Beta (vs. Universe)	0.73	0.66	0.69	0.79	1.30	NA	0.78
Alpha (vs. Universe)	0.06	0.06	0.05	0.03	−0.05	NA	0.04
Average Portfolio Size	247	247	247	247	248	NA	NA
Average Number of Companies *Outperforming*	116	117	112	111	96	NA	NA
Average Number of Companies *Underperforming*	121	121	124	124	136	NA	NA
Median Portfolio Value – Econ. Profits – (ROIC, Beta)	12.6%	1.4%	−1.6%	−5.2%	−21.6%	−2.7%	−0.1%
Average Market Capitalization	$9,807	$5,295	$3,444	$2,915	$2,512	NA	NA

* Equal-weighted average of S&P 500 returns. ** Annual holding period run quarterly for a larger sample size; arithmetic average excess returns.
Source: Standard & Poor's Compustat Point in Time Database; Charter Oak Investment Systems, Inc., Venues® Data Engine

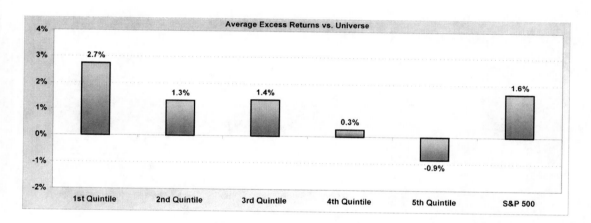

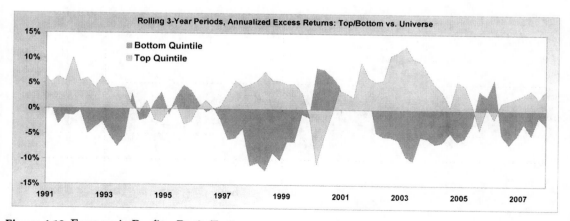

Figure 4.18 Economic Profits: Basic Test

1988 ~ 2007	1st Quintile	2nd Quintile	3rd Quintile	4th Quintile	5th Quintile	Universe	S&P 500*
CAGR – Annual Rebalance	14.7%	12.5%	13.4%	11.5%	9.4%	11.2%	12.9%
Average Excess Return vs. Universe**	2.7%	1.0%	1.1%	0.5%	−1.4%	NA	1.6%
Value of $10,000 Invested (20 Years)	$155,439	$104,937	$122,843	$87,532	$60,826	$83,161	$112,895
% of 1-Year Periods Strategy Outperforms the Universe	66.2%	55.8%	57.1%	58.4%	36.4%	NA	59.7%
% Rolling 3-Year Periods Strategy Outperforms	76.8%	55.1%	59.4%	55.1%	23.2%	NA	71.0%
Maximum Gain	57.7%	53.5%	53.3%	54.4%	80.3%	59.2%	54.1%
Maximum Loss	−22.5%	−21.7%	−22.9%	−27.5%	−37.6%	−24.9%	−25.9%
Sharpe Ratio	0.74	0.64	0.68	0.62	0.30	0.49	0.69
Standard Deviation of Returns	0.15	0.14	0.14	0.14	0.22	0.16	0.14
Beta (vs. Universe)	0.80	0.73	0.70	0.75	1.27	NA	0.78
Alpha (vs. Universe)	0.05	0.04	0.05	0.04	−0.05	NA	0.04
Average Portfolio Size	260	260	261	260	261	NA	NA
Average Number of Companies *Outperforming*	122	118	121	116	102	NA	NA
Average Number of Companies *Underperforming*	127	132	130	131	142	NA	NA
Median Portfolio Value — Econ. Profits – (ROIC, No Beta)	11.5%	0.5%	−2.3%	−5.3%	−21.2%	−2.7%	−1.0%
Average Market Capitalization	$8,843	$5,264	$3,238	$3,271	$2,591	NA	NA

* Equal-weighted average of S&P 500 returns. ** Annual holding period run quarterly for a larger sample size; arithmetic average excess returns.
Source: Standard & Poor's Compustat Point in Time Database; Charter Oak Investment Systems, Inc., Venues® Data Engine

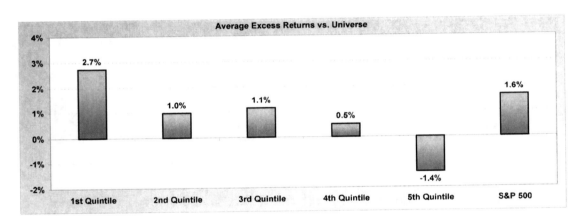

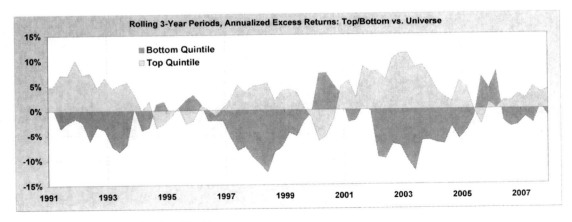

Figure 4.19 Economic Profits: No Beta

Materials, a large U.S. maker of silicon wafers for the semiconductor industry, soared from $13 in late 2004 to $94 at the end of 2007, as it recorded strong earnings growth due to increasing sales of silicon wafers to the solar energy industry. In early 2008, however, the stock fell by over 30% to about $62, as investors began to worry about share prices in the solar energy industry. The problem was overly high expectations: MEMC shares sold at 15× forward earnings estimates at the end of 2004 but were selling at over 27× estimates by the end of 2007. To see if valuation would work in the capital asset pricing model, we replaced a stock's Beta with its price-to-sales (P/S) ratio.[14] (Like Beta, the average P/S ratio is about 1.0, so it works well in the CAPM equation.) The result was an improvement in excess returns, particularly for the bottom quintile.

Using price to sales in place of Beta, the top quintile outperforms by an average of 3.2% versus 2.7% with Beta (see Figure 4.20). Consistency of returns remains about the same. The bottom quintile of economic profits using price to sales underperforms by 3.2%, on average, a strong improvement over the 0.9% underperformance for economic profits with Beta. The consistency of this underperformance also improves. I believe these results, especially the greatly improved results for the bottom quintile, show that Beta is a poor proxy for risk. In the economic profits test that follows this one, we're going to stick with price to sales in place of Beta. In addition, we'll replace ROIC with cash ROIC in our calculation of profitability. You'll see that this replacement even further increases excess returns and consistency.

Economic Profits: Cash ROIC and Price to Sales in Place of Beta

For our final economic profits test, we throw out income statement–based ROIC and replace it with cash flow–based ROIC, which is defined simply as 12-month free cash flow (cash from operations minus capital expenses) divided by invested capital. Again, we used the average rate for the 10-year Treasury note as our risk-free rate, in calculating the cost of common equity, and a company's P/S ratio in place of Beta. The results are very strong.

The top quintile outperforms by 5.1%, on average, and does so for 76% of one-year and 88% of rolling three-year periods (see Figure 4.21). The top quintile significantly underperforms only in 1999–2000 and 2003–2004. The maximum loss remains a low 22%, and the Sharpe ratio increases to 0.87 from 0.78 for our original economic

---

[14] The formula for the cost of common equity (Figure 4.17) using price to sales in place of Beta is the risk-free interest rate (7.5%) plus the P/S ratio multiplied by the equity risk premium (9.0%). The P/S ratio was limited to no higher than 2.0 and no lower than 0.2 to keep extreme values from unduly affecting a company's cost of capital.

1988 ~ 2007	1st Quintile	2nd Quintile	3rd Quintile	4th Quintile	5th Quintile	Universe	S&P 500*
CAGR – Annual Rebalance	15.4%	13.1%	13.3%	12.5%	7.1%	11.2%	12.9%
Average Excess Return vs. Universe**	3.2%	1.9%	1.7%	0.3%	−3.2%	NA	1.6%
Value of $10,000 Invested (20 Years)	$174,389	$117,082	$120,879	$105,044	$39,624	$83,161	$112,895
% of 1-Year Periods Strategy Outperforms the Universe	64.9%	58.4%	62.3%	45.5%	36.4%	NA	59.7%
% Rolling 3-Year Periods Strategy Outperforms	76.8%	75.4%	68.1%	53.6%	11.6%	NA	71.0%
Maximum Gain	59.4%	56.7%	49.3%	54.6%	73.5%	59.2%	54.1%
Maximum Loss	−23.8%	−22.5%	−23.8%	−23.6%	−44.9%	−24.9%	−25.9%
Sharpe Ratio	0.73	0.66	0.75	0.60	0.21	0.49	0.69
Standard Deviation of Returns	0.16	0.15	0.13	0.14	0.23	0.16	0.14
Beta (vs. Universe)	0.79	0.71	0.67	0.80	1.28	NA	0.78
Alpha (vs. Universe)	0.06	0.05	0.06	0.03	−0.07	NA	0.04
Average Portfolio Size	260	260	261	260	261	NA	NA
Average Number of Companies *Outperforming*	124	120	122	116	98	NA	NA
Average Number of Companies *Underperforming*	124	129	129	132	147	NA	NA
Median Portfolio Value – Econ. Profits (ROIC, P/S)	9.7%	−0.2%	−3.6%	−7.9%	−26.6%	−5.3%	−2.2%
Average Market Capitalization	$5,962	$4,929	$4,600	$4,257	$3,449	NA	NA

* Equal-weighted average of S&P 500 returns. ** Annual holding period run quarterly for a larger sample size; arithmetic average excess returns.
Source: Standard & Poor's Compustat Point in Time Database; Charter Oak Investment Systems, Inc., Venues® Data Engine

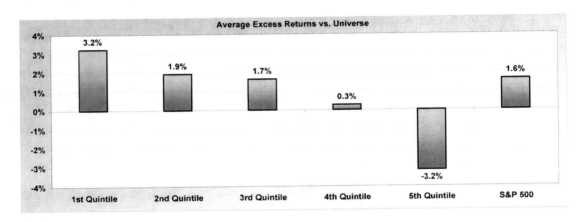

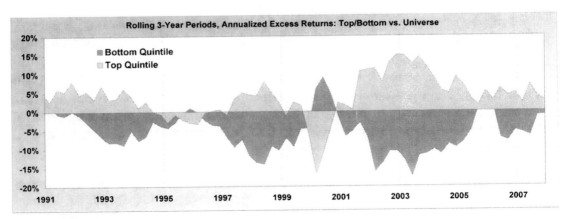

Figure 4.20 Economic Profits: Price to Sales in Place of Beta

1990 ~ 2007	1st Quintile	2nd Quintile	3rd Quintile	4th Quintile	5th Quintile	Universe	S&P 500*
CAGR – Annual Rebalance	16.2%	12.9%	11.5%	9.9%	5.0%	10.3%	12.0%
Average Excess Return vs. Universe**	5.1%	2.3%	1.0%	−1.1%	−5.5%	NA	1.5%
Value of $10,000 Invested (18 Years)	$149,233	$88,440	$71,006	$54,302	$24,101	$58,670	$76,297
% of 1-Year Periods Strategy Outperforms the Universe	76.4%	61.1%	50.0%	44.4%	25.0%	NA	56.9%
% Rolling 3-Year Periods Strategy Outperforms	87.5%	76.6%	64.1%	37.5%	15.6%	NA	68.8%
Maximum Gain	54.2%	52.6%	62.1%	57.3%	68.9%	59.2%	54.1%
Maximum Loss	−21.6%	−26.7%	−23.7%	−28.5%	−48.0%	−24.9%	−25.9%
Sharpe Ratio	0.87	0.69	0.60	0.41	0.10	0.46	0.64
Standard Deviation of Returns	0.15	0.15	0.14	0.16	0.23	0.17	0.14
Beta (vs. Universe)	0.71	0.71	0.76	0.92	1.25	NA	0.78
Alpha (vs. Universe)	0.09	0.06	0.04	0.00	−0.09	NA	0.04
Average Portfolio Size	222	223	223	223	223	NA	NA
Average Number of Companies *Outperforming*	109	106	99	92	83	NA	NA
Average Number of Companies *Underperforming*	103	108	112	119	129	NA	NA
Median Portfolio Value – Econ. Profits – (Cash ROIC, P/S)	11.9%	−3.6%	−9.1%	−15.9%	−37.0%	−10.4%	−6.5%
Average Market Capitalization	$5,900	$5,826	$6,042	$4,947	$3,554	NA	NA

* Equal-weighted average of S&P 500 returns. ** Annual holding period run quarterly for a larger sample size; arithmetic average excess returns.
Source: Standard & Poor's Compustat Point in Time Database; Charter Oak Investment Systems, Inc., Venues® Data Engine

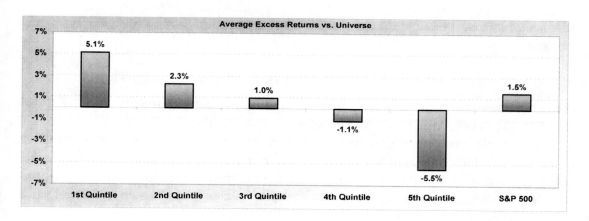

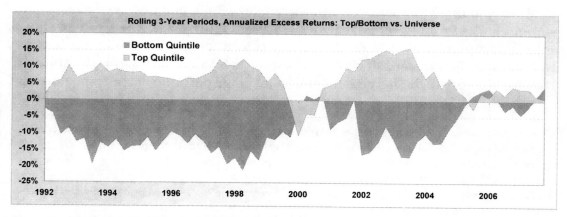

Figure 4.21 Economic Profits: Cash ROIC and Price to Sales in Place of Beta

profits test.[15] Average portfolio values for economic profits based on cash ROIC range from 8% to over 13%.

The bottom quintile underperforms by 5.5%, on average, and does so for 75% of one-year and 84% of rolling three-year periods. Average portfolio values for economic profits for the bottom quintile range from −29% to −47%.

Economic Profits (Cash ROIC/Price to Sales) by Economic Sector

The economic profits strategy using cash ROIC and price to sales in place of Beta works extremely well across economic sectors. In fact, it works for almost every sector across the board. In particular, I'd point out the health care sector, where the top quintile out-performs by an average of 8.6% and does so for 100% of rolling three-year periods, and the bottom quintile underperforms by 9.4% and does so for 94% of rolling three-year periods (see Figure 4.22). The strategy also works very well in the information technol-ogy sector. Its only weakness is in the bottom quintiles of the telecom services and util-ities sectors. However, note that the utilities sector test contains an average of only three companies in the bottom quintile and hence may not be reliable.

Economic Profits (Cash ROIC/Price to Sales) and Enterprise Value to EBITDA

As you've seen earlier in this chapter, profitability and valuation tests work very well together. This test combines the strongest of the profitability tests with one of the strongest valuation tests.[16] Also note that by combining a cash flow–based profitability strategy with an income statement–based valuation strategy, we get a better view of the company as a whole. The strategy considers data from all three financial statements— the income statement, balance sheet, and cash flow statement—as well as market price. The results are very strong.

The top quintile outperforms by an average of 8.1%, and does so for 76% of one-year and 88% of rolling three-year periods (see Figure 4.23). The strategy signifi-cantly underperforms only in 1999–2000 and in 2003. The maximum loss is a low 18%, and the standard deviation of returns is 0.16 versus 0.17 for the Universe, resulting in a very high Sharpe ratio of 0.98. Average portfolio values range from 8%

---

[15] One might reasonably ask why I use the Sharpe ratio in presenting the strategies in this book, while I eschew the use of Beta (at least in the cost of capital calculation), since both are related to the same university professor (William Sharpe). The answer is primarily that the Sharpe ratio is a measure of risk-adjusted returns that is widely used by money managers.

[16] You'll see in Chapter 5 that enterprise value to EBITDA and free cash flow to price are by far the two strongest valuation factors we tested.

Top Quintile

1990 ~ 2007	Energy	Materials	Industrials	Consumer Discretionary	Consumer Staples	Health Care	Financials	Information Technology	Telecom Services	Utilities	Universe	S&P 500*
CAGR – Quintile	17.6%	13.9%	14.8%	13.6%	14.1%	20.5%	18.9%	20.5%	11.5%	22.0%	10.3%	12.0%
CAGR – Sector	11.9%	9.7%	10.7%	7.3%	10.8%	11.9%	14.1%	8.1%	5.6%	11.9%	NA	NA
Excess Return vs. Sector	5.6%	4.1%	4.2%	6.2%	3.3%	8.6%	4.8%	12.5%	6.0%	10.1%	NA	NA
Value of $10,000	$184,335	$103,324	$120,638	$98,995	$107,988	$287,365	$225,113	$288,840	$71,356	$360,422	$58,670	$76,297
% 1-Year Outperformance	66.7%	77.8%	83.3%	77.8%	66.7%	66.7%	55.6%	72.2%	72.2%	50.0%	NA	NA
% 3-Year Outperformance	75.0%	87.5%	93.8%	93.8%	81.3%	100.0%	68.8%	87.5%	68.8%	87.5%	NA	NA
Maximum Gain	70.4%	42.0%	40.0%	58.5%	46.6%	78.6%	56.5%	122.3%	52.6%	200.6%	44.0%	41.4%
Maximum Loss	−24.6%	−19.2%	−14.8%	−18.2%	−12.8%	−16.6%	−15.0%	−33.3%	−28.8%	−20.1%	−19.1%	−18.1%
Standard Deviation	0.26	0.17	0.16	0.20	0.16	0.24	0.24	0.32	0.24	0.49	0.17	0.15
Beta (vs. Sector)	0.89	1.02	0.98	0.93	1.04	0.82	0.85	0.76	0.43	1.65	NA	NA
Alpha (vs. Sector)	0.07	0.04	0.04	0.07	0.03	0.11	0.07	0.14	0.09	0.07	NA	NA
Portfolio Size	18	25	47	53	15	31	26	37	6	2	NA	NA

Bottom Quintile

1990 ~ 2007	Energy	Materials	Industrials	Consumer Discretionary	Consumer Staples	Health Care	Financials	Information Technology	Telecom Services	Utilities	Universe	S&P 500*
CAGR – Quintile	6.9%	5.0%	2.9%	3.7%	6.0%	2.5%	11.0%	−0.2%	4.1%	15.1%	10.3%	12.0%
CAGR – Sector	11.9%	9.7%	10.7%	7.3%	10.8%	11.9%	14.1%	8.1%	5.6%	11.9%	NA	NA
Excess Return vs. Sector	−5.0%	−4.7%	−7.8%	−3.7%	−4.8%	−9.4%	−3.1%	−8.2%	−1.5%	3.2%	NA	NA
Value of $10,000	$33,406	$24,022	$16,674	$19,094	$28,731	$15,472	$65,577	$9,697	$20,483	$126,488	$58,670	$76,297
% 1-Year Outperformance	38.9%	44.4%	16.7%	27.8%	22.2%	22.2%	27.8%	22.2%	55.6%	61.1%	NA	NA
% 3-Year Outperformance	12.5%	12.5%	18.8%	25.0%	6.3%	6.3%	18.8%	12.5%	37.5%	75.0%	NA	NA
Maximum Gain	68.6%	49.3%	40.9%	55.0%	36.3%	89.1%	56.7%	215.4%	151.2%	149.3%	44.0%	41.4%
Maximum Loss	−50.8%	−25.5%	−32.8%	−26.5%	−18.9%	−38.4%	−19.1%	−65.7%	−66.2%	−42.3%	−19.1%	−18.1%
Standard Deviation	0.31	0.18	0.17	0.21	0.15	0.30	0.22	0.58	0.47	0.39	0.17	0.15
Beta (vs. Sector)	1.19	1.02	1.05	1.02	0.97	1.13	0.88	1.42	1.17	1.76	NA	NA
Alpha (vs. Sector)	−0.06	0.00	−0.05	−0.06	0.01	−0.09	0.01	−0.14	−0.06	0.03	NA	NA
Portfolio Size	19	25	50	58	18	32	29	39	7	3	NA	NA

* Equal-weighted average of S&P 500 returns.
Source: Standard & Poor's Compustat Point in Time Database; Charter Oak Investment Systems, Inc., Venues® Data Engine

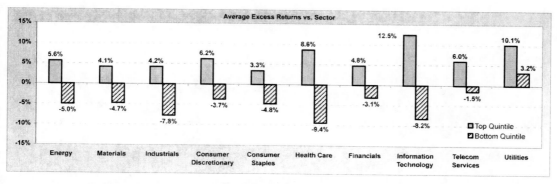

Figure 4.22 Economic Profits (Cash ROIC / Price to Sales) by Economic Sector

1990 ~ 2007	1st Quintile	2nd Quintile	3rd Quintile	4th Quintile	5th Quintile	Universe	S&P 500*
CAGR − Annual Rebalance	17.9%	11.5%	9.9%	7.3%	1.0%	10.3%	12.0%
Average Excess Return vs. Universe**	8.1%	1.9%	−1.7%	−2.5%	−6.0%	NA	1.5%
Value of $10,000 Invested (18 Years)	$193,951	$70,732	$54,406	$35,431	$11,862	$58,670	$76,297
% of 1-Year Periods Strategy Outperforms the Universe	76.4%	52.8%	44.4%	33.3%	23.6%	NA	56.9%
% Rolling 3-Year Periods Strategy Outperforms	87.5%	75.0%	37.5%	15.6%	12.5%	NA	68.8%
Maximum Gain	56.1%	60.7%	54.1%	58.9%	139.3%	59.2%	54.1%
Maximum Loss	−17.6%	−25.2%	−26.9%	−32.4%	−70.1%	−24.9%	−25.9%
Sharpe Ratio	0.98	0.59	0.41	0.28	0.04	0.46	0.64
Standard Deviation of Returns	0.16	0.16	0.15	0.19	0.42	0.17	0.14
Beta (vs. Universe)	0.65	0.74	0.68	1.02	1.77	NA	0.78
Alpha (vs. Universe)	0.12	0.05	0.02	−0.03	−0.15	NA	0.04
Average Portfolio Size	52	52	52	52	53	NA	NA
Average Number of Companies *Outperforming*	26	25	24	20	16	NA	NA
Average Number of Companies *Underperforming*	23	26	26	30	33	NA	NA
Median Portfolio Value − Economic Profits	13.7%	−3.3%	−8.9%	−16.8%	−51.6%	−10.6%	−6.3%
Median Portfolio Value − EV-to-EBITDA	3.4	6.9	9.2	14.3	−13.6	10.7	9.1
Average Market Capitalization	$3,095	$3,392	$4,800	$5,390	$1,063	NA	NA

* Equal-weighted average of S&P 500 returns. ** Annual holding period run quarterly for a larger sample size; arithmetic average excess returns.
Source: Standard & Poor's Compustat Point in Time Database; Charter Oak Investment Systems, Inc., Venues® Data Engine

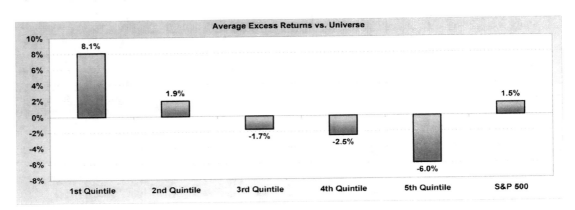

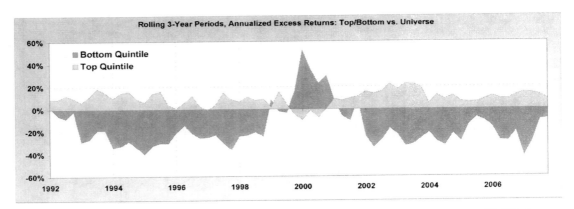

Figure 4.23 Economic Profits (Cash ROIC / Price to Sales) and Enterprise Value to EBITDA

to 27% for economic profits and from 3× to 5× for enterprise value (EV) to EBITDA, so companies in the top quintile are both very profitable (remember that 8% to 27% signifies cash profits *above* the average cost of capital) and very inexpensive on an operating earnings basis.

The bottom quintile underperforms by an average of 6%, and does so for 76% of one-year and 87% of rolling three-year periods. The bottom quintile significantly out-performs in only three periods: 1990–1991, 1999–2000, and 2003. Average portfolio val-ues are in the high negative numbers for economic profits and range from −3× to −26× for EV to EBITDA, so companies in this quintile have both cash outflows and negative operating earnings (before depreciation).

Economic Profits (Cash ROIC/Price to Sales) and Capital Expenditures to Property, Plant, and Equipment

I'll discuss the capex to property, plant, and equipment (PP&E) strategy in detail in Chapter 10. It is a "red flag" that can indicate trouble for the companies that appear in the bottom quintile. Specifically, capex to PP&E serves as a barometer of *capital intensity*, the degree that a company must rely on capital assets, such as machinery, factories, and office equipment, to produce goods or render services. Capital intensity is directly related to economic profits—the reason is that the more capital required by a business (to purchase additional capital assets), the more profits the business must generate in order produce an economic profit (a profit above the business's cost of capital). Companies in the top quintile of this strategy have low capital expenditures relative to their existing capital asset base and are also generating strong economic profits. In con-trast, companies in the bottom quintile are seeing their capital investment rate increase and are generating economic losses.

The top quintile outperforms by 5.3%, on average, and does so for 78% of one-year and 88% of rolling three-year periods (see Figure 4.24). The top quintile significantly underperforms in only three periods: 1990–1991, 1999–2000, and 2003. The one fault of the top quintile is that its returns are slightly volatile, with a standard deviation of 0.18 versus 0.14 for the S&P 500. The result is only a moderate Sharpe ratio of 0.73 versus a ratio of 0.64 for the S&P 500. Average portfolio values range from 8% to 25% for economic profits and from 2% to 9% for capex to PP&E, the latter indicating that com-panies in the top quintile must spend only modest amounts on capex relative to their existing capital asset base.

The bottom quintile underperforms by 12.4%, on average, and does so for 76% of one-year and 95% of rolling three-year periods, making it very consistent. It signifi-cantly outperforms only in 1999–2000 and in 2003. Average portfolio values are in the high negatives for economic profits and range from 71% to over 100% for capex to

1990 ~ 2007	1st Quintile	2nd Quintile	3rd Quintile	4th Quintile	5th Quintile	Universe	S&P 500*
CAGR – Annual Rebalance	16.9%	12.0%	10.5%	11.1%	−4.4%	10.3%	12.0%
Average Excess Return vs. Universe**	5.3%	1.2%	0.0%	−0.5%	−12.4%	NA	1.5%
Value of $10,000 Invested (18 Years)	$166,193	$76,574	$60,611	$66,891	$4,447	$58,670	$76,297
% of 1-Year Periods Strategy Outperforms the Universe	77.8%	58.3%	54.2%	40.3%	23.6%	NA	56.9%
% Rolling 3-Year Periods Strategy Outperforms	87.5%	67.2%	59.4%	29.7%	4.7%	NA	68.8%
Maximum Gain	62.9%	52.6%	59.0%	65.3%	92.0%	59.2%	54.1%
Maximum Loss	−22.6%	−29.8%	−37.2%	−30.7%	−85.0%	−24.9%	−25.9%
Sharpe Ratio	0.73	0.60	0.49	0.39	−0.14	0.46	0.64
Standard Deviation of Returns	0.18	0.15	0.16	0.19	0.34	0.17	0.14
Beta (vs. Universe)	0.83	0.70	0.76	1.01	1.66	NA	0.78
Alpha (vs. Universe)	0.07	0.05	0.03	−0.01	−0.20	NA	0.04
Average Portfolio Size	54	53	53	53	53	NA	NA
Average Number of Companies *Outperforming*	27	25	24	22	16	NA	NA
Average Number of Companies *Underperforming*	25	27	27	29	35	NA	NA
Median Portfolio Value – Economic Profits	13.2%	−3.2%	−9.1%	−17.3%	−48.7%	−10.6%	−6.3%
Median Portfolio Value – Capex to PP&E	6%	14%	20%	33%	89%	35%	23%
Average Market Capitalization	$3,126	$4,567	$7,188	$4,829	$1,409	NA	NA

* Equal-weighted average of S&P 500 returns. ** Annual holding period run quarterly for a larger sample size; arithmetic average excess returns.
Source: Standard & Poor's Compustat Point in Time Database; Charter Oak Investment Systems, Inc., Venues® Data Engine

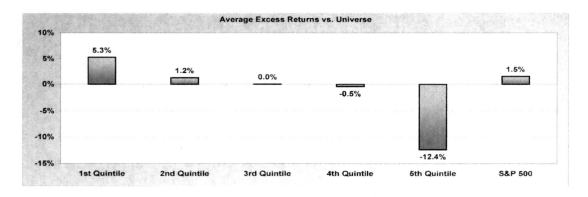

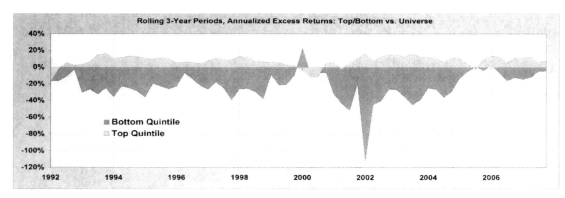

Figure 4.24 Economic Profits (Cash ROIC/Price to Sales) and Capital Expenditures to Property, Plant, and Equipment

PP&E; this means that companies in the bottom quintile are both generating economic losses and spending enough on capital expenditures in a single year to nearly replace their entire existing capital asset base (at depreciated book value).[17] Thus, they are not only destroying shareholder value in the present, they are likely increasing the rate (through large capital additions) at which they will destroy shareholder value in the future.

SUMMARY

- Profitability strategies as a group work well quantitatively—they're predictive of excess stock market returns. One reason for this is that past profitability often serves as a barometer of a company's potential for future success, since it indicates the results that might be expected if current and future profits are reinvested in the business.
- Profitability should be viewed as a strong combining factor—an important *basic*—in constructing quantitative tests or stock screens.
- Profitability strategies act as strong *building blocks* in combination with valuation strategies: the profitability factor measures the quality of the company's assets, while the valuation factor indicates the price the investor must pay to obtain those assets.
- Return on invested capital (ROIC) is a strong profitability factor. It compares a firm's after-tax operating income to the total investment in the firm (both debt and equity). ROIC is also very consistent across economic sectors.
- Like other profitability strategies, companies in the top quintile by ROIC tend to be large caps. Large cap companies often have both the competitive strength and economies of scale necessary to achieve strong profitability.
- While ROIC is calculated using the income statement, cash ROIC is based on income as measured by cash flow (from the statement of cash flows). ROIC and cash ROIC make a strong two-factor strategy.
- Unprofitable companies that are issuing large amounts of shares should be avoided or sold short. The bottom quintile of the ROIC and one-year reduction in shares outstanding strategy can provide a list of such short-sale candidates.
- A simpler measure of return on capital that is just as effective as ROIC, is operating income to invested capital. Earnings before interest and taxes (EBIT) or earnings before interest, taxes, depreciation and amortization (EBITDA)

---

[17] If the replacement value of existing PP&E was considered, capital expenditures would likely appear less dramatic but still high.

minus capital expenditures can both be used to approximate operating income in calculating this ratio. Use the same denominator—invested capital—used in calculating ROIC.

- Combining profitability and valuation factors works particularly well when the profitability measure is income statement-based and the valuation measure is cash flow statement-based, or vice versa. One such strong two-factor strategy is EBITDA minus capital expenditures to invested capital and free cash flow to price.

- Return on equity (ROE) is another simple profitability strategy that works well. Return on assets (ROA) *doesn't* work as well, perhaps because assets is too broad a measure of a company's invested capital.

- A combination of ROE and ROA works very well to identify stocks that should be avoided or sold short. Stocks in the bottom quintile of this strategy underperform significantly.

- The ROE and price to book value strategy combines two investment factors that share a similar denominator (common equity/stockholders' equity). The strategy provides strong and consistent excess returns.

- The economic profits strategy seeks to calculate the difference between the income generated by a firm and the real or implied cost of invested capital (debt plus equity). It is one of the most effective profitability strategies we tested.

- To arrive at economic profits, we begin with ROIC (profitability) and then subtract the cost of capital that has been contributed to, or reinvested in, the business.

- The cost of capital calculation, sometimes called the *weighted average cost of capital*, is detailed in Figure 4.17. It includes the cost of debt plus an implied cost of equity, which is calculated as Beta times the equity risk premium plus the risk free rate of return. Beta is used to represent the risk (volatility) of the individual security and the equity risk premium represents the return of stocks over Treasury, or "risk free," securities over an extended period of time.

- The economic profits test can be improved simply by leaving out Beta. It can further be improved by substituting a company's price-to-sales (P/S) ratio for Beta. The P/S ratio is used to capture a company's valuation, the level of which represents an important risk factor.

- A final improvement to the economic profits test can be made by substituting cash ROIC for ROIC. Cash ROIC uses free cash flow (cash flow from operations minus capital expenditures) in place of operating income, and results in a very strong test.

- One of the strongest two-factor strategies presented in this book is economic profits (cash ROIC/price-to-sales) and enterprise value to EBITDA. It combines a cash flow-based profitability measure with an income statement-based valuation measure.

CHAPTER 5

Valuation

[How] does one decide what's "attractive?" In answering this question, most analysts feel they must choose between two approaches customarily thought to be in opposition: "value" and "growth." Indeed, many investment professionals see any mixing of the two terms as a form of intellectual cross-dressing.

> Warren Buffett, from *The Essays of Warren Buffett* (selected and arranged by Lawrence Cunningham)

Intrinsic value is the investment concept on which our views of security analysis are founded. Without some defined standards of value for judging whether securities are over- or underpriced in the marketplace, the analyst is a potential victim of the tides of pessimism and euphoria which sweep the security markets.

> Sidney Cottle, Roger F. Murray, Frank E. Block, *Graham and Dodd's Security Analysis*

Value in the stock market, as in the markets for anything from real estate to works of art to baseball cards, derives from purchasing an asset at a price below that at which it can readily be resold later. It would seem, then, that value must not be easy to discover, for if it were, many investors would rush to buy the assets of "value," but few would be willing to sell (supermarkets often do this with a few advertised items—called *loss leaders*—but only with the idea that once customers are in the store, they will purchase more expensive items as well). Yet without value, an investor can only hope that someone else will be willing to pay an even higher price for the asset. This is the "greater fools" theory of investment—the theory that an investment can always be sold above its purchase price as long as there are investors who are even greater fools than the original purchaser. The prudent investor strives to purchase shares at a discount to fair value, providing what Benjamin Graham called a *margin of safety*. If, after purchasing stock at such a discount and watching it rise toward fair value, the fools and greater fools do come along, then so much the better.

Just because a stock is cheap doesn't guarantee that it brings with it value. Penny stocks derive their name from their low price, but they often prove a trap for the inexperienced investor (and a boon to promoters). A company whose business model isn't working can stay cheap for a very long time. Sun Microsystems, for example, soared to over $250 during the 1999 Internet boom. Following the Internet bust, from 2003 through early 2008, shares traded in a range from about $12 to $26,[1] while valuations on a price-to-sales basis ranged from 0.6× to 1.5×, well below the technology sector average of 1.6× to 2.8× for the period. On the other hand, stocks that have high price-to-earnings (P/E) or even price-to-sales (P/S) ratios aren't necessarily overvalued. Over the past 20 years, McDonald's ratio of price to trailing earnings per share has averaged over 21× (a P/E ratio many would consider to be high), but its stock has far outpaced the returns on the S&P 500 over this period.

Valuation can be approached in a variety of ways. Many investors seek to determine the approximate value of the returns they can expect on an investment, whether in cash inflows to the business or in dividends paid to owners, discounted at some appropriate rate to account for (1) the riskiness of the investment and (2) the rate of return readily available on a less risky investment, such as U.S. Treasury securities. Others simply seek to determine the price that an informed private investor, such as an industry competitor or investment firm, would pay for the assets of the corporation. Both of these approaches involve making qualitative judgments (e.g., what is the relationship between the fair value of a firm's assets and their book value?) and/or projections about the future (e.g., is a company's current competitive advantage likely to be sustainable?). Making such qualitative or future trend-related judgments is not easily done with quantitative analysis.

In this chapter, we take a rather simple approach to valuation: we just compare the cost of one company to the cost of every other company in our Universe, based on some historical measurement of profitability or asset value, and assume a purchase of the cheapest stocks and a sale of the most expensive. It is a testament to the power of valuation that such crude tests generate the strong results you will see in the following pages. What you will also see is that the combination of valuation and other basics, such as profitability, price momentum, and growth, results in some of the strongest two-factor tests that we recorded. In particular, when we combine valuation and growth factors, it becomes obvious that far from being distinct approaches, growth and value complement each other. Value protects the investor from the excesses of growth,

[1] As of May 2008, shares of Sun Microsystems (JAVA) traded near $13.

primarily that growth stocks become too popular and hence overvalued, often just at the time that growth itself is peaking. On the other hand, growth helps protect the investor from the primary pitfall of value—buying a stock "just because it is cheap." Many investors have had the experience of buying a so-called cheap stock, only to see it remain cheap for year after year, due to a lack of a fundamental catalyst likely to turn the business, or the investment, around.

FREE CASH FLOW TO PRICE

Free cash flow to price is defined as a company's cash flow from operations minus capital expenditures over the past 12 months (both from the statement of cash flows) as a percent of the company's current market capitalization (common shares outstanding multiplied by the current price).[2] As you'll see in Chapter 6, cash flow strategies in general have worked very well since the statement of cash flows was widely adopted in 1989. However, in recent years (2003–2007) cash flow–based strategies have not worked as well. To some extent, the free cash flow to price strategy lacks this defect (it outperforms moderately in 2003 through 2006 but underperforms in 2007). Free cash flow to price is an excellent building block, combining well with profitability, technical, other cash flow, and even other valuation factors. In addition, free cash flow to price works well across industries. Because of its strength, consistency, and versatility, unusual for a quantitative strategy, I consider free cash flow to price to be the king of the valuation strategies.

Note that, as with all valuation strategies presented in this chapter, the free cash flow-to-price strategy simply compares the ratio for each company in our Universe to that of every other company in the Universe. Valuation tests could be refined somewhat by comparing individual company valuations to industry group averages or to their own historical averages (although this would necessarily shorten the testing period). However, in evaluating the strength of a given valuation strategy, the tests presented in this chapter work well. Additionally, sector tests serve to show how each single-factor test works according to broad economic sector categories (energy, materials, industrials, health care, etc.). Note that banks are excluded from all cash flow–based tests, as the Compustat database does not contain cash flow values for them.

The top quintile of the free cash flow-to-price strategy outperforms by 5.6%, on average, and does so for 78% of one-year and 88% of rolling three-year periods (see Figure 5.1). It significantly underperforms only in 1990, 1999–2000, and 2007. Average portfolio values for the top quintile for free cash flow to price are consistently above 10% and get as high as 25% to 30% at bear market bottoms (e.g., 1990 and 2002). The maximum

---

[2] Alternatively, one could use 12-month free cash flow from operations minus capital expenditures divided by common shares outstanding as a percent of current price.

1990 ~ 2007	1st Quintile	2nd Quintile	3rd Quintile	4th Quintile	5th Quintile	Universe	S&P 500*
CAGR – Annual Rebalance	16.6%	13.2%	10.9%	4.9%	5.4%	10.3%	12.0%
Average Excess Return vs. Universe**	5.6%	2.7%	0.3%	−3.7%	−4.5%	NA	1.5%
Value of $10,000 Invested (18 Years)	$158,514	$93,826	$64,466	$23,740	$25,973	$58,670	$76,297
% of 1-Year Periods Strategy Outperforms the Universe	77.8%	63.9%	47.2%	23.6%	19.4%	NA	56.9%
% Rolling 3-Year Periods Strategy Outperforms	87.5%	81.3%	37.5%	9.4%	12.5%	NA	68.8%
Maximum Gain	67.6%	51.8%	49.9%	62.4%	81.7%	59.2%	54.1%
Maximum Loss	−22.6%	−19.3%	−30.1%	−50.3%	−40.4%	−24.9%	−25.9%
Sharpe Ratio	0.78	0.79	0.48	0.19	0.14	0.46	0.64
Standard Deviation of Returns	0.17	0.13	0.17	0.22	0.23	0.17	0.14
Beta (vs. Universe)	0.80	0.73	0.96	1.19	1.31	NA	0.78
Alpha (vs. Universe)	0.08	0.06	0.01	−0.06	−0.08	NA	0.04
Average Portfolio Size	333	333	333	333	333	NA	NA
Average Number of Companies *Outperforming*	166	155	141	124	125	NA	NA
Average Number of Companies *Underperforming*	150	163	177	192	191	NA	NA
Median Portfolio Value – FCF to Price	16.7%	5.5%	2.5%	−0.4%	−14.9%	2.1%	3.3%
Average Market Capitalization	$3,599	$5,907	$7,528	$4,623	$2,178	NA	NA

* Equal-weighted average of S&P 500 returns. ** Annual holding period run quarterly for a larger sample size; arithmetic average excess returns.
Source: Standard & Poor's Compustat Point in Time Database; Charter Oak Investment Systems, Inc., Venues® Data Engine

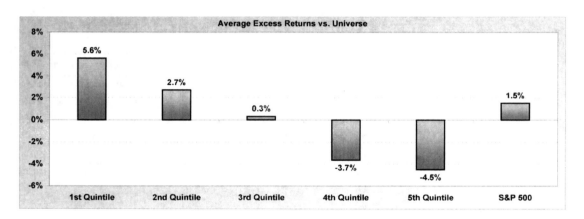

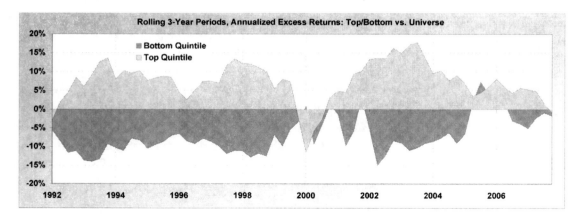

Figure 5.1 Free Cash Flow to Price

loss is a low 23%, and the Sharpe ratio is 0.78, well above the 0.64 value for the S&P 500 and relatively high for a single-factor strategy. On average, 166 of the companies in the top quintile outperform, versus 150 that underperform, a strong showing.

The bottom quintile underperforms by 4.5%, and does so for 81% of one-year and 87% of rolling three-year periods. It significantly outperforms in 1999–2000, 2003–2004, and 2006. Average portfolio values for free cash flow to price for the bottom quintile are consistently negative, meaning these companies had net outflows of cash over the 12 months prior to portfolio formation, and range from −8% to −24%. An average of 191 companies in the bottom quintile underperforms versus 125 that outperform.

Free Cash Flow to Price by Economic Sector

As mentioned above, the free cash flow-to-price strategy is very versatile, working across most of the economic sectors tested. The strategy works very well in the energy, industrials, consumer discretionary, consumer staples, health care, information technology, and utilities sectors. It also works consistently in financials (which excludes banks) and for the top quintile of materials and telecom services. The strategy shines for the health care sector: the top quintile outperforms over 100% of the rolling three-year periods tested and has a maximum loss of just 14% (see Figure 5.2).

Free Cash Flow to Price and External Financing to Assets

The external financing strategy juxtaposes companies that, on balance, are repurchasing shares and reducing debt with companies that are issuing shares and/or debt. Guess who loses? Our research shows that companies that access the capital markets, in particular the equity markets, consistently underperform over the following 12 months, whereas companies that reduce shares and reduce debt consistently outperform. By combining free cash flow to price (a valuation factor) with external financing (a capital allocation factor), we come up with an exceedingly strong strategy. The top quintile contains low-valuation companies with excess cash flow that are reducing shares and debt, and the bottom quintile contains high-valuation companies with cash outflows that are issuing large amounts of shares and/or debt. By issuing shares, corporations dilute the holdings of existing stockholders, and by issuing debt, corporations increase risk and may reduce the earnings available to stockholders.[3] Companies that generate excess

---

[3] Although it is true that in a good economic period, corporations can use debt to invest in profitable projects and thereby enhance returns to shareholders, the converse is also true: in an economic downturn when profits contract, large amounts of debt can severely constrain profitability and in some cases cause bankruptcy.

Top Quintile

1990 ~ 2007	Energy	Materials	Industrials	Consumer Discretionary	Consumer Staples	Health Care	Financials	Information Technology	Telecom Services	Utilities	Universe	S&P 500*
CAGR – Quintile	18.0%	14.4%	14.5%	13.3%	17.4%	21.3%	18.1%	19.5%	10.7%	21.5%	10.3%	12.0%
CAGR – Sector	11.9%	9.7%	10.7%	7.3%	10.8%	11.9%	14.1%	8.1%	5.6%	11.9%	NA	NA
Excess Return vs. Sector	6.1%	4.7%	3.9%	6.0%	6.6%	9.4%	4.0%	11.5%	5.2%	9.6%	NA	NA
Value of $10,000	$197,397	$112,505	$114,667	$95,125	$178,198	$322,946	$199,294	$247,594	$62,822	$335,030	$58,670	$76,297
% 1-Year Outperformance	66.7%	72.2%	72.2%	77.8%	72.2%	72.2%	61.1%	66.7%	66.7%	77.8%	NA	NA
% 3-Year Outperformance	81.3%	87.5%	93.8%	93.8%	93.8%	100.0%	81.3%	81.3%	62.5%	81.3%	NA	NA
Maximum Gain	67.5%	46.0%	46.2%	50.9%	60.9%	82.6%	55.7%	67.5%	55.9%	202.0%	44.0%	41.4%
Maximum Loss	−26.9%	−13.2%	−19.3%	−20.2%	−19.9%	−14.0%	−19.9%	−30.5%	−41.9%	−80.6%	−19.1%	−18.1%
Standard Deviation	0.23	0.17	0.17	0.19	0.19	0.25	0.25	0.24	0.23	0.59	0.17	0.15
Beta (vs. Sector)	0.79	1.01	1.04	0.93	1.23	0.81	0.98	0.51	0.32	1.47	NA	NA
Alpha (vs. Sector)	0.08	0.05	0.04	0.06	0.05	0.12	0.05	0.15	0.10	0.17	NA	NA
Portfolio Size	21	28	55	66	19	40	30	55	8	3	NA	NA

Bottom Quintile

1990 ~ 2007	Energy	Materials	Industrials	Consumer Discretionary	Consumer Staples	Health Care	Financials	Information Technology	Telecom Services	Utilities	Universe	S&P 500*
CAGR – Quintile	8.2%	8.7%	3.9%	3.3%	6.9%	3.2%	8.5%	2.0%	5.7%	5.0%	10.3%	12.0%
CAGR – Sector	11.9%	9.7%	10.7%	7.3%	10.8%	11.9%	14.1%	8.1%	5.6%	11.9%	NA	NA
Excess Return vs. Sector	−3.7%	−1.1%	−6.8%	−4.0%	−3.9%	−8.7%	−5.7%	−6.1%	0.2%	−6.9%	NA	NA
Value of $10,000	$41,407	$44,669	$19,761	$18,081	$32,992	$17,573	$43,075	$14,325	$27,296	$24,065	$58,670	$76,297
% 1-Year Outperformance	38.9%	50.0%	11.1%	27.8%	33.3%	22.2%	33.3%	16.7%	38.9%	33.3%	NA	NA
% 3-Year Outperformance	12.5%	31.3%	12.5%	25.0%	6.3%	12.5%	12.5%	18.8%	56.3%	37.5%	NA	NA
Maximum Gain	60.3%	41.2%	43.6%	56.3%	37.4%	67.0%	62.5%	213.8%	268.1%	122.1%	44.0%	41.4%
Maximum Loss	−50.7%	−13.1%	−32.5%	−36.2%	−19.3%	−39.7%	−24.0%	−63.9%	−70.0%	−62.2%	−19.1%	−18.1%
Standard Deviation	0.30	0.17	0.19	0.25	0.16	0.26	0.22	0.59	0.69	0.39	0.17	0.15
Beta (vs. Sector)	1.12	1.03	1.17	1.25	0.99	0.98	0.87	1.47	1.69	1.78	NA	NA
Alpha (vs. Sector)	−0.04	0.03	−0.06	−0.08	0.01	−0.06	−0.01	−0.13	−0.04	−0.05	NA	NA
Portfolio Size	22	29	57	69	21	41	33	57	9	3	NA	NA

* Equal-weighted average of S&P 500 returns.
Source: Standard & Poor's Compustat Point in Time Database, Charter Oak Investment Systems

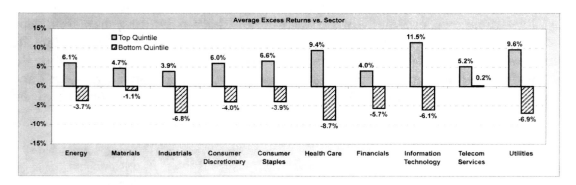

Figure 5.2 Free Cash Flow to Price by Economic Sector

capital, on the other hand (their financing is internally funded), are able to increase the ownership stakes of existing shareholders (by buying back shares) and reduce financial risk (by retiring debt).

The numerator of external financing is calculated as cash received from share issuance minus cash spent on share repurchases plus cash received from debt issuance minus cash spent on debt retirement.[4] This net value is then divided by total assets. All data necessary for the calculation of this ratio are available from the financing section of a company's cash flow statement, except for total assets, which is from the balance sheet. The top quintile outperforms by 7.1%, on average, and is consistent, outperforming for 72% of one-year and 89% of rolling three-year periods. It significantly underperforms only in 1990, 1999–2000, and 2007 (see Figure 5.3). Average portfolio values for free cash flow to price vary from 11% to 33%, and average values for external financing to assets range from −11% to −17%. The latter figures mean that companies in the top quintile have made net share repurchases and/or debt reductions equal to 11% to 17% of total assets.

The bottom quintile of this strategy has the highest negative excess returns of any two-factor strategy presented in this book and would make an excellent short-sale strategy. It underperforms by an average of 15.3%, and does so for 86% of one-year and 100% of rolling three-year periods. It significantly outperforms only in 1999–2000, 2003, and 2007. An average of 44 companies in the bottom quintile underperform for every 19 that outperform. This is a decidedly small-cap strategy with an average market capitalization of $1.2 billion. Companies in this quintile issue shares and/or debt equal to an average of about 50% of assets and have negative free cash flows.

Free Cash Flow to Price and Seven-Month Relative Strength

Combining valuation with capital allocation, in the previous strategy resulted in very strong underperformance for the bottom quintile. The free cash flow to price and seven-month relative strength strategy combines valuation with price momentum and results in a more "balanced" test, with strong excess returns for the top and bottom quintiles and linear returns in between. Price momentum strategies, often called "technical" strategies, tell us one thing: that the supply/demand balance has turned in favor of a stock (for the top quintile) or against a stock (for the bottom quintile).

Our research found that valuation and price momentum strategies make consistently strong combinations. Why should valuation and technical analysis work so well together? I believe the answer is relatively simple. A consistent problem with buying

---

[4] In our calculation we also include changes in short-term debt. However, including short-term debt makes little practical difference in terms of excess returns for the strategy.

1990 ~ 2007	1st Quintile	2nd Quintile	3rd Quintile	4th Quintile	5th Quintile	Universe	S&P 500*
CAGR – Annual Rebalance	19.0%	14.7%	14.2%	0.8%	−8.5%	10.3%	12.0%
Average Excess Return vs. Universe**	7.1%	2.8%	2.5%	−5.9%	−15.3%	NA	1.5%
Value of $10,000 Invested (18 Years)	$230,131	$117,226	$109,341	$11,614	$2,003	$58,670	$76,297
% of 1-Year Periods Strategy Outperforms the Universe	72.2%	58.3%	59.7%	20.8%	13.9%	NA	56.9%
% Rolling 3-Year Periods Strategy Outperforms	89.1%	73.4%	67.2%	12.5%	0.0%	NA	68.8%
Maximum Gain	59.7%	46.4%	56.1%	57.2%	88.9%	59.2%	54.1%
Maximum Loss	−28.8%	−20.1%	−36.4%	−70.3%	−74.0%	−24.9%	−25.9%
Sharpe Ratio	0.86	0.83	0.58	0.08	−0.24	0.46	0.64
Standard Deviation of Returns	0.17	0.13	0.18	0.23	0.31	0.17	0.14
Beta (vs. Universe)	0.76	0.61	0.98	1.22	1.61	NA	0.78
Alpha (vs. Universe)	0.10	0.08	0.03	−0.09	−0.23	NA	0.04
Average Portfolio Size	67	67	67	67	66	NA	NA
Average Number of Companies *Outperforming*	32	33	30	23	19	NA	NA
Average Number of Companies *Underperforming*	31	31	34	40	44	NA	NA
Median Portfolio Value – FCF to Price	14.9%	5.5%	2.5%	−0.6%	−15.3%	2.1%	3.3%
Median Portfolio Value – Extern. Fin. to Assets	−13.4%	−4.0%	0.3%	7.8%	52.3%	5.4%	0.3%
Average Market Capitalization	$3,080	$7,316	$7,651	$4,166	$1,220	NA	NA

* Equal-weighted average of S&P 500 returns. ** Annual holding period run quarterly for a larger sample size; arithmetic average excess returns.
Source: Standard & Poor's Compustat Point in Time Database; Charter Oak Investment Systems Inc., Venues® Data Engine

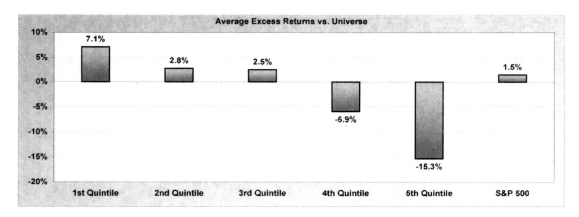

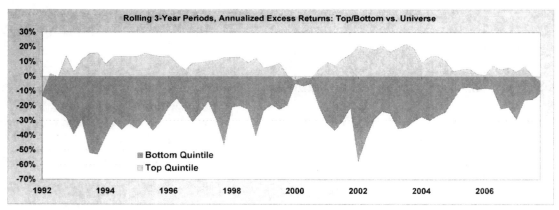

Figure 5.3 Free Cash Flow to Price and External Financing to Assets

so-called value stocks is that some stocks are cheap for a reason. Competition is eroding their business model, the industry is going through an extended downturn, operating efficiency is deteriorating, and so on. Stocks that are cheap for a reason can stay cheap for a long time. Often, however, when a fundamental situation starts to improve (a company becomes more competitive, its industry improves, its operating efficiency begins to increase) the supply/demand picture for a stock indicates that some investors realize that a change is taking place. Put another way, price strength may indicate the presence of a *catalyst*, some fundamental change with regard to the company that is likely to unlock the value of the stock. Price weakness, on the other hand, may mean that investors see signs that a strong fundamental situation is beginning to deteriorate.

Relative strength is simply the price change of one stock over a given period relative to the price change of a group of other stocks over the same period. Relative strength for a stock can be calculated versus the S&P 500, all of the stocks in the New York Stock Exchange, and so on. Relative strength numbers, which are often expressed as percentiles, can be found in periodicals such as *Investors Business Daily*, and in financial databases. For the quantitative tests shown here, we calculate relative strength simply by comparing the seven-month price change for one stock to the seven-month price change of every other stock in our Universe.[5] So, the median portfolio values for seven-month relative strength, shown in Figure 5.4, are expressed as the median seven-month price change for a given quintile. Chapter 9 will explain in detail why we chose seven months as our calculation period.

The top quintile outperforms by 9.5%, on average, and does so for 76% of one-year and 94% of rolling three-year periods (see Figure 5.4). The strategy significantly underperforms in only two periods, 1999–2000 and 2003–2004. Average portfolio values for the top quintile vary from 10% to 27% for free cash flow to price and from 7% (in 2002) to well over 60% for seven-month price change. The Sharpe ratio for the strategy is a very high 0.97, and Alpha versus the Universe is 0.11 versus 0.04 for the S&P 500.

The bottom quintile underperforms by an average of 8.6%, and does so for 79% of one-year and 91% of rolling three-year periods. It significantly outperforms only in 1999–2000 and 2003–2004. It has a huge maximum loss of 81%, suffered from September 2000 to September 2001. An average of 40 portfolio companies underperforms for every 24 that outperform. Average portfolio values range from −7% to −31% for free cash flow to price and from −8% to −61% for seven-month price change.

---

[5] The seven-month price change is calculated simply as the current price of the stock divided by the price seven months ago minus 1.

1990 ~ 2007	1st Quintile	2nd Quintile	3rd Quintile	4th Quintile	5th Quintile	Universe	S&P 500*
CAGR – Annual Rebalance	20.8%	12.5%	8.7%	3.0%	2.8%	10.3%	12.0%
Average Excess Return vs. Universe**	9.5%	2.4%	-2.1%	-5.3%	-8.6%	NA	1.5%
Value of $10,000 Invested (18 Years)	$301,427	$83,749	$44,564	$16,958	$16,528	$58,670	$76,297
% of 1-Year Periods Strategy Outperforms the Universe	76.4%	63.9%	41.7%	18.1%	20.8%	NA	56.9%
% Rolling 3-Year Periods Strategy Outperforms	93.8%	68.8%	20.3%	7.8%	9.4%	NA	68.8%
Maximum Gain	65.0%	54.9%	43.1%	49.3%	125.6%	59.2%	54.1%
Maximum Loss	-24.3%	-19.0%	-27.2%	-49.6%	-81.2%	-24.9%	-25.9%
Sharpe Ratio	0.97	0.79	0.39	0.13	-0.03	0.46	0.64
Standard Deviation of Returns	0.18	0.13	0.14	0.18	0.33	0.17	0.14
Beta (vs. Universe)	0.86	0.63	0.77	0.99	1.57	NA	0.78
Alpha (vs. Universe)	0.11	0.07	0.01	-0.05	-0.15	NA	0.04
Average Portfolio Size	66	66	66	66	67	NA	NA
Average Number of Companies *Outperforming*	32	30	27	25	24	NA	NA
Average Number of Companies *Underperforming*	29	33	37	39	40	NA	NA
Median Portfolio Value – FCF to Price	15.8%	5.5%	2.5%	-0.5%	-17.5%	2.1%	3.3%
Median Portfolio Value – 7-Month Price Change	53.6%	18.2%	10.9%	-1.6%	-32.4%	20.5%	5.6%
Average Market Capitalization	$3,519	$6,332	$9,439	$6,312	$1,400	NA	NA

* Equal-weighted average of S&P 500 returns. ** Annual holding period run quarterly for a larger sample size; arithmetic average excess returns.
Source: Standard & Poor's Compustat Point in Time Database; Charter Oak Investment Systems, Inc., Venues® Data Engine

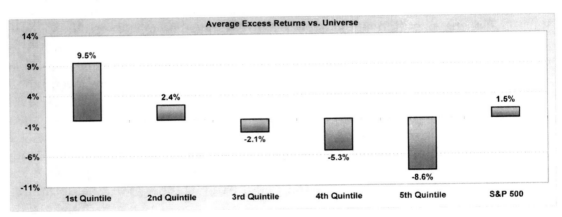

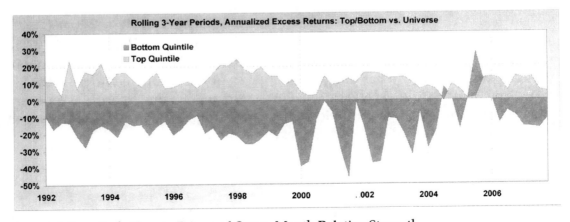

Figure 5.4 Free Cash Flow to Price and Seven-Month Relative Strength

ENTERPRISE VALUE TO EBITDA

Enterprise value (EV) to EBITDA (earnings before interest, taxes, depreciation, and amortization) is a widely used valuation measure, and our tests show it is used for a good reason. We've already seen the EV-to-EBITDA ratio in Chapter 4. It consists of total EV (market value of common stock plus total debt minus cash and cash equivalents)[6] divided by EBITDA. EBITDA is roughly equivalent to operating income before depreciation.[7] Enterprise value represents the theoretical price that an acquirer would have to pay (excluding a takeover premium) to buy the entire firm, while EBITDA represents the profit-making capability of the firm, before depreciation, financing expenses, and taxes.

Professional investors use EV to EBITDA as a valuation tool in a number of industries, to compare the relative value of one company's earnings stream to another's. Corporate managers and private investors seeking to gain corporate control often use EV to EBITDA when valuing potential acquisitions. One weakness of EBITDA as a measure of profitability is that by excluding depreciation the cost of previously purchased property, plant, and equipment (PP&E) is also excluded. The cost of existing PP&E can be captured by including depreciation (using EBIT), or the cost of maintaining and replacing PP&E can be captured by subtracting capital expenditures. However, testing on EBIT (earnings before interest and taxes but after depreciation) and EBITDA minus capital expenditures showed little difference versus using EBITDA alone.[8]

Together with free cash flow to price, enterprise value to EBITDA is the strongest of the valuation ratios we tested. Like free cash flow to price, quintile returns are very linear (a diagonal line can be drawn through the excess returns graph in Figure 5.5, connecting all the returns from Q1 through Q5), indicating a strong correlation between the strategy and excess returns. Also, like free cash flow to price, EV to EBITDA is a versatile *building block*, combining well with nearly every other category of strategy presented in this book. In general, I believe valuation should form a part of every quantitative stock selection model or screen.

The top quintile outperforms by 5.3%, on average, and does so for 75% of one-year and 88% of rolling three-year periods (see Figure 5.5). It significantly underperforms

---

[6] A more complete definition of enterprise value is market value of common stock plus total debt plus minority interest plus preferred stock minus cash and cash equivalents. We tested EV calculated in a number of ways, and from a quantitative point of view there is little difference between the method we chose and alternative methods.

[7] The proper calculation of EBITDA also includes nonoperating income, such as dividend income and royalty income. However, from the viewpoint of a quantitative test, the difference is academic.

[8] Using EBITDA minus capex in the denominator of EV to EBITDA slightly reduced the returns on the top quintile but increased the consistency of the bottom quintile.

1988 ~ 2007	1st Quintile	2nd Quintile	3rd Quintile	4th Quintile	5th Quintile	Universe	S&P 500*
CAGR – Annual Rebalance	16.6%	12.8%	12.4%	9.4%	3.0%	11.2%	12.9%
Average Excess Return vs. Universe**	5.3%	1.9%	0.3%	−2.3%	−4.9%	NA	1.6%
Value of $10,000 Invested (20 Years)	$215,153	$112,057	$103,073	$60,518	$18,010	$83,161	$112,895
% of 1-Year Periods Strategy Outperforms the Universe	75.3%	57.1%	48.1%	36.4%	28.6%	NA	59.7%
% Rolling 3-Year Periods Strategy Outperforms	88.4%	73.9%	56.5%	17.4%	8.7%	NA	71.0%
Maximum Gain	66.6%	57.2%	52.4%	48.2%	103.5%	59.2%	54.1%
Maximum Loss	−20.9%	−23.5%	−18.7%	−40.2%	−74.0%	−24.9%	−25.9%
Sharpe Ratio	0.84	0.71	0.61	0.35	0.10	0.49	0.69
Standard Deviation of Returns	0.16	0.14	0.14	0.17	0.32	0.16	0.14
Beta (vs. Universe)	0.76	0.72	0.77	0.96	1.61	NA	0.78
Alpha (vs. Universe)	0.08	0.05	0.03	−0.02	−0.12	NA	0.04
Average Portfolio Size	385	386	386	386	386	NA	NA
Average Number of Companies Outperforming	188	180	174	157	134	NA	NA
Average Number of Companies Underperforming	178	189	193	208	230	NA	NA
Median Portfolio Value – EV to EBITDA	5.4	7.9	10.1	14.1	−13.6	10.4	10.4
Average Market Capitalization	$3,163	$3,627	$4,588	$6,400	$3,265	NA	NA

* Equal-weighted average of S&P 500 returns. ** Annual holding period run quarterly for a larger sample size; arithmetic average excess returns.
Source: Standard & Poor's Compustat Point in Time Database; Charter Oak Investment Systems, Inc., Venues® Data Engine

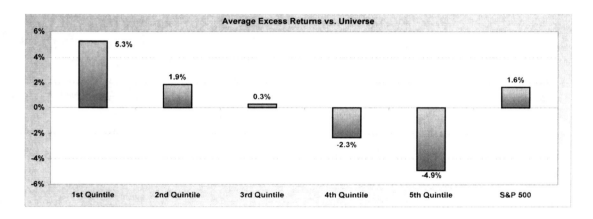

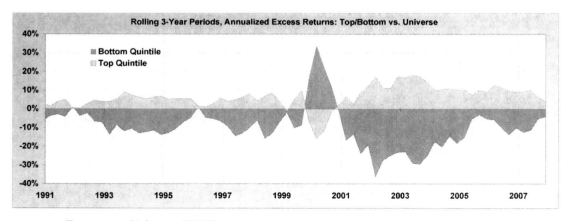

Figure 5.5 Enterprise Value to EBITDA

only in 1999–2000. Average portfolio values for EV to EBITDA range from 4× to 6×, and an average of 188 companies outperforms for every 178 that underperform (a strong showing for a top quintile). The maximum loss is a low 21%, and the standard deviation of returns is 0.16, in line with the standard deviation for the Universe, resulting in a Sharpe ratio of 0.84, the second-highest Sharpe ratio for a single-factor strategy recorded in this book.

The bottom quintile underperforms by an average of 4.9%, and does so for 71% of one-year and 91% of rolling three-year periods. The bottom quintile is quite volatile, with a Beta of 1.6 and a standard deviation of returns of 0.32 versus 0.14 for the S&P 500. As a result, it outperforms periodically, but the primary periods of outperformance are 1996, 1998–2000, and 2003–2004. Note that, like the free cash flow-to-price strategy, EV to EBITDA selects small to midcap stocks in both the top and bottom quintiles. Companies in the bottom quintile either have very little EBITDA, resulting in very high EV-to-EBITDA ratios, or have losses, resulting in negative ratios.

Enterprise Value to EBITDA by Economic Sector

The strength of this strategy is verified by how well it works over the different economic sectors. The four sectors that stand out as having exceptionally strong excess returns for the EV-to-EBITDA strategy are energy, materials, health care, and information technology (see Figure 5.6). These are all sectors in which EV to EBITDA is used widely by both minority investors (e.g., professional money managers) and control-oriented investors (e.g., corporate managers or private investment funds) seeking to purchase large stakes or entire companies. The strategy also works well for the industrials and consumer discretionary sectors. It is less consistent for consumer staples, telecom services, and financial stocks, for the latter of which there is no good definition for EBITDA (interest expense is usually part of a financial company's cost of doing business).

Enterprise Value to EBITDA and Return on Invested Capital

We saw the return on invested capital (ROIC) strategy in Chapter 4. As a stand-alone strategy, ROIC is moderately strong, but not nearly as strong as EV to EBITDA. Combining a valuation strategy (EV to EBITDA) with a profitability strategy (ROIC) makes good investment sense. However, this strategy shows that the emphasis quantitatively should be on the valuation factor. The strategy shown here selects companies by EV to EBITDA first and only secondarily by ROIC. The same strategy with the factors reversed isn't nearly as strong or consistent. Note that, like the EV-to-EBITDA strategy alone, the returns on this strategy are very symmetrical, a sign of quantitative strength.

Top Quintile

1988 ~ 2007	Energy	Materials	Industrials	Consumer Discretionary	Consumer Staples	Health Care	Financials	Information Technology	Telecom Services	Utilities	Universe	S&P 500*
CAGR – Quintile	21.6%	15.7%	14.7%	12.6%	17.4%	19.4%	15.2%	14.1%	14.3%	15.3%	11.2%	12.9%
CAGR – Sector	13.5%	10.2%	11.2%	8.8%	12.6%	12.3%	14.5%	7.6%	9.2%	13.0%	NA	NA
Excess Return vs. Sector	8.1%	5.5%	3.5%	3.8%	4.8%	7.1%	0.8%	6.5%	5.0%	2.4%	NA	NA
Value of $10,000	$501,388	$183,933	$155,694	$106,998	$245,359	$347,567	$169,930	$138,845	$143,739	$173,287	$83,161	$112,895
% 1-Year Outperformance	90.0%	80.0%	85.0%	80.0%	60.0%	75.0%	60.0%	70.0%	60.0%	80.0%	NA	NA
% 3-Year Outperformance	83.3%	100.0%	94.4%	94.4%	72.2%	88.9%	66.7%	83.3%	83.3%	83.3%	NA	NA
Maximum Gain	86.1%	45.6%	47.2%	48.2%	72.2%	85.3%	65.4%	58.2%	54.6%	39.9%	44.0%	41.4%
Maximum Loss	−34.4%	−14.2%	−14.0%	−28.4%	−21.7%	−18.6%	−32.4%	−31.8%	−36.7%	−11.9%	−19.1%	−18.1%
Standard Deviation	0.27	0.16	0.16	0.20	0.23	0.25	0.26	0.21	0.23	0.15	0.16	0.14
Beta (vs. Sector)	1.00	1.00	1.02	1.02	1.33	0.82	1.18	0.42	0.52	0.85	NA	NA
Alpha (vs. Sector)	0.08	0.06	0.03	0.04	0.02	0.10	−0.01	0.11	0.09	0.04	NA	NA
Portfolio Size	24	31	56	68	20	39	52	55	9	25	NA	NA

Bottom Quintile

1988 ~ 2007	Energy	Materials	Industrials	Consumer Discretionary	Consumer Staples	Health Care	Financials	Information Technology	Telecom Services	Utilities	Universe	S&P 500*
CAGR – Quintile	5.2%	2.6%	6.5%	5.6%	9.6%	5.2%	11.6%	2.5%	10.0%	11.2%	11.2%	12.9%
CAGR – Sector	13.5%	10.2%	11.2%	8.8%	12.6%	12.3%	14.5%	7.6%	9.2%	13.0%	NA	NA
Excess Return vs. Sector	−8.3%	−7.6%	−4.7%	−3.1%	−2.9%	−7.1%	−2.8%	−5.1%	0.8%	−1.8%	NA	NA
Value of $10,000	$27,609	$16,720	$35,165	$29,876	$63,059	$27,700	$90,227	$16,335	$67,161	$83,157	$83,161	$112,895
% 1-Year Outperformance	20.0%	30.0%	30.0%	30.0%	45.0%	30.0%	35.0%	50.0%	55.0%	40.0%	NA	NA
% 3-Year Outperformance	5.6%	16.7%	11.1%	16.7%	16.7%	11.1%	22.2%	33.3%	55.6%	33.3%	NA	NA
Maximum Gain	66.9%	42.1%	42.9%	50.3%	36.6%	116.6%	54.6%	231.6%	220.2%	68.9%	44.0%	41.4%
Maximum Loss	−57.2%	−34.9%	−28.1%	−33.7%	−17.2%	−41.2%	−28.9%	−62.8%	−67.7%	−25.5%	−19.1%	−18.1%
Standard Deviation	0.32	0.21	0.18	0.22	0.15	0.37	0.22	0.62	0.61	0.22	0.16	0.14
Beta (vs. Sector)	1.21	1.21	1.12	1.02	0.91	1.37	1.00	1.62	1.52	1.28	NA	NA
Alpha (vs. Sector)	−0.10	−0.03	−0.04	−0.06	0.04	−0.09	0.01	−0.13	−0.05	0.04	NA	NA
Portfolio Size	24	31	58	72	22	40	55	57	10	25	NA	NA

* Equal-weighted average of S&P 500 returns.
Source: Standard & Poor's Compustat Point in Time Database; Charter Oak Investment Systems, Inc., Venues® Data Engine

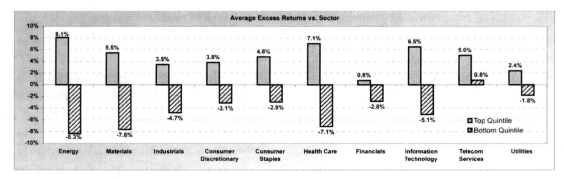

Figure 5.6 Enterprise Value to EBITDA by Economic Sector

The top quintile outperforms by 6.8%, on average, and does so for 78% of one-year and 88% of rolling three-year periods (see Figure 5.7). It only significantly underperforms in 1998–2000. The top quintile has a moderate maximum loss of 24% and a high Sharpe ratio of 0.90 (vs. 0.69 for the S&P 500). Average portfolio values range from 3× to 5× for EV to EBITDA and 22% to over 30% for ROIC, so these are highly profitable companies that are relatively inexpensive.

The bottom quintile underperforms by an average of 7.4%, and does so for 77% of one-year and 88% of rolling three-year periods. It is very volatile, with a maximum loss of 75%, a maximum gain of 141%, and a standard deviation of returns of 0.41 versus 0.14 for the S&P 500; it outperforms significantly in 1991–1992, 1996, 1999–2000, and 2003. Average portfolio values range from −2× to −53× for EV to EBITDA and in the high negative values for ROIC, indicating that companies in the bottom quintile have sizable operating losses.

Enterprise Value to EBITDA and Free Cash Flow to Operating Income

This strategy combines a valuation factor with a cash flow factor. The denominator of both of these factors is similar: on the one hand, we essentially look at operating income before depreciation (EBITDA), and on the other, we look at operating income after depreciation. So, this strategy considers both the price being paid for operating income and the amount of cash being generated as a percent of operating income. The top quintile contains companies that are selling at low prices relative to earnings (EBITDA) and have high quality earnings—they are generating more than a dollar of cash for each dollar of accounting earnings. The bottom quintile contains companies that are expensive on an operating income basis and are generating even less cash than they are operating income. As with the previous EV-to-EBITDA strategies, the excess returns on this strategy are both symmetrical and consistent.

The top quintile outperforms by 7.9%, on average, and does so for 75% of one-year and 89% of rolling three-year periods (see Figure 5.8). It underperforms significantly only in 1990–1991 and 1999–2000. The maximum loss is a low 20%, and the Sharpe ratio is 0.87 versus 0.64 for the S&P 500. Average portfolio values range from 1× to 5× for EV to EBITDA and from 150% to over 200% for free cash flow to operating income, so these are inexpensive companies with high-quality earnings.

The bottom quintile underperforms by an average of 7.9%, making it perfectly symmetrical with the top quintile, and does so for 74% of one-year and 91% of rolling three-year periods. Like the bottom quintile of the preceding strategy, it is quite volatile, and outperforms strongly in 1999–2000 and 2003–2004. Average portfolio values range from high positive to high negative numbers for EV to EBITDA and very high negative numbers for free cash flow to operating income: companies in the bottom quintile have little or no EBITDA and have cash outflows.

1988 ~ 2007	1st Quintile	2nd Quintile	3rd Quintile	4th Quintile	5th Quintile	Universe	S&P 500*
CAGR – Annual Rebalance	18.5%	12.5%	13.2%	7.7%	−3.9%	11.2%	12.9%
Average Excess Return vs. Universe**	6.8%	2.2%	−0.1%	−2.2%	−7.4%	NA	1.6%
Value of $10,000 Invested (20 Years)	$297,147	$105,265	$119,661	$44,478	$4,549	$83,161	$112,895
% of 1-Year Periods Strategy Outperforms the Universe	77.9%	55.8%	49.4%	44.2%	23.4%	NA	59.7%
% Rolling 3-Year Periods Strategy Outperforms	88.4%	69.6%	49.3%	34.8%	11.6%	NA	71.0%
Maximum Gain	66.5%	59.8%	46.8%	46.5%	141.2%	59.2%	54.1%
Maximum Loss	−23.5%	−28.9%	−21.5%	−36.9%	−75.2%	−24.9%	−25.9%
Sharpe Ratio	0.90	0.69	0.57	0.33	0.02	0.49	0.69
Standard Deviation of Returns	0.17	0.15	0.14	0.18	0.41	0.16	0.14
Beta (vs. Universe)	0.78	0.75	0.74	0.96	1.82	NA	0.78
Alpha (vs. Universe)	0.10	0.05	0.03	−0.02	−0.18	NA	0.04
Average Portfolio Size	74	74	75	74	75	NA	NA
Average Number of Companies Outperforming	36	35	34	30	21	NA	NA
Average Number of Companies Underperforming	34	36	37	40	49	NA	NA
Median Portfolio Value – EV-to-EBITDA	4.0	7.8	10.0	13.8	−15.7	10.5	9.1
Median Portfolio Value – ROIC	26.7%	13.1%	10.6%	7.1%	−52.1%	9.4%	11.4%
Average Market Capitalization	$4,098	$4,061	$4,262	$5,797	$1,043	NA	NA

* Equal-weighted average of S&P 500 returns. ** Annual holding period run quarterly for a larger sample size; arithmetic average excess returns.
Source: Standard & Poor's Compustat Point in Time Database; Charter Oak Investment Systems, Inc., Venues® Data Engine

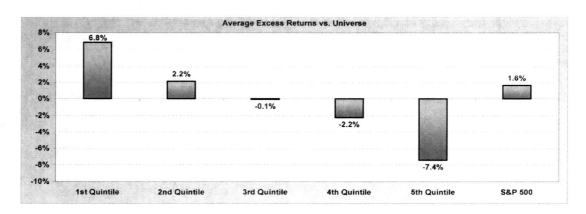

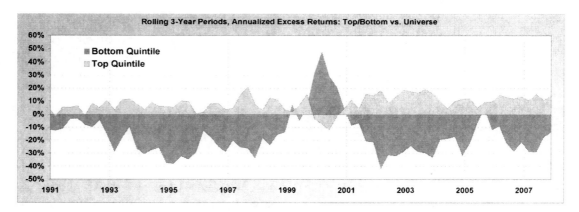

Figure 5.7 Enterprise Value to EBITDA and Return on Invested Capital

1990 ~ 2007	1st Quintile	2nd Quintile	3rd Quintile	4th Quintile	5th Quintile	Universe	S&P 500*
CAGR – Annual Rebalance	17.6%	11.6%	10.1%	6.3%	−0.2%	10.3%	12.0%
Average Excess Return vs. Universe**	7.9%	2.4%	−0.8%	−3.9%	−7.9%	NA	1.5%
Value of $10,000 Invested (18 Years)	$185,969	$72,551	$56,816	$29,918	$9,585	$58,670	$76,297
% of 1-Year Periods Strategy Outperforms the Universe	75.0%	51.4%	44.4%	25.0%	26.4%	NA	56.9%
% Rolling 3-Year Periods Strategy Outperforms	89.1%	68.8%	40.6%	6.3%	9.4%	NA	68.8%
Maximum Gain	58.4%	50.4%	45.8%	45.6%	128.2%	59.2%	54.1%
Maximum Loss	−19.9%	−24.3%	−24.1%	−43.8%	−74.6%	−24.9%	−25.9%
Sharpe Ratio	0.87	0.69	0.50	0.21	0.00	0.46	0.64
Standard Deviation of Returns	0.18	0.15	0.14	0.19	0.36	0.17	0.14
Beta (vs. Universe)	0.74	0.68	0.72	0.98	1.65	NA	0.78
Alpha (vs. Universe)	0.11	0.06	0.03	−0.04	−0.16	NA	0.04
Average Portfolio Size	62	63	63	63	63	NA	NA
Average Number of Companies *Outperforming*	31	30	29	24	20	NA	NA
Average Number of Companies *Underperforming*	27	31	32	35	39	NA	NA
Median Portfolio Value – EV-to-EBITDA	4.2	8.0	10.4	14.3	62.6	10.7	9.1
Median Portfolio Value – FCF-to-Operating Income	184%	61%	41%	−62%	−748%	−17%	9%
Average Market Capitalization	$2,492	$5,026	$6,317	$6,857	$1,794	NA	NA

* Equal-weighted average of S&P 500 returns. ** Annual holding period run quarterly for a larger sample size; arithmetic average excess returns.
Source: Standard & Poor's Compustat Point in Time Database; Charter Oak Investment Systems, Inc., Venues® Data Engine

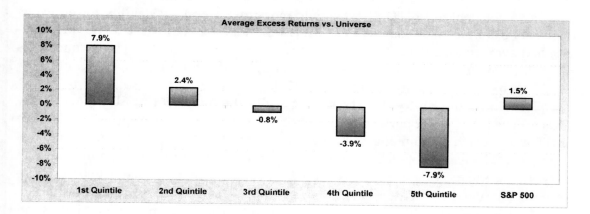

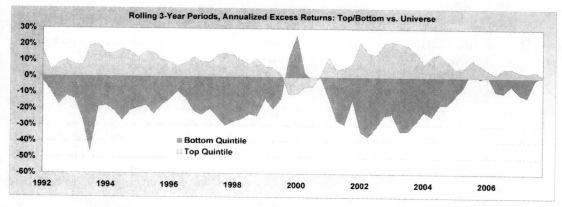

Figure 5.8 Enterprise Value to EBITDA and Free Cash Flow to Operating Income

Enterprise Value to EBITDA and Total Debt to EBITDA

One thing that you will find in Chapter 10, Red Flags, is that, over the short term (the 12-month holding periods tested here), the market rewards companies that take risk and punishes those it deems too conservative.[9] Companies that take on large amounts of debt increase both opportunities and risks for shareholders. In a good business cycle, these companies can use added leverage to expand their businesses and thus increase after-tax returns to equity holders. As a result, financial *leverage* strategies, such as debt to equity, do not work quantitatively, with low-debt companies underperforming and high-debt companies outperforming. Debt *payback* ratios, such as total debt to EBITDA, on the other hand, work better, since they also consider profitability.

The top quintile of this strategy contains companies that have both low valuations and low total debt (long-term debt plus debt in current liabilities).[10] The strategy uses a common denominator (EBITDA), looking for companies that are both inexpensive relative to EBITDA and have a low debt-to-EBITDA ratio. Corporate managers and credit analysts favor debt to EBITDA as a way to measure a company's ability to service its debts. For example, debt issuers rated AAA by Standard & Poor's (the highest debt rating) had average total debt to EBITDA ratios of 3.3× over the last 17 years, companies rated BBB (the lowest "investment-grade" rating) had ratios of 3.9×, and companies rated B (a speculative rating) had ratios of 13.0×.

Combining the EV-to-EBTIDA strategy with the total debt-to-EBITDA strategy adds a little bit of extra performance to both the top and bottom quintiles of EV to EBITDA alone, while maintaining strong consistency. It also slightly reduces the maximum loss and volatility of returns for the top quintile, increases the maximum gain, and increases the Sharpe ratio from 0.84 for the EV-to-EBITDA strategy alone to 0.91 for the combined strategy (see Figure 5.9). Interestingly, the average market cap for the top quintile falls from $3.2 billion (EV to EBITDA alone) to $2.2 billion (the combined strategy), so the combined strategy selects smaller-cap stocks.

Average portfolio values for the top quintile range from 1× to 5× for EV to EBITDA and from 0.1× to 0.4× for total debt to EBITDA. So, top quintile companies are selling at very low valuations and have almost no debt.

---

[9] This is the opposite of what one might expect. It seems intuitive that investors would prefer less risky investments. However, over the short term, stock investors chase high business returns, and such high returns are only possible in some cases by adding significant amounts of debt. However, over the long term, it appears that conservatively financed businesses fare better, and are thus likely to provide superior long-term results.

[10] Debt in current liabilities consists of short-term notes payable and the portion of long-term debt that is due within one year.

1988 ~ 2007	1st Quintile	2nd Quintile	3rd Quintile	4th Quintile	5th Quintile	Universe	S&P 500*
CAGR – Annual Rebalance	17.4%	11.7%	12.8%	9.3%	4.3%	11.2%	12.9%
Average Excess Return vs. Universe**	6.0%	1.0%	−0.3%	−3.0%	−5.6%	NA	1.6%
Value of $10,000 Invested (20 Years)	$245,683	$91,394	$111,794	$59,127	$23,250	$83,161	$112,895
% of 1-Year Periods Strategy Outperforms the Universe	75.3%	51.9%	51.9%	36.4%	28.6%	NA	59.7%
% Rolling 3-Year Periods Strategy Outperforms	89.9%	63.8%	50.7%	13.0%	17.4%	NA	71.0%
Maximum Gain	70.1%	47.2%	46.1%	45.8%	69.3%	59.2%	54.1%
Maximum Loss	−17.6%	−27.0%	−17.8%	−39.1%	−72.6%	−24.9%	−25.9%
Sharpe Ratio	0.91	0.66	0.58	0.30	0.10	0.49	0.69
Standard Deviation of Returns	0.15	0.14	0.13	0.17	0.25	0.16	0.14
Beta (vs. Universe)	0.75	0.68	0.70	0.91	1.41	NA	0.78
Alpha (vs. Universe)	0.09	0.05	0.03	−0.02	−0.11	NA	0.04
Average Portfolio Size	78	77	77	77	77	NA	NA
Average Number of Companies *Outperforming*	35	36	34	31	28	NA	NA
Average Number of Companies *Underperforming*	38	39	39	41	44	NA	NA
Median Portfolio Value – EV-to-EBITDA	4.1	7.9	10.1	13.9	40.9	10.5	9.1
Median Portfolio Value – Total Debt-to-EBITDA	0.2	1.1	1.8	3.7	29.7	2.5	2.6
Average Market Capitalization	$2,190	$5,292	$5,766	$4,234	$3,749	NA	NA

* Equal-weighted average of S&P 500 returns. ** Annual holding period run quarterly for a larger sample size; arithmetic average excess returns.
Source: Standard & Poor's Compustat Point in Time Database; Charter Oak Investment Systems, Inc., Venues® Data Engine

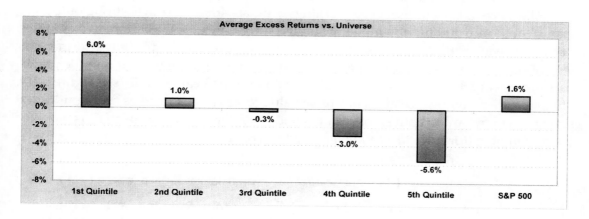

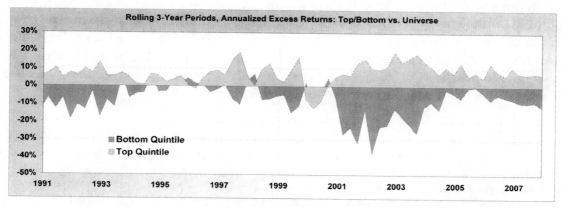

Figure 5.9 Enterprise Value to EBITDA and Total Debt to EBITDA

PRICE TO EARNINGS (CURRENT FISCAL YEAR EPS ESTIMATE)

The P/E ratio is the most widely known stock valuation measure, used by amateur and professional investors alike. We tested the price-to-earnings strategy in a variety of ways: using trailing 12-month earnings (diluted and basic), current fiscal year analyst earnings per share (EPS) estimates, one-year forward EPS estimates, and total EV in place of market price. All measures worked moderately well, with little difference in excess returns. However, a P/E ratio using current fiscal year EPS estimates[11] was the most consistent, and I'll present it here. One note of interest: we found that, for high P/E stocks (the bottom quintile), the further out the EPS estimate used, the greater the underperformance of the quintile. That is, for the bottom quintile, trailing EPS underperformed less than estimates, and current year estimates underperformed less than one-year forward estimates. The reason, I believe, is that all projections of future events are uncertain, and the further into the future one projects, the higher that uncertainty. The lesson: beware of stocks selling at high multiples of expected future earnings.

The price to current fiscal year earnings estimate strategy shows strong outperformance for the top quintile and moderate underperformance for the bottom two quintiles. The consistency of the strategy is about average, with the top quintile outperforming for 66% of one-year and 83% of rolling three-year periods, and the bottom quintile underperforming for 58% of one-year and 83% of rolling three-year periods (see Figure 5.10). The free cash flow-to-price and enterprise value-to-EBITDA strategies are significantly stronger with regard to both excess returns and consistency. Average portfolio values for the top quintile (for price to earnings) range from 6× to 12×.

Price to Earnings (Current Fiscal Year EPS Estimates) by Economic Sector

The price-to-earnings strategy works primarily with four economic sectors: consumer discretionary, health care, information technology, and telecom services. The bottom quintile for the energy sector works well, but the top quintile is inconsistent. The strategy also works with the consumer staples sector, but results are inconsistent. The sector tests highlight the moderate strength of the P/E ratio as a quantitative factor: while free cash flow to price and EV to EBITDA work broadly across economic sectors, P/E ratio works well only for specific sectors (see Figure 5.11).[12]

---

[11] We use I/B/E/S analysts' consensus EPS estimates for the current fiscal year. These estimates represent the average of all the forecast firms, including the major Wall Street brokerage firms, that contribute estimates to I/B/E/S. The I/B/E/S database is now owned by Thomson Reuters Corporation.

[12] However, as I mentioned in the introduction, great investors, such as John Neff of the Vanguard Windsor Fund, have used P/E ratios as a profitable investment tool, so its value should not be discounted. Quantitatively, however, it is not our strongest valuation factor.

1988 ~ 2007	1st Quintile	2nd Quintile	3rd Quintile	4th Quintile	5th Quintile	Universe	S&P 500*
CAGR – Annual Rebalance	14.8%	12.7%	12.2%	9.0%	4.2%	11.2%	12.9%
Average Excess Return vs. Universe**	4.7%	1.2%	0.0%	−1.9%	−2.2%	NA	1.6%
Value of $10,000 Invested (20 Years)	$156,764	$109,857	$100,781	$56,350	$22,924	$83,161	$112,895
% of 1-Year Periods Strategy Outperforms the Universe	66.2%	55.8%	54.5%	31.2%	41.6%	NA	59.7%
% Rolling 3-Year Periods Strategy Outperforms	82.6%	71.0%	52.2%	23.2%	17.4%	NA	71.0%
Maximum Gain	70.5%	48.9%	46.4%	49.0%	117.1%	59.2%	54.1%
Maximum Loss	−31.4%	−21.4%	−22.1%	−48.9%	−72.9%	−24.9%	−25.9%
Sharpe Ratio	0.67	0.66	0.59	0.32	0.17	0.49	0.69
Standard Deviation of Returns	0.19	0.14	0.14	0.19	0.34	0.16	0.14
Beta (vs. Universe)	0.82	0.68	0.79	1.07	1.67	NA	0.78
Alpha (vs. Universe)	0.07	0.05	0.03	−0.03	−0.11	NA	0.04
Average Portfolio Size	389	389	389	389	390	NA	NA
Average Number of Companies *Outperforming*	197	179	173	158	144	NA	NA
Average Number of Companies *Underperforming*	178	193	197	212	222	NA	NA
Median Portfolio Value – Price to Earnings	9.5	14.6	18.7	25.6	−38.1	20.9	18.8
Average Market Capitalization	$3,637	$3,962	$5,694	$5,688	$2,524	NA	NA

* Equal-weighted average of S&P 500 returns. ** Annual holding period run quarterly for a larger sample size; arithmetic average excess returns.
Source: Standard & Poor's Compustat Point in Time Database; Thomson Reuters I/B/E/S Estimates; Charter Oak Investment Systems, Inc., Venues® Data Engine

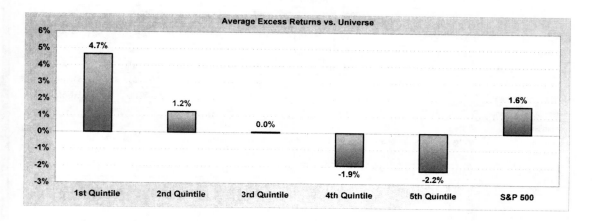

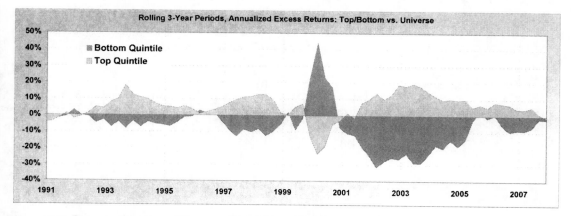

Figure 5.10 Price to Earnings (Current Fiscal Year EPS Estimates)

Top Quintile

1988 ~ 2007	Energy	Materials	Industrials	Consumer Discretionary	Consumer Staples	Health Care	Financials	Information Technology	Telecom Services	Utilities	Universe	S&P 500*
CAGR – Quintile	16.4%	7.9%	11.9%	11.5%	15.2%	16.9%	14.1%	10.7%	13.0%	12.9%	11.2%	12.9%
CAGR – Sector	13.5%	10.2%	11.2%	8.8%	12.6%	12.3%	14.5%	7.6%	9.2%	13.0%	NA	NA
Excess Return vs. Sector	2.9%	−2.3%	0.7%	2.8%	2.6%	4.6%	−0.4%	3.2%	3.7%	0.0%	NA	NA
Value of $10,000	$209,791	$45,931	$94,500	$88,659	$169,576	$226,794	$139,316	$76,723	$114,543	$113,639	$83,161	$112,895
% 1-Year Outperformance	45.0%	25.0%	55.0%	75.0%	50.0%	70.0%	45.0%	65.0%	65.0%	50.0%	NA	NA
% 3-Year Outperformance	66.7%	33.3%	66.7%	88.9%	61.1%	88.9%	33.3%	61.1%	66.7%	61.1%	NA	NA
Maximum Gain	52.6%	36.3%	46.9%	59.5%	68.4%	77.7%	58.0%	106.6%	60.8%	64.3%	44.0%	41.4%
Maximum Loss	−45.3%	−19.3%	−18.1%	−19.5%	−20.5%	−15.7%	−24.7%	−32.2%	−38.5%	−27.9%	−19.1%	−18.1%
Standard Deviation	0.24	0.14	0.15	0.18	0.22	0.24	0.22	0.30	0.26	0.19	0.16	0.14
Beta (vs. Sector)	0.90	0.86	1.00	0.96	1.39	0.89	0.97	0.77	0.40	1.16	NA	NA
Alpha (vs. Sector)	0.04	−0.01	0.01	0.03	−0.01	0.06	0.00	0.04	0.10	−0.02	NA	NA
Portfolio Size	24	31	58	68	20	41	62	59	8	25	NA	NA

Bottom Quintile

1988 ~ 2007	Energy	Materials	Industrials	Consumer Discretionary	Consumer Staples	Health Care	Financials	Information Technology	Telecom Services	Utilities	Universe	S&P 500*
CAGR – Quintile	9.9%	6.5%	8.7%	4.3%	10.1%	5.8%	15.9%	5.0%	6.5%	13.4%	11.2%	12.9%
CAGR – Sector	13.5%	10.2%	11.2%	8.8%	12.6%	12.3%	14.5%	7.6%	9.2%	13.0%	NA	NA
Excess Return vs. Sector	−3.6%	−3.7%	−2.5%	−4.4%	−2.5%	−6.6%	1.4%	−2.6%	−2.8%	0.4%	NA	NA
Value of $10,000	$66,637	$35,067	$53,372	$23,412	$67,899	$30,617	$191,319	$26,549	$34,956	$122,617	$83,161	$112,895
% 1-Year Outperformance	30.0%	40.0%	40.0%	50.0%	45.0%	30.0%	65.0%	40.0%	50.0%	50.0%	NA	NA
% 3-Year Outperformance	22.2%	22.2%	16.7%	16.7%	33.3%	11.1%	66.7%	44.4%	33.3%	72.2%	NA	NA
Maximum Gain	76.4%	51.6%	55.2%	51.1%	33.8%	84.2%	63.7%	215.0%	182.2%	56.2%	44.0%	41.4%
Maximum Loss	−50.1%	−35.1%	−24.5%	−43.5%	−25.0%	−32.8%	−35.4%	−61.3%	−77.8%	−24.4%	−19.1%	−18.1%
Standard Deviation	0.35	0.22	0.18	0.24	0.16	0.31	0.25	0.58	0.51	0.19	0.16	0.14
Beta (vs. Sector)	1.31	1.36	1.18	1.24	1.03	1.18	1.09	1.52	1.28	1.09	NA	NA
Alpha (vs. Sector)	−0.06	0.01	−0.03	−0.07	0.05	−0.06	0.05	−0.11	−0.03	0.05	NA	NA
Portfolio Size	25	31	61	72	23	42	65	61	9	26	NA	NA

* Equal-weighted average of S&P 500 returns.
Source: Standard & Poor's Compustat Point in Time Database; Thomson Reuters I/B/E/S Estimates; Charter Oak Investment Systems, Inc., Venues® Data Engine

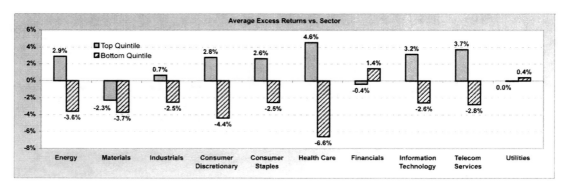

Figure 5.11 Price to Earnings (Current Fiscal Year EPS Estimates) by Economic Sector

Price to Earnings and Enterprise Value to EBITDA

This two-factor valuation-only strategy evaluates companies in two slightly different ways. First, it looks simply at price to net income on a per share basis (EPS); next, it looks at the total value of the company (EV) relative to operating income before depreciation (or EBITDA). In addition, the strategy looks backward (historical EBITDA) and forward (estimated EPS). I view this strategy as a more complete price-to-earnings evaluation, one that takes into account total EV, historical operating income, and projected earnings per share, all at the same time. It works very well.

The top quintile outperforms by 7.1%, on average, and does so for 73% of one-year and 86% of rolling three-year periods (see Figure 5.12). It significantly underperforms in 1990–1991, 1996, 1999–2000, and 2007. An average of 35 companies in the top quintile outperforms versus 31 that underperform, a strong showing. Average portfolio values for the top quintile vary from 6× to 10× for price to estimated earnings and 1× to 4× for EV to EBITDA.

The bottom quintile underperforms by an average of 5%, and does so for 73% of one-year periods and 87% of rolling three-year periods. However, the bottom quintile is extremely volatile, outperforming strongly during several periods (particularly 1999–2000). Its Beta versus the Universe is 1.9, and its maximum annual gain is a huge 162%. Average portfolio values are negative for both P/E and EV to EBITDA ratios.

Price to Earnings and EPS Score

This strategy is the first presented to combine valuation and growth. As you saw in Chapter 3, earning per share growth strategies alone don't predict future stock market returns. I believe that there are two reasons for this: (1) earnings growth is highly visible, and companies with the strongest earnings growth command the highest valuations (and thus are subject to a fall on a slight disappointment); and (2) high rates of earnings growth are hard to maintain, and earnings growth tends to revert toward the mean (the disappointment).

We've solved this problem, in part, by creating a combined score that looks at both the growth and linearity (consistency) of earnings. The EPS score measures quarterly earnings over the past 10 quarters. We use a formula called the Relative Strength Index (RSI) to calculate a company's EPS growth trend, based on 10 quarters of earnings.[13] The EPS score is a weighted factor consisting of 80% RSI

---

[13] RSI is a technical (price momentum–based) concept developed by J. Welles Wilder. It is discussed in depth in Chapter 7, as it is applied to the EPS score, and in Chapter 9, as it is applied to price momentum.

1988 ~ 2007	1st Quintile	2nd Quintile	3rd Quintile	4th Quintile	5th Quintile	Universe	S&P 500*
CAGR – Annual Rebalance	18.3%	13.1%	13.7%	8.4%	1.3%	11.2%	12.9%
Average Excess Return vs. Universe**	7.1%	1.2%	0.5%	−3.2%	−5.0%	NA	1.6%
Value of $10,000 Invested (20 Years)	$287,415	$117,164	$130,259	$50,093	$12,998	$83,161	$112,895
% of 1-Year Periods Strategy Outperforms the Universe	72.7%	54.5%	45.5%	36.4%	27.3%	NA	59.7%
% Rolling 3-Year Periods Strategy Outperforms	85.5%	55.1%	59.4%	20.3%	13.0%	NA	71.0%
Maximum Gain	63.7%	52.9%	41.1%	68.1%	161.8%	59.2%	54.1%
Maximum Loss	−26.4%	−22.7%	−20.2%	−53.3%	−70.8%	−24.9%	−25.9%
Sharpe Ratio	0.82	0.66	0.70	0.23	0.07	0.49	0.69
Standard Deviation of Returns	0.18	0.14	0.12	0.21	0.43	0.16	0.14
Beta (vs. Universe)	0.78	0.64	0.68	1.12	1.88	NA	0.78
Alpha (vs. Universe)	0.10	0.06	0.05	−0.05	−0.16	NA	0.04
Average Portfolio Size	68	69	69	69	69	NA	NA
Average Number of Companies Outperforming	35	33	32	27	21	NA	NA
Average Number of Companies Underperforming	31	34	34	38	44	NA	NA
Median Portfolio Value – Price to Earnings	8.6	14.6	18.9	26.4	−12.9	20.9	18.8
Median Portfolio Value – EV to EBITDA	3.4	7.1	9.7	15.7	−14.8	10.5	9.1
Average Market Capitalization	$3,232	$4,025	$4,824	$8,286	$902	NA	NA

* Equal-weighted average of S&P 500 returns. ** Annual holding period run quarterly for a larger sample size; arithmetic average excess returns.
Source: Standard & Poor's Compustat Point in Time Database; Thomson Reuters I/B/E/S Estimates; Charter Oak Investment Systems, Inc., Venues® Data Engine

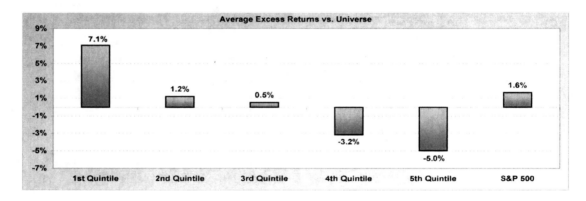

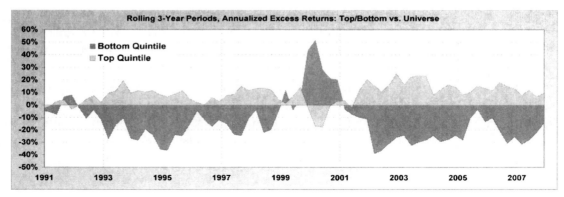

Figure 5.12 Price to Earnings and Enterprise Value to EBITDA

(growth trend) and 20% EPS linearity.[14] Companies with the strongest 10-quarter EPS growth and the highest linearity are placed in the top quintile, and companies with the highest negative EPS growth and the greatest earnings volatility are placed in the bottom quintile. Earnings per share scores in our database range from 0 to 95, with the highest score indicating both the highest level of EPS growth and the lowest volatility.

The price-to-earnings and EPS score strategy is an intuitive combination. The top quintile of this strategy contains companies that are seeing strong growth in earnings per share, along with low volatility of those earnings, and whose earnings are cheap relative to the P/E ratios of other companies. The bottom quintile contains companies whose earnings are seeing rapid declines and/or are volatile and whose P/E ratio is high relative to other stocks.

The top quintile outperforms by 5.5%, on average, and does so for 68% of one-year and 81% of rolling three-year periods (see Figure 5.13). Although the consistency of the strategy is a little weaker than I'd like, it has the virtue of having performed well recently. The strategy is also moderately volatile, with a maximum loss of 28%, versus 25% for the Universe, and a standard deviation of returns of 0.20, versus 0.16. This volatility results in a Sharpe ratio of just 0.66, slightly below the 0.69 ratio for the S&P 500. Average portfolio values range from 5× to 12× for the P/E ratio and 60 to 82 for the EPS score.

The bottom quintile of this strategy does not significantly underperform. Despite this problem, I presented the strategy because the top quintile works and the strategy illustrates a combination of factors—EPS growth and P/E ratio—that is commonly used by investors on Wall Street and Main Street alike. In Chapter 7, you'll see how the EPS score can be combined effectively with other valuation and fundamental factors to form strong tests that use growth as a primary factor.

Price to Earnings Plus Dividends and 52-Week Price Range

The price-to-earnings-plus-dividends strategy simply divides the current stock price of a company by the current fiscal year EPS estimate plus the past 12 months' dividends per share. Dividends are not a separate source of income to the shareholders; rather, they represent the portion of income (EPS) that is actually paid out to the shareholders. Adding dividends to earnings, therefore, doesn't significantly improve the P/E ratio

---

[14] Linearity is calculated based on the standard deviation of the 10 quarters of earnings. For a more complete explanation, see Chapter 7.

1988 ~ 2007	1st Quintile	2nd Quintile	3rd Quintile	4th Quintile	5th Quintile	Universe	S&P 500*
CAGR – Annual Rebalance	15.1%	12.5%	11.5%	9.5%	9.1%	11.2%	12.9%
Average Excess Return vs. Universe**	5.5%	1.5%	0.1%	−0.8%	0.0%	NA	1.6%
Value of $10,000 Invested (20 Years)	$166,160	$105,736	$88,061	$61,431	$57,490	$83,161	$112,895
% of 1-Year Periods Strategy Outperforms the Universe	67.5%	58.4%	49.4%	41.6%	45.5%	NA	59.7%
% Rolling 3-Year Periods Strategy Outperforms	81.2%	65.2%	42.0%	36.2%	33.3%	NA	71.0%
Maximum Gain	71.7%	49.6%	42.0%	45.7%	115.9%	59.2%	54.1%
Maximum Loss	−28.1%	−21.7%	−16.7%	−38.6%	−61.2%	−24.9%	−25.9%
Sharpe Ratio	0.66	0.66	0.65	0.45	0.25	0.49	0.69
Standard Deviation of Returns	0.20	0.15	0.13	0.16	0.33	0.16	0.14
Beta (vs. Universe)	0.89	0.66	0.61	0.89	1.69	NA	0.78
Alpha (vs. Universe)	0.07	0.06	0.05	0.01	−0.09	NA	0.04
Average Portfolio Size	66	66	66	66	67	NA	NA
Average Number of Companies *Outperforming*	33	30	28	26	25	NA	NA
Average Number of Companies *Underperforming*	30	33	35	36	36	NA	NA
Median Portfolio Value − Price to Earnings	9.6	14.7	18.2	23.9	−23.7	20.9	18.9
Median Portfolio Value – EPS Score	65	52	45	34	5	40	40
Average Market Capitalization	$3,522	$4,568	$6,492	$7,836	$2,037	NA	NA

* Equal-weighted average of S&P 500 returns. ** Annual holding period run quarterly for a larger sample size; arithmetic average excess returns.
Source: Standard & Poor's Compustat Point in Time Database; Thomson Reuters I/B/E/S Estimates; Charter Oak Investment Systems, Inc., Venues® Data Engine

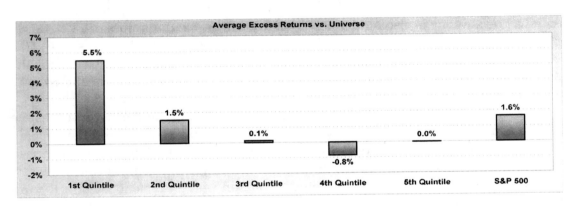

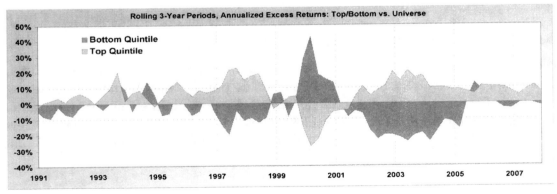

Figure 5.13 Price to Earnings and EPS Score

strategy, but it changes it to favor companies that pay significant dividends (in the top quintile) and to avoid companies with high P/E ratios and no dividends (in the bottom quintile). As in the previous strategy, we use current fiscal year analysts' average earnings estimates to calculate the P/E ratios.

As previously mentioned, valuation and price momentum (technical) factors work well together. The valuation factor selects stocks that appear cheap, whereas the technical factor suggests that the market believes the company has a "catalyst"—some business or industry improvement or other factor, such as a potential takeover offer, that will help boost the company's stock market valuation. The 52-week price range strategy calculates the range between a stock's past 52-week high and 52-week low and determines whether the current stock price is closer to the high end or the low end of this range.[15]

The top quintile of this strategy contains stocks that have low valuations on a price-to-earnings-plus-dividend basis *and* are at the high end of their 52-week price range (i.e., are close to their 52-week highs)—stocks that are cheap and have been moving up in price. The bottom quintile contains stocks with high valuations that are near the low end of their 52-week price range (close to their 52-week lows)—stocks that are expensive and have been moving down in price.

The strategy is very symmetrical, a sign of a strong strategy, with the top quintile outperforming by 6% and the bottom quintile underperforming by 6.5% (see Figure 5.14). The top quintile outperforms for 69% of one-year and 84% of rolling three-year periods, and the bottom quintile underperforms for 65% of one-year and 90% of rolling three-year periods. The bottom quintile is volatile, outperforming significantly in 1999 and in 2003. Average portfolio values for the top quintile range from 5× to 11× for price to earnings plus dividends per share and 40% to 98% for the 52-week price range. Average values for the bottom quintile are consistently negative for price to earnings plus dividends (meaning that portfolio companies have estimated losses per share) and have 52-week price range values of 3% to 46%. Note that the top quintile, with an average market cap of $5.4 billion, tends to choose large cap stocks, whereas the bottom quintile (average $1.6 billion) tends to select small caps. The addition of dividends skews the top quintile toward larger caps, as small, faster growing companies tend not to pay dividends.

---

[15] The formula for the 52-week price range is (current price – 52-week low) / (52-week high – 52-week low). A stock's 52-week price range can be found in certain financial newspapers (*Investor's Business Daily* is one), as well as financial Web sites, such as Yahoo! Finance.

1988 ~ 2007	1st Quintile	2nd Quintile	3rd Quintile	4th Quintile	5th Quintile	Universe	S&P 500*
CAGR – Annual Rebalance	16.7%	13.6%	13.2%	4.5%	−1.8%	11.2%	12.9%
Average Excess Return vs. Universe**	6.0%	2.7%	1.4%	−3.9%	−6.5%	NA	1.6%
Value of $10,000 Invested (20 Years)	$221,239	$128,286	$119,695	$24,104	$6,944	$83,161	$112,895
% of 1-Year Periods Strategy Outperforms the Universe	68.8%	62.3%	57.1%	29.9%	35.1%	NA	59.7%
% Rolling 3-Year Periods Strategy Outperforms	84.1%	68.1%	66.7%	17.4%	10.1%	NA	71.0%
Maximum Gain	58.6%	54.9%	43.6%	51.0%	113.0%	59.2%	54.1%
Maximum Loss	−29.8%	−16.1%	−18.5%	−54.7%	−77.3%	−24.9%	−25.9%
Sharpe Ratio	0.79	0.71	0.70	0.20	0.04	0.49	0.69
Standard Deviation of Returns	0.18	0.15	0.14	0.21	0.38	0.16	0.14
Beta (vs. Universe)	0.77	0.62	0.73	1.12	1.91	NA	0.78
Alpha (vs. Universe)	0.09	0.07	0.05	−0.05	−0.18	NA	0.04
Average Portfolio Size	75	75	76	75	76	NA	NA
Average Number of Companies *Outperforming*	38	37	35	29	26	NA	NA
Average Number of Companies *Underperforming*	33	35	37	43	46	NA	NA
Median Portfolio Value – Price to EPS + Divs.	8.7	12.8	16.2	23.1	−12.0	17.1	14.5
Median Portfolio Value − 52-week Price Range	90%	79%	69%	57%	18%	60%	59%
Average Market Capitalization	$5,402	$5,710	$4,505	$4,766	$1,584	NA	NA

* Equal-weighted average of S&P 500 returns. ** Annual holding period run quarterly for a larger sample size; arithmetic average excess returns.
Source: Standard & Poor's Compustat Point in Time Database; Thomson Reuters I/B/E/S Estimates; Charter Oak Investment Systems, Inc., Venues® Data Engine

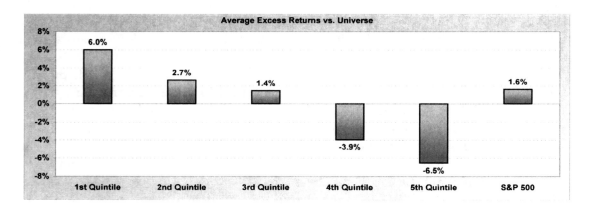

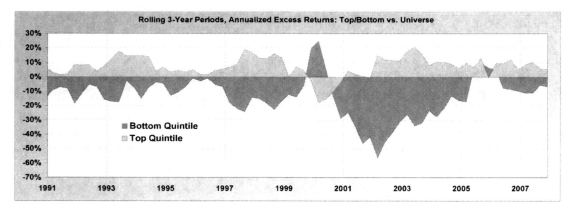

Figure 5.14 Price to Earnings Plus Dividends and 52-Week Price Range

ENTERPRISE VALUE TO SALES

EV to sales is another widely used valuation strategy. Investors usually use a company's common stock market value instead of EV (called the price to sales ratio), but we found that use of EV instead of market capitalization alone made the strategy more consistent.[16] EV to sales (or P/S) has two distinct advantages as a valuation ratio: it is usable with companies that temporarily have no earnings (cyclical companies during an economic downturn, new technology companies spending a lot on R&D, etc.), and since sales fluctuate less than earnings, it is a more stable ratio. However, there have been plenty of companies throughout stock market history that have generated strong sales growth and very little profitability—airlines have been a great example of this.[17] So, the EV-to-sales strategy is best used in combination with another valuation, profitability, or technical factor.

The top quintile of this strategy outperforms by an average of 3.6%, and does so for 64% of one-year and 78% of rolling three-year periods (see Figure 5.15). The bottom quintile underperforms by 4.7%, on average, and does so for 69% of one-year and 90% of three-year periods. Average portfolio values for EV to sales range from 0.2× to 0.5× for the top quintile, and from 3.4× to over 8.0× for the bottom quintile. (I'm excluding from these ranges average EV to sales values for the bottom quintile of 29× and 15×, which occurred in 1999 and 2000, respectively.)

Enterprise Value to Sales by Economic Sector

The EV-to-sales strategy works particularly well for the energy, health care, and information technology sectors. Information technology tends to be a cyclical and R&D-intensive industry, so in economic downturns, technology companies often have little or no earnings. Thus, the EV-to-sales ratio can be used to compare companies with losses to their own valuation histories and to other companies in the sector, which may or may not have earnings. Note that this strategy also works fairly well for the materials and financial sectors. For financial companies, *sales* are defined as net interest income plus noninterest income minus noninterest (operating) expenses (see Figure 5.16).

Enterprise Value to Sales and Free Cash Flow to Price

You might think that combining two strategies that measure similar things won't increase the strength of a strategy. Sometimes this is true, and sometimes it isn't. In Chapter 4, we saw the ROIC and cash ROIC strategy, which measures two different

---

[16] Our definition of enterprise value is market value of common equity plus long-term debt minus cash and short-term investments.

[17] One experienced investor's advice: "Never buy anything with wings or wheels."

1988 ~ 2008	1st Quintile	2nd Quintile	3rd Quintile	4th Quintile	5th Quintile	Universe	S&P 500*
CAGR – Annual Rebalance	14.6%	12.7%	12.0%	11.6%	3.4%	11.2%	12.9%
Average Excess Return vs. Universe**	3.6%	1.3%	0.3%	0.0%	−4.7%	NA	1.6%
Value of $10,000 Invested (20 Years)	$152,710	$109,989	$96,170	$89,191	$19,547	$83,161	$112,895
% of 1-Year Periods Strategy Outperforms the Universe	63.6%	53.2%	57.1%	49.4%	31.2%	NA	59.7%
% Rolling 3-Year Periods Strategy Outperforms	78.3%	69.6%	58.0%	44.9%	10.1%	NA	71.0%
Maximum Gain	71.8%	59.1%	54.3%	52.7%	81.7%	59.2%	54.1%
Maximum Loss	−27.8%	−23.9%	−23.6%	−31.7%	−75.7%	−24.9%	−25.9%
Sharpe Ratio	0.68	0.63	0.57	0.49	0.12	0.49	0.69
Standard Deviation of Returns	0.17	0.15	0.15	0.17	0.28	0.16	0.14
Beta (vs. Universe)	0.83	0.81	0.87	0.98	1.42	NA	0.78
Alpha (vs. Universe)	0.06	0.04	0.02	0.00	−0.10	NA	0.04
Average Portfolio Size	412	412	412	412	413	NA	NA
Average Number of Companies *Outperforming*	183	178	174	172	140	NA	NA
Average Number of Companies *Underperforming*	190	197	197	200	230	NA	NA
Median Portfolio Value – EV to Sales	0.4	1.2	1.9	3.4	7.6	1.3	1.2
Average Market Capitalization	$2,280	$3,700	$4,372	$6,336	$5,358	NA	NA

* Equal-weighted average of S&P 500 returns. ** Annual holding period run quarterly for a larger sample size; arithmetic average excess returns.
Source: Standard & Poor's Compustat Point in Time Database; Charter Oak Investment Systems, Inc., Venues® Data Engine

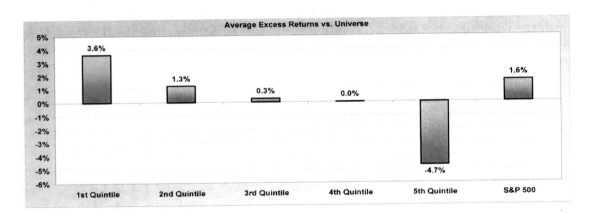

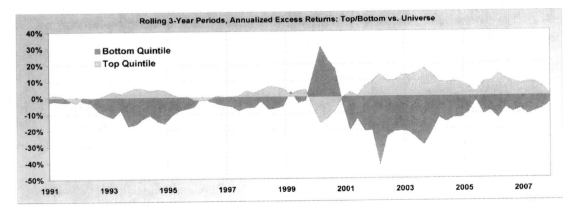

Figure 5.15 Enterprise Value to Sales

Top Quintile

1988 ~ 2007	Energy	Materials	Industrials	Consumer Discretionary	Consumer Staples	Health Care	Financials	Information Technology	Telecom Services	Utilities	Universe	S&P 500*
CAGR – Quintile	18.2%	13.1%	12.3%	9.5%	13.9%	20.9%	16.8%	15.2%	4.2%	13.0%	11.2%	12.9%
CAGR – Sector	13.5%	10.2%	11.3%	8.8%	12.6%	12.3%	14.5%	7.5%	9.2%	13.0%	NA	NA
Excess Return vs. Sector	4.7%	2.9%	1.1%	0.8%	1.3%	8.6%	2.3%	7.7%	−5.0%	0.0%	NA	NA
Value of $10,000	$282,781	$117,068	$102,071	$61,623	$133,934	$444,595	$222,306	$169,807	$22,939	$115,238	$83,161	$112,895
% 1-Year Outperformance	55.0%	65.0%	55.0%	55.0%	65.0%	85.0%	70.0%	75.0%	35.0%	55.0%	NA	NA
% 3-Year Outperformance	88.9%	83.3%	66.7%	55.6%	72.2%	88.9%	83.3%	83.3%	38.9%	55.6%	NA	NA
Maximum Gain	52.1%	48.1%	50.3%	49.4%	48.5%	88.5%	70.7%	75.9%	43.6%	66.1%	44.0%	41.4%
Maximum Loss	−17.4%	−18.2%	−25.5%	−33.7%	−25.0%	−17.1%	−27.2%	−37.4%	−64.3%	−34.7%	−19.1%	−18.1%
Standard Deviation	0.19	0.19	0.18	0.21	0.19	0.24	0.26	0.26	0.29	0.20	0.16	0.14
Beta (vs. Sector)	0.67	1.19	1.19	1.00	1.22	0.76	1.17	0.57	0.57	1.18	NA	NA
Alpha (vs. Sector)	0.09	0.01	−0.01	0.01	−0.01	0.12	0.00	0.11	0.01	−0.02	NA	NA
Portfolio Size	24	32	59	71	21	40	60	59	9	25	NA	NA

Bottom Quintile

1988 ~ 2007	Energy	Materials	Industrials	Consumer Discretionary	Consumer Staples	Health Care	Financials	Information Technology	Telecom Services	Utilities	Universe	S&P 500*
CAGR – Quintile	5.6%	5.0%	7.6%	6.1%	8.1%	1.2%	11.4%	1.0%	3.6%	12.2%	11.2%	12.9%
CAGR – Sector	13.5%	10.2%	11.3%	8.8%	12.6%	12.3%	14.5%	7.5%	9.2%	13.0%	NA	NA
Excess Return vs. Sector	−8.0%	−5.2%	−3.6%	−2.6%	−4.5%	−11.1%	−3.0%	−6.5%	−5.7%	−0.8%	NA	NA
Value of $10,000	$29,558	$26,437	$43,377	$32,983	$47,300	$12,737	$87,069	$12,312	$20,107	$100,006	$83,161	$112,895
% 1-Year Outperformance	20.0%	40.0%	20.0%	40.0%	30.0%	15.0%	20.0%	40.0%	60.0%	40.0%	NA	NA
% 3-Year Outperformance	22.2%	16.7%	16.7%	16.7%	16.7%	5.6%	22.2%	27.8%	55.6%	27.8%	NA	NA
Maximum Gain	67.5%	36.9%	39.9%	51.7%	43.2%	102.3%	70.4%	225.5%	185.1%	34.1%	44.0%	41.4%
Maximum Loss	−56.5%	−27.5%	−24.0%	−38.0%	−22.1%	−49.5%	−26.9%	−63.8%	−70.8%	−12.0%	−19.1%	−18.1%
Standard Deviation	0.29	0.17	0.17	0.20	0.16	0.34	0.23	0.60	0.57	0.15	0.16	0.14
Beta (vs. Sector)	1.10	0.90	1.00	0.96	0.99	1.28	0.98	1.55	1.53	0.85	NA	NA
Alpha (vs. Sector)	−0.08	0.01	−0.01	−0.04	0.03	−0.12	0.02	−0.14	−0.12	0.07	NA	NA
Portfolio Size	25	32	62	75	24	42	62	62	10	26	NA	NA

* Equal-weighted average of S&P 500 returns.
Source: Standard & Poor's Compustat Point in Time Database; Charter Oak Investment Systems, Inc., Venues® Data Engine

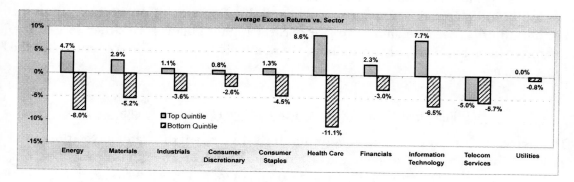

Figure 5.16 Enterprise Value to Sales by Economic Sector

aspects of profitability and works very well. If two strategies are too closely related, they usually do not add to each other (and sometimes even subtract from each other). But when the strategies measure different aspects of the same investment approach, particularly if it is a strong approach like valuation, they often work quite well together. This is the case with EV to sales and free cash flow to price. This strategy looks at a company's valuation in terms of both sales generation and cash flow generation. Both sales and cash flow are important, but they're also to some extent independent of each other (it's quite common for companies that are growing sales and earnings rapidly to have low free cash flows, as cash is used to fund growth), and the combined strategy works much better than either of the single factors alone.

The top quintile outperforms by 7.6%, on average, and does so for 73% of one-year and 87% of rolling three-year periods (see Figure 5.17). It underperformed slightly in 1994–1995 and significantly in 1999–2000 and 2003. The primary flaw of this strategy is that it is somewhat volatile: the maximum loss is 33% (vs. 26% for the S&P 500), and the standard deviation of returns is 0.20 (vs. 0.15). The result is a Sharpe ratio of 0.77, only moderately above the 0.64 ratio for the S&P 500. Average portfolio values for the top quintile range from 0.1× to 0.5× for EV to sales and 16% to 50% for free cash flow to price.

The bottom quintile underperforms by 8.9%, on average, and does so for 76% of one-year and 89% of rolling three-year periods. The bottom quintile significantly outperforms in 1999–2000 and in 2003–2004. Average portfolio values range from 5× to over 11× for EV to sales and from −8% to −33% for free cash flow to price. An average of 41 companies in the bottom quintile underperforms, versus an average of 21 that outperforms.

Valuation strategies in general tend to favor small and midcap stocks in the top quintile. Combining two valuation factors into one test intensifies this small/midcap focus. The average market cap for the top quintile is just $1.8 billion, one of the smallest we've seen yet in this quintile. This is also one of the few tests we've seen so far in which the top quintile contains smaller market capitalization stocks, on average, than the bottom quintile. Because small-cap stocks carry higher business risk than large caps, they tend to be more volatile, explaining the relatively high volatility of returns for the top quintile.

Enterprise Value to Sales and Seven-Month Relative Strength

The free cash flow to price and seven-month relative strength strategy was presented earlier in this chapter. EV to sales and seven-month relative strength is nearly as strong and as consistent, even though EV to sales, on its own, is a much weaker strategy than free cash flow to price. The combined strength that occurs when a valuation strategy is

1990 ~ 2007	1st Quintile	2nd Quintile	3rd Quintile	4th Quintile	5th Quintile	Universe	S&P 500*
CAGR – Annual Rebalance	16.9%	13.3%	8.9%	5.9%	−1.6%	10.3%	12.0%
Average Excess Return vs. Universe**	7.6%	3.6%	−0.8%	−2.2%	−8.9%	NA	1.5%
Value of $10,000 Invested (18 Years)	$166,180	$95,206	$46,781	$28,099	$7,493	$58,670	$76,297
% of 1-Year Periods Strategy Outperforms the Universe	73.2%	57.7%	47.9%	31.0%	23.9%	NA	56.3%
% Rolling 3-Year Periods Strategy Outperforms	87.3%	74.6%	38.1%	20.6%	11.1%	NA	68.3%
Maximum Gain	78.1%	51.9%	52.8%	70.5%	122.0%	59.2%	54.1%
Maximum Loss	−32.6%	−24.4%	−24.9%	−49.6%	−67.4%	−24.9%	−25.9%
Sharpe Ratio	0.77	0.72	0.47	0.25	−0.03	0.46	0.64
Standard Deviation of Returns	0.20	0.16	0.15	0.23	0.35	0.17	0.15
Beta (vs. Universe)	0.80	0.73	0.81	1.20	1.63	NA	0.78
Alpha (vs. Universe)	0.10	0.07	0.02	−0.05	−0.17	NA	0.04
Average Portfolio Size	65	65	65	65	65	NA	NA
Average Number of Companies *Outperforming*	32	31	27	25	21	NA	NA
Average Number of Companies *Underperforming*	30	31	35	36	41	NA	NA
Median Portfolio Value – EV to Sales	0.4	1.1	1.7	3.0	8.6	1.4	1.2
Median Portfolio Value – FCF to Price	25.2%	7.2%	3.1%	−0.1%	−21.2%	2.1%	3.3%
Average Market Capitalization	$1,805	$4,008	$5,061	$5,556	$2,355	NA	NA

* Equal-weighted average of S&P 500 returns.** Annual holding period run quarterly for a larger sample size; arithmetic average excess returns.
Source: Standard & Poor's Compustat Point in Time Database; Charter Oak Investment Systems, Inc., Venues® Data Engine

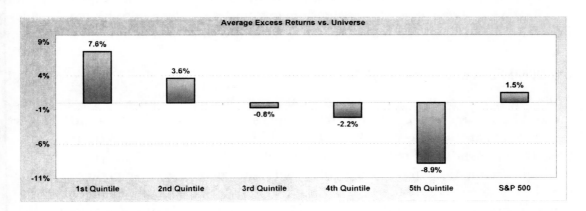

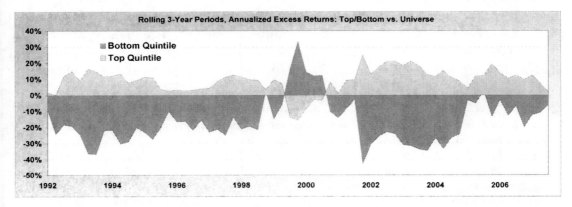

Figure 5.17 Enterprise Value to Sales and Free Cash Flow to Price

paired with a technical strategy shows that such a combination has sound underpin-
nings in investment theory. Specifically, technical strategies "point out" when undervalued stocks are likely to move higher (i.e., to see an increase in their valuation levels)
due to favorable trends in supply and demand.

The top quintile outperforms by 6.1%, on average, and does so for 78% of one-year
and 81% of rolling three-year periods (see Figure 5.18). It significantly underperforms
only in 1995, 1999–2000, and in 2003. Volatility is relatively low, with a maximum loss
of 25% and a standard deviation of returns of 0.16 (vs. 0.14 for the S&P 500), resulting in
a moderately high Sharpe ratio of 0.86. Average portfolio values for the top quintile
range from 0.1× to 0.6× for EV to sales and from 3% (1987) to well over 100% for seven-
month price change.[18]

The bottom quintile underperforms by 12.9%, on average, and is very consistent,
making it a strong short-sale strategy. It underperforms for 86% of one-year and 97% of
rolling three-year periods. An average of 51 companies in the bottom quintile underperforms for every 27 that outperform, one of the best ratios for the bottom quintile
we've seen yet. Average portfolio values range from 4× to over 8× for EV to sales and
from −3% to less than −50% for the seven-month price change.

DIVIDEND PLUS REPURCHASE YIELD

Dividend yield is another widely used valuation strategy. Some investors, particularly
those who are income conscious, favor stocks with high dividend yields. Other
investors and analysts use a stock's historical dividend yield to judge its current valuation. The dividend yield strategy has one problem, however: dividend yields that are
too high often indicate there is a problem with the company, and sometimes indicate
that the dividend is likely to be cut.[19] Thus, the top quintile of the dividend yield strategy (not shown) actually underperforms the second quintile. Even the second quintile,
which consists of stocks with a median dividend yield of 2.3%, only outperforms modestly (1.8%) and with average consistency (outperforming for 62% of one-year and 74%
of rolling three-year periods). A stronger strategy can be created by combining dividend
yield with share repurchase "yield." Dividend plus repurchase yield is calculated by

---

[18] Recall that we compute seven-month relative strength by simply comparing the seven-month price
change of one stock to that of every other stock in our Universe.

[19] Corporations are not obligated to pay dividends on common stocks. The best firms seek to at least
maintain a dividend, as a sign of corporate financial strength as well as a token of management's
fiduciary duty to shareholders. However, debt covenants often restrict dividend payments if certain
financial criteria are not met, and if the choice is between the survival of the corporation and the
payment of the dividend, you can guess what takes first priority.

1988 ~ 2007	1st Quintile	2nd Quintile	3rd Quintile	4th Quintile	5th Quintile	Universe	S&P 500*
CAGR – Annual Rebalance	16.6%	13.6%	13.0%	9.3%	−3.1%	11.2%	12.9%
Average Excess Return vs. Universe**	6.1%	0.7%	1.3%	−0.5%	−12.9%	NA	1.6%
Value of $10,000 Invested (20 Years)	$216,882	$129,024	$114,452	$59,347	$5,351	$83,161	$112,895
% of 1-Year Periods Strategy Outperforms the Universe	77.9%	55.8%	57.1%	41.6%	14.3%	NA	59.7%
% Rolling 3-Year Periods Strategy Outperforms	81.2%	60.9%	63.8%	42.0%	2.9%	NA	71.0%
Maximum Gain	60.4%	57.1%	48.1%	42.8%	64.4%	59.2%	54.1%
Maximum Loss	−24.7%	−20.6%	−18.8%	−24.3%	−80.9%	−24.9%	−25.9%
Sharpe Ratio	0.86	0.60	0.70	0.52	−0.18	0.49	0.69
Standard Deviation of Returns	0.16	0.15	0.13	0.15	0.27	0.16	0.14
Beta (vs. Universe)	0.82	0.76	0.71	0.77	1.43	NA	0.78
Alpha (vs. Universe)	0.08	0.04	0.05	0.02	−0.18	NA	0.04
Average Portfolio Size	80	81	81	81	81	NA	NA
Average Number of Companies *Outperforming*	37	38	38	34	27	NA	NA
Average Number of Companies *Underperforming*	37	40	40	44	51	NA	NA
Median Portfolio Value – EV to Sales	0.4	1.1	1.9	3.0	6.9	1.4	1.2
Median Portfolio Value – 7-Month Price Change	51%	16%	7%	−1%	−17%	19%	5%
Average Market Capitalization	$1,910	$3,948	$5,254	$7,832	$4,408	NA	NA

* Equal-weighted average of S&P 500 returns. ** Annual holding period run quarterly for a larger sample size; arithmetic average excess returns.
Source: Standard & Poor's Compustat Point in Time Database; Charter Oak Investment Systems, Inc., Venues® Data Engine

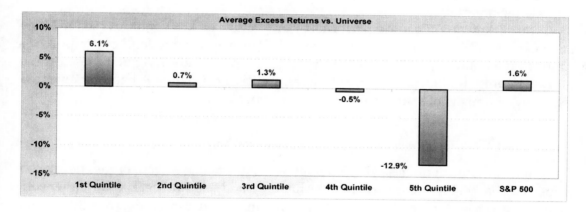

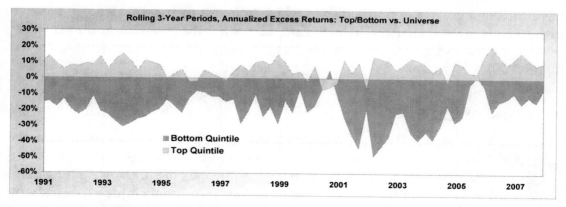

Figure 5.18 Enterprise Value to Sales and Seven-Month Relative Strength

taking the past 12 months' dividends paid on common shares and adding the past 12 months' cash share repurchases (net of cash received from share issuance). All of this data can be found in the financing section of a company's statement of cash flows. Cash dividends plus net share repurchases are then divided by market capitalization to arrive at dividend plus repurchase yield. This strategy provides higher excess returns than the dividend yield strategy alone.

The top quintile of this strategy outperforms by an average of 2.4%, and does so for 52% of one-year and 71% of rolling three-year periods (see Figure 5.19). The top quintile has an average market cap of $6.6 billion, meaning it is a large-cap strategy. Large-cap companies often generate a lot of cash and, since opportunities for growth are limited, can use that cash to pay dividends and repurchase shares. The average dividend plus share repurchase yield for the top quintile ranges from 6% to over 15%, but it has come down significantly since the late 1980s. Also note that the strategy has low volatility, with a standard deviation of returns of 0.14 for the top quintile, in line with the standard deviation for the S&P 500, and a Sharpe ratio of 0.75, which is strong for a single-factor strategy.

The bottom quintile underperforms by an average of 4.3%, and does so for 74% of one-year and 87% of rolling three-year periods. The average dividend plus repurchase yield for the bottom quintile ranges from −7% to −19%, indicating that these companies are issuing significant amounts of shares. We'll see in Chapter 8 that companies that issue large numbers of shares consistently underperform.

Dividend Plus Repurchase Yield by Economic Sector

The dividend-and-repurchase yield strategy works particularly well for the energy, consumer staples, health care, information technology, and telecom sectors. The larger companies in these sectors tend to be mature companies in mature industries that do not have sufficient growth opportunities in which to invest their cash. Hence, a return of cash strategy is a good one for them. In particular, this is the strongest consumer staples strategy we have seen so far. The strategy also works well for the industrials sector (see Figure 5.20).

PRICE TO BOOK VALUE

Like enterprise value to sales, price to book value is not among the strongest valuation strategies. Excess returns and consistency are moderate. There are a couple factors at work here. First, like EV to sales, price to book value tells the investor nothing about price relative to *profitability*. A stock with a low price-to-book value ratio is simply "cheap" based on the price of acquiring its assets—just because the assets are cheap

1988 ~ 2007	1st Quintile	2nd Quintile	3rd Quintile	4th Quintile	5th Quintile	Universe	S&P 500*
CAGR – Annual Rebalance	14.0%	13.0%	11.7%	9.9%	6.0%	11.2%	12.9%
Average Excess Return vs. Universe**	2.4%	1.4%	0.0%	−0.1%	−4.3%	NA	1.6%
Value of $10,000 Invested (20 Years)	$138,023	$114,824	$91,657	$65,617	$31,901	$83,161	$112,895
% of 1-Year Periods Strategy Outperforms the Universe	51.9%	59.7%	50.6%	40.3%	26.0%	NA	59.7%
% Rolling 3-Year Periods Strategy Outperforms	71.0%	75.4%	49.3%	36.2%	13.0%	NA	71.0%
Maximum Gain	54.5%	53.7%	57.1%	62.2%	76.8%	59.2%	54.1%
Maximum Loss	−21.4%	−22.5%	−23.7%	−43.0%	−54.9%	−24.9%	−25.9%
Sharpe Ratio	0.75	0.70	0.51	0.37	0.15	0.49	0.69
Standard Deviation of Returns	0.14	0.14	0.16	0.21	0.25	0.16	0.14
Beta (vs. Universe)	0.68	0.73	0.95	1.22	1.40	NA	0.78
Alpha (vs. Universe)	0.06	0.05	0.01	−0.03	−0.09	NA	0.04
Average Portfolio Size	347	348	348	347	348	NA	NA
Average Number of Companies *Outperforming*	164	159	177	141	128	NA	NA
Average Number of Companies *Underperforming*	169	175	178	185	201	NA	NA
Median Portfolio Value – Dividend + Repurchase Yield	7.9%	2.3%	0.4%	−0.5%	−9.0%	0.3%	2.7%
Average Market Capitalization	$6,563	$6,878	$4,380	$2,621	$1,702	NA	NA

* Equal-weighted average of S&P 500 returns. ** Annual holding period run quarterly for a larger sample size; arithmetic average excess returns.
Source: Standard & Poor's Compustat Point in Time Database; Charter Oak Investment Systems, Inc., Venues® Data Engine

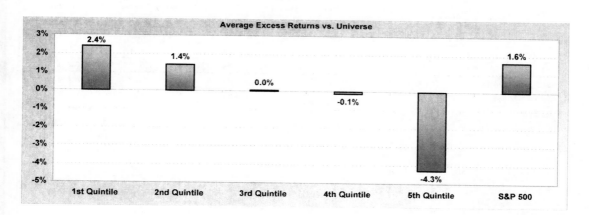

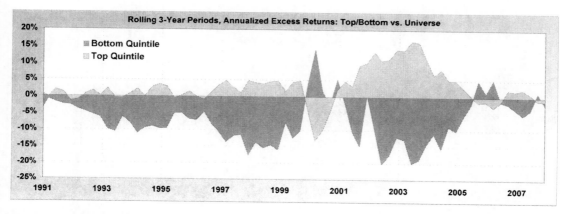

Figure 5.19 Dividend plus Repurchase Yield

Top Quintile

1988 ~ 2007	Energy	Materials	Industrials	Consumer Discretionary	Consumer Staples	Health Care	Financials	Information Technology	Telecom Services	Utilities	Universe	S&P 500*
CAGR – Quintile	18.9%	12.5%	13.7%	10.6%	19.4%	17.5%	13.9%	13.6%	15.0%	15.6%	11.2%	12.9%
CAGR – Sector	13.5%	10.2%	11.3%	8.8%	12.6%	12.3%	14.5%	7.5%	9.2%	13.0%	NA	NA
Excess Return vs. Sector	5.4%	2.3%	2.4%	1.9%	6.8%	5.2%	−0.5%	6.1%	5.8%	2.6%	NA	NA
Value of $10,000	$319,368	$105,963	$129,432	$75,630	$347,324	$252,985	$135,976	$127,914	$163,213	$180,986	$83,161	$112,895
% 1-Year Outperformance	75.0%	60.0%	65.0%	65.0%	85.0%	75.0%	50.0%	65.0%	60.0%	30.0%	NA	NA
% 3-Year Outperformance	83.3%	61.1%	83.3%	66.7%	100.0%	83.3%	33.3%	83.3%	61.1%	66.7%	NA	NA
Maximum Gain	48.9%	36.7%	37.9%	34.1%	72.9%	66.5%	55.9%	78.4%	80.0%	105.0%	44.0%	41.4%
Maximum Loss	−18.4%	−15.8%	−12.6%	−22.6%	−12.5%	−15.3%	−23.8%	−36.7%	−41.2%	−14.3%	−19.1%	−18.1%
Standard Deviation	0.18	0.13	0.14	0.16	0.20	0.21	0.23	0.26	0.28	0.25	0.16	0.14
Beta (vs. Sector)	0.62	0.81	0.88	0.82	1.28	0.79	0.98	0.65	0.69	0.98	NA	NA
Alpha (vs. Sector)	0.10	0.04	0.04	0.03	0.04	0.08	0.00	0.08	0.08	0.04	NA	NA
Portfolio Size	22	31	58	69	21	39	30	55	8	3	NA	NA

Bottom Quintile

1988 ~ 2007	Energy	Materials	Industrials	Consumer Discretionary	Consumer Staples	Health Care	Financials	Information Technology	Telecom Services	Utilities	Universe	S&P 500*
CAGR – Quintile	6.7%	2.8%	5.9%	7.2%	8.0%	7.9%	10.2%	5.1%	−3.1%	1.4%	11.2%	12.9%
CAGR – Sector	13.5%	10.2%	11.3%	8.8%	12.6%	12.3%	14.5%	7.5%	9.2%	13.0%	NA	NA
Excess Return vs. Sector	−6.9%	−7.4%	−5.3%	−1.6%	−4.6%	−4.4%	−4.3%	−2.5%	−12.4%	−11.5%	NA	NA
Value of $10,000	$36,419	$17,512	$31,618	$40,156	$46,351	$45,807	$69,550	$26,834	$5,296	$13,275	$83,161	$112,895
% 1-Year Outperformance	15.0%	20.0%	30.0%	50.0%	30.0%	35.0%	25.0%	40.0%	35.0%	45.0%	NA	NA
% 3-Year Outperformance	11.1%	5.6%	11.1%	22.2%	11.1%	22.2%	22.2%	33.3%	16.7%	55.6%	NA	NA
Maximum Gain	74.4%	41.7%	41.7%	60.3%	35.5%	98.8%	37.4%	188.3%	204.2%	85.7%	44.0%	41.4%
Maximum Loss	−59.1%	−32.0%	−28.5%	−30.3%	−18.9%	−39.2%	−34.8%	−56.8%	−65.4%	−91.3%	−19.1%	−18.1%
Standard Deviation	0.31	0.18	0.17	0.23	0.15	0.29	0.19	0.49	0.56	0.37	0.16	0.14
Beta (vs. Sector)	1.19	1.10	1.09	1.13	1.00	1.11	0.78	1.27	1.36	1.57	NA	NA
Alpha (vs. Sector)	−0.08	−0.02	−0.04	−0.05	0.02	−0.06	0.02	−0.11	−0.17	−0.04	NA	NA
Portfolio Size	23	32	61	73	23	41	33	57	9	4	NA	NA

* Equal-weighted average of S&P 500 returns.
Source: Standard & Poor's Compustat Point in Time Database; Charter Oak Investment Systems, Inc., Venues® Data Engine

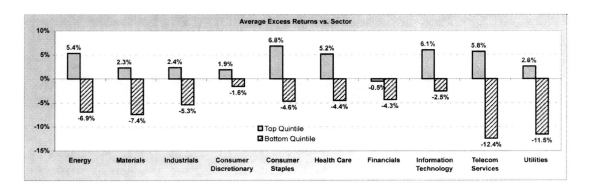

Figure 5.20 Dividend and Repurchase Yield by Economic Sector

doesn't mean the company can earn a good return on those assets (this is why return on equity and price to book combine so well, see Chapter 4). Second, book value is subject to a number of factors that can cause it to diverge significantly from the fair value of the assets of the company: historical price accounting,[20] the inclusion of intangible assets in book value, and so on. Despite these problems, price to book can make an excellent combining factor, working well with profitability factors (return on equity, economic profits), other valuation factors (EV to EBITDA, free cash flow to price), and technical strategies (seven-month relative strength, 52-week price range).

In addition to the straight price-to-book value ratio, we tested price to tangible book value, enterprise value to book value, and so on. Price to tangible book value provided a little extra outperformance (about 0.3%) and consistency for the top quintile, but the bottom quintile didn't work as well. So, the tests that follow are all based simply on price to book value. The top quintile of the strategy outperforms by an average of 3.6% and is moderately consistent, outperforming for 62% of one-year and 80% of rolling three-year periods (see Figure 5.21). Like most valuation strategies, it is small cap, with an average market cap of $2.2 billion. The bottom two quintiles underperform moderately (2.4% for the fourth quintile and 1.9% for the fifth), and are also moderately consistent. They tend to include larger cap stocks, with an average market cap of $5.6 billion to $5.9 billion. Average portfolio values for price to book value range from 0.6× to 1.4× for the top quintile and 7× to over 20× for the bottom quintile.

Price to Book Value by Economic Sector

Price to book value works moderately well for the energy, industrials, consumer staples, health care, and financials sectors. It works very well, in terms of excess returns, for the information technology and telecom services sectors, but returns are only moderately consistent. It is also a strong negative strategy for the materials sector. It can be used as a valuation factor in the utilities sector, a sector in which set sizes for quantitative factors often tend to be small (see Figure 5.22).

Price to Book Value and Economic Profits

This test combines a valuation factor with a profitability factor, in this case the economic profits strategy from Chapter 4. The version of economic profits we use employs cash

---

[20] Under U.S. generally accepted accounting principles (GAAP), assets are generally recorded in a company's financial statements at the value at which they were acquired less associated depreciation or amortization charges. Certain assets, such as land, may have fair values well above their recorded book values. Other assets may be worth significantly less than their recorded book values.

1988 ~ 2007	1st Quintile	2nd Quintile	3rd Quintile	4th Quintile	5th Quintile	Universe	S&P 500*
CAGR – Annual Rebalance	14.5%	12.9%	11.2%	8.9%	7.1%	11.2%	12.9%
Average Excess Return vs. Universe**	3.6%	1.5%	−0.3%	−2.4%	−1.9%	NA	1.6%
Value of $10,000 Invested (20 Years)	$150,779	$112,494	$83,018	$55,296	$39,686	$83,161	$112,895
% of 1-Year Periods Strategy Outperforms the Universe	62.3%	55.8%	53.2%	28.6%	40.3%	NA	59.7%
% Rolling 3-Year Periods Strategy Outperforms	79.7%	71.0%	43.5%	15.9%	15.9%	NA	71.0%
Maximum Gain	82.7%	60.2%	47.4%	50.3%	85.6%	59.2%	54.1%
Maximum Loss	−29.2%	−21.1%	−22.9%	−39.5%	−65.3%	−24.9%	−25.9%
Sharpe Ratio	0.61	0.63	0.54	0.33	0.24	0.49	0.69
Standard Deviation of Returns	0.19	0.15	0.14	0.17	0.26	0.16	0.14
Beta (vs. Universe)	0.94	0.81	0.85	1.00	1.32	NA	0.78
Alpha (vs. Universe)	0.04	0.04	0.02	−0.02	−0.06	NA	0.04
Average Portfolio Size	425	425	425	425	426	NA	NA
Average Number of Companies *Outperforming*	204	196	180	174	165	NA	NA
Average Number of Companies *Underperforming*	200	206	221	230	240	NA	NA
Median Portfolio Value – Price-to-Book	1.1	1.9	2.6	4.1	15.2	2.3	2.3
Average Market Capitalization	$2,179	$3,012	$4,045	$5,694	$5,992	NA	NA

* Equal-weighted average of S&P 500 returns. ** Annual holding period run quarterly for a larger sample size; arithmetic average excess returns.
Source: Standard & Poor's Compustat Point in Time Database; Charter Oak Investment Systems, Inc., Venues® Data Engine

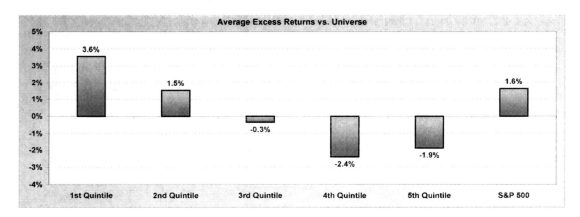

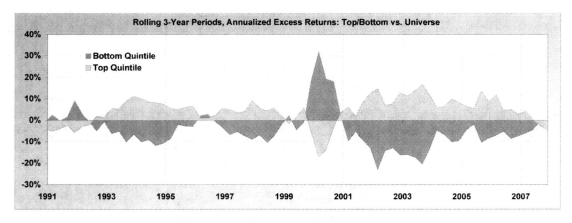

Figure 5.21 Price to Book Value

Top Quintile

1988 ~ 2007	Energy	Materials	Industrials	Consumer Discretionary	Consumer Staples	Health Care	Financials	Information Technology	Telecom Services	Utilities	Universe	S&P 500*
CAGR – Quintile	16.4%	10.7%	13.3%	8.1%	16.2%	15.0%	16.6%	12.3%	15.6%	15.4%	11.2%	12.9%
CAGR – Sector	13.5%	10.2%	11.2%	8.8%	12.6%	12.3%	14.5%	7.6%	9.2%	13.0%	NA	NA
Excess Return vs. Sector	2.9%	0.5%	2.1%	−0.7%	3.6%	2.7%	2.1%	4.7%	6.3%	2.5%	NA	NA
Value of $10,000	$210,276	$76,561	$122,536	$47,407	$200,813	$163,402	$215,264	$101,556	$180,106	$176,673	$83,161	$112,895
% 1-Year Outperformance	65.0%	40.0%	75.0%	45.0%	60.0%	70.0%	70.0%	60.0%	50.0%	55.0%	NA	NA
% 3-Year Outperformance	66.7%	61.1%	72.2%	55.6%	72.2%	72.2%	72.2%	77.8%	77.8%	66.7%	NA	NA
Maximum Gain	71.3%	69.6%	57.6%	51.2%	73.3%	86.7%	70.5%	96.2%	156.6%	69.7%	44.0%	41.4%
Maximum Loss	−37.7%	−27.8%	−21.6%	−30.5%	−15.2%	−27.6%	−41.2%	−51.3%	−50.6%	−17.5%	−19.1%	−18.1%
Standard Deviation	0.27	0.23	0.19	0.21	0.21	0.24	0.31	0.33	0.42	0.20	0.16	0.14
Beta (vs. Sector)	0.98	1.34	1.24	1.05	1.19	0.83	1.34	0.80	1.02	1.14	NA	NA
Alpha (vs. Sector)	0.03	−0.02	0.00	−0.01	0.02	0.05	−0.01	0.06	0.07	0.01	NA	NA
Portfolio Size	25	33	61	74	21	42	64	61	10	25	NA	NA

Bottom Quintile

1988 ~ 2007	Energy	Materials	Industrials	Consumer Discretionary	Consumer Staples	Health Care	Financials	Information Technology	Telecom Services	Utilities	Universe	S&P 500*
CAGR – Quintile	6.9%	5.6%	8.6%	6.9%	10.4%	7.7%	12.1%	5.5%	2.6%	11.3%	11.2%	12.9%
CAGR – Sector	13.5%	10.2%	11.2%	8.8%	12.6%	12.3%	14.5%	7.6%	9.2%	13.0%	NA	NA
Excess Return vs. Sector	−6.6%	−4.6%	−2.7%	−1.9%	−2.2%	−4.6%	−2.4%	−2.1%	−6.6%	−1.7%	NA	NA
Value of $10,000	$38,187	$29,694	$51,786	$37,717	$72,693	$44,041	$97,757	$29,103	$16,763	$84,984	$83,161	$112,895
% 1-Year Outperformance	30.0%	35.0%	25.0%	40.0%	35.0%	35.0%	25.0%	50.0%	50.0%	35.0%	NA	NA
% 3-Year Outperformance	16.7%	16.7%	5.6%	38.9%	22.2%	27.8%	27.8%	38.9%	33.3%	27.8%	NA	NA
Maximum Gain	51.4%	38.0%	37.0%	55.3%	47.8%	95.7%	48.6%	175.1%	187.2%	65.1%	44.0%	41.4%
Maximum Loss	−56.3%	−18.6%	−20.8%	−46.9%	−19.6%	−39.6%	−20.5%	−49.8%	−68.6%	−28.6%	−19.1%	−18.1%
Standard Deviation	0.26	0.17	0.16	0.22	0.16	0.32	0.17	0.48	0.57	0.20	0.16	0.14
Beta (vs. Sector)	0.99	1.03	1.02	1.01	1.04	1.25	0.74	1.24	1.47	1.13	NA	NA
Alpha (vs. Sector)	−0.06	0.00	−0.01	−0.03	0.04	−0.05	0.03	−0.09	−0.11	0.07	NA	NA
Portfolio Size	26	34	63	78	24	44	67	63	10	26	NA	NA

* Equal-weighted average of S&P 500 returns.
Source: Standard & Poor's Compustat Point in Time Database; Charter Oak Investment Systems, Inc., Venues® Data Engine

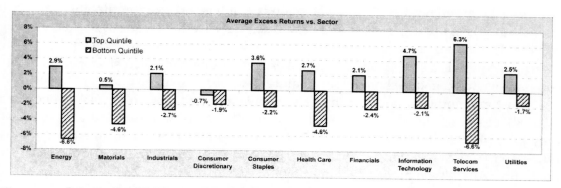

Figure 5.22 Price to Book Value by Economic Sector

ROIC in determining the profitability side of the equation and the stock's P/S ratio in place of Beta, as a proxy for risk, in determining the cost of equity. (Recall that the economic profits strategy seeks to determine a company's true, or economic, profitability to shareholders by subtracting its cost of capital from its return on capital.) The result is a very strong and consistent two-factor strategy that takes into account, on the one hand, a simple book value comparison and, on the other, an involved profitability assessment that looks at cash flow, the cost of capital, and price to sales. This is a complex approach, but it works.

The top quintile outperforms by 8.1%, on average, and does so for 74% of one-year and 86% of rolling three-year periods (see Figure 5.23). It significantly underperforms in 1999–2000, 2003, and 2006–2007. Volatility is somewhat high, with a maximum loss of 31% and a standard deviation of returns of 0.22 versus 0.14 for the S&P 500. The result is a Sharpe ratio of 0.74, moderately higher than the 0.64 ratio for the S&P 500. Average portfolio values for the top quintile range from 0.6× to 1.3× for price to book value and from 6% to well over 20% for economic profits, so the companies in this quintile are selling at their book values, on average, and are generating very strong cash returns on capital.

The bottom quintile underperforms by an average of 9.9%, and does so for 74% of one-year and 91% of rolling three-year periods. However, the bottom quintile is quite volatile, significantly outperforming in 1990, 1996, 1999–2000, 2003, and 2007. Average portfolio values range from 6× to 11× for price to book value and in the very high negative numbers for economic profits.

Price to Book Value and Operating Cash Flow to Equity

This strategy is similar to the return on equity and price to book value strategy presented in Chapter 4. In both cases, the strategies use a common denominator—stockholders' (or common) equity—and in both cases a profitability strategy is paired with a valuation strategy. The difference here is that valuation is emphasized over profitability, and that profitability is expressed in terms of cash (cash flow from operations) instead of net income. The second factor in this strategy could be called "cash return on equity." Cash return on equity is a strong factor that makes for a strong combined strategy. Note that companies with negative shareholders' equity have been excluded.

The top quintile outperforms by 6.6%, on average, and does so for 74% of one-year and 88% of rolling three-year periods (see Figure 5.24). It significantly underperforms only in 1990–1991, 1999–2000, and 2007. Average portfolio values for the top quintile range from 0.6× to 1.3× for price to book value and from 39% to over 50% for cash return on equity. Volatility is moderately high, with a maximum loss of 30% and a standard deviation of returns of 0.20 versus 0.14 for the S&P 500. The result is only a moderate Sharpe ratio of 0.72 versus 0.64 for the S&P 500.

1990 ~ 2007	1st Quintile	2nd Quintile	3rd Quintile	4th Quintile	5th Quintile	Universe	S&P 500*
CAGR – Annual Rebalance	18.7%	11.8%	11.0%	6.9%	−1.7%	10.3%	12.0%
Average Excess Return vs. Universe**	8.1%	2.0%	−1.1%	−3.1%	−9.9%	NA	1.5%
Value of $10,000 Invested (18 Years)	$217,728	$74,469	$65,540	$32,980	$7,307	$58,670	$76,297
% of 1-Year Periods Strategy Outperforms the Universe	73.6%	51.4%	50.0%	27.8%	26.4%	NA	56.9%
% Rolling 3-Year Periods Strategy Outperforms	85.9%	62.5%	45.3%	14.1%	9.4%	NA	68.8%
Maximum Gain	86.3%	58.4%	49.9%	50.2%	120.3%	59.2%	54.1%
Maximum Loss	−31.0%	−32.3%	−22.0%	−48.5%	−70.0%	−24.9%	−25.9%
Sharpe Ratio	0.74	0.58	0.50	0.23	−0.06	0.46	0.64
Standard Deviation of Returns	0.22	0.17	0.13	0.20	0.35	0.17	0.14
Beta (vs. Universe)	0.80	0.72	0.63	1.09	1.47	NA	0.78
Alpha (vs. Universe)	0.10	0.05	0.03	−0.04	−0.16	NA	0.04
Average Portfolio Size	54	54	54	54	55	NA	NA
Average Number of Companies *Outperforming*	28	26	24	21	16	NA	NA
Average Number of Companies *Underperforming*	24	26	27	31	35	NA	NA
Median Portfolio Value – Price-to-Book	1.0	2.0	2.7	3.9	8.4	2.4	2.4
Median Portfolio Value – Economic Profits	14.5%	−3.6%	−8.9%	−18.2%	−55.4%	−10.6%	−6.3%
Average Market Capitalization	$2,268	$2,878	$4,807	$5,066	$2,399	NA	NA

* Equal-weighted average of S&P 500 returns. ** Annual holding period run quarterly for a larger sample size; arithmetic average excess returns.
Source: Standard & Poor's Compustat Point in Time Database; Charter Oak Investment Systems, Inc., Venues® Data Engine

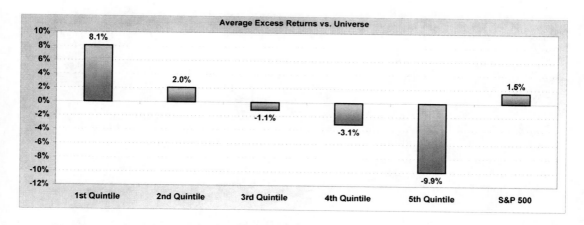

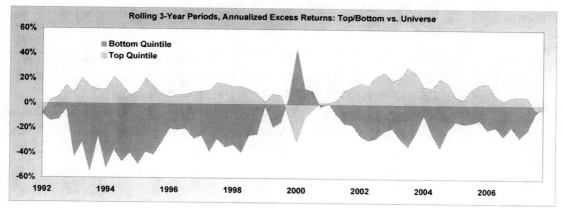

Figure 5.23 Price to Book Value and Economic Profits

1990 ~ 2007	1st Quintile	2nd Quintile	3rd Quintile	4th Quintile	5th Quintile	Universe	S&P 500*
CAGR – Annual Rebalance	17.7%	15.4%	10.4%	7.1%	−5.8%	10.3%	12.0%
Average Excess Return vs. Universe**	6.6%	4.3%	−0.5%	−3.6%	−13.2%	NA	1.5%
Value of $10,000 Invested (18 Years)	$187,703	$131,232	$59,648	$34,353	$3,409	$58,670	$76,297
% of 1-Year Periods Strategy Outperforms the Universe	73.6%	69.4%	50.0%	30.6%	20.8%	NA	56.9%
% Rolling 3-Year Periods Strategy Outperforms	87.5%	84.4%	42.2%	6.3%	7.8%	NA	68.8%
Maximum Gain	74.5%	55.8%	54.0%	53.4%	117.2%	59.2%	54.1%
Maximum Loss	−29.6%	−22.8%	−23.3%	−55.6%	−75.1%	−24.9%	−25.9%
Sharpe Ratio	0.72	0.78	0.53	0.18	−0.16	0.46	0.64
Standard Deviation of Returns	0.20	0.16	0.14	0.22	0.34	0.17	0.14
Beta (vs. Universe)	0.86	0.74	0.74	1.15	1.49	NA	0.78
Alpha (vs. Universe)	0.08	0.08	0.03	−0.05	−0.19	NA	0.04
Average Portfolio Size	67	67	67	67	68	NA	NA
Average Number of Companies Outperforming	33	33	30	26	18	NA	NA
Average Number of Companies Underperforming	30	31	34	38	46	NA	NA
Median Portfolio Value – Price-to-Book	1.1	2.1	2.8	4.1	9.4	2.4	2.4
Median Portfolio Value – Operating Cash Flow-to-Equity	44.3%	27.4%	22.4%	16.1%	−50.7%	24.8%	31.7%
Average Market Capitalization	$2,490	$3,027	$3,616	$4,703	$1,728	NA	NA

* Equal-weighted average of S&P 500 returns. ** Annual holding period run quarterly for a larger sample size; arithmetic average excess returns.
Source: Standard & Poor's Compustat Point in Time Database; Charter Oak Investment Systems, Inc., Venues® Data Engine

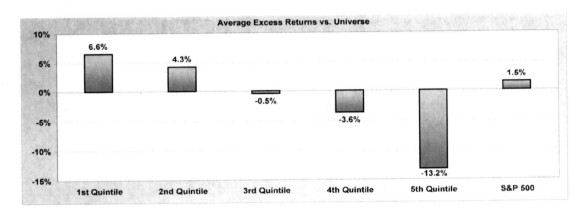

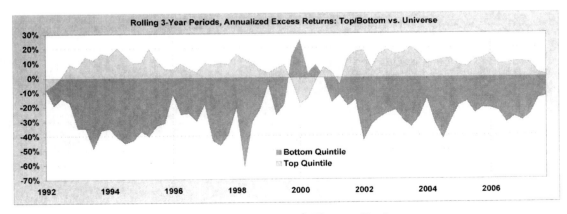

Figure 5.24 Price to Book Value and Operating Cash Flow to Equity

The bottom quintile underperforms by a very high 13.2%, on average, and does so for 79% of one-year and 92% of rolling three-year periods. It significantly outperforms only in 1999–2000 and 2003–2004. High negative excess returns and strong consistency make the bottom quintile a strong short-sale strategy. Average portfolio values range from 6× to over 13× for price to book value and in the high negative numbers for operating cash flow to equity, indicating that companies in this quintile are expensive relative to assets and have large cash outflows. Note that the strategy even works for the second and fourth quintiles, with the second quintile outperforming by an average of 4.3% and doing so for 84% of rolling three-year periods and the fourth quintile underperforming by 3.6% and doing so for 94% of rolling three-year periods. On average, 46 portfolio companies in the bottom quintile underperform versus 18 that outperform.

SUMMARY

- Valuation strategies in general work well quantitatively. A simple strategy of comparing the cost of one company to the cost of a number of other companies, based on some historical measure of profitability or asset value, works effectively, providing strong and consistent excess returns.
- Valuation is one of our most powerful *basics* and valuation factors should be used liberally as building blocks in quantitative screens and models.
- Combining valuation and other basics, such as cash flow, profitability, price momentum, and growth, results in some of the strongest two-factor strategies that we tested.
- Two of the strongest valuation approaches we tested are free cash flow to price and enterprise value (EV) to EBITDA. The free-cash-flow-to-price ratio is calculated as 12-month cash flows from operations minus 12-month capital expenditures, all divided by market capitalization.
- EV to EBTIDA is calculated as current enterprise value (the market value of common equity plus long-term debt minus cash and short-term investments) divided by 12-month earnings before interest, taxes, depreciation, and amortization (which can be approximated as operating income before depreciation).
- The free cash flow to price strategy generates strong and consistent excess returns, and is quite versatile, combining well with almost all quantitative factors we tested. Free cash flow to price also works well across economic sectors, and lacks the major defect of most cash flow-based strategies—that they haven't worked well recently.

- The free cash flow to price and external financing strategy combines a valuation factor with a capital allocation factor (share repurchases and debt reduction), with strong and consistent results. The bottom quintile of this strategy underperforms by an average of 15% and does so for 100% of rolling three-year periods, making it the strongest short sale strategy presented in this book.
- Valuation and price momentum-based, or technical, factors combine very well. The valuation factor tells the investor that the stock is attractively priced, while the price momentum factor indicates that investors expect some fundamental improvement at the company. Free cash flow to price and seven-month relative strength is an example of such a combination.
- Unlike profitability strategies, valuation strategies generally select small to mid-cap stocks in their top quintiles (with the exception of dividend yield strategies, which select large-cap stocks). The emphasis on small-cap stocks in the top quintile can be accentuated by combining *two* valuation factors in a single test, for example, EV to sales and free cash flow to price. However, reducing the average market cap size of a portfolio generally increases the volatility of returns for that portfolio.
- The combination of a valuation factor and a profitability factor is a strong one, since it captures two essentials in investing. However, valuation is the stronger of the two factors and should be place first (if the quantitative test emphasizes the first factor).
- The forward price-to-earnings (P/E) ratio works moderately well quantitatively. The current-year's analysts' earnings estimate works slightly better quantitatively than trailing (actual) 12-month earnings or next-year's estimated earnings. For the bottom quintile, however, using next-year's estimated EPS provides the strongest underperformance. That is, stocks selling at the highest multiples of projected future earnings underperform the most.
- However, the forward P/E strategy is not as strong or as consistent as EV to EBITDA and free cash flow to price, and does not work as consistently across economic sectors.
- The EV to sales ratio works moderately well and has the advantage of being usable with companies that temporarily have no earnings. It works particularly well with the energy, health care, and information technology sectors.
- Strategies based on dividend yield suffer from a couple problems. One is that dividend yields that are too high often indicate lower earnings at a company

and sometimes foreshadow a dividend *cut*. Another is that excess returns for the strategy are neither strong nor consistent.

- A stronger strategy that favors stocks with generous dividend yields is the dividend plus share repurchase yield strategy. This ratio is calculated by adding 12-month common dividends to 12-month net share repurchases and dividing the sum by a company's market capitalization.

- The dividend plus share repurchase yield strategy works particularly well for the consumer staples sector, a sector for which many other quantitative factors don't work.

- The price to book value ratio works only moderately well as a single-factor strategy. However, price to book value makes a strong building block, working well with profitability factors, other valuation factors, and technical factors.

- In particular, the price to book value and economics profits strategy makes a strong combination, with average excess returns for the top quintile above 8%.

- The bottom quintile of the price to book value and cash return on equity strategy underperforms by over 13%, on average, and is very consistent, making it a strong short-sale strategy.

CHAPTER 6

Cash Flow

A cash-flow survey of forty-four high P/E companies a few years ago pointed to twenty-six as worrisome; eleven months later, the stock prices of the twenty-six had fallen an average of 15%, while the others' prices were up 1.5%. The analysis pointed to trouble in seven companies ... all of which within a year were in bankruptcy. So, the analysis is worth running, if only for the bargains they steer you away from.

John C. Boland, *Wall Street's Insiders*

Cash flow allows a troubled company to keep paying that fat 5-percent dividend, or to buy back shares to placate disgruntled shareholders and support the stock price. Cash flow gives the company maneuvering room to pull clear of its problems. And cash flow lets it rebuild existing businesses, acquire other promising companies, or even start new ones. Cash flow is raw power. Cash flow is king.

Anthony M. Gallea & William Patalon III, *Contrarian Investing*

In 1987 the Financial Accounting Standards Board mandated that U.S. corporations provide cash flow statements. Most companies began implementing this rule in 1989. The standard, SFAS 95, requires that companies classify cash flows by operating, investing, and financing activities.[1] The standard greatly improved the consistency of cash flow reporting, and thus gave investors greater insight as to how companies were generating cash and how they were using it. In this chapter, we focus on cash from operating activities as well as one specific use of cash from investing activities—capital

---

[1] *Cash* is narrowly defined as cash and cash equivalents. Cash includes currency on hand and demand deposits with financial institutions, while cash equivalents are short-term investments that are readily convertible into cash.

expenditures (also referred to as purchases of property, plant, and equipment). Operating cash flow consists of cash received from the sale of goods and services less cash outflows required to produce those goods and render services, including cash taxes paid on profits and interest paid on debt financing. Our research shows that the level of operating cash flow a company generates is a strong indicator of future stock market returns.

Because cash accounting is volatile (one company may make large investments in new production equipment or working capital in a given year that are expected to pay off in the future, while another may see cash flows rise substantially as past investments bear fruit), cash flow ratios vary greatly by company and even over different time periods for the same company. Operating cash flow-to-sales ratios in the Compustat database for calendar year 2005, for example, varied from over 300% to less than −1,000%. Stock market returns aren't always linked to cash flow levels. For example, Intermune Inc., a biotechnology company, had a net operating cash outflow of $71 million in 2005 on sales of $110 million but recorded a stock market return of 33% over the following 12 months. Obviously, Intermune was being valued much more on future product expectations, and hence future cash flows, than on current results.[2]

However, a quick look at the list of the highest stock market performers in the following year (2006) shows that most had 2005 operating cash flow-to-sales ratios of 10% or greater, and a number had exceptionally high cash flow to sales (in the range of 20% to 60%). On the other hand, many of the following year's losers had very low or negative operating cash flows. If accounting earnings are so important, why do cash flows have such a noticeable affect on investment returns? One reason is that most investors have a visceral understanding that cash represents a reality—purchasing power—while accounting earnings are at least one step removed from that reality.

A look at the difference between accrual-basis accounting and cash-basis accounting is in order here. You'll recall from Chapter 3 that under accrual accounting, expenses are matched with their associated revenues whenever reasonable and practical. In addition, accrual accounting revenues generally aren't recognized until fully earned, whether or not partial cash has been received. As a result, there are significant timing differences between actual cash inflows and outflows, as reported on the statement of cash flows, and accrual accounting–based earnings, as reported on the income statement.

U.S.-based companies follow generally accepted accounting principles (GAAP) to establish accounting policies used to record financial results. While GAAP outlines standards, conventions, and rules that companies are expected to follow in reporting financial results, the specific applications of these guidelines are often left to company

---

[2] Or, perhaps, perceived takeover value.

accountants. Companies that use conservative accounting policies apply GAAP in ways that most accurately portray income, expense, and asset values. In making estimates, they err on the side of understating financial values rather than overstating them. Companies that apply accounting standards aggressively, on the other hand, select policies that present the best possible picture to shareholders and potential investors. Aggressive accounting tactics include "techniques" such as frequent changes of accounting policy, failure to take sufficient depreciation expense, use of one-time accounting gains to boost earnings, use of so-called special charges to shift expenses from one period to another, and failure to take necessary write-downs and impairment charges.

The point is that in subtle and sometimes not so subtle ways accrual accounting–based earnings can be manipulated to present a more favorable view of a company's results than business reality warrants. One item that cannot be so easily manipulated, however, is corporate cash flow.[3] Cash flow represents the actual inflow and outflow of cash that occurs during a period and result in either a net increase or net decrease in cash and cash equivalents at the end of the period. Our research shows that investors place significantly more value on actual cash inflows and outflows over time than on income statement–based earnings, and that accrual accounting earnings when not backed up by at least some degree of cash flow can often be considered suspect. In this chapter we'll look at cash flow in three different ways: as a measure of the quality of accrual accounting earnings, as a cash-based profitability measure, and as a combined cash flow/capital allocation valuation measure.

FREE CASH FLOW TO OPERATING INCOME

One way of looking at the quality of a company's earnings is to look at the amount of cash a company generates over time relative to its earnings. If accounting earnings aren't eventually realized in cash, they merely represent numbers printed quarterly on paper. Companies with high levels of free cash flow for each dollar of accounting earnings can generally be said to have high-quality earnings: each dollar of accounting earnings is backed by a dollar or more of cash.

In this chapter, we primarily look at free cash flow (FCF), defined as the past 12 months' cash flow from operations less capital expenditures. The reason we subtract capital expenditures is that they represent a nondiscretionary expense that a company must incur to maintain its manufacturing and other operating capabilities. In the income statement, depreciation is used to allocate the cost of existing property, plant,

---

[3] This is not to say that reported cash flows cannot be manipulated, just that because cash flows involve fewer judgments and estimates to measure, they are less susceptible to manipulation.

and equipment (PP&E) over its productive life. When working with operating cash flows, where depreciation (a noncash operating expense) is added back, capital expenses should be subtracted to account for capital maintenance and expansion needs.[4] Companies that do not spend sufficiently on capex cannot remain competitive. Test results bear out this statement: excess returns achieved in tests using operating cash flow alone are less than those in which free cash flow is used. In addition, we tested a variety of denominators for the free cash flow-to-operating income ratio, including net income, EBITDA (earnings before interest, taxes, depreciation, and amortization), and sales. However, the combination of FCF and operating income worked the best in terms of excess returns and consistency of the strategy.

At the outset of this chapter, I'd like to point out that cash flow strategies have one major flaw: while cash flow strategies worked extremely well for the first decade after the introduction of the cash flow statement, they haven't worked well recently. For example, the top quintile of the FCF-to-operating income strategy didn't work in 2004–2005 or in late 2006 through 2007. The cash return on invested capital (ROIC) strategy, which you'll see later, is slightly more consistent, but excess returns in recent years have been weak. I believe that the reason is that investors have increasingly focused on companies that generate significant amounts of cash, and hence easily available excess returns have diminished. We can overcome this defect to some extent by combining cash flow strategies with other strategies, particularly with valuation strategies. You'll see two-factor strategies in this chapter that have worked well in recent years. Ultimately, however, it's important to recognize that cash generation is much of what makes a business valuable, and while excess returns on cash flow–based quantitative tests may fluctuate, cash flow strategies should continue to remain important.

The top quintile of this strategy outperforms by an average of 5%, and does so consistently, as mentioned above, until 2004. However, despite recent weakness, the strategy still manages to outperform by 75% of one-year and 84% of rolling three-year periods. Companies in the top quintile generate a large amount of FCF per dollar of operating income, with average portfolio values in the range of 200% to above 500%.

The bottom quintile underperforms by 3.8%, and does so for 78% of one-year and 84% of rolling three-year periods (see Figure 6.1). It outperforms significantly in 1999–2000, 2003–2004, and 2006–2007. Companies in the bottom quintile have large negative cash flows relative to operating income.[5]

---

[4] Just as we subtracted capital expenses from EBITDA, in Chapter 4, when measuring profitability.

[5] Handling negative values can be problematic. We use the following formula to establish the correct relationship between free cash flow (FCF) and operating income (OI): if $FCF/OI \geq 0$, then $FCF/@abs(OI)$, otherwise $(FCF - OI)/@abs(OI)$. @abs is a function that returns the absolute value.

1990–2007	1st Quintile	2nd Quintile	3rd Quintile	4th Quintile	5th Quintile	Universe	S&P 500*
CAGR – Annual Rebalance	15.7%	12.9%	10.8%	6.2%	6.5%	10.3%	12.0%
Average Excess Return vs. Universe**	5.0%	2.6%	0.1%	−2.9%	−3.8%	NA	1.5%
Value of $10,000 Invested (18 Years)	$137,147	$89,029	$63,171	$29,755	$30,847	$58,670	$76,297
% of 1-Year Periods Strategy Outperforms the Universe	75.0%	61.1%	50.0%	29.2%	22.2%	NA	56.9%
% Rolling 3-Year Periods Strategy Outperforms	84.4%	76.6%	46.9%	18.8%	15.6%	NA	68.8%
Maximum Gain	64.8%	49.6%	50.6%	58.6%	81.2%	59.2%	54.1%
Maximum Loss	−26.7%	−20.0%	−25.8%	−37.1%	−40.8%	−24.9%	−25.9%
Sharpe Ratio	0.68	0.74	0.57	0.25	0.17	0.46	0.64
Standard Deviation of Returns	0.19	0.14	0.14	0.19	0.23	0.17	0.14
Beta (vs. Universe)	1.04	0.78	0.77	1.10	1.27	NA	0.78
Alpha (vs. Universe)	0.04	0.05	0.03	−0.04	−0.07	NA	0.04
Average Portfolio Size	316	317	317	317	317	NA	NA
Average Number of Companies *Outperforming*	147	144	140	125	121	NA	NA
Average Number of Companies *Underperforming*	152	156	163	178	180	NA	NA
Median Portfolio Value – FCF-to-Operating Income	306%	60%	33%	−51%	−434%	−17%	9.0%
Average Market Capitalization	$4,386	$6,840	$6,009	$4,063	$2,507	NA	NA

* Equal-weighted average of S&P 500 returns. ** Annual holding period run quarterly for a larger sample size; arithmetic average excess returns.
Source: Standard & Poor's Compustat Point in Time Database; Charter Oak Investment Systems, Inc., Venues® Data Engine

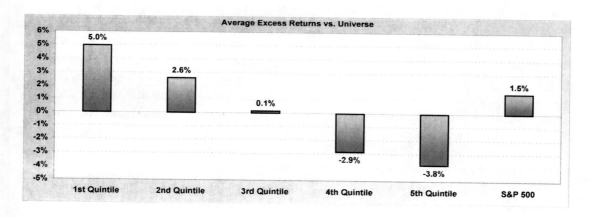

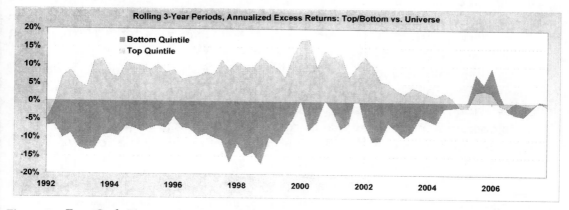

Figure 6.1 Free Cash Flow to Operating Income

Free Cash Flow to Operating Income by Economic Sector

The FCF-to-operating income strategy works well across economic sectors. It is particularly strong for the energy, consumer discretionary, health care, and information technology sectors. It also works for the industrials, consumer staples, and telecom services sectors. The strategy doesn't work for the financial sector, which is not surprising, as financial services businesses use cash differently than other industries. For the utilities industry, set sizes are too small for the test to be considered valid (see Figure 6.2).

Free Cash Flow to Operating Income and Acquisitions to Invested Capital

The top quintile of this test contains companies that have a high level of FCF and that refrain from using that cash for business acquisitions. The bottom quintile contains companies with negative cash flows that are making significant cash acquisitions. This test shows that, at least over the short term (the following 12 months), acquisitions significantly decrease shareholder value. There are many possible problems with acquisitions, but two stand out. First, corporate managers often pay too much for acquisitions, a result of the drive toward empire building (management salaries often go up as the size of their empire increases) and of the failure to properly account for the amount of shareholder value being given in exchange for the acquired company. Second, acquisitions usually increase expenses over the short term: corporations often have difficulty integrating acquired companies, getting profit margins up to desired levels, and achieving expected cost savings. While many large U.S. corporations have grown successfully by acquisition, General Electric and United Technologies to name two, on average shareholders should be wary of large acquisitions.[6]

The top quintile of this strategy outperforms by 5.9%, on average, and does so for 70% of one-year and 92% of rolling three-year periods (see Figure 6.3). This strategy significantly underperforms only in 1999–2000 and 2006–2007, but outside these two periods, it has a much better recent track record than the FCF-to-operating income strategy alone. Average portfolio values range from 150% to over 500% for FCF to operating income and are zero for cash acquisitions to invested capital.

The bottom quintile underperforms by 8.8%, on average, and does so for 86% of both one-year and rolling three-year periods. Bottom quintile companies tend to be small caps, with an average market cap of $1.9 billion. They have high negative FCF, relative to operating income, and make acquisitions that range from 9% to nearly 40% of total invested capital. The bottom quintile significantly outperformed only in 2003–2004, 2006, and 2007. Note the strong linearity of returns for this strategy.

---

[6] This is attested to by the large number of acquisitions that within a few years of purchase suddenly become "divestitures." Management is rarely held to account for such failures.

Top Quintile

1990– 2007	Energy	Materials	Industrials	Consumer Discretionary	Consumer Staples	Health Care	Financials	Information Technology	Telecom Services	Utilities	Universe	S&P 500*
CAGR – Quintile	16.9%	9.9%	13.6%	14.3%	14.9%	20.4%	13.2%	18.5%	9.2%	13.5%	10.3%	12.0%
CAGR – Sector	11.9%	9.7%	10.7%	7.3%	10.8%	11.9%	14.1%	8.1%	5.6%	11.9%	NA	NA
Excess Return vs. Sector	5.0%	0.2%	2.9%	6.9%	4.1%	8.6%	−0.9%	10.4%	3.6%	1.6%	NA	NA
Value of $10,000	$166,338	$54,611	$99,132	$110,361	$120,891	$284,067	$93,711	$212,404	$48,617	$98,284	$58,670	$76,297
% 1-Year Outperformance	72.2%	50.0%	77.8%	77.8%	66.7%	77.8%	55.6%	77.8%	72.2%	50.0%	NA	NA
% 3-Year Outperformance	68.8%	68.8%	100.0%	100.0%	87.5%	100.0%	37.5%	93.8%	68.8%	62.5%	NA	NA
Maximum Gain	81.5%	57.4%	43.3%	45.9%	45.6%	94.7%	44.9%	131.6%	66.8%	181.6%	44.0%	41.4%
Maximum Loss	−22.7%	−23.2%	−8.5%	−12.6%	−6.5%	−21.7%	−22.8%	−34.8%	−41.9%	−20.0%	−19.1%	−18.1%
Standard Deviation	0.27	0.18	0.15	0.18	0.15	0.28	0.21	0.37	0.25	0.43	0.17	0.15
Beta (vs. Sector)	0.94	1.02	0.98	0.89	0.89	0.98	0.82	0.89	0.27	1.57	NA	NA
Alpha (vs. Sector)	0.06	0.00	0.03	0.08	0.05	0.09	0.02	0.11	0.09	−0.02	NA	NA
Portfolio Size	20	27	52	63	18	38	29	52	7	2	NA	NA

Bottom Quintile

1990– 2007	Energy	Materials	Industrials	Consumer Discretionary	Consumer Staples	Health Care	Financials	Information Technology	Telecom Services	Utilities	Universe	S&P 500*
CAGR – Quintile	9.0%	4.6%	4.0%	2.9%	7.0%	7.7%	11.2%	4.4%	−2.9%	8.2%	10.3%	12.0%
CAGR – Sector	11.9%	9.7%	10.7%	7.3%	10.8%	11.9%	14.1%	8.1%	5.6%	11.9%	NA	NA
Excess Return vs. Sector	−3.0%	−5.2%	−6.6%	−4.4%	−3.8%	−4.2%	−2.9%	−3.6%	−8.5%	−3.8%	NA	NA
Value of $10,000	$46,990	$22,350	$20,315	$16,829	$34,021	$37,779	$67,391	$21,865	$5,853	$41,079	$58,670	$76,297
% 1-Year Outperformance	33.3%	22.2%	11.1%	22.2%	27.8%	27.8%	38.9%	33.3%	50.0%	50.0%	NA	NA
% 3-Year Outperformance	25.0%	12.5%	12.5%	18.8%	12.5%	18.8%	18.8%	25.0%	25.0%	56.3%	NA	NA
Maximum Gain	76.3%	41.5%	45.6%	51.5%	33.8%	73.8%	67.0%	194.2%	150.9%	138.5%	44.0%	41.4%
Maximum Loss	−52.4%	−21.4%	−30.7%	−31.3%	−21.6%	−36.5%	−17.0%	−53.2%	−67.8%	−62.2%	−19.1%	−18.1%
Standard Deviation	0.31	0.18	0.19	0.23	0.15	0.27	0.23	0.53	0.53	0.42	0.17	0.15
Beta (vs. Sector)	1.15	1.09	1.18	1.18	0.95	1.00	0.91	1.32	1.37	1.92	NA	NA
Alpha (vs. Sector)	−0.04	−0.01	−0.06	−0.08	0.02	−0.01	0.02	−0.10	−0.18	−0.03	NA	NA
Portfolio Size	21	28	54	67	20	39	32	54	8	3	NA	NA

* Equal-weighted average of S&P 500 returns.
Source: Standard & Poor's Compustat Point in Time Database; Charter Oak Investment Systems, Inc., Venues® Data Engine

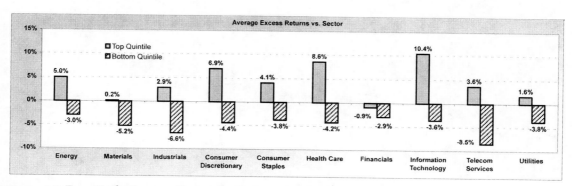

Figure 6.2 Free Cash Flow to Operating Income by Economic Sector

1990–2007	1st Quintile	2nd Quintile	3rd Quintile	4th Quintile	5th Quintile	Universe	S&P 500*
CAGR – Annual Rebalance	17.3%	12.2%	8.3%	4.3%	−1.3%	10.3%	12.0%
Average Excess Return vs. Universe**	5.9%	3.1%	−0.6%	−5.6%	−8.8%	NA	1.5%
Value of $10,000 Invested (18 Years)	$177,259	$79,390	$41,869	$21,514	$7,879	$58,669	$76,297
% of 1-Year Periods Strategy Outperforms the Universe	70.4%	64.8%	39.4%	25.4%	14.1%	NA	56.3%
% Rolling 3-Year Periods Strategy Outperforms	92.1%	76.2%	36.5%	15.9%	14.3%	NA	68.3%
Maximum Gain	63.4%	49.9%	52.4%	60.7%	94.5%	59.2%	54.1%
Maximum Loss	−27.2%	−16.9%	−25.2%	−41.3%	−43.1%	−24.9%	−25.9%
Sharpe Ratio	0.79	0.69	0.45	0.11	−0.04	0.46	0.64
Standard Deviation of Returns	0.17	0.16	0.16	0.21	0.25	0.17	0.15
Beta (vs. Universe)	0.88	0.85	0.81	1.11	1.30	NA	0.78
Alpha (vs. Universe)	0.07	0.05	0.02	−0.07	−0.12	NA	0.04
Average Portfolio Size	59	58	58	58	58	NA	NA
Average Number of Companies Outperforming	29	26	25	23	20	NA	NA
Average Number of Companies Underperforming	27	29	31	33	35	NA	NA
Median Portfolio Value – FCF to Operating Income	245%	59%	33%	−54%	−317%	−18%	9%
Median Portfolio Value – Acquisitions to Inv. Cap.	0.0%	0.0%	0.4%	2.2%	18.1%	5.0%	4.2%
Average Market Capitalization	$7,710	$1,194	$4,839	$5,208	$1,923	NA	NA

* Equal-weighted average of S&P 500 returns. ** Annual holding period run quarterly for a larger sample size; arithmetic average excess returns.
Source: Standard & Poor's Compustat Point in Time Database; Charter Oak Investment Systems, Inc., Venues® Data Engine

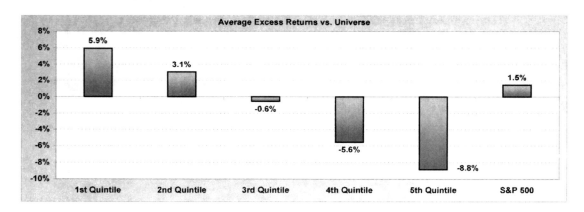

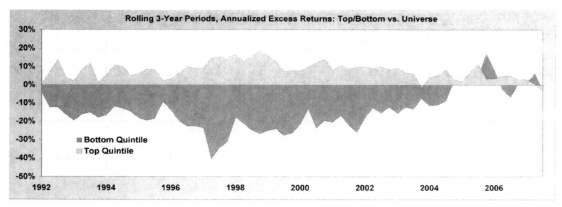

Figure 6.3 Free Cash Flow to Operating Income and Acquisitions to Invested Capital

Free Cash Flow to Operating Income and External Financing to Assets

Related to acquisitions to invested capital is the external financing-to-assets strategy, which we saw in Chapter 5. External financing is calculated as cash received from share issuance net of cash spent on share repurchases and cash received from debt issuance net of cash spent on debt reduction, all as a percent of total assets.[7] Companies that make sizable business acquisitions must often issue large amounts of shares and debt.[8] However, share and debt issuance can also be used for other purposes, such as business expansion, recapitalization, or just to infuse necessary capital into poorly performing or development-stage companies. Whatever the reason, companies that significantly increase their capital base consistently underperform, whereas those that reduce their capital base, through share repurchases and debt reductions, outperform.

The top quintile of this strategy contains companies that generate large amounts of cash relative to income and use excess cash to reduce outstanding shares and pay off debt. The bottom quintile contains companies with large operating cash outflows that are also issuing large amounts of shares and/or debt.

The top quintile outperforms by an average of 7%, and does so for 73% of one-year and 83% of rolling three-year periods (see Figure 6.4). The strategy's main flaw is that it hasn't worked recently, underperforming in all but a few periods during 2004 through 2007. Average portfolio values for companies in this quintile range from 140% to well over 500% for FCF to operating income and from −11% to −18% for external financing to assets (reflecting the percentage of cash relative to assets used to buy back shares and reduce debt).

The bottom quintile underperforms by a very high 14.4%, on average, and does so for 82% of one-year and 100% of rolling three-year periods. It significantly outperforms in only three periods, 1999–2000, 2003–2004, and 2007. This consistency makes it a strong short-sale strategy. Companies in the bottom portfolio have high negative FCF and issue debt and shares equal to an average of 35% to 71% of assets. The strategy favors small caps, with an average market capitalization of $1.5 billion.

Free Cash Flow to Operating Income and Price to Sales

This strategy combines a cash quality of earnings measure with a valuation measure. The FCF-to-operating income ratio ensures that the companies in the top quintile of this

---

[7] Share issuance/repurchase and debt issuance/reduction figures can be found in the financing section of a company's cash flow statement.

[8] Companies typically don't receive cash for shares issued to complete an acquisition, so such share issuance isn't captured in the external financing-to-assets strategy. Acquisition-related share issuance *is* captured in the one-year share reduction/increase strategy, which is presented in Chapter 8.

1990–2007	1st Quintile	2nd Quintile	3rd Quintile	4th Quintile	5th Quintile	Universe	S&P 500*
CAGR – Annual Rebalance	19.6%	13.6%	13.8%	2.7%	−5.6%	10.3%	12.0%
Average Excess Return vs. Universe**	7.0%	3.0%	1.8%	−6.3%	−14.4%	NA	1.5%
Value of $10,000 Invested (18 Years)	$251,814	$98,778	$102,085	$16,292	$3,536	$58,669	$76,297
% of 1-Year Periods Strategy Outperforms the Universe	73.2%	54.9%	62.0%	21.1%	18.3%	NA	56.3%
% Rolling 3-Year Periods Strategy Outperforms	82.5%	69.8%	66.7%	15.9%	0.0%	NA	68.3%
Maximum Gain	64.4%	51.4%	51.6%	59.8%	92.1%	59.2%	54.1%
Maximum Loss	−25.1%	−20.2%	−20.0%	−62.8%	−75.2%	−24.9%	−25.9%
Sharpe Ratio	0.81	0.79	0.69	0.07	−0.20	0.46	0.64
Standard Deviation of Returns	0.18	0.14	0.14	0.21	0.33	0.17	0.15
Beta (vs. Universe)	0.94	0.66	0.73	1.08	1.62	NA	0.78
Alpha (vs. Universe)	0.08	0.07	0.05	−0.07	−0.22	NA	0.04
Average Portfolio Size	64	63	63	63	63	NA	NA
Average Number of Companies Outperforming	31	30	29	25	19	NA	NA
Average Number of Companies Underperforming	30	31	32	36	41	NA	NA
Median Portfolio Value – FCF to Oper. Income	278.0%	60.4%	33.1%	−57.5%	−554.5%	−17.6%	9.0%
Median Portfolio Value – Extern.Fin. to Assets	−13.7%	−4.1%	−0.3%	7.5%	50.5%	5.4%	0.3%
Average Market Capitalization	$4,175	$8,776	$6,872	$4,006	$1,454	NA	NA

* Equal-weighted average of S&P 500 returns. ** Annual holding period run quarterly for a larger sample size; arithmetic average excess returns.
Source: Standard & Poor's Compustat Point in Time Database; Charter Oak Investment Systems, Inc., Venues® Data Engine

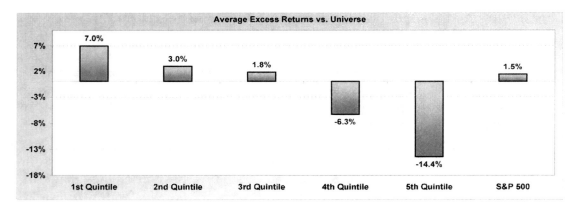

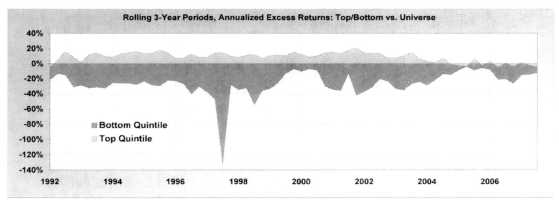

Figure 6.4 Free Cash Flow to Operating Income and External Financing to Assets

strategy are generating both income statement–based earnings and cash flow, while the price-to-sales (P/S) ratio ensures that these companies are purchased at the lowest possible price relative to sales. The strategy is both strong and consistent, and excess returns are quite linear, a sign that the strategy works for real fundamental reasons.

The top quintile outperforms by 7.9%, on average, and does so for 72% of one-year and 89% of rolling three-year periods (see Figure 6.5). It significantly underperforms in 1995, 1999–2000, 2003, and the end of 2007. The strategy is moderately volatile, with a maximum loss of 29% versus 25% for the Universe, and a standard deviation of returns of 0.19 versus 0.17 for the Universe. Nevertheless, the Sharpe ratio is a moderately high 0.82. Average portfolio values range from 160% to over 1,000% for FCF to operating income and from 0.2× to 0.5× for price to sales, so companies in the top quintile generate cash well in excess of operating earnings and are relatively cheap.

The bottom portfolio underperforms by an average of 8.4%, and does so for 76% of one-year and 95% of rolling three-year periods. It significantly outperforms in 1990, 1996, 1999–2000, and at the end of 2007. An average of 42 portfolio companies underperforms for every 19 that outperform. Average portfolio values range from −150% to less than −800% for FCF to operating income and 4× to over 20× for price to sales, indicating these companies have negative cash flows and are very expensive relative to sales.

CASH RETURN ON INVESTED CAPITAL

The previous strategy compared FCF to income. The cash ROIC strategy simply compares FCF to total capital. While FCF to operating profit can be considered a "quality of earnings" strategy, which looks at cash flow from an income statement point of view, cash ROIC is a profitability strategy that looks at cash flow in relationship to the balance sheet, specifically in relationship to both equity and long-term liability accounts. We've seen cash ROIC in Chapter 4, within the economic profits strategy, in which cash ROIC was compared with the cost of capital to determine economic profitability.[9] Here, we simply look at cash profitability relative to total capital, without reference to capital costs. The strategy is simple but works very well. *Invested capital* is defined as the book value of common equity plus long-term debt, minority interest, and preferred stock. Note that a cash return on equity (ROE) strategy is also possible. In fact, we used cash ROE in Chapter 5—price to book value and operating cash flow to equity. We don't present cash ROE as a single-factor strategy in this book.

---

[9] Economic profits can be defined as profits available to shareholders after deducting a charge, or "rental fee," for the use of capital.

1990–2007	1st Quintile	2nd Quintile	3rd Quintile	4th Quintile	5th Quintile	Universe	S&P 500*
CAGR – Annual Rebalance	20.2%	13.2%	10.9%	2.3%	−3.0%	10.3%	12.0%
Average Excess Return vs. Universe**	7.9%	2.4%	−0.4%	−5.3%	−8.4%	NA	1.5%
Value of $10,000 Invested (18 Years)	$273,632	$93,175	$64,483	$15,146	$5,782	$58,669	$76,297
% of 1-Year Periods Strategy Outperforms the Universe	72.2%	56.9%	44.4%	29.2%	23.6%	NA	56.9%
% Rolling 3-Year Periods Strategy Outperforms	89.1%	65.6%	43.8%	20.3%	4.7%	NA	68.8%
Maximum Gain	90.1%	52.6%	54.9%	67.2%	144.6%	59.2%	54.1%
Maximum Loss	−29.1%	−22.3%	−23.1%	−68.5%	−73.1%	−24.9%	−25.9%
Sharpe Ratio	0.82	0.70	0.50	0.09	−0.02	0.46	0.64
Standard Deviation of Returns	0.19	0.15	0.15	0.26	0.37	0.17	0.14
Beta (vs. Universe)	0.82	0.69	0.74	1.29	1.56	NA	0.78
Alpha (vs. Universe)	0.10	0.06	0.03	−0.09	−0.15	NA	0.04
Average Portfolio Size	63	63	63	63	64	NA	NA
Average Number of Companies *Outperforming*	32	30	28	23	19	NA	NA
Average Number of Companies *Underperforming*	28	30	33	37	42	NA	NA
Median Portfolio Value – FCF to Oper. Income	245%	59%	34%	−52%	−490%	−18%	9%
Median Portfolio Value – Price to Sales	0.3	0.9	1.3	2.5	8.2	1.0	0.9
Average Market Capitalization	$2,281	$4,576	$6,718	$5,211	$1,874	NA	NA

* Equal-weighted average of S&P 500 returns. ** Annual holding period run quarterly for a larger sample size; arithmetic average excess returns.
Source: Standard & Poor's Compustat Point in Time Database; Charter Oak Investment Systems, Inc., Venues® Data Engine

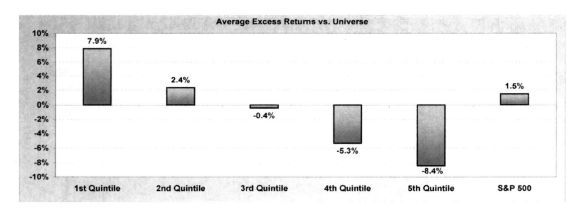

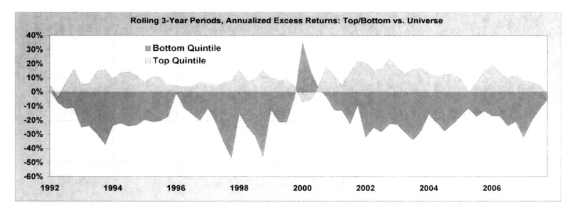

Figure 6.5 Free Cash Flow to Operating Income and Price to Sales

The cash ROIC strategy is very strong, and excess returns are linear; it only suffers from the single flaw described earlier (it hasn't worked well recently)—admittedly a serious one, but one that can be corrected by combining it with other factors. The top quintile outperforms by an average of 5%, and does so for 79% of one-year and 83% of rolling three-year periods (see Figure 6.6). The strategy underperformed in 2003, as low-profitability stocks outperformed coming out of the bear market, and showed slight underperformance in 2005 and 2007. Average cash ROIC values for the top quintile range from 26% to over 30%. Note that cash ROIC is a large-cap strategy, with an average market capitalization of $7.6 billion for the top quintile.[10] Large-cap companies tend to generate more excess cash than smaller companies, which need their cash to grow.

The bottom quintile underperforms by 5.9%, on average, and does so for 76% of one-year and 91% of rolling three-year periods. The bottom quintile significantly outperforms in 1999–2000, 2003–2004, 2006, and 2007. Average cash ROIC portfolio values for the bottom quintile range from −13% to −30%.[11] The bottom quintile tends to contain smaller cap companies, with an average market capitalization of $2.2 billion.

Cash Return on Invested Capital by Economic Sector

Like the FCF-to-operating income strategy, the cash ROIC strategy works very well with the energy, consumer discretionary, health care, and information technology sectors. Cash ROIC also works well for consumer staples, a sector known for its ability to generate strong cash flows. The strategy works moderately well for the materials and utilities sectors (see Figure 6.7).

Cash Return on Invested Capital and Capital Expenditures to Property, Plant & Equipment

We saw the capex-to-PP&E strategy in Chapter 4, in conjunction with the economic profits test. Here we pair it with cash ROIC alone. The test combines a cash profitability measure with a factor that measures capital intensity (capex to PP&E). As mentioned previously, capital intensity refers to the amount of capital assets, such as factories or machinery, necessary to produce goods or render services. Oil exploration and development and airlines are examples of capital-intensive industries, while financial firms

---

[10] The market capitalization of the top quintile averaged $11 billion in 2006 and $13 billion in 2007. Note that the market cap figure shown in the table is averaged over the entire test period, so it does not account for increases in market cap over the years that have occurred due to inflation.

[11] For the cash ROIC strategy, we require that invested capital be greater than zero, so companies with both negative free cash flow and negative invested capital will not be incorrectly ranked due to the resulting positive value that would occur in calculating ROIC.

1990–2007	1st Quintile	2nd Quintile	3rd Quintile	4th Quintile	5th Quintile	Universe	S&P 500*
CAGR – Annual Rebalance	15.3%	14.0%	10.4%	8.3%	3.3%	10.3%	12.0%
Average Excess Return vs. Universe**	5.0%	2.4%	0.3%	−1.4%	−5.9%	NA	1.5%
Value of $10,000 Invested (18 Years)	$129,541	$105,376	$59,064	$42,332	$17,819	$58,670	$76,297
% of 1-Year Periods Strategy Outperforms the Universe	79.2%	61.1%	44.4%	36.1%	23.6%	NA	56.9%
% Rolling 3-Year Periods Strategy Outperforms	82.8%	76.6%	60.9%	23.4%	9.4%	NA	68.8%
Maximum Gain	53.3%	56.5%	53.5%	62.5%	81.8%	59.2%	54.1%
Maximum Loss	−18.8%	−23.0%	−25.2%	−31.7%	−55.2%	−24.9%	−25.9%
Sharpe Ratio	0.83	0.71	0.53	0.36	0.07	0.46	0.64
Standard Deviation of Returns	0.15	0.14	0.15	0.17	0.26	0.17	0.14
Beta (vs. Universe)	0.87	0.80	0.87	1.00	1.45	NA	0.78
Alpha (vs. Universe)	0.07	0.05	0.02	−0.02	−0.11	NA	0.04
Average Portfolio Size	332	332	332	332	333	NA	NA
Average Number of Companies *Outperforming*	157	153	143	137	118	NA	NA
Average Number of Companies *Underperforming*	160	164	171	179	197	NA	NA
Median Portfolio Value – Cash ROIC	30.0%	11.2%	5.1%	−1.0%	−21.0%	4.3%	8.4%
Average Market Capitalization	$7,614	$5,458	$4,598	$3,963	$2,244	NA	NA

* Equal-weighted average of S&P 500 returns. ** Annual holding period run quarterly for a larger sample size; arithmetic average excess returns.
Source: Standard & Poor's Compustat Point in Time Database; Charter Oak Investment Systems, Inc., Venues® Data Engine

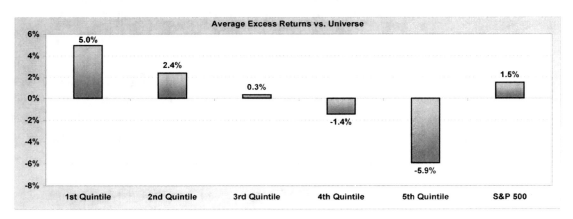

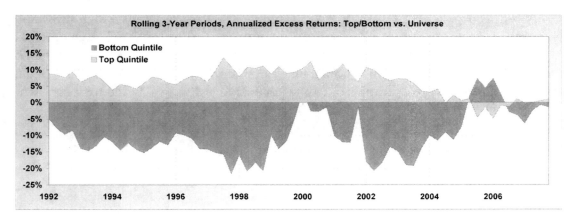

Figure 6.6 Cash Return on Invested Capital

Top Quintile

1990–2007	Energy	Materials	Industrials	Consumer Discretionary	Consumer Staples	Health Care	Financials	Information Technology	Telecom Services	Utilities	Universe	S&P 500*
CAGR – Quintile	17.5%	12.2%	13.6%	13.7%	17.4%	18.2%	17.2%	15.0%	8.4%	15.3%	10.3%	12.0%
CAGR – Sector	11.9%	9.7%	10.7%	7.3%	10.8%	11.9%	14.1%	8.0%	5.6%	11.9%	NA	NA
Excess Return vs. Sector	5.6%	2.5%	2.9%	6.4%	6.6%	6.4%	3.1%	7.0%	2.8%	3.4%	NA	NA
Value of $10,000	$182,494	$79,447	$98,779	$101,583	$178,409	$203,572	$174,475	$124,638	$42,514	$130,547	$58,670	$76,297
% 1-Year Outperformance	72.2%	72.2%	55.6%	83.3%	83.3%	66.7%	50.0%	66.7%	61.1%	61.1%	NA	NA
% 3-Year Outperformance	68.8%	81.3%	81.3%	93.8%	93.8%	93.8%	56.3%	75.0%	62.5%	68.8%	NA	NA
Maximum Gain	62.9%	38.4%	37.3%	49.5%	70.5%	95.1%	54.1%	88.6%	50.7%	143.3%	44.0%	41.4%
Maximum Loss	−27.1%	−23.3%	−7.3%	−9.5%	−14.4%	−16.7%	−16.3%	−30.9%	−42.0%	−24.4%	−19.1%	−18.1%
Standard Deviation	0.22	0.15	0.14	0.16	0.20	0.27	0.21	0.28	0.23	0.37	0.17	0.15
Beta (vs. Sector)	0.77	0.82	0.90	0.79	1.29	0.91	0.84	0.66	0.32	1.39	NA	NA
Alpha (vs. Sector)	0.08	0.04	0.04	0.08	0.04	0.08	0.05	0.09	0.07	0.02	NA	NA
Portfolio Size	21	28	55	65	19	40	30	54	8	3	NA	NA

Bottom Quintile

1990–2007	Energy	Materials	Industrials	Consumer Discretionary	Consumer Staples	Health Care	Financials	Information Technology	Telecom Services	Utilities	Universe	S&P 500*
CAGR – Quintile	4.8%	5.5%	2.5%	2.1%	6.6%	1.8%	10.4%	0.3%	4.9%	−0.2%	10.3%	12.0%
CAGR – Sector	11.9%	9.7%	10.7%	7.3%	10.8%	11.9%	14.1%	8.0%	5.6%	11.9%	NA	NA
Excess Return vs. Sector	−7.1%	−4.2%	−8.2%	−5.2%	−4.2%	−10.1%	−3.7%	−7.7%	−0.7%	−12.1%	NA	NA
Value of $10,000	$23,243	$26,417	$15,504	$14,559	$31,354	$13,770	$59,465	$10,596	$23,477	$9,722	$58,670	$76,297
% 1-Year Outperformance	27.8%	33.3%	11.1%	27.8%	38.9%	16.7%	44.4%	16.7%	50.0%	38.9%	NA	NA
% 3-Year Outperformance	6.3%	31.3%	0.0%	6.3%	12.5%	6.3%	31.3%	18.8%	37.5%	12.5%	NA	NA
Maximum Gain	58.4%	43.7%	41.3%	55.6%	36.8%	76.6%	59.3%	212.6%	229.5%	119.0%	44.0%	41.4%
Maximum Loss	−52.3%	−20.3%	−32.2%	−29.5%	−20.5%	−37.4%	−24.4%	−62.5%	−70.2%	−70.5%	−19.1%	−18.1%
Standard Deviation	0.30	0.18	0.18	0.24	0.16	0.29	0.23	0.59	0.64	0.45	0.17	0.15
Beta (vs. Sector)	1.13	1.08	1.16	1.23	0.99	1.06	0.91	1.47	1.59	1.71	NA	NA
Alpha (vs. Sector)	−0.08	0.00	−0.07	−0.10	0.02	−0.09	0.01	−0.14	−0.06	−0.06	NA	NA
Portfolio Size	22	29	57	69	21	41	33	57	9	3	NA	NA

* Equal-weighted average of S&P 500 returns.
Source: Standard & Poor's Compustat Point in Time Database; Charter Oak Investment Systems, Inc., Venues® Data Engine

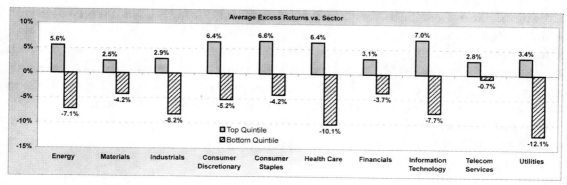

Figure 6.7 Cash Return on Invested Capital by Economic Sector

are not usually capital intensive. This test approaches capital intensity by measuring how much capital a company must contribute in a given year to maintain and grow its productive capacity (capex) relative to its *existing* capital asset base (PP&E).[12] Companies that generate a lot of cash relative to invested capital and whose capital spending needs are declining outperform, whereas companies that are net users of cash but have increasing capital spending needs—which they may struggle to fund—significantly underperform.

The top quintile outperforms by an average of 4.7%, and does so for 74% of one-year and 86% of rolling three-year periods (see Figure 6.8). It significantly underperforms only in 1991, 1999–2000, and 2003–2004. The maximum loss for the top quintile is a very low 16%, and the maximum loss increases linearly by quintile, which indicates that risk increases as you move down the quintiles. Average portfolio values for the top quintile range from 24% to 31% for cash ROIC and from 4% to 11% for capex to PP&E, indicating that these are cash-rich companies that require low levels of capital spending relative to their existing capital asset base in order to remain competitive.

The bottom quintile makes a strong short-sale strategy, underperforming by 12.9% on average. It underperforms for 78% of one-year and 97% of rolling three-year periods. The bottom quintile outperforms significantly only in 1999–2000, 2003–2004, and 2005. Average portfolio values range from −20% to −44% for cash ROIC and 71% to 121% for capex to PP&E—meaning that portfolio companies have cash outflows and are spending about 1× their existing capital base on capex in a year.

Cash Return on Invested Capital and Capital Spending to Invested Capital

While this test and the preceding test may seem similar, in actuality they are very different. The preceding test puts companies with the lowest levels of capex (relative to PP&E) in the top quintile and those with the highest levels of capex in the bottom. This test puts companies with the highest levels of capex (relative to invested capital) in the top quintile and those with the lowest levels in the bottom. So, we have two tests in which similar criteria are used for the second factor (capex), but the ranking for that criterion is reversed (low to high in the preceding test, high to low in this one). Yet both tests work well. The reason? The preceding test looked at capital intensity, whereas this test looks at capital spending adequacy. Having to spend ever increasing amounts on capex in order to stay competitive is a bad thing, since profitability suffers. But companies that do not spend adequately on PP&E cannot stay competitive. Also note that the top quintile of this test contains companies that have strong cash flows that are

---

[12] We use net PP&E in the calculation (i.e., gross PP&E less accumulated depreciation).

1990–2007	1st Quintile	2nd Quintile	3rd Quintile	4th Quintile	5th Quintile	Universe	S&P 500*
CAGR – Annual Rebalance	16.5%	12.8%	11.9%	10.8%	−7.1%	10.3%	12.0%
Average Excess Return vs. Universe**	4.7%	1.9%	0.5%	−1.1%	−12.9%	NA	1.5%
Value of $10,000 Invested (18 Years)	$156,258	$87,064	$76,043	$62,992	$2,678	$58,670	$76,297
% of 1-Year Periods Strategy Outperforms the Universe	73.6%	56.9%	51.4%	38.9%	22.2%	NA	56.9%
% Rolling 3-Year Periods Strategy Outperforms	85.9%	68.8%	62.5%	34.4%	3.1%	NA	68.8%
Maximum Gain	58.0%	53.5%	55.3%	67.7%	95.4%	59.2%	54.1%
Maximum Loss	−16.3%	−22.5%	−28.4%	−35.0%	−83.9%	−24.9%	−25.9%
Sharpe Ratio	0.82	0.72	0.56	0.34	−0.15	0.46	0.64
Standard Deviation of Returns	0.15	0.13	0.15	0.20	0.34	0.17	0.14
Beta (vs. Universe)	0.74	0.67	0.74	1.05	1.68	NA	0.78
Alpha (vs. Universe)	0.08	0.06	0.04	−0.02	−0.21	NA	0.04
Average Portfolio Size	64	64	64	64	64	NA	NA
Average Number of Companies *Outperforming*	32	31	29	27	18	NA	NA
Average Number of Companies *Underperforming*	30	31	32	34	42	NA	NA
Median Portfolio Value – Cash ROIC	28.1%	11.0%	5.0%	−1.6%	−29.9%	4.3%	8.4%
Median Portfolio Value – Capex-to-PP&E	7.6%	14.5%	19.2%	29.7%	89.6%	29.9%	22.3%
Average Market Capitalization	$6,329	$6,629	$5,458	$4,756	$1,254	NA	NA

* Equal-weighted average of S&P 500 returns. ** Annual holding period run quarterly for a larger sample size; arithmetic average excess returns.
Source: Standard & Poor's Compustat Point in Time Database, Charter Oak Investment Systems, Inc., Venues® Data Engine

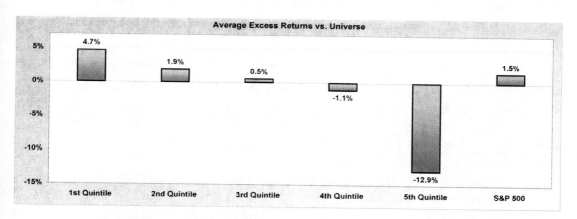

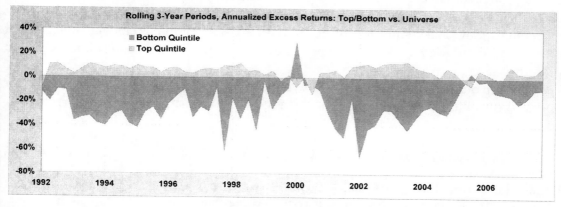

Figure 6.8 Cash ROIC and Capital Expenditures to Property, Plant & Equipment

spending significantly on capex; capital expenditures may be high, but these companies have the profitability to afford them.

The top quintile outperforms by 6.6%, on average, and does so for 79% of one-year and 84% of rolling three-year periods (see Figure 6.9). It underperforms significantly only in 1992–1993, 2003–2004, and 2006. The top quintile has a low maximum loss of 16% and a Sharpe ratio of 0.88, nearly double that of the Universe. Average portfolio values for the top quintile range from 27% to 52% for cash ROIC and from 16% to 24% for capex to invested capital, so these companies not only are generating a lot of cash but also are using this cash to significantly expand their productive capabilities.

The bottom quintile underperforms by an average of 10.4%, and does so for 82% of one-year and 98% of rolling three-year periods. It outperforms significantly only in 1991, 2000, and 2003–2004. Average portfolio values for the bottom quintile range from −17% to −40% for cash ROIC and from 1% to 5% for capex to invested capital. Not only do bottom quintile companies have large cash outflows after accounting for capex, but they are spending very low amounts of cash on maintenance and replacement of PP&E and may become noncompetitive.

Cash Return on Invested Capital and Price to Invested Capital

Price to invested capital is a valuation metric that is similar to price to book value, except here we include the total capital invested in the corporation instead of just stockholders' equity. You'll recall from Chapter 4 that the combination of ROE and price to book value worked well. It combined a profitability and a valuation metric and used a similar denominator for each (common equity/shareholders' equity[13]). In the current strategy, we use the same principle by combining cash ROIC (a profitability metric) with price to invested capital (a valuation metric) and using the same denominator (invested capital) for each. We are in effect asking What kind of cash return can a company generate on its invested capital? and What price does the investor have to pay for that invested capital? The results are strong. Price to invested capital is calculated as market capitalization divided by common equity plus long-term debt, minority interest,[14] and preferred stock.

The top quintile outperforms by an average of 6.7%, and does so for 72% of one-year and 89% of rolling three-year periods (see Figure 6.10). It significantly underperforms

---

[13] Total common equity is used for price to book value, and total shareholder's equity, including preferred equity, is used for return on equity.

[14] Minority interest is a liability representing the ownership stake of outside shareholders in a consolidated business unit of a company, such as a subsidiary in which the company owns 85%, and outside stockholders own 15%.

1990–2007	1st Quintile	2nd Quintile	3rd Quintile	4th Quintile	5th Quintile	Universe	S&P 500*
CAGR – Annual Rebalance	16.4%	12.1%	12.5%	6.9%	−3.6%	10.3%	12.0%
Average Excess Return vs. Universe**	6.6%	2.8%	0.7%	−2.4%	−10.4%	NA	1.5%
Value of $10,000 Invested (18 Years)	$153,961	$78,470	$83,527	$33,123	$5,123	$58,670	$76,297
% of 1-Year Periods Strategy Outperforms the Universe	79.2%	62.5%	45.8%	31.9%	18.1%	NA	56.9%
% Rolling 3-Year Periods Strategy Outperforms	84.4%	70.3%	48.4%	26.6%	1.6%	NA	68.8%
Maximum Gain	59.0%	58.7%	60.7%	77.7%	88.8%	59.2%	54.1%
Maximum Loss	−15.7%	−24.2%	−27.9%	−33.6%	−53.0%	−24.9%	−25.9%
Sharpe Ratio	0.88	0.71	0.50	0.28	−0.10	0.46	0.64
Standard Deviation of Returns	0.16	0.15	0.17	0.19	0.28	0.17	0.14
Beta (vs. Universe)	0.84	0.80	0.88	1.05	1.50	NA	0.78
Alpha (vs. Universe)	0.09	0.05	0.02	−0.03	−0.16	NA	0.04
Average Portfolio Size	66	66	66	66	67	NA	NA
Average Number of Companies *Outperforming*	31	30	29	26	22	NA	NA
Average Number of Companies *Underperforming*	31	34	34	37	42	NA	NA
Median Portfolio Value – Cash ROIC	31.6%	11.2%	5.2%	−1.0%	−24.2%	4.3%	8.4%
Median Portfolio Value – Capex-to-Invested Capital	18.6%	10.0%	7.7%	6.3%	2.4%	10.8%	11.0%
Average Market Capitalization	$9,500	$5,722	$4,369	$2,724	$2,937	NA	NA

* Equal-weighted average of S&P 500 returns. ** Annual holding period run quarterly for a larger sample size; arithmetic average excess returns.
Source: Standard & Poor's Compustat Point in Time Database, Charter Oak Investment Systems, Inc., Venues® Data Engine

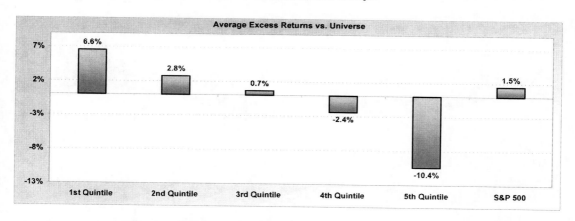

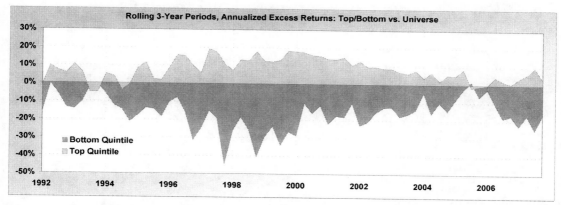

Figure 6.9 Cash Return on Invested Capital and Capex to Invested Capital

1990–2007	1st Quintile	2nd Quintile	3rd Quintile	4th Quintile	5th Quintile	Universe	S&P 500*
CAGR – Annual Rebalance	17.1%	14.3%	9.5%	5.7%	−4.3%	10.3%	12.0%
Average Excess Return vs. Universe**	6.7%	3.1%	0.1%	−3.0%	−9.2%	NA	1.5%
Value of $10,000 Invested (18 Years)	$172,358	$110,980	$51,602	$27,049	$4,545	$58,670	$76,297
% of 1-Year Periods Strategy Outperforms the Universe	72.2%	55.6%	50.0%	27.8%	26.4%	NA	56.9%
% Rolling 3-Year Periods Strategy Outperforms	89.1%	76.6%	59.4%	14.1%	6.3%	NA	68.8%
Maximum Gain	68.8%	57.3%	46.8%	50.7%	114.5%	59.2%	54.1%
Maximum Loss	−27.4%	−20.4%	−31.0%	−41.8%	−72.1%	−24.9%	−25.9%
Sharpe Ratio	0.71	0.77	0.51	0.25	−0.04	0.46	0.64
Standard Deviation of Returns	0.20	0.14	0.15	0.19	0.37	0.17	0.14
Beta (vs. Universe)	0.82	0.68	0.70	0.98	1.57	NA	0.78
Alpha (vs. Universe)	0.09	0.07	0.04	−0.03	−0.16	NA	0.04
Average Portfolio Size	66	66	67	66	67	NA	NA
Average Number of Companies *Outperforming*	33	32	29	25	20	NA	NA
Average Number of Companies *Underperforming*	29	32	34	37	44	NA	NA
Median Portfolio Value – Cash ROIC	28.2%	11.0%	5.1%	−1.3%	−36.5%	4.3%	8.4%
Median Portfolio Value – Price to Invested Capital	0.9	1.4	1.5	2.1	7.6	1.33	1.23
Average Market Capitalization	$3,850	$3,702	$4,606	$4,239	$1,917	NA	NA

* Equal-weighted average of S&P 500 returns. ** Annual holding period run quarterly for a larger sample size; arithmetic average excess returns.
Source: Standard & Poor's Compustat Point in Time Database, Charter Oak Investment Systems, Inc., Venues® Data Engine

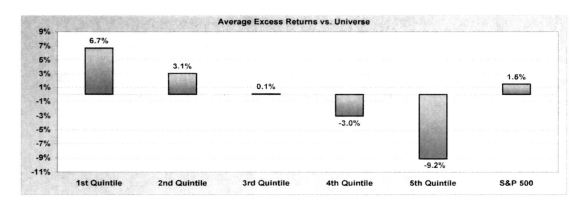

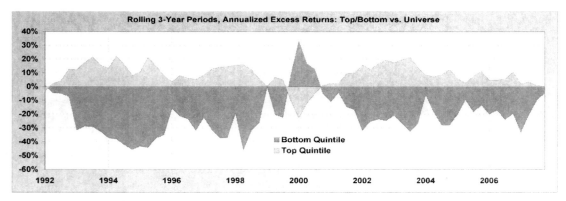

Figure 6.10 Cash Return on Invested Capital and Price to Invested Capital

only in 1990, 1999–2000, and 2007. Average portfolio values for the top quintile range from 24% to 34% for cash ROIC and from 0.5× to 1.2× for price to invested capital, so these are highly profitable but inexpensive companies.

The bottom quintile underperforms by 9.2%, on average, and does so for 74% of one-year and 94% of rolling three-year periods. It significantly outperforms in 1990–1991, 1999–2000, and 2003–2004. Average portfolio values for the bottom quintile range from −22% to −49% for cash ROIC and 3.7× to 32.0× for price to invested capital. Note that the quintiles are nearly perfectly symmetrical, with the second quintile outperforming by 3%, the third quintile flat, and the fourth quintile underperforming by 3%, a sign of a very strong strategy.

FREE CASH FLOW PLUS NET SHARE REPURCHASE PLUS DIVIDEND TO PRICE

FCF plus net share repurchase plus dividend to price is a hybrid test that combines three separate elements into one: cash flow, capital allocation, and valuation. The ratio is calculated by taking 12-month FCF (net cash from operating activities minus capital expenditures) and adding to that net cash received from share repurchase (or subtracting net cash paid for share issuance) and dividends, both from the financing section of the cash flow statement, and dividing everything by market capitalization. In reality, share repurchases and dividends do not "add" to FCF; to the contrary, they are usually paid out of the current year's cash flow. However, like the price to earnings plus dividends strategy presented in Chapter 5, this strategy emphasizes sound capital allocation by favoring companies that repurchase shares and pay dividends (in the top quintile) and avoiding companies that issue large amounts of shares and pay no dividends (in the bottom quintile). The performance isn't significantly different than the FCF-to-price strategy alone, but it selects slightly different companies in the top and bottom quintiles, and we use it as a building block to construct two-factor strategies that emphasize both valuation and capital allocation.

The top quintile of this strategy outperforms by an average of 5.1%, and does so for 76% of one-year and 88% of rolling three-year periods (see Figure 6.11). The strategy significantly underperforms only in 1999–2000 and 2007. Both the maximum loss (22%) and the standard deviation of returns (0.16) are low, the latter resulting in a high Sharpe ratio for a single-factor strategy of 0.79. Average portfolio values for FCF plus share repurchases plus dividend to price range from 15% to 41%. This compares to 11% to 31% for the FCF-to-price strategy alone, so companies in the top quintile of this strategy are repurchasing significant amounts of shares and/or paying large dividends.

1990–2007	1st Quintile	2nd Quintile	3rd Quintile	4th Quintile	5th Quintile	Universe	S&P 500*
CAGR – Annual Rebalance	15.9%	12.9%	11.0%	6.7%	4.4%	10.3%	12.0%
Average Excess Return vs. Universe**	5.1%	2.1%	0.4%	−2.0%	−5.2%	NA	1.5%
Value of $10,000 Invested (18 Years)	$143,088	$88,504	$64,961	$31,975	$21,849	$58,670	$76,297
% of 1-Year Periods Strategy Outperforms the Universe	76.4%	61.1%	50.0%	29.2%	16.7%	NA	56.9%
% Rolling 3-Year Periods Strategy Outperforms	87.5%	73.4%	51.6%	14.1%	12.5%	NA	68.8%
Maximum Gain	64.3%	49.7%	48.8%	72.6%	82.0%	59.2%	54.1%
Maximum Loss	−21.7%	−21.9%	−29.5%	−47.5%	−48.2%	−24.9%	−25.9%
Sharpe Ratio	0.79	0.76	0.51	0.25	0.10	0.46	0.64
Standard Deviation of Returns	0.16	0.13	0.16	0.23	0.25	0.17	0.14
Beta (vs. Universe)	0.75	0.68	0.94	1.23	1.40	NA	0.78
Alpha (vs. Universe)	0.08	0.06	0.01	−0.05	−0.10	NA	0.04
Average Portfolio Size	332	333	333	333	333	NA	NA
Average Number of Companies *Outperforming*	165	155	142	127	122	NA	NA
Average Number of Companies *Underperforming*	153	164	174	188	193	NA	NA
Median Portfolio Value – FCF + Repur.+ Div. to Prc.	21.2%	7.5%	3.0%	−1.2%	−21.5%	1.8%	6.2%
Average Market Capitalization	$4,623	$7,176	$6,741	$3,554	$1,761	NA	NA

* Equal-weighted average of S&P 500 returns. ** Annual holding period run quarterly for a larger sample size; arithmetic average excess returns.
Source: Standard & Poor's Compustat Point in Time Database, Charter Oak Investment Systems, Inc., Venues® Data Engine

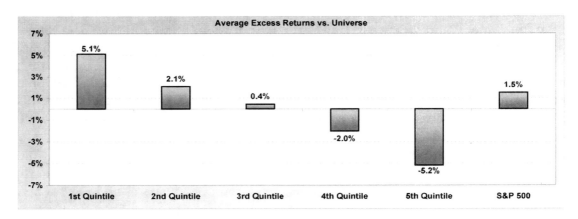

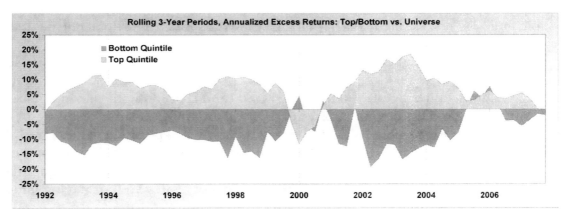

Figure 6.11 Free Cash Flow Plus Net Share Repurchase Plus Dividend to Price

The bottom quintile underperforms by 5.2%, on average, 0.7% more than the FCF-to-price strategy alone. The extra performance is gained by including companies in the bottom quintile that are issuing large numbers of shares.[15] The bottom quintile underperforms for 83% of one-year and 87% of rolling three-year periods. It significantly outperforms in three periods: 1999–2000, 2003–2004, and 2006. Average portfolio values for the bottom quintile range from −12% to −27%, indicating that these companies have cash outflows and/or are issuing large amounts of shares.

Free Cash Flow Plus Net Share Repurchase Plus Dividend to Price by Economic Sector

The sector test is very similar to the sector test for FCF to price alone, except that the energy, industrials, and consumer staples sectors all show significantly higher outperformance and are more consistent. The energy, industrials, and consumer staples sectors all represent mature industries (although the energy industry has seen strong growth in recent years). A strategy of returning cash to shareholders, through dividends and share repurchases, makes sense for mature industries where growth opportunities might not be as great as in other areas. Note that, with the exception of telecom services, this strategy is strong across the board (see Figure 6.12).

Free Cash Flow Plus Net Share Repurchase Plus Dividend to Price and One-Year Reduction in Shares Outstanding

This strategy combines two factors that seem redundant: share repurchase to price (contained in the first factor) and one-year reduction in shares outstanding. However, the first factor, which represents net cash received from share repurchases, does not guarantee that companies are reducing shares or even repurchasing significant amounts of shares. Since many companies issue large number of shares to cover employee stock option exercises, and options are usually exercised at prices well below the current share price, a company often has to spend a lot more cash on share repurchases than it receives from share issuance to options holders just to keep the share count flat. The one-year reduction in shares figure, on the other hand, calculates the actual reduction (or increase) in share count based on the common shares outstanding number from the balance sheet. Using this ratio as the second factor of this strategy guarantees that companies that are spending cash on share repurchases are also reducing their shares outstanding.

The companies in the top quintile of this strategy have positive cash flow and are repurchasing shares, paying dividends, and seeing their actual share count decline—

---

[15] We'll see in Chapter 8 that companies that issue large amounts of shares significantly underperform.

Top Quintile

1990–2007	Energy	Materials	Industrials	Consumer Discretionary	Consumer Staples	Health Care	Financials	Information Technology	Telecom Services	Utilities	Universe	S&P 500*
CAGR – Quintile	19.5%	12.9%	15.8%	13.1%	18.9%	19.7%	19.0%	17.6%	7.7%	20.5%	10.3%	12.0%
CAGR – Sector	11.9%	9.7%	10.7%	7.3%	10.8%	11.9%	14.1%	8.0%	5.6%	11.9%	NA	NA
Excess Return vs. Sector	7.5%	3.2%	5.1%	5.8%	8.1%	7.9%	4.9%	9.6%	2.1%	8.6%	NA	NA
Value of $10,000	$246,502	$89,275	$140,341	$92,219	$225,863	$256,273	$228,589	$186,148	$37,977	$286,045	$58,670	$76,297
% 1-Year Outperformance	77.8%	72.2%	88.9%	72.2%	83.3%	72.2%	61.1%	66.7%	61.1%	66.7%	NA	NA
% 3-Year Outperformance	81.3%	87.5%	93.8%	93.8%	100.0%	93.8%	93.8%	87.5%	56.3%	81.3%	NA	NA
Maximum Gain	68.7%	42.4%	43.5%	47.4%	73.0%	75.6%	59.4%	54.2%	49.0%	120.9%	44.0%	41.4%
Maximum Loss	−19.3%	−14.6%	−13.5%	−18.9%	−11.1%	−16.5%	−18.6%	−30.6%	−41.9%	−14.3%	−19.1%	−18.1%
Standard Deviation	0.22	0.17	0.16	0.19	0.20	0.25	0.25	0.21	0.24	0.34	0.17	0.15
Beta (vs. Sector)	0.76	0.99	0.98	0.94	1.25	0.86	1.00	0.44	0.41	1.55	NA	NA
Alpha (vs. Sector)	0.10	0.04	0.05	0.06	0.06	0.10	0.05	0.13	0.06	0.04	NA	NA
Portfolio Size	21	28	55	66	19	40	30	55	8	2	NA	NA

Bottom Quintile

1990–2007	Energy	Materials	Industrials	Consumer Discretionary	Consumer Staples	Health Care	Financials	Information Technology	Telecom Services	Utilities	Universe	S&P 500*
CAGR – Quintile	7.6%	5.4%	4.1%	3.6%	6.9%	3.6%	8.3%	3.8%	4.4%	−1.0%	10.3%	12.0%
CAGR – Sector	11.9%	9.7%	10.7%	7.3%	10.8%	11.9%	14.1%	8.0%	5.6%	11.9%	NA	NA
Excess Return vs. Sector	−4.3%	−4.3%	−6.6%	−3.8%	−3.9%	−8.3%	−5.9%	−4.2%	−1.2%	−12.9%	NA	NA
Value of $10,000	$37,551	$25,962	$20,512	$18,771	$33,111	$18,891	$41,824	$19,617	$21,700	$8,317	$58,670	$76,297
% 1-Year Outperformance	38.9%	33.3%	16.7%	38.9%	27.8%	27.8%	22.2%	27.8%	44.4%	22.2%	NA	NA
% 3-Year Outperformance	25.0%	12.5%	6.3%	25.0%	18.8%	12.5%	12.5%	25.0%	43.8%	37.5%	NA	NA
Maximum Gain	81.2%	47.7%	44.6%	53.4%	38.8%	81.7%	51.3%	224.9%	226.6%	154.7%	44.0%	41.4%
Maximum Loss	−57.7%	−22.9%	−31.6%	−35.2%	−19.8%	−38.7%	−26.3%	−65.0%	−65.2%	−91.3%	−19.1%	−18.1%
Standard Deviation	0.34	0.19	0.19	0.25	0.16	0.29	0.20	0.60	0.62	0.56	0.17	0.15
Beta (vs. Sector)	1.30	1.16	1.21	1.23	0.97	1.08	0.79	1.49	1.54	2.58	NA	NA
Alpha (vs. Sector)	−0.06	0.01	−0.06	−0.08	0.02	−0.09	0.00	−0.12	−0.07	−0.05	NA	NA
Portfolio Size	22	29	57	70	21	41	33	57	9	3	NA	NA

* Equal-weighted average of S&P 500 returns.
Source: Standard & Poor's Compustat Point in Time Database; Charter Oak Investment Systems, Inc., Venues® Data Engine

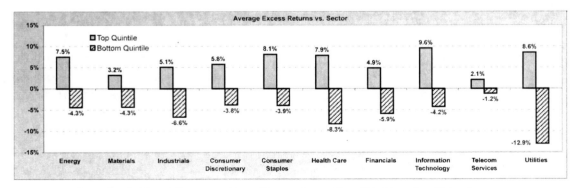

Figure 6.12 Free Cash Flow Plus Net Share Repurchase Plus Dividend to Price by Economic Sector

and they are attractively priced. The companies in the bottom quintile, in contrast, have negative cash flows and are issuing large numbers of shares, a potent combination in terms of causing stock price underperformance.

The top quintile of this strategy outperforms by 5.6% on average, and does so for 72% of one-year and 86% of rolling three-year periods (see Figure 6.13). It significantly underperforms only in 1990, 1999–2000, and 2006. Its maximum loss is a relatively low 22%, and its standard deviation of returns is quite low (0.15), resulting in a strong Sharpe ratio of 0.88. Average portfolio values are 16% to 37% for FCF plus repurchase plus dividend to price and 6% to 13% for one-year reduction in shares.

The bottom quintile underperforms by an average of 12.1% and is very consistent, underperforming for 81% of one-year and 100% of rolling three-year periods, making it a strong short-sale strategy. It significantly outperforms only in 1990, 1999, and 2007. Average portfolio values range from −13% to −32% for FCF plus repurchase plus dividend to price and from −49% to less than −150% for one-year share reduction (representing a 50% to 150% share increase).

Free Cash Flow Plus Dividend Yield and Return on Equity

In this strategy, we look only at FCF plus dividends as a percent of price and ignore share repurchases. Companies in the top quintile have strong cash flows relative to price, generally pay dividends, and are very profitable in terms of ROE. Companies in the bottom quintile have negative cash flows, do not pay dividends (generally), and have high negative returns on equity; that is, they have large income statement losses in addition to their cash losses.

The strategy performs very well, and is both consistent and linear in its pattern of excess returns. The top quintile outperforms by an average of 6.7% and does so for 78% of one-year and 91% of rolling three-year periods (see Figure 6.14). It significantly underperforms only in 1999–2000 and 2003–2004, and has worked very well recently. It has a low maximum loss of 18%, and a high Sharpe ratio of 0.89. Average portfolio values range from 12% to 32% for FCF plus dividend yield[16] and 31% to 78% for ROE, so these are very profitable companies that are cheap on an FCF basis.

The bottom quintile underperforms by an average of 9.7%, and does so for 78% of one-year and 92% of rolling three-year periods. It significantly outperforms only in 1999–2000 and 2003–2004. Average portfolio values range from −8% to −23% for FCF plus dividend yield and from −30% to less than −160% for ROE.

---

[16] The formula for free cash flow plus dividend yield is 12-month operating cash flows minus 12-month capital expenditures plus 12-month cash dividends paid, all divided by market capitalization.

1990–2007	1st Quintile	2nd Quintile	3rd Quintile	4th Quintile	5th Quintile	Universe	S&P 500*
CAGR – Annual Rebalance	16.4%	13.8%	10.5%	1.8%	−4.2%	10.3%	12.0%
Average Excess Return vs. Universe**	5.6%	1.7%	0.3%	−2.2%	−12.1%	NA	1.5%
Value of $10,000 Invested (18 Years)	$154,383	$102,629	$60,352	$13,742	$4,608	$58,670	$76,297
% of 1-Year Periods Strategy Outperforms the Universe	72.2%	56.9%	47.2%	33.3%	19.4%	NA	56.9%
% Rolling 3-Year Periods Strategy Outperforms	85.9%	62.5%	50.0%	15.6%	0.0%	NA	68.8%
Maximum Gain	59.6%	46.1%	54.0%	107.6%	77.3%	59.2%	54.1%
Maximum Loss	−22.1%	−21.0%	−29.7%	−64.5%	−62.1%	−24.9%	−25.9%
Sharpe Ratio	0.88	0.79	0.45	0.18	−0.16	0.46	0.64
Standard Deviation of Returns	0.15	0.12	0.18	0.31	0.27	0.17	0.14
Beta (vs. Universe)	0.66	0.60	1.00	1.42	1.38	NA	0.78
Alpha (vs. Universe)	0.10	0.06	0.00	−0.07	−0.17	NA	0.04
Average Portfolio Size	66	66	66	66	65	NA	NA
Average Number of Companies *Outperforming*	31	32	28	23	21	NA	NA
Average Number of Companies *Underperforming*	32	32	34	39	40	NA	NA
Median Portfolio Value – FCF + Repur. + Div. to Prc.	24.3%	7.6%	2.9%	−1.4%	−24.1%	1.8%	6.2%
Median Portfolio Value – 1 Yr. Reduction in Shares	10.0%	0.6%	−0.9%	−5.6%	−121.8%	−75.8%	−2.9%
Average Market Capitalization	$3,894	$10,121	$5,906	$3,375	$1,253	NA	NA

* Equal-weighted average of S&P 500 returns. ** Annual holding period run quarterly for a larger sample size; arithmetic average excess returns.
Source: Standard & Poor's Compustat Point in Time Database, Charter Oak Investment Systems, Inc., Venues® Data Engine

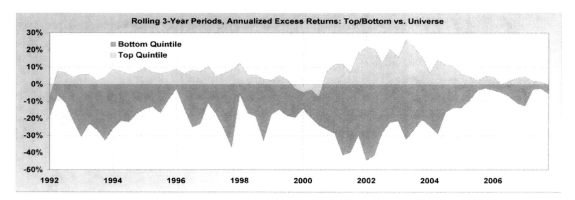

Figure 6.13 Free Cash Flow Plus Net Share Repurchase Plus Dividend to Price and One-Year Reduction in Shares Outstanding

1990–2007	1st Quintile	2nd Quintile	3rd Quintile	4th Quintile	5th Quintile	Universe	S&P 500*
CAGR – Annual Rebalance	17.0%	11.7%	12.7%	5.1%	−3.3%	10.3%	12.0%
Average Excess Return vs. Universe**	6.7%	2.8%	0.7%	−3.1%	−9.7%	NA	1.5%
Value of $10,000 Invested (18 Years)	$167,687	$73,735	$85,476	$24,494	$5,418	$58,670	$76,297
% of 1-Year Periods Strategy Outperforms the Universe	77.8%	63.9%	52.8%	29.2%	22.2%	NA	56.9%
% Rolling 3-Year Periods Strategy Outperforms	90.6%	67.2%	64.1%	25.0%	7.8%	NA	68.8%
Maximum Gain	59.9%	52.8%	53.9%	107.7%	105.2%	59.2%	54.1%
Maximum Loss	−18.3%	−18.9%	−31.5%	−67.7%	−76.1%	−24.9%	−25.9%
Sharpe Ratio	0.89	0.75	0.52	0.18	−0.05	0.46	0.64
Standard Deviation of Returns	0.16	0.14	0.16	0.26	0.38	0.17	0.14
Beta (vs. Universe)	0.76	0.71	0.90	1.29	1.74	NA	0.78
Alpha (vs. Universe)	0.10	0.06	0.02	−0.07	−0.19	NA	0.04
Average Portfolio Size	64	64	64	64	65	NA	NA
Average Number of Companies *Outperforming*	32	30	28	23	19	NA	NA
Average Number of Companies *Underperforming*	29	31	34	37	42	NA	NA
Median Portfolio Value – FCF + Div. to Price	17.6%	6.9%	3.4%	0.1%	−11.6%	3.5%	5.3%
Median Portfolio Value – ROE	44.7%	20.7%	15.5%	7.5%	−127.4%	9.4%	15.0%
Average Market Capitalization	$7,426	$8,623	$5,413	$3,013	$1,147	NA	NA

* Equal-weighted average of S&P 500 returns. ** Annual holding period run quarterly for a larger sample size; arithmetic average excess returns.
Source: Standard & Poor's Compustat Point in Time Database, Charter Oak Investment Systems, Inc., Venues® Data Engine

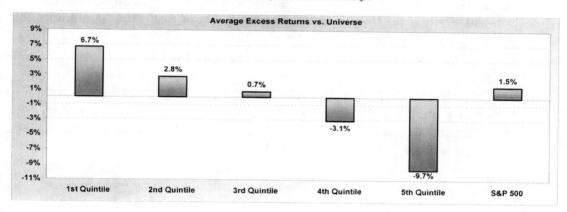

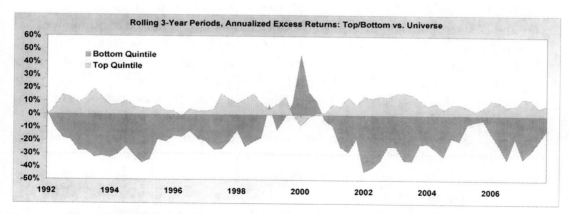

Figure 6.14 Free Cash Flow Plus Dividend Yield and Return on Equity

SUMMARY

- Together with valuation and profitability, cash flow is one of the most predictive *basics*. Our research shows that the level of operating cash flow a company generates over time is a strong indicator of future stock market returns.
- Although accrual accounting-based earnings are important, cash flow is also important because cash represents a reality—purchasing power—while accounting earnings are at least one step removed from that reality.
- The free cash flow (FCF) to operating income ratio assesses the quality of a company's earnings by determining how much of a company's accounting earnings are actually realized in cash. Companies with high levels of FCF for each dollar of operating earnings can generally be said to have high-quality earnings and vice versa.
- Free cash flow is defined as 12-month cash flows from operating activities minus 12-month capital expenditures. Capital expenditures are subtracted because we consider them a nondiscretionary use of cash, since companies that do not maintain and expand plant and equipment cannot remain competitive.
- The FCF to operating income strategy is strong and works well across economic sectors, but like other cash flow-based strategies, it hasn't worked well in recent years. The likely reason: investors have increasingly focused on cash flow generation and easily available excess returns have diminished. However, this defect can be overcome by combining cash flow based building blocks with other factors, particularly with valuation factors.
- The free cash flow to operating income and acquisitions to invested capital strategy generates strong results, in the top quintile, simply by including companies that generate significant amounts of cash, relative to income, and that avoid using that cash to make business acquisitions.
- The FCF to operating income and external financing strategy considers not only how much cash a company generates and but also what it does with that cash, in terms of share and debt issuance or reduction. Companies with strong cash flows that repurchase shares and reduce debt outperform. Companies with negative cash flows that issue large amounts of shares and/or debt underperform (by an average of over 14%) and do so consistently.
- The FCF to operating income and price to sales strategy results in a combined cash flow/valuation measure that generates strong and consistent excess returns. Unlike cash flow strategies alone, it works well in recent years.
- The cash return on invested capital (ROIC) strategy simply compares a company's FCF to total invested capital. Invested capital is defined as the

book value of common equity plus long-term debt plus preferred stock and minority interest. A cash return on equity strategy is also possible.

- The top quintile of the cash ROIC strategy tends to select large cap companies, since large companies often generate more excess cash than smaller peers, which need their cash to grow. The strategy generates strong excess returns and works well across economic sectors.

- The cash ROIC and capex to property plant & equipment backtest shows that companies with strong FCF generation and declining capital spending needs outperform, while companies that have cash outflows and increasing capital spending needs strongly underperform. The bottom quintile of this test would make a good short-sale strategy.

- The cash ROIC and price to invested capital backtest seeks to answer two questions: What level of cash return does a company earn on invested capital? and What price must be paid for that invested capital? Excess returns are strong, consistent, and nearly perfectly symmetrical among quintiles, indicating a well-founded strategy.

- The FCF plus share repurchase plus dividend to price strategy a hybrid that combines cash flow, capital allocation, and valuation into a single-factor. The ratio is calculated by taking the last 12 months' FCF and adding to that net cash paid for share repurchase (or subtracting net cash received from share issuance) plus dividends, and dividing everything by market capitalization. This strategy is a useful building block in constructing two-factor strategies that emphasize both valuation and capital allocation.

- The bottom quintile of the FCF plus net share repurchase plus dividend to price and one-year reduction in shares outstanding strategy underperforms strongly (by over 12%) and consistently, making it a strong short-sale strategy. It selects stocks of companies that have cash outflows and also issue large numbers of shares.

- The free cash flow plus dividend yield and return on equity strategy combines cash generation, valuation, profitability, and dividend yield into a single test. It generates strong, consistent, and linear excess returns.

CHAPTER 7

Growth

One of the cardinal sins of investing, I have learned, is treating the greatest companies just like all the other investments you own.

Frederick R. Kobrick, *The Big Money: Seven Steps to Picking Great Stocks and Finding Financial Security*

No one can see ahead three years, let alone five or ten. Competition, new inventions—all kinds of things—can change the situation in twelve months.

T. Rowe Price, from John Train's *Money Masters of Our Time*

Although stock market history is replete with great value investors, growth stocks have also had their champions. One early proponent of growth stock investing and a great investor was Thomas Rowe Price, Jr., the late founder of the multibillion-dollar investment management firm that still bears his name (T. Rowe Price). Mr. Price's basic tenet was that "investors could earn superior returns by investing in well-managed companies in fertile fields whose earnings and dividends could be expected to grow faster than inflation and the overall economy."[1] T. Rowe Price's philosophy of growth stock investing was, essentially, *own great companies in great industries, and ignore the ups and downs of the economy and stock market.*[2] To find great companies, investors must be able to identify great management teams with strong business models and strategic vision (e.g., Microsoft, Wal-Mart, Cisco Systems, Nike, McDonald's, and Merck in their heydays). To find great industries,

---

[1] From the T. Rowe Price corporate Web site: www.troweprice.com.

[2] Price defined growth companies as ones that have reached new highs in earnings per share at the peak of each major business cycle and that show signs of continuing this trend during the next business cycle.

investors must determine major trends in the United States or the global economy that are not likely to go away: the economic swells versus the smaller waves that break against the shore and disappear. Thus, of all investing approaches, growth stock investing is perhaps the most dependent on art and the least amenable to quantitative analysis.

Growth investors face two significant problems. First, they must identify growth companies that are still in the early to middle stages of their growth cycles—those companies that still have long stretches of growth ahead of them. Second, they must find companies that have some strategic advantage that enables them to stay well ahead of the competition. In their early stages, rapidly growing companies with great leaders in expanding industries often have wonderful futures ahead, and their stock prices often do not fully reflect this growth potential (think of Microsoft in the late 1980s and early 1990s). However, very few companies can maintain high rates of sales and earnings growth for extended periods. The primary reason is that high growth and strong profitability attract competition; most often, the greater the perceived opportunities in an industry, the greater the competition. So, the truly great growth stocks—those that have been able to maintain high growth levels year after year—have all had some important competitive edge that allowed them to stay well ahead of rivals:[3] Coca-Cola had a great brand name, Wal-Mart had strategic vision and a new retail concept, Cisco was a pioneer in a burgeoning industry, Microsoft controlled the operating system. For every Coca-Cola, Wal-Mart, Cisco, and Microsoft, however, there have been thousands of companies that generated strong earnings growth for a few years but were not able to sustain high growth rates over the long term.

Because true long-term growth companies represent the few not the many, growth is difficult if not impossible to model quantitatively. Most quantitative strategies take a "value" approach simply because value factors work well (Chapter 5), and growth factors are usually weak, at best. From a quantitative perspective, companies with high growth rates suffer from the phenomenon of reversion to the mean. Figure 7.1 shows the growth rates of S&P 500 companies with the highest and lowest rates of three-year average earnings growth.[4] The $Y0$ at the bottom of the graph represents the point at which the top and bottom portfolios were formed. The points labeled $Y-1$, $Y-2$, $Y-3$, and so on, represent the growth rates of these same portfolios (i.e., the portfolios formed in year $Y0$) during the periods one year, two years, three years, and so on, *prior to* portfolio formation. The points labeled $Y+1$, $Y+2$, $Y+3$, and so on, represent the same portfolio growth rates one, two, three years, and so on, *following* portfolio formation. This graph illustrates quite clearly the primary problem with

---

[3] This is what business consultants aptly refer to as *sustainable competitive advantage*.

[4] Specifically, the graph shows the median growth rate of the top and bottom quintiles of the S&P 500 selected by three-year compound annual earnings per share (EPS) growth.

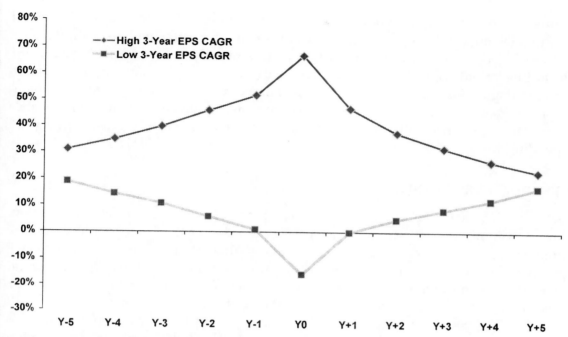

Figure 7.1 Earnings Growth Rates of High and Low Earnings Growth S&P 500 Companies: Five Years Prior to and Five Years Following Portfolio Formation

growth stock investing: over time, high earnings growth rates slow (on average), and low earnings growth rates increase.[5]

Another problem with high growth companies from a quantitative point of view is that they tend to carry both high investor expectations and high valuations, which make growth stocks particularly sensitive to disappointments. The combination of high growth that tends to revert to the mean and high valuations is a volatile one and is the reason so many growth "momentum" investors get burnt. The growth stock investor must have confidence that he or she can separate the few true long-term growth stories from the many high flyers that sooner or later come back to earth.

So, what is the answer to this puzzle from a quantitative point of view? We can answer it in a few ways. First, as we saw in Chapter 3, while some growth factors (sales, earnings) are not predictive, other growth factors (free cash flow) are. The beginning of this chapter focuses on free cash flow (FCF) growth, which is a moderately predictive single-factor strategy. Second, although earnings growth alone is not predictive, earnings growth combined with earnings linearity (a measure the consistency of earnings)

---

[5] This statistical phenomenon is sometimes called *reversion to the mean.*

is predictive. We have created an earnings score that provides a combined ranking for companies on earnings growth and earnings consistency (as well as a similar FCF score). Third, we'll combine the growth factors presented here with other factors, including valuation, profitability, capital allocation, and price-momentum factors, to form strong two-factor strategies. In particular, the combination of growth and valuation generates strong and consistent excess returns. Finally, we'll look at an instance where low growth results in positive excess returns, specifically growth in capital spending.

FREE CASH FLOW PER SHARE SCORE

Before we look at the FCF per share score, which is a somewhat complicated calculation, I want to give you an alternative: one-year FCF per share growth, alone (not shown), is predictive and works almost as well as the FCF score presented here. To calculate FCF per share growth, take a company's 12-month operating cash flows minus capital expenditures and divide by the number of common shares outstanding. Then, divide this amount by the FCF per share figure for the prior year and subtract 1.[6]

The FCF per share score, on the other hand, is calculated based on a company's rank on two factors: a growth index and a measure of growth linearity. The calculation begins with 10 consecutive quarters of FCF per share figures. The growth index is calculated by dividing the most recent 3 quarters of cash flow by the last (oldest) 3 quarters of cash flow in the 10-quarter series. The higher the percentage change, the higher the score. Linearity is calculated as the standard deviation of the 10 quarterly cash flow per share numbers divided by the average of the cash flow numbers.[7] The lower the adjusted standard deviation, the higher the score (i.e., we're looking for consistent quarterly cash flows). The two factors are then combined by weighting the growth index by 70% and the linearity by 30%. The result is a combined score that tells us something about both the growth and the consistency of quarterly cash flows over the past two and one-half years.

The FCF per share score (see Figure 7.2) generates moderately high excess returns for a single-factor strategy and is relatively consistent. Although the bottom quintile of the strategy hasn't worked well in recent years, the top quintile slightly outperformed the market each year from mid–2004 through 2006, unlike other FCF-based strategies.

---

[6] We use a somewhat more complex calculation that handles negative free cash flow values: $(fcfps[y0] - fcfps[y-1])/@abs(fcfps[y-1])$, where $fcfps$ is free cash flow per share, @abs calculates the absolute value, and y0 equals the past 12 month period and y–1 equals the preceding 12 month period.

[7] This is done to prevent companies with low cash flow numbers from receiving higher linearity scores than companies with high cash flow numbers.

1991–2007	1st Quintile	2nd Quintile	3rd Quintile	4th Quintile	5th Quintile	Universe	S&P 500*
CAGR – Annual Rebalance	16.2%	13.7%	12.6%	12.3%	8.6%	12.1%	13.5%
Average Excess Return vs. Universe**	3.5%	1.9%	1.0%	−0.6%	−2.7%	NA	1.3%
Value of $10,000 Invested (17 Years)	$127,905	$88,071	$75,097	$71,803	$40,496	$69,381	$86,051
% of 1-Year Periods Strategy Outperforms the Universe	80.3%	59.1%	57.6%	36.4%	31.8%	NA	57.6%
% Rolling 3-Year Periods Strategy Outperforms	86.2%	75.9%	72.4%	36.2%	20.7%	NA	69.0%
Maximum Gain	53.2%	61.1%	59.6%	59.2%	67.6%	59.2%	54.1%
Maximum Loss	−22.0%	−25.7%	−24.2%	−28.2%	−34.7%	−24.9%	−25.9%
Sharpe Ratio	0.81	0.68	0.67	0.55	0.33	0.55	0.74
Standard Deviation of Returns	0.15	0.16	0.15	0.15	0.19	0.17	0.14
Beta (vs. Universe)	0.91	0.96	0.87	0.90	1.11	NA	0.76
Alpha (vs. Universe)	0.05	0.02	0.03	0.01	−0.04	NA	0.05
Average Portfolio Size	291	291	291	291	291	NA	NA
Average Number of Companies *Outperforming*	134	127	129	124	118	NA	NA
Average Number of Companies *Underperforming*	142	149	148	154	159	NA	NA
Median Portfolio Value – Free Cash Flow Per Share Score	49	41	34	23	9	32	33
Average Market Capitalization	$7,382	$5,896	$5,720	$4,144	$3,509	NA	NA

* Equal-weighted average of S&P 500 returns. ** Annual holding period run quarterly for a larger sample size; arithmetic average excess returns.
Source: Standard & Poor's Compustat Point in Time Database; Charter Oak Investment Systems, Inc., Venues® Data Engine

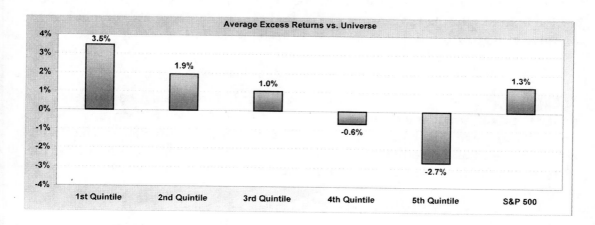

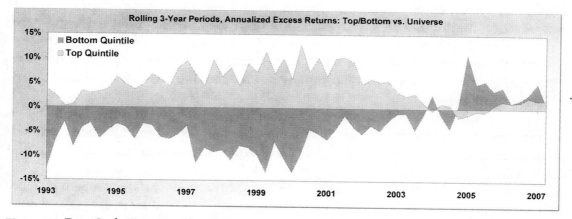

Figure 7.2 Free Cash Flow Per Share Score

The top quintile outperforms by 3.5%, on average, and does so for 80% of one-year and 86% of rolling three-year periods. It significantly underperforms only in 1992 and 2003–2004. It has a relatively low maximum loss of 22% and a high Sharpe ratio for a single-factor strategy, of 0.81. With an average market cap of $7.4 billion, the strategy tends to select large-cap stocks. Average portfolio values for the top quintile of the FCF per share score strategy range from 45 to 61. The highest FCF per share score in our database over the period tested is 71, and the lowest is 0. It is interesting to note that FCF scores for all quintiles have gradually improved over the years tested, probably a sign that corporations, along with investors, are focusing on improved cash flow generation.

The bottom quintile underperforms by 2.7%, on average, and has average consistency, underperforming for 68% of one-year and 79% of rolling three-year periods. Unfortunately, the bottom quintile seems to have stopped working since 2003. However, we'll see that it becomes more consistent when combined with another factor, such as a valuation or profitability factor. Average portfolio values for FCF score for the bottom quintile range from 9 to 11, indicating that these are companies with negative FCF growth and low consistency of cash flows.

Free Cash Flow Per Share Score by Economic Sector

The FCF score strategy works particularly well for the industrials, consumer discretionary, and information technology sectors. It also works well for consumer staples. The best companies in all four of these sectors generate very strong FCFs. The strategy also works well as a negative strategy in the financials and telecom services sectors. Note that banks are not included in the financials results (see Figure 7.3).

Free Cash Flow Per Share Score and Enterprise Value to EBITDA

This strategy combines a cash flow–based growth metric with an accrual accounting–based valuation metric. The results are both very strong and very consistent. Adding a valuation factor to a growth factor helps ensure that the investor does not overpay for growth. On the other hand, the growth factor helps ensure that the company is not simply a low-valuation company destined to stay low valuation (due to lack of meaningful growth).

The top quintile of this strategy is particularly impressive. It outperforms by an average of over 8%, and does so for 76% of one-year and 90% of rolling three-year periods (see Figure 7.4). The strategy significantly underperforms only in 1999–2000 and 2003–2004. The maximum loss is a relatively low 21%, and the Sharpe ratio is 1.03, the highest for a two-factor strategy in this book. In addition, the strategy's Beta is a low 0.65, indicating low volatility, while its Alpha is a high 0.13, and an average of 29 portfolio companies outperform versus only 22 that underperform, a very strong showing.

Top Quintile

1991–2007	Energy	Materials	Industrials	Consumer Discretionary	Consumer Staples	Health Care	Financials	Information Technology	Telecom Services	Universe	S&P 500*
CAGR – Quintile	17.4%	11.7%	15.2%	14.3%	14.9%	14.5%	19.7%	14.5%	7.9%	12.1%	13.5%
CAGR – Sector	13.8%	11.6%	12.5%	9.7%	11.8%	12.2%	17.0%	9.0%	7.4%	NA	NA
Excess Return vs. Sector	3.6%	0.2%	2.7%	4.6%	3.2%	2.3%	2.6%	5.4%	0.5%	NA	NA
Value of $10,000	$153,785	$66,005	$111,118	$97,077	$106,639	$100,364	$211,713	$99,191	$36,308	$69,381	$86,051
% 1-Year Outperformance	58.8%	58.8%	64.7%	76.5%	64.7%	52.9%	70.6%	70.6%	52.9%	NA	NA
% 3-Year Outperformance	53.3%	53.3%	80.0%	73.3%	93.3%	80.0%	60.0%	80.0%	40.0%	NA	NA
Maximum Gain	63.0%	40.3%	37.9%	48.8%	68.3%	67.3%	52.0%	119.0%	63.2%	44.0%	41.4%
Maximum Loss	−27.6%	−9.3%	−8.5%	−12.9%	−8.3%	−22.0%	−12.4%	−38.5%	−38.3%	−19.1%	−18.1%
Standard Deviation	0.24	0.14	0.15	0.17	0.19	0.22	0.19	0.35	0.22	0.16	0.14
Beta (vs. Sector)	0.84	0.94	0.96	0.89	1.03	0.78	0.85	0.85	0.32	NA	NA
Alpha (vs. Sector)	0.06	0.01	0.03	0.06	0.03	0.05	0.05	0.06	0.06	NA	NA
Portfolio Size	18	25	49	58	17	34	26	47	6	NA	NA

Bottom Quintile

1990–2007	Energy	Materials	Industrials	Consumer Discretionary	Consumer Staples	Health Care	Financials	Information Technology	Telecom Services	Universe	S&P 500*
CAGR – Quintile	10.3%	10.5%	9.8%	6.5%	10.3%	14.2%	10.8%	4.0%	0.4%	12.1%	13.5%
CAGR – Sector	13.8%	11.6%	12.5%	9.7%	11.8%	12.2%	17.0%	9.0%	7.4%	NA	NA
Excess Return vs. Sector	−3.4%	−1.1%	−2.7%	−3.1%	−1.5%	2.0%	−6.2%	−5.0%	−7.0%	NA	NA
Value of $10,000	$53,325	$54,663	$48,779	$29,386	$52,871	$95,799	$57,576	$19,474	$10,741	$69,381	$86,051
% 1-Year Outperformance	47.1%	29.4%	29.4%	35.3%	41.2%	64.7%	35.3%	29.4%	41.2%	NA	NA
% 3-Year Outperformance	40.0%	20.0%	13.3%	26.7%	40.0%	73.3%	20.0%	20.0%	26.7%	NA	NA
Maximum Gain	62.2%	39.7%	48.2%	49.7%	39.2%	87.7%	44.5%	98.4%	56.3%	44.0%	41.4%
Maximum Loss	−47.9%	−17.3%	−23.2%	−17.7%	−20.3%	−26.8%	−20.7%	−54.2%	−65.0%	−19.1%	−18.1%
Standard Deviation	0.30	0.17	0.16	0.18	0.14	0.30	0.19	0.35	0.31	0.16	0.14
Beta (vs. Sector)	1.07	1.09	1.16	0.95	0.90	1.05	0.68	0.83	0.65	NA	NA
Alpha (vs. Sector)	−0.03	0.04	−0.01	−0.04	0.08	0.00	0.05	−0.11	−0.12	NA	NA
Portfolio Size	19	25	51	62	19	36	30	49	7	NA	NA

* Equal-weighted average of S&P 500 returns.
Source: Standard & Poor's Compustat Point in Time Database; Charter Oak Investment Systems, Inc., Venues® Data Engine

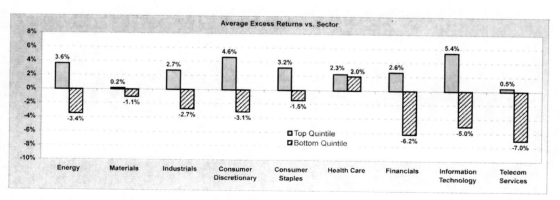

Figure 7.3 Free Cash Flow Per Share Score by Economic Sector

1991–2007	1st Quintile	2nd Quintile	3rd Quintile	4th Quintile	5th Quintile	Universe	S&P 500*
CAGR – Annual Rebalance	22.2%	15.4%	13.5%	9.7%	1.6%	12.1%	13.5%
Average Excess Return vs. Universe**	8.1%	3.1%	0.8%	−2.7%	−6.7%	NA	1.3%
Value of $10,000 Invested (17 Years)	$302,073	$114,923	$86,124	$47,987	$13,116	$69,381	$86,051
% of 1-Year Periods Strategy Outperforms the Universe	75.8%	54.5%	54.5%	30.3%	27.3%	NA	57.6%
% Rolling 3-Year Periods Strategy Outperforms	89.7%	67.2%	65.5%	15.5%	6.9%	NA	69.0%
Maximum Gain	62.4%	73.5%	50.9%	54.3%	126.3%	59.2%	54.1%
Maximum Loss	−21.1%	−24.4%	−20.6%	−34.2%	−69.1%	−24.9%	−25.9%
Sharpe Ratio	1.03	0.73	0.71	0.36	0.07	0.55	0.74
Standard Deviation of Returns	0.17	0.17	0.14	0.18	0.36	0.17	0.14
Beta (vs. Universe)	0.65	0.79	0.69	0.97	1.86	NA	0.76
Alpha (vs. Universe)	0.13	0.06	0.05	−0.02	−0.18	NA	0.05
Average Portfolio Size	54	55	55	55	55	NA	NA
Average Number of Companies *Outperforming*	29	26	27	23	19	NA	NA
Average Number of Companies *Underperforming*	22	27	26	30	33	NA	NA
Median Portfolio Value – FCF Per Share Score	49	41	34	24	10	32	33
Median Portfolio Value – EV to EBITDA	4.6	8.3	10.1	12.9	−77.3	10.8	9.2
Average Market Capitalization	$5,588	$4,484	$5,810	$6,161	$3,092	NA	NA

* Equal-weighted average of S&P 500 returns. ** Annual holding period run quarterly for a larger sample size; arithmetic average excess returns.
Source: Standard & Poor's Compustat Point in Time Database; Charter Oak Investment Systems, Inc., Venues® Data Engine

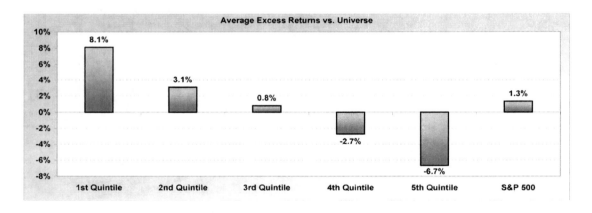

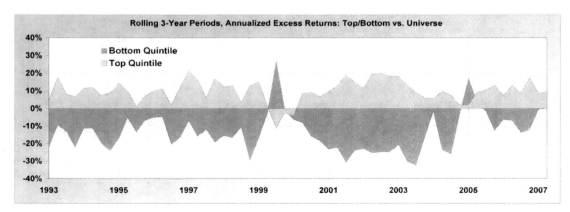

Figure 7.4 Free Cash Flow Per Share Score and Enterprise Value to EBITDA

With an average market cap of $5.6 billion, the strategy selects mid- to large-cap stocks (the average market cap ranged from $7 billion in 2003 to $19 billion in 2006). Average portfolio values for the top quintile range from 46 to 61 for FCF per share score and 4× to 5× for enterprise value (EV) to EBITDA (earnings before interest, taxes, depreciation, and amortization), so these are companies with strong and consistent cash flow growth that are selling at low multiples of operating income.

The bottom quintile is only a little less impressive. It underperforms by 6.7%, on average, and does so for 73% of one-year and 93% of rolling three-year periods. It significantly outperforms in 1991, 1996, 1999–2000, and 2003, and is a very volatile strategy, with a Beta of 1.9. An average of 33 portfolio companies underperforms versus only 19 that outperform. Average portfolio values range from 8 to 12 for FCF per share score and from high positive numbers (50× to 80×) to high negatives for EV to EBITDA.

One-Year Free Cash Flow Per Share Growth and 28/16-Week Relative Strength Index

This test combines a growth factor—FCF growth—with a price-action based, or technical, factor—the Relative Strength Index. (I'll cover the RSI in Chapter 9, Price Momentum, and we'll also see it later in this chapter, where we apply it to earnings per share growth.) Growth factors and technical factors typically work well together but make for a volatile combination: technical factors typically measure price momentum,[8] and growth factors measure cash flow or earnings momentum. When the stock market and the economy are strong, this combination of price and fundamental (earnings or cash flow) momentum often works well. However, when a good stock market starts to unravel, stocks of companies that have recorded high price and fundamental momentum can fall fast. This strategy is not immune from this defect. As you can see from the three-year rolling average returns graph in Figure 7.5, it can be quite volatile. In fact, from April 2000 to March 2001, the top quintile of this strategy fell by 51% (the maximum loss for this quintile) as the former high flyers of the preceding Internet and telecom bubble were deflated. However, the strategy has strong excess returns, is consistent over time, and despite its volatility has a Sharpe ratio of 0.78, well above the Sharpe ratios for the Universe or the S&P 500.

The 28/16-week Relative Strength Index should not be confused with the seven-month relative strength strategy seen in Chapter 5 (although the names are easy to confuse). The seven-month relative strength calculation is based on the absolute rate of

---

[8] To understand the concept of price momentum, consider its simplest form: the rate of change. Rate of change simply calculates the price increase or decrease of a stock over a specified period of time. Stocks with low rates of change are considered to have low momentum, and stocks with high rates of change to have high momentum.

1993–2007	1st Quintile	2nd Quintile	3rd Quintile	4th Quintile	5th Quintile	Universe	S&P 500*
CAGR – Annual Rebalance	17.2%	13.1%	6.9%	8.2%	4.4%	8.5%	9.6%
Average Excess Return vs. Universe**	8.9%	4.4%	−1.1%	−2.0%	−4.9%	NA	0.2%
Value of $10,000 Invested (16 Years)	$126,369	$71,577	$28,934	$35,448	$20,010	$37,137	$43,383
% of 1-Year Periods Strategy Outperforms the Universe	73.0%	66.7%	36.5%	42.9%	23.8%	NA	44.4%
% Rolling 3-Year Periods Strategy Outperforms	83.6%	81.8%	36.4%	20.0%	12.7%	NA	49.1%
Maximum Gain	83.0%	114.1%	39.1%	45.9%	91.0%	50.7%	42.3%
Maximum Loss	−51.0%	−33.6%	−28.6%	−31.9%	−50.3%	−27.2%	−27.4%
Sharpe Ratio	0.78	0.57	0.56	0.41	0.13	0.54	0.69
Standard Deviation of Returns	0.22	0.22	0.12	0.14	0.22	0.15	0.12
Beta (vs. Universe)	1.21	1.21	0.72	0.87	1.19	NA	0.69
Alpha (vs. Universe)	0.06	0.02	0.02	0.00	−0.07	NA	0.04
Average Portfolio Size	61	61	62	61	62	NA	NA
Average Number of Companies *Outperforming*	30	31	28	28	26	NA	NA
Average Number of Companies *Underperforming*	27	28	31	32	34	NA	NA
Median Portfolio Value – FCF PS 1Yr Growth	868.2%	68.1%	12.4%	−40.5%	−383.0%	94.2%	128.7%
Median Portfolio Value – 28/16-Week RSI	74.7	64.0	57.0	48.0	33.0	55.4	54.4
Average Market Capitalization	$3,547	$6,800	$8,262	$5,577	$2,846	NA	NA

* Equal-weighted average of S&P 500 returns. ** Annual holding period run quarterly for a larger sample size; arithmetic average excess returns.
Source: Standard & Poor's Compustat Point in Time Database; Charter Oak Investment Systems, Inc., Venues® Data Engine

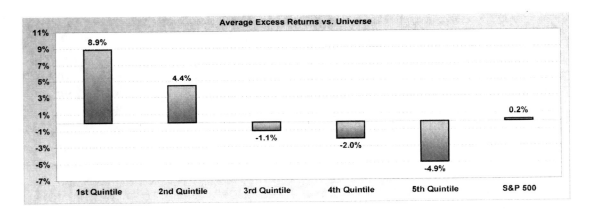

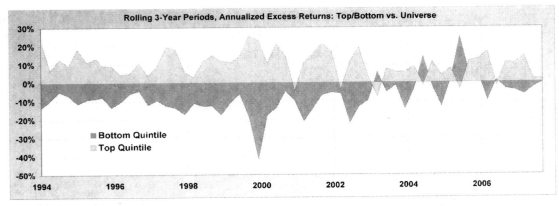

Figure 7.5 One-Year Free Cash Flow Per Share Growth and 28/16-Week Relative Strength Index

price change of an individual stock versus a group of stocks. The 28/16-week RSI calculates a stock's momentum by considering the *average trend* in price changes over a given period of time, and it indexes those price changes, so that the investor has an absolute measure of when momentum is high (over 70) or low (below 30).[9] We use a 28-week period to calculate RSI for the top three quintiles and 16 weeks to calculate RSI for the bottom two quintiles. (I'll explain why when we discuss RSI more fully in Chapter 9.) We use one-year FCF per share growth here to show how it can be used as an alternative to the FCF per share score.

The top quintile of this strategy outperforms by almost 9%, on average, and does so for 73% of one-year and 84% of rolling three-year periods. It significantly underperforms only in 2000 and 2003–2004, and briefly in 2006 and 2007. Volatility is high, with the above-mentioned maximum loss of 51% and a maximum gain of 83%. Beta versus the Universe is also high (1.2), and the standard deviation of returns is 0.22 for the top quintile versus 0.15 for the Universe. The result is a moderate Sharpe ratio of 0.78. Average portfolio values range from 400% to over 1,000% for one-year FCF per share growth (cash flow numbers are typically volatile from year to year) and from 63 to 77 for 28-week RSI.[10]

The bottom quintile underperforms by an average of 4.9%, and does so for 76% of one-year and 87% of rolling three-year periods. It significantly outperforms in 1999–2000 and 2003–2004, and more moderately in 2007. The bottom quintile is equal to the top quintile in volatility, with a Beta of 1.2 and a standard deviation of returns of 0.22. Average portfolio values range from −200% to less than −500% for one-year FCF per share growth and from 19 to 46 for 16-week RSI.

Free Cash Flow Per Share Score and Return on Equity

This strategy combines a cash flow–based growth factor with an accrual accounting–based profitability factor (return on equity). It is easy to confuse growth and profitability, but in reality they are separate indicators of corporate performance. A company can be highly profitable but show little growth. For example, if we change the top quintile of the FCF per share score and ROE strategy to look for companies with the highest level of cash flow growth but the lowest level of profitability (ROE), then run this screen as of December 2006, we come up with 62 companies. Integrated Device Technologies, for example, a maker of semiconductors, had a FCF per share score of

---

[9] The formula for RSI is $100 - 100/(1 + RS)$, where RS equals the sum of the price changes on up weeks divided by the sum of the price changes on down weeks (both expressed as positive numbers).

[10] Because RSI is indexed, RSI values range from 0 (the highest negative price momentum) to 100 (the highest positive price momentum).

62 (and strong FCF growth) but had negative ROE. Other companies have high levels of profitability but little growth. Hershey Co., for example, had ROE of 63% in a port-folio formed as of December 2006 but had a FCF per share score of 19 (and declining cash flow growth).

Ideally, a common stock investor would like to see both growth and profitability in potential investments (and acquire both for a reasonable price). The top quintile of this strategy selects companies with the highest cash flow growth and linearity and the highest profitability, in terms of ROE. The bottom quintile selects companies with low or negative FCF growth, high volatility of cash flows, and negative returns on equity. The results are strong and relatively consistent.

The top quintile outperforms by 7%, on average, and does so for 71% of one-year and 83% of rolling three-year periods (see Figure 7.6). It underperforms significantly only in 1992–1994 and 2003–2004. The maximum loss is a relatively low 20%, and the Sharpe ratio is a high 0.85. Average portfolio values for the top quintile range from 46 to 61 for FCF per share score and from 34% to 59% for ROE, so these are *very* profitable companies with high and consistent FCF growth. Note that companies in the top quin-tile tend to be mega-caps, with an average market cap of $14 billion. Large companies with multiple product lines, brand loyalty, and economies of scale are the most likely to provide both strong cash flow growth and strong profitability.

The bottom quintile underperforms by 4.8%, on average, and does so for 66% of one-year and 82% of rolling three-year periods. However, it is somewhat volatile, out-performing significantly in 1994, 1996, 1998–2000, 2003–2004, and 2007. Average port-folio values for the bottom quintile range from 9 to 12 for FCF per share score and −22% to −130% for ROE.

EARNINGS PER SHARE SCORE

The EPS score is an earnings-based growth factor that actually works. It doesn't work well as a single factor—consistency is only moderate, and excess returns are weak. However, it works very well in combination with other fundamental and market-based factors, significantly enhancing returns and adding consistency. In particular, it com-bines well with valuation factors, as we saw with the FCF per share score. The EPS score is based on 10 quarters of earnings and is a weighted average of two factors: the EPS growth trend and the linearity (volatility) of EPS. To calculate the EPS growth trend, we use a modified version of the RSI. In Chapter 9, I'll present the traditional version of the RSI, which is an oscillator used to measure stock price momentum. Here we use it to calculate earnings momentum.

The formula for the modified RSI used to calculate the EPS score is

$$RSI \text{ (shortened)} = U/D,$$

1991–2007	1st Quintile	2nd Quintile	3rd Quintile	4th Quintile	5th Quintile	Universe	S&P 500*
CAGR – Annual Rebalance	19.3%	12.9%	12.2%	15.5%	2.7%	12.1%	13.5%
Average Excess Return vs. Universe**	7.0%	1.2%	2.1%	1.5%	−4.8%	NA	1.4%
Value of $10,000 Invested (17 Years)	$199,539	$78,114	$71,123	$115,162	$15,662	$69,381	$86,051
% of 1-Year Periods Strategy Outperforms the Universe	70.8%	61.5%	66.2%	55.4%	33.8%	NA	56.9%
% Rolling 3-Year Periods Strategy Outperforms	82.5%	68.4%	75.4%	57.9%	17.5%	NA	68.4%
Maximum Gain	67.7%	48.5%	50.8%	75.3%	94.6%	59.2%	54.1%
Maximum Loss	−20.2%	−27.4%	−19.6%	−28.4%	−54.3%	−24.9%	−25.9%
Sharpe Ratio	0.85	0.69	0.75	0.57	0.13	0.53	0.73
Standard Deviation of Returns	0.18	0.14	0.14	0.18	0.30	0.16	0.14
Beta (vs. Universe)	0.93	0.77	0.67	0.93	1.61	NA	0.75
Alpha (vs. Universe)	0.08	0.04	0.06	0.02	−0.13	NA	0.05
Average Portfolio Size	56	56	56	56	57	NA	NA
Ave rage Number of Companies *Outperforming*	28	25	26	24	20	NA	NA
Average Number of Companies *Underperforming*	26	29	28	29	33	NA	NA
Median Portfolio Value – FCF PS Score	50	41	34	23	10	32	33
Median Portfolio Value – Return on Equity	45.6%	18.0%	13.0%	8.0%	−40.8%	11.5%	14.4%
Average Market Capitalization	$14,009	$7,356	$4,410	$3,373	$2,632	NA	NA

* Equal-weighted average of S&P 500 returns. ** Annual holding period run quarterly for a larger sample size; arithmetic average excess returns.
Source: Standard & Poor's Compustat Point in Time Database; Charter Oak Investment Systems, Inc., Venues® Data Engine

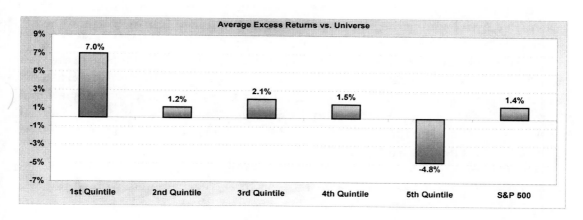

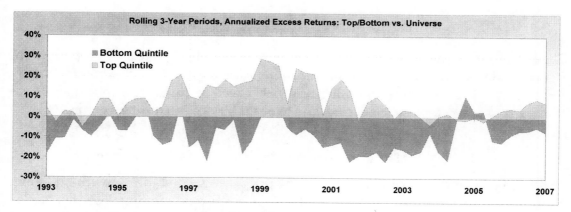

Figure 7.6 Free Cash Flow Per Share Score and Return on Equity

where U is the sum of the total EPS dollar increases for the quarters in which EPS rises, and D is the sum of the total EPS dollar decreases for the quarters in which EPS falls (expressed as a positive number).

An example of the calculation is as follows (for illustrative purposes, I'll use 5 quarters of EPS for the calculation instead of 10): Company A records sequential EPS over the past five quarters of $0.50, $0.70, $0.40, $0.90, and $0.80. The sum of the dollar increases for the "up" quarters is $0.20 + $0.50, or a total of $0.70. The sum of the dollar decreases for the "down" quarters is −$0.30 + −$0.10, or −$0.40, which expressed as a positive number is $0.40. So, our shortened RSI calculation is $0.70/$0.40, or 1.75. This means that the ratio of quarterly EPS increases versus quarterly EPS decreases over the period is 1.75 to 1.

EPS linearity is calculated as the standard deviation of the 10 quarterly EPS figures divided by the average value of those earnings. Dividing the standard deviation by the average EPS figure "normalizes" the standard deviation and prevents look-ahead bias that can occur in the calculation due to split adjustment. The EPS score for a company is calculated by weighting the EPS growth trend, or shortened RSI, by 80% and the EPS linearity by 20%. EPS scores in our database range from 0 to 95.

The top quintile outperforms by 1.9%, on average, and does so for 56% of one-year and 77% of rolling three-year periods (see Figure 7.7), giving it rather weak consistency. The strategy has a low maximum loss (23%) and a moderate standard deviation of returns (0.17), resulting in a Sharpe ratio of 0.58, below the Sharpe ratio for the S&P 500 (0.69) but above the ratio for the Universe (0.49). Average portfolio values for EPS score for the top quintile range from 58 to 79.

The bottom quintile is weak, underperforming by only 0.3%, on average, and doing so for 57% of one-year and 64% of rolling three-year periods. Average portfolio values for EPS score for the bottom quintile range from 10 to 15.

Earnings Per Share Score by Economic Sector

The EPS score strategy works poorly in our sector test, only significantly outperforming in the consumer discretionary and information technology sectors. The bottom quintile works a little better, underperforming reasonably well in the energy, consumer discretionary, consumer staples, health care, and telecom services sectors (see Figure 7.8).

Earnings Per Share Score and Free Cash Flow Plus Dividend to Price

The EPS score and FCF plus dividend to price strategy combines growth and value factors and also accrual accounting (EPS) and cash-based accounting (FCF) factors in a single strategy. We've already seen that growth and value work together well: growth

1988–2007	1st Quintile	2nd Quintile	3rd Quintile	4th Quintile	5th Quintile	Universe	S&P 500*
CAGR – Annual Rebalance	13.1%	11.8%	11.9%	11.3%	10.3%	11.2%	12.9%
Average Excess Return vs. Universe**	1.9%	0.7%	0.6%	−0.3%	−0.3%	NA	1.6%
Value of $10,000 Invested (20 Years)	$116,366	$92,511	$95,524	$85,418	$71,596	$83,161	$112,895
% of 1-Year Periods Strategy Outperforms the Universe	55.8%	53.2%	46.8%	39.0%	42.9%	NA	59.7%
% Rolling 3-Year Periods Strategy Outperforms	76.8%	65.2%	55.1%	40.6%	36.2%	NA	71.0%
Maximum Gain	55.2%	56.3%	53.2%	60.2%	69.7%	59.2%	54.1%
Maximum Loss	−22.7%	−20.2%	−22.8%	−25.7%	−38.0%	−24.9%	−25.9%
Sharpe Ratio	0.58	0.61	0.63	0.53	0.39	0.49	0.69
Standard Deviation of Returns	0.17	0.14	0.14	0.15	0.20	0.16	0.14
Beta (vs. Universe)	0.99	0.86	0.79	0.86	1.17	NA	0.78
Alpha (vs. Universe)	0.02	0.02	0.03	0.01	−0.02	NA	0.04
Average Portfolio Size	370	371	371	371	371	NA	NA
Average Number of Companies *Outperforming*	166	164	163	162	151	NA	NA
Average Number of Companies *Underperforming*	186	189	189	191	197	NA	NA
Median Portfolio Value – EPS Score	65	54	43	29	11	40	40
Average Market Capitalization	$4,463	$5,070	$5,254	$4,451	$2,706	NA	NA

* Equal-weighted average of S&P 500 returns. ** Annual holding period run quarterly for a larger sample size; arithmetic average excess returns.
Source: Standard & Poor's Compustat Point in Time Database; Charter Oak Investment Systems, Inc., Venues® Data Engine

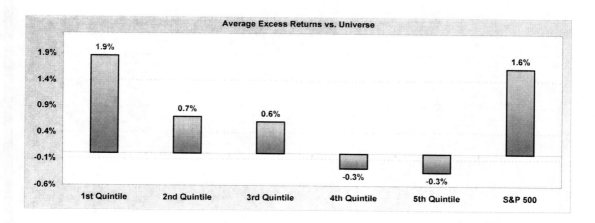

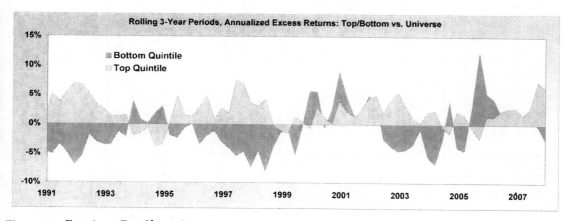

Figure 7.7 Earnings Per Share Score

Top Quintile

1988–2007	Energy	Materials	Industrials	Consumer Discretionary	Consumer Staples	Health Care	Financials	Information Technology	Telecom Services	Utilities	Universe	S&P 500*
CAGR – Quintile	14.2%	10.8%	10.1%	9.8%	12.5%	11.1%	15.1%	11.8%	6.3%	11.9%	11.2%	12.9%
CAGR – Sector	13.5%	10.2%	11.3%	8.8%	12.6%	12.3%	14.5%	7.5%	9.2%	13.0%	NA	NA
Excess Return vs. Sector	0.7%	0.5%	−1.2%	1.1%	−0.1%	−1.3%	0.6%	4.2%	−2.9%	−1.1%	NA	NA
Value of $10,000	$142,316	$77,076	$68,538	$64,955	$105,518	$81,462	$165,642	$92,533	$33,893	$94,335	$83,161	$112,895
% 1-Year Outperformance	55.0%	60.0%	55.0%	60.0%	40.0%	50.0%	55.0%	65.0%	70.0%	55.0%	NA	NA
% 3-Year Outperformance	61.1%	44.4%	38.9%	66.7%	33.3%	44.4%	72.2%	66.7%	55.6%	50.0%	NA	NA
Maximum Gain	66.8%	38.7%	37.6%	50.6%	73.1%	85.0%	55.3%	123.1%	58.2%	63.3%	44.0%	41.4%
Maximum Loss	−56.5%	−16.4%	−13.3%	−23.7%	−12.6%	−20.9%	−27.9%	−44.3%	−50.9%	−30.1%	−19.1%	−18.1%
Standard Deviation	0.29	0.16	0.15	0.19	0.19	0.25	0.22	0.34	0.31	0.20	0.16	0.14
Beta (vs. Sector)	1.10	0.96	1.00	0.99	0.99	0.95	0.99	0.86	0.42	1.20	NA	NA
Alpha (vs. Sector)	0.00	0.01	−0.01	0.01	0.00	0.00	0.01	0.05	0.05	−0.03	NA	NA
Portfolio Size	22	28	54	63	19	37	55	52	8	24	NA	NA

Bottom Quintile

1988–2007	Energy	Materials	Industrials	Consumer Discretionary	Consumer Staples	Health Care	Financials	Information Technology	Telecom Services	Utilities	Universe	S&P 500*
CAGR – Quintile	8.5%	11.0%	11.0%	6.9%	10.0%	9.0%	14.3%	9.5%	−1.9%	12.3%	11.2%	12.9%
CAGR – Sector	13.5%	10.2%	11.3%	8.8%	12.6%	12.3%	14.5%	7.5%	9.2%	13.0%	NA	NA
Excess Return vs. Sector	−5.0%	0.8%	−0.3%	−1.9%	−2.6%	−3.4%	−0.1%	2.0%	−11.1%	−0.7%	NA	NA
Value of $10,000	$51,339	$81,297	$80,620	$37,640	$67,417	$55,643	$145,455	$61,738	$6,785	$101,827	$83,161	$112,895
% 1-Year Outperformance	35.0%	60.0%	65.0%	45.0%	45.0%	35.0%	60.0%	65.0%	40.0%	55.0%	NA	NA
% 3-Year Outperformance	11.1%	50.0%	50.0%	27.8%	33.3%	38.9%	50.0%	66.7%	11.1%	33.3%	NA	NA
Maximum Gain	73.7%	57.3%	47.7%	47.0%	31.5%	94.9%	60.3%	110.2%	83.5%	60.5%	44.0%	41.4%
Maximum Loss	−43.8%	−27.9%	−22.1%	−39.0%	−21.2%	−27.2%	−30.0%	−56.3%	−70.6%	−25.7%	−19.1%	−18.1%
Standard Deviation	0.30	0.19	0.16	0.21	0.14	0.28	0.25	0.37	0.43	0.19	0.16	0.14
Beta (vs. Sector)	1.12	1.16	1.04	1.11	0.93	1.09	1.08	0.97	1.10	1.10	NA	NA
Alpha (vs. Sector)	−0.06	0.05	0.01	−0.04	0.04	−0.01	0.04	−0.07	−0.14	0.04	NA	NA
Portfolio Size	22	29	56	67	22	38	58	54	8	25	NA	NA

* Equal-weighted average of S&P 500 returns.
Source: Standard & Poor's Compustat Point in Time Database; Charter Oak Investment Systems, Inc., Venues® Data Engine

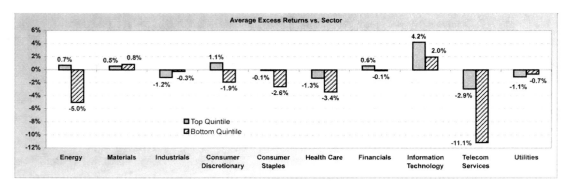

Figure 7.8 Earnings Per Share Score by Economic Sector

tells the investor that a company is capable of expanding its business and that its assets are productive, while value ensures that the investor doesn't overpay for those assets (or, in this case, cash profits). The top quintile of this strategy contains companies whose EPS are increasing and consistent[11] and whose cash flows are both positive and attractively priced. Companies in the top quintile may also be paying significant dividends. The bottom quintile, in contrast, contains companies with declining earnings ("negative growth") and cash outflows after accounting for capital expenditures.

The top quintile outperforms by 7%, on average, and does so for 79% of one-year and 92% of rolling three-year periods (see Figure 7.9). The top quintile significantly underperforms only in 1990, 1999–2000, and 2003–2004, making it very consistent. The maximum loss is a low 19% and the Sharpe ratio a moderately high 0.80. Average portfolio values range from 58 to 78 for the EPS score and from 14% to 27% for FCF plus dividend to price, indicating that these companies have relatively high EPS growth and linearity, have positive FCF and/or significant dividends, and are inexpensive relative to cash flow and dividends. With an average market capitalization of $5.0 billion, the strategy tends to consist of mid- to large-cap stocks.

The bottom quintile underperforms by 3.4%, on average, and does so for 75% of one-year and 80% of rolling three-year periods. Volatility is high, with a standard deviation of returns of 0.29 and a Beta of 1.5. Average portfolio values range from 8 to 12 for the EPS score and from −8% to −38% for FCF plus dividend to price. These are companies with declining and/or volatile earnings that have negative FCFs and generally pay no dividends.

Earnings Per Share Score and Operating Cash Flow Per Share to Current-Year EPS Estimate

This strategy combines the EPS score with a cash flow factor, specifically one that measures the quality of earnings by comparing cash-based EPS to income statement–based EPS. In addition, the strategy compares current cash flow per share to estimated EPS, so in the top quintile, it selects companies that have both growing earnings and significant cash flow even relative to future (estimated) earnings. The bottom quintile contains companies with declining earnings trends that have low or negative current cash flows relative to earnings. The strategy works very well.

The top quintile outperforms by an average of 6.1%, and does so for 78% of one-year and 91% of rolling three-year periods (see Figure 7.10). The top quintile significantly underperforms only in 1999–2000 and 2003. The maximum loss is a

---

[11] Because the growth portion of the EPS score simply looks at the growth trend, it is possible that a company with a high EPS score could still have negative earnings, as long as those earnings are rapidly becoming less negative.

1990–2007	1st Quintile	2nd Quintile	3rd Quintile	4th Quintile	5th Quintile	Universe	S&P 500*
CAGR – Annual Rebalance	17.2%	13.2%	13.4%	7.0%	6.5%	10.3%	12.0%
Average Excess Return vs. Universe**	7.0%	2.6%	1.5%	−1.9%	−3.4%	NA	1.5%
Value of $10,000 Invested (18 Years)	$173,608	$93,875	$95,648	$33,612	$30,881	$58,670	$76,297
% of 1-Year Periods Strategy Outperforms the Universe	79.2%	63.9%	52.8%	34.7%	25.0%	NA	56.9%
% Rolling 3-Year Periods Strategy Outperforms	92.2%	71.9%	59.4%	18.8%	20.3%	NA	68.8%
Maximum Gain	65.5%	50.4%	43.1%	56.2%	94.5%	59.2%	54.1%
Maximum Loss	−18.8%	−18.9%	−20.3%	−38.4%	−47.2%	−24.9%	−25.9%
Sharpe Ratio	0.80	0.75	0.69	0.29	0.15	0.46	0.64
Standard Deviation of Returns	0.18	0.14	0.13	0.20	0.29	0.17	0.14
Beta (vs. Universe)	0.85	0.71	0.67	1.10	1.52	NA	0.78
Alpha (vs. Universe)	0.09	0.06	0.05	−0.03	−0.10	NA	0.04
Average Portfolio Size	60	61	61	61	61	NA	NA
Average Number of Companies Outperforming	31	30	26	23	22	NA	NA
Average Number of Companies Underperforming	26	29	32	34	36	NA	NA
Median Portfolio Value – EPS Score	67	55	44	28	10	41	40
Median Portfolio Value – FCF + Dividend to Price	18.4%	6.6%	4.4%	1.1%	−18.8%	3.5%	5.3%
Average Market Capitalization	$4,968	$7,618	$9,212	$5,257	$1,472	NA	NA

* Equal-weighted average of S&P 500 returns. ** Annual holding period run quarterly for a larger sample size; arithmetic average excess returns
Source: Standard & Poor's Compustat Point in Time Database; Charter Oak Investment Systems, Inc., Venues® Data Engine

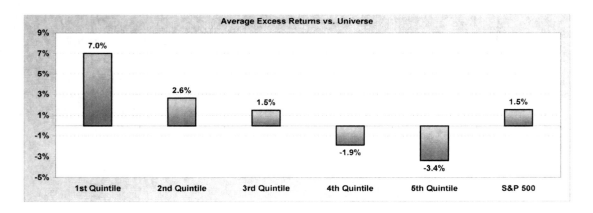

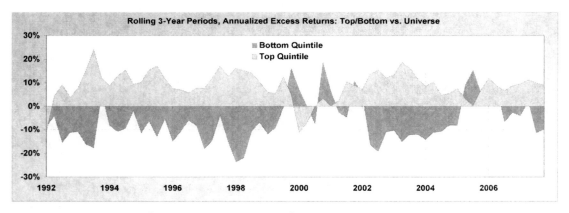

Figure 7.9 Earnings Per Share Score and Free Cash Flow Plus Dividend to Price

1990–2007	1st Quintile	2nd Quintile	3rd Quintile	4th Quintile	5th Quintile	Universe	S&P 500*
CAGR – Annual Rebalance	16.8%	14.3%	13.2%	10.1%	2.6%	10.3%	12.0%
Average Excess Return vs. Universe**	6.1%	2.1%	2.5%	−0.3%	−6.0%	NA	1.5%
Value of $10,000 Invested (18 Years)	$162,668	$110,690	$92,820	$56,910	$15,873	$58,670	$76,297
% of 1-Year Periods Strategy Outperforms the Universe	77.8%	65.3%	56.9%	40.3%	25.0%	NA	56.9%
% Rolling 3-Year Periods Strategy Outperforms	90.6%	71.9%	65.6%	32.8%	9.4%	NA	68.8%
Maximum Gain	62.9%	56.5%	48.7%	59.8%	91.1%	59.2%	54.1%
Maximum Loss	−22.5%	−20.2%	−21.1%	−24.7%	−52.3%	−24.9%	−25.9%
Sharpe Ratio	0.76	0.70	0.78	0.48	0.06	0.46	0.64
Standard Deviation of Returns	0.18	0.14	0.13	0.15	0.29	0.17	0.14
Beta (vs. Universe)	0.97	0.76	0.67	0.82	1.60	NA	0.78
Alpha (vs. Universe)	0.06	0.05	0.06	0.02	−0.13	NA	0.04
Average Portfolio Size	56	56	56	56	57	NA	NA
Average Number of Companies *Outperforming*	27	27	26	24	19	NA	NA
Average Number of Companies *Underperforming*	26	28	28	30	34	NA	NA
Median Portfolio Value – EPS Score	66	55	44	30	9	41	40
Median Portfolio Value – Oper. CF PS to Est. EPS	3.9	1.9	1.4	1.1	−2.1	3.3	2.6
Average Market Capitalization	$4,535	$5,885	$8,644	$6,732	$1,916	NA	NA

* Equal-weighted average of S&P 500 returns. ** Annual holding period run quarterly for a larger sample size; arithmetic average excess returns.
Source: Standard & Poor's Compustat Point in Time Database; Thomson Reuters I/B/E/S; Charter Oak Investment Systems, Inc., Venues® Data Engine

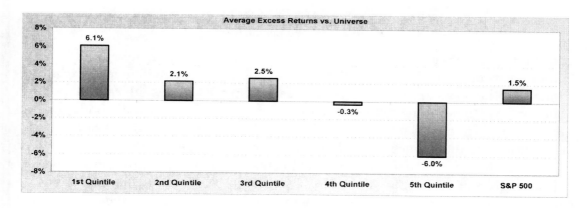

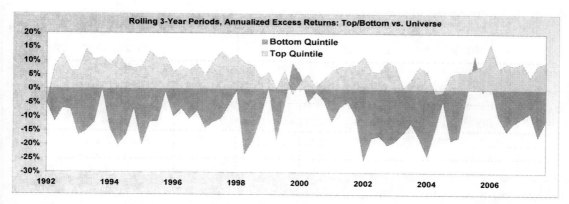

Figure 7.10 Earnings Per Share Score and Operating Cash Flow Per Share to Current-Year EPS Estimate

relatively low 23%, but the standard deviation of returns is a little higher than average (0.18 vs. 0.14 for the S&P 500), resulting in a moderate Sharpe ratio of 0.76. Average portfolio values for the top quintile range from 57 to 77 for the EPS score and 2.9× to 7.8× for operating cash flow per share to estimated EPS, indicating that these companies are growing earnings significantly and have strong cash flows relative to those earnings.

The bottom quintile underperforms by an average of 6%, and does so for 75% of one-year and 91% of rolling three-year periods. It significantly outperforms in 1991, 1993, 1999–2000, and 2003. The bottom quintile is quite volatile, with a maximum loss of 52%, a maximum gain of 91%, and a Beta of 1.6 versus the Universe. Average portfolio values range from 8 to 15 for the EPS score and from −0.5× to −5.0× for operating cash flow per share to estimated EPS, so these companies have both volatile and declining earnings and negative cash flows.

Earnings Per Share Score and One-Year Free Cash Flow Growth to One-Year Invested Capital Growth

This strategy combines an earnings growth factor with a profitability growth factor. Our calculation for one-year growth in FCF to one-year growth in invested capital is similar to the year-to-year change in cash return on invested capital (ROIC). Therefore, the top quintile of this strategy contains companies that are both growing EPS and increasing their profitability on a cash basis, while the bottom quintile contains companies that have both declining EPS trends and declining cash profitability. A company that is growing earnings isn't necessarily increasing profitability—often, earnings growth can come at the expense of profitability, for example, when a company lowers prices to boost unit volume growth. This strategy tells us that both things are going well (or poorly) for a company.

The top quintile outperforms by 5.3%, on average, and does so for 60% of one-year and 85% of rolling three-year periods (see Figure 7.11), making it moderately consistent. The top quintile significantly underperformed in 1992, 1999–2000, and 2003–2004. The maximum loss is a low 18%, and the Sharpe ratio is relatively high, at 0.81. Average portfolio values range from 57 to 77 for the EPS score and from about 80× to over 150× for the FCF growth to invested capital growth ratio.

The bottom quintile underperforms by 1.9%, on average, and does so for 53% of one-year and 62% of rolling three-year periods. The major flaw in this strategy is the lack of strength and consistency in the bottom quintile. This is partly because low profitability companies tend to outperform coming out of bear markets and at speculative tops in bull markets.

1991–2007	1st Quintile	2nd Quintile	3rd Quintile	4th Quintile	5th Quintile	Universe	S&P 500*
CAGR – Annual Rebalance	17.5%	15.3%	11.8%	9.9%	8.9%	12.1%	13.5%
Average Excess Return vs. Universe**	5.3%	2.1%	−0.2%	−1.1%	−1.9%	NA	1.4%
Value of $10,000 Invested (17 Years)	$154,313	$113,135	$66,795	$49,991	$42,592	$69,381	$86,051
% of 1-Year Periods Strategy Outperforms the Universe	60.3%	52.9%	45.6%	36.8%	47.1%	NA	55.9%
% Rolling 3-Year Periods Strategy Outperforms	85.0%	63.3%	38.3%	28.3%	38.3%	NA	68.3%
Maximum Gain	62.7%	53.8%	54.7%	66.8%	67.7%	59.2%	54.1%
Maximum Loss	−18.2%	−17.7%	−26.2%	−28.5%	−47.5%	−24.9%	−25.9%
Sharpe Ratio	0.81	0.69	0.57	0.40	0.33	0.54	0.73
Standard Deviation of Returns	0.18	0.16	0.15	0.19	0.21	0.16	0.14
Beta (vs. Universe)	0.85	0.84	0.83	1.05	1.09	NA	0.76
Alpha (vs. Universe)	0.07	0.04	0.02	−0.02	−0.03	NA	0.04
Average Portfolio Size	58	58	58	58	59	NA	NA
Average Number of Companies *Outperforming*	28	27	26	24	23	NA	NA
Average Number of Companies *Underperforming*	27	30	30	32	32	NA	NA
Median Portfolio Value – EPS Score	68	56	44	29	10	42	40
Median Portfolio Value – FCF 1Yr Gr.-to-Inv. Cap. 1Yr Gr.	119.1	6.0	0.5	−4.3	−136.5	85.8	44.2
Average Market Capitalization	$3,819	$7,240	$7,599	$4,530	$2,538	NA	NA

* Equal-weighted average of S&P 500 returns. ** Annual holding period run quarterly for a larger sample size; arithmetic average excess returns.
Source: Standard & Poor's Compustat Point in Time Database; Charter Oak Investment Systems, Inc., Venues® Data Engine

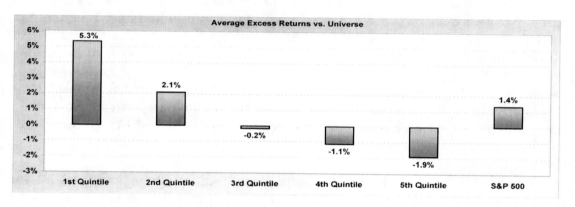

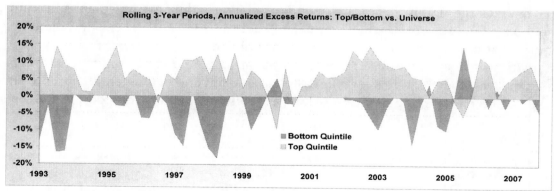

Figure 7.11 Earnings Per Share Score and One-Year Free Cash Flow Growth to One-Year Invested Capital Growth

TWO-YEAR AVERAGE CAPITAL EXPENDITURES PER SHARE GROWTH

Our research shows that cash spent on capital expenditures is a little bit like what occurred to Goldilocks: too little is no good, and too much is no good, but perhaps there is a level that is "just right." If one considers both the purpose of capital expenditures and the effects of capex on the income statement and balance sheet, the reasons become clear. Capital expenditures represent cash spent by businesses to purchase long-lived assets, such as land, buildings, factory and other heavy machinery, and office equipment:[12] capex represents a company's investments in productive capacity needed to create products or render services and may be used either to maintain existing productive capacity or to add new capacity. Therefore, companies that spend too little on capex risk becoming inefficient and losing market share to competitors as production equipment and facilities become obsolete or wear down.

However, capital expenditures are also a significant business expense. Capital spending for the companies in our backtest Universe has averaged 6.7% of total assets per year over the past 20 years, a very large sum when one considers that total assets per company over the same period averaged $7.6 billion. Capital expenditures not only represent an immediate cash outflow, they also result in periodic depreciation charges that appear as a (noncash) expense on the income statement.[13] Depreciation is a significant expense, averaging 4.4% of assets and about 10% of sales per year for the companies in our Universe over the past 20 years. So, companies that spend too much on capital expenditures are punished in two ways: their cash flows are immediately reduced, and their profit margins decline due to high depreciation charges.

In Chapters 4 and 6, we saw the capital expenditures to property, plant, and equipment strategy. The capex to PP&E strategy measures *capital intensity*: companies that record large amounts of capital spending relative to their existing plant and equipment base underperform, while companies that can sustain their existing plant and equipment base with small amounts of capital spending outperform, on average. Industries such as automobile manufacturing, airlines, and steel production are capital intensive—they require a lot of investment in plant and equipment in order to create products and provide services. As long as profits adequately compensate investors

---

[12] From an accounting point of view, capital assets also include mineral deposits, timber reserves, patents, trademarks, leaseholds, and investments in affiliated companies.

[13] Because capital assets are by definition capitalized (they are recorded in an asset account on the balance sheet and not immediately expensed), their costs must be written off over their useful lives through depreciation charges.

for capital contributed, capital intensive industries can reward shareholders. However, high capital intensity and low profitability, which often go together, and are a bad combination. So, going back to Goldilocks, capital spending is "too much" when investors are not sufficiently rewarded for capital committed.

In Chapter 6, we also saw the capital spending to invested capital strategy (in conjunction with cash ROIC). This strategy worked in opposition to the capex to PP&E strategy—companies that recorded the lowest levels of capex, relative to invested capital, underperformed, and companies that recorded the highest levels outperformed. This strategy suggests that a certain amount of money generated by the corporation must be reinvested in capex each year in order for a company to stay competitive. According to our Goldilocks analogy, companies that spend "too little" on capex fall behind.

This brings us back to the current strategy. Like capex to PP&E, the two-year growth in capital expenditures per share strategy tells us something about capital intensity. Companies with the highest levels of growth in capex may be becoming more capital intensive, particularly if their business isn't growing as fast as their capital expenditures. Companies with the lowest levels of capital expenditure growth may be becoming less capital intensive, particularly if sales and earnings are growing faster than capital expenditures. So, although we're including the capex growth strategy along with FCF growth and EPS growth, it's actually used in reverse: companies with the lowest growth in capex are put in the top quintile, while companies with the highest capex growth are put in the bottom. Capex growth doesn't make a strong single-factor strategy, but it works well in combination with valuation and cash flow strategies.

The top quintile of this strategy outperforms by an average of 2.1% and is moderately consistent, outperforming for 64% of one-year and 73% of rolling three-year periods (see Figure 7.12). It significantly underperforms in 1990–1991, 1995–1996, 2004–2005, and 2007. Average portfolio values for two-year average capex per share growth range from −16% to −45%, so these are companies that are cutting back on capex significantly. Notice that the second quintile also outperforms by 2% and is almost as consistent as the first quintile. The second quintile contains companies that, on average, slightly increase or slightly reduce capex each year (average portfolio values range from +8% to −18%).

The bottom quintile underperforms by 3.1%, on average, and does so for 73% of one-year and 84% of rolling three-year periods. It significantly outperforms in 1999–2000, 2003, 2006, and 2007. Companies in this quintile increase annual capex by an average of 140% to over 300% annually, so they represent extremes in capital spending growth.

1988–2007	1st Quintile	2nd Quintile	3rd Quintile	4th Quintile	5th Quintile	Universe	S&P 500*
CAGR – Annual Rebalance	13.3%	13.4%	12.0%	12.0%	7.6%	11.2%	12.9%
Average Excess Return vs. Universe**	2.1%	2.0%	0.8%	0.6%	−3.1%	NA	1.6%
Value of $10,000 Invested (20 Years)	$122,338	$122,916	$96,917	$95,987	$43,221	$83,160	$112,895
% of 1-Year Periods Strategy Outperforms the Universe	63.6%	61.0%	58.4%	49.4%	27.3%	NA	59.7%
% Rolling 3-Year Periods Strategy Outperforms	72.5%	75.4%	56.5%	53.6%	15.9%	NA	71.0%
Maximum Gain	72.3%	62.2%	51.5%	52.9%	59.4%	59.2%	54.1%
Maximum Loss	−23.9%	−26.1%	−25.8%	−24.4%	−35.4%	−24.9%	−25.9%
Sharpe Ratio	0.58	0.68	0.65	0.59	0.26	0.49	0.69
Standard Deviation of Returns	0.18	0.15	0.14	0.15	0.19	0.16	0.14
Beta (vs. Universe)	1.03	0.86	0.79	0.88	1.13	NA	0.78
Alpha (vs. Universe)	0.02	0.04	0.04	0.02	−0.05	NA	0.04
Average Portfolio Size	280	280	280	280	279	NA	NA
Average Number of Companies *Outperforming*	122	128	126	119	108	NA	NA
Average Number of Companies *Underperforming*	142	139	141	147	157	NA	NA
Median Portfolio Value – 2Yr Avg. Capex Growth	−27%	0%	16%	38%	187%	45%	17%
Average Market Capitalization	$3,292	$7,041	$6,258	$4,792	$2,708	NA	NA

* Equal-weighted average of S&P 500 returns.** Annual holding period run quarterly for a larger sample size; arithmetic average excess returns.
Source: Standard & Poor's Compustat Point in Time Database; Charter Oak Investment Systems, Inc., Venues® Data Engine

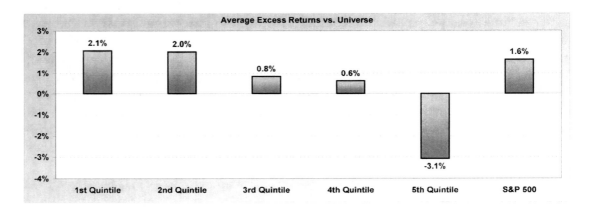

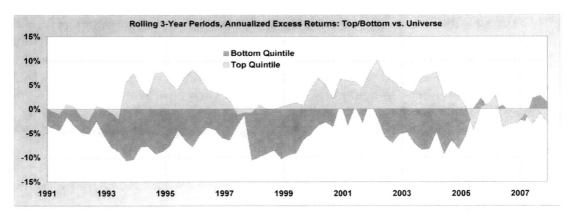

Figure 7.12 Two-Year Average Capital Expenditures Per Share Growth

Two-Year Average Capex Per Share Growth by Economic Sector

The strategy works well for the industrials, consumer discretionary, consumer staples, and information technology sectors, particularly in the top quintile. Decreases in capital spending in these sectors, which, with the possible exception of technology, represent mature industries, may indicate that that the companies showing the decreases are becoming less capital intensive—a good thing in any industry, but particularly good in a mature industry, where growth prospects are low. Telecom services companies with the highest growth in capex show strong underperformance, of about 7%. Telecom services is a capital-intensive sector to begin with, and often, as in 1998–1999, companies make the largest capital investments just prior to a peak in the business cycle (see Figure 7.13).

Two-Year Average Capex Per Share Growth and Free Cash Flow to Price

This strategy considers both capital intensity (capex per share growth) and valuation, and works very well. One reason may be that the two factors used in this strategy share a common element: because capital expenditures usually require large cash outlays, growth or decline in capex often has a significant effect on the level of FCF (which you'll recall is calculated as cash flow from operating activities minus capital expenditures). So, in the top quintile this strategy contains companies that are lowering capital expenditures, thus aiding FCF generation, and that are selling at low multiples of that cash flow. The bottom quintile contains companies that are raising capital expenditures, resulting in significant cash outflows, and are thus expensive on an FCF-to-price basis.

The top quintile outperforms by 8%, on average, and does so for 79% of one-year and 87% of rolling three-year periods (see Figure 7.14). The top quintile significantly underperforms only in two periods: 1999–2000 and 2007. Average portfolio values range from −21% to −42% for two-year average capex per share growth and from 14% to 28% for FCF to price, so top quintile companies are making large reductions in capital expenditures and selling at low valuations relative to cash flow after capex. The top quintile's only weakness is slight volatility, with a standard deviation of returns of 0.20 vs. 0.15 for the S&P 500, resulting in a moderately Sharpe ratio of 0.79 (versus 0.64 for the S&P 500).

The bottom quintile underperforms by an average of 6.6%, and does so for 80% of one-year and 89% of rolling three-year periods. Average portfolio values range from 140% to well over 300% for capex per share growth and from −10% to −37% for FCF to price (indicating large cash outflows). Overall quintile returns are very linear, the sign of a strong strategy, with the second quintile outperforming by 3.5%, on average, and the fourth quintile underperforming by 2.6%.

Top Quintile

1988–2007	Energy	Materials	Industrials	Consumer Discretionary	Consumer Staples	Health Care	Financials	Information Technology	Telecom Services	Utilities	Universe	S&P 500*
CAGR – Quintile	12.1%	9.3%	13.7%	11.8%	17.3%	13.0%	14.6%	13.4%	12.2%	12.5%	11.2%	12.9%
CAGR – Sector	13.5%	10.2%	11.3%	8.7%	12.6%	12.3%	14.5%	7.5%	9.2%	13.0%	NA	NA
Excess Return vs. Sector	−1.5%	−0.9%	2.5%	3.1%	4.8%	0.6%	0.1%	5.9%	3.0%	−0.4%	NA	NA
Value of $10,000	$97,816	$59,712	$130,849	$92,578	$245,239	$114,366	$152,055	$122,987	$100,337	$106,139	$83,160	$112,895
% 1-Year Outperformance	45.0%	45.0%	80.0%	70.0%	75.0%	55.0%	50.0%	60.0%	45.0%	55.0%	NA	NA
% 3-Year Outperformance	44.4%	44.4%	94.4%	94.4%	100.0%	44.4%	50.0%	72.2%	66.7%	61.1%	NA	NA
Maximum Gain	68.7%	52.2%	48.1%	59.9%	56.7%	64.1%	60.8%	103.0%	80.4%	138.5%	44.0%	41.4%
Maximum Loss	−26.7%	−23.0%	−16.0%	−27.6%	−12.8%	−28.9%	−21.9%	−30.0%	−40.2%	−45.0%	−19.1%	−18.1%
Standard Deviation	0.27	0.18	0.16	0.21	0.18	0.22	0.22	0.32	0.33	0.37	0.16	0.14
Beta (vs. Sector)	0.99	1.09	1.01	1.11	1.18	0.78	0.90	0.79	0.66	1.35	NA	NA
Alpha (vs. Sector)	−0.01	−0.01	0.02	0.02	0.03	0.04	0.02	0.07	0.07	−0.01	NA	NA
Portfolio Size	19	28	53	61	20	33	19	45	7	3	NA	NA

Bottom Quintile

1988–2007	Energy	Materials	Industrials	Consumer Discretionary	Consumer Staples	Health Care	Financials	Information Technology	Telecom Services	Utilities	Universe	S&P 500*
CAGR – Quintile	12.2%	8.0%	9.0%	7.7%	11.1%	8.5%	12.4%	5.4%	1.9%	10.3%	11.2%	12.9%
CAGR – Sector	13.5%	10.2%	11.3%	8.7%	12.6%	12.3%	14.5%	7.5%	9.2%	13.0%	NA	NA
Excess Return vs. Sector	−1.3%	−2.2%	−2.2%	−1.0%	−1.5%	−3.8%	−2.1%	−2.1%	−7.3%	−2.7%	NA	NA
Value of $10,000	$99,911	$46,938	$56,230	$44,296	$81,958	$51,305	$104,261	$28,523	$14,688	$70,979	$83,160	$112,895
% 1-Year Outperformance	45.0%	55.0%	35.0%	45.0%	50.0%	35.0%	50.0%	40.0%	25.0%	60.0%	NA	NA
% 3-Year Outperformance	38.9%	33.3%	16.7%	38.9%	50.0%	22.2%	33.3%	38.9%	11.1%	55.6%	NA	NA
Maximum Gain	82.1%	42.7%	38.7%	47.3%	30.8%	79.4%	62.3%	90.9%	308.7%	143.3%	44.0%	41.4%
Maximum Loss	−47.3%	−22.2%	−15.5%	−22.6%	−15.5%	−46.1%	−23.7%	−49.1%	−72.1%	−80.6%	−19.1%	−18.1%
Standard Deviation	0.33	0.18	0.15	0.19	0.12	0.29	0.21	0.31	0.74	0.47	0.16	0.14
Beta (vs. Sector)	1.19	1.11	0.97	1.01	0.69	1.08	0.84	0.80	1.78	2.22	NA	NA
Alpha (vs. Sector)	−0.03	0.02	0.00	−0.03	0.07	−0.03	0.04	−0.09	−0.11	0.09	NA	NA
Portfolio Size	18	27	51	57	18	31	16	43	6	2	NA	NA

* Equal-weighted average of S&P 500 returns.
Source: Standard & Poor's Compustat Point in Time Database; Charter Oak Investment Systems, Inc., Venues® Data Engine

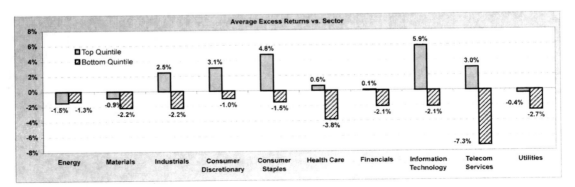

Figure 7.13 Two-Year Average Capex Per Share Growth by Economic Sector

1990–2007	1st Quintile	2nd Quintile	3rd Quintile	4th Quintile	5th Quintile	Universe	S&P 500*
CAGR – Annual Rebalance	18.5%	14.6%	10.7%	6.4%	3.6%	10.3%	12.0%
Average Excess Return vs. Universe**	8.0%	3.5%	0.6%	−2.6%	−6.6%	NA	1.5%
Value of $10,000 Invested (18 Years)	$213,425	$115,412	$62,526	$30,597	$18,890	$58,669	$76,297
% of 1-Year Periods Strategy Outperforms the Universe	78.9%	62.0%	57.7%	29.6%	19.7%	NA	56.3%
% Rolling 3-Year Periods Strategy Outperforms	87.3%	73.0%	50.8%	17.5%	11.1%	NA	68.3%
Maximum Gain	79.4%	54.1%	39.2%	49.1%	80.8%	59.2%	54.1%
Maximum Loss	−27.3%	−19.9%	−21.9%	−27.4%	−43.8%	−24.9%	−25.9%
Sharpe Ratio	0.79	0.81	0.66	0.29	0.05	0.46	0.64
Standard Deviation of Returns	0.20	0.14	0.13	0.18	0.25	0.17	0.15
Beta (vs. Universe)	0.90	0.69	0.67	0.94	1.35	NA	0.78
Alpha (vs. Universe)	0.09	0.07	0.05	−0.02	−0.11	NA	0.04
Average Portfolio Size	54	55	55	55	55	NA	NA
Average Number of Companies *Outperforming*	27	27	25	22	19	NA	NA
Average Number of Companies *Underperforming*	25	26	28	31	33	NA	NA
Median Portfolio Value – 2Yr Avg. Capex Growth	−28%	0%	17%	37%	201%	42%	17%
Median Portfolio Value – FCF to Price	18.9%	6.3%	3.2%	−1.0%	−16.7%	2.1%	3.3%
Average Market Capitalization	$2,844	$7,775	$9,918	$5,994	$1,491	NA	NA

* Equal-weighted average of S&P 500 returns. ** Annual holding period run quarterly for a larger sample size; arithmetic average excess returns.
Source: Standard & Poor's Compustat Point in Time Database; Charter Oak Investment Systems, Inc., Venues® Data Engine

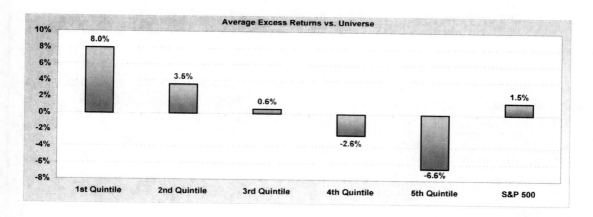

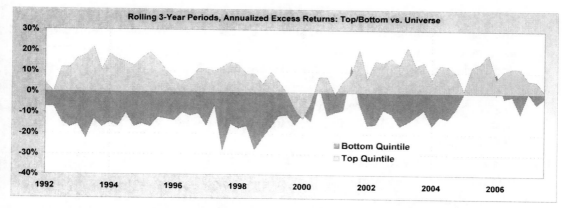

Figure 7.14 Two-Year Average Capex Per Share Growth and Free Cash Flow to Price

Two-Year Average Capex Per Share Growth and Operating Cash Flow to Invested Capital

This strategy examines both capital intensity and cash profitability (cash ROE). We use operating cash flow instead of FCF to invested capital to avoid choosing companies that are increasing profitability simply by reducing capital expenditures. Companies with high cash profitability have the option of increasing or decreasing capital expenditures as business needs and potential returns on new projects dictate. In contrast, companies with negative operating cash flows that are showing large increases in capital expenditures are both further hurting profitability (through increases in capex) and taking on significant liquidity risks (e.g., the risk of not being able to satisfy creditors).

The top quintile outperforms by 6.7%, on average, and does so for 78% of one-year and 89% of rolling three-year periods (see Figure 7.15). It significantly underperforms primarily in 2003–2004. The maximum loss is a low 21%, and the Sharpe ratio is a moderately high 0.80. Average portfolio values range from −19% to −40% for two-year average capex per share growth and 30% to 42% for operating cash flow to invested capital. So, the top quintile contains companies with very high levels of cash profitability that are able to significantly cut back on capital spending.

The bottom quintile underperforms by 9.5%, on average, and does so for 81% of one-year and 92% of rolling three-year periods. The strategy is very consistent, showing significant outperformance only in 1990, 1999–2000, and 2003–2004. Average portfolio values range from 150% to well over 200% for two-year average capex growth and from −4% to −26% for operating cash flow to invested capital. So, companies in the bottom quintile have both negative cash flows and rapidly expanding capital spending needs—a bad combination.

SUMMARY

- Growth investing is an approach that isn't easily accessible to quantitative analysis. True long-term growth stocks represent the few rather than the many, and the combination of high growth rates that tend to revert toward the mean and high associated valuation multiples is a volatile one that often leads to disappointment.

- However, this chapter presented a variety of approaches to growth investing that *can be* successful quantitatively, particularly when growth is combined with valuation.

- The free cash flow per share score is calculated based on a company's rank on two factors: a growth index and a measure of growth linearity.

- The FCF per share score generates moderately high excess returns for a single-factor strategy and is relatively consistent. The top quintile slightly

1990–2007	1st Quintile	2nd Quintile	3rd Quintile	4th Quintile	5th Quintile	Universe	S&P 500*
CAGR – Annual Rebalance	17.2%	12.9%	14.1%	12.7%	0.1%	10.3%	12.0%
Average Excess Return vs. Universe**	6.7%	3.0%	1.8%	1.3%	−9.5%	NA	1.5%
Value of $10,000 Invested (18 Years)	$172,792	$88,276	$107,801	$85,735	$10,233	$58,669	$76,297
% of 1-Year Periods Strategy Outperforms the Universe	77.8%	59.7%	52.8%	48.6%	19.4%	NA	56.9%
% Rolling 3-Year Periods Strategy Outperforms	89.1%	75.0%	64.1%	54.7%	7.8%	NA	68.8%
Maximum Gain	65.2%	55.2%	47.4%	52.2%	86.2%	59.2%	54.1%
Maximum Loss	−21.2%	−26.1%	−25.2%	−26.1%	−62.0%	−24.9%	−25.9%
Sharpe Ratio	0.80	0.74	0.68	0.59	−0.06	0.46	0.64
Standard Deviation of Returns	0.18	0.15	0.14	0.15	0.30	0.17	0.14
Beta (vs. Universe)	0.93	0.76	0.74	0.82	1.57	NA	0.78
Alpha (vs. Universe)	0.08	0.06	0.05	0.04	−0.16	NA	0.04
Average Portfolio Size	54	55	55	55	55	NA	NA
Average Number of Companies *Outperforming*	26	26	26	24	18	NA	NA
Average Number of Companies *Underperforming*	26	27	26	28	35	NA	NA
Median Portfolio Value – 2Yr Avg. Capex Growth	−25%	0%	16%	37%	212%	42%	17%
Median Portfolio Value – Oper. CF to Inv. Cap.	38.0%	21.9%	16.4%	10.3%	−13.8%	14.7%	19.2%
Average Market Capitalization	$5,301	$8,170	$4,914	$2,934	$1,761	NA	NA

* Equal-weighted average of S&P 500 returns. ** Annual holding period run quarterly for a larger sample size; arithmetic average excess returns.
Source: Standard & Poor's Compustat Point in Time Database; Charter Oak Investment Systems, Inc., Venues® Data Engine

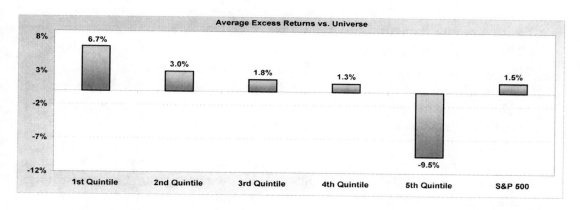

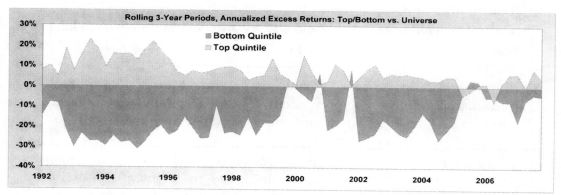

Figure 7.15 Two-Year Average Capex Per Share Growth and Operating Cash Flow to Invested Capital

outperformed the market each year from mid–2004 through 2006, unlike other FCF-based strategies.

- A simpler although slightly less effective growth measure can be obtained by using one-year FCF per share growth, alone.
- The FCF per share score and enterprise value to EBITDA strategy combines a cash flow statement-based growth metric with an income statement-based valuation metric, resulting in excess returns that are strong, linear, and consistent. The top quintile of this strategy has the highest Sharpe ratio (1.03) for a two-factor strategy in this book.
- Valuation and growth are two *basics* that work very well together: the valuation factor keeps the investor from overpaying for growth and the growth factor prevents the selection of low valuation stocks that are destined to stay low valuation.
- The EPS score is an earnings-based growth factor that actually works. Although it is weak as a single-factor strategy, it works well in combination with other fundamental and market-based factors.
- The EPS score is based on 10 quarters of earnings and is a weighted average of two factors: the EPS growth trend and EPS linearity.
- The EPS score and FCF plus dividend to price strategy combines growth and value factors and also accrual accounting (EPS) and cash-based accounting (FCF) factors in a single strategy, resulting in strong and consistent excess returns.
- The EPS score and operating cash flow per share to current-year EPS estimate strategy combines EPS growth with a cash flow factor that measures earnings quality by comparing cash-based EPS to income statement-based EPS. Excess returns are strong and consistent.
- Capital expenditures (capex) represent a company's investments in long-lived assets, such as factories and equipment, needed to create products and provide services.
- Capital spending becomes "too much" when investors are not sufficiently rewarded, through strong profitability, for capital committed. Capital spending is "too little" when companies become unable to maintain production efficiency or stay competitive.
- The top quintile of the two-year average capex per share growth strategy contains companies that may be becoming less capital intensive—they are seeing declines in capital expenditures. The bottom quintile contains

companies that may be becoming more capital intensive—they are seeing rising growth in capex.

- The two-year average capex per share growth and FCF to price strategy considers both capital intensity (capex per share growth) and valuation. Excess returns are strong, linear, and very consistent.

CHAPTER 8

Capital Allocation

As I see it, the tendency in this country is to overreach for new business, and usually at the wrong time. . . . [T]o expand during a boom is fatal unless the anticipated profits after-tax will amortize the added capacity in the very briefest time. . . .

Gerald M. Loeb, *The Battle for Investment Survival*

Capital allocation involves a corporation's use of capital resources, primarily cash. Sources of cash (cash inflows) include income from business operations, asset and investment sales, issuance of stock, and issuance of debt. Uses of cash (cash outflows) include the operating expenses of the business, investments in the business (through capital expenditures, research and development,[1] etc.), business acquisitions, investments in businesses or securities, cash dividends, repayments of debt, and repurchases of shares. Business managers face capital allocation decisions every day: Do they invest in this project or that one? Should plant capacity be added or retired? Should a new office be opened in a new location? Should debt be refinanced? The list goes on. Many corporate executives got where they are because they were star sales or marketing people, had experience running a successful division, or worked their way up through accounting and finance. However, sales, marketing, management, or even finance and accounting experience doesn't necessarily translate into experience in making sound

---

[1] According to U.S. generally accepted accounting principles, research and development (R&D) costs are treated as expenses and are not typically capitalized. However, R&D funds, properly used, represent an investment in a business that can be expected to pay off, in terms of increased revenues and profits, at a later date. Hence, I categorize R&D costs with capital expenditures, and not as operating expenses.

capital allocation decisions. And as we'll see in this chapter, the way corporations allocate their capital can have a strong effect on their stock market valuations.

A corporation's level of profitability significantly affects its capital allocation choices. Companies that generate low levels of profitability must retain cash to fund business needs and to provide a margin of safety in the event of a business downturn. Companies that generate cash well in excess of business needs, however, must decide how best to deploy that cash. Corporate executives with access to excess cash (and even some without it) often exhibit a tendency toward entering new businesses lines in which the company has little experience or competitive advantage, making large acquisitions, and so on. Generally speaking, the larger the business, the larger upper management's expected paycheck and the greater their personal influence and prestige.

Capital expenditures necessary to support existing operations, so-called maintenance capex, must be made. Businesses that fall short of cash and become unable to maintain and replace existing capital assets will more than likely fall behind competitors—and watch their businesses erode. On the other hand, businesses that have excess cash can increase capital investments and R&D investments in profitable projects and thereby increase potential future revenues and profits. From a quantitative point of view, capital expenditures are tricky. While moderately high funding of capital investments is good (as you'll see in this chapter), companies that increase capital spending too quickly underperform (Chapter 7), and in particular companies that show sharp increases in capital intensity underperform (Chapter 10).

Companies with excess cash can also pay or increase dividends. The 2003 Jobs and Growth Tax Relief Act lowered the tax rate on qualified dividends for most taxpayers to 15%. The number of companies in our Universe paying a dividend rose from 768 in 2002 to 1,046 in 2006, a 36% increase in just four years. However, the average payout ratio (dividends divided by pretax income) remained about flat during that period, at 16% to 18%, down from payout ratios of 23% to 25% in the late 1980s. At the same time, the number of companies in our Universe repurchasing stock (net of stock issuance) increased from 568 in 2002 to over 900 in 2006, a 58% increase, and the value of those repurchases increased from 3.5% of invested capital in 2002 to almost 7% in 2006.

There are a few likely reasons that corporate managers have favored share repurchases over dividends in recent years. One is simply that dividend yields have fallen so low, in general,[2] that many investors have come to see a healthy dividend as a "plus" rather than a "must have." Another reason is that, although companies do not have a legal obligation to pay dividends, many companies view dividends, once instituted, as an unspoken obligation to shareholders. Companies that cut their dividends often see

---

[2] The average dividend yield for our Universe fell from near 3% in the late 1980s to just 1% in 2003.

significant declines in share prices. Stock repurchases, on the other hand, can be short term in nature and discretionary as to timing or even as to whether a repurchase plan is completed at all.

Finally, and perhaps most importantly, a large part of executive compensation is paid in stock options, and the higher a company's stock price, the greater the value of existing stock options. Since dividends represent a divestiture of corporate profits—the company pays out part of its net worth to shareholders—large dividend payments usually result in declines in stock prices. Share repurchases, in contrast, can be used as a tool to bolster stock prices. The math works this way: if a company repurchases 10% of its outstanding shares, annual earnings per share automatically rise by 11%. If the company's price to earnings (P/E) multiple remains the same, this means that the stock price also goes up by 11%, something that is very good for large holders of stock options.

Of course, like dividends, share repurchases represent a divestiture of retained earnings, so perhaps in our repurchase example the P/E multiple would go down, and the market value of the company would decrease. Overall, however, our research shows that it doesn't work out this way. Companies that raise their annual dividends show very low or no excess stock market returns. However (as you'll see), companies that repurchase large amounts of shares, and in particular those that actually reduce shares outstanding, outperform significantly, while companies that issue large amounts of shares significantly underperform.

Our research also shows that the valuation at which shares are repurchased (or issued) matters. This makes sense, since a share repurchase by a company is essentially an investment in its own shares. If a firm buys its own shares at a discount to their fair value, it has both increased the ownership stake of existing shareholders and done so at an attractive price. If, however, a corporation repurchases its shares significantly above their intrinsic value, it is using shareholder funds for a poor investment, and in the end, shareholders suffer as a result. Unfortunately, the calculation of intrinsic value often plays little role in a company's share repurchase plan. As one experienced investor I know put it: "CEO's and CFO's never think the price is too dear. Then when tough times hit and the stocks get cheaper, they quit the buybacks!"

Another potential use of excess cash is to reduce debt. Debt reduction, like capital expenditures, is a tricky subject from a quantitative point of view. The reason is that, over the short term (our 12-month portfolio holding period), the stock market rewards companies that take risks and punishes those that are too conservative. Thus, over the short term, companies with high cash balances and low debt-to-capital ratios underperform, and those with little cash and high debt outperform. Companies in the latter group provide greater financial leverage, enabling equity investors to better profit from periods of strong economic growth. Over the long term, companies with low debt and adequate cash balances have a much better chance of surviving the ups and downs of the economy than their more highly leveraged and less liquid peers. However, stock market logic often changes with the length of one's investment horizon.

In this chapter, we ignore a company's debt level and look simply at the effects of debt reduction or increase. By reducing debt, companies not only reduce risk but also decrease interest payments, thus increasing earnings available to equity holders. The strategy works well when combined with other strategies, particularly with a share repurchase strategy (and adds conservatism, in my view). Companies that add large amounts of debt, significantly underperform and should be avoided.

Finally, we'll take a look at business acquisitions, specifically cash acquisitions as a percentage of invested capital. Companies that make large acquisitions tend to underperform, whereas those that avoid acquisitions outperform. A number of highly successful U.S. corporations have grown significantly through acquisition. United Technologies, for example, has built a world-class aerospace-industrial business by acquiring companies such as Otis, Carrier, Sundstrand Corp., Chubb plc, Kidde, and Rocketdyne. However, many other companies have made ill-informed acquisitions, at too high a price, and/or have found integrating the acquired companies to be more difficult than planned. As a result, acquisitions in general don't work, particularly over the 12-month holding period we use to tabulate results.

Although we will reference capital allocation activities in this chapter that are "shareholder friendly"—including capital expenditures and other types of investment (when undertaken wisely), dividend payments, share repurchases, and debt reduction— the investor must always keep in mind that he or she is not the only constituent that a company must satisfy. In particular, a company must satisfy the requirements of its debt holders and other corporate creditors, which are specified legally in bond indentures and other credit agreements. Dividend policy, share repurchases, and other cash payouts may all be restricted by credit agreements. As mentioned above, the needs and desires of management sometimes come first, as do the basic cash needs of the company. However, to the extent that a company is able to undertake capital allocation decisions that are friendly to shareholders, in preference to those that are friendly to debt holders, common stock investors can expect to see improved returns on their investments.

One additional footnote: most experienced investors understand that cash generation and capital allocation vary markedly from stage to stage of the corporate life cycle. Mature companies with dominant market share positions in slow-growing industries often generate a lot of excess cash and use much of that cash to reduce debt, repurchase shares, and pay dividends. Rapid-growth companies in expanding markets with prospects for strong profitability would be foolish to return large amounts of cash to shareholders. Most of the cash such companies generate is needed to fund business development and future growth. If such companies become highly profitable, shareholders are well served by reinvestment of cash, since returns generated on cash reinvested in the business are likely to be far higher than returns available in, say, corporate bonds should the company return cash to shareholders. To a certain extent, quantitative tests can take into account both a company's growth profile and its capital allocation decisions, for example, by combining growth or the amount of cash flow generation with share repurchase and debt reduction levels. However, the investor in individual securities would do well to view capital allocation decisions in light of a corporation's profitable growth opportunities: the greater the opportunities for profitable growth, the higher the optimal reinvestment rate, while the lower the profitable growth opportunities, the higher the expected payout rate.

SHARE REPURCHASES AND SHARE REDUCTION

Net Share Repurchase to Invested Capital

The net share repurchase strategy looks at two figures from the financing section of a company's cash flow statement: purchase of common and preferred stock[3] and issuance of common and preferred stock. (Note that companies sometimes provide only stock purchases net of stock sales, or vice versa, rather than listing each item separately.) Net cash spent on share repurchases (or received from share issuance) is then compared to total invested capital.[4] Companies with the highest levels of net share repurchases are included in the top quintile; those with the highest levels of share issuance are included in the bottom quintile. As mentioned above, mature companies that have dominant market shares in slow-growing industries often have excess cash available for uses such as share repurchase, while fast-growing smaller companies in less mature industries need excess cash to fund growth. This is reflected in the average market capitalization by quintile for this strategy: companies in the top quintile have an average market capitalization of $7.7 billion (a large-cap strategy), while companies in the bottom three quintiles have average market capitalizations of between $2.3 and $3.4 billion (small- to mid-cap strategies).

The top quintile outperforms by 2.5%, on average, and does so for 68% of one-year and 73% of rolling three-year periods (see Figure 8.1). It significantly underperforms in four periods: 1993, 1999–2000, 2003–2004, and 2005–2006. However, excess returns are generally low. Volatility is also low, with a Beta of 0.8 and a standard deviation of returns of 0.14 versus 0.16 for the Universe. The result is a Sharpe ratio of 0.78, moderately high

---

[3] Sometimes called "purchases of treasury stock."

[4] Book value of common equity plus long-term debt plus preferred stock and minority interest.

1988–2007	1st Quintile	2nd Quintile	3rd Quintile	4th Quintile	5th Quintile	Universe	S&P 500*
CAGR – Annual Rebalance	14.2%	13.2%	11.8%	10.8%	4.6%	11.2%	12.9%
Average Excess Return vs. Universe**	2.5%	1.7%	0.6%	−0.5%	−4.9%	NA	1.6%
Value of $10,000 Invested (20 Years)	$142,568	$118,765	$93,777	$77,727	$24,637	$83,161	$112,895
% of 1-Year Periods Strategy Outperforms the Universe	67.5%	49.4%	51.9%	49.4%	27.3%	NA	59.7%
% Rolling 3-Year Periods Strategy Outperforms	72.5%	65.2%	60.9%	42.0%	10.1%	NA	71.0%
Maximum Gain	53.4%	59.7%	62.7%	61.0%	91.3%	59.2%	54.1%
Maximum Loss	−20.9%	−24.5%	−25.2%	−45.3%	−63.5%	−24.9%	−25.9%
Sharpe Ratio	0.78	0.68	0.56	0.39	0.12	0.49	0.69
Standard Deviation of Returns	0.14	0.14	0.16	0.20	0.27	0.16	0.14
Beta (vs. Universe)	0.76	0.79	0.89	1.16	1.41	NA	0.78
Alpha (vs. Universe)	0.06	0.04	0.02	−0.02	−0.10	NA	0.04
Average Portfolio Size	350	354	345	349	349	NA	NA
Average Number of Companies *Outperforming*	162	160	152	145	126	NA	NA
Average Number of Companies *Underperforming*	174	176	174	186	205	NA	NA
Median Portfolio Value – Share Repurch. to Inv. Cap.	11.3%	0.6%	−0.2%	−1.7%	−29.7%	−4.4%	2.8%
Average Market Capitalization	$7,702	$5,647	$3,072	$3,414	$2,250	NA	NA

* Equal-weighted average of S&P 500 returns. ** Annual holding period run quarterly for a larger sample size; arithmetic average excess returns.
Source: Standard & Poor's Compustat Point in Time Database, Charter Oak Investment Systems, Inc., Venues® Data Engine

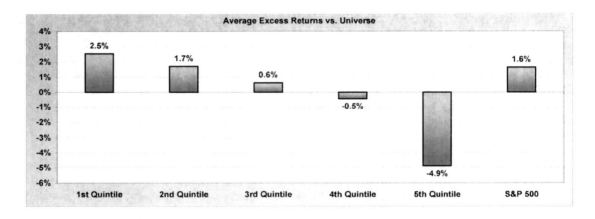

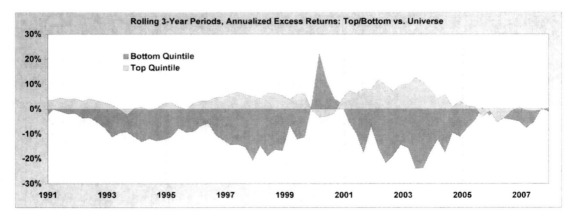

Figure 8.1 Net Share Repurchase to Invested Capital

for a single-factor strategy. Average portfolio values for net share repurchases to invested capital range from 5% to over 20%.

Performance for the bottom quintile is much stronger. It underperforms by an average of 4.9% and does so for 73% of one-year and 90% of rolling three-year periods. It significantly outperforms in 1990–1991, 1999–2000, 2003, and 2007. Average portfolio values for net share repurchase to invested capital range from −15% to less than −50%, so companies in this quintile are issuing large amounts of shares.

One-Year Reduction in Shares Outstanding

The one-year reduction in shares outstanding strategy works a bit better than the net share repurchase-to-invested capital strategy, and it is the one we'll use more frequently in this chapter. This strategy simply compares the number of shares outstanding for a company for the most recent quarter with the number of shares outstanding four quarters ago. Common shares outstanding can be found on the balance sheet or in the notes to the shareholders' equity section of the financial statements.

The reduction in shares outstanding strategy is stronger than the net share repurchase strategy because it is possible for a company to spend a lot of cash on share repurchases but still not reduce shares outstanding. This results from the fact that companies often issue large amounts of shares when employees exercise stock options. Because stock option exercises take place at a price below the current market price, and because shares are repurchased at the current market price, cash received from stock options often results in a larger amount of shares issued than the amount of shares that can be repurchased with the same amount of cash. For example, let's say that a company issues one million shares for stock options with an average exercise price of $20, receiving $20 million in cash. If the average market price of the stock during the year was $40, and if repurchases were made at this average price, then the company would have to spend $40 million just to keep its share count even. This would result in a net cash repurchase value for the year of $20 million but a year-to-year change in shares outstanding of 0%. By looking at shares outstanding alone, we can tell whether a company's share repurchase strategy is to reduce its equity base or simply to offset the dilutive effect of option exercises.

The top quintile of this strategy outperforms by 3.1%, on average, and does so for 69% of one-year and 75% of rolling three-year periods (see Figure 8.2). It has a low maximum loss of 19%, versus 25% for the Universe, and a Sharpe ratio of 0.81, versus 0.49 for the Universe. Average portfolio values for one-year share reduction range from 2% to 7%. Companies in this portfolio tend to be large caps, with an average market value of $6.0 billion, and market values over the 2003 to 2006 period of $12 billion to $13 billion. Note that the average market cap for this strategy ($6.0 billion) is lower than the $7.7 billion for the share repurchase-to-invested cap strategy. This is because large cap companies often

1988–2007	1st Quintile	2nd Quintile	3rd Quintile	4th Quintile	5th Quintile	Universe	S&P 500*
CAGR – Annual Rebalance	14.4%	13.0%	13.1%	12.2%	5.5%	11.2%	12.9%
Average Excess Return vs. Universe**	3.1%	1.1%	1.7%	1.5%	−5.2%	NA	1.6%
Value of $10,000 Invested (20 Years)	$148,640	$114,727	$117,762	$99,988	$29,238	$83,161	$112,895
% of 1-Year Periods Strategy Outperforms the Universe	68.8%	53.2%	70.1%	59.7%	20.8%	NA	59.7%
% Rolling 3-Year Periods Strategy Outperforms	75.4%	59.4%	81.2%	66.7%	2.9%	NA	71.0%
Maximum Gain	53.4%	52.8%	58.8%	62.3%	66.7%	59.2%	54.1%
Maximum Loss	−18.9%	−21.1%	−24.1%	−44.0%	−48.9%	−24.9%	−25.9%
Sharpe Ratio	0.81	0.73	0.64	0.46	0.14	0.49	0.69
Standard Deviation of Returns	0.14	0.13	0.15	0.21	0.22	0.16	0.14
Beta (vs. Universe)	0.70	0.70	0.92	1.19	1.27	NA	0.78
Alpha (vs. Universe)	0.07	0.05	0.03	−0.01	−0.09	NA	0.04
Average Portfolio Size	400	399	402	400	400	NA	NA
Average Number of Companies *Outperforming*	185	182	181	171	151	NA	NA
Average Number of Companies *Underperforming*	195	197	200	206	227	NA	NA
Median Portfolio Value – 1-Year Reduction in Shares	4.5%	0.0%	−0.9%	−3.4%	−45.0%	−9.1%	−2.8%
Average Market Capitalization	$6,045	$5,251	$4,041	$3,300	$3,120	NA	NA

* Equal-weighted average of S&P 500 returns. ** Annual holding period run quarterly for a larger sample size; arithmetic average excess returns.
Source: Standard & Poor's Compustat Point in Time Database, Charter Oak Investment Systems, Inc., Venues® Data Engine

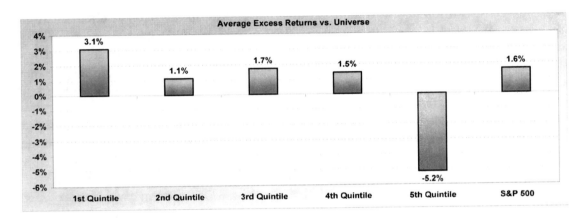

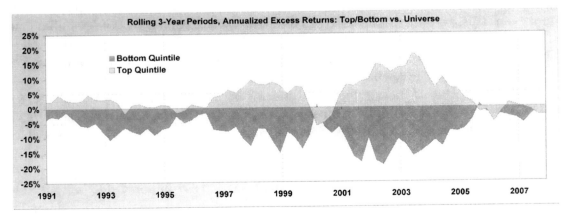

Figure 8.2 One-Year Reduction in Shares Outstanding

issue large numbers of stock options, and large share repurchases must be undertaken just to keep share count from increasing. However, as you can see from the results of this strategy, actual reductions in share count result in stronger and more linear excess returns.

The bottom quintile underperforms by over 5%, on average, and does so for 79% of one-year and 97% of rolling three-year periods. Average portfolio values for share reduction for the bottom quintile range from −26% to almost −60%, indicating these companies are issuing shares at a high rate. One reason that companies issue large numbers of shares is to make stock-based business acquisitions, and, as we'll see later in this chapter, companies that make large acquisitions significantly underperform companies that do not, on average.

One-Year Reduction in Shares Outstanding by Economic Sector

The reduction in shares strategy works very well for the energy, consumer staples, health care, and information technology sectors. In particular, the top quintile of the information technology sector outperforms by over 7%, and the bottom quintile underperforms by almost 8%, making both very consistent (see Figure 8.3). In past years, info tech companies have issued large numbers of stock options to compensate employees. As a result, technology companies that substantially reduce shares outstanding often have to undertake large share repurchase programs, backed by a lot of cash. This strategy is telling us that the market rewards technology companies that control their share counts and punishes those that significantly increase share counts, most likely for acquisitions. The strategy also works moderately well for the consumer discretionary, financials, and telecom services sector (much of the losses in the bottom quintile of the telecom services sector occurred in 2000, following the preceding telecom boom). In all, the strategy works well across sectors.

One-Year Reduction in Shares Outstanding and Enterprise Value to EBITDA

As mentioned in the introduction to this chapter, our research shows that the share repurchase strategy generates excess returns in proportion to the valuation at which shares are repurchased. Companies that repurchase shares at valuations well above a company's intrinsic value are essentially giving a few shareholders (the selling shareholders) a good deal at the expense of the rest of the shareholders. Companies that repurchase shares when their stock is selling at a significant discount to fair value, in contrast, are purchasing more than $1 of value for each dollar of shareholder funds spent on the repurchase. In this test, we don't bother trying to calculate intrinsic value, which is difficult or impossible to approximate quantitatively. Instead, we calculate valuation simply by looking at the current enterprise value (EV) to EBITDA (earnings

Top Quintile

1988–2007	Energy	Materials	Industrials	Consumer Discretionary	Consumer Staples	Health Care	Financials	Information Technology	Telecom Services	Utilities	Universe	S&P 500*
CAGR – Quintile	17.2%	10.7%	11.6%	11.3%	17.4%	18.1%	17.2%	14.9%	12.9%	14.3%	11.2%	12.9%
CAGR – Sector	13.5%	10.2%	11.3%	8.8%	12.6%	12.3%	14.5%	7.5%	9.2%	13.0%	NA	NA
Excess Return vs. Sector	3.7%	0.5%	0.4%	2.6%	4.8%	5.7%	2.7%	7.3%	3.7%	1.3%	NA	NA
Value of $10,000	$238,745	$76,901	$90,338	$85,235	$246,830	$276,799	$238,217	$160,087	$113,037	$144,446	$83,161	$112,895
% 1-Year Outperformance	80.0%	55.0%	55.0%	65.0%	85.0%	75.0%	70.0%	70.0%	55.0%	65.0%	NA	NA
% 3-Year Outperformance	83.3%	55.6%	77.8%	72.2%	94.4%	88.9%	72.2%	88.9%	72.2%	77.8%	NA	NA
Maximum Gain	60.0%	31.4%	33.3%	41.0%	57.1%	61.1%	73.4%	78.1%	99.4%	44.9%	44.0%	41.4%
Maximum Loss	−26.5%	−12.4%	−12.2%	−22.1%	−5.1%	−24.9%	−18.2%	−33.7%	−42.4%	−14.2%	−19.1%	−18.1%
Standard Deviation	0.24	0.14	0.14	0.17	0.17	0.21	0.24	0.28	0.34	0.15	0.16	0.14
Beta (vs. Sector)	0.92	0.88	0.88	0.87	1.07	0.77	1.06	0.67	0.87	0.92	NA	NA
Alpha (vs. Sector)	0.04	0.02	0.02	0.04	0.04	0.09	0.02	0.09	0.05	0.02	NA	NA
Portfolio Size	24	32	60	74	23	41	65	58	9	26	NA	NA

Bottom Quintile

1988–2007	Energy	Materials	Industrials	Consumer Discretionary	Consumer Staples	Health Care	Financials	Information Technology	Telecom Services	Utilities	Universe	S&P 500*
CAGR – Quintile	6.8%	3.6%	6.0%	3.9%	8.1%	3.8%	11.2%	−0.3%	−3.9%	9.7%	11.2%	12.9%
CAGR – Sector	13.5%	10.2%	11.3%	8.8%	12.6%	12.3%	14.5%	7.5%	9.2%	13.0%	NA	NA
Excess Return vs. Sector	−6.7%	−6.6%	−5.3%	−4.9%	−4.5%	−8.5%	−3.3%	−7.8%	−13.1%	−3.2%	NA	NA
Value of $10,000	$37,242	$20,372	$31,775	$21,457	$47,346	$21,213	$83,678	$9,476	$4,556	$64,006	$83,161	$112,895
% 1-Year Outperformance	30.0%	15.0%	25.0%	30.0%	30.0%	10.0%	30.0%	20.0%	30.0%	45.0%	NA	NA
% 3-Year Outperformance	11.1%	5.6%	11.1%	16.7%	5.6%	0.0%	22.2%	5.6%	16.7%	33.3%	NA	NA
Maximum Gain	69.9%	49.0%	44.9%	51.7%	32.7%	60.9%	47.4%	106.5%	82.9%	63.3%	44.0%	41.4%
Maximum Loss	−59.1%	−25.2%	−29.8%	−32.1%	−21.4%	−35.6%	−41.3%	−54.0%	−66.6%	−37.7%	−19.1%	−18.1%
Standard Deviation	0.32	0.20	0.18	0.22	0.13	0.26	0.23	0.35	0.38	0.22	0.16	0.14
Beta (vs. Sector)	1.26	1.25	1.20	1.13	0.80	0.98	1.02	0.91	0.95	1.30	NA	NA
Alpha (vs. Sector)	−0.09	−0.03	−0.03	−0.08	0.04	−0.06	0.02	−0.15	−0.17	0.04	NA	NA
Portfolio Size	23	31	58	70	21	40	61	56	8	25	NA	NA

* Equal-weighted average of S&P 500 returns.
Source: Standard & Poor's Compustat Point in Time Database; Charter Oak Investment Systems, Venues® Data Engine

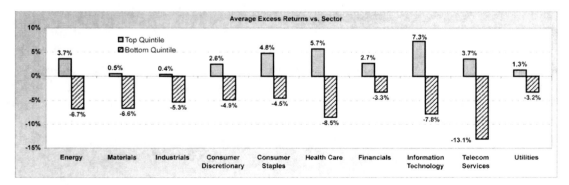

Figure 8.3 One-Year Reduction in Shares Outstanding by Economic Sector

before interest, taxes, depreciation, and amortization) multiple of the shares relative to the EV-to-EBITDA multiple of all other companies in the Universe. As you can see from the results, the strategy works very well.

The top quintile outperforms by 6%, on average, and does so for 73% of one-year and 86% of rolling three-year periods (see Figure 8.4). The top quintile significantly underperforms only in 1998–2000, 2006, and 2007. It has a low maximum loss (22%) and a high Sharpe ratio (0.90). It also has very low volatility, with a Beta of just 0.7 relative to the Universe. Note that the Alpha values, or risk-adjusted excess returns, for the quintiles are quite linear, ranging from 0.10 for the top quintile all the way down to −0.20 for the bottom (reflecting linearity in both Beta and in excess returns). Average portfolio values for the top quintile vary from 2% to 7% for one-year share reduction and from 3× to 5× for EV to EBITDA, so these are very low valuation companies that are significantly reducing their share counts.

The bottom quintile underperforms by almost 10%, on average, and does so for 73% of one-year and 93% of rolling three-year periods. The bottom quintile is very volatile, with a maximum loss of 79%, a maximum gain of 165%, and a Beta of 1.8 relative to the Universe. It significantly outperforms in 1991, 1996, 1999–2000, and 2003–2004. Average portfolio values range from −19% to less than −100% for one-year reduction in shares and high positive to high negative values for EV to EBITDA, indicating these companies have low earnings or losses and are issuing large amounts of shares. This strategy would make a good short-sale strategy.

One-Year Reduction in Shares Outstanding and Seven-Month Relative Strength

This strategy combines a capital allocation factor (reduction in shares) with a technical, or price momentum, factor (relative strength). Generally, our testing shows that "payout" strategies, such as share reductions, in which corporations are divesting capital, combine very well with price momentum strategies (relative strength, 52-week price range). Not only are excess returns high, but performance is relatively consistent. The reason may be that corporations sometimes undertake large share repurchases when they feel their shares have been unduly punished by the market. If, following the repurchases, the shares subsequently show price strength, this is a sign that the market also believes that the shares have been unduly punished and that the share repurchase is having the desired affect (of reviving the stock). On the other hand, if a company is issuing large numbers of shares, weak relative strength represents the market's vote of no-confidence in the company's financial position or strategic plan (e.g., an acquisition). The seven-month relative strength strategy compares a stock's rate of change (percent increase or decrease) over the past seven months to the rate of change of every other stock in our Universe.

1988–2007	1st Quintile	2nd Quintile	3rd Quintile	4th Quintile	5th Quintile	Universe	S&P 500*
CAGR – Annual Rebalance	17.3%	12.4%	13.2%	6.2%	−4.8%	11.2%	12.9%
Average Excess Return vs. Universe**	6.0%	1.9%	1.3%	−1.7%	−9.7%	NA	1.6%
Value of $10,000 Invested (20 Years)	$242,229	$103,501	$120,378	$33,430	$3,729	$83,161	$112,895
% of 1-Year Periods Strategy Outperforms the Universe	72.7%	57.1%	49.4%	37.7%	27.3%	NA	59.7%
% Rolling 3-Year Periods Strategy Outperforms	85.5%	71.0%	58.0%	34.8%	7.2%	NA	71.0%
Maximum Gain	59.2%	52.6%	45.2%	63.7%	165.0%	59.2%	54.1%
Maximum Loss	−22.1%	−27.2%	−18.8%	−66.7%	−78.9%	−24.9%	−25.9%
Sharpe Ratio	0.90	0.73	0.66	0.26	−0.04	0.49	0.69
Standard Deviation of Returns	0.16	0.14	0.14	0.25	0.40	0.16	0.14
Beta (vs. Universe)	0.66	0.60	0.77	1.27	1.82	NA	0.78
Alpha (vs. Universe)	0.10	0.07	0.04	−0.05	−0.20	NA	0.04
Average Portfolio Size	73	73	74	74	74	NA	NA
Average Number of Companies *Outperforming*	35	33	34	29	22	NA	NA
Average Number of Companies *Underperforming*	35	36	35	41	47	NA	NA
Median Portfolio Value – 1 Yr Reduction in Shares	5.2%	0.0%	−0.8%	−3.2%	−41.2%	−9.1%	−2.8%
Median Portfolio Value – EV-to-EBITDA	4.1	7.3	9.6	15.8	−33.8	10.5	9.1
Average Market Capitalization	$4,598	$3,524	$3,751	$5,028	$1,452	NA	NA

* Equal-weighted average of S&P 500 returns. ** Annual holding period run quarterly for a larger sample size; arithmetic average excess returns.
Source: Standard & Poor's Compustat Point in Time Database, Charter Oak Investment Systems, Inc., Venues® Data Engine

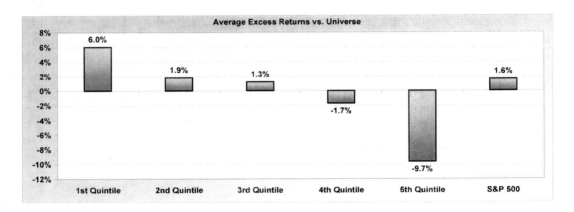

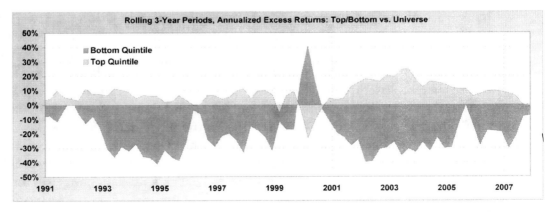

Figure 8.4 One-Year Reduction in Shares Outstanding and Enterprise Value to EBITDA

The top quintile outperforms by nearly 6%, on average, and does so for 70% of one-year and 86% of rolling three-year periods (see Figure 8.5). The top quintile significantly underperforms in 1992–1993, 1995, 2000, 2003, and 2006. It has a low maximum loss (20%) and a moderately high Sharpe ratio (0.81). Average portfolio values range from 3% to 11% for one-year share reduction and from 11% to over 100% for seven-month relative strength, meaning that average portfolio prices increased from 11% to 100% over a seven-month period.[5]

The bottom quintile underperforms by nearly 11%, on average, and does so for 86% of one-year and 96% of rolling three-year periods, making this a very effective and consistent strategy. It significantly outperforms only in 1998 and 2001 (during one quarterly period for each year) and in 2003–2004. The strategy has a moderately low Beta (for a bottom quintile) of 1.5 and a strong negative Alpha of −0.16. On average 50 portfolio companies underperform versus only 26 that outperform. Average portfolio values vary from −18% to −79% for one-year reduction in shares (meaning companies are increasing shares by this amount) and −7% to −57% for seven-month relative strength, meaning that average portfolio prices decreased by 7% to 57% over a seven-month period.

One-Year Reduction in Shares Outstanding and Depreciation Expense to Invested Capital

We'll look at the depreciation-to-invested capital strategy in depth in Chapter 10. For now, I'll describe it as a measure of how conservative or aggressive a company is in its accounting practices. Accountants use depreciation to recognize the cost of a capital asset, such as a building or machinery, over the course of its useful life. Because depreciation is recorded as an expense on the income statement, the more depreciation a company recognizes in any one period, the lower its reported earnings. However, accountants must make a number of estimates in determining depreciation expense, and can also choose from a variety of depreciation methods. Thus, depreciation policy can serve as a barometer of how liberally or conservatively a firm accounts for its expenses. The depreciation-to-invested capital strategy looks at how much depreciation expense a company records in a given year relative to its total invested capital. The top quintile of the strategy presented here contains companies with large one-year reductions in share count (a conservative use of shareholder capital) that also recognize a lot of depreciation expense (implying conservative accounting). The bottom quintile contains companies that significantly increase shares outstanding (an aggressive use of capital) that recognize a minimum of depreciation relative to invested capital (implying aggressive accounting). Although not the strongest two-factor strategy we present, the strategy works well.

---

[5] The seven-month relative strength strategy is explained in detail in Chapter 9.

1988–2007	1st Quintile	2nd Quintile	3rd Quintile	4th Quintile	5th Quintile	Universe	S&P 500*
CAGR – Annual Rebalance	16.5%	12.4%	13.9%	7.9%	−0.9%	11.2%	12.9%
Average Excess Return vs. Universe**	5.8%	0.0%	1.8%	−0.7%	−10.7%	NA	1.6%
Value of $10,000 Invested (20 Years)	$211,195	$102,881	$134,096	$45,716	$8,273	$83,161	$112,895
% of 1-Year Periods Strategy Outperforms the Universe	70.1%	54.5%	51.9%	44.2%	14.3%	NA	59.7%
% Rolling 3-Year Periods Strategy Outperforms	85.5%	53.6%	68.1%	36.2%	4.3%	NA	71.0%
Maximum Gain	71.5%	43.0%	49.4%	62.5%	99.2%	59.2%	54.1%
Maximum Loss	−19.5%	−19.2%	−22.7%	−47.1%	−71.3%	−24.9%	−25.9%
Sharpe Ratio	0.81	0.64	0.71	0.40	−0.09	0.49	0.69
Standard Deviation of Returns	0.17	0.13	0.14	0.19	0.28	0.16	0.14
Beta (vs. Universe)	0.91	0.61	0.77	1.03	1.46	NA	0.78
Alpha (vs. Universe)	0.07	0.05	0.05	−0.01	−0.16	NA	0.04
Average Portfolio Size	80	80	81	80	81	NA	NA
Average Number of Companies *Outperforming*	36	37	38	33	26	NA	NA
Average Number of Companies *Underperforming*	37	40	39	43	50	NA	NA
Median Portfolio Value – 1-Year Reduction in Shares	5.0%	0.0%	−0.8%	−3.3%	−37.5%	−9.1%	−2.8%
Median Portfolio Value – 7-Month Price Change	50%	16%	7%	−3%	−27%	19%	5%
Average Market Capitalization	$5,558	$5,882	$4,884	$3,691	$1,916	NA	NA

* Equal-weighted average of S&P 500 returns. ** Annual holding period run quarterly for a larger sample size; arithmetic average excess returns.
Source: Standard & Poor's Compustat Point in Time Database, Charter Oak Investment Systems, Inc., Venues® Data Engine

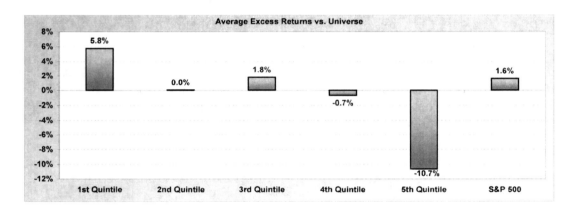

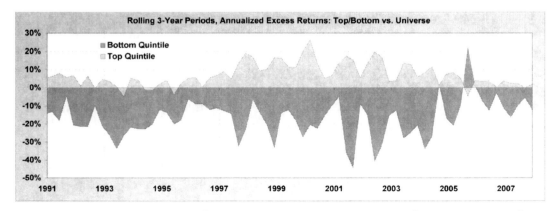

Figure 8.5 One-Year Reduction in Shares Outstanding and Seven-Month Relative Strength

The top quintile outperforms by 3.8%, on average, and does so for 66% of one-year and 83% of rolling three-year periods (see Figure 8.6). It significantly underperforms in two types of periods: during the early stages of bull markets (1991–1992 and 2003–2004) and market tops (2000 and 2007), both periods when more speculative and less conservative companies outperform. The top quintile has a low maximum loss (19%), and a low standard deviation of returns (0.14), resulting in a high Sharpe ratio (0.86 versus 0.69 for the S&P 500). It is a large-cap strategy, with an average market cap of $8.1 billion. Average portfolio values range from 2% to 10% for one-year reduction in shares and from 12% to 19% for depreciation to invested capital.

The bottom quintile underperforms by an average of just over 7%, and does so for 73% of one-year and 94% of rolling three-year periods. It significantly outperforms in 1991, 1995–1996, 2000, and 2003–2004. Average portfolio values range from −23% to less than −60% for one-year reduction in shares (corresponding to large share issuance) and about 1% to 3% for depreciation to invested capital. So, the bottom quintile contains companies that are showing large increases in share count and are recording very little depreciation expense.

ONE-YEAR REDUCTION IN LONG-TERM DEBT

As mentioned in the introduction, strategies based on the level of a company's debt have not worked as expected quantitatively, at least over the past 20 years. Part of the explanation may be due to the steady decline in interest rates, and hence the cost of debt, over that 20-year period. However, I believe the main explanation has to do with how the market values risk. Over the short term (our 12-month portfolio holding periods), the market seems to place a higher valuation on companies with higher financial leverage (and higher risk) than those with lower leverage (lower risk). The reason, I believe, is that companies with higher leverage are able to generate more profits for stockholders during good economic periods than more conservatively financed companies. The market responds positively to such financial engineering—at least over the short term.

As you'll see in Chapter 10, companies with the highest total debt to capital levels show positive excess returns, while those with the lowest debt levels show negative excess returns, the opposite of what one might expect. Debt payback ratios, such as EBITDA to total debt and operating cash flow to total debt, work somewhat better. These ratios measure the level of debt relative to profitability, and by implication the ability to make interest and principal payments. The long-term debt reduction strategy, shown here, also works modestly well. I present it not only for completeness but also because it makes a useful combining factor, especially for investors interested in more conservative investment strategies.

1988–2007	1st Quintile	2nd Quintile	3rd Quintile	4th Quintile	5th Quintile	Universe	S&P 500*
CAGR – Annual Rebalance	14.7%	12.1%	13.8%	10.7%	0.8%	11.2%	12.9%
Average Excess Return vs. Universe**	3.8%	1.6%	2.7%	−1.3%	−7.2%	NA	1.6%
Value of $10,000 Invested (20 Years)	$156,446	$99,024	$133,388	$76,190	$11,685	$83,161	$112,895
% of 1-Year Periods Strategy Outperforms the Universe	66.2%	50.6%	59.7%	36.4%	27.3%	NA	59.7%
% Rolling 3-Year Periods Strategy Outperforms	82.6%	66.7%	68.1%	30.4%	5.8%	NA	71.0%
Maximum Gain	47.8%	62.4%	54.3%	64.4%	76.6%	59.2%	54.1%
Maximum Loss	−18.6%	−27.1%	−20.1%	−43.6%	−63.1%	−24.9%	−25.9%
Sharpe Ratio	0.86	0.69	0.69	0.35	0.03	0.49	0.69
Standard Deviation of Returns	0.14	0.14	0.16	0.19	0.25	0.16	0.14
Beta (vs. Universe)	0.66	0.74	0.86	1.10	1.43	NA	0.78
Alpha (vs. Universe)	0.08	0.05	0.04	−0.03	−0.13	NA	0.04
Average Portfolio Size	61	62	62	62	62	NA	NA
Average Number of Companies *Outperforming*	28	29	29	26	21	NA	NA
Average Number of Companies *Underperforming*	30	30	30	32	39	NA	NA
Median Portfolio Value – 1 Year Reduction in Shares	5.1%	−0.1%	−0.8%	−2.8%	−28.8%	−9.1%	−2.8%
Median Portfolio Value – Depreciation to Inv. Capital	14.3%	8.5%	6.5%	4.4%	1.7%	7.3%	8.1%
Average Market Capitalization	$8,143	$4,631	$4,546	$3,438	$3,083	NA	NA

* Equal-weighted average of S&P 500 returns. ** Annual holding period run quarterly for a larger sample size; arithmetic average excess returns.
Source: Standard & Poor's Compustat Point in Time Database, Charter Oak Investment Systems, Inc., Venues® Data Engine

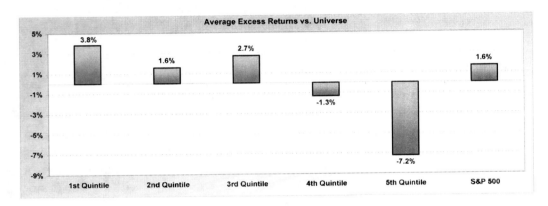

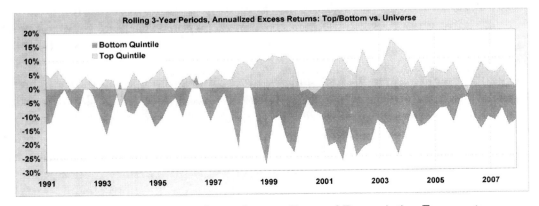

Figure 8.6 One-Year Reduction in Shares Outstanding and Depreciation Expense to Invested Capital

In this single-factor strategy, the second quintile turns out to be the strongest, so I'll use the second and fifth quintiles in the strategy discussion and in the rolling three-year returns graph (see Figure 8.7). The top quintile contains companies that have had very large reductions in debt, by an average of about 50%. Companies in this quintile neither outperform nor underperform. The second quintile, in contrast, contains companies that have reduced debt by about 10% (average portfolio values range from 5% to 14% annual reductions). The second quintile outperforms by 2.7%, on average, and does so for 68% of one-year and 87% of rolling three-year periods, making it a relatively consistent strategy. It significantly underperforms only in 1995–1996, 1999–2000, and 2003. The strategy has a low maximum loss (23%) and a low standard deviation of returns (0.14), resulting in a moderately high Sharpe ratio (0.76).

The bottom quintile underperforms by 2.8%, on average, and does so for 88% of one-year and 97% of rolling three-year periods, making it a very consistent strategy. It significantly outperforms only in 2000–2001 and 2004. Volatility is relatively low for the fifth quintile, with a maximum loss of 27%, a maximum gain of 59%, and a standard deviation of returns of just 0.16, unusual for a bottom quintile. Average portfolio values range from about −250% to less than −500%, meaning that companies in this quintile doubled to quintupled, on average, their long-term debt over a one-year period.

One-Year Reduction in Long-Term Debt by Economic Sector

The one-year reduction in debt strategy works fairly well across sectors. Note that we use the second quintile and the bottom quintile instead of the top quintile and bottom quintile in presenting this test (see Figure 8.8). The strategy works particularly well for the industrials, consumer discretionary, health care, information technology, and telecom services sectors. It also works as a negative strategy for the consumer staples sector. It is not consistent for the energy, materials, financials, or utilities sectors.

Net Debt Reduction to Invested Capital and Net Share Repurchase to Invested Capital

This strategy would be more accurately called net debt reduction/issuance to invested capital and net share reduction/issuance to invested capital. The top quintile contains companies that are spending large amounts of cash on both debt reduction (net of debt issuance) and share repurchases (net of share issuance). The bottom quintile contains companies that are large net issuers of both debt and equity. This strategy has a common denominator—invested capital—and matches one type of company payout of capital (debt reduction) to another (share repurchase). Considering that the strategy takes into account *only* capital allocation, it generates relatively high excess returns and is consistent. (Note that this strategy considers cash spent on debt reduction and share issuance

1988–2007	1st Quintile	2nd Quintile	3rd Quintile	4th Quintile	5th Quintile	Universe	S&P 500*
CAGR – Annual Rebalance	10.7%	14.4%	13.9%	12.3%	8.5%	11.2%	12.9%
Average Excess Return vs. Universe**	0.0%	2.7%	2.1%	0.5%	−2.8%	NA	1.6%
Value of $10,000 Invested (20 Years)	$75,935	$147,674	$134,442	$101,747	$51,382	$83,161	$112,895
% of 1-Year Periods Strategy Outperforms the Universe	49.4%	67.5%	68.8%	41.6%	11.7%	NA	59.7%
% Rolling 3-Year Periods Strategy Outperforms	40.6%	87.0%	85.5%	53.6%	2.9%	NA	71.0%
Maximum Gain	62.9%	58.0%	58.6%	53.1%	59.1%	59.2%	54.1%
Maximum Loss	−29.1%	−22.6%	−24.3%	−24.8%	−27.0%	−24.9%	−25.9%
Sharpe Ratio	0.46	0.76	0.69	0.60	0.33	0.49	0.69
Standard Deviation of Returns	0.18	0.14	0.15	0.14	0.16	0.16	0.14
Beta (vs. Universe)	1.06	0.82	0.84	0.81	0.97	NA	0.78
Alpha (vs. Universe)	−0.01	0.05	0.04	0.03	−0.02	NA	0.04
Average Portfolio Size	353	352	352	352	352	NA	NA
Average Number of Companies *Outperforming*	145	164	163	159	144	NA	NA
Average Number of Companies *Underperforming*	187	170	171	177	191	NA	NA
Median Portfolio Value – 1 Year Reduction in LT Debt	54.2%	10.0%	−0.7%	−18.5%	−390.6%	−67.2%	−37.1%
Average Market Capitalization	$2,915	$4,593	$4,945	$6,255	$4,274	NA	NA

* Equal-weighted average of S&P 500 returns. ** Annual holding period run quarterly for a larger sample size; arithmetic average excess returns.
Source: Standard & Poor's Compustat Point in Time Database, Charter Oak Investment Systems, Inc., Venues® Data Engine

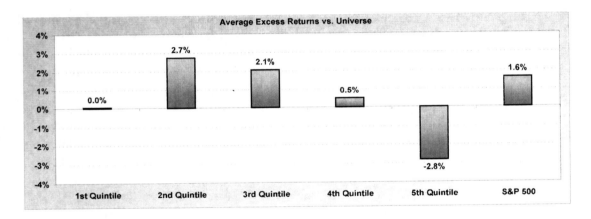

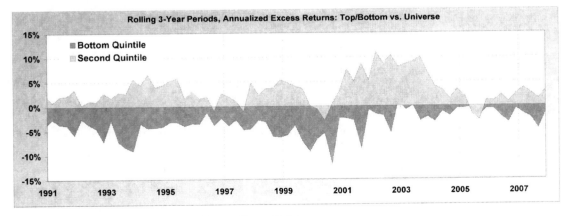

Figure 8.7 One-Year Reduction in Long-Term Debt

Second Quintile

1988–2007	Energy	Materials	Industrials	Consumer Discretionary	Consumer Staples	Health Care	Financials	Information Technology	Telecom Services	Utilities	Universe	SP 500*
CAGR – Quintile	15.4%	11.6%	13.1%	11.1%	11.3%	16.1%	14.8%	9.3%	13.9%	12.6%	11.2%	12.9%
CAGR – Sector	13.5%	10.2%	11.3%	8.7%	12.6%	12.3%	14.5%	7.5%	9.2%	13.0%	NA	NA
Excess Return vs. Sector	1.9%	1.4%	1.9%	2.4%	−1.3%	3.7%	0.3%	1.8%	4.7%	−0.3%	NA	NA
Value of $10,000	$176,584	$90,476	$117,525	$82,298	$85,565	$197,280	$158,066	$58,963	$135,182	$107,618	$83,160	$112,895
% 1-Year Outperformance	65.0%	50.0%	70.0%	75.0%	35.0%	65.0%	45.0%	60.0%	70.0%	55.0%	NA	NA
% 3-Year Outperformance	50.0%	55.6%	83.3%	88.9%	27.8%	83.3%	38.9%	72.2%	83.3%	50.0%	NA	NA
Maximum Gain	53.9%	32.3%	35.0%	58.3%	34.7%	74.9%	57.3%	84.6%	105.3%	42.9%	44.0%	41.4%
Maximum Loss	−31.1%	−17.4%	−18.9%	−28.3%	−13.8%	−27.1%	−21.5%	−48.4%	−43.3%	−22.6%	−19.1%	−18.1%
Standard Deviation	0.23	0.14	0.14	0.20	0.15	0.24	0.23	0.30	0.34	0.16	0.16	0.14
Beta (vs. Sector)	0.81	0.85	0.97	1.03	1.03	0.92	1.06	0.63	0.88	0.96	NA	NA
Alpha (vs. Sector)	0.04	0.03	0.02	0.02	−0.02	0.05	0.00	0.05	0.05	0.00	NA	NA
Portfolio Size	22	30	54	65	20	32	55	39	9	26	NA	NA

Bottom Quintile

1988–2007	Energy	Materials	Industrials	Consumer Discretionary	Consumer Staples	Health Care	Financials	Information Technology	Telecom Services	Utilities	Universe	SP 500*
CAGR – Quintile	12.2%	9.2%	8.0%	5.3%	10.2%	9.0%	12.7%	3.6%	−0.6%	13.3%	11.2%	12.9%
CAGR – Sector	13.5%	10.2%	11.3%	8.7%	12.6%	12.3%	14.5%	7.5%	9.2%	13.0%	NA	NA
Excess Return vs. Sector	−1.3%	−1.0%	−3.3%	−3.4%	−2.4%	−3.4%	−1.8%	−3.8%	−9.8%	0.4%	NA	NA
Value of $10,000	$100,285	$58,650	$46,641	$27,945	$69,648	$55,835	$108,767	$20,479	$8,931	$121,752	$83,160	$112,895
% 1-Year Outperformance	45.0%	40.0%	25.0%	35.0%	35.0%	25.0%	40.0%	25.0%	30.0%	50.0%	NA	NA
% 3-Year Outperformance	44.4%	33.3%	11.1%	11.1%	33.3%	22.2%	44.4%	22.2%	16.7%	72.2%	NA	NA
Maximum Gain	72.3%	42.9%	39.5%	46.6%	40.9%	78.1%	63.7%	141.0%	68.8%	71.5%	44.0%	41.4%
Maximum Loss	−45.2%	−20.4%	−23.2%	−31.2%	−26.5%	−25.0%	−36.2%	−50.7%	−69.3%	−19.6%	−19.1%	−18.1%
Standard Deviation	0.30	0.19	0.15	0.21	0.17	0.25	0.24	0.39	0.37	0.19	0.16	0.14
Beta (vs. Sector)	1.17	1.21	1.00	1.07	1.01	0.92	1.11	1.03	0.87	1.13	NA	NA
Alpha (vs. Sector)	−0.03	0.02	0.00	−0.05	0.06	0.03	0.03	−0.10	−0.15	0.08	NA	NA
Portfolio Size	22	30	53	62	19	31	53	38	8	25	NA	NA

* Equal-weighted average of S&P 500 returns.
Source: Standard & Poor's Compustat Point in Time Database; Charter Oak Investment Systems, Inc., Venues® Data Engine

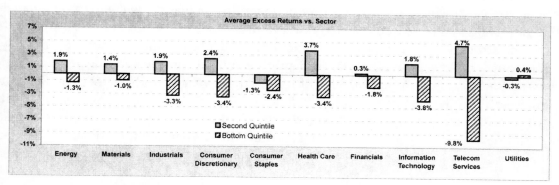

Figure 8.8 One-Year Reduction in Long-Term Debt by Economic Sector

relative to invested capital and not the actual reduction or increase in debt and shares in percentage terms.)

The top quintile outperforms by an average of 4.2%, and does so for 65% of one-year and 84% of rolling three-year periods (see Figure 8.9). It significantly underperforms only in 1999–2000 and 2003–2004. The strategy has a low maximum loss (20%) and a relatively high Sharpe ratio (0.83). Average portfolio values range from 11% to 22% for net debt reduction to invested capital and from 2% to over 15% for net share repurchases to invested capital, so companies in this quintile are making significant redemptions/repurchases of both debt and shares. The average market cap is $6.4 billion, so this tends to be a large-cap strategy.

The bottom quintile underperforms by over 8%, on average, and does so for 80% of one-year and 93% of rolling three-year periods, making it very consistent. It significantly outperforms only in 1989, 1999–2000, and 2003–2004. Average portfolio values range from -26% to -49% for net debt reduction to invested capital and -10% to -37% for net share repurchase to invested capital, so companies in this quintile are receiving a large amount of cash from both debt and share issuance.

One-Year Reduction in Long-Term Debt and Economic Profits

You'll recall the economic profits strategy from Chapter 4. The concept of economic profits is that capital is not free, and that the real or implied cost of capital should be subtracted from profits in order to arrive at true or "economic" profits available to shareholders. The economic profits factor used here employs cash return on invested capital to measure profitability and a company's price-to-sales (P/S) ratio, in place of Beta, to calculate the equity risk premium used in the cost of capital calculation.[6] A cash-based profitability measure, such as the one used here, combines well with capital allocation strategies, since it serves as an indicator of the amount of excess cash being generated by a business. The higher the level of cash generation, the more cash available to reduce debt or buy back shares. Also, by including P/S in the economic profits calculation, we help to ensure that the companies in the top quintile aren't overvalued.

The strategy works very well, particularly considering that the weaker factor—debt reduction—is selected first. The top quintile outperforms by 7.3%, on average, and does so for 75% of one-year and 91% of rolling three-year periods (see Figure 8.10). It significantly underperforms only in 1990 and 2003–2004. The strategy is somewhat volatile, with a maximum loss of 29% and a standard deviation of returns of 0.18 versus 0.14 for the S&P 500. This lowers the Sharpe ratio somewhat, but it is still a respectable

---

[6] See Chapter 4 for a complete discussion of economic profits and the calculation of the cost of capital.

1988–2007	1st Quintile	2nd Quintile	3rd Quintile	4th Quintile	5th Quintile	Universe	S&P 500*
CAGR – Annual Rebalance	14.9%	14.8%	9.9%	10.9%	2.6%	11.2%	12.9%
Average Excess Return vs. Universe**	4.2%	3.7%	−2.5%	−0.1%	−8.4%	NA	1.6%
Value of $10,000 Invested (20 Years)	$159,563	$157,326	$66,204	$79,043	$16,870	$83,161	$112,895
% of 1-Year Periods Strategy Outperforms the Universe	64.9%	64.9%	36.4%	46.8%	19.5%	NA	59.7%
% Rolling 3-Year Periods Strategy Outperforms	84.1%	79.7%	24.6%	46.4%	7.2%	NA	71.0%
Maximum Gain	53.5%	55.1%	52.2%	50.9%	79.3%	59.2%	54.1%
Maximum Loss	−19.5%	−24.1%	−46.5%	−30.9%	−65.6%	−24.9%	−25.9%
Sharpe Ratio	0.83	0.79	0.29	0.49	−0.01	0.49	0.69
Standard Deviation of Returns	0.15	0.15	0.19	0.16	0.28	0.16	0.14
Beta (vs. Universe)	0.75	0.79	1.03	0.88	1.51	NA	0.78
Alpha (vs. Universe)	0.07	0.06	−0.03	0.01	−0.15	NA	0.04
Average Portfolio Size	69	69	75	66	69	NA	NA
Average Number of Companies *Outperforming*	33	33	32	28	26	NA	NA
Average Number of Companies *Underperforming*	33	33	40	34	40	NA	NA
Median Portfolio Value – Debt Reduct. to Inv. Cap.	14.2%	2.0%	−0.1%	−4.6%	−33.0%	−2.9%	−2.8%
Median Portfolio Value – Stock Repur. to Inv. Cap.	7.2%	0.5%	−0.4%	−0.8%	−24.8%	−4.4%	2.8%
Average Market Capitalization	$6,445	$4,969	$2,809	$3,670	$2,523	NA	NA

* Equal-weighted average of S&P 500 returns. ** Annual holding period run quarterly for a larger sample size; arithmetic average excess returns.
Source: Standard & Poor's Compustat Point in Time Database, Charter Oak Investment Systems, Inc., Venues® Data Engine

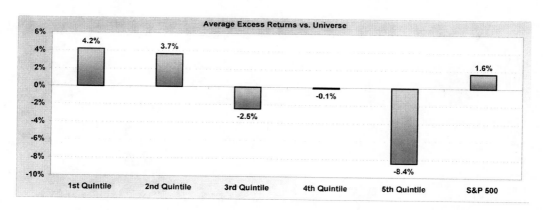

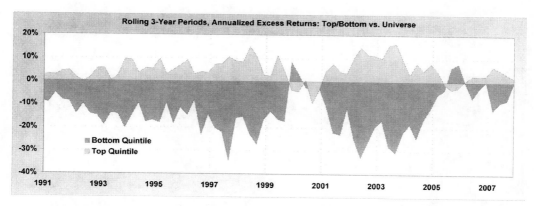

Figure 8.9 Net Debt Reduction to Invested Capital and Net Share Repurchase to Invested Capital

1990–2007	1st Quintile	2nd Quintile	3rd Quintile	4th Quintile	5th Quintile	Universe	S&P 500*
CAGR – Annual Rebalance	16.9%	14.6%	15.2%	8.8%	0.1%	10.3%	12.0%
Average Excess Return vs. Universe**	7.3%	3.8%	3.6%	−0.3%	−9.4%	NA	1.5%
Value of $10,000 Invested (18 Years)	$165,880	$115,515	$128,675	$45,344	$10,212	$58,669	$76,297
% of 1-Year Periods Strategy Outperforms the Universe	75.0%	66.7%	63.9%	47.2%	26.4%	NA	56.9%
% Rolling 3-Year Periods Strategy Outperforms	90.6%	78.1%	73.4%	46.9%	4.7%	NA	68.8%
Maximum Gain	58.9%	59.2%	68.4%	57.2%	84.6%	59.2%	54.1%
Maximum Loss	−29.4%	−19.2%	−24.7%	−33.0%	−70.4%	−24.9%	−25.9%
Sharpe Ratio	0.84	0.76	0.76	0.42	−0.06	0.46	0.64
Standard Deviation of Returns	0.18	0.15	0.15	0.18	0.29	0.17	0.14
Beta (vs. Universe)	0.94	0.69	0.71	0.96	1.44	NA	0.78
Alpha (vs. Universe)	0.08	0.08	0.07	0.00	−0.15	NA	0.04
Average Portfolio Size	51	51	51	51	51	NA	NA
Average Number of Companies *Outperforming*	24	25	25	22	18	NA	NA
Average Number of Companies *Underperforming*	23	23	23	26	31	NA	NA
Median Portfolio Value – 1 Year Reduction in LT Debt	48.9%	11.2%	0.3%	−19.1%	−615.7%	−62.1%	−31.8%
Median Portfolio Value – Economic Profits	15.4%	−1.6%	−7.6%	−15.9%	−47.0%	−11.2%	−6.5%
Average Market Capitalization	$3,637	$4,792	$5,315	$5,662	$2,814	NA	NA

* Equal-weighted average of S&P 500 returns. ** Annual holding period run quarterly for a larger sample size; arithmetic average excess returns.
Source: Standard & Poor's Compustat Point in Time Database; Charter Oak Investment Systems, Inc., Venues® Data Engine

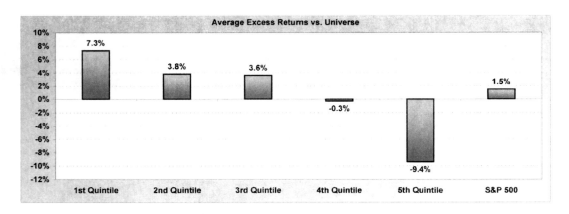

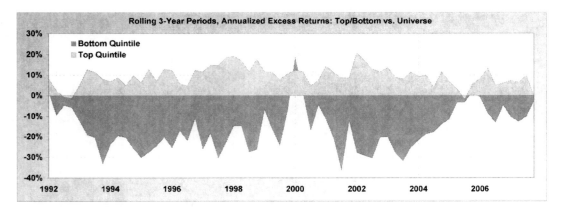

Figure 8.10 One-Year Reduction in Long-Term Debt and Economic Profits

0.84 versus 0.64 for the S&P 500. Average portfolio values for the top quintile range from 41% to 55% for one-year debt reduction and from 13% to over 20% for economic profits. These are companies that are generating large amounts of cash (well above their cost of capital) and that are using at least some of that cash to make big debt reductions. Note that while the top quintile of the one-year debt reduction strategy, alone, shows no excess returns, this strategy shows very large excess returns in the top quintile. This is the magic of effectively combining strategies.

The bottom quintile underperforms by 9.4%, on average, and does so for 74% of one-year and 95% of rolling three-year periods. It significantly outperforms in 1990–1991, 1999–2000, 2003–2004, and 2007. Average portfolio values vary from about −200% to −900% for one-year debt reduction (signaling huge debt increases) and from −36% to less than −60% for economic profits, indicating operating cash outflows. On average 31 portfolio companies underperform versus only 18 that outperform. Bottom quintile companies have high cash outflows at the same time that they are adding significant amounts of debt, a bad combination.

EXTERNAL FINANCING TO ASSETS

The external financing strategy brings the net debt reduction and net share repurchase strategy, presented earlier in this chapter (see Figure 8.9), together into a single factor. The external financing test contrasts companies that must access the debt and equity markets for their financing needs (the bottom quintile) with those that generate excess capital and use that capital to repurchase shares and reduce debt (the top quintile). The test is calculated as the past 12 month cash received from share issuance and long-term debt issuance minus cash paid out for share repurchase and debt reduction plus the change in short-term debt,[7] all as a percent of total assets. Companies with the highest amounts of net cash received from share issuance, long-term debt issuance, and/or increases in short-term debt—those with high external financing needs—are put in the bottom quintile. Companies with the highest amount of net cash paid out for share repurchases, long-term debt reductions, and/or reductions in short-term debt—those that generate excess cash and use it to reduce their capital base—are put in the top quintile.

Because external financing is a strong factor, particularly in combination with other investment factors, we tested it in a variety of ways. The strategy worked best when a firm's total assets, instead of invested capital, were used as the denominator.

---

[7] Cash received from debt issuance or share issuance, cash used for share repurchase or debt reduction, and changes in short-term debt can all be found in the financing section of a company's statement of cash flows.

Also, we found that including changes in short-term debt significantly improved the consistency of the strategy. A strategy of just combining the one-year percent changes in both shares outstanding and long-term debt worked, but not as well as the external financing formula outlined above.

External financing works well with a number of other *basics*, including cash generation, valuation, other capital allocation strategies, profitability, technical strategies, and growth (i.e., every major type of strategy presented in this book). Additionally, because it is so strong, it can be used almost equally well as the first factor of a two-factor strategy or as the second factor.

The top quintile outperforms by 3.1%, on average, and does so for 68% of one-year and 81% of rolling three-year periods (see Figure 8.11). It underperforms significantly in 1999–2000 and in 2003–2006. Although excess returns on the top quintile for the external financing strategy alone have been weak since 2003, we'll look at some two-factor combinations that correct this problem. Volatility is low, with a standard deviation of 0.15 versus 0.14 for the S&P 500, resulting in a Sharpe ratio of 0.77 (vs. 0.69). Average portfolio values range from −8% to −14%, meaning that companies in the top quintile are spending 8% to 14% of cash relative to total assets to repurchase shares and reduce debt. The average market cap for this strategy is $5.4 billion, indicating these are mid- to large-cap stocks.

The bottom quintile underperforms by an average of 6.7%, and does so for 79% of one-year and 94% of rolling three-year periods. It outperforms significantly only in 1999–2000, 2003–2004, and 2007. Average portfolio values range from 22% to 57%, meaning that companies in the bottom quintile received 22% to 57% in cash relative to assets (on average) from share and debt issuance (i.e., they are issuing a lot of shares and/or debt). With an average market cap of $2.2 billion, the strategy tends to contain small- to mid-cap stocks.

External Financing to Assets by Economic Sector

Like the share reduction and debt reduction strategies, external financing is strong across economic sectors. It works particularly well in the energy, consumer discretionary, consumer staples, health care, information technology, and utilities sectors. It also works moderately well in industrials. Results show that a strategy of preferring companies that generate excess income internally and return capital to shareholders over companies that increase their existing capital base by accessing the financial markets, potentially diluting existing shareholders, is broadly applicable (see Figure 8.12).

External Financing to Assets and Acquisitions to Invested Capital

This strategy combines two capital allocation strategies—its top quintile contains companies that are repurchasing shares, reducing debt, and refraining from cash business

1988–2007	1st Quintile	2nd Quintile	3rd Quintile	4th Quintile	5th Quintile	Universe	S&P 500*
CAGR – Annual Rebalance	14.9%	13.4%	13.4%	10.1%	3.2%	11.2%	12.9%
Average Excess Return vs. Universe**	3.1%	2.3%	1.8%	−0.9%	−6.7%	NA	1.6%
Value of $10,000 Invested (20 Years)	$161,577	$122,903	$122,741	$68,769	$18,875	$83,161	$112,895
% of 1-Year Periods Strategy Outperforms the Universe	67.5%	64.9%	67.5%	32.5%	20.8%	NA	59.7%
% Rolling 3-Year Periods Strategy Outperforms	81.2%	79.7%	71.0%	29.0%	5.8%	NA	71.0%
Maximum Gain	55.2%	58.3%	59.9%	60.7%	70.5%	59.2%	54.1%
Maximum Loss	−22.9%	−22.6%	−27.6%	−29.6%	−61.8%	−24.9%	−25.9%
Sharpe Ratio	0.77	0.75	0.58	0.43	0.06	0.49	0.69
Standard Deviation of Returns	0.15	0.14	0.17	0.17	0.24	0.16	0.14
Beta (vs. Universe)	0.83	0.78	1.02	0.99	1.39	NA	0.78
Alpha (vs. Universe)	0.05	0.05	0.02	−0.01	−0.12	NA	0.04
Average Portfolio Size	351	350	350	350	350	NA	NA
Average Number of Companies *Outperforming*	159	161	153	145	127	NA	NA
Average Number of Companies *Underperforming*	173	171	179	188	205	NA	NA
Median Portfolio Value – External Financing-to-Assets	−10.6%	−1.6%	0.9%	5.3%	32.5%	5.4%	0.3%
Average Market Capitalization	$5,398	$5,016	$4,747	$4,692	$2,224	NA	NA

* Equal-weighted average of S&P 500 returns. ** Annual holding period run quarterly for a larger sample size; arithmetic average excess returns.
Source: Standard & Poor's Compustat Point in Time Database, Charter Oak Investment Systems, Inc., Venues® Data Engine

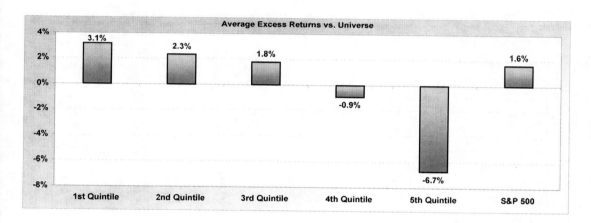

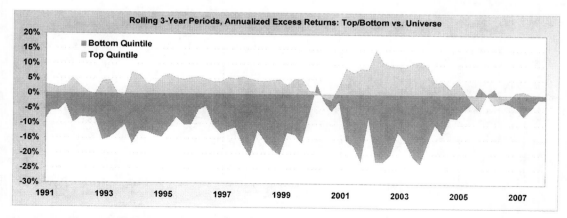

Figure 8.11 External Financing to Assets

Top Quintile

1988–2007	Energy	Materials	Industrials	Consumer Discretionary	Consumer Staples	Health Care	Financials	Information Technology	Telecom Services	Utilities	Universe	S&P 500*
CAGR – Quintile	17.4%	10.0%	13.7%	14.2%	17.5%	19.3%	15.6%	15.0%	10.7%	18.2%	11.2%	12.9%
CAGR – Sector	13.5%	10.2%	11.3%	8.8%	12.6%	12.3%	14.5%	7.5%	9.2%	13.0%	NA	NA
Excess Return vs. Sector	3.9%	−0.2%	2.4%	5.4%	4.9%	7.0%	1.2%	7.4%	1.5%	5.2%	NA	NA
Value of $10,000	$247,869	$67,502	$129,957	$141,617	$251,620	$341,118	$182,341	$163,317	$76,946	$282,662	$83,161	$112,895
% 1-Year Outperformance	85.0%	60.0%	70.0%	75.0%	65.0%	75.0%	55.0%	75.0%	65.0%	70.0%	NA	NA
% 3-Year Outperformance	83.3%	61.1%	77.8%	83.3%	88.9%	100.0%	50.0%	83.3%	61.1%	72.2%	NA	NA
Maximum Gain	60.7%	33.4%	42.1%	51.0%	63.8%	93.7%	69.1%	81.1%	65.5%	105.0%	44.0%	41.4%
Maximum Loss	−36.3%	−14.4%	−9.4%	−20.6%	−8.2%	−21.7%	−15.5%	−38.3%	−37.7%	−41.8%	−19.1%	−18.1%
Standard Deviation	0.26	0.14	0.14	0.18	0.19	0.25	0.22	0.26	0.27	0.34	0.16	0.14
Beta (vs. Sector)	0.96	0.83	0.94	0.91	1.18	0.94	0.88	0.61	0.53	1.68	NA	NA
Alpha (vs. Sector)	0.05	0.02	0.03	0.06	0.03	0.08	0.03	0.10	0.06	−0.01	NA	NA
Portfolio Size	23	32	61	74	23	42	34	58	9	4	NA	NA

Bottom Quintile

1988–2007	Energy	Materials	Industrials	Consumer Discretionary	Consumer Staples	Health Care	Financials	Information Technology	Telecom Services	Utilities	Universe	S&P 500*
CAGR – Quintile	5.2%	4.9%	4.6%	3.6%	5.9%	3.8%	8.7%	−0.5%	4.0%	0.2%	11.2%	12.9%
CAGR – Sector	13.5%	10.2%	11.3%	8.8%	12.6%	12.3%	14.5%	7.5%	9.2%	13.0%	NA	NA
Excess Return vs. Sector	−8.3%	−5.3%	−6.6%	−5.2%	−6.7%	−8.5%	−5.7%	−8.0%	−5.2%	−12.8%	NA	NA
Value of $10,000	$27,491	$26,136	$24,631	$20,170	$31,670	$21,198	$53,429	$9,024	$22,025	$10,374	$83,161	$112,895
% 1-Year Outperformance	25.0%	30.0%	20.0%	25.0%	20.0%	20.0%	30.0%	20.0%	40.0%	40.0%	NA	NA
% 3-Year Outperformance	22.2%	22.2%	5.6%	0.0%	0.0%	5.6%	22.2%	11.1%	44.4%	38.9%	NA	NA
Maximum Gain	74.6%	47.1%	38.3%	51.7%	33.8%	105.0%	46.8%	167.9%	98.1%	114.9%	44.0%	41.4%
Maximum Loss	−61.5%	−25.5%	−23.2%	−34.8%	−25.2%	−40.4%	−26.9%	−57.8%	−70.3%	−80.6%	−19.1%	−18.1%
Standard Deviation	0.33	0.20	0.16	0.22	0.15	0.32	0.20	0.45	0.39	0.40	0.16	0.14
Beta (vs. Sector)	1.27	1.23	1.01	1.14	0.81	1.24	0.83	1.18	0.81	1.93	NA	NA
Alpha (vs. Sector)	−0.10	−0.02	−0.04	−0.08	0.04	−0.08	−0.01	−0.15	−0.08	−0.03	NA	NA
Portfolio Size	22	32	58	70	21	40	30	55	8	3	NA	NA

* Equal-weighted average of S&P 500 returns.
Source: Standard & Poor's Compustat Point in Time Database; Charter Oak Investment Systems, Inc., Venues® Data Engine

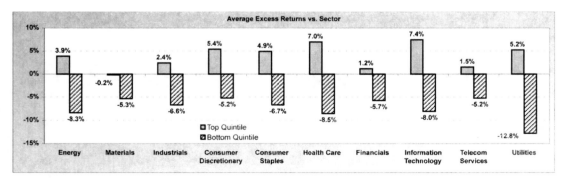

Figure 8.12 External Financing to Assets by Economic Sector

acquisitions; the bottom quintile contains companies that are issuing shares, issuing debt, and spending large amounts of cash on business acquisitions. The strategy works well: quintile returns are very linear and volatility for the top two quintiles is low. However, negative excess returns for the bottom quintile are not as strong as those for the external financing strategy alone.

The top quintile outperforms by 4.3%, on average, and does so for 68% of one-year and 83% of rolling three-year periods (see Figure 8.13). It significantly underperforms only in 1991, 1999–2000, and 2003–2004. Volatility is very low, and the Sharpe ratio is a moderately high 0.82. Average portfolio values for the top quintile range from −7% to −13% for external financing to assets (indicating significant share repurchases and debt reductions) and are 0% for cash acquisitions to invested capital. With an average market capitalization of $9.5 billion, the strategy selects large-cap stocks.

The bottom quintile underperforms by an average of 4.9%, and does so for 71% of one-year and 77% of rolling three-year periods. Note that negative excess returns for the bottom quintile can be increased significantly by combining the one-year share reduction factor with cash acquisitions to invested capital. The reason is that, in the external financing strategy, companies are issuing shares for cash, while the reduction in shares strategy also includes companies that are issuing shares to make acquisitions (thus, the one-year reduction in shares and cash acquisitions to invested capital strategy covers both cash and stock-based acquisitions). The bottom quintile also has not been consistent in recent years, outperforming in 2002 and 2004–2007. Average portfolio values range from 23% to 50% for external financing to assets and 37% to 72% for cash acquisitions to invested capital, meaning that companies in this quintile are issuing large amounts of shares and debt and using a good portion of the cash received to make acquisitions.

External Financing to Assets and Price to Book Value

As we saw in the one-year reduction in shares and the EV-to-EBITDA test, capital allocation and valuation strategies work well together. A primary reason for this is that share repurchases are an effective use of shareholder capital to the extent that a company's stock market value is below the company's fair, or intrinsic, value when the company buys back the shares. This strategy considers share repurchase and valuation, on a price-to-book value basis, as well as debt reduction. Note that large share repurchases reduce book value, since repurchased shares are usually held as treasury stock, which represents stock that has been reacquired by the company and is available for retirement or reissue. Treasury stock is subtracted from stockholder's equity to arrive at total book value. So, companies in the top quintile look cheap even on the basis of the reduced book value resulting from share repurchases.

1988–2007	1st Quintile	2nd Quintile	3rd Quintile	4th Quintile	5th Quintile	Universe	S&P 500*
CAGR – Annual Rebalance	16.7%	14.0%	9.6%	8.5%	5.5%	11.2%	12.9%
Average Excess Return vs. Universe**	4.3%	2.9%	1.4%	−3.4%	−4.9%	NA	1.6%
Value of $10,000 Invested (20 Years)	$219,492	$137,168	$62,422	$50,716	$28,968	$83,161	$112,895
% of 1-Year Periods Strategy Outperforms the Universe	67.5%	61.0%	51.9%	35.1%	28.6%	NA	59.7%
% Rolling 3-Year Periods Strategy Outperforms	82.6%	71.0%	47.8%	23.2%	23.2%	NA	71.0%
Maximum Gain	62.7%	55.0%	89.7%	62.8%	55.4%	59.2%	54.1%
Maximum Loss	−25.4%	−19.4%	−33.8%	−31.4%	−46.6%	−24.9%	−25.9%
Sharpe Ratio	0.82	0.74	0.43	0.27	0.17	0.49	0.69
Standard Deviation of Returns	0.15	0.15	0.22	0.17	0.19	0.16	0.14
Beta (vs. Universe)	0.80	0.76	1.14	0.95	1.03	NA	0.78
Alpha (vs. Universe)	0.07	0.06	0.00	−0.03	−0.05	NA	0.04
Average Portfolio Size	65	64	64	64	64	NA	NA
Average Number of Companies *Outperforming*	30	29	25	26	25	NA	NA
Average Number of Companies *Underperforming*	31	32	37	35	36	NA	NA
Median Portfolio Value – Extern. Fin. to Assets	−9.4%	−1.7%	0.6%	4.9%	32.4%	5.4%	0.3%
Median Portfolio Value – Acquisitions to Inv. Cap.	0.0%	0.0%	0.0%	3.8%	50.1%	5.0%	4.3%
Average Market Capitalization	$9,456	$1,174	$2,766	$5,237	$2,313	NA	NA

* Equal-weighted average of S&P 500 returns.** Annual holding period run quarterly for a larger sample size; arithmetic average excess returns.
Source: Standard & Poor's Compustat Point in Time Database, Charter Oak Investment Systems, Inc., Venues® Data Engine

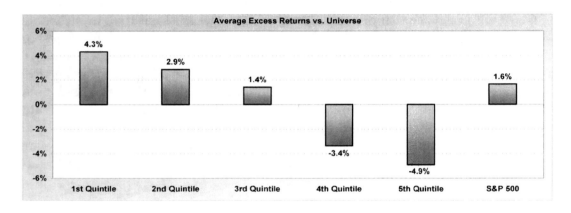

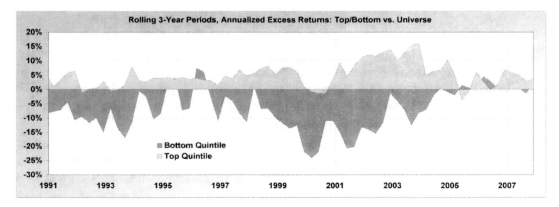

Figure 8.13 External Financing to Assets and Acquisitions to Invested Capital

The top quintile outperforms by 6.0%, on average, and does so for 69% of one-year and 83% of rolling three-year periods (see Figure 8.14). It underperforms significantly only in 1990, 1998–2000, and 2007. The strategy is somewhat volatile, with a maximum loss of 30% and a standard deviation of returns of 0.19, above the 0.16 value for the Universe, resulting in a moderate Sharpe ratio of 0.75. By combining the external financing strategy with a valuation strategy, we significantly reduce the average market cap of the top quintile, which goes from $5.4 billion for external financing alone down to $1.8 billion for the combined strategy. Average portfolio values range from −7% to −12% for external financing to assets (representing net share repurchases and debt reductions) and 0.6× to 1.5× for price to book value.

The bottom quintile underperforms by 6.3%, on average, and does so for 77% of one-year and 93% of rolling three-year periods. It significantly outperforms in 1991, 1996, 1999–2000, 2003, and 2007. Outperformance during 1999 was a huge 168%, making this a volatile strategy. Average portfolio values range from 38% to over 100% for external financing to assets and from very high positive values to high negative values for price to book value, so companies in the bottom quintile are issuing large amounts of shares and/or debt and are expensive relative to asset (book) values.

External Financing to Assets and Free Cash Flow Plus Dividend Yield

External financing and free cash flow (FCF) plus dividend yield combines a strong capital allocation strategy with our strongest valuation strategy (FCF to price). We add dividend yield to FCF yield in this case, to emphasize companies that also pay significant dividends in the top quintile. So, the top quintile of this strategy contains companies that are repurchasing shares and reducing debt, have significant FCFs, pay dividends, and are cheap relative to FCF and dividends. The bottom quintile contains companies that are issuing shares and debt, have negative FCFs, and generally pay low or no dividends. The strategy is both strong and consistent.

The top quintile outperforms by 7.3%, on average, and does so for 76% of one-year and 86% of rolling three-year periods (see Figure 8.15). It significantly underperforms in 1990, 1996, 1999–2000, 2003, and 2007. The Sharpe ratio is a relatively high 0.85, and the maximum loss is 30%, about 5% above the maximum loss for the Universe. Average portfolio values for the top quintile range from −9% to −13% for external financing to assets (signifying share repurchases and/or debt reduction) and from 15% to over 30% for FCF plus dividend to price.

The bottom quintile underperforms by 8.5%, on average, and does so for 77% of one-year and 92% of rolling three-year periods. It significantly outperforms only in 1999–2000, 2003–2004, and 2005. Average portfolio values range from 20% to 48% for

1988–2007	1st Quintile	2nd Quintile	3rd Quintile	4th Quintile	5th Quintile	Universe	S&P 500*
CAGR – Annual Rebalance	18.0%	13.4%	13.2%	7.8%	−1.3%	11.2%	12.9%
Average Excess Return vs. Universe**	6.0%	2.4%	1.6%	−3.0%	−6.3%	NA	1.6%
Value of $10,000 Invested (20 Years)	$275,597	$122,859	$120,168	$44,640	$7,682	$83,161	$112,895
% of 1-Year Periods Strategy Outperforms the Universe	68.8%	61.0%	55.8%	32.5%	23.4%	NA	59.7%
% Rolling 3-Year Periods Strategy Outperforms	82.6%	65.2%	56.5%	20.3%	7.2%	NA	71.0%
Maximum Gain	83.1%	62.6%	78.9%	59.8%	194.1%	59.2%	54.1%
Maximum Loss	−30.3%	−26.3%	−26.1%	−39.4%	−77.5%	−24.9%	−25.9%
Sharpe Ratio	0.75	0.67	0.56	0.30	0.04	0.49	0.69
Standard Deviation of Returns	0.19	0.16	0.17	0.17	0.41	0.16	0.14
Beta (vs. Universe)	0.88	0.78	0.93	0.95	1.74	NA	0.78
Alpha (vs. Universe)	0.07	0.05	0.02	−0.02	−0.16	NA	0.04
Average Portfolio Size	70	70	70	70	70	NA	NA
Average Number of Companies *Outperforming*	32	33	30	28	22	NA	NA
Average Number of Companies *Underperforming*	33	33	36	39	45	NA	NA
Median Portfolio Value – External Financing to Assets	−9.6%	−1.6%	0.8%	5.1%	52.2%	5.4%	0.3%
Median Portfolio Value – Price to Book	1.1	1.7	2.4	4.1	48.1	2.3	2.3
Average Market Capitalization	$1,779	$3,009	$4,402	$5,989	$2,939	NA	NA

* Equal-weighted average of S&P 500 returns. ** Annual holding period run quarterly for a larger sample size; arithmetic average excess returns.
Source: Standard & Poor's Compustat Point in Time Database; Charter Oak Investment Systems, Inc., Venues® Data Engine

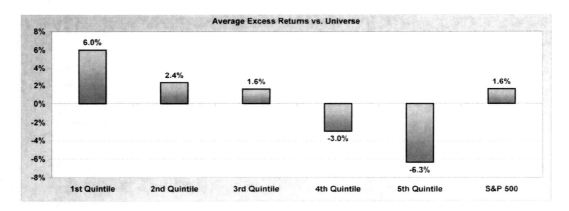

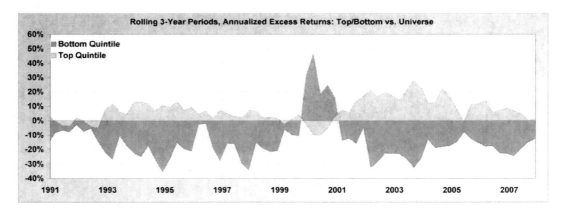

Figure 8.14 External Financing to Assets and Price to Book Value

1990–2007	1st Quintile	2nd Quintile	3rd Quintile	4th Quintile	5th Quintile	Universe	S&P 500*
CAGR – Annual Rebalance	19.3%	12.6%	14.1%	6.8%	1.2%	10.3%	12.0%
Average Excess Return vs. Universe**	7.3%	2.4%	1.3%	−3.5%	−8.5%	NA	1.5%
Value of $10,000 Invested (18 Years)	$238,451	$84,960	$106,626	$32,470	$12,463	$58,670	$76,297
% of 1-Year Periods Strategy Outperforms the Universe	76.1%	54.9%	47.9%	35.2%	22.5%	NA	56.3%
% Rolling 3-Year Periods Strategy Outperforms	85.7%	73.0%	47.6%	12.7%	7.9%	NA	68.3%
Maximum Gain	69.4%	54.1%	55.0%	59.5%	92.6%	59.2%	54.1%
Maximum Loss	−29.9%	−24.1%	−44.4%	−41.9%	−64.4%	−24.9%	−25.9%
Sharpe Ratio	0.85	0.77	0.50	0.20	−0.02	0.46	0.64
Standard Deviation of Returns	0.18	0.13	0.18	0.21	0.30	0.17	0.15
Beta (vs. Universe)	0.76	0.60	0.95	1.11	1.58	NA	0.78
Alpha (vs. Universe)	0.10	0.07	0.02	−0.05	−0.16	NA	0.04
Average Portfolio Size	66	67	67	67	67	NA	NA
Average Number of Companies *Outperforming*	33	31	30	26	24	NA	NA
Average Number of Companies *Underperforming*	31	33	34	38	40	NA	NA
Median Portfolio Value – External Financing to Assets	−10.4%	−1.8%	0.7%	5.2%	29.8%	5.4%	0.3%
Median Portfolio Value – Free Cash Flow + Dividend Yield	20.7%	8.1%	3.5%	−1.9%	−30.6%	3.0%	5.0%
Average Market Capitalization	$3,955	$6,278	$6,451	$3,430	$1,462	NA	NA

* Equal-weighted average of S&P 500 returns. ** Annual holding period run quarterly for a larger sample size; arithmetic average excess returns.
Source: Standard & Poor's Compustat Point in Time Database; Charter Oak Investment Systems, Inc., Venues® Data Engine

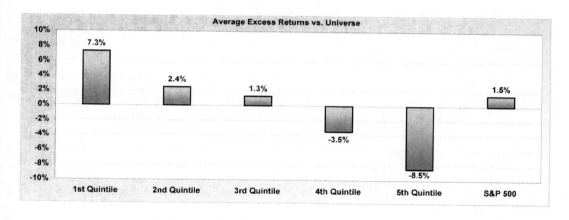

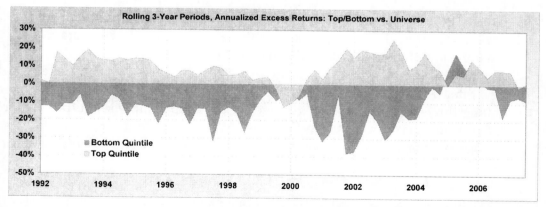

Figure 8.15 External Financing to Assets and Free Cash Flow Plus Dividend Yield

external financing to assets (signifying large share and debt issuance) and from −15% to −52% for FCF plus dividend to price (indicating high negative cash flows).

External Financing to Assets and 52-Week Price Range

In Chapter 5, we combined a valuation factor (price to earnings plus dividends) with 52-week price range and found that the two worked well together. Here we combine a capital allocation factor and 52-week price range—a price momentum factor—and get even stronger results. Price momentum tells the investor whether demand for a given stock strong is strong, weak, or indifferent. Strong demand for a stock may indicate that the market believes that something is improving fundamentally at the company, whereas weak demand may indicate that the market believes something is not well. While the opinions of market participants are certainly not always right, the market's "opinion" is *often* right, and this is where price momentum indicators come in handy.

As you'll recall, 52-week price range indicates how close a stock is to its 52-week high (the top quintile) or its 52-week low (the bottom quintile).[8] In the top quintile of this strategy, we have companies that are repurchasing shares and reducing debt and whose stock prices are near their 52-week highs. The price action of these stocks indicates that investors believe these companies are doing something right. The bottom quintile contains companies that are issuing shares and debt and whose stock prices are near their 52-week lows. The price action of these stocks is a vote of no confidence in the company's actions. As you'll see, the companies in this quintile are punished severely.

The top quintile outperforms by 5.7%, on average, and does so for 71% of one-year and 90% of rolling three-year periods (see Figure 8.16). It has a low maximum loss of 22%, a relatively low standard deviation of 0.16, and a strong Sharpe ratio of 0.84. The strategy's main weakness is that it didn't work in recent years: 2003–2004 and 2006–2007. Average portfolio values range from −8% to −13% for external financing to assets (indicating significant share repurchases and/or debt reduction) and 62% to 98% for 52-week price range, indicating stocks of these companies are an average of 38% to 2% below the top of their 52-week price ranges.

The bottom quintile underperforms by over 13%, on average, making it a strong short-sale strategy. It is also very consistent, underperforming for 82% of one-year and 96% of rolling three-year periods. On average, 47 portfolio companies outperform for every 22 that underperform, a strong showing. Average portfolio values range from 19% to 93% for external financing to assets (indicating large share and/or debt issuance)

---

[8] The formula is (current price − 52-week low)/(52-week high − 52-week low). The 52-week price range strategy is discussed in depth in Chapter 9.

1988–2007	1st Quintile	2nd Quintile	3rd Quintile	4th Quintile	5th Quintile	Universe	S&P 500*
CAGR – Annual Rebalance	16.3%	13.1%	11.1%	7.3%	−4.3%	11.2%	12.9%
Average Excess Return vs. Universe**	5.7%	3.4%	1.4%	−3.3%	−13.1%	NA	1.6%
Value of $10,000 Invested (20 Years)	$205,338	$116,889	$82,727	$41,265	$4,171	$83,160	$112,895
% of 1-Year Periods Strategy Outperforms the Universe	71.4%	67.5%	48.1%	35.1%	18.2%	NA	62.3%
% Rolling 3-Year Periods Strategy Outperforms	89.6%	88.3%	57.1%	19.5%	3.9%	NA	76.6%
Maximum Gain	57.4%	52.7%	55.3%	68.2%	96.9%	59.2%	54.1%
Maximum Loss	−22.0%	−21.1%	−26.5%	−35.3%	−67.8%	−24.9%	−25.9%
Sharpe Ratio	0.84	0.83	0.57	0.27	−0.18	0.49	0.69
Standard Deviation of Returns	0.16	0.14	0.17	0.18	0.29	0.16	0.14
Beta (vs. Universe)	0.87	0.75	0.95	0.98	1.52	NA	0.78
Alpha (vs. Universe)	0.07	0.06	0.02	−0.03	−0.20	NA	0.04
Average Portfolio Size	70	70	70	70	71	NA	NA
Average Number of Companies *Outperforming*	32	32	29	28	22	NA	NA
Average Number of Companies *Underperforming*	32	35	37	40	47	NA	NA
Median Portfolio Value – Extern. Finan. to Assets	−10.6%	−1.7%	0.8%	5.1%	31.1%	5.4%	0.3%
Median Portfolio Value – 52-Week Price Range	96%	85%	64%	37%	16%	60%	59%
Average Market Capitalization	$6,238	$5,861	$5,219	$3,988	$1,745	NA	NA

* Equal-weighted average of S&P 500 returns. ** Annual holding period run quarterly for a larger sample size; arithmetic average excess returns.
Source: Standard & Poor's Compustat Point in Time Database; Charter Oak Investment Systems, Inc., Venues® Data Engine

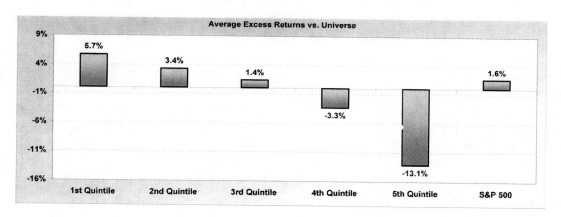

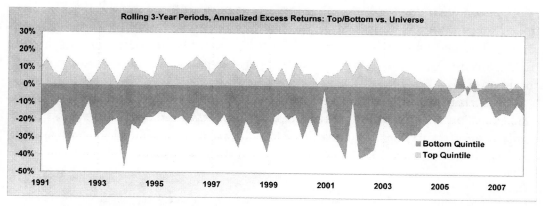

Figure 8.16 External Financing to Assets and 52-Week Price Range

and 3% to 29% for 52-week price range. The strategy significantly outperformed only in 1991, 1999, and 2003–2004. Two of these periods, 1991 and 2003–2004, correspond to the end of a bear market/beginning of a new bull market when beaten down stocks of low-quality companies usually outperform.

THREE-YEAR AVERAGE CAPITAL EXPENDITURES TO INVESTED CAPITAL

In the two-year average capex per share growth strategy, in Chapter 7, we saw that companies that grow capital expenditures too rapidly (by an average of over 100% each year for two consecutive years) significantly underperform. One reason for this is that companies often expand their businesses the most just prior to a peak in their business cycles. On the other hand, we saw that companies that decreased capital spending significantly (by an average of 15% or more per year over two consecutive years) outperform. The ability to decrease capital spending may indicate that productivity is improving (i.e., that these corporations are getting the same or better output from a decreased investment in plant, machinery, equipment, etc.).

This strategy looks at capital spending adequacy. Companies that spend low amounts on capital expenditures relative to their total capital base over a three-year period underperform, while companies that spend high amounts relative to capital tend to outperform. This test doesn't take into account whether a company is in a capital-intensive industry or not, or whether it earns a strong return on its capital investment or not. However, it does show, using a very broad brush stroke, that companies that spend too little on capex often run into problems. Note that the first quintile has only minor excess returns. These are companies that are spending the highest amounts on capex relative to capital, and in some cases perhaps overspending.[9]

Companies in the *second* quintile outperform by an average of 1.9%, and do so for 66% of one-year and 74% of rolling three-year periods (see Figure 8.17). The Sharpe ratio for this strategy is a moderate 0.65. Average portfolio values for three-year capex to invested capital range from 8% to 14%, indicating that these companies are spending a significant amount on capital maintenance and expansion relative to their invested capital base.

The bottom quintile underperforms by 1.3% on average, and does so for 66% of one-year and 64% of rolling three-year periods. Average portfolio values for this quintile range from 1% to 3%, meaning that companies in this quintile are spending very little on capital expenditures relative to invested capital.

---

[9] Note that banks and most utility companies are excluded from this calculation, as they do not have quarterly values for capital expenditures in the Compustat database.

1988–2007	1st Quintile	2nd Quintile	3rd Quintile	4th Quintile	5th Quintile	Universe	S&P 500*
CAGR – Annual Rebalance	11.6%	13.5%	13.0%	10.9%	9.5%	11.2%	12.9%
Average Excess Return vs. Universe**	1.0%	1.9%	1.3%	−0.4%	−1.3%	NA	1.6%
Value of $10,000 Invested (20 Years)	$89,302	$126,673	$115,070	$79,875	$61,439	$83,161	$112,895
% of 1-Year Periods Strategy Outperforms the Universe	59.7%	66.2%	61.0%	39.0%	33.8%	NA	59.7%
% Rolling 3-Year Periods Strategy Outperforms	49.3%	73.9%	75.4%	30.4%	36.2%	NA	71.0%
Maximum Gain	59.7%	57.3%	57.6%	60.6%	61.4%	59.2%	54.1%
Maximum Loss	−24.2%	−26.9%	−26.4%	−28.5%	−26.6%	−24.9%	−25.9%
Sharpe Ratio	0.59	0.65	0.61	0.47	0.38	0.49	0.69
Standard Deviation of Returns	0.15	0.15	0.16	0.16	0.18	0.16	0.14
Beta (vs. Universe)	0.89	0.91	0.93	0.96	1.03	NA	0.78
Alpha (vs. Universe)	0.02	0.03	0.02	0.00	−0.02	NA	0.04
Average Portfolio Size	293	294	294	294	294	NA	NA
Average Number of Companies *Outperforming*	125	132	131	121	125	NA	NA
Average Number of Companies *Underperforming*	154	148	148	158	154	NA	NA
Median Portfolio Value – 3Yr Av Capex to Inv Cap	21.7%	11.6%	8.1%	5.3%	1.8%	9.7%	10.8%
Average Market Capitalization	$5,781	$5,584	$4,897	$3,748	$3,963	NA	NA

* Equal-weighted average of S&P 500 returns. ** Annual holding period run quarterly for a larger sample size; arithmetic average excess returns.
Source: Standard & Poor's Compustat Point in Time Database, Charter Oak Investment Systems, Inc., Venues® Data Engine

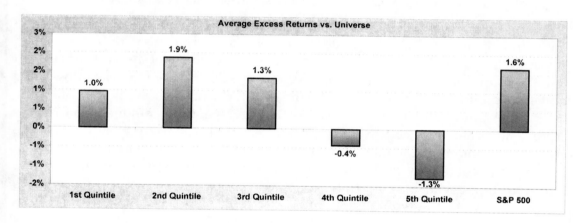

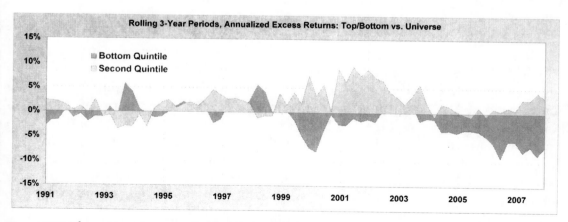

Figure 8.17 Three-Year Average Capital Expenditures to Invested Capital

Three-Year Average Capital Expenditures to Invested Capital by Economic Sector

Sector results in Figure 8.18 use the second and the fifth (bottom) quintile of the three-year average capital expenditures-to-invested capital strategy. As you saw in the non-sector backtest summary (Figure 8.17) the second quintile outperforms the first quintile, on average. The sector test shows that the second quintile of this test is driven by the information technology and telecom services sectors. The strongest outperformance for these two sectors takes place during 1998 and 1999—precisely the period we *don't* want a strategy to outperform. So, the sector test indicates that the capex-to-invested capital strategy alone is biased by sector results occurring in 1998 and 1999. Despite this fact, we'll see in the next test that this bias can be removed simply by combining the capex-to-invested capital strategy with a valuation strategy.

Three-Year Average Capital Expenditures to Invested Capital and Free Cash Flow to Price

Note, first of all, that unlike the capex to invested capital strategy alone, which outperforms strongly in 1999–2000, this strategy *does not* work during this period. The companies in the top quintile of this strategy are spending significant amounts of cash on capital improvements and expansion, have positive FCFs (operating cash flows *after* capital expenditures), and do not require the investor to pay a lot for those cash flows. The bottom quintile contains companies that are spending minimally on capital improvements and have negative FCFs. These companies are likely spending too little on capital expenditures and may have a liquidity problem (not enough cash coming in). The strategy works very well and has generated very high returns in recent years, in contrast to the FCF-to-price strategy alone, which has not generated high returns in recent years. Also note that the returns for this strategy are quite linear, as is the maximum loss, indicating that the correlation between the strategy, returns, and risk is a strong one.

The top quintile outperforms by 5.7%, on average, and does so for 68% of one-year and 86% of rolling three-year periods (see Figure 8.19). It significantly underperforms only in 1991, 1999–2000, and 2003–2004. The strategy has a very low maximum loss (18%) and a low standard deviation of returns (0.14), with the latter aiding its very high Sharpe ratio of 0.96. Note that the top quintile of the FCF-to-price strategy alone outperforms by 5.6%, on average and has a standard deviation of returns of 0.17 and a resulting Sharpe ratio of just 0.78. So, although the excess returns for the top quintile of the current strategy are about equal to those for the top quintile of FCF to price alone, the volatility of the current strategy is less, and the resulting Sharpe ratio is significantly higher. Average portfolio values range from 15% to 24% for three-year average capex to invested capital and 6% to 13% for FCF to price.

Second Quintile

1988–2007	Energy	Materials	Industrials	Consumer Discretionary	Consumer Staples	Health Care	Financials	Information Technology	Telecom Services	Utilities	Universe	SP 500*
CAGR – Quintile	11.1%	10.5%	12.7%	9.0%	11.1%	12.5%	14.0%	14.4%	16.4%	7.1%	11.2%	12.9%
CAGR – Sector	13.5%	10.2%	11.3%	8.7%	12.6%	12.3%	14.5%	7.5%	9.2%	13.0%	NA	NA
Excess Return vs. Sector	−2.5%	0.3%	1.5%	0.2%	−1.5%	0.2%	−0.5%	6.9%	7.2%	−5.8%	NA	NA
Value of $10,000	$81,392	$73,813	$109,537	$55,594	$82,147	$105,258	$137,481	$147,680	$207,902	$39,686	$83,160	$112,895
% 1-Year Outperformance	35.0%	30.0%	60.0%	50.0%	40.0%	65.0%	50.0%	80.0%	55.0%	55.0%	NA	NA
% 3-Year Outperformance	27.8%	38.9%	83.3%	66.7%	33.3%	44.4%	38.9%	88.9%	72.2%	55.6%	NA	NA
Maximum Gain	75.4%	40.8%	41.9%	57.2%	37.7%	49.4%	61.3%	174.7%	223.8%	147.2%	44.0%	41.4%
Maximum Loss	−44.4%	−15.3%	−11.4%	−24.7%	−17.4%	−32.6%	−30.2%	−43.0%	−38.0%	−84.2%	−19.1%	−18.1%
Standard Deviation	0.27	0.15	0.14	0.19	0.14	0.19	0.23	0.45	0.55	0.47	0.16	0.14
Beta (vs. Sector)	1.03	1.00	0.91	0.99	0.96	0.69	1.01	1.17	1.37	2.38	NA	NA
Alpha (vs. Sector)	−0.03	0.00	0.02	0.00	−0.01	0.04	0.00	0.06	0.05	−0.15	NA	NA
Portfolio Size	19	28	53	61	20	33	24	46	7	3	NA	NA

Bottom Quintile

1988–2007	Energy	Materials	Industrials	Consumer Discretionary	Consumer Staples	Health Care	Financials	Information Technology	Telecom Services	Utilities	Universe	SP 500*
CAGR – Quintile	15.8%	10.7%	10.2%	7.5%	10.7%	9.0%	12.3%	5.9%	5.6%	11.8%	11.2%	12.9%
CAGR – Sector	13.5%	10.2%	11.3%	8.7%	12.6%	12.3%	14.5%	7.5%	9.2%	13.0%	NA	NA
Excess Return vs. Sector	2.3%	0.5%	−1.1%	−1.2%	−1.9%	−3.3%	−2.2%	−1.6%	−3.6%	−1.2%	NA	NA
Value of $10,000	$188,036	$75,935	$69,572	$42,187	$76,231	$56,244	$101,459	$31,291	$29,888	$92,951	$83,160	$112,895
% 1-Year Outperformance	60.0%	50.0%	40.0%	45.0%	40.0%	25.0%	40.0%	45.0%	30.0%	45.0%	NA	NA
% 3-Year Outperformance	77.8%	50.0%	44.4%	50.0%	33.3%	22.2%	27.8%	27.8%	27.8%	44.4%	NA	NA
Maximum Gain	54.1%	35.3%	34.6%	46.3%	30.5%	69.5%	46.7%	96.1%	88.0%	153.9%	44.0%	41.4%
Maximum Loss	−48.7%	−18.7%	−14.2%	−27.5%	−30.5%	−29.9%	−33.4%	−40.6%	−49.7%	−62.2%	−19.1%	−18.1%
Standard Deviation	0.27	0.16	0.14	0.20	0.16	0.25	0.22	0.30	0.36	0.44	0.16	0.14
Beta (vs. Sector)	1.00	1.00	0.90	1.00	1.02	0.94	0.94	0.78	0.81	1.06	NA	NA
Alpha (vs. Sector)	0.03	0.04	0.02	−0.02	0.07	−0.01	0.04	−0.09	−0.07	−0.01	NA	NA
Portfolio Size	20	29	54	63	21	34	32	47	7	3	NA	NA

* Equal-weighted average of S&P 500 returns.
Source: Standard & Poor's Compustat Point in Time Database; Charter Oak Investment Systems, Venues® Data Engine

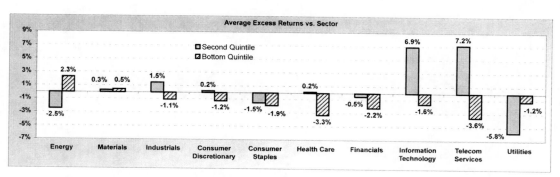

Figure 8.18 Three-Year Average Capital Expenditures to Invested Capital by Economic Sector

1990–2007	1st Quintile	2nd Quintile	3rd Quintile	4th Quintile	5th Quintile	Universe	S&P 500*
CAGR – Annual Rebalance	15.9%	13.0%	12.2%	5.7%	1.1%	10.3%	12.0%
Average Excess Return vs. Universe**	5.7%	3.6%	1.1%	−4.5%	−7.1%	NA	1.5%
Value of $10,000 Invested (18 Years)	$141,314	$90,371	$79,148	$27,074	$12,267	$58,670	$76,297
% of 1-Year Periods Strategy Outperforms the Universe	67.6%	64.8%	52.1%	21.1%	21.1%	NA	56.3%
% Rolling 3-Year Periods Strategy Outperforms	85.7%	76.2%	58.7%	9.5%	1.6%	NA	68.3%
Maximum Gain	52.4%	45.5%	52.5%	73.1%	88.6%	59.2%	54.1%
Maximum Loss	−17.5%	−20.5%	−29.7%	−49.6%	−39.4%	−24.9%	−25.9%
Sharpe Ratio	0.96	0.83	0.55	0.15	0.03	0.46	0.64
Standard Deviation of Returns	0.14	0.14	0.16	0.22	0.25	0.17	0.15
Beta (vs. Universe)	0.62	0.70	0.88	1.13	1.36	NA	0.78
Alpha (vs. Universe)	0.10	0.07	0.03	−0.06	−0.12	NA	0.04
Average Portfolio Size	57	57	57	57	58	NA	NA
Average Number of Companies *Outperforming*	27	27	25	21	22	NA	NA
Average Number of Companies *Underperforming*	27	28	30	34	33	NA	NA
Median Portfolio Value – 3Yr Av Capex to Inv Cap	20.2%	11.5%	8.0%	5.3%	1.8%	9.7%	10.9%
Median Portfolio Value – FCF to Price	9.0%	4.7%	3.5%	1.0%	−15.2%	2.1%	3.3%
Average Market Capitalization	$7,795	$7,960	$8,337	$5,176	$3,567	NA	NA

* Equal-weighted average of S&P 500 returns. ** Annual holding period run quarterly for a larger sample size; arithmetic average excess returns.
Source: Standard & Poor's Compustat Point in Time Database; Charter Oak Investment Systems, Inc., Venues® Data Engine

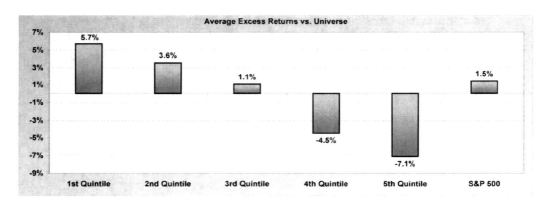

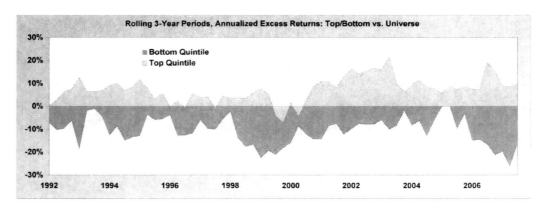

Figure 8.19 Three-Year Average Capital Expenditures to Invested Capital and Free Cash Flow to Price

The bottom quintile underperforms by an average of 7.1% (vs. 4.5% for the FCF-to-price strategy alone), and does so for 79% of one-year and 98% of rolling three-year periods, making it very consistent. It significantly outperforms in 1990–1991, 1996, 2000, and 2003–2004. Note that the fourth quintile also generates significant negative excess returns (−4.5%, on average) and is nearly as consistent as the fifth quintile. The companies in the bottom two quintiles of this strategy should be sold or avoided. Average portfolio values for the bottom quintile range from 1% to 3% for three-year average capital expenditures to invested capital and −7% to −34% for FCF to price, so these are companies that are spending very little on maintaining their capital assets and are not even generating sufficient cash to pay for existing capital expenditures.

ACQUISITIONS TO INVESTED CAPITAL

You've already seen the acquisitions to invested capital strategy in Chapter 6, as well as earlier in this chapter. The test would be better called *cash acquisitions* to invested capital, as it only takes into account cash outflows related to acquisitions, as reported in the investing section of a company's statement of cash flows. (It therefore does *not* include stock-based business acquisitions; we capture stock-based acquisitions through the one-year reduction/increase in shares strategy.) Acquisitions as defined in the Compustat database include cash outflows used to purchase the net assets or property, plant, and equipment (PP&E) of an acquired business; long-term debt assumed in an acquisition; costs in excess of the net assets of businesses acquired (goodwill); additional investment in consolidated subsidiaries; and other increases in business ownership.

Because so many companies have no cash acquisitions in a given year, and we require that set sizes be equal among the five quintiles, we use a little trick to differentiate among these companies. If a company has had no acquisitions, we set the value for acquisitions to 0.1 (instead of 0) and divide this by invested capital. Although artificial, the trick works. Since they have larger amounts of invested capital, larger-cap companies that have made no cash acquisitions end up in the top quintile. Notice that the average market cap of the top quintile is $7.2 billion.

Smaller cap companies that have made no cash acquisitions are put in the second quintile. The average market cap of the second quintile is $1.1 billion. Notice that large-cap companies that avoid cash acquisitions (the first quintile) outperform more than small-cap companies that avoid cash acquisitions (the second quintile). This may be because small-cap companies can gain market share and scale by judiciously made acquisitions, while large caps generally already have the necessary scale to compete well.

The top quintile of this strategy (large-cap companies that avoid cash acquisitions) outperforms by an average of 2.9%, and does so for 75% of one-year and 81% of rolling three-year periods (see Figure 8.20). The top quintile significantly underperforms only

1988–2007	1st Quintile	2nd Quintile	3rd Quintile	4th Quintile	5th Quintile	Universe	S&P 500*
CAGR – Annual Rebalance	14.5%	12.6%	10.3%	10.0%	7.6%	11.2%	12.9%
Average Excess Return vs. Universe**	2.9%	1.3%	−0.5%	−1.5%	−3.0%	NA	1.6%
Value of $10,000 Invested (20 Years)	$149,105	$106,684	$70,832	$67,852	$43,300	$83,160	$112,895
% of 1-Year Periods Strategy Outperforms the Universe	75.3%	62.3%	40.3%	35.1%	24.7%	NA	59.7%
% Rolling 3-Year Periods Strategy Outperforms	81.2%	65.2%	30.4%	24.6%	7.2%	NA	71.0%
Maximum Gain	64.3%	60.4%	65.8%	59.5%	54.4%	59.2%	54.1%
Maximum Loss	−25.3%	−25.7%	−36.0%	−28.9%	−29.0%	−24.9%	−25.9%
Sharpe Ratio	0.69	0.53	0.38	0.40	0.32	0.49	0.69
Standard Deviation of Returns	0.16	0.18	0.20	0.16	0.16	0.16	0.14
Beta (vs. Universe)	0.93	1.03	1.15	0.97	0.92	NA	0.78
Alpha (vs. Universe)	0.04	0.01	−0.02	−0.01	−0.02	NA	0.04
Average Portfolio Size	322	321	321	321	321	NA	NA
Average Number of Companies *Outperforming*	148	138	129	137	132	NA	NA
Average Number of Companies *Underperforming*	159	165	174	169	173	NA	NA
Median Portfolio Value – Acquisitions to Inv. Cap.	−0.7%	0.0%	0.1%	2.3%	22.2%	4.8%	4.2%
Average Market Capitalization	$7,226	$1,124	$3,027	$5,257	$3,627	NA	NA

* Equal-weighted average of S&P 500 returns. ** Annual holding period run quarterly for a larger sample size; arithmetic average excess returns.
Source: Standard & Poor's Compustat Point in Time Database; Charter Oak Investment Systems, Inc., Venues® Data Engine

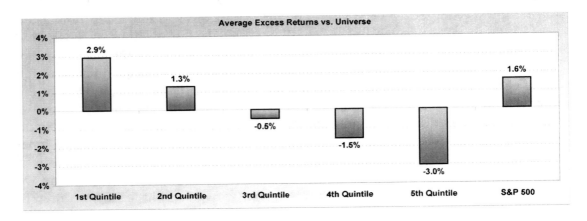

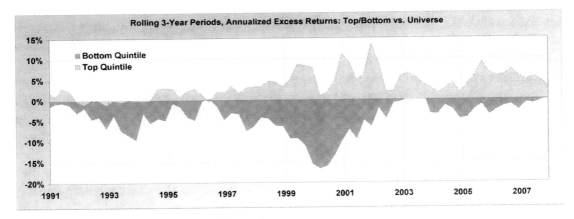

Figure 8.20 Acquisitions to Invested Capital

during 1991–1992 and briefly in 2000. It has a maximum loss of 25% and a Sharpe ratio of 0.69, both in line with the S&P 500. Average portfolio values are slightly negative, indicating that a few of these companies acquired assets that resulted in a net inflow of cash.[10] However, the vast majority of companies in the top quintile had a cash acquisitions value of zero or close to zero.

The bottom quintile underperforms by 3%, on average, and does so for 75% of one-year and 93% of rolling three-year periods. The bottom quintile significantly outperforms only in 1994, 2000–2001, and 2007. Average portfolio values for acquisitions to invested capital range from 11% to 33%, so companies in this quintile are making significant cash acquisitions relative to their existing capital bases.

Acquisitions to Invested Capital by Economic Sector

The strategy works well for the industrials, consumer discretionary, consumer staples, and information technology sectors, as well as the top quintile of the health care sector. It also works well as a negative strategy for financials, telecom services, and utilities; however, the strong negative results for the last two of these sectors primarily occurred during the 2000–2003 bear market. So, overall, the acquisitions-to-invested capital strategy is moderately consistent by sector (see Figure 8.21).

Acquisitions to Invested Capital and Capital Expenditures to Property, Plant, and Equipment

This strategy combines a capital allocation factor with a factor that measures capital intensity—how much capital investment a company must make each year to produce goods and/or provide services competitively. We've already seen the capex-to-PP&E strategy in previous chapters, and I'll cover it in detail in Chapter 10. For now, let's say that companies with high capex relative to existing PP&E may be seeing capital investments required to stay competitive increase (capital intensity is rising), while companies with low capital spending to PP&E may be becoming more productive and efficient (capital intensity is declining). Thus, the top quintile of this strategy selects companies that are not making cash acquisitions and that may be experiencing declining capital intensity, perhaps due to increasing productivity made possible by previous technology investments, outsourcing of manufacturing, and so on. Companies in the bottom quintile are making large cash acquisitions and are also making large investments in PP&E relative to their existing capital asset base. These two factors suggest that companies in the bottom quintile are struggling to remain competitive. The results of this test bear out these conclusions.

---

[10] Acquisitions are often reported on the cash flow statement as "net of cash acquired."

Top Quintile

1988–2007	Energy	Materials	Industrials	Consumer Discretionary	Consumer Staples	Health Care	Financials	Information Technology	Telecom Services	Utilities	Universe	SP 500*
CAGR – Quintile	14.3%	10.8%	15.2%	10.7%	15.1%	16.6%	15.7%	13.0%	11.7%	17.0%	11.2%	12.9%
CAGR – Sector	13.5%	10.2%	11.3%	8.7%	12.6%	12.3%	14.5%	7.5%	9.2%	13.0%	NA	NA
Excess Return vs. Sector	0.8%	0.6%	4.0%	2.0%	2.5%	4.3%	1.2%	5.5%	2.5%	4.0%	NA	NA
Value of $10,000	$145,630	$77,953	$170,267	$76,031	$166,507	$216,367	$184,834	$114,302	$92,025	$229,184	$83,160	$112,895
% 1-Year Outperformance	50.0%	55.0%	75.0%	70.0%	60.0%	70.0%	60.0%	70.0%	55.0%	45.0%	NA	NA
% 3-Year Outperformance	50.0%	44.4%	100.0%	72.2%	83.3%	94.4%	61.1%	77.8%	50.0%	61.1%	NA	NA
Maximum Gain	52.8%	42.5%	55.1%	44.0%	37.6%	66.6%	51.4%	154.5%	103.5%	135.6%	44.0%	41.4%
Maximum Loss	−24.5%	−20.6%	−17.4%	−32.7%	−14.5%	−23.3%	−23.3%	−49.4%	−40.1%	−40.4%	−19.1%	−18.1%
Standard Deviation	0.20	0.16	0.16	0.20	0.14	0.22	0.22	0.41	0.34	0.38	0.16	0.14
Beta (vs. Sector)	0.72	0.94	1.09	1.04	0.90	0.84	0.97	1.05	0.86	1.27	NA	NA
Alpha (vs. Sector)	0.04	0.02	0.03	0.02	0.04	0.06	0.02	0.05	0.04	0.04	NA	NA
Portfolio Size	22	29	56	69	21	38	31	52	8	3	NA	NA

Bottom Quintile

1988–2007	Energy	Materials	Industrials	Consumer Discretionary	Consumer Staples	Health Care	Financials	Information Technology	Telecom Services	Utilities	Universe	SP 500*
CAGR – Quintile	13.6%	9.8%	8.5%	5.4%	8.1%	12.6%	9.9%	3.8%	1.0%	−9.1%	11.2%	12.9%
CAGR – Sector	13.5%	10.2%	11.3%	8.7%	12.6%	12.3%	14.5%	7.5%	9.2%	13.0%	NA	NA
Excess Return vs. Sector	0.1%	−0.4%	−2.7%	−3.3%	−4.5%	0.2%	−4.6%	−3.7%	−8.2%	−22.1%	NA	NA
Value of $10,000	$128,864	$64,804	$51,310	$28,571	$47,750	$106,962	$65,781	$21,123	$12,158	$1,618	$83,160	$112,895
% 1-Year Outperformance	50.0%	45.0%	35.0%	30.0%	25.0%	65.0%	35.0%	35.0%	40.0%	42.1%	NA	NA
% 3-Year Outperformance	44.4%	50.0%	22.2%	11.1%	16.7%	61.1%	16.7%	16.7%	16.7%	38.9%	NA	NA
Maximum Gain	61.2%	33.3%	35.3%	46.1%	33.6%	63.9%	39.6%	60.8%	77.4%	88.8%	44.0%	41.4%
Maximum Loss	−54.0%	−21.1%	−22.8%	−25.0%	−21.7%	−23.1%	−22.0%	−49.3%	−52.1%	−80.6%	−19.1%	−18.1%
Standard Deviation	0.29	0.17	0.14	0.20	0.14	0.23	0.19	0.24	0.29	0.40	0.16	0.14
Beta (vs. Sector)	1.11	1.06	0.92	1.04	0.89	0.84	0.74	0.54	0.65	2.13	NA	NA
Alpha (vs. Sector)	−0.01	0.01	0.01	−0.05	0.04	0.07	0.03	−0.09	−0.10	−0.17	NA	NA
Portfolio Size	21	29	54	65	19	36	28	50	7	3	NA	NA

* Equal-weighted average of S&P 500 returns.
Source: Standard & Poor's Compustat Point in Time Database; Charter Oak Investment Systems, Inc., Venues® Data Engine

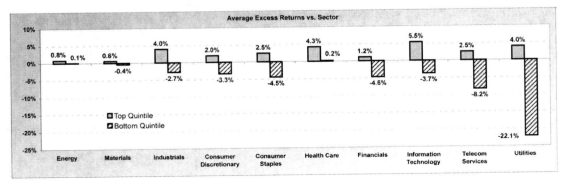

Figure 8.21 Acquisitions to Invested Capital by Economic Sector

1988–2007	1st Quintile	2nd Quintile	3rd Quintile	4th Quintile	5th Quintile	Universe	S&P 500*
CAGR – Annual Rebalance	17.2%	12.3%	11.2%	10.3%	−1.5%	11.2%	12.9%
Average Excess Return vs. Universe**	5.5%	2.2%	−0.2%	−1.3%	−11.8%	NA	1.6%
Value of $10,000 Invested (20 Years)	$237,273	$101,731	$84,163	$70,885	$7,433	$83,160	$112,895
% of 1-Year Periods Strategy Outperforms the Universe	70.1%	50.6%	41.6%	41.6%	13.0%	NA	59.7%
% Rolling 3-Year Periods Strategy Outperforms	87.0%	72.5%	30.4%	30.4%	1.4%	NA	71.0%
Maximum Gain	74.4%	59.6%	64.1%	68.0%	47.9%	59.2%	54.1%
Maximum Loss	−27.6%	−24.1%	−28.4%	−39.8%	−57.0%	−24.9%	−25.9%
Sharpe Ratio	0.81	0.64	0.46	0.36	−0.17	0.49	0.69
Standard Deviation of Returns	0.17	0.16	0.17	0.19	0.21	0.16	0.14
Beta (vs. Universe)	0.82	0.84	0.97	1.10	1.15	NA	0.78
Alpha (vs. Universe)	0.08	0.04	0.00	−0.03	−0.14	NA	0.04
Average Portfolio Size	61	61	61	61	60	NA	NA
Average Number of Companies *Outperforming*	31	25	25	27	19	NA	NA
Average Number of Companies *Underperforming*	28	32	33	32	38	NA	NA
Median Portfolio Value – Acquisitions to Inv. Cap.	−0.8%	0.0%	0.1%	2.6%	20.6%	4.8%	4.2%
Median Portfolio Value – Capex to PP&E	6.0%	16.0%	28.4%	33.3%	61.0%	29.4%	22.3%
Average Market Capitalization	$3,809	$974	$3,523	$5,567	$1,813	NA	NA

* Equal-weighted average of S&P 500 returns. ** Annual holding period run quarterly for a larger sample size; arithmetic average excess returns.
Source: Standard & Poor's Compustat Point in Time Database; Charter Oak Investment Systems, Inc., Venues® Data Engine

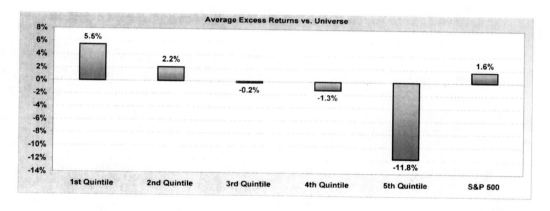

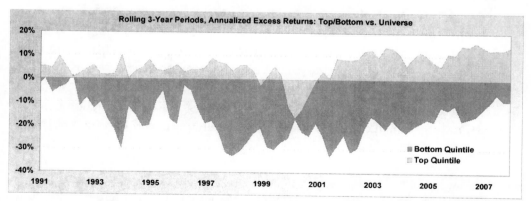

Figure 8.22 Acquisitions to Invested Capital and Capital Expenditures to Property, Plant, and Equipment

The top quintile outperforms by 5.5%, on average, and does so for 70% of one-year and 87% of rolling three-year periods (see Figure 8.22). The strategy significantly underperforms in only one period, 1998–2000, a period when many sound strategies failed to work.[11] Volatility is moderate, with a standard deviation of returns of 0.17, resulting in a moderately high Sharpe ratio of 0.81. Average portfolio values range from 0% to −3% for acquisitions to invested capital and from 3% to 9% for capex to PP&E.

The bottom quintile underperforms by 11.8%, on average, and does so for 87% of one-year and 99% of rolling three-year periods, making it extremely consistent. It significantly outperforms only in one period: 1990–1991. The maximum loss is a high 57%, while the maximum gain is only 48%. The Sharpe ratio of −0.17 is one of the lowest we've seen. In a word, this would make an excellent short-sale strategy. Average portfolio values range from 12% to 32% for cash acquisitions to invested capital and from 55% to 76% for capex to PP&E, so these are companies that are both making large acquisitions and making large additions to their existing capital asset base.

SUMMARY

- Our research shows that capital allocation is an important *basic*, combining well with almost every other basic presented in this book. In particular, capital allocation strategies show the investor what to avoid, and should be included in most short-sale strategies. The bottom quintiles of strategies that include capital allocation factors have the highest negative excess returns shown in this book.

- In general, companies with excess cash that use that cash in "shareholder friendly" ways, including judicious capital expenditures, dividend payments, share repurchases, and debt reduction, outperform, while companies that are short of cash that make large acquisitions and issue shares and debt underperform.

- The net share repurchase to invested capital strategy looks at the amount of cash spent on stock repurchases, net of cash received from share issuance. It works moderately well, but excess returns are generally low.

- A stronger share repurchase/issuance strategy is one-year reduction in shares outstanding, which compares the number of shares currently outstanding to

---

[11] Famed value investor Julian Robertson, founder of the hedge fund Tiger Management Corp. and possessor of one of the best long-term track records in investment history, was forced to close the fund in March 2000, as value-oriented investments were simply not performing.

shares outstanding four quarters ago. Companies that significantly reduce shares outstanding outperform, and those that issue large numbers of shares strongly underperform (by an average of over 5%).

- Our research shows that share repurchases work in proportion to the valuation at which the shares are bought back: companies that significantly reduce shares outstanding and do so at low valuations realize nearly twice the excess returns (outperformance) as do companies that significantly reduce share count regardless of valuation.

- The one-year reduction in shares outstanding and enterprise value to EBITDA strategy combines a share repurchase/issuance factor with a valuation factor, resulting in strong and consistent excess returns for both top and bottom quintiles. The bottom quintile contains over-priced companies that are issuing large numbers of shares; it would make a good short-sale strategy.

- Share repurchase strategies also combine well with technical, or price momentum-based, strategies (relative strength, 52-week price range).

- The one-year reduction in long-term debt strategy shows modest excess returns for the *second* quintile (companies reducing debt) and modest negative excess returns for the bottom quintile (companies issuing debt). It makes a useful building block, especially for investors interested in more conservative investment strategies.

- The net debt reduction to invested capital and net share repurchase to invested capital strategy contains, in the top quintile, companies that are spending significant amounts of cash on both debt reduction and share repurchase. Although the strategy considers *only* capital allocation, it generates moderately strong excess returns and is consistent.

- The top quintile of the one-year reduction in long-term debt and economic profits strategy contains companies that are generating very strong cash profits, relative to their cost of capital, and that are using excess cash to significantly reduce debt. It generates strong and consistent excess returns.

- The external financing to assets strategy brings the net debt reduction and net share repurchase strategies together into a single factor. It is calculated as cash received from share and debt issuance minus cash paid for stock repurchase and debt reduction plus the change in short-term (current) debt, all divided by total assets.

- External financing to assets combines well with every major type of strategy (all of the *basics*) presented in this book. In particular, it makes a good short-sale factor.

- The external financing to assets and price to book value strategy combines capital allocation with valuation—a strong combination—resulting in high, linear, and consistent excess returns.
- The external financing and FCF plus dividend yield strategy combines our best capital allocation strategy with our best valuation strategy (FCF to price). Excess returns are strong, linear, and consistent.
- The external financing to assets and 52-week price range strategy combines capital allocation and price momentum. The bottom quintile would make a good short-sale strategy.
- Results of the three-year average capex to invested capital strategy show that companies that spend too little on capital expenditures often run into problems, while companies that spend moderately-high amounts on capex outperform on average. However, the strategy is biased by results occurring in 1998 and 1999. This bias can be removed by combining the strategy with a valuation factor.
- The three-year average capex to invested capital and FCF to price strategy generates strong excess returns. Companies in the top quintile of this strategy have the cash flow to fund necessary capital expenditures, while those in the bottom do not.
- From a quantitative point of view, investors can enhance returns simply by avoiding companies that make large cash business acquisitions. In particular, large-cap companies that avoid cash acquisitions significantly outperform.
- The bottom quintile of the acquisitions to invested capital and capex to property, plant & equipment (PP&E) strategy contains companies that have made large cash acquisitions and are also making large investments in PP&E relative to their existing capital asset base. These two factors suggest that these companies are struggling to remain competitive. This quintile underperforms by almost 12%, on average, and is very consistent.

CHAPTER 9

Price Momentum

The skill in investing is distinguishing between what's going up and what's going down.

John Murphy, www.stockcharts.com

The hard-to-accept great paradox in the stock market is that what seems too high and risky to the majority usually goes higher and what seems low and cheap usually goes lower.

William J. O'Neil, *How to Make Money in Stocks*

We all know that prices move up and down. They always have and they always will. My theory is that behind these major movements there is an irresistible force. That is all one needs to know.

Jesse L. Livermore, *How to Trade in Stocks*

Price momentum strategies fall squarely under a type of investment strategy called *technical analysis*. The technical analyst seeks to predict future stock price movements by studying a stock's historical market action, the patterns and trends formed by changes in a stock's price and in its trading volume.[1] Put more simply, technical analysts read charts. The technical analyst often believes that "the chart tells the whole story," that is, that all available information relevant to valuing a stock, from company fundamentals to industry dynamics to economic conditions and psychological factors, are built into a stock's price and thus into its chart. By analyzing a stock's chart, the technician seeks to determine changes in the supply/demand balance for a stock that are likely to lead to further price movements, up or down, in the future.

---

[1] Technical analysis is not limited to analysis of common stocks. It is also applied to commodities, currencies, bonds, and so on. However, technical analysis as discussed here will focus on strategies that can be applied successfully to stocks.

Some on Wall Street and elsewhere look at technical analysis as a form of financial superstition, something akin to divining the future in patterns made by tea leaves or coffee grounds. The Random Walk theory, popularized by Burton Malkiel in his book *A Random Walk Down Wall Street*, tells us that price movements are random, unpredictable, and independent of each other, and therefore that a stock's past price movement can't be used to predict future trends. However, professional "tape readers" like Jesse Livermore proved the Random Walk theory wrong long before its birth. Livermore amassed millions of dollars in the stock market (at a time when a millionaire was *very* wealthy) just by watching minute-to-minute and day-to-day stock price patterns and "listening" to what these patterns were telling him about the condition of a stock or the market in general.

Every experienced investor knows instinctively that markets, and individual stocks, move in trends. Late in the nineteenth century Charles Dow identified three basic types of price movements underlying the stock market averages: primary movements, lasting from months to years; secondary movements, lasting from weeks to months; and minor fluctuations, lasting from a few hours to a few days.[2] Primary movements in the market are analogous to large swells in the ocean that go on for miles and are so large as to be imperceptible to the ship that is floating on them. Secondary movements are analogous to breaking waves that can be treacherous to ships caught in them, and daily price fluctuations are simply the minor ripples that occur constantly and mean little. The tests in this chapter aim to capture the primary trends in stocks, those that will drive them for several months (and with a little luck for our 12-month holding period).

So, if we are to believe that technical analysis is not financial sorcery, what are the market phenomena that make it work? Market technicians believe that changes in price action foreshadow changes in fundamentals. That is, they view changes in price as a leading indicator of something that is affecting company fundamentals that will become widely known only later. This is quite plausible. As discussed in Chapter 1, the market is often very efficient (it's just not *always* efficient). This means that relevant news about a company, industry, and so on, is quickly incorporated into a stock's price. If a company's order growth has suddenly started to slow, for example, it may not be immediately announced to the public. However, company employees, suppliers to the company, or competitors may notice the trend and act on it by selling shares in the stock market or by telling others, who then sell shares.[3] The average investor may have no

---

[2] Dow's theory was later more fully developed in books by William Peter Hamilton (*The Stock Market Barometer*) and Robert Rhea (*The Dow Theory*).

[3] Of course, it is illegal for corporate employees to trade company stock based on material inside information. However, cases of insider trading have occurred frequently throughout stock market history.

way to know what is fundamentally affecting the company at the time but can see that the stock's price action has suddenly begun to change for the worse.

It's also important to keep in mind that stock market participants attempt to anticipate future events. The economy may be growing rapidly, and business profits piling up, but if investors sense that the business cycle is overheating, stocks will go down, not up, in anticipation of a business slowdown that is likely to occur as credit is tightened to prevent inflation. The future is inherently unpredictable, so the opinions of market participants will be wrong at times. However, stock market participants include some very intelligent people, and market action tends to be "right" in anticipating future trends and events more often than it is wrong.

In addition, there are two more subtle reasons why technical analysis works. First, technical analysis reflects market psychology, as well as changes in company fundamentals; and market psychology affects the behavior of investors. Human psychology has been "grooved in" over the years and represents the one aspect of investing that can be counted on to repeat itself. Individual stocks and markets often bottom in a selling crescendo, when fear dominates and investors have given up hope; stocks and markets peak when investors ignore the value and quality of the assets they are purchasing, when the public believes the bull market will go on forever, and when speculative fervor is rampant. Technical indicators provide clues as to where we are in a stock or market cycle with regard to investor psychology, and hence what is likely to happen next. Second, technical analysis works to some extent simply because it has so many adherents who look for the same types of price patterns. Positive supply/demand trends tend to attract buyers, whereas negative trends cause selling. Thus, to the extent that technical analysts think in similar ways, technical analysis is self-fulfilling.

The price momentum strategies presented in this chapter are perhaps the simplest of technical strategies, and thus the strategies that lend themselves most readily to quantitative testing. *Price momentum* refers to the velocity[4] of price movement, or the rate of change of price over a specified time period. Since volume is necessary to push stock prices upward, positive price momentum tells us that an increased number of buyers have entered the market for a given stock: demand currently outweighs supply. Downward (negative) price momentum, in contrast, tells us that the supply/demand balance for a stock has tipped in favor of sellers: either selling has significantly increased, or there is simply an absence of buyers. Price momentum sounds too simple to work, yet our tests show that it does. Stocks that are high do indeed move higher, and

---

[4] *Velocity* can be defined as the speed with which an object moves in a given direction over a given period of time.

stocks that are low often move lower. In particular, we'll see that when price momentum is combined with fundamental factors—including valuation, profitability, cash generation, growth, and capital allocation—it yields quantitative results that are both strong and consistent over time. The results of these combinations provide concrete evidence of the benefits to the investor of an integrated approach to investment analysis that considers technical factors as well as fundamentals.

RELATIVE STRENGTH

Relative strength measures the price momentum of one stock, group of stocks, market index, and so on, relative to the price momentum of another stock, group of stocks, or market index. In this case, we are interested in the strength of each stock in our Universe relative to the strength of every other stock in the Universe. We calculate relative strength by simply ranking stocks according to their rate of change[5] over a specified period of time. The 20% of stocks with the highest rate of change go into the top quintile, the 20% with the lowest rate of change go into the bottom quintile, and so on. Relative strength tells us which stocks have been the best performers over a given period, and which stocks have been the worst. In general, we expect the best performing stocks to continue to perform strongly and the worst performers to continue to perform poorly.

Relative Strength: Top Quintile—Various Calculation Periods

Relative strength must be calculated over a certain time period, whether it is just the rate of change for a single day or for several months. In order to choose the optimal time period from a quantitative point of view—the time period with the most excess returns and highest consistency—we ran the relative strength test using a variety of time periods. Figure 9.1 shows the results for the top quintile of stocks by relative strength, run over various periods from 2 months through 80 months. Excess returns are shown in the middle column, and the percentage of one-year periods that the top quintile outperforms are shown in the third column. The holding period for each test was kept constant at 12 months. Portfolios are formed quarterly from 1987 through 2006, and excess returns are averaged across these periods.

---

[5] *Rate of change* is simply the percent change in a stock's price over a given period. It is calculated by dividing the most recent closing price for a security by the closing price X number of periods ago, where X represents the time period to be used in the rate of change calculation (7 months, 15 weeks, 25 days, etc.).

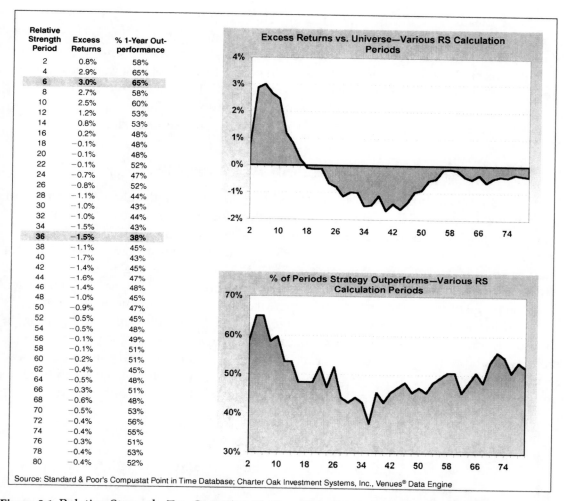

Figure 9.1 Relative Strength: Top Quintile—Various Calculation Periods in Months (12-Month Holding Periods)

Note that excess returns for the top quintile of the relative strength strategy tend to peak rather quickly. The six-month relative strength calculation period has the highest excess returns, at 3.0%, and the highest percentage of one-year periods that the strategy outperforms, at 65%. Note that after the 16-month calculation period excess returns turn negative. The lowest negative excess returns then occur at 40 months, at −1.7%. However, the percentage of underperformance (1 minus the percentage of outperformance) is highest at 36 months, where excess returns are −1.5% and the percentage of underperformance is 62% (1 − 38%).

From this test, we'll choose two relative strength periods, a short-term and a long-term calculation period. We'll choose seven-month relative strength for the top quintile of our short-term relative strength test. (Our testing shows that seven-month relative strength has slightly better performance than six months.) We expect that the top quintile by seven-month relative strength will outperform. For the bottom quintile of our long-term relative strength test, we'll choose a 36-month calculation period. We expect that the bottom quintile by 36-month relative strength will underperform.

Relative Strength: Bottom Quintile—Various Calculation Periods

Figure 9.2 shows the bottom quintile of stocks by relative strength calculation period for our backtest Universe. Like Figure 9.1, 12-month holding periods are used for all calculation periods. Notice that six-month relative strength shows the highest negative excess returns for the bottom quintile, at −3.6%, and the next-to-highest percentage of one-year periods of *under*performance, at 74% (1 – 26%). Following 14 months, excess returns turn positive, and excess returns don't peak until 90 months, at 3.7%. However, the percentage of one-year periods of outperformance peaks at 88 months, at 69%.

For our short-term relative strength measure for the bottom quintile, we'll again choose 7-month relative strength (which our testing shows works slightly better than six months), and for the top quintile of our long-term relative strength indicator we'll choose 88 months, or $7^1/_3$ years. We expect the bottom quintile by 7-month relative strength to underperform and the top quintile by 88-month relative strength to outperform.

Seven-Month Relative Strength

Our first full relative strength test uses seven-month relative strength for all quintiles. Testing showed that seven months was the optimum calculation period for a short-term relative strength strategy, in terms of both excess returns and consistency of those returns. When relative strength is expressed as a number (vs. a line on a stock chart), it is often expressed as a percentile, a number ranging from 1 to 100. A relative strength percentile of 85, for example, would signify that a stock had a relative strength ranking equal to or higher than 85% of its peers. In this test, we do not calculate the relative strength percentile ranking of the stocks, but simply the absolute seven-month rate of change. Stocks with the highest seven-month rates of change are put in the top quintile, and those with the lowest are put in the bottom quintile.

Note that the relative strength strategy by itself is volatile and somewhat inconsistent. The top quintile of this strategy outperforms by an average of 3.3%, and does so for 60% of one-year and 65% of rolling three-year periods (see Figure 9.3). It is quite volatile, with a maximum loss of 66%, the highest for a top quintile we've seen so far,

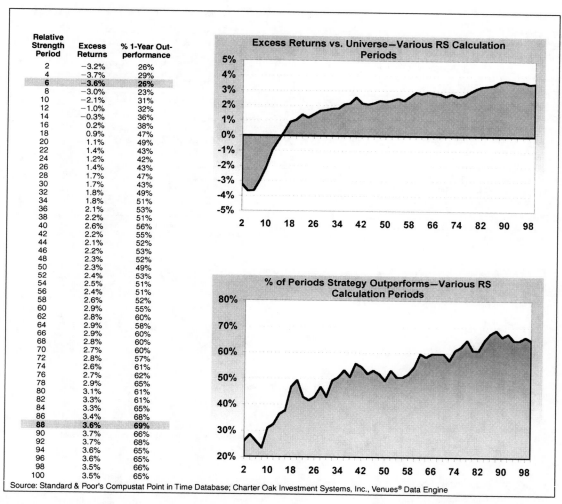

Relative Strength Period	Excess Returns	% 1-Year Out-performance
2	−3.2%	26%
4	−3.7%	29%
6	−3.6%	26%
8	−3.0%	23%
10	−2.1%	31%
12	−1.0%	32%
14	−0.3%	36%
16	0.2%	38%
18	0.9%	47%
20	1.1%	49%
22	1.4%	43%
24	1.2%	42%
26	1.4%	43%
28	1.7%	47%
30	1.7%	43%
32	1.8%	49%
34	1.8%	51%
36	2.1%	53%
38	2.2%	51%
40	2.6%	56%
42	2.2%	55%
44	2.1%	52%
46	2.2%	53%
48	2.3%	52%
50	2.3%	49%
52	2.4%	53%
54	2.5%	51%
56	2.4%	51%
58	2.6%	52%
60	2.9%	55%
62	2.8%	60%
64	2.9%	58%
66	2.9%	60%
68	2.8%	60%
70	2.7%	60%
72	2.8%	57%
74	2.6%	61%
76	2.7%	62%
78	2.9%	65%
80	3.1%	61%
82	3.3%	61%
84	3.3%	65%
86	3.4%	68%
88	3.6%	69%
90	3.7%	66%
92	3.7%	68%
94	3.6%	65%
96	3.6%	65%
98	3.5%	66%
100	3.5%	65%

Source: Standard & Poor's Compustat Point in Time Database; Charter Oak Investment Systems, Inc., Venues® Data Engine

Figure 9.2 Relative Strength: Bottom Quintile—Various Calculation Periods in Months (12-Month Holding Periods)

and a standard deviation of returns of 0.26, resulting in a Sharpe ratio of just 0.44, the lowest top-quintile Sharpe ratio recorded in this book. Average portfolio values for seven-month price change vary from 13% to well over 100%.

Note that the top quintile outperformed by over 50% in 1999–2000, resulting in the big bump seen on the rolling three-year returns graph. As we'll see later, this defect can be overcome by combining this factor with almost any valuation factor—just as growth and valuation make a natural pair, momentum and valuation do also.

1988–2007	1st Quintile	2nd Quintile	3rd Quintile	4th Quintile	5th Quintile	Universe	S&P 500*
CAGR – Annual Rebalance	12.3%	12.1%	12.6%	10.9%	8.4%	11.2%	12.9%
Average Excess Return vs. Universe**	3.3%	0.7%	0.5%	−0.1%	−3.4%	NA	1.6%
Value of $10,000 Invested (20 Years)	$101,219	$98,721	$107,933	$78,606	$49,854	$83,161	$112,895
% of 1-Year Periods Strategy Outperforms the Universe	59.7%	64.9%	55.8%	45.5%	26.0%	NA	59.7%
% Rolling 3-Year Periods Strategy Outperforms	65.2%	65.2%	60.9%	46.4%	11.6%	NA	71.0%
Maximum Gain	115.2%	50.1%	54.1%	51.6%	74.5%	59.2%	54.1%
Maximum Loss	−66.3%	−34.0%	−18.7%	−23.2%	−51.9%	−24.9%	−25.9%
Sharpe Ratio	0.44	0.60	0.62	0.54	0.22	0.49	0.69
Standard Deviation of Returns	0.26	0.15	0.14	0.15	0.22	0.16	0.14
Beta (vs. Universe)	1.29	0.85	0.79	0.80	1.15	NA	0.78
Alpha (vs. Universe)	0.00	0.03	0.03	0.02	−0.05	NA	0.04
Average Portfolio Size	429	430	430	430	430	NA	NA
Average Number of Companies *Outperforming*	175	192	198	190	175	NA	NA
Average Number of Companies *Underperforming*	217	215	215	223	236	NA	NA
Median Portfolio Value – 7-Month Price Change	91%	21%	7%	−5%	−24%	19%	5%
Average Market Capitalization	$3,113	$4,949	$5,295	$4,719	$2,999	NA	NA

* Equal-weighted average of S&P 500 returns. ** Annual holding period run quarterly for a larger sample size; arithmetic average excess returns.
Source: Standard & Poor's Compustat Point in Time Database; Charter Oak Investment Systems, Inc., Venues® Data Engine

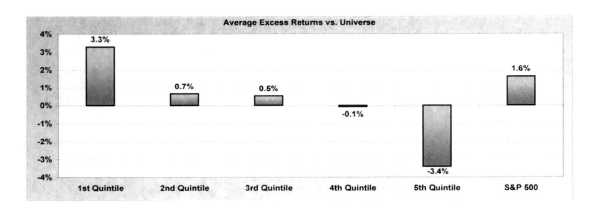

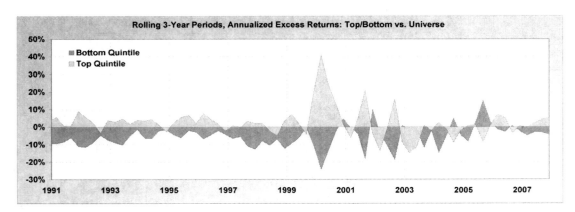

Figure 9.3 Seven-Month Relative Strength

The bottom quintile underperforms by 3.4%, on average, and does so for 74% of one-year and 88% of rolling three-year periods. It is also volatile, but not quite as volatile as the top quintile, with a maximum loss of 52% and a standard deviation of returns of 0.22. Average portfolio values for seven-month price change range from −3% to −46%.

Seven-Month Relative Strength by Economic Sector

The seven-month relative strength strategy works particularly well for the telecom and utilities sectors. Otherwise, the top quintile of this strategy alone is weak by sector. Seven-month relative strength also works well as a negative strategy for the energy, materials, industrials, and consumer discretionary sectors (see Figure 9.4).

88/36-Month Relative Strength

This test combines two long-term relative strength factors from our calculation period tests (Figures 9.1 and 9.2). We use 88-month relative strength for the top three quintiles and 36-month relative strength for the bottom two quintiles. The results are less strong, but not as volatile, as the seven-month relative strength strategy. The companies in the top quintile of this strategy have stock prices that have underperformed over a seven-year period, while the companies in the bottom quintile have *outperformed* for three years. The strategy works because negative and positive sentiment both get taken too far, and beaten down stocks eventually become value investments, while high flyers eventually fall back to earth.

The top quintile outperforms by 2.6%, on average, and does so for 55% of one-year and 61% of rolling three-year periods, making it less consistent than we'd like (see Figure 9.5). The maximum loss is 34%, almost half the 66% maximum loss of the top quintile of the seven-month relative strength strategy, and the Sharpe ratio is 0.55 (vs. 0.44). Average portfolio values for 88-month price change vary from −8% to −64%. If inflation is factored in, these are investments that have suffered large losses over the past seven years.

The bottom quintile underperforms by 1.5%, on average, and does so for 62% of one-year and 71% of rolling three-year periods. Average portfolio values for 36-month price change vary from 150% to well over 500%.

The major weakness of this strategy, as you can see from the three-year rolling returns graph, is its inconsistency over time. Strong excess returns primarily occurred in 1991–1995 and 1999–2004. However, we will see later that this flaw can be overcome by simply adding a valuation factor.

Top Quintile

1988–2007	Energy	Materials	Industrials	Consumer Discretionary	Consumer Staples	Health Care	Financials	Information Technology	Telecom Services	Utilities	Universe	S&P 500*
CAGR – Quintile	11.2%	12.0%	12.0%	9.6%	11.9%	10.6%	14.0%	8.5%	12.5%	15.4%	11.2%	12.9%
CAGR – Sector	13.5%	10.2%	11.3%	8.8%	12.6%	12.3%	14.5%	7.5%	9.2%	13.0%	NA	NA
Excess Return vs. Sector	−2.3%	1.8%	0.7%	0.9%	−0.7%	−1.7%	−0.5%	0.9%	3.3%	2.5%	NA	NA
Value of $10,000	$84,173	$95,782	$95,632	$62,876	$94,601	$75,094	$136,278	$50,873	$105,304	$176,740	$83,161	$112,895
% 1-Year Outperformance	50.0%	55.0%	55.0%	55.0%	50.0%	50.0%	35.0%	55.0%	65.0%	65.0%	NA	NA
% 3-Year Outperformance	50.0%	55.6%	44.4%	66.7%	55.6%	33.3%	38.9%	55.6%	72.2%	77.8%	NA	NA
Maximum Gain	66.2%	59.7%	44.7%	56.0%	54.3%	130.9%	54.1%	185.3%	122.7%	68.1%	44.0%	41.4%
Maximum Loss	−54.6%	−18.6%	−12.8%	−31.9%	−25.5%	−32.3%	−19.8%	−45.9%	−57.2%	−19.5%	−19.1%	−18.1%
Standard Deviation	0.30	0.19	0.16	0.22	0.17	0.36	0.22	0.48	0.43	0.18	0.16	0.14
Beta (vs. Sector)	1.16	1.03	1.01	1.05	1.01	1.32	0.97	1.23	0.94	1.00	NA	NA
Alpha (vs. Sector)	−0.03	0.02	0.01	0.01	0.00	−0.04	0.00	0.00	0.07	0.03	NA	NA
Portfolio Size	25	33	60	73	21	41	71	59	9	27	NA	NA

Bottom Quintile

1988–2007	Energy	Materials	Industrials	Consumer Discretionary	Consumer Staples	Health Care	Financials	Information Technology	Telecom Services	Utilities	Universe	S&P 500*
CAGR – Quintile	9.0%	6.9%	9.4%	4.2%	15.0%	11.2%	12.0%	7.5%	3.3%	10.4%	11.2%	12.9%
CAGR – Sector	13.5%	10.2%	11.3%	8.8%	12.6%	12.3%	14.5%	7.5%	9.2%	13.0%	NA	NA
Excess Return vs. Sector	−4.6%	−3.3%	−1.8%	−4.5%	2.4%	−1.1%	−2.4%	0.0%	−6.0%	−2.6%	NA	NA
Value of $10,000	$55,799	$37,834	$60,788	$22,837	$162,856	$83,957	$97,120	$42,393	$19,032	$71,752	$83,161	$112,895
% 1-Year Outperformance	25.0%	35.0%	45.0%	35.0%	55.0%	50.0%	45.0%	50.0%	35.0%	45.0%	NA	NA
% 3-Year Outperformance	22.2%	27.8%	22.2%	22.2%	50.0%	55.6%	44.4%	44.4%	38.9%	33.3%	NA	NA
Maximum Gain	66.9%	47.8%	46.7%	52.6%	62.6%	64.4%	53.9%	110.8%	156.9%	65.5%	44.0%	41.4%
Maximum Loss	−49.9%	−24.6%	−31.1%	−39.4%	−17.6%	−38.2%	−45.2%	−59.8%	−63.0%	−48.9%	−19.1%	−18.1%
Standard Deviation	0.29	0.19	0.18	0.22	0.21	0.26	0.26	0.38	0.46	0.23	0.16	0.14
Beta (vs. Sector)	1.05	1.19	1.11	1.08	1.25	0.95	1.13	0.96	1.11	1.27	NA	NA
Alpha (vs. Sector)	−0.04	0.00	−0.01	−0.05	0.10	0.01	0.02	−0.08	−0.08	0.01	NA	NA
Portfolio Size	25	34	62	77	24	43	74	62	10	28	NA	NA

* Equal-weighted average of S&P 500 returns.
Source: Standard & Poor's Compustat Point in Time Database; Charter Oak Investment Systems, Inc., Venues® Data Engine

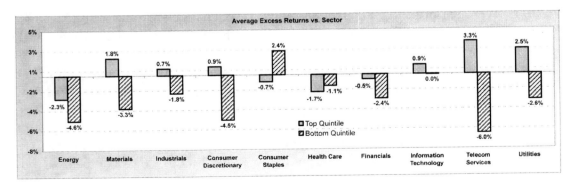

Figure 9.4 Seven-Month Relative Strength by Economic Sector

1988–2007	1st Quintile	2nd Quintile	3rd Quintile	4th Quintile	5th Quintile	Universe	S&P 500*
CAGR – Annual Rebalance	13.8%	12.4%	12.5%	12.8%	8.7%	11.2%	12.9%
Average Excess Return vs. Universe**	2.6%	1.1%	0.9%	1.0%	−1.5%	NA	1.6%
Value of $10,000 Invested (20 Years)	$133,549	$103,706	$106,140	$111,379	$52,587	$83,161	$112,895
% of 1-Year Periods Strategy Outperforms the Universe	54.5%	42.9%	53.2%	68.8%	37.7%	NA	59.7%
% Rolling 3-Year Periods Strategy Outperforms	60.9%	62.3%	65.2%	68.1%	29.0%	NA	71.0%
Maximum Gain	90.3%	51.7%	46.3%	50.0%	60.7%	59.2%	54.1%
Maximum Loss	−33.5%	−21.9%	−20.0%	−20.0%	−53.8%	−24.9%	−25.9%
Sharpe Ratio	0.55	0.66	0.70	0.63	0.30	0.49	0.69
Standard Deviation of Returns	0.20	0.14	0.13	0.14	0.22	0.16	0.14
Beta (vs. Universe)	0.98	0.70	0.69	0.84	1.24	NA	0.78
Alpha (vs. Universe)	0.03	0.05	0.05	0.03	−0.04	NA	0.04
Average Portfolio Size	366	365	365	371	371	NA	NA
Average Number of Companies *Outperforming*	161	167	165	167	150	NA	NA
Average Number of Companies *Underperforming*	185	182	184	185	199	NA	NA
Median Portfolio Value – 88/36-Month Price Change	−32.1%	12.6%	46.3%	80.9%	422.8%	118.2%	57.0%
Average Market Capitalization	$3,367	$4,992	$4,850	$5,400	$4,349	NA	NA

* Equal-weighted average of S&P 500 returns. ** Annual holding period run quarterly for a larger sample size; arithmetic average excess returns.
Source: Standard & Poor's Compustat Point in Time Database; Charter Oak Investment Systems, Inc., Venues® Data Engine

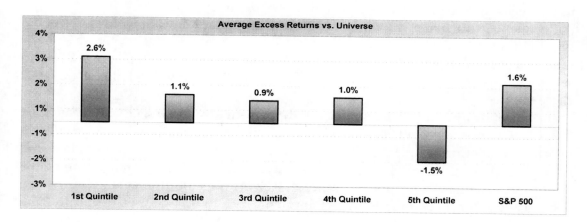

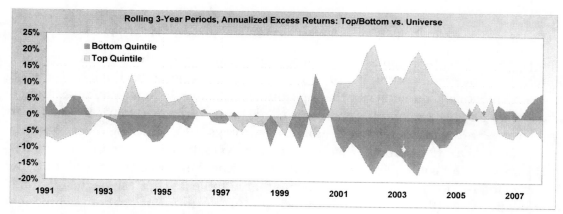

Figure 9.5 88/36-Month Relative Strength

Seven-Month Relative Strength and Free Cash Flow Plus Dividend Plus Share Repurchase to Price

As we saw in Chapter 5, valuation and price momentum strategies work well together. The valuation factor helps ensure that the investor is not overpaying for a stock, while the technical factor can indicate the presence of an underlying fundamental catalyst, seen by some investors but not widely known, that is likely to drive the stock higher. Generally speaking, I'd like to emphasize the valuation factor in a valuation/price momentum strategy, by selecting it first. However, in this chapter we'll look at how price momentum and valuation combine when the technical factor is emphasized. The strategy presented here combines valuation (FCF to price) and capital allocation (dividend plus share repurchase to price) with price momentum. It is both strong and consistent.

The top quintile outperforms by 8.3%, on average, and does so for 79% of one-year and 81% of rolling three-year periods (see Figure 9.6). The top quintile significantly underperforms during only two periods: 1999–2000 and 2003–2004. The strategy is quite volatile, with a maximum loss of 57% and a standard deviation of returns of 0.21 (vs. 0.14 for the S&P 500), resulting in a moderate Sharpe ratio of 0.76, versus a Sharpe ratio of 0.64 for the S&P 500. Average portfolio values range from 9% to over 150% for seven-month price change and from 3% to 25% for FCF plus dividend plus share repurchase to price.

The bottom quintile of this strategy underperforms by an average of 10%, and does so for 82% of one-year and 94% of rolling three-year periods. The bottom quintile significantly outperforms in 1999, 2001, 2003–2004, and 2006. The bottom quintile is even more volatile than the top quintile, with a maximum loss of 64%, a maximum gain of 109%, and a standard deviation of returns of 0.32. Average portfolio values range from −9% to −55% for seven-month price change and −9% to −51% for FCF plus dividend plus share repurchase to price.

88/36-Month Relative Strength and Enterprise Value to EBITDA

This strategy combines a long-term relative strength measure with a valuation measure. In terms of price momentum, it works in reverse of the seven-month relative strength test shown above. Companies in the top quintile have *low* 88-month relative strength and low valuations: top quintile companies have underperformed for over seven years and have very low prices relative to EBITDA (earnings before interest, taxes, depreciation, and amortization). In other words, they are oversold and underpriced. The 2006 portfolio included companies such as Gap Inc., Alcoa, Verizon Communications, and Navistar International. Companies in the bottom quintile, in contrast, have high three-year relative strength and very high valuations: these companies are both overbought and overpriced.

1990–2007	1st Quintile	2nd Quintile	3rd Quintile	4th Quintile	5th Quintile	Universe	S&P 500*
CAGR – Annual Rebalance	16.8%	12.1%	9.5%	6.3%	0.1%	10.3%	12.0%
Average Excess Return vs. Universe**	8.3%	1.7%	−0.8%	−2.8%	−10.0%	NA	1.5%
Value of $10,000 Invested (18 Years)	$164,763	$78,248	$50,830	$29,906	$10,252	$58,669	$76,297
% of 1-Year Periods Strategy Outperforms the Universe	79.2%	59.7%	48.6%	25.0%	18.1%	NA	56.9%
% Rolling 3-Year Periods Strategy Outperforms	81.3%	65.6%	35.9%	18.8%	6.3%	NA	68.8%
Maximum Gain	68.2%	47.6%	45.2%	57.4%	109.4%	59.2%	54.1%
Maximum Loss	−57.0%	−28.3%	−20.3%	−45.1%	−64.2%	−24.9%	−25.9%
Sharpe Ratio	0.76	0.66	0.56	0.28	−0.07	0.46	0.64
Standard Deviation of Returns	0.21	0.14	0.12	0.18	0.32	0.17	0.14
Beta (vs. Universe)	1.03	0.69	0.60	0.93	1.56	NA	0.78
Alpha (vs. Universe)	0.08	0.05	0.04	−0.02	−0.17	NA	0.04
Average Portfolio Size	66	66	66	67	67	NA	NA
Average Number of Companies *Outperforming*	31	31	27	26	23	NA	NA
Average Number of Companies *Underperforming*	29	32	36	38	41	NA	NA
Median Portfolio Value – 7-Month Price Change	61.6%	23.5%	9.6%	−6.2%	−26.3%	20.5%	5.6%
Median Portfolio Value – FCF + Div. + Repur. to Price	17.4%	8.5%	5.1%	−0.3%	−33.4%	1.8%	6.2%
Average Market Capitalization	$4,698	$8,073	$7,724	$5,194	$1,254	NA	NA

* Equal-weighted average of S&P 500 returns. ** Annual holding period run quarterly for a larger sample size; arithmetic average excess returns.
Source: Standard & Poor's Compustat Point in Time Database; Charter Oak Investment Systems, Inc., Venues® Data Engine

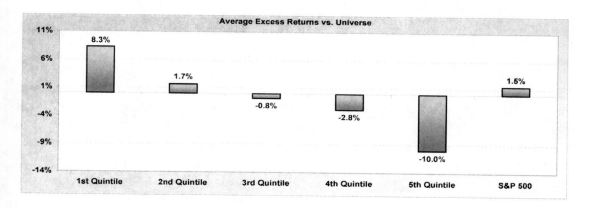

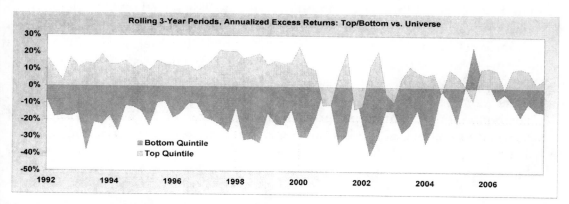

Figure 9.6 Seven-Month Relative Strength and Free Cash Flow Plus Dividend Plus Share Repurchase to Price

The top quintile outperforms by 7.7%, on average, and does so for 69% of one-year and 77% of rolling three-year periods (see Figure 9.7). The top quintile significantly underperforms in 1990–1991, 1995–1996, and 1999–2000. It has a moderate maximum loss of 28%, a standard deviation of returns of 0.19, and a moderately-strong Sharpe ratio of 0.83. Average portfolio values range from 12% to −46% for 88-month price change and 1× to 6× for enterprise value (EV) to EBITDA. Note that 27 portfolio companies outperform, on average, versus 23 that underperform, a strong showing for a top quintile.

The bottom quintile underperforms by 3.5%, on average, and does so for 62% of one-year and 81% of rolling three-year periods. The bottom quintile is very volatile, with a huge maximum gain of 174%, a standard deviation of returns of 0.40, and a Beta of 1.6 versus the Universe. Average portfolio values range from 250% to well over 500% for 36-month price change and very high positive to negative values for EV to EBITDA, indicating little or negative operating income. Note that the bottom quintile outperformed by an average of 71% in 1999–2000, so excluding this period, negative excess returns would have been significantly higher.

Seven-Month Relative Strength and Price to Earnings Plus Dividends

The top quintile of this strategy emphasizes companies that have strong short-term price momentum and low valuations on a price-to-estimated earnings basis[6] and that pay significant dividends. The bottom quintile contains companies with very low price momentum that are expensive on a price-to-forward earnings basis and generally pay no dividends. The strategy works moderately well, and the top quintile has been particularly consistent in recent years.

The top quintile outperforms by 4.8%, on average, and does so for 69% of one-year and 80% of rolling three-year periods (see Figure 9.8). It's relatively volatile, with a maximum loss of 46% and a standard deviation of returns of 0.20. The Sharpe ratio is 0.65, slightly below the Sharpe ratio of 0.69 for the S&P 500. Average portfolio values range from 4% to well over 100% for seven-month price change and from 9× to 12× (excluding 1998 and 1999, which were significantly higher) for price to earnings plus dividends.

The bottom quintile underperforms by 4.7%, on average, and does so for 67% of one-year and 84% of rolling three-year periods. It is quite volatile, outperforming by 70% in 1999 and 46% in 2003. Average portfolio values range from −9% to −54% for seven-month price change and are negative for price to earnings plus dividends.

---

[6] All price-to-earnings tests in this book use Thomson Reuters I/B/E/S average analysts' EPS estimates for a company's current fiscal year.

1988–2007	1st Quintile	2nd Quintile	3rd Quintile	4th Quintile	5th Quintile	Universe	S&P 500*
CAGR – Annual Rebalance	19.8%	14.2%	11.1%	11.3%	1.5%	11.2%	12.9%
Average Excess Return vs. Universe**	7.7%	2.3%	0.1%	−0.2%	−3.5%	NA	1.6%
Value of $10,000 Invested (20 Years)	$369,550	$142,719	$82,691	$84,435	$13,459	$83,160	$112,895
% of 1-Year Periods Strategy Outperforms the Universe	68.8%	54.5%	49.4%	50.6%	37.7%	NA	59.7%
% Rolling 3-Year Periods Strategy Outperforms	76.8%	65.2%	47.8%	47.8%	18.8%	NA	71.0%
Maximum Gain	82.0%	53.8%	46.0%	49.7%	174.7%	59.2%	54.1%
Maximum Loss	−27.5%	−19.5%	−16.3%	−22.2%	−65.2%	−24.9%	−25.9%
Sharpe Ratio	0.83	0.75	0.64	0.55	0.12	0.49	0.69
Standard Deviation of Returns	0.19	0.14	0.13	0.15	0.40	0.16	0.14
Beta (vs. Universe)	0.77	0.57	0.64	0.79	1.60	NA	0.78
Alpha (vs. Universe)	0.11	0.08	0.05	0.02	−0.11	NA	0.04
Average Portfolio Size	52	53	53	66	66	NA	NA
Average Number of Companies *Outperforming*	27	26	23	29	22	NA	NA
Average Number of Companies *Underperforming*	23	25	27	34	40	NA	NA
Median Portfolio Value – 88/36-Month Price Change	−24.9%	44.6%	112.9%	83.2%	523.9%	246.3%	176.5%
Median Portfolio Value – EV-to-EBITDA	4.0	6.8	9.1	13.1	110.3	10.0	8.8
Average Market Capitalization	$2,806	$3,605	$5,362	$6,960	$3,346	NA	NA

* Equal-weighted average of S&P 500 returns. ** Annual holding period run quarterly for a larger sample size; arithmetic average excess returns.
Source: Standard & Poor's Compustat Point in Time Database; Charter Oak Investment Systems, Inc., Venues® Data Engine

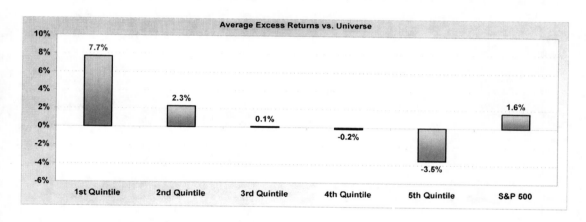

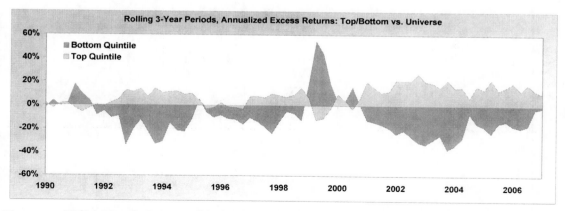

Figure 9.7 88/36-Month Relative Strength and Enterprise Value to EBITDA

1988–2007	1st Quintile	2nd Quintile	3rd Quintile	4th Quintile	5th Quintile	Universe	S&P 500*
CAGR – Annual Rebalance	14.8%	12.7%	12.3%	10.4%	6.6%	11.2%	12.9%
Average Excess Return vs. Universe**	4.8%	1.3%	1.0%	−0.5%	−4.7%	NA	1.6%
Value of $10,000 Invested (20 Years)	$157,498	$109,220	$101,274	$72,455	$36,237	$83,160	$112,895
% of 1-Year Periods Strategy Outperforms the Universe	68.8%	58.4%	57.1%	46.8%	32.5%	NA	59.7%
% Rolling 3-Year Periods Strategy Outperforms	79.7%	60.9%	59.4%	44.9%	15.9%	NA	71.0%
Maximum Gain	58.8%	50.7%	50.7%	57.7%	117.0%	59.2%	54.1%
Maximum Loss	−46.3%	−19.5%	−17.5%	−26.8%	−65.6%	−24.9%	−25.9%
Sharpe Ratio	0.65	0.65	0.70	0.48	0.10	0.49	0.69
Standard Deviation of Returns	0.20	0.15	0.13	0.16	0.33	0.16	0.14
Beta (vs. Universe)	0.96	0.66	0.57	0.81	1.67	NA	0.78
Alpha (vs. Universe)	0.05	0.06	0.06	0.02	−0.13	NA	0.04
Average Portfolio Size	73	74	74	74	74	NA	NA
Average Number of Companies *Outperforming*	34	34	34	32	28	NA	NA
Average Number of Companies *Underperforming*	34	36	37	39	43	NA	NA
Median Portfolio Value – 7-Month Price Change	45.6%	20.0%	7.5%	−5.0%	−26.4%	18.9%	4.9%
Median Portfolio Value – Price to Earnings + Dividends	10.1	11.6	13.1	17.3	−13.0	16.7	13.9
Average Market Capitalization	$3,593	$4,561	$6,283	$5,363	$1,588	NA	NA

* Equal-weighted average of S&P 500 returns. ** Annual holding period run quarterly for a larger sample size; arithmetic average excess returns.
Source: Standard & Poor's Compustat Point in Time Database; Thomson Reuters I/B/E/S Estimates; Charter Oak Investment Systems, Inc., Venues® Data Engine

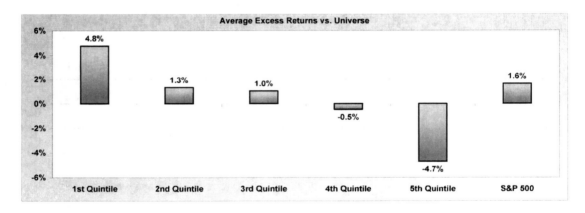

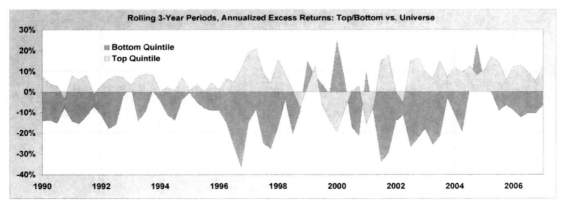

Figure 9.8 Seven-Month Relative Strength and Price to Earnings Plus Dividends

52-WEEK PRICE RANGE

Almost any beginning investor, as well as many noninvestors, can repeat an often heard maxim of Wall Street: buy low and sell high. Indeed, in order to make money in any business venture, the entrepreneur must follow some form of this advice, purchasing goods or providing services at a lesser price than that at which they're ultimately sold. The 52-week price range strategy stands this maxim on its head. The strategy measures the proximity of a stock to its 52-week high or 52-week low. Stocks near their 52-week highs are purchased, while stocks nearer their 52-week lows are sold. The gist of this strategy might be expressed more accurately as buy high and sell higher, and sell low and buy (back) lower. The strategy illustrates a truth about investing that is not widely understood: the common stock investor should buy into strength and sell (i.e., sell short) into weakness.

We calculate 52-week price range as (current price – 52-week low)/(52-week high – 52-week low). The strategy is much stronger and less volatile than the seven-month relative strength strategy. It is also more consistent. In addition, returns on this strategy are almost perfectly linear (the first quintile has higher excess returns than the second quintile, which has higher excess returns than the third quintile, etc.), a sign that there is a strong correlation between the strategy and excess returns.

The top quintile outperforms by 4.3%, on average, and does so for 75% of one-year and 86% of rolling three-year periods (see Figure 9.9). The strategy significantly underperforms in 1994, 1999, 2000, 2003–2004, and 2007. The maximum loss is a low 20%, and the Sharpe ratio, at 0.69, is equal to the Sharpe ratio for the S&P 500. While this equality is not good in and of itself, the 52-week price range strategy makes an excellent building block, significantly boosting returns, consistency, and Sharpe ratios when paired with fundamental factors. Average portfolio values for 52-week price range vary from 61% to 98%.[7]

The bottom quintile underperforms by 3.9%, on average, and does so for 79% of one-year and 93% of rolling three-year periods. It significantly outperforms in 1991, 1999–2000, 2003–2004, and 2006–2007. Average portfolio values for 52-week price range vary from 8% to 53%.

52-Week Price Range by Economic Sector

The 52-week price range strategy (see Figure 9.10) is relatively consistent across sectors, working well for the materials, industrials, consumer discretionary, and telecom services sectors. It also works as a negative strategy in the energy, health care, and utilities sectors.

---

[7] A value of 61% signifies that a stock is 61% above the bottom of its 52-week range. A value of 98% indicates that a stock is 2% below the top of its 52-week range.

1988–2007	1st Quintile	2nd Quintile	3rd Quintile	4th Quintile	5th Quintile	Universe	S&P 500*
CAGR – Annual Rebalance	14.5%	12.7%	11.6%	9.0%	7.2%	11.2%	12.9%
Average Excess Return vs. Universe**	4.3%	2.1%	0.0%	−2.2%	−3.9%	NA	1.6%
Value of $10,000 Invested (20 Years)	$151,122	$109,764	$90,094	$56,402	$39,922	$83,161	$112,895
% of 1-Year Periods Strategy Outperforms the Universe	75.3%	68.8%	50.6%	24.7%	20.8%	NA	59.7%
% Rolling 3-Year Periods Strategy Outperforms	85.5%	71.0%	46.4%	7.2%	7.2%	NA	71.0%
Maximum Gain	69.3%	50.4%	56.1%	61.8%	74.5%	59.2%	54.1%
Maximum Loss	−20.2%	−33.5%	−29.1%	−26.9%	−38.7%	−24.9%	−25.9%
Sharpe Ratio	0.69	0.60	0.52	0.36	0.20	0.49	0.69
Standard Deviation of Returns	0.18	0.17	0.16	0.16	0.21	0.16	0.14
Beta (vs. Universe)	0.99	0.97	0.95	0.97	1.14	NA	0.78
Alpha (vs. Universe)	0.04	0.02	0.01	−0.02	−0.06	NA	0.04
Average Portfolio Size	446	447	447	447	447	NA	NA
Average Number of Companies *Outperforming*	198	201	198	188	180	NA	NA
Average Number of Companies *Underperforming*	209	224	229	241	251	NA	NA
Median Portfolio Value – 52-Week Price Range	96%	83%	63%	41%	17%	60%	59%
Average Market Capitalization	$4,934	$4,658	$4,030	$3,780	$3,109	NA	NA

* Equal-weighted average of S&P 500 returns. ** Annual holding period run quarterly for a larger sample size; arithmetic average excess returns.
Source: Standard & Poor's Compustat Point in Time Database; Charter Oak Investment Systems, Inc., Venues® Data Engine

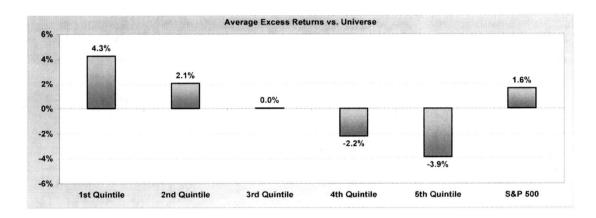

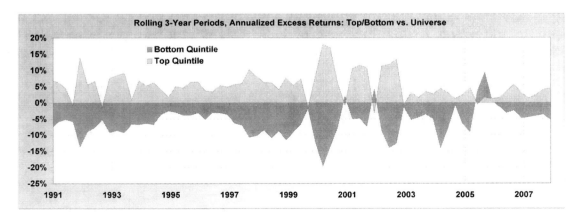

Figure 9.9 52-Week Price Range

Top Quintile

1990–2007	Energy	Materials	Industrials	Consumer Discretionary	Consumer Staples	Health Care	Financials	Information Technology	Telecom Services	Utilities	Universe	S&P 500*
CAGR – Quintile	13.9%	14.3%	15.2%	12.1%	10.0%	13.7%	14.0%	8.3%	15.8%	14.0%	11.2%	12.9%
CAGR – Sector	13.5%	10.2%	11.3%	8.8%	12.6%	12.3%	14.5%	7.5%	9.2%	13.0%	NA	NA
Excess Return vs. Sector	0.3%	4.1%	4.0%	3.4%	-2.6%	1.4%	-0.5%	0.8%	6.6%	1.0%	NA	NA
Value of $10,000	$134,211	$144,403	$169,971	$98,483	$67,643	$131,033	$136,268	$49,555	$188,459	$136,458	$83,161	$112,895
% 1-Year Outperformance	50.0%	70.0%	85.0%	70.0%	35.0%	45.0%	40.0%	65.0%	70.0%	50.0%	NA	NA
% 3-Year Outperformance	66.7%	77.8%	94.4%	77.8%	16.7%	61.1%	44.4%	61.1%	88.9%	61.1%	NA	NA
Maximum Gain	51.5%	60.5%	45.4%	61.1%	43.0%	79.6%	53.8%	84.5%	106.3%	64.6%	44.0%	41.4%
Maximum Loss	-30.7%	-15.6%	-15.7%	-24.8%	-8.8%	-26.0%	-19.8%	-40.9%	-51.1%	-12.6%	-19.1%	-18.1%
Standard Deviation	0.24	0.18	0.17	0.20	0.14	0.26	0.21	0.31	0.37	0.17	0.16	0.14
Beta (vs. Sector)	0.86	1.07	1.09	0.98	0.77	0.98	0.93	0.78	0.95	0.98	NA	NA
Alpha (vs. Sector)	0.02	0.04	0.03	0.04	0.00	0.02	0.01	0.02	0.08	0.01	NA	NA
Portfolio Size	26	34	62	76	22	44	73	64	10	27	NA	NA

Bottom Quintile

1990–2007	Energy	Materials	Industrials	Consumer Discretionary	Consumer Staples	Health Care	Financials	Information Technology	Telecom Services	Utilities	Universe	S&P 500*
CAGR – Quintile	9.4%	9.8%	6.4%	3.7%	14.7%	10.5%	13.8%	5.1%	5.1%	9.5%	11.2%	12.9%
CAGR – Sector	13.5%	10.2%	11.3%	8.8%	12.6%	12.3%	14.5%	7.5%	9.2%	13.0%	NA	NA
Excess Return vs. Sector	-4.1%	-0.4%	-4.9%	-5.0%	2.1%	-1.9%	-0.6%	-2.4%	-4.2%	-3.5%	NA	NA
Value of $10,000	$60,571	$64,784	$34,313	$20,867	$155,406	$73,298	$133,768	$27,257	$26,876	$61,136	$83,161	$112,895
% 1-Year Outperformance	25.0%	35.0%	20.0%	35.0%	45.0%	40.0%	55.0%	45.0%	35.0%	40.0%	NA	NA
% 3-Year Outperformance	16.7%	50.0%	11.1%	27.8%	50.0%	38.9%	55.6%	44.4%	33.3%	33.3%	NA	NA
Maximum Gain	59.8%	44.1%	42.9%	53.1%	72.6%	68.8%	61.2%	122.7%	160.2%	65.4%	44.0%	41.4%
Maximum Loss	-47.5%	-23.3%	-26.4%	-36.1%	-18.7%	-35.2%	-37.6%	-61.6%	-58.8%	-46.7%	-19.1%	-18.1%
Standard Deviation	0.27	0.17	0.18	0.22	0.23	0.27	0.26	0.41	0.45	0.24	0.16	0.14
Beta (vs. Sector)	0.98	0.96	1.15	1.08	1.32	1.01	1.13	1.07	1.10	1.39	NA	NA
Alpha (vs. Sector)	-0.03	0.04	-0.05	-0.06	0.11	0.01	0.04	-0.10	-0.07	0.00	NA	NA
Portfolio Size	26	35	65	80	24	45	76	66	11	28	NA	NA

* Equal-weighted average of S&P 500 returns.
Source: Standard & Poor's Compustat Point in Time Database; Charter Oak Investment Systems, Inc., Venues® Data Engine

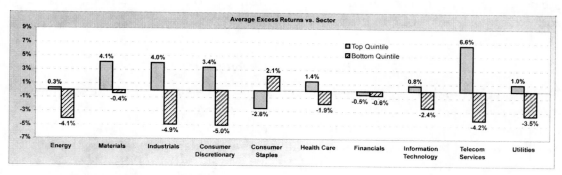

Figure 9.10 52-Week Price Range by Economic Sector

Interestingly, the sector does not work well in the information technology sector. The returns for this sector indicate that the 52-week price range strategy worked only in years where technology-stock speculation was strong (1993–1994, 1998–1999), but otherwise it doesn't help investors pick stocks in this sector. In the consumer staples sector, the strategy actually works in reverse, with the top quintile underperforming and the bottom quintile outperforming. The consumer staples sector appears to be the exception to the rule: these are stodgy, mature companies, and strong momentum should be sold and not bought.

52-Week Price Range and Free Cash Flow to Price

The 52-week price range and FCF-to-price strategy matches a very strong technical factor with a very strong valuation factor. Companies in the top quintile are generating positive FCFs, selling at low prices relative to those cash flows, and advancing toward their 52-week highs. Companies in the bottom quintile have negative FCFs, are expensive, and are pushing down toward their 52-week lows. The results are both strong and consistent. In particular, notice the strong linearity of excess returns and of the maximum loss.

The top quintile outperforms by 6.9%, on average, and does so for 75% of one-year and 84% of rolling three-year periods (see Figure 9.11). The top quintile underperforms in 1999–2000, 2003–2004, and 2007. It has a low maximum loss of 19%, a moderate standard deviation of returns of 0.17, and a relatively high Sharpe ratio of 0.84. An average of 32 portfolio stocks outperforms for every 29 that underperform, a strong showing. Average portfolio values vary from 75% to 97% for 52-week price range and 7% to 26% for FCF to price.

The bottom portfolio underperforms by 9.5%, on average, and does so for 82% of one-year and 92% of rolling three-year periods. The fourth quintile also significantly underperforms (by 7.8%), and is also very consistent. An average of 42 out of 67 stocks in the bottom quintile and 39 out of 67 in the fourth quintile underperform. Average portfolio values for the bottom quintile vary from 8% to 50% for 52-week price range and −9% to −37% for FCF to price.

52-Week Price Range and Return on Equity

This strategy combines a price momentum factor with a profitability factor. Since this strategy does *not* include a valuation factor, the companies in the top quintile tend to be growth-oriented, selling at relatively high multiples of cash flow or earnings. However, the high returns these companies generate on shareholders' capital plus the fact that their stocks are advancing toward their 52-week highs indicate that they are strong potential investments. Note that the majority of companies that show up on this list

1990–2007	1st Quintile	2nd Quintile	3rd Quintile	4th Quintile	5th Quintile	Universe	S&P 500*
CAGR – Annual Rebalance	15.4%	11.9%	10.3%	1.7%	0.4%	10.3%	12.0%
Average Excess Return vs. Universe**	6.9%	2.5%	−1.2%	−7.8%	−9.5%	NA	1.5%
Value of $10,000 Invested (18 Years)	$132,295	$75,713	$58,236	$13,583	$10,743	$58,670	$76,297
% of 1-Year Periods Strategy Outperforms the Universe	75.0%	56.9%	38.9%	20.8%	18.1%	NA	56.9%
% Rolling 3-Year Periods Strategy Outperforms	84.4%	65.6%	32.8%	9.4%	7.8%	NA	68.8%
Maximum Gain	54.1%	48.3%	56.0%	65.0%	101.1%	59.2%	54.1%
Maximum Loss	−19.1%	−20.3%	−41.7%	−51.4%	−58.7%	−24.9%	−25.9%
Sharpe Ratio	0.84	0.75	0.39	0.00	−0.06	0.46	0.64
Standard Deviation of Returns	0.17	0.14	0.17	0.22	0.31	0.17	0.14
Beta (vs. Universe)	0.79	0.70	0.91	1.14	1.55	NA	0.78
Alpha (vs. Universe)	0.09	0.06	0.00	−0.09	−0.16	NA	0.04
Average Portfolio Size	66	67	67	67	67	NA	NA
Average Number of Companies *Outperforming*	32	31	28	25	23	NA	NA
Average Number of Companies *Underperforming*	29	32	36	39	42	NA	NA
Median Portfolio Value – 52-Week Price Range	96%	84%	67%	44%	15%	60%	60%
Median Portfolio Value – FCF to Price	15.3%	5.7%	3.2%	−1.1%	−24.0%	2.1%	3.3%
Average Market Capitalization	$3,798	$7,151	$6,565	$4,554	$1,343	NA	NA

* Equal-weighted average of S&P 500 returns. ** Annual holding period run quarterly for a larger sample size; arithmetic average excess returns.
Source: Standard & Poor's Compustat Point in Time Database; Charter Oak Investment Systems, Inc., Venues® Data Engine

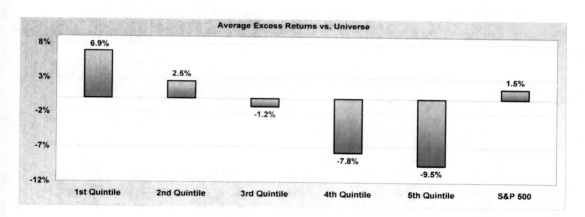

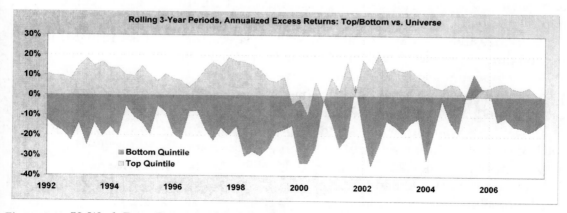

Figure 9.11 52-Week Price Range and Free Cash Flow to Price

generate positive FCFs, so they have cash-based earnings as well as accrual account-ing–based earnings. Despite the lack of a valuation factor, the strategy is very consistent over time—significantly more consistent than just using a profitability strategy alone.

The top quintile outperforms by 6.3%, on average, and does so for 78% of one-year and 93% of rolling three-year periods (see Figure 9.12). The top quintile significantly underperforms only in 1992–1993, 2003–2004, and 2007. The maximum loss is a low 21%, but volatility is moderately high, with a standard deviation of returns of 0.19, resulting in a moderate Sharpe ratio of 0.76. Average portfolio values for the top quin-tile vary from 61% to 98% for 52-week price range and from 30% to well over 50% for return on equity (ROE). With an average market capitalization of $10 billion, this is pri-marily a large-cap strategy.

The bottom quintile underperforms by an average of 9.1%, and does so for 77% of one-year and 94% of rolling three-year periods. The bottom quintile significantly out-performs only in 1994, 1999–2000, and 2003–2004. During 2003–2004, the beginning of a bull market, it outperformed by an average of almost 40%, as beaten down, low-prof-itability stocks strongly outperformed. The bottom quintile is quite volatile, with a maximum loss of 77%, a standard deviation of returns of 0.33, and a Beta of 1.7. Average portfolio values vary from 7% to 51% for 52-week price range and −12% to less than −100% for ROE. On average 50 portfolio companies underperform versus 28 that outperform.

52-Week Price Range and Price to Book Value

The 52-week price range and price to book value strategy is consistent and also very simple, combining in the top quintile stocks that are nearing new highs and that are low priced relative to the book value of equity. Notice the relationship between this strategy and the preceding one. The 52-week price range and ROE strategy looked at the amount of profitability a company was generating on book value, while this strategy looks at the price the investor must pay for that book value. A strong three-factor screen would com-bine all three: 52-week price range, ROE, and price to book value.

The top quintile outperforms by an average or 4.5%, and does so for 64% of one-year and 84% of rolling three-year periods (see Figure 9.13). It underperforms signifi-cantly in 1991, 1994–1995, 1999–2000, and 2003. The strategy has a low maximum loss of 23% and low volatility, with a standard deviation of returns of 0.16 and a Beta versus the Universe of just 0.7. As a result, the Sharpe ratio is a strong 0.81 (vs. 0.69 for the S&P 500). Average portfolio values vary from 58% to 99% for 52-week price range and from 0.9× to 2.2× for price to book value. Note that the preceding strategy, which empha-sized profitability, was a decidedly large-cap strategy, while this strategy, by emphasiz-ing valuation, is a small- to mid-cap strategy, with an average market cap of $2.9 billion.

1988–2007	1st Quintile	2nd Quintile	3rd Quintile	4th Quintile	5th Quintile	Universe	S&P 500*
CAGR – Annual Rebalance	17.0%	14.0%	11.2%	8.8%	0.6%	11.2%	12.9%
Average Excess Return vs. Universe**	6.3%	1.7%	0.2%	−2.0%	−9.1%	NA	1.6%
Value of $10,000 Invested (20 Years)	$231,675	$136,379	$84,079	$54,217	$11,352	$83,161	$112,895
% of 1-Year Periods Strategy Outperforms the Universe	77.9%	55.8%	53.2%	45.5%	23.4%	NA	59.7%
% Rolling 3-Year Periods Strategy Outperforms	92.8%	58.0%	49.3%	27.5%	5.8%	NA	71.0%
Maximum Gain	65.9%	55.0%	49.8%	61.1%	109.5%	59.2%	54.1%
Maximum Loss	−20.8%	−18.4%	−21.6%	−32.0%	−77.2%	−24.9%	−25.9%
Sharpe Ratio	0.76	0.66	0.56	0.36	−0.03	0.49	0.69
Standard Deviation of Returns	0.19	0.15	0.15	0.17	0.33	0.16	0.14
Beta (vs. Universe)	1.04	0.75	0.78	0.92	1.70	NA	0.78
Alpha (vs. Universe)	0.06	0.05	0.03	−0.01	−0.18	NA	0.04
Average Portfolio Size	81	81	81	81	82	NA	NA
Average Number of Companies *Outperforming*	38	38	37	34	28	NA	NA
Average Number of Companies *Underperforming*	37	40	42	43	50	NA	NA
Median Portfolio Value – 52-Week Price Range	96%	83%	62%	41%	16%	60%	59%
Median Portfolio Value – Return on Equity	43.1%	18.0%	13.3%	8.1%	−35.8%	11.7%	14.7%
Average Market Capitalization	$10,033	$5,739	$3,935	$2,535	$1,574	NA	NA

* Equal-weighted average of S&P 500 returns. ** Annual holding period run quarterly for a larger sample size; arithmetic average excess returns.
Source: Standard & Poor's Compustat Point in Time Database; Charter Oak Investment Systems, Inc., Venues® Data Engine

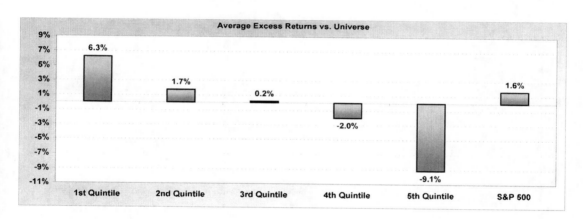

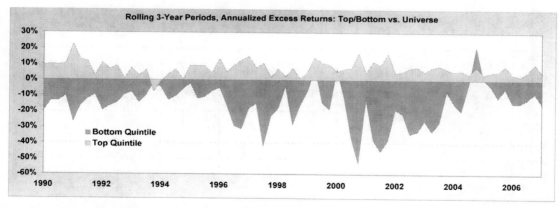

Figure 9.12 52-Week Price Range and Return on Equity

1988–2007	1st Quintile	2nd Quintile	3rd Quintile	4th Quintile	5th Quintile	Universe	S&P 500*
CAGR – Annual Rebalance	16.1%	13.6%	12.5%	7.5%	0.4%	11.2%	12.9%
Average Excess Return vs. Universe**	4.5%	2.7%	0.0%	−4.9%	−9.3%	NA	1.6%
Value of $10,000 Invested (20 Years)	$197,293	$127,944	$105,640	$42,416	$10,867	$83,161	$112,895
% of 1-Year Periods Strategy Outperforms the Universe	63.6%	63.6%	53.2%	20.8%	16.9%	NA	59.7%
% Rolling 3-Year Periods Strategy Outperforms	84.1%	72.5%	47.8%	13.0%	2.9%	NA	71.0%
Maximum Gain	61.0%	49.7%	53.4%	63.7%	57.7%	59.2%	54.1%
Maximum Loss	−22.5%	−17.9%	−23.6%	−40.1%	−62.6%	−24.9%	−25.9%
Sharpe Ratio	0.81	0.70	0.53	0.16	−0.05	0.49	0.69
Standard Deviation of Returns	0.16	0.15	0.15	0.20	0.24	0.16	0.14
Beta (vs. Universe)	0.69	0.79	0.86	1.05	1.28	NA	0.78
Alpha (vs. Universe)	0.08	0.05	0.02	−0.06	−0.13	NA	0.04
Average Portfolio Size	84	85	85	85	85	NA	NA
Average Number of Companies *Outperforming*	39	39	38	33	29	NA	NA
Average Number of Companies *Underperforming*	37	40	44	48	54	NA	NA
Median Portfolio Value – 52-Week Price Range	96%	83%	63%	42%	19%	60%	59%
Median Portfolio Value – Price to Book Value	1.4	2.0	2.6	3.4	9.8	2.3	2.3
Average Market Capitalization	$2,896	$4,313	$4,074	$5,248	$5,050	NA	NA

* Equal-weighted average of S&P 500 returns. ** Annual holding period run quarterly for a larger sample size; arithmetic average excess returns.
Source: Standard & Poor's Compustat Point in Time Database; Charter Oak Investment Systems, Inc., Venues® Data Engine

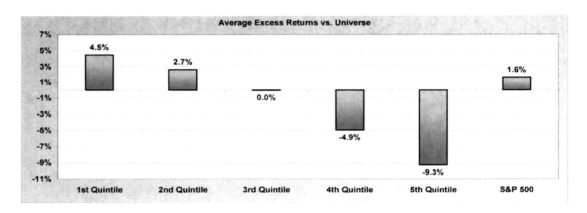

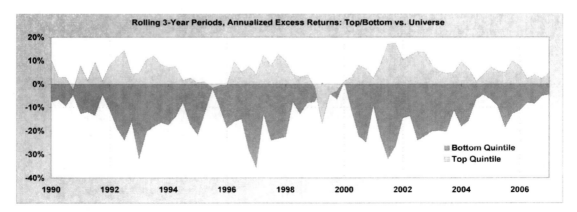

Figure 9.13 52-Week Price Range and Price to Book Value

The bottom quintile underperforms by an average of 9.3%, and does so for 83% of one-year and 97% of rolling three-year periods. It significantly outperformed only in 1991, 1995, 1999, and 2003. Average portfolio values vary from 9% to 53% for 52-week price range and from 3× to well over 20× for price to book value.

RELATIVE STRENGTH INDEX

Although relative strength and the Relative Strength Index share similar names, they're actually quite different strategies. The Relative Strength Index (RSI), developed by J. Welles Wilder,[8] is widely used among traders and other technicians. If you'll recall, we calculate relative strength (*not* RSI) by simply comparing one stock's rate of change over a given period with the rate of change of every other stock in our Universe. While rate of change measures momentum by simply comparing the beginning price over the calculation period with the ending price, RSI uses *all* the price changes that occur within the calculation period to determine the average price change over the period. By using the average price change, RSI provides a more accurate measure of overall price movement that is less subject to large "bumps" due to the beginning and ending price used rather than rate of change. Technicians often calculate RSI using a 14-day or 14-week period, depending on whether it will be used on a daily or weekly chart. Also, since RSI is an index whose values can range from 0 to 100, technicians use RSI as an oscillator. Readings above 70 are generally considered overbought (a potential selling point), and readings below 30 are considered oversold (a potential buying point).

We'll calculate RSI as an index, so that it can be easily compared to RSI readings you will find on technical charts. However, we won't use it as an overbought/oversold oscillator. Rather, we'll use it as we used relative strength: to indicate when momentum for a stock is positive and likely to continue upward over the next 12 months, or when momentum is negative and likely to continue downward. The formula for RSI is

$$RSI = 100 - (100 / (1 + U/D)),$$

where U is the sum of the total price points gained on up days, and D is the sum of the total price points lost on down days (expressed as a positive number).

Relative Strength Index: Top Quintile—Various Calculation Periods

As with relative strength, RSI can be calculated over any time period. Since we are not interested in short-term outperformance (our portfolio holding periods are always 12 months), we use weekly instead of daily calculation periods for RSI. This means that

---

[8] For more information on RSI, see J. Welles Wilder Jr.'s book *New Concepts in Technical Trading Systems.*

weekly closing prices are used in the RSI calculation. Figure 9.14 shows the results of RSI calculation periods ranging from 2 weeks to 48 weeks for the top quintile of stocks by RSI in our test Universe.[9] We find that excess returns peak at 6.6% at a calculation period of 32 weeks, while the percentage of one-year outperformance peaks at 78% at a calculation period of 28 weeks. I prefer to sacrifice a little bit of excess return for an increase in consistency, so we'll choose 28 weeks as the calculation period for our top quintile.

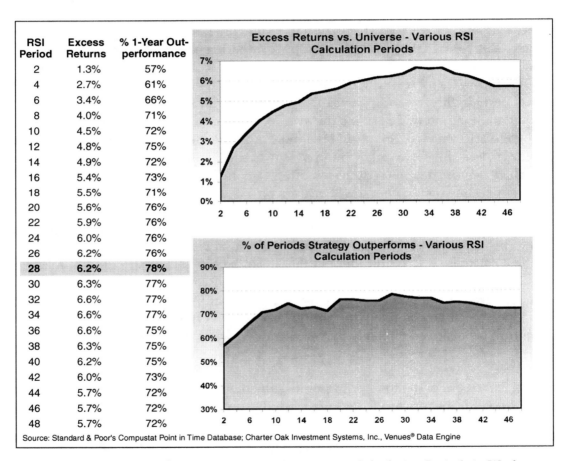

RSI Period	Excess Returns	% 1-Year Out-performance
2	1.3%	57%
4	2.7%	61%
6	3.4%	66%
8	4.0%	71%
10	4.5%	72%
12	4.8%	75%
14	4.9%	72%
16	5.4%	73%
18	5.5%	71%
20	5.6%	76%
22	5.9%	76%
24	6.0%	76%
26	6.2%	76%
28	6.2%	78%
30	6.3%	77%
32	6.6%	77%
34	6.6%	77%
36	6.6%	75%
38	6.3%	75%
40	6.2%	75%
42	6.0%	73%
44	5.7%	72%
46	5.7%	72%
48	5.7%	72%

Source: Standard & Poor's Compustat Point in Time Database; Charter Oak Investment Systems, Inc., Venues® Data Engine

Figure 9.14 Relative Strength Index: Top Quintile—Various Calculation Periods in Weeks (12-Month Holding Periods)

[9] Calculations are performed from 1991 through 2006, due to limitations on the pricing data available.

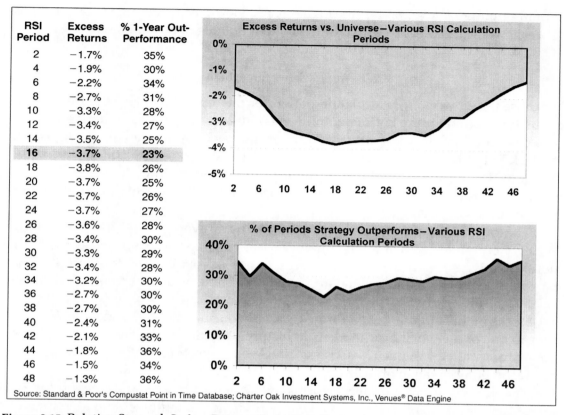

RSI Period	Excess Returns	% 1-Year Out-Performance
2	−1.7%	35%
4	−1.9%	30%
6	−2.2%	34%
8	−2.7%	31%
10	−3.3%	28%
12	−3.4%	27%
14	−3.5%	25%
16	−3.7%	23%
18	−3.8%	26%
20	−3.7%	25%
22	−3.7%	26%
24	−3.7%	27%
26	−3.6%	28%
28	−3.4%	30%
30	−3.3%	29%
32	−3.4%	28%
34	−3.2%	30%
36	−2.7%	30%
38	−2.7%	30%
40	−2.4%	31%
42	−2.1%	33%
44	−1.8%	36%
46	−1.5%	34%
48	−1.3%	36%

Source: Standard & Poor's Compustat Point in Time Database; Charter Oak Investment Systems, Inc., Venues® Data Engine

Figure 9.15 Relative Strength Index: Bottom Quintile—Various Calculation Periods in Weeks (12-Month Holding Periods)

Relative Strength Index: Bottom Quintile—Various Calculation Periods (12-Month Holding Periods)

Figure 9.15 shows calculation periods from 2 through 48 weeks for the bottom quintile of the RSI strategy. One characteristic that we found with momentum-based strategies is that calculation periods for negative momentum tests (those in which you want a stock's price to continue to go down) are shorter than calculation periods for positive momentum tests (in which you want the stock to continue going up). The reason is likely that stocks often move downward more quickly than they move upward. In any case, this relationship holds true for RSI. While positive excess returns peak using a calculation period of 32 weeks for the top quintile by RSI, negative excess returns reach a trough using a period of 18 weeks for the bottom quintile. However, the percentage of one-year underperformance for the bottom quintile reaches a high of at 77% (1 − 23%) at 16 weeks. (Recall that we are interested in underperformance and not outperformance for the bottom quintile.) Since I prefer to weight consistency over excess return, we'll choose 16 weeks as the calculation period for the bottom quintile of our RSI test.

28/16-Week Relative Strength Index

We chose the 28-week RSI calculation period for the top quintile and the 16-week RSI calculation period for the bottom quintile of the RSI strategy because they provide the best combination of excess returns and consistency. For convenience, we use the 28-week RSI calculation for the top three quintiles and the 16-week RSI for the bottom two quintiles. As mentioned above, longer calculation periods work best for price momentum strategies that involve buying stocks, and shorter calculation periods work best for short-sale strategies.

The top quintile of this strategy outperforms by an average of 6.2%, and does so for 70% of one-year and 80% of rolling three-year periods (see Figure 9.16). Like the seven-month relative strength strategy, the RSI strategy is volatile. The top quintile has a maximum loss of 47% and a standard deviation of returns of 0.20, versus 0.12 for the S&P 500, resulting in a Sharpe ratio of 0.70, just above the 0.67 Sharpe ratio for the S&P 500. Stocks in this quintile outperformed strongly during late 1999 and early 2000, just prior to one of the worst bear markets in history. This shows the danger of relying on momentum strategies alone to choose stocks. Average portfolio values for 28-week RSI for the top quintile range from 55 to 74.

The bottom quintile underperforms by 3.2%, on average, and does so for 77% of one-year and 79% of rolling three-year periods. It is slightly less volatile than the top quintile, with a standard deviation of returns of 0.17. Average portfolio values for 16-week RSI range from 29 to 45.

28/16-Week Relative Strength Index by Economic Sector

The 28-week RSI strategy, used for the top quintile, works only for the consumer discretionary, information technology, and telecom services sectors (see Figure 9.17). For the technology sector, the test is biased by very strong results occurring in 1998 and 1999. The consumer discretionary and telecom services sectors work more consistently, with the telecom sector in particular outperforming in recent years.

The 16-week RSI strategy, which we use for the bottom quintile, shows good consistency and excess returns for the energy, materials, industrials, telecom, and utilities sectors. Here results do not seem to be biased by one or two years.

Note that, as we saw with the 52-week price range strategy, the top quintile of consumer staples works well as a negative strategy, indicating that price strength in staples should be sold and not bought.

1992–2007	1st Quintile	2nd Quintile	3rd Quintile	4th Quintile	5th Quintile	Universe	S&P 500*
CAGR – Annual Rebalance	16.7%	11.5%	8.8%	9.7%	8.8%	10.8%	11.1%
Average Excess Return vs. Universe**	6.2%	1.8%	−0.6%	−1.3%	−3.2%	NA	0.7%
Value of $10,000 Invested (16 Years)	$118,325	$56,681	$38,717	$44,287	$38,329	$51,436	$53,765
% of 1-Year Periods Strategy Outperforms the Universe	70.3%	68.8%	45.3%	43.8%	23.4%	NA	56.3%
% Rolling 3-Year Periods Strategy Outperforms	80.4%	73.2%	35.7%	37.5%	21.4%	NA	60.7%
Maximum Gain	72.6%	62.3%	66.8%	61.4%	59.0%	50.7%	59.6%
Maximum Loss	−46.5%	−34.4%	−25.2%	−29.8%	−40.3%	−27.2%	−28.0%
Sharpe Ratio	0.70	0.60	0.50	0.43	0.26	0.52	0.67
Standard Deviation of Returns	0.20	0.16	0.14	0.15	0.17	0.15	0.12
Beta (vs. Universe)	1.02	1.01	0.87	0.85	0.95	NA	0.66
Alpha (vs. Universe)	0.06	0.02	0.01	0.01	−0.03	NA	0.05
Average Portfolio Size	416	416	416	423	424	NA	NA
Average Number of Companies *Outperforming*	187	184	178	186	179	NA	NA
Average Number of Companies *Underperforming*	196	212	220	220	229	NA	NA
Median Portfolio Value – 28/16-Week RSI	71	61	54	47	33	54	54
Average Market Capitalization	$5,320	$5,390	$5,297	$4,822	$4,065	NA	NA

* Equal-weighted average of S&P 500 returns. ** Annual holding period run quarterly for a larger sample size; arithmetic average excess returns.
Source: Standard & Poor's Compustat Point in Time Database; Charter Oak Investment Systems, Inc., Venues® Data Engine

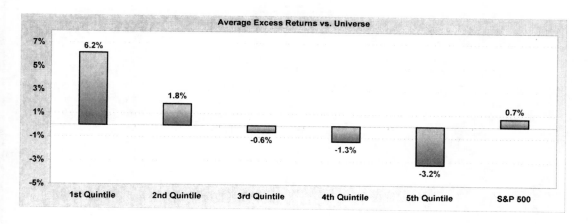

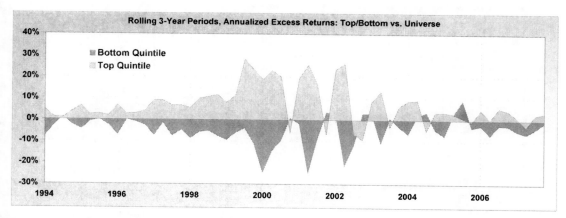

Figure 9.16 28/16-Week Relative Strength Index

Top Quintile

1988–2007	Energy	Materials	Industrials	Consumer Discretionary	Consumer Staples	Health Care	Financials	Information Technology	Telecom Services	Utilities	Universe	S&P 500*
CAGR – Quintile	12.3%	11.2%	12.0%	10.7%	3.9%	7.3%	11.1%	10.3%	11.3%	7.7%	10.4%	12.3%
CAGR – Sector	15.2%	10.5%	11.1%	7.3%	10.4%	8.3%	14.9%	7.1%	6.4%	12.6%	NA	NA
Excess Return vs. Sector	−2.9%	0.7%	0.9%	3.3%	−6.5%	−1.0%	−3.7%	3.2%	4.8%	−4.9%	NA	NA
Value of $10,000	$64,271	$54,566	$61,405	$50,674	$18,407	$31,073	$54,210	$47,794	$55,219	$32,580	$48,418	$63,697
% 1-Year Outperformance	43.8%	56.3%	50.0%	68.8%	31.3%	43.8%	25.0%	56.3%	62.5%	25.0%	NA	NA
% 3-Year Outperformance	42.9%	42.9%	50.0%	78.6%	0.0%	50.0%	14.3%	64.3%	64.3%	14.3%	NA	NA
Maximum Gain	55.5%	49.4%	37.7%	36.5%	34.9%	43.1%	46.3%	100.3%	83.7%	32.2%	44.0%	41.4%
Maximum Loss	−37.9%	−18.8%	−11.7%	−21.7%	−29.4%	−25.5%	−12.5%	−36.0%	−42.8%	−19.1%	−19.1%	−18.1%
Standard Deviation	0.26	0.18	0.14	0.16	0.16	0.20	0.16	0.32	0.28	0.15	0.15	0.13
Beta (vs. Sector)	0.92	1.06	0.93	0.92	0.98	0.90	0.82	0.76	0.51	0.75	NA	NA
Alpha (vs. Sector)	−0.02	0.00	0.02	0.04	−0.06	0.00	−0.01	0.04	0.09	−0.02	NA	NA
Portfolio Size	25	30	57	71	20	44	66	64	9	22	NA	NA

Bottom Quintile

1988–2007	Energy	Materials	Industrials	Consumer Discretionary	Consumer Staples	Health Care	Financials	Information Technology	Telecom Services	Utilities	Universe	S&P 500*
CAGR – Quintile	10.8%	6.4%	7.2%	5.6%	7.8%	10.2%	13.2%	6.8%	−4.8%	6.5%	10.4%	12.3%
CAGR – Sector	15.2%	10.5%	11.1%	7.3%	10.4%	8.3%	14.9%	7.1%	6.4%	12.6%	NA	NA
Excess Return vs. Sector	−4.4%	−4.1%	−3.9%	−1.7%	−2.6%	1.8%	−1.7%	−0.3%	−11.2%	−6.0%	NA	NA
Value of $10,000	$51,759	$27,006	$30,559	$24,077	$33,206	$47,018	$72,680	$28,642	$4,559	$27,553	$48,418	$63,697
% 1-Year Outperformance	25.0%	31.3%	25.0%	56.3%	37.5%	68.8%	25.0%	43.8%	18.8%	12.5%	NA	NA
% 3-Year Outperformance	21.4%	28.6%	14.3%	28.6%	28.6%	57.1%	14.3%	50.0%	0.0%	28.6%	NA	NA
Maximum Gain	64.8%	34.4%	34.2%	41.9%	53.2%	81.4%	61.3%	98.9%	123.2%	28.7%	44.0%	41.4%
Maximum Loss	−34.5%	−23.4%	−21.1%	−12.8%	−16.4%	−26.7%	−16.4%	−48.7%	−60.6%	−29.9%	−19.1%	−18.1%
Standard Deviation	0.25	0.18	0.15	0.15	0.18	0.28	0.21	0.34	0.41	0.18	0.15	0.13
Beta (vs. Sector)	0.94	1.08	1.07	0.88	1.18	1.20	0.99	0.79	1.01	0.97	NA	NA
Alpha (vs. Sector)	−0.04	0.04	−0.01	−0.01	0.04	0.06	0.07	−0.08	−0.16	0.00	NA	NA
Portfolio Size	26	31	60	76	22	46	70	69	10	23	NA	NA

* Equal-weighted average of S&P 500 returns.
Source: Standard & Poor's Compustat Point in Time Database; Charter Oak Investment Systems, Inc., Venues® Data Engine

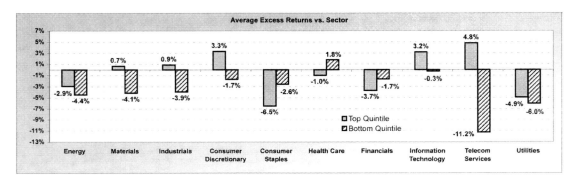

Figure 9.17 28/16-Week Relative Strength Index by Sector

28/16-Week Relative Strength Index and 52-Week Price Range

This strategy combines two different price momentum factors. The RSI strategy simply looks at the average trend of a stock over the past 28 weeks (or 16 weeks for the bottom two quintiles), while the 52-week price range looks at where the stock is relative to its performance over the past year. It is quite possible for a stock to have a low RSI score but to be near its 52-week high, for example, a stock that ran up to its 52-week high but then stalled at this level. Conversely, it is possible for a stock to have a relatively strong RSI reading but be nowhere near a 52-week high; an example would be a stock that fell to its 52-week low but suddenly began to regain price momentum. This test ensures that stocks have strong (or weak) price momentum on both measures. Like single-factor price momentum strategies, this strategy is quite volatile and outperforms most in overheated markets, such as in 1999. (So, don't be overly impressed by the extreme returns in the top quintile. They are driven in part by very high returns in late 1999 and early 2000.) However, it is also much more consistent than a single-factor momentum strategy, and excess returns are strong even if 1999 and 2000 are excluded. I would not necessarily recommend using a strategy such as this alone, but I would definitely recommend it in concert with a valuation, profitability, or other fundamental strategy.

The top quintile of this strategy outperforms by almost 11%, on average, and does so for 80% of one-year and 91% of rolling three-year periods, making it very consistent (see Figure 9.18). The major flaw of this strategy, and one that can be overcome by combining it with a fundamental or valuation strategy, is its great volatility. The top quintile has a maximum loss of 33%, a maximum gain of 151%, and a standard deviation of returns of 0.25, well above the 0.12 value for the S&P 500. However, the Sharpe ratio is relatively strong, at 0.78, versus 0.67 for the S&P 500. Average portfolio values for 28-week RSI vary from 58 to 77, meaning that these stocks are in uptrends. Average values for 52-week price range vary from 93% to 100%, indicating they are also close to their 52-week highs.

The bottom quintile underperforms by 9.6%, on average, and does so for 84% of one-year and 96% of rolling three-year periods. Average portfolio values vary from 24 to 42 for 16-week RSI and from 2% to 29% for 52-week price range. The stocks in this quintile have been in downtrends, with prices near their 52-week lows.

28/16-Week Relative Strength Index and Economic Profits

This strategy combines price momentum, cash flow, profitability, and valuation all in one, with good results. As you'll recall, we calculate economic profits as the difference between a company's cash return on capital (cash ROIC) and its cost of capital. In calculating the cost of capital, we use a company's price-to-sales (P/S) ratio in place of Beta

1992–2007	1st Quintile	2nd Quintile	3rd Quintile	4th Quintile	5th Quintile	Universe	S&P 500*
CAGR – Annual Rebalance	24.4%	13.1%	9.9%	8.1%	3.1%	10.8%	11.1%
Average Excess Return vs. Universe**	10.7%	3.9%	−1.0%	−4.5%	−9.6%	NA	−0.4%
Value of $10,000 Invested (16 Years)	$331,037	$71,773	$45,060	$34,964	$16,298	$51,436	$53,765
% of 1-Year Periods Strategy Outperforms the Universe	79.7%	71.9%	42.2%	23.4%	15.6%	NA	42.2%
% Rolling 3-Year Periods Strategy Outperforms	91.1%	89.3%	35.7%	7.1%	3.6%	NA	48.2%
Maximum Gain	150.5%	77.7%	74.3%	68.4%	103.1%	66.6%	59.6%
Maximum Loss	−33.1%	−23.4%	−25.9%	−33.2%	−49.2%	−26.9%	−28.0%
Sharpe Ratio	0.78	0.74	0.51	0.24	−0.04	0.56	0.67
Standard Deviation of Returns	0.25	0.17	0.15	0.18	0.23	0.16	0.12
Beta (vs. Universe)	1.11	0.98	0.87	0.93	1.15	NA	0.66
Alpha (vs. Universe)	0.09	0.04	0.01	−0.04	−0.12	NA	0.04
Average Portfolio Size	83	83	83	85	85	NA	NA
Average Number of Companies *Outperforming*	35	37	36	35	35	NA	NA
Average Number of Companies *Underperforming*	36	42	44	46	47	NA	NA
Median Portfolio Value – 28/16-Week RSI	72	61	54	47	29	54	54
Median Portfolio Value – 52-Week Price Range	99%	92%	69%	36%	7%	62%	61%
Average Market Capitalization	$5,063	$6,228	$4,486	$4,304	$4,154	NA	NA

* Equal-weighted average of S&P 500 returns. ** Annual holding period run quarterly for a larger sample size; arithmetic average excess returns.
Source: Standard & Poor's Compustat Point in Time Database; Charter Oak Investment Systems, Inc., Venues® Data Engine

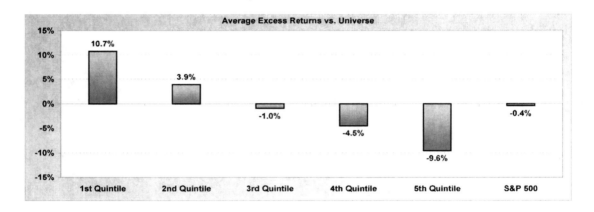

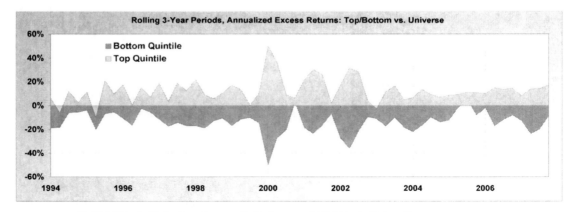

Figure 9.18 28/16-Week Relative Strength Index and 52-Week Price Range

1992–2007	1st Quintile	2nd Quintile	3rd Quintile	4th Quintile	5th Quintile	Universe	S&P 500*
CAGR – Annual Rebalance	17.4%	10.8%	7.5%	10.1%	0.0%	10.8%	11.1%
Average Excess Return vs. Universe**	7.7%	1.0%	−1.7%	−2.4%	−10.3%	NA	−0.4%
Value of $10,000 Invested (16 Years)	$129,527	$51,865	$32,016	$46,955	$9,925	$51,436	$53,765
% of 1-Year Periods Strategy Outperforms the Universe	71.9%	56.3%	42.2%	32.8%	21.9%	NA	42.2%
% Rolling 3-Year Periods Strategy Outperforms	85.7%	64.3%	32.1%	28.6%	10.7%	NA	48.2%
Maximum Gain	70.6%	57.6%	58.1%	73.9%	117.0%	66.6%	59.6%
Maximum Loss	−24.0%	−22.8%	−26.6%	−37.0%	−58.3%	−26.9%	−28.0%
Sharpe Ratio	0.97	0.70	0.53	0.35	−0.06	0.56	0.67
Standard Deviation of Returns	0.17	0.14	0.13	0.18	0.28	0.16	0.12
Beta (vs. Universe)	0.85	0.65	0.72	0.96	1.44	NA	0.66
Alpha (vs. Universe)	0.10	0.06	0.02	−0.02	−0.16	NA	0.04
Average Portfolio Size	54	54	54	54	55	NA	NA
Average Number of Companies *Outperforming*	26	25	24	23	20	NA	NA
Average Number of Companies *Underperforming*	25	27	28	29	34	NA	NA
Median Portfolio Value – 28/16-Week RSI	70	60	55	46	33	54	54
Median Portfolio Value – Economic Profits	15.5%	−2.1%	−9.5%	−15.7%	−39.5%	−11.5%	−6.6%
Average Market Capitalization	$8,221	$6,802	$7,880	$5,397	$2,594	NA	NA

* Equal-weighted average of S&P 500 returns. ** Annual holding period run quarterly for a larger sample size; arithmetic average excess returns.
Source: Standard & Poor's Compustat Point in Time Database; Charter Oak Investment Systems, Inc., Venues® Data Engine

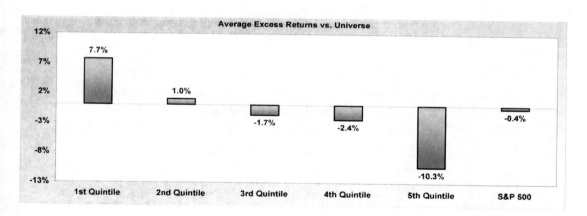

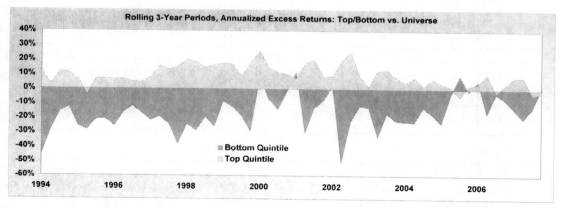

Figure 9.19 28/16-Week Relative Strength Index and Economic Profits

to determine the risk premium that should be placed on equity, the theory being the higher the P/S valuation, the greater the risk.

The top quintile outperforms by 7.7%, on average, and does so for 72% of one-year and 86% of rolling three-year periods (see Figure 9.19). Volatility is relatively low, with a maximum loss of 24%, a standard deviation of returns of 0.17, and a Beta of 0.9 versus the Universe. The result is a very high Sharpe ratio of 0.97, versus a Sharpe ratio of 0.67 for the S&P 500. The strategy's one weakness is that, like many cash flow–based strategies, it hasn't worked well recently. Average excess returns for the top quintile were 1% in 2006 and −1% in 2007. Average portfolio values vary from 54 to 75 for 28-week RSI and from 10% to 30% for economic profits. The strategy tends to select large-cap stocks, with an average market value of $8.2 billion.

The bottom quintile underperforms by 10.3%, on average, and does so for 78% of one-year and 89% of rolling three-year periods. The bottom quintile significantly outperforms in 1999–2000, 2003–2004, and 2006. Average portfolio values vary from 25 to 45 for 16-week RSI and from −24% to −59% for economic profits.

SUMMARY

- Market technicians believe that changes in price action, what we classify in this chapter as *price momentum,* foreshadow changes in fundamentals. Our research shows that price momentum-based quantitative strategies work, with stocks showing the strongest price momentum outperforming and those showing the weakest momentum underperforming.

- Not only can price momentum give investors clues as to fundamental changes that are taking place at a company that may not yet be widely known, but price momentum also reflects the psychology of market participants—investor sentiment—and human psychology is a strong factor in influencing stock price movements.

- Price momentum refers to the *velocity* of price movement, or the rate of change of price over a specified period of time. Positive (upward) price momentum tells us that demand currently outweighs supply, while negative (downward) price momentum tells us that supply outweighs demand.

- Research on price momentum proves a simple, but not widely understood, fact: over our 12-month holding period, stocks that are high tend to move higher, while stocks that are low often move lower.

- Because price momentum is to a large extent independent from fundamentals and valuations, price momentum factors combine well with almost every other *basic* presented in this book: profitability, valuation, cash flow, growth, capital allocation, and red flags (risk).

- Relative strength is a simple price-momentum strategy that works. We calculate relative strength simply by ranking all stocks in our Universe according to their rate of price change over a specified period of time. Research shows that seven-month relative strength provides the highest excess returns and best consistency of returns over our 12-month holding period.
- The relative strength strategy by itself is volatile; however, this volatility can be overcome simply by combining relative strength with a valuation factor.
- Valuation and price momentum strategies work well together. Valuation helps ensure that the investor does not overpay for a hot stock, while price momentum can indicate the presence of an underlying fundamental catalyst likely to propel the shares higher (or lower).
- The seven-month relative strength and free cash flow plus dividend plus share repurchase to price strategy combines price momentum, cash flow, capital allocation, and valuation into a single strategy. It is both strong and consistent.
- The 52-week price range strategy shows clearly that, in general, the common stock investor should buy into strength and sell (i.e., sell short) into weakness.
- The formula for 52-week price range is (current price – 52-week low)/(52-week high – 52-week low). Excess returns for the strategy are stronger and more consistent than those for the seven-month relative strength strategy. The strategy is also consistent across economic sectors.
- The consumer staples sector appears to be an exception to the rule with regard to price momentum: strong price momentum in consumer staples stocks should be sold, not bought, and vice versa.
- The 52-week price range and FCF to price strategy matches our strongest technical factor with one of our strongest valuation factors. Excess returns are strong, linear, and consistent. Stocks in the bottom two quintiles of this strategy consistently underperform, and should be avoided.
- The 52-week price range and return on equity (ROE) strategy combines price momentum with profitability and also works well. Despite the lack of a valuation factor, this strategy is very consistent over time. An even stronger, three-factor strategy could be constructed by simply adding a valuation factor, such as price to book value, to 52-week price range and ROE.
- Unlike relative strength, the Relative Strength Index (RSI) uses all the price changes that occur within the calculation period to determine the average price trend over the period. RSI is calculated using the formula $100 - (100 / (1 + U/D))$, where U is the sum of the total price points gained on up days, and D is the sum of the total price points lost on down days (expressed as a positive number).

- One characteristic of price momentum is that optimal calculation periods for negative momentum tests (in which you want a stock's price to go down) are often shorter than those for positive momentum tests (in which you want a stock's price to go up). The reason is likely that stocks move downward more quickly than they move upward.
- This relationship holds true for RSI: while positive excess returns peak near a period of 28 weeks, negative excess returns peak near 16 weeks.
- The 28/16-week RSI & 52-week price range strategy combines two different price momentum factors. It generates strong and consistent returns, but has high volatility. The addition of a valuation factor (as a third factor) would help offset volatility and further strengthen consistency.
- The 28/16-week RSI and economic profits strategy combines price momentum, cash flow, profitability, and valuation all into one, with good results. In particular, the Sharpe ratio for the top quintile of the strategy is a high 0.97.

CHAPTER 10

Red Flags

The worst sort of business is one that grows rapidly, requires significant capital to engender the growth, and then earns little or no money. Think airlines. Here a *durable* competitive advantage has proven elusive ever since the days of the Wright [b]rothers. Indeed, if a farsighted capitalist had been present at Kitty Hawk, he would have done his successors a huge favor by shooting Orville down.

Warren Buffett, 2007 Annual Report to Shareholders

So far in this book, I've identified six primary types of investment strategies that drive future stock market returns from a quantitative point of view. I call these primary drivers the *basics*, since they represent the essentials of common stock investment. Chapters 4 through 9,[1] covered many of the basic drivers of *future* stock market returns, including profitability, valuation, cash flow, growth, capital allocation, and price momentum. A quantitative investor, or an investor simply seeking to become better at picking stocks, can count on these six fundamental drivers to provide a solid foundation for building an effective quantitative screen or model or in qualitatively choosing a winning portfolio of stocks.[2] The various *building blocks* that I've presented under these six basic categories— return on invested capital, return on equity, and economic profits, for example, under profitability—can be mixed and matched to form complex quantitative models or

---

[1] Chapter 3 covers the basic drivers of day-to-day returns in the stock market. Chapters 4 through 9, as well as this chapter, cover the basic drivers of future returns.

[2] Although qualitative stock analysis isn't the primary subject of this book, I believe few investors would argue that the basic drivers presented here don't apply equally to quantitative and qualitative analysis.

screens. I'll provide suggestions on how to best combine these factors and how to incorporate them into your investment process in Chapters 12 and 13.

However, outside of these six basics, there are a number of important investment factors that can be used effectively in quantitative models and that can further expand one's understanding of how the stock market works. It would be impossible in terms of both time and space to cover all of them in this book. However, this chapter contains five such strategies, grouped under the rather general title of "red flags." The title is perhaps not apt, since stocks in the bottom quintile of many of the strategies in this book can be seen as waving a red flag, warning of likely underperformance to come. However, the strategies presented in this chapter have been traditionally viewed as measures of risk: leverage and debt payback, capital intensity, capital investment coverage, working capital efficiency, and accounting conservatism. While none of these factors are unusually strong in and of themselves, each points out an aspect of a company's financial and/or business condition that is indicative of corporate health or disease. Moreover, most of these strategies form individual building blocks that are more or less independent of the six major categories of basics presented in the preceding chapters, and thus can add significant investment value to a multifactor model or screen.

FINANCIAL LEVERAGE AND DEBT PAYBACK

Financial leverage ratios measure the amount of debt a company has relative to capital or assets and give an indication of how significant the risk of insolvency may be for the firm. Often used ratios include long-term debt to equity, total debt to assets, and total debt to invested capital. Since a lower leverage ratio means that a company carries less financial risk, you might expect that a quantitative test based on financial leverage would show companies with low leverage outperforming and companies with high leverage underperforming. If so, you would be disappointed. At least over the short term (our 12-month holding period), the market rewards companies that take financial risk and punishes those that are more fiscally conservative (those with low debt).

Why should this be so? One reason is that in a good economy companies with high financial leverage can use debt to ratchet up their ability to generate income (one of the goals of leverage). Interest expense is generally fixed, and returns in excess of the cost of debt accrue to shareholders. Another factor is that interest rates have generally declined over our 20-year test period, so financial leverage has become less and less costly (and therefore less risky) to carry. However, although the market rewards financial risk takers over the short term, the long-term picture is likely quite different. In an economic downturn, companies with high levels of debt are sometimes unable to make debt service payments—or such contractually obligated payments prevent them from making necessary investments in their businesses. Thus, we looked for another method to reduce financial risk in quantitative portfolios that doesn't detract from excess returns.

In Chapter 5, I presented the enterprise value (EV) to EBITDA (earnings before interest, taxes, depreciation, and amortization) and total debt to EBITDA strategy. The top quintile of that strategy contains companies with low valuations *and* low total debt relative to income. The total debt-to-EBITDA factor increased excess returns, reduced the maximum loss, and reduced the volatility of returns. The difference between total debt to EBITDA and a leverage strategy like debt to equity is that total debt to EBITDA considers not only financial leverage but also profitability.[3] A company with high debt and high profitability will have a lower debt to income value than a company with high debt and low profitability. This is important because high debt companies with low profitability are likely to have trouble servicing debt. In this section, we look at a company's ratio of free cash flow to long-term debt, a debt-related strategy that considers cash profitability and makes a good debt-related building block.

Total Debt to Invested Capital

First, we'll start by looking at a simple financial leverage ratio. The total debt-to-invested capital strategy contains companies with the highest debt to capital values in the top quintile and the lowest debt to capital values in the bottom quintile. Total debt equals long-term debt plus debt in current liabilities, and invested capital is the book value of common equity plus long-term debt plus preferred stock and minority interest. I present this strategy just to show that, over the short term, the market rewards companies that take financial risk and does not reward companies that are too financially conservative. However, we won't use this strategy as a building block because we're seeking to decrease risk with debt-based strategies, not to increase it.

The top quintile (high debt companies) outperforms by 2.3%, on average, and does so for 65% of one-year and 81% of rolling three-year periods (see Figure 10.1). The bottom two quintiles (low debt companies) underperform slightly and are moderately consistent. Companies in the top quintile have short-term plus long-term debt equal to 100% or more of invested capital, while companies in the bottom quintile have little or no debt. The results of this test show that, except for certain periods, the market has rewarded companies with high debt-to-capital ratios, at least over our 12-month test period.

---

[3] Because total debt to EBITDA considers debt relative to income generation, it is considered a debt *payback* ratio.

1988–2007	1st Quintile	2nd Quintile	3rd Quintile	4th Quintile	5th Quintile	Universe	S&P 500*
CAGR – Annual Rebalance	13.3%	12.3%	12.2%	9.7%	7.8%	11.2%	12.9%
Average Excess Return vs. Universe**	2.3%	0.6%	0.2%	−1.5%	−1.3%	NA	1.6%
Value of $10,000 Invested (20 Years)	$122,344	$101,145	$100,556	$63,310	$45,066	$83,161	$112,895
% of 1-Year Periods Strategy Outperforms the Universe	64.9%	50.6%	51.9%	33.8%	40.3%	NA	59.7%
% Rolling 3-Year Periods Strategy Outperforms	81.2%	44.9%	56.5%	17.4%	23.2%	NA	71.0%
Maximum Gain	65.2%	56.7%	54.2%	57.9%	82.6%	59.2%	54.1%
Maximum Loss	−37.4%	−24.2%	−23.7%	−38.5%	−55.7%	−24.9%	−25.9%
Sharpe Ratio	0.57	0.61	0.57	0.37	0.27	0.49	0.69
Standard Deviation of Returns	0.18	0.14	0.14	0.18	0.25	0.16	0.14
Beta (vs. Universe)	1.02	0.75	0.85	1.05	1.32	NA	0.78
Alpha (vs. Universe)	0.02	0.04	0.02	−0.02	−0.05	NA	0.04
Average Portfolio Size	409	410	410	410	410	NA	NA
Average Number of Companies Outperforming	188	187	182	170	158	NA	NA
Average Number of Companies Underperforming	197	202	209	221	232	NA	NA
Median Portfolio Value – Total Debt to Invested Capital	118%	54%	36%	17%	1%	45%	55%
Average Market Capitalization	$5,561	$4,114	$4,681	$4,597	$2,629	NA	NA

* Equal-weighted average of S&P 500 returns. ** Annual holding period run quarterly for a larger sample size; arithmetic average excess returns.
Source: Standard & Poor's Compustat Point in Time Database; Charter Oak Investment Systems, Inc., Venues® Data Engine

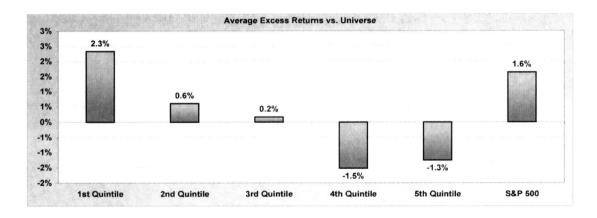

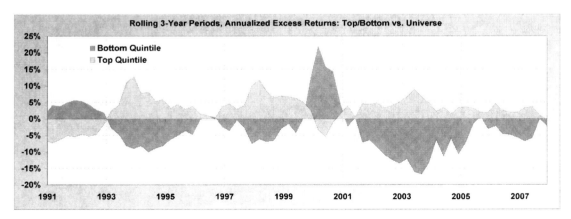

Figure 10.1 Total Debt to Invested Capital (High to Low)

Note that we also ran this test without financial companies, since financials use debt to fund their operating activities[4] and often have large amounts of debt, putting a large number of financial companies in the top quintile. Although removing financials does reduce the excess returns of the top quintile significantly (financial stocks outperformed over our test period), it does not change the overall results of the test.

Free Cash Flow to Long-Term Debt

Free cash flow (FCF) to long-term debt is a debt *payback* ratio. This ratio indicates how long it might take a company to pay back its outstanding debt, given current FCF levels. The ratio also serves as a barometer reading of the financial health of the company.[5] Companies in the top quintile of this strategy have very high FCF (cash from operating activities after capital expenditures) relative to long-term debt. Companies in the bottom quintile generally have cash outflows and therefore are not generating cash flow with which they can service debt.

The top quintile outperforms by 3.5%, on average, and does so for 65% of one-year and 70% of rolling three-year periods (see Figure 10.2). It has a low maximum loss of 22% and a moderately-high Sharpe ratio for a single-factor strategy of 0.71. Average portfolio values for FCF to long-term debt range from 11× to over 100×. The top quintile tends to select large-cap companies, with an average market capitalization of $6.7 billion.

The bottom quintile underperforms by 5.9%, on average, and does so for 75% of one-year and 91% of rolling three-year periods. Average portfolio values for FCF to long-term debt range from −6× to over −100×, indicating cash outflows.

Free Cash Flow to Long-Term Debt by Economic Sector

FCF to long-term debt works well as a strategy across economic sectors. It shows particularly strong excess returns in the energy, consumer discretionary, health care, financials, and telecom services sectors. Note that the strategy works in the financial sector, even though most financial companies use debt and cash as a part of their businesses. The strategy also appears to work for utilities, although the set size is too small to form a reliable test (see Figure 10.3).

---

[4] For example, banks and other lending institutions often use significant amounts of debt to provide funding for loans. Thus, debt for banks can be considered as similar to working capital or inventory for industrial companies.

[5] We exclude companies with no long-term debt when calculating this ratio, as it improves the consistency of the single-factor test. However, including companies with no long-term debt in the two-factor strategies does not significantly change results.

1990–2007	1st Quintile	2nd Quintile	3rd Quintile	4th Quintile	5th Quintile	Universe	S&P 500*
CAGR – Annual Rebalance	13.9%	13.3%	12.1%	9.7%	3.5%	10.3%	12.0%
Average Excess Return vs. Universe**	3.5%	2.5%	1.2%	−0.7%	−5.9%	NA	1.5%
Value of $10,000 Invested (18 Years)	$104,724	$94,626	$78,109	$52,865	$18,531	$58,669	$76,297
% of 1-Year Periods Strategy Outperforms the Universe	65.3%	66.7%	54.2%	41.7%	25.0%	NA	56.9%
% Rolling 3-Year Periods Strategy Outperforms	70.3%	79.7%	73.4%	34.4%	9.4%	NA	68.8%
Maximum Gain	54.3%	50.4%	54.8%	62.1%	83.4%	59.2%	54.1%
Maximum Loss	−22.0%	−20.7%	−29.3%	−30.4%	−55.4%	−24.9%	−25.9%
Sharpe Ratio	0.71	0.73	0.60	0.41	0.07	0.46	0.64
Standard Deviation of Returns	0.16	0.14	0.15	0.17	0.26	0.17	0.14
Beta (vs. Universe)	0.89	0.76	0.78	0.95	1.43	NA	0.78
Alpha (vs. Universe)	0.05	0.05	0.04	0.00	−0.11	NA	0.04
Average Portfolio Size	289	290	290	290	290	NA	NA
Average Number of Companies *Outperforming*	132	134	133	124	105	NA	NA
Average Number of Companies *Underperforming*	144	144	141	151	171	NA	NA
Median Portfolio Value – FCF to Long-Term Debt	65.3	0.4	0.1	0.0	−24.6	5.0	2.6
Average Market Capitalization	$6,699	$6,239	$5,524	$4,228	$2,388	NA	NA

* Equal-weighted average of S&P 500 returns. ** Annual holding period run quarterly for a larger sample size; arithmetic average excess returns.
Source: Standard & Poor's Compustat Point in Time Database; Charter Oak Investment Systems, Inc., Venues® Data Engine

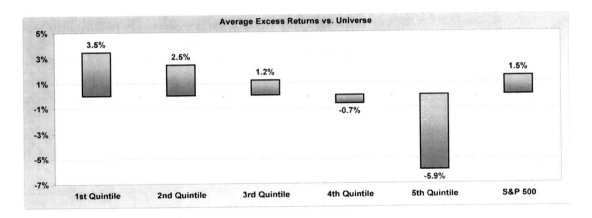

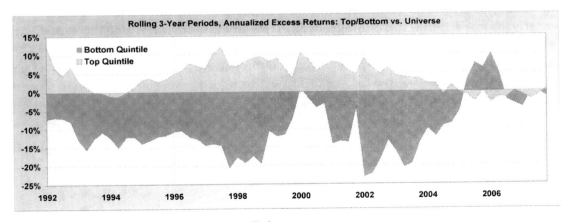

Figure 10.2 Free Cash Flow to Long-Term Debt

Top Quintile

1990–2007	Energy	Materials	Industrials	Consumer Discretionary	Consumer Staples	Health Care	Financials	Information Technology	Telecom Services	Utilities	Universe	S&P 500*
CAGR – Quintile	16.7%	10.9%	12.5%	12.1%	12.1%	15.2%	18.4%	8.7%	9.1%	15.0%	10.3%	12.0%
CAGR – Sector	11.9%	9.7%	10.7%	7.3%	10.8%	11.9%	14.2%	8.0%	5.6%	11.9%	NA	NA
Excess Return vs. Sector	4.8%	1.1%	1.9%	4.8%	1.3%	3.3%	4.2%	0.7%	3.6%	3.0%	NA	NA
Value of $10,000	$161,053	$64,167	$83,725	$78,405	$77,583	$127,904	$208,063	$45,186	$48,164	$123,193	$58,669	$76,297
% 1-Year Outperformance	72.2%	44.4%	44.4%	66.7%	50.0%	55.6%	66.7%	55.6%	55.6%	55.6%	NA	NA
% 3-Year Outperformance	75.0%	56.3%	56.3%	75.0%	81.3%	75.0%	56.3%	56.3%	62.5%	68.8%	NA	NA
Maximum Gain	50.5%	40.0%	37.9%	60.4%	35.1%	83.0%	55.6%	66.7%	63.8%	105.0%	44.0%	41.4%
Maximum Loss	−26.0%	−22.4%	−6.5%	−11.8%	−9.3%	−21.3%	−13.7%	−32.0%	−42.0%	−24.4%	−19.1%	−18.1%
Standard Deviation	0.21	0.16	0.13	0.18	0.14	0.23	0.22	0.26	0.24	0.29	0.17	0.15
Beta (vs. Sector)	0.76	0.84	0.78	0.87	0.97	0.78	0.83	0.62	0.29	1.09	NA	NA
Alpha (vs. Sector)	0.07	0.03	0.04	0.06	0.02	0.06	0.07	0.03	0.09	0.04	NA	NA
Portfolio Size	20	27	49	59	17	33	26	38	8	2	NA	NA

Bottom Quintile

1990–2007	Energy	Materials	Industrials	Consumer Discretionary	Consumer Staples	Health Care	Financials	Information Technology	Telecom Services	Utilities	Universe	S&P 500*
CAGR – Quintile	6.6%	6.0%	3.9%	3.6%	6.1%	3.7%	10.7%	−0.2%	−9.7%	7.3%	10.3%	12.0%
CAGR – Sector	11.9%	9.7%	10.7%	7.3%	10.8%	11.9%	14.2%	8.0%	5.6%	11.9%	NA	NA
Excess Return vs. Sector	−5.4%	−3.7%	−6.7%	−3.7%	−4.7%	−8.1%	−3.5%	−8.2%	−15.3%	−4.6%	NA	NA
Value of $10,000	$31,512	$28,738	$20,012	$18,986	$28,825	$19,373	$62,385	$9,668	$1,583	$35,535	$58,669	$76,297
% 1-Year Outperformance	27.8%	33.3%	16.7%	33.3%	27.8%	27.8%	38.9%	27.8%	16.7%	33.3%	NA	NA
% 3-Year Outperformance	18.8%	18.8%	18.8%	18.8%	6.3%	0.0%	31.3%	12.5%	12.5%	31.3%	NA	NA
Maximum Gain	61.5%	38.3%	41.4%	57.0%	30.1%	85.9%	58.3%	175.8%	94.1%	156.4%	44.0%	41.4%
Maximum Loss	−54.1%	−17.2%	−32.5%	−24.9%	−21.3%	−42.9%	−22.6%	−62.1%	−80.2%	−45.0%	−19.1%	−18.1%
Standard Deviation	0.31	0.17	0.19	0.23	0.16	0.30	0.22	0.53	0.41	0.46	0.17	0.15
Beta (vs. Sector)	1.17	1.00	1.21	1.14	0.88	1.12	0.89	1.32	1.05	1.56	NA	NA
Alpha (vs. Sector)	−0.06	0.01	−0.06	−0.08	0.02	−0.06	0.01	−0.16	−0.19	−0.05	NA	NA
Portfolio Size	21	28	52	63	20	34	30	41	8	3	NA	NA

* Equal-weighted average of S&P 500 returns.
Source: Standard & Poor's Compustat Point in Time Database; Charter Oak Investment Systems, Inc., Venues® Data Engine

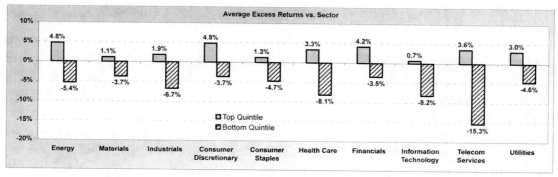

Figure 10.3 Free Cash Flow to Long-Term Debt by Economic Sector

Free Cash Flow to Long-Term Debt and Economic Profits

This strategy looks at FCF in two complementary ways. We've already seen the economic profits strategy several times. It uses cash return on invested capital (ROIC) to determine a company's cash-based profitability and subtracts from that a "rental charge" to account for the cost of capital contributed to the company. So, on the one hand the strategy presented here looks at cash adequacy relative only to debt (FCF to long-term debt), and on the other hand, it looks at cash return on total capital, after deducting a charge for the cost of capital. The results are both strong and consistent.

The top quintile outperforms by 7.5%, on average, and does so for 74% of one-year and 91% of rolling three-year periods (see Figure 10.4). The top quintile significantly underperforms only in 1992, 1999–2000, 2003, and 2007. It has a low maximum loss of 25% and a strong Sharpe ratio of 0.88, versus 0.64 for the S&P 500. Average portfolio values range from 4× to over 100× for FCF to long-term debt and from 26% to 48% for economic profits, so these are highly profitable companies that would have no problem paying off their long-term debt out of a single year's cash flow.

The bottom quintile underperforms by 13%, on average, and does so for 78% of one-year and 95% of rolling three-year periods. It is quite volatile, with a maximum loss of 66%, a maximum gain of 73%, and a standard deviation of returns of 0.30 (vs. 0.14 for the S&P 500). Although the strategy provides strong underperformance, suitable for a short-sale strategy, it tends to outperform significantly coming out of bear markets and at speculative tops in bull markets. Average portfolio values are negative for FCF to debt and range from −58% to −96% for economic profits, so the bottom quintile contains companies with large cash outflows.

Free Cash Flow to Long-Term Debt and Return on Equity

This strategy compares a company's cash adequacy (relative to its long-term debt) to a company's income statement–based profitability. In so doing, it looks at a company's balance sheet, income statement, and cash flow statement, all at once. In this sense, the strategy is similar to the ROIC and cash ROIC strategy presented in Chapter 4.

The top quintile outperforms by 6%, on average, and does so for 65% of one-year and 75% of rolling three-year periods (see Figure 10.5). The strategy significantly underperforms during only three periods: 1992–1993, 1999–2000, and 2003–2004. The maximum loss is a low 17%, and the Sharpe ratio is a moderately-strong 0.81. Average portfolio values range from 5× to over 100× for FCF to long-term debt and from 35% to over 50% for return on equity (ROE). The average market capitalization for this strategy is $14.7 billion, making it the largest cap strategy we've seen. Companies in the top quintile in 2006 included such behemoths as 3M, Exxon Mobil, Johnson & Johnson, Pepsico, and Coca-Cola.

1990–2007	1st Quintile	2nd Quintile	3rd Quintile	4th Quintile	5th Quintile	Universe	S&P 500*
CAGR – Annual Rebalance	18.5%	16.1%	13.1%	9.8%	−2.2%	10.3%	12.0%
Average Excess Return vs. Universe**	7.5%	5.1%	2.5%	−1.3%	−13.0%	NA	1.5%
Value of $10,000 Invested (18 Years)	$212,820	$145,835	$91,928	$54,131	$6,650	$58,669	$76,297
% of 1-Year Periods Strategy Outperforms the Universe	73.6%	69.4%	58.3%	43.1%	22.2%	NA	56.9%
% Rolling 3-Year Periods Strategy Outperforms	90.6%	79.7%	73.4%	37.5%	4.7%	NA	68.8%
Maximum Gain	69.1%	50.5%	51.8%	46.1%	73.0%	59.2%	54.1%
Maximum Loss	−24.9%	−23.2%	−22.7%	−32.3%	−65.9%	−24.9%	−25.9%
Sharpe Ratio	0.88	0.91	0.65	0.36	−0.18	0.46	0.64
Standard Deviation of Returns	0.17	0.14	0.16	0.18	0.30	0.17	0.14
Beta (vs. Universe)	0.85	0.67	0.72	0.90	1.39	NA	0.78
Alpha (vs. Universe)	0.09	0.09	0.06	0.00	−0.18	NA	0.04
Average Portfolio Size	52	52	53	52	53	NA	NA
Average Number of Companies *Outperforming*	26	26	25	22	15	NA	NA
Average Number of Companies *Underperforming*	25	25	26	28	35	NA	NA
Median Portfolio Value – FCF to Long-Term Debt	19.0	0.5	0.1	−0.1	−66.8	5.0	2.6
Median Portfolio Value – Economic Profits	32.5%	2.5%	−5.0%	−15.7%	−69.2%	−11.2%	−6.5%
Average Market Capitalization	$6,156	$6,325	$5,716	$3,457	$1,610	NA	NA

* Equal-weighted average of S&P 500 returns. ** Annual holding period run quarterly for a larger sample size; arithmetic average excess returns.
Source: Standard & Poor's Compustat Point in Time Database; Charter Oak Investment Systems, Inc., Venues® Data Engine

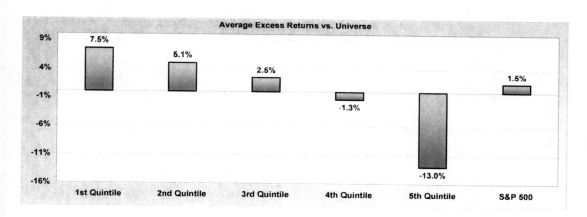

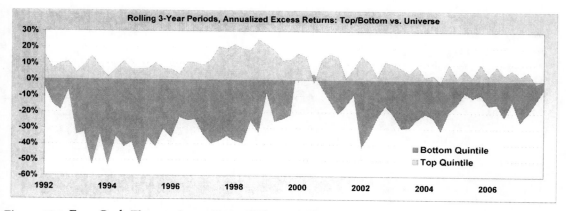

Figure 10.4 Free Cash Flow to Long-Term Debt and Economic Profits

1990–2007	1st Quintile	2nd Quintile	3rd Quintile	4th Quintile	5th Quintile	Universe	S&P 500*
CAGR – Annual Rebalance	15.0%	13.4%	12.7%	9.2%	−3.8%	10.3%	12.0%
Average Excess Return vs. Universe**	6.0%	2.0%	1.1%	−1.8%	−10.1%	NA	1.5%
Value of $10,000 Invested (18 Years)	$123,174	$96,105	$85,369	$48,607	$4,992	$58,669	$76,297
% of 1-Year Periods Strategy Outperforms the Universe	65.3%	61.1%	58.3%	47.2%	19.4%	NA	56.9%
% Rolling 3-Year Periods Strategy Outperforms	75.0%	57.8%	62.5%	51.6%	7.8%	NA	68.8%
Maximum Gain	58.9%	48.8%	53.4%	69.6%	111.3%	59.2%	54.1%
Maximum Loss	−16.9%	−21.9%	−25.4%	−36.4%	−75.6%	−24.9%	−25.9%
Sharpe Ratio	0.81	0.68	0.59	0.33	−0.06	0.46	0.64
Standard Deviation of Returns	0.17	0.14	0.15	0.18	0.38	0.17	0.14
Beta (vs. Universe)	0.79	0.74	0.68	0.87	1.71	NA	0.78
Alpha (vs. Universe)	0.08	0.05	0.05	0.00	−0.19	NA	0.04
Average Portfolio Size	55	56	56	56	56	NA	NA
Average Number of Companies *Outperforming*	27	27	26	23	16	NA	NA
Average Number of Companies *Underperforming*	27	28	27	29	37	NA	NA
Median Portfolio Value – FCF to Long-Term Debt	36.0	0.5	0.1	0.0	−42.7	5.0	2.6
Median Portfolio Value – Return on Equity	43.2%	20.2%	12.5%	4.5%	−129.9%	9.4%	15.0%
Average Market Capitalization	$14,701	$7,024	$4,456	$3,325	$1,207	NA	NA

* Equal-weighted average of S&P 500 returns. ** Annual holding period run quarterly for a larger sample size; arithmetic average excess returns.
Source: Standard & Poor's Compustat Point in Time Database; Charter Oak Investment Systems, Inc., Venues® Data Engine

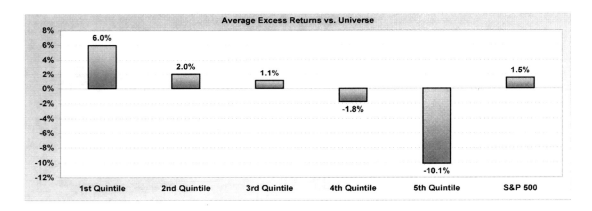

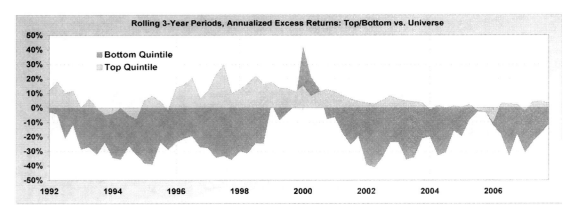

Figure 10.5 Free Cash Flow to Long-Term Debt and Return on Equity

The bottom quintile underperforms by about 10%, on average, and does so for 81% of one-year and 92% of rolling three-year periods. The bottom quintile significantly out-performs only in 1990–1991, 1999–2000, and 2003–2004. Average portfolio values are in the high negatives for both FCF to long-term debt and ROE, indicating operating losses on both a cash flow and income statement basis.

CAPITAL EXPENDITURES TO PROPERTY, PLANT, AND EQUIPMENT

We've seen the capex to property, plant, and equipment (PP&E) strategy before in Chapters 4, 6, and 8. Capex to PP&E has to do with *capital intensity,* or the amount of investment in capital assets, such as machinery, office equipment, and buildings, neces-sary to manufacture products or render services. Examples of capital-intensive indus-tries include automobile manufacturing, airlines, steel production, oil production and refining, and chemicals production. In each of these industries, large capital invest-ments are required to manufacture products or to provide services. Capital intensity may simply be a fact of life in a given industry, and if a company is able to generate a sufficient amount of profit on capital employed, capital intensity is not necessarily a negative. However, some capital-intensive businesses, for example, airlines, regularly fail to do this. As capital spending rises, cash flow decreases, and the amount of income necessary to generate an adequate return on the expanded capital base also rises.

The capex-to-PP&E strategy looks at changes in capital intensity at a company by comparing the current year's capital expenditures to the historical value of PP&E.[6] Companies that make annual capital expenditures equal to half or more of the histori-cal cost of existing PP&E are likely becoming more capital intensive than they were in the past, and, as a result, their stocks underperform. Companies that are spending just a fraction of existing historical costs on PP&E may be becoming less capital intensive. For example, they may have outsourced manufacturing or increased the efficiency of capital equipment through the addition of technology. However, they may also be underspending on repair and maintenance of existing PP&E. Overall, however, compa-nies whose capital spending is low relative to existing PP&E values outperform.

The top quintile of this strategy outperforms by 2.1%, on average, and does so for 62% of one-year and 67% of rolling three-year periods (see Figure 10.6), making it only moderately consistent. The strategy significantly underperforms in three periods: 1990–1992, 1995, and 1998–2000. It has a low maximum loss of 23% and a Sharpe ratio of 0.67, about equal to the Sharpe ratio for the S&P 500 (0.69). Average portfolio values

---

[6] The denominator we use in this strategy is *net* property, plant, & equipment, or gross PP&E minus accumulated depreciation.

1988–2007	1st Quintile	2nd Quintile	3rd Quintile	4th Quintile	5th Quintile	Universe	S&P 500*
CAGR – Annual Rebalance	13.4%	12.4%	12.3%	10.9%	5.1%	11.2%	12.9%
Average Excess Return vs. Universe**	2.1%	1.0%	0.5%	−0.2%	−3.8%	NA	1.6%
Value of $10,000 Invested (20 Years)	$123,690	$103,742	$102,196	$78,992	$27,084	$83,161	$112,895
% of 1-Year Periods Strategy Outperforms the Universe	62.3%	51.9%	46.8%	41.6%	31.2%	NA	59.7%
% Rolling 3-Year Periods Strategy Outperforms	66.7%	62.3%	52.2%	31.9%	13.0%	NA	71.0%
Maximum Gain	67.2%	55.1%	54.0%	62.0%	98.5%	59.2%	54.1%
Maximum Loss	−23.0%	−23.5%	−25.5%	−34.6%	−64.5%	−24.9%	−25.9%
Sharpe Ratio	0.67	0.64	0.57	0.43	0.15	0.49	0.69
Standard Deviation of Returns	0.15	0.14	0.15	0.18	0.28	0.16	0.14
Beta (vs. Universe)	0.81	0.80	0.90	1.07	1.48	NA	0.78
Alpha (vs. Universe)	0.04	0.04	0.02	−0.01	−0.10	NA	0.04
Average Portfolio Size	332	331	331	331	331	NA	NA
Average Number of Companies *Outperforming*	153	146	146	139	119	NA	NA
Average Number of Companies *Underperforming*	161	170	169	177	193	NA	NA
Median Portfolio Value – Capex to PP&E	7.6%	16.2%	22.3%	32.7%	69.5%	29.4%	22.3%
Average Market Capitalization	$3,447	$5,499	$5,788	$4,655	$2,527	NA	NA

* Equal-weighted average of S&P 500 returns. ** Annual holding period run quarterly for a larger sample size; arithmetic average excess returns.
Source: Standard & Poor's Compustat Point in Time Database; Charter Oak Investment Systems, Inc., Venues® Data Engine

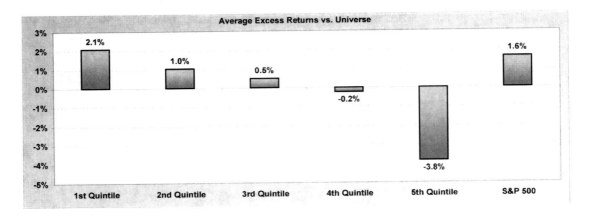

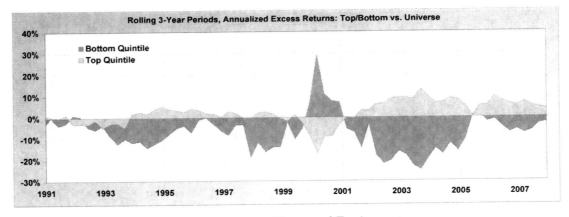

Figure 10.6 Capital Expenditures to Property, Plant, and Equipment

for capex to PP&E range from 7% to 10%, so these companies are "replacing" their existing capital asset base every 10 to 14 years.[7]

The bottom quintile underperforms by 3.8%, on average, and does so for 69% of one-year and 87% of rolling three-year periods. The bottom quintile is highly volatile, outperforming in 1991–1992, 1995, 1999–2000, and 2003–2004. Average portfolio values for capex to PP&E range from 54% to 84%, so these companies are replacing half or more of their existing capital asset base (at depreciated book value) in a single year.

Capital Expenditures to Property, Plant, and Equipment by Economic Sector

The strategy works well for the materials, industrials, consumer staples, financials, and information technology sectors. The telecom services sector shows underperformance of about 11% for the bottom quintile, but this is primarily driven by extremely low returns in 2000 through 2002, following the preceding telecom boom. The strategy also works for the health care sector, but the top quintile for health care is inconsistent (see Figure 10.7).

Capital Expenditures to Property, Plant, and Equipment and Return on Invested Capital

This strategy is similar to the cash ROIC and capex-to-PP&E strategy presented in Chapter 6, except here we look at income statement–based ROIC. Companies in the top quintile of this strategy have low capex needs relative to their existing PP&E base, but are also very profitable. Companies in the bottom quintile must make very large capital investments to stay competitive and are unprofitable—a bad combination.

The top quintile outperforms by 4.4%, on average, and does so for 64% of one-year and 80% of rolling three-year periods (see Figure 10.8). The top quintile significantly underperforms only in 1994–1995, 1998–2000, and 2003–2004. The maximum loss is low (18%), and the standard deviation of returns is also low (0.14), resulting in a high Sharpe ratio of 0.88. Average portfolio values for the top quintile range from 4% to 11% for capex to PP&E and from 18% to 29% for ROIC. These are companies with strong profitability that do not need large additions to their capital asset base to remain competitive.

The bottom quintile underperforms by 7.3%, on average, and does so for 67% of one-year and 90% of rolling three-year periods. The bottom quintile significantly outperforms in 1990–1991, 1995–1996, 1998–2000, and 2003–2004. Average portfolio values range from 56% to 111% for capex to PP&E and from −5% to −41% for ROIC, so these

---

[7] For example, at a 7% capex-to-PP&E rate, a company will spend an amount equal to the book value of its current net PP&E in 14.3 years. This is likely a significant understatement, however, since it doesn't take into account inflation, money spent on maintenance, or money spent on business expansion.

Top Quintile

1988–2007	Energy	Materials	Industrials	Consumer Discretionary	Consumer Staples	Health Care	Financials	Information Technology	Telecom Services	Utilities	Universe	S&P 500*
CAGR – Quintile	13.2%	11.8%	14.7%	9.8%	16.4%	14.0%	16.6%	14.1%	11.0%	5.2%	11.2%	12.9%
CAGR – Sector	13.5%	10.2%	11.3%	8.8%	12.6%	12.3%	14.5%	7.5%	9.2%	13.0%	NA	NA
Excess Return vs. Sector	−0.3%	1.6%	3.5%	1.0%	3.8%	1.7%	2.2%	6.6%	1.7%	−7.7%	NA	NA
Value of $10,000	$120,351	$93,839	$155,649	$64,557	$208,947	$137,771	$216,217	$139,607	$80,084	$26,355	$83,161	$112,895
% 1-Year Outperformance	55.0%	65.0%	70.0%	65.0%	65.0%	60.0%	70.0%	65.0%	65.0%	52.6%	NA	NA
% 3-Year Outperformance	33.3%	66.7%	94.4%	61.1%	88.9%	50.0%	61.1%	83.3%	55.6%	27.8%	NA	NA
Maximum Gain	55.2%	43.6%	47.8%	41.3%	50.1%	62.9%	60.8%	86.1%	95.6%	170.6%	44.0%	41.4%
Maximum Loss	−29.9%	−27.5%	−18.5%	−31.3%	−11.2%	−25.6%	−20.6%	−36.6%	−46.9%	−20.4%	−19.1%	−18.1%
Standard Deviation	0.25	0.18	0.16	0.19	0.18	0.21	0.22	0.29	0.34	0.39	0.16	0.14
Beta (vs. Sector)	0.89	1.16	1.09	1.02	1.12	0.77	0.91	0.71	0.67	−0.29	NA	NA
Alpha (vs. Sector)	0.01	0.00	0.03	0.01	0.03	0.04	0.04	0.08	0.06	0.23	NA	NA
Portfolio Size	22	31	60	72	23	40	23	57	9	4	NA	NA

Bottom Quintile

1988–2007	Energy	Materials	Industrials	Consumer Discretionary	Consumer Staples	Health Care	Financials	Information Technology	Telecom Services	Utilities	Universe	S&P 500*
CAGR – Quintile	7.7%	6.9%	5.4%	5.8%	8.6%	5.5%	10.5%	2.1%	−1.4%	5.9%	11.2%	12.9%
CAGR – Sector	13.5%	10.2%	11.3%	8.8%	12.6%	12.3%	14.5%	7.5%	9.2%	13.0%	NA	NA
Excess Return vs. Sector	−5.8%	−3.3%	−5.8%	−2.9%	−4.0%	−6.8%	−3.9%	−5.5%	−10.7%	−7.0%	NA	NA
Value of $10,000	$44,454	$38,097	$28,899	$30,997	$52,006	$29,359	$73,971	$15,090	$7,474	$31,539	$83,161	$112,895
% 1-Year Outperformance	45.0%	35.0%	20.0%	35.0%	25.0%	30.0%	35.0%	45.0%	40.0%	55.0%	NA	NA
% 3-Year Outperformance	16.7%	33.3%	0.0%	33.3%	27.8%	5.6%	27.8%	22.2%	16.7%	44.4%	NA	NA
Maximum Gain	60.1%	30.8%	34.4%	51.5%	32.4%	90.1%	44.1%	148.0%	97.1%	135.0%	44.0%	41.4%
Maximum Loss	−60.7%	−15.3%	−19.3%	−24.1%	−22.0%	−39.0%	−25.4%	−58.5%	−72.2%	−80.6%	−19.1%	−18.1%
Standard Deviation	0.32	0.12	0.13	0.19	0.16	0.29	0.19	0.43	0.41	0.45	0.16	0.14
Beta (vs. Sector)	1.22	0.73	0.82	0.97	1.01	1.10	0.62	1.10	0.95	1.82	NA	NA
Alpha (vs. Sector)	−0.07	0.02	−0.02	−0.04	0.04	−0.06	0.01	−0.11	−0.16	0.03	NA	NA
Portfolio Size	22	31	57	68	20	39	20	54	8	3	NA	NA

* Equal-weighted average of S&P 500 returns.
Source: Standard & Poor's Compustat Point in Time Database; Charter Oak Investment Systems, Inc., Venues® Data Engine

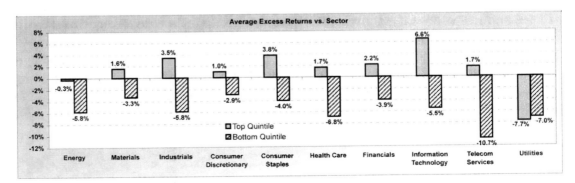

Figure 10.7 Capital Expenditures to Property, Plant, and Equipment by Economic Sector

1988–2007	1st Quintile	2nd Quintile	3rd Quintile	4th Quintile	5th Quintile	Universe	S&P 500*
CAGR – Annual Rebalance	15.9%	12.6%	14.1%	8.8%	−5.0%	11.2%	12.9%
Average Excess Return vs. Universe**	4.4%	2.1%	1.2%	−1.3%	−7.3%	NA	1.6%
Value of $10,000 Invested (20 Years)	$190,573	$107,112	$138,871	$54,079	$3,586	$83,161	$112,895
% of 1-Year Periods Strategy Outperforms the Universe	63.6%	57.1%	51.9%	42.9%	32.5%	NA	59.7%
% Rolling 3-Year Periods Strategy Outperforms	79.7%	62.3%	53.6%	31.9%	10.1%	NA	71.0%
Maximum Gain	54.7%	52.4%	48.4%	62.7%	134.6%	59.2%	54.1%
Maximum Loss	−17.6%	−19.2%	−26.8%	−38.0%	−82.1%	−24.9%	−25.9%
Sharpe Ratio	0.88	0.73	0.62	0.39	0.02	0.49	0.69
Standard Deviation of Returns	0.14	0.14	0.15	0.17	0.41	0.16	0.14
Beta (vs. Universe)	0.70	0.68	0.77	1.00	1.85	NA	0.78
Alpha (vs. Universe)	0.08	0.06	0.04	−0.01	−0.18	NA	0.04
Average Portfolio Size	62	62	62	62	63	NA	NA
Average Number of Companies *Outperforming*	30	29	29	24	17	NA	NA
Average Number of Companies *Underperforming*	30	31	31	35	41	NA	NA
Median Portfolio Value – Capex to PP&E	8.3%	16.4%	22.3%	33.2%	76.9%	29.4%	22.3%
Median Portfolio Value – ROIC	21.4%	13.1%	10.8%	7.5%	−28.7%	9.3%	11.6%
Average Market Capitalization	$5,115	$5,623	$5,009	$3,180	$1,198	NA	NA

* Equal-weighted average of S&P 500 returns.** Annual holding period run quarterly for a larger sample size; arithmetic average excess returns.
Source: Standard & Poor's Compustat Point in Time Database; Charter Oak Investment Systems, Inc., Venues® Data Engine

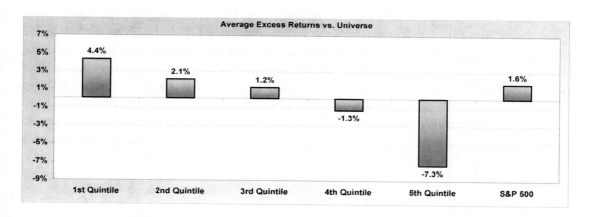

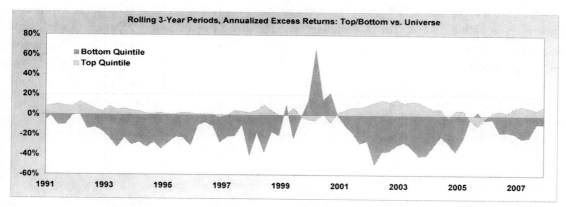

Figure 10.8 Capital Expenditures to Property, Plant, and Equipment and Return on Invested Capital

are companies that are experiencing losses but are also seeing capital spending require-ments increase significantly. An average of 41 portfolio companies outperforms versus 17 that underperform, indicating that the strategy is a strong one.

Capital Expenditures to Property, Plant, and Equipment and 52-Week Price Range

This strategy is very simple yet works well. It combines a capital intensity factor with a price momentum factor. The top quintile contains companies that require decreasing amounts of capital investment to remain competitive and that are at or near 52-week highs. The bottom quintile contains companies that require large increases in capital investment to maintain competitiveness and are falling toward 52-week lows.

The top quintile outperforms by an average of 4.9%, and does so for 75% of one-year and 83% of rolling three-year periods (see Figure 10.9). The top quintile signifi-cantly underperforms in 1991, 1995–1996, 1999–2000, and 2003. It has a low maximum loss of 18% and a relatively high Sharpe ratio of 0.85. Average portfolio values range from 5% to 10% for capex to PP&E and from 63% to 98% for 52-week price range.

The bottom quintile underperforms by an average of 9%, and does so for 79% of one-year and 94% of rolling three-year periods. The bottom quintile significantly out-performs only in 1995, 1999–2000, and 2003–2004. Average portfolio values range from 53% to 126% for PP&E to capex and from 2% to 41% for 52-week price range. An aver-age of 42 portfolio companies underperforms versus 22 that outperform.

Note that overall excess returns for this strategy, as well as quintile maximum losses, are quite linear, indicating that the strategy is strong and that risk increases as one moves down the quintiles.

OPERATING CASH FLOW TO CAPITAL EXPENDITURES

Since at least a certain level of capital expenditures is necessary for companies to repair and replace PP&E, capex can be considered a required use of cash.[8] Operating cash flow to capital expenditures looks at how much cash a company has available to fund this very necessary expense. Companies that generate high operating cash flow relative to capital spending needs have excess cash that can be used to pay dividends, repurchase shares, reduce debt, make business acquisitions, or expand the business through increased capital spending. They are also less likely to have problems meeting debt ser-vice needs. On the other hand, companies that do not even generate sufficient cash flow

---

[8] Companies also use capital expenditures to expand their productive capacity, but because we can't easily distinguish between maintenance capex and expenditures made to expand a business, we consider capex as a unit in all of our quantitative tests.

1988–2007	1st Quintile	2nd Quintile	3rd Quintile	4th Quintile	5th Quintile	Universe	S&P 500*
CAGR – Annual Rebalance	17.3%	13.9%	13.5%	9.4%	−2.0%	11.2%	12.9%
Average Excess Return vs. Universe**	4.9%	2.1%	1.5%	−3.3%	−9.0%	NA	1.6%
Value of $10,000 Invested (20 Years)	$243,032	$134,697	$124,800	$60,175	$6,646	$83,161	$112,895
% of 1-Year Periods Strategy Outperforms the Universe	75.3%	70.1%	49.4%	29.9%	20.8%	NA	59.7%
% Rolling 3-Year Periods Strategy Outperforms	82.6%	68.1%	60.9%	17.4%	5.8%	NA	71.0%
Maximum Gain	48.6%	54.9%	62.5%	68.9%	82.3%	59.2%	54.1%
Maximum Loss	−17.5%	−22.0%	−25.1%	−43.0%	−73.9%	−24.9%	−25.9%
Sharpe Ratio	0.85	0.70	0.58	0.25	−0.03	0.49	0.69
Standard Deviation of Returns	0.15	0.15	0.16	0.19	0.29	0.16	0.14
Beta (vs. Universe)	0.79	0.78	0.90	1.05	1.49	NA	0.78
Alpha (vs. Universe)	0.08	0.05	0.03	−0.04	−0.15	NA	0.04
Average Portfolio Size	66	66	66	66	67	NA	NA
Average Number of Companies *Outperforming*	32	30	30	28	22	NA	NA
Average Number of Companies *Underperforming*	28	33	34	36	42	NA	NA
Median Portfolio Value – Capex to PP&E	8.4%	16.4%	22.4%	32.7%	67.8%	29.4%	22.3%
Median Portfolio Value – 52-Week Price Range	96%	83%	65%	42%	16%	60%	59%
Average Market Capitalization	$4,317	$7,046	$5,732	$4,358	$1,626	NA	NA

* Equal-weighted average of S&P 500 returns. ** Annual holding period run quarterly for a larger sample size; arithmetic average excess returns.
Source: Standard & Poor's Compustat Point in Time Database; Charter Oak Investment Systems, Inc., Venues® Data Engine

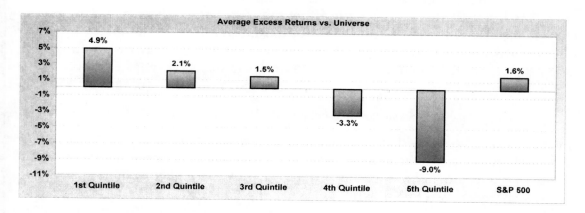

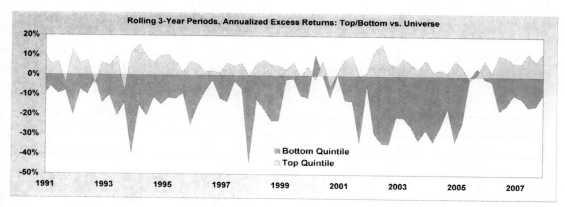

Figure 10.9 Capital Expenditures to Property, Plant, and Equipment and 52-Week Price Range

to meet capital spending requirements may have very limited financial flexibility and run the risk of becoming noncompetitive.

This strategy puts companies that have high cash flows relative to capital expenditures in the top quintile and companies that have negative cash flows, and thus that may have trouble paying for capital expenditures, in the bottom quintile. The strategy is relatively consistent, has low volatility (in the top quintile), and makes a strong building block.

The top quintile outperforms by 4.2%, on average, and does so for 74% of one-year and 77% of rolling three-year periods (see Figure 10.10). The top quintile underperforms in only four years (unfortunately, like most cash flow strategies, all of them are recent): 2004 through 2007. The maximum loss is a low 22%, and the Sharpe ratio is 0.71, significantly above the S&P 500 Sharpe ratio of 0.64. Average portfolio values for operating cash flow to capital expenditures range from 9× to well over 20×, so these are companies that can easily fund current capex needs and still have a lot of cash left over.

The bottom quintile underperforms by 7.2%, on average, and does so for 79% of one-year and 91% of rolling three-year periods. It significantly outperforms only in 1999–2000, 2003–2004, and 2006. Average portfolio values for operating cash flow to capex range from −3× to −16×, so these companies have significant cash outflows and, as a result, may fall behind on maintenance or replacement of capital assets.

Operating Cash Flow to Capital Expenditures by Economic Sector

Like other cash flow-based strategies, the operating cash flow-to-capex strategy works very well by sector. The top quintile works for every sector except the financials and utilities sectors. Since cash is often used as part of a financial company's business (to make loans, etc.), cash flow is not a typically used measure for financials; in addition, capital expenditures are not usually significant for financial companies. The utility sector has an average set size of only two companies, making this test unreliable. The bottom quintile of this test works for every sector, without exception (see Figure 10.11). I believe this fact reflects the importance of positive cash flows and the need to adequately fund capital expenditures for most types of businesses.

Operating Cash Flow to Capital Expenditures Plus Interest and Price to Capital Expenditures

This strategy combines a measure of cash coverage of financial and business expenses with a valuation factor. We use operating cash flow to capital expenses plus interest expense because we found that including interest expense made excess returns more consistent and less volatile. A high operating cash flow to capex plus interest ratio indicates a company should have little problem in meeting either need. A low or negative

1990–2007	1st Quintile	2nd Quintile	3rd Quintile	4th Quintile	5th Quintile	Universe	S&P 500*
CAGR – Annual Rebalance	14.9%	12.8%	10.9%	9.8%	2.0%	10.3%	12.0%
Average Excess Return vs. Universe**	4.2%	2.4%	0.9%	−0.4%	−7.2%	NA	1.5%
Value of $10,000 Invested (18 Years)	$122,047	$87,348	$64,522	$53,850	$14,298	$58,670	$76,297
% of 1-Year Periods Strategy Outperforms the Universe	73.6%	65.3%	54.2%	43.1%	20.8%	NA	56.9%
% Rolling 3-Year Periods Strategy Outperforms	76.6%	75.0%	59.4%	28.1%	9.4%	NA	68.8%
Maximum Gain	54.9%	51.1%	56.0%	59.9%	81.0%	59.2%	54.1%
Maximum Loss	−22.2%	−19.8%	−25.3%	−28.6%	−61.6%	−24.9%	−25.9%
Sharpe Ratio	0.71	0.73	0.58	0.43	0.02	0.46	0.64
Standard Deviation of Returns	0.17	0.14	0.15	0.17	0.28	0.17	0.14
Beta (vs. Universe)	0.97	0.79	0.85	0.97	1.52	NA	0.78
Alpha (vs. Universe)	0.05	0.05	0.03	0.00	−0.13	NA	0.04
Average Portfolio Size	325	326	326	326	326	NA	NA
Average Number of Companies *Outperforming*	151	147	141	138	113	NA	NA
Average Number of Companies *Underperforming*	158	164	168	172	195	NA	NA
Median Portfolio Value – Op. Cash Flow to Capex	19.7	2.5	1.5	0.9	−5.1	3.2	3.3
Average Market Capitalization	$5,334	$6,031	$5,770	$4,347	$2,141	NA	NA

* Equal-weighted average of S&P 500 returns. ** Annual holding period run quarterly for a larger sample size; arithmetic average excess returns.
Source: Standard & Poor's Compustat Point in Time Database; Charter Oak Investment Systems, Inc., Venues® Data Engine

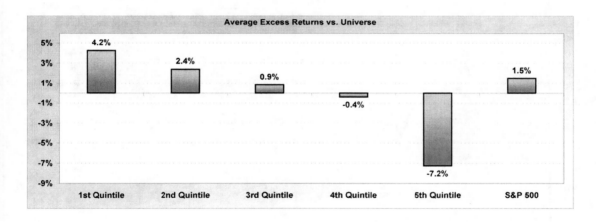

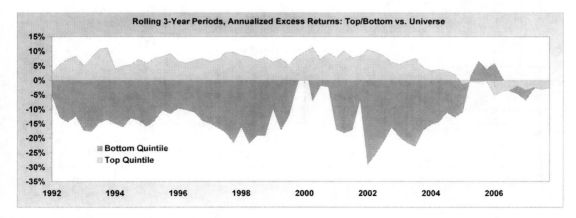

Figure 10.10 Operating Cash Flow to Capital Expenditures

								Top Quintile				
				Consumer	Consumer	Health		Information	Telecom			S&P
1990–2007	Energy	Materials	Industrials	Discretionary	Staples	Care	Financials	Technology	Services	Utilities	Universe	500*
CAGR – Quintile	16.8%	12.2%	14.5%	13.4%	16.3%	20.3%	15.5%	14.9%	9.0%	5.7%	10.3%	12.0%
CAGR – Sector	11.9%	9.7%	10.7%	7.3%	10.8%	11.9%	14.2%	8.0%	5.6%	11.9%	NA	NA
Excess Return vs. Sector	4.9%	2.5%	3.8%	6.1%	5.5%	8.5%	1.3%	6.9%	3.4%	−6.2%	NA	NA
Value of $10,000	$163,671	$79,984	$114,904	$95,668	$151,925	$280,027	$133,996	$121,349	$46,862	$25,578	$58,669	$76,297
% 1-Year Outperformance	61.1%	44.4%	88.9%	83.3%	77.8%	77.8%	44.4%	61.1%	66.7%	35.3%	NA	NA
% 3-Year Outperformance	81.3%	75.0%	93.8%	100.0%	81.3%	93.8%	37.5%	75.0%	62.5%	25.0%	NA	NA
Maximum Gain	53.6%	39.9%	42.1%	51.9%	70.5%	99.0%	68.8%	82.4%	58.2%	193.9%	44.0%	41.4%
Maximum Loss	−30.9%	−17.5%	−8.7%	−14.5%	−15.1%	−14.1%	−18.4%	−33.2%	−41.9%	−42.1%	−19.1%	−18.1%
Standard Deviation	0.23	0.16	0.14	0.18	0.20	0.26	0.23	0.28	0.24	0.49	0.17	0.15
Beta (vs. Sector)	0.83	0.87	0.94	0.91	1.23	0.95	0.91	0.67	0.35	−0.13	NA	NA
Alpha (vs. Sector)	0.07	0.04	0.04	0.07	0.04	0.09	0.03	0.09	0.08	0.18	NA	NA
Portfolio Size	21	28	55	66	19	40	20	56	8	2	NA	NA

								Bottom Quintile				
				Consumer	Consumer	Health		Information	Telecom			S&P
1990–2007	Energy	Materials	Industrials	Discretionary	Staples	Care	Financials	Technology	Services	Utilities	Universe	500*
CAGR – Quintile	3.2%	6.0%	3.2%	0.6%	7.2%	0.4%	9.7%	0.4%	−5.9%	−1.9%	10.3%	12.0%
CAGR – Sector	11.9%	9.7%	10.7%	7.3%	10.8%	11.9%	14.2%	8.0%	5.6%	11.9%	NA	NA
Excess Return vs. Sector	−8.8%	−3.8%	−7.5%	−6.7%	−3.6%	−11.5%	−4.4%	−7.7%	−11.5%	−13.8%	NA	NA
Value of $10,000	$17,491	$28,330	$17,632	$11,044	$35,152	$10,747	$53,353	$10,661	$3,320	$7,086	$58,669	$76,297
% 1-Year Outperformance	27.8%	33.3%	11.1%	27.8%	44.4%	27.8%	33.3%	22.2%	33.3%	44.4%	NA	NA
% 3-Year Outperformance	12.5%	31.3%	18.8%	12.5%	12.5%	0.0%	25.0%	6.3%	31.3%	31.3%	NA	NA
Maximum Gain	56.0%	40.5%	47.2%	55.2%	35.0%	98.4%	53.6%	197.8%	223.0%	156.4%	44.0%	41.4%
Maximum Loss	−57.5%	−26.2%	−31.9%	−32.4%	−20.0%	−36.9%	−29.7%	−62.2%	−80.6%	−84.2%	−19.1%	−18.1%
Standard Deviation	0.32	0.18	0.19	0.24	0.16	0.33	0.21	0.56	0.71	0.55	0.17	0.15
Beta (vs. Sector)	1.21	1.07	1.22	1.22	1.00	1.22	0.82	1.40	1.81	2.47	NA	NA
Alpha (vs. Sector)	−0.10	0.01	−0.06	−0.10	0.02	−0.12	0.01	−0.14	−0.19	−0.07	NA	NA
Portfolio Size	22	29	58	70	22	42	23	58	9	3	NA	NA

* Equal-weighted average of S&P 500 returns.
Source: Standard & Poor's Compustat Point in Time Database; Charter Oak Investment Systems, Inc., Venues® Data Engine

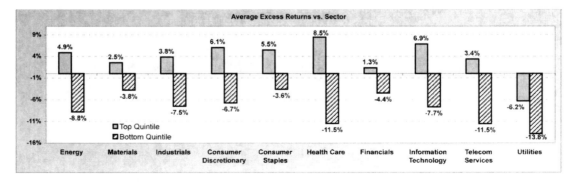

Figure 10.11 Operating Cash Flow to Capital Expenditures by Economic Sector

ratio may indicate that a company is at risk of missing debt service payments or may have trouble funding adequate capital expenditures. Price to capital expenditures is an unorthodox valuation factor that I have never seen used elsewhere. However, it makes sense in the context of this strategy. While the cash flow to capex plus interest ratio tells investors that companies in the top quintile have more than ample cash flow to meet interest and capital spending needs, the price-to-capex factor tells investors just how much investment in both maintenance and future business growth they are getting for each dollar they invest in the company. Companies with high capex relative to price offer investors the opportunity to benefit from substantial future business growth, if capital investments produce the desired results.

The top quintile of this strategy outperforms by 5.9%, on average, and does so for 74% of one-year and 83% of rolling three-year periods (see Figure 10.12). It significantly underperforms only in 1990–1991, 1999–2000, and 2004–2005. The top quintile has a low maximum loss of 24% and a low standard deviation of returns of 0.15, resulting in a high Sharpe ratio of 0.90. Average portfolio values range from 2× to 7× for operating cash flow to capex plus interest expense and from 10× to about 50× for price to capex.

The bottom quintile underperforms by an average of about 9%, and does so for 79% of one-year and 98% of rolling three-year periods, making it a very consistent strategy. The bottom quintile significantly outperforms in four periods: 1990–1991, 1995–1996, 1999–2000, and 2003–2004. An average of 33 stocks in the bottom quintile underperforms versus 18 that outperform. Average portfolio values range from −3× to less than −20× for operating cash flow to capex plus interest, indicating large cash outflows, and from 90× to over 500× for price to capex. Note that both the top and bottom quintiles tend to select midcap stocks.

Operating Cash Flow to Capital Expenditures and Depreciation to Invested Capital

This strategy considers both the cash a company has available to fund necessary investments in its business and how conservatively or aggressively a company accounts for the expenses related to those capital investments. The depreciation-to-invested capital strategy is discussed in depth below. For now, let's say that companies that recognize high amounts of depreciation expense relative to their invested capital base may be considered to be conservative in their accounting. On the other hand, companies that take a minimum of depreciation expense relative to invested capital can be viewed as suspect of using aggressive accounting techniques. Companies that have lots of cash to back up their capital spending and take sufficient depreciation expense to recognize the cost of those capital investments outperform. Companies that do not have sufficient cash flow to back up capital spending and are applying "liberal" depreciation policies to existing capital assets, perhaps to hide their lack of income, underperform.

1990–2007	1st Quintile	2nd Quintile	3rd Quintile	4th Quintile	5th Quintile	Universe	S&P 500*
CAGR – Annual Rebalance	19.0%	13.3%	10.4%	11.4%	0.2%	10.3%	12.0%
Average Excess Return vs. Universe**	5.9%	2.9%	0.4%	0.2%	−9.1%	NA	1.5%
Value of $10,000 Invested (18 Years)	$230,542	$93,982	$59,193	$70,211	$10,328	$58,670	$76,297
% of 1-Year Periods Strategy Outperforms the Universe	73.6%	56.9%	51.4%	45.8%	20.8%	NA	56.9%
% Rolling 3-Year Periods Strategy Outperforms	82.8%	79.7%	57.8%	40.6%	1.6%	NA	68.8%
Maximum Gain	56.4%	52.9%	55.1%	55.5%	78.7%	59.2%	54.1%
Maximum Loss	−24.3%	−20.6%	−25.9%	−28.2%	−52.9%	−24.9%	−25.9%
Sharpe Ratio	0.90	0.74	0.56	0.48	−0.05	0.46	0.64
Standard Deviation of Returns	0.15	0.14	0.14	0.17	0.28	0.17	0.14
Beta (vs. Universe)	0.70	0.63	0.67	0.87	1.40	NA	0.78
Alpha (vs. Universe)	0.10	0.07	0.04	0.02	−0.14	NA	0.04
Average Portfolio Size	52	53	53	53	53	NA	NA
Average Number of Companies *Outperforming*	26	25	24	22	18	NA	NA
Average Number of Companies *Underperforming*	23	26	26	27	33	NA	NA
Median Portfolio Value – Op. CF to Capex + Interest	3.2	1.7	1.1	0.6	−7.2	2.0	2.2
Median Portfolio Value – Price to Capex	23.5	19.1	15.0	18.0	277.6	14.7	13.6
Average Market Capitalization	$3,674	$5,846	$7,056	$5,288	$3,343	NA	NA

* Equal-weighted average of S&P 500 returns. ** Annual holding period run quarterly for a larger sample size; arithmetic average excess returns.
Source: Standard & Poor's Compustat Point in Time Database; Charter Oak Investment Systems, Inc., Venues® Data Engine

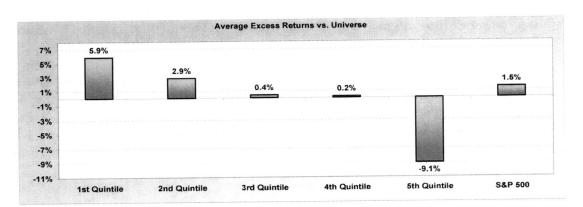

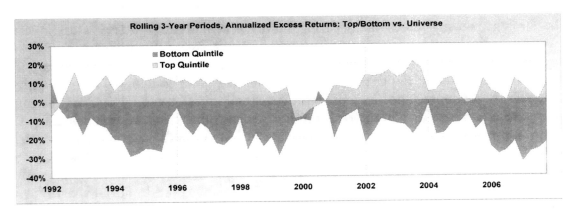

Figure 10.12 Operating Cash Flow to Capital Expenditures Plus Interest and Price to Capital Expenditures

The top quintile outperforms by 7.5% on average, and does so for 78% of one-year and 84% of rolling three-year periods (see Figure 10.13). Unfortunately, the top quintile underperformed recently: from 2004 through 2007. It has a low maximum loss of 18% and a relatively high Sharpe ratio of 0.84. Average portfolio values range from 5× to over 15× for operating cash flow to capex and from 9% to 20% for depreciation to invested capital.

The bottom quintile underperforms by an average of 7.4%, and does so for 78% of one-year and 100% of rolling three-year periods, making this a very consistent strategy. The bottom quintile significantly outperforms only in 1990–1991, 1999–2000, and 2003–2004. Average portfolio values range from −7× to less than −30× for operating cash flow to capex and from 1% to 3% for depreciation to invested capital, so companies in this quintile have cash outflows and are recognizing very little depreciation expense relative to their invested capital base.

ONE-YEAR CHANGE IN INVENTORY PLUS RECEIVABLES TURNOVER

The one-year change in inventory plus receivables turnover strategy measures a company's working capital efficiency. Working capital represents cash used to finance a company's short-term operating activities. Specifically, it represents the financing necessary to maintain a company's *cash conversion cycle*, the amount of time necessary for a company to go from the purchase of raw materials to the sale of goods and the final receipt of cash from goods purchased on credit (accounts receivable). A company that is able to shorten its cash conversion cycle, by more efficient handling of inventory and faster collection of receivables, is able to free up cash that can be invested in the business or returned to shareholders. A company that sees its cash conversion cycle lengthen, because it is holding increased inventory and/or taking longer to collect receivables, must use more cash to meet current business needs.[9]

Our research indicates that the one-year change in inventory plus receivables turnover ratio is the best quantitative measure of working capital efficiency. Inventory plus receivables turnover is calculated by dividing 12-month sales by the 12-month average of inventory plus accounts receivable. A higher ratio of inventory plus receivables turnover indicates more efficient use of working capital (more sales generated per dollar

---

[9] The cash conversion cycle measures the elapsed time, usually in days, from cash payments to suppliers for materials necessary to manufacture products to receipt of cash from customers in exchange for the sale of those products. Since suppliers usually do not receive cash upon delivery and customers usually do not pay cash upon sale, both accounts payable and accounts receivable are usually taken into account in calculating cash conversion. Here, however, we'll ignore the accounts payable portion.

1990–2007	1st Quintile	2nd Quintile	3rd Quintile	4th Quintile	5th Quintile	Universe	S&P 500*
CAGR – Annual Rebalance	16.3%	15.8%	12.6%	10.3%	−0.5%	10.3%	12.0%
Average Excess Return vs. Universe**	7.5%	5.1%	0.4%	−0.5%	−7.4%	NA	1.5%
Value of $10,000 Invested (18 Years)	$152,656	$140,543	$85,328	$58,347	$9,213	$58,669	$76,297
% of 1-Year Periods Strategy Outperforms the Universe	77.8%	66.7%	56.9%	44.4%	22.2%	NA	56.9%
% Rolling 3-Year Periods Strategy Outperforms	84.4%	81.3%	56.3%	45.3%	0.0%	NA	68.8%
Maximum Gain	70.9%	53.3%	59.5%	61.7%	80.0%	59.2%	54.1%
Maximum Loss	−18.4%	−23.1%	−31.6%	−28.3%	−56.1%	−24.9%	−25.9%
Sharpe Ratio	0.84	0.91	0.50	0.46	0.01	0.46	0.64
Standard Deviation of Returns	0.18	0.14	0.16	0.16	0.28	0.17	0.14
Beta (vs. Universe)	0.93	0.70	0.84	0.83	1.49	NA	0.78
Alpha (vs. Universe)	0.08	0.09	0.02	0.02	−0.13	NA	0.04
Average Portfolio Size	54	54	54	54	54	NA	NA
Average Number of Companies *Outperforming*	25	26	24	24	18	NA	NA
Average Number of Companies *Underperforming*	26	26	27	28	34	NA	NA
Median Portfolio Value – Oper. CF to Capex	7.5	2.4	1.5	0.9	−12.4	3.2	3.3
Median Portfolio Value – Depreciation to Inv. Cap.	13.1%	8.8%	7.9%	6.1%	1.6%	7.4%	8.2%
Average Market Capitalization	$4,388	$6,943	$3,655	$5,542	$3,147	NA	NA

* Equal-weighted average of S&P 500 returns. ** Annual holding period run quarterly for a larger sample size; arithmetic average excess returns.
Source: Standard & Poor's Compustat Point in Time Database; Charter Oak Investment Systems, Inc., Venues® Data Engine

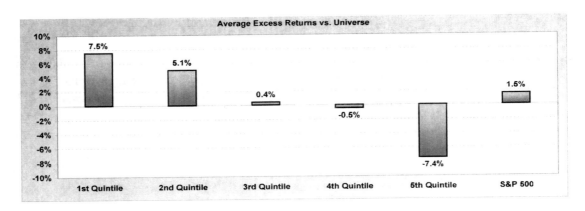

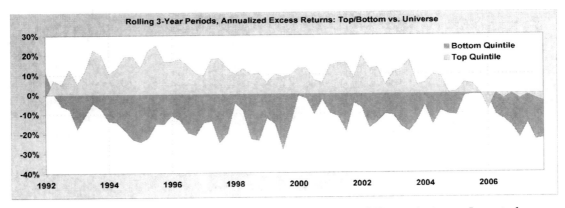

Figure 10.13 Operating Cash Flow to Capital Expenditures and Depreciation to Invested Capital

of inventories and receivables), while a lower ratio indicates less efficient working capital use. The one-year percentage change ratio is calculated by dividing the current year's inventory plus receivables turnover ratio by the same ratio for the year earlier and subtracting 1. A positive number indicates that turnover is increasing and the company is becoming more efficient, whereas a negative number indicates that turnover is decreasing and the company is becoming less efficient.

The top three quintiles of this strategy outperform; however, we'll look at the second quintile, since it has the best combination of outperformance and consistency. The second quintile outperforms by an average of 1.8%, and does so for 69% of one-year and 90% of rolling three-year periods (see Figure 10.14). The second quintile significantly underperforms only in 1991–1992, 1996, 1999–2000, and 2003. It has a low maximum loss (20%), a low standard deviation of returns (0.15), and a moderate Sharpe ratio of 0.68, slightly less than the Sharpe ratio for the S&P 500 (0.69). Average portfolio values for one-year change in inventory plus receivables turnover range from 4% to well over 10%, so these are companies that are significantly improving working capital efficiency and as a result improving operating cash flow.[10]

Companies in the bottom quintile underperform by an average of 3.7%, and do so for 75% of one-year and 88% of rolling three-year periods. Average portfolio values range from −16% to −26%, indicating that these companies are seeing turnover ratios decline significantly, and thus are becoming less efficient in working capital usage. Since investments in working capital are a use of cash, companies in the bottom quintile are also seeing their operating cash flow reduced due to the decrease in working capital efficiency.

One-Year Change in Inventory Plus Receivables Turnover by Economic Sector

The strategy works well by sector. In the sector test, as in the test above, we use the second quintile in place of the top quintile because of its higher positive excess returns and consistency. The strategy works for the energy, industrials, consumer discretionary, consumer staples, health care, and information technology sectors. Surprisingly, it even seems to work in the financials sector (see Figure 10.15). The top quintile works better than the second quintile for the telecom services and utilities sectors. This consistency across sectors shows the importance of efficient working capital management, and why poor working capital efficiency is a red flag. The strategy does not work in the materials sector.

---

[10] Working capital needs vary with the business cycle, as a company needs more inventory and must grant more receivables when business is expanding and can significantly reduce inventories and sees decreased receivables when business is contracting.

1988–2007	1st Quintile	2nd Quintile	3rd Quintile	4th Quintile	5th Quintile	Universe	S&P 500*
CAGR – Annual Rebalance	12.2%	13.6%	13.2%	11.7%	7.0%	11.2%	12.9%
Average Excess Return vs. Universe**	1.3%	1.8%	1.9%	0.2%	−3.7%	NA	1.6%
Value of $10,000 Invested (20 Years)	$99,865	$128,663	$120,012	$91,167	$38,816	$83,160	$112,895
% of 1-Year Periods Strategy Outperforms the Universe	51.9%	68.8%	63.6%	44.2%	24.7%	NA	59.7%
% Rolling 3-Year Periods Strategy Outperforms	59.4%	89.9%	79.7%	43.5%	11.6%	NA	71.0%
Maximum Gain	62.5%	57.3%	54.0%	57.6%	58.8%	59.2%	54.1%
Maximum Loss	−27.4%	−19.8%	−21.5%	−24.1%	−33.9%	−24.9%	−25.9%
Sharpe Ratio	0.51	0.68	0.72	0.58	0.25	0.49	0.69
Standard Deviation of Returns	0.18	0.15	0.14	0.14	0.18	0.16	0.14
Beta (vs. Universe)	1.08	0.86	0.80	0.84	1.05	NA	0.78
Alpha (vs. Universe)	0.00	0.03	0.04	0.02	−0.04	NA	0.04
Average Portfolio Size	347	347	347	347	348	NA	NA
Average Number of Companies *Outperforming*	144	158	160	150	137	NA	NA
Average Number of Companies *Underperforming*	182	172	173	179	192	NA	NA
Median Portfolio Value – 1Yr Chg. Invt. + Rcvbl. Turn.	48.8%	5.7%	0.6%	−4.7%	−19.9%	6.2%	2.6%
Average Market Capitalization	$3,708	$4,850	$5,104	$4,124	$3,757	NA	NA

* Equal-weighted average of S&P 500 returns. ** Annual holding period run quarterly for a larger sample size; arithmetic average excess returns.
Source: Standard & Poor's Compustat Point in Time Database; Charter Oak Investment Systems, Inc., Venues® Data Engine

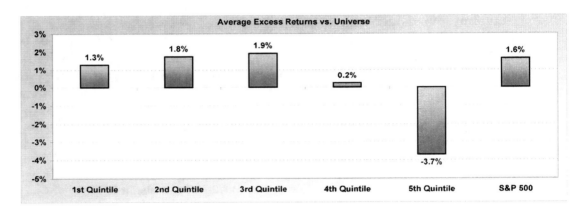

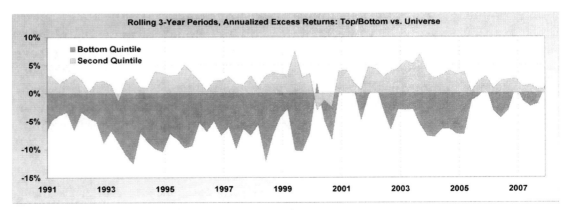

Figure 10.14 One-Year Change in Inventory Plus Receivables Turnover

Second Quintile

1990–2007	Energy	Materials	Industrials	Consumer Discretionary	Consumer Staples	Health Care	Financials	Information Technology	Telecom Services	Utilities	Universe	S&P 500*
CAGR – Quintile	15.6%	10.1%	12.3%	10.2%	15.1%	16.5%	15.7%	11.?%	3.5%	11.2%	11.2%	12.9%
CAGR – Sector	13.5%	10.2%	11.3%	8.7%	12.6%	12.3%	14.5%	7.5%	9.2%	13.0%	NA	NA
Excess Return vs. Sector	2.0%	−0.1%	1.0%	1.5%	2.5%	4.2%	1.2%	3.9%	−5.8%	−1.8%	NA	NA
Value of $10,000	$180,678	$68,861	$100,886	$69,877	$167,404	$212,583	$185,773	$86,198	$19,747	$82,922	$83,160	$112,895
% 1-Year Outperformance	60.0%	40.0%	55.0%	55.0%	75.0%	65.0%	65.0%	55.0%	35.0%	50.0%	NA	NA
% 3-Year Outperformance	61.1%	50.0%	88.9%	77.8%	66.7%	83.3%	66.7%	72.2%	33.3%	33.3%	NA	NA
Maximum Gain	49.9%	39.7%	43.3%	45.0%	49.9%	66.0%	55.1%	153.4%	118.5%	42.5%	44.0%	41.4%
Maximum Loss	−38.1%	−19.0%	−16.8%	−31.0%	−25.7%	−20.1%	−21.4%	−46.7%	−52.6%	−20.4%	−19.1%	−18.1%
Standard Deviation	0.25	0.16	0.15	0.19	0.18	0.21	0.22	0.40	0.39	0.16	0.16	0.14
Beta (vs. Sector)	0.93	1.03	0.99	0.99	1.19	0.81	0.90	1.04	1.06	0.85	NA	NA
Alpha (vs. Sector)	0.03	0.00	0.01	0.02	0.01	0.06	0.03	0.03	−0.05	0.00	NA	NA
Portfolio Size	21	30	56	65	21	35	43	54	7	16	NA	NA

Bottom Quintile

1990–2007	Energy	Materials	Industrials	Consumer Discretionary	Consumer Staples	Health Care	Financials	Information Technology	Telecom Services	Utilities	Universe	S&P 500*
CAGR – Quintile	12.6%	10.1%	7.1%	2.3%	8.5%	5.7%	10.2%	3.0%	6.2%	10.9%	11.2%	12.9%
CAGR – Sector	13.5%	10.2%	11.3%	8.7%	12.6%	12.3%	14.5%	7.5%	9.2%	13.0%	NA	NA
Excess Return vs. Sector	−1.0%	−0.1%	−4.2%	−6.5%	−4.0%	−6.6%	−4.3%	−4.5%	−3.1%	−2.0%	NA	NA
Value of $10,000	$106,852	$68,254	$39,081	$15,637	$51,485	$30,496	$70,247	$18,128	$33,082	$79,798	$83,160	$112,895
% 1-Year Outperformance	45.0%	40.0%	25.0%	20.0%	25.0%	25.0%	40.0%	35.0%	45.0%	35.0%	NA	NA
% 3-Year Outperformance	44.4%	38.9%	11.1%	0.0%	16.7%	11.1%	33.3%	33.3%	44.4%	38.9%	NA	NA
Maximum Gain	53.9%	52.4%	38.3%	43.1%	27.0%	87.2%	53.7%	80.9%	95.1%	56.2%	44.0%	41.4%
Maximum Loss	−42.0%	−19.4%	−26.2%	−33.0%	−18.4%	−37.4%	−47.1%	−52.4%	−48.7%	−16.8%	−19.1%	−18.1%
Standard Deviation	0.25	0.20	0.15	0.21	0.15	0.26	0.24	0.32	0.35	0.20	0.16	0.14
Beta (vs. Sector)	0.98	1.24	0.97	1.11	0.93	1.01	1.05	0.79	0.73	1.15	NA	NA
Alpha (vs. Sector)	−0.01	0.04	−0.01	−0.09	0.03	−0.03	0.00	−0.12	−0.08	0.05	NA	NA
Portfolio Size	21	30	57	67	22	36	45	54	8	16	NA	NA

* Equal-weighted average of S&P 500 returns.
Source: Standard & Poor's Compustat Point in Time Database; Charter Oak Investment Systems, Inc., Venues® Data Engine

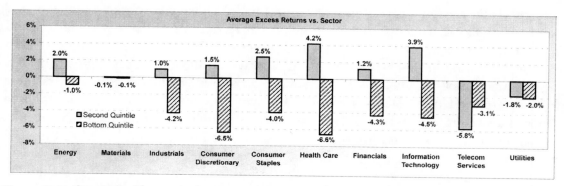

Figure 10.15 One-Year Change in Inventory Plus Receivables Turnover by Economic Sector

One-Year Change in Inventory Plus Receivables Turnover and Free Cash Flow to Price

This strategy combines a working capital efficiency factor with a cash flow–based valuation factor. Companies that increase working capital efficiency by definition improve cash generation: less cash is tied up in inventory and accounts receivable, and more is available to pay dividends, repurchase shares, make business investments, and so on. The top quintile of this strategy contains companies that are generating increased operating cash flow through working capital improvements and that have a low market valuation placed on that cash flow (after deducting capital expenditures). The bottom quintile contains companies that are becoming less efficient in their use of cash and that have high valuations on an FCF-to-price basis. The strategy is very strong, very linear, and consistent.

The top portfolio outperforms by 7.3%, on average, and does so for 74% of one-year and 81% of rolling three-year periods (see Figure 10.16). The top quintile significantly underperforms in only three periods: 1998–1999, 2003, and 2006–2007. It has a low maximum loss of 22% and a relatively high Sharpe ratio of 0.83, versus 0.64 for the S&P 500. Average portfolio values range from 21% to 45% for one-year change in inventory plus receivables turnover and from 15% to over 30% for FCF to price, so companies in the bottom quintile are making large improvements in operating efficiency and are attractively priced on a cash flow basis.

The bottom quintile underperforms by an average of 8%, and does so for 83% of one-year and 92% of rolling three-year periods. It significantly outperforms only in 1990, 1999–2000, and 2003–2004. Average portfolio values range from -18% to -31% for one-year change in inventory plus receivables turnover and -12% to -35% for FCF to price, indicating that these companies are becoming less efficient in their use of working capital and are seeing large cash outflows, perhaps as a result.

DEPRECIATION TO INVESTED CAPITAL

U.S. generally accepted accounting principles (GAAP) leave corporate managers and accountants a lot of leeway in determining proper accounting policies, making accounting estimates, and applying standards and principles. This was done purposely, since creating an entirely rule-based accounting code would have been unwieldy, considering the many types of business entities and the various ways of conducting business that exist in the United States. However, the very leeway that allows accountants to choose the accounting measures they feel most accurately reflect their financial results also allows others to "bend the rules" or even to intentionally misrepresent financial results.

Depreciation policy is one area of accounting that is subject to a lot of judgment. GAAP require that companies spread the cost of an asset over its useful life "as equitably

1990–2007	1st Quintile	2nd Quintile	3rd Quintile	4th Quintile	5th Quintile	Universe	S&P 500*
CAGR – Annual Rebalance	16.5%	13.4%	11.6%	5.1%	1.4%	10.3%	12.0%
Average Excess Return vs. Universe**	7.3%	3.0%	1.5%	−4.0%	−8.0%	NA	1.5%
Value of $10,000 Invested (18 Years)	$156,731	$96,853	$72,680	$24,561	$12,948	$58,669	$76,297
% of 1-Year Periods Strategy Outperforms the Universe	73.6%	63.9%	56.9%	19.4%	16.7%	NA	56.9%
% Rolling 3-Year Periods Strategy Outperforms	81.3%	76.6%	59.4%	6.3%	7.8%	NA	68.8%
Maximum Gain	63.7%	50.6%	46.9%	74.8%	85.4%	59.2%	54.1%
Maximum Loss	−22.3%	−18.2%	−22.6%	−34.1%	−52.6%	−24.9%	−25.9%
Sharpe Ratio	0.83	0.73	0.63	0.20	−0.01	0.46	0.64
Standard Deviation of Returns	0.18	0.15	0.15	0.19	0.26	0.17	0.14
Beta (vs. Universe)	0.80	0.67	0.78	0.99	1.35	NA	0.78
Alpha (vs. Universe)	0.10	0.07	0.04	−0.04	−0.12	NA	0.04
Average Portfolio Size	60	60	60	60	61	NA	NA
Average Number of Companies *Outperforming*	29	29	27	23	22	NA	NA
Average Number of Companies *Underperforming*	28	29	32	34	36	NA	NA
Median Portfolio Value – 1Yr Chng. Invt. + Rcvbl. Turn.	31.8%	5.5%	0.5%	−4.8%	−23.6%	6.7%	2.6%
Median Portfolio Value – FCF to Price	20.5%	6.6%	3.4%	−0.3%	−21.8%	2.1%	3.3%
Average Market Capitalization	$3,179	$5,015	$8,049	$4,141	$1,848	NA	NA

* Equal-weighted average of S&P 500 returns. ** Annual holding period run quarterly for a larger sample size; arithmetic average excess returns.
Source: Standard & Poor's Compustat Point in Time Database; Charter Oak Investment Systems, Inc., Venues® Data Engine

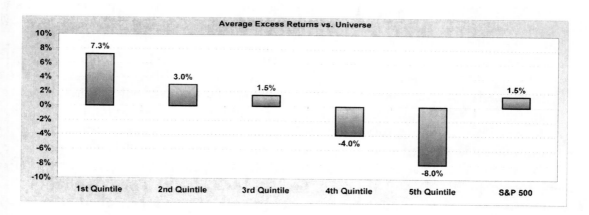

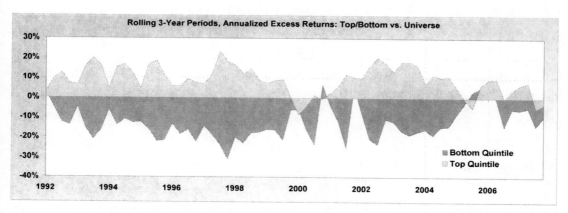

Figure 10.16 One-Year Change in Inventory Plus Receivables Turnover and Free Cash Flow to Price

as possible." Estimates must be made as to an asset's useful life as well as its residual value.[11] Also, an accounting method must be chosen to best allocate an asset's depreciable cost (its actual cost minus its estimated residual value) over its useful life. Depreciation methods vary from simple straight-line depreciation, which subtracts an equal amount of cost over each year of the asset's useful life, to so-called accelerated methods, in which more depreciation expense is recorded in the early years of an asset's useful life, and less depreciation is recorded in later years.[12] Since there is so much latitude in recording depreciation expense for a tangible asset, a company's depreciation practices can serve as a good barometer of how conservative or aggressive a company is in its choice of accounting policies.

Companies that apply accounting conventions conservatively seek to accurately estimate financial values, and where estimates might be called into question to err on the side of understatement. Companies that apply accounting conventions aggressively seek to portray financial data in the best possible light, and in the worst cases to mislead or defraud investors. Since a company can significantly improve its financial results simply by reducing its depreciation expense, we use depreciation to invested capital as a barometer of conservatism in accounting.[13]

Companies in the top quintile of this strategy outperform by 1.7%, on average, and do so for 68% of one-year periods but only 58% of rolling three-year periods (see Figure 10.17). The second quintile provides nearly equal results to the first quintile, with less volatility. Average portfolio values for depreciation to invested capital range from 14% to over 16% for the top quintile and from 7% to 9% for the second quintile. The bottom quintile underperforms by 2.2%, on average, and does so for 74% of one-year and 85% of rolling three-year periods, making this a consistent strategy and truly a red flag—companies that do not take enough depreciation expense relative to their invested capital base consistently underperform. Average portfolio values for depreciation to invested capital for the bottom quintile range from 1% to 3%.

Depreciation to Invested Capital by Economic Sector

Not surprisingly, the depreciation to invested capital strategy works best in sectors that are capital intensive and thus require the recognition of a lot of depreciation expense. The

---

[11] *Residual value* is also referred to as *salvage value* or *scrap value*. It is the value that a company expects to receive upon disposition of a fixed asset no longer needed in its business.

[12] Depreciation can also be based on the actual use (activity) of the asset, for example, how many miles a truck is driven.

[13] Depreciation expense to net PP&E might seem like a more intuitive measure; however, it didn't test as well quantitatively.

1988–2007	1st Quintile	2nd Quintile	3rd Quintile	4th Quintile	5th Quintile	Universe	S&P 500*
CAGR – Annual Rebalance	12.1%	13.6%	13.1%	10.9%	8.3%	11.2%	12.9%
Average Excess Return vs. Universe**	1.7%	1.8%	0.5%	−0.8%	−2.2%	NA	1.6%
Value of $10,000 Invested (20 Years)	$98,390	$128,539	$117,481	$78,536	$48,888	$83,160	$112,895
% of 1-Year Periods Strategy Outperforms the Universe	67.5%	59.7%	55.8%	33.8%	26.0%	NA	59.7%
% Rolling 3-Year Periods Strategy Outperforms	58.0%	69.6%	49.3%	27.5%	14.5%	NA	71.0%
Maximum Gain	63.1%	63.1%	55.8%	57.5%	59.0%	59.2%	54.1%
Maximum Loss	−28.8%	−24.6%	−24.1%	−24.8%	−30.1%	−24.9%	−25.9%
Sharpe Ratio	0.59	0.62	0.59	0.47	0.33	0.49	0.69
Standard Deviation of Returns	0.17	0.16	0.15	0.16	0.18	0.16	0.14
Beta (vs. Universe)	0.96	0.94	0.86	0.93	1.05	NA	0.78
Alpha (vs. Universe)	0.02	0.03	0.02	0.00	−0.03	NA	0.04
Average Portfolio Size	322	322	322	322	323	NA	NA
Average Number of Companies *Outperforming*	140	144	144	137	132	NA	NA
Average Number of Companies *Underperforming*	164	164	163	169	175	NA	NA
Median Portfolio Value – Depreciation to Invested Capital	15.1%	8.5%	6.3%	4.6%	2.1%	7.4%	8.1%
Average Market Capitalization	$5,160	$4,174	$4,435	$3,865	$3,814	NA	NA

* Equal-weighted average of S&P 500 returns. ** Annual holding period run quarterly for a larger sample size; arithmetic average excess returns.
Source: Standard & Poor's Compustat Point in Time Database; Charter Oak Investment Systems, Inc., Venues® Data Engine

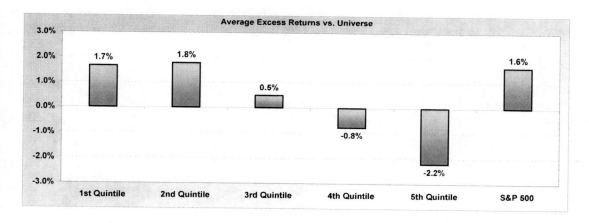

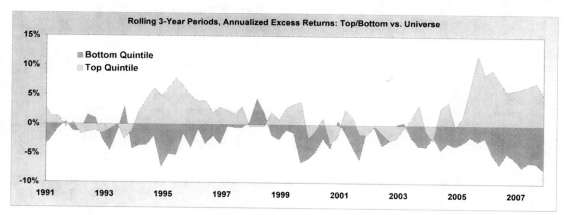

Figure 10.17 Depreciation to Invested Capital

Top Quintile

1990–2007	Energy	Materials	Industrials	Consumer Discretionary	Consumer Staples	Health Care	Financials	Information Technology	Telecom Services	Utilities	Universe	S&P 500*
CAGR – Quintile	15.4%	12.3%	13.2%	11.4%	12.5%	12.0%	11.9%	7.3%	5.0%	13.1%	11.2%	12.9%
CAGR – Sector	13.5%	10.2%	11.3%	8.7%	12.6%	12.3%	14.5%	7.5%	9.2%	13.0%	NA	NA
Excess Return vs. Sector	1.8%	2.1%	1.9%	2.7%	−0.1%	−0.3%	−2.6%	−0.2%	−4.2%	0.1%	NA	NA
Value of $10,000	$173,936	$102,529	$118,406	$86,104	$104,685	$97,127	$95,540	$41,202	$26,416	$116,838	$83,160	$112,895
% 1-Year Outperformance	60.0%	65.0%	60.0%	65.0%	65.0%	50.0%	40.0%	60.0%	45.0%	55.0%	NA	NA
% 3-Year Outperformance	61.1%	83.3%	77.8%	72.2%	61.1%	55.6%	38.9%	55.6%	27.8%	61.1%	NA	NA
Maximum Gain	89.3%	38.8%	45.1%	45.9%	39.1%	54.7%	58.6%	82.6%	54.2%	49.0%	44.0%	41.4%
Maximum Loss	−40.3%	−23.9%	−12.3%	−21.2%	−17.2%	−26.6%	−39.4%	−59.0%	−44.9%	−15.5%	−19.1%	−18.1%
Standard Deviation	0.30	0.16	0.15	0.19	0.16	0.21	0.22	0.33	0.25	0.16	0.16	0.14
Beta (vs. Sector)	1.13	0.93	0.97	0.98	1.03	0.78	0.84	0.79	0.42	0.98	NA	NA
Alpha (vs. Sector)	0.00	0.03	0.02	0.03	0.00	0.03	0.00	0.03	0.02	0.01	NA	NA
Portfolio Size	23	28	48	61	16	33	26	45	8	24	NA	NA

Bottom Quintile

1990 ~ 2007	Energy	Materials	Industrials	Consumer Discretionary	Consumer Staples	Health Care	Financials	Information Technology	Telecom Services	Utilities	Universe	S&P 500*
CAGR – Quintile	10.7%	5.9%	7.0%	7.1%	8.8%	7.6%	12.6%	3.2%	7.3%	10.8%	11.2%	12.9%
CAGR – Sector	13.5%	10.2%	11.3%	8.7%	12.6%	12.3%	14.5%	7.5%	9.2%	13.0%	NA	NA
Excess Return vs. Sector	−2.9%	−4.3%	−4.2%	−1.6%	−3.8%	−4.8%	−1.9%	−4.3%	−2.0%	−2.1%	NA	NA
Value of $10,000	$76,027	$31,718	$39,038	$39,578	$53,614	$43,089	$108,106	$18,827	$40,661	$78,388	$83,160	$112,895
% 1-Year Outperformance	40.0%	25.0%	20.0%	40.0%	30.0%	25.0%	45.0%	30.0%	50.0%	35.0%	NA	NA
% 3-Year Outperformance	33.3%	0.0%	11.1%	38.9%	16.7%	11.1%	27.8%	27.8%	44.4%	33.3%	NA	NA
Maximum Gain	41.4%	39.6%	36.7%	49.3%	35.4%	83.0%	68.8%	112.9%	98.5%	69.8%	44.0%	41.4%
Maximum Loss	−44.1%	−24.5%	−21.0%	−24.6%	−26.7%	−39.9%	−21.9%	−45.0%	−75.7%	−31.4%	−19.1%	−18.1%
Standard Deviation	0.23	0.16	0.16	0.19	0.14	0.28	0.22	0.36	0.42	0.21	0.16	0.14
Beta (vs. Sector)	0.84	1.04	1.06	1.00	0.92	1.07	0.98	0.94	0.95	1.23	NA	NA
Alpha (vs. Sector)	−0.01	−0.01	−0.02	−0.03	0.05	−0.05	0.02	−0.11	−0.05	0.05	NA	NA
Portfolio Size	24	29	50	65	19	35	29	48	9	25	NA	NA

* Equal-weighted average of S&P 500 returns.
Source: Standard & Poor's Compustat Point in Time Database; Charter Oak Investment Systems, Inc., Venues® Data Engine

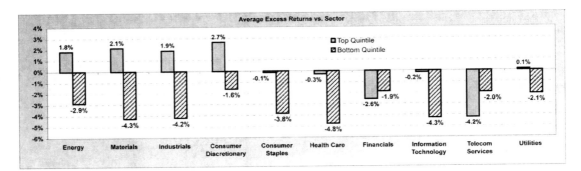

Figure 10.18 Depreciation to Invested Capital by Economic Sector

energy, materials, industrials, and consumer discretionary sectors work best. The first three of these sectors require large amounts of machinery and other equipment to extract, mine, and produce their products. Companies in the consumer discretionary sector sometimes require large investments in buildings, such as retail stores, in order to do business. It is also important to note that depreciation to invested capital works as a negative strategy in every sector except financials, where capital expenses are minimal, and telecom services, where results are biased by the huge telecom boom that took place in 1998–1999 (see Figure 10.18). The consistency of the bottom quintile across sectors suggests that, in general, companies that fail to record sufficient depreciation expense are likely trying to cover up poor operating performance with an aggressive application of accounting policy.

Depreciation to Invested Capital and Free Cash Flow Plus Net Share Repurchase Plus Dividend to Price

This strategy combines a measure of accounting conservatism (depreciation to invested capital), a valuation measure (FCF to price), and capital allocation factors (share repurchases and dividends). Companies in the top quintile are taking large amounts of depreciation expense relative to their invested capital base (an indicator of accounting conservatism), are selling at high multiples of FCF to price, and are repurchasing significant amounts of shares and/or paying dividends. Companies in the bottom quintile are recognizing very little depreciation expense, and have one or more of the following characteristics: negative FCF, no cash dividends, and/or significant share issuance. In short, these companies lack cash, are aggressive in their accounting, and are making capital allocation choices that are not shareholder friendly.

The top quintile of this strategy outperforms by 6.4%, on average, and does so for 75% of one-year and 88% of rolling three-year periods (see Figure 10.19). The top quintile significantly underperforms in 1990–1991, 1995–1996, 1999–2000, and 2003–2004. It has a relatively high maximum loss (33%) but a low standard deviation of returns (0.15), resulting in a high Sharpe ratio of 0.91. Average portfolio values for the bottom quintile range from 12% to 22% for depreciation to invested capital and from 15% to 22% for FCF plus net share repurchase plus dividend to price. As a result of the emphasis on share repurchases and dividends, the strategy tends to be large cap, with an average market capitalization of $6.7 billion.

The bottom quintile underperforms by 9.7%, on average, and does so for 83% of one-year and 98% of rolling three-year periods, making it a very consistent strategy. The bottom quintile significantly outperforms only in 1990–1991, 1996, 1998, and 2003–2004. An average of 34 companies in the bottom quintile underperforms versus 19 that outperform. Average portfolio values range from 1% to 3% for depreciation to invested capital and −14% to −45% for FCF plus net share repurchase plus dividend to price.

1990–2007	1st Quintile	2nd Quintile	3rd Quintile	4th Quintile	5th Quintile	Universe	S&P 500*
CAGR – Annual Rebalance	17.1%	12.3%	11.9%	4.8%	−2.8%	10.3%	12.0%
Average Excess Return vs. Universe**	6.4%	2.5%	1.0%	−4.2%	−9.7%	NA	1.5%
Value of $10,000 Invested (18 Years)	$171,176	$80,341	$75,258	$23,249	$5,975	$58,669	$76,297
% of 1-Year Periods Strategy Outperforms the Universe	75.0%	56.9%	61.1%	22.2%	16.7%	NA	56.9%
% Rolling 3-Year Periods Strategy Outperforms	87.5%	62.5%	64.1%	12.5%	1.6%	NA	68.8%
Maximum Gain	63.3%	48.5%	55.2%	76.7%	71.6%	59.2%	54.1%
Maximum Loss	−32.9%	−26.0%	−26.1%	−38.4%	−52.1%	−24.9%	−25.9%
Sharpe Ratio	0.91	0.73	0.56	0.16	−0.08	0.46	0.64
Standard Deviation of Returns	0.15	0.14	0.16	0.22	0.26	0.17	0.14
Beta (vs. Universe)	0.63	0.65	0.87	1.14	1.40	NA	0.78
Alpha (vs. Universe)	0.11	0.07	0.03	−0.06	−0.14	NA	0.04
Average Portfolio Size	55	55	55	55	56	NA	NA
Average Number of Companies *Outperforming*	27	27	25	21	19	NA	NA
Average Number of Companies *Underperforming*	25	26	27	31	34	NA	NA
Median Portfolio Value – Depreciation to Inv. Cap.	14.8%	8.7%	6.6%	4.7%	2.1%	7.4%	8.2%
Median Portfolio Value – FCF + Repur. + Div. to Prc.	17.3%	7.6%	3.9%	−1.7%	−28.3%	1.8%	6.2%
Average Market Capitalization	$6,742	$6,004	$6,578	$3,650	$1,998	NA	NA

* Equal-weighted average of S&P 500 returns. ** Annual holding period run quarterly for a larger sample size; arithmetic average excess returns.
Source: Standard & Poor's Compustat Point in Time Database; Charter Oak Investment Systems, Inc., Venues® Data Engine

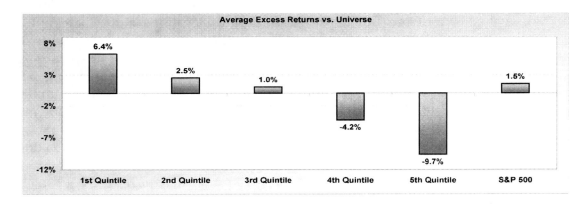

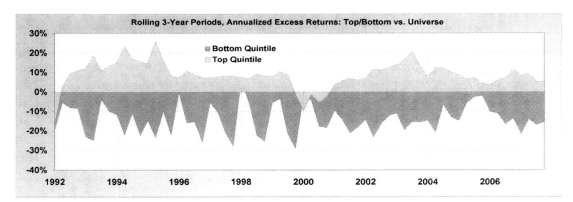

Figure 10.19 Depreciation to Invested Capital and Free Cash Flow Plus Net Share Repurchase Plus Dividend to Price

1988–2007	1st Quintile	2nd Quintile	3rd Quintile	4th Quintile	5th Quintile	Universe	S&P 500*
CAGR – Annual Rebalance	17.8%	14.4%	14.5%	10.6%	−3.2%	11.2%	12.9%
Average Excess Return vs. Universe**	4.7%	2.7%	1.8%	−1.8%	−9.7%	NA	1.6%
Value of $10,000 Invested (20 Years)	$264,949	$148,415	$151,202	$74,545	$5,226	$83,160	$112,895
% of 1-Year Periods Strategy Outperforms the Universe	74.0%	59.7%	55.8%	32.5%	18.2%	NA	59.7%
% Rolling 3-Year Periods Strategy Outperforms	82.6%	75.4%	62.3%	23.2%	5.8%	NA	71.0%
Maximum Gain	49.3%	54.3%	57.4%	51.7%	82.9%	59.2%	54.1%
Maximum Loss	−17.7%	−20.9%	−22.9%	−26.0%	−64.0%	−24.9%	−25.9%
Sharpe Ratio	0.90	0.77	0.66	0.37	−0.05	0.49	0.69
Standard Deviation of Returns	0.14	0.14	0.15	0.17	0.29	0.16	0.14
Beta (vs. Universe)	0.69	0.74	0.83	0.94	1.61	NA	0.78
Alpha (vs. Universe)	0.09	0.06	0.04	−0.01	−0.17	NA	0.04
Average Portfolio Size	57	57	57	57	56	NA	NA
Average Number of Companies *Outperforming*	27	26	24	23	18	NA	NA
Average Number of Companies *Underperforming*	27	28	29	30	35	NA	NA
Median Portfolio Value – Depreciation to Inv. Cap.	16.6%	8.8%	6.6%	4.8%	2.1%	7.3%	8.1%
Median Portfolio Value – Extern. Finan. to Inv. Cap.	−22.8%	−4.4%	1.2%	9.2%	62.4%	6.7%	0.4%
Average Market Capitalization	$5,988	$5,039	$4,083	$4,592	$2,252	NA	NA

* Equal-weighted average of S&P 500 returns. ** Annual holding period run quarterly for a larger sample size; arithmetic average excess returns.
Source: Standard & Poor's Compustat Point in Time Database; Charter Oak Investment Systems, Inc., Venues® Data Engine

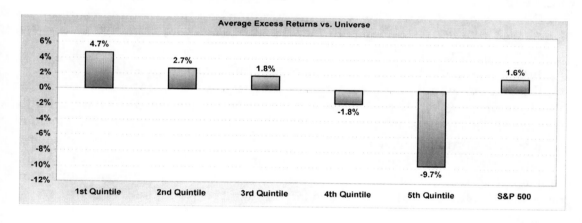

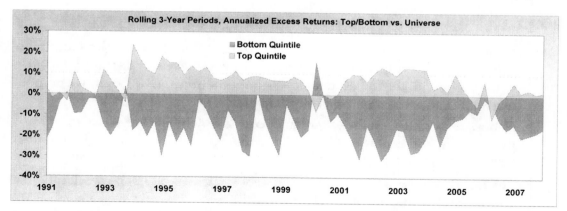

Figure 10.20 Depreciation to Invested Capital and External Financing to Invested Capital

Depreciation to Invested Capital and External Financing to Invested Capital

Depreciation to invested capital and external financing to invested capital looks at two forms of conservatism: conservatism in accounting policy and conservatism in capital allocation. Quantitatively viewed, the market rewards conservatism in both these areas and punishes aggressiveness in accounting and in the use of capital. In addition, this strategy employs a common denominator—invested capital—a technique that often results in a stronger strategy. The top quintile of this strategy contains companies that record high amounts of depreciation expense relative to capital and are using large amounts of cash to repurchase shares and/or reduce debt. The bottom quintile contains companies that take very low amounts of depreciation expense relative to invested capital and are issuing large amounts of shares and/or debt.

The top quintile outperforms by an average of 4.7%, and does so for 74% of one-year and 83% of rolling three-year periods (see Figure 10.20). The top quintile significantly underperforms in 1988–1989, 1991, 1999–2000, 2003–2004, and 2006. It has a low maximum loss of 18% and a low standard deviation of returns of 0.14, resulting in a high Sharpe ratio of 0.90. Average portfolio values range from 13% to 23% for depreciation to invested capital and from −17% to −48% for external financing to invested capital, indicating significant share repurchases and/or debt reductions.

The bottom quintile underperforms by almost 10%, on average, and does so for 82% of one-year and 94% of rolling three-year periods. The bottom quintile significantly outperforms only in 1991–1992, 1999–2000, and 2003–2004. An average of 35 companies in the bottom portfolio underperforms, versus 18 that outperform, a strong showing. Average portfolio values vary from 1% to 3% for depreciation to invested capital and from 46% to over 100% for external financing to invested capital, indicating that companies in the bottom quintile are issuing large amounts of shares and/or debt.

SUMMARY

- Financial leverage ratios, such as total debt to capital, don't work as one might expect quantitatively: companies with the highest levels of debt outperform, while those with the lowest debt levels underperform. As a result, we do not use financial leverage ratios as building blocks to control for risk.
- Debt *payback* ratios, on the other hand, consider debt levels relative to profitability, and can be used as building blocks to reduce risk in quantitative models and screens.
- The free cash flow (FCF) to long-term debt strategy is a debt payback ratio that looks at cash flow adequacy relative to debt levels. It works well across sectors and combines well with profitability, valuation, and price-momentum factors.

- The capex to property, plant, & equipment (PP&E) strategy attempts to provide a measure of capital intensity. In general, companies that are making large capital expenditures relative to the book value of existing PP&E (those that may be becoming more capital intensive) underperform, while companies making small capital investments relative to existing PP&E (those that may be becoming less capital intensive) outperform.

- The capex to PP&E and 52-week price range strategy combines a capital intensity measure with a price-momentum measure and generates strong excess returns. Companies in the top quintile of this strategy require decreasing amounts of capital investment and are at or near 52-week highs, while companies in the bottom quintile require large increases in capex to remain competitive and are near 52-week lows.

- The operating cash flow to capex strategy puts companies that have more than ample cash to fund capital spending needs in the top quintile and those that have cash outflows and thus may have trouble meeting capital spending needs in the bottom quintile. Excess returns are strong and relatively consistent, and the factor makes a good building block. It also works well across sectors.

- A two-factor strategy of operating cash flow to capex plus interest and price to capex generates strong and consistent excess returns. The addition of interest expense to the operating cash flow to capex factor makes excess returns more consistent and less volatile. Price to capex is an unorthodox valuation factor, but it works well in this context.

- The operating cash flow to capex and depreciation to invested capital strategy considers both excess cash relative to capital spending needs and how conservatively or aggressively a company accounts for the costs of its capital investments (depreciation). Excess returns are strong and linear.

- The one-year change in inventory plus receivables turnover strategy, looks at how efficiently companies manage their working capital, which represents investment needed to finance a company's short-term operating activities (inventory, accounts receivable, etc.). Companies that moderately improve working capital efficiency outperform, while those that see their working capital efficiency deteriorate underperform. The strategy is consistent across sectors.

- The top quintile of the one-year change in inventory plus receivables turnover and free cash flow to price strategy contains companies that are generating increased operating cash flow through working capital improvements and that have a low market valuation placed on that cash flow. The bottom quintile contains companies that are becoming less efficient in their working capital management and are expensive. Excess returns are strong, linear, and consistent.

- The depreciation to invested capital strategy seeks to separate companies that apply accounting conventions conservatively from those that employ aggressive accounting techniques. Because businesses have wide latitude in accounting for depreciation, a company's depreciation policy serves as a good barometer of accounting conservatism or aggressiveness. Companies that take the lowest amounts of depreciation expense, relative to invested capital, underperform, while those that take the highest amounts of depreciation expense outperform.

- The depreciation to invested capital strategy works best in sectors that are capital intensive, and thus require the recognition of significant amounts of depreciation expense, including the energy, materials, industrials, and consumer discretionary sectors.

- The depreciation to invested capital and free cash flow plus net share repurchase plus dividend to price strategy considers accounting conservatism or aggressiveness, cash flow generation, valuation, and capital allocation, all in a single strategy. Excess returns are strong, linear, and consistent.

CHAPTER 11

Collected Wisdom

> Simplicity is the final achievement. After one has played a vast quantity of notes and more notes, it is simplicity that emerges as the crowning reward of art.
>
> Frédéric Chopin

In Chapter 1, I stated my goals for this book: to determine and present empirically the major drivers of stock market returns and thus to provide investors with a map of the market from a quantitative point of view. However, my intention was not to write a work of reference. Although reference books can provide readers with valuable information, they usually do little to help practitioners expand their mastery of a field of study. On the other hand, an educational work that shows readers how to apply the lessons and data it contains *can* help them advance their understanding of a field. This chapter and the two that follow will enable you to understand, synthesize, and apply all the lessons of the various quantitative tests presented in this book. In so doing, I believe they will help you to become a better investor, one who understands empirically what works and what doesn't in common stock investing and who knows how to put that knowledge to profitable use by identifying strong potential investments, conducting in-depth research, and putting your money to work successfully in the stock market.

This chapter will help you put together the investment *mosaic* discussed in Chapter 1, by summarizing all of the lessons learned from the individual quantitative tests presented in this book. The mosaic, thus formed, should provide you with a mental picture of the qualities and characteristics that make an investment attractive or unattractive, as well as the relative importance of each factor. Chapter 12 will show you how to effectively combine the individual investment factors, or building blocks, and how to structure multifactor strategies to form more comprehensive stock selection models and screens. Finally, Chapter 13 will show you how to integrate the strategies presented in this book into your own investment process, whether that means integrating the ideas presented into your day-to-day stock analysis, creating strong stock selection screens to identify potential investments, or building your own quantitative models and portfolios.

THE ART OF INVESTMENT

Sound investment thinking is not complex or cluttered; instead, it focuses on identifying the essential factors of a potential investment, based on the available facts. Wall Street analysts write research reports on individual companies that sometimes fill 100 pages or more (referred to as *doorstoppers*), describing every product line in detail, exhaustively examining competitive position, and providing detailed valuation analyses. Such in-depth analysis helps to sell research reports to institutional money managers;[1] however, it isn't necessary to choose winning stocks. To be successful, the common stock investor must answer three essential questions about any potential investment, with a relatively high degree of certainty: (1) Is the business doing well? (2) Is the valuation attractive? and (3) Is the timing, in terms of overall stock market and individual stock supply/demand trends, right? Let's look at each of these questions individually.[2]

Usually, it is relatively easy to determine if a business is doing well. The investor should first of all look at how the business's products or services are selling in the marketplace. If a business has a competitive edge—something definitely to be desired—strong sales should translate into healthy profit margins and relatively high returns on capital. Moderate profit growth is also preferable, although not essential.[3] Strong free cash flow (FCF) generation is usually desirable, unless a company has a lot of profitable growth opportunities and is reinvesting cash in its business to take advantage of these. The investor might also form an opinion on the outlook for the industry or market in which the company competes. Are there reasons to believe industry demand is likely to

---

[1] Brokerage firms, such as Merrill Lynch and Morgan Stanley, generally do not sell their research directly; rather, they provide research to investment firms in exchange for trading commissions from those firms, a practice known as soft dollaring.

[2] This discussion will focus on how to *buy* stocks, since most investors are interested in this topic. For those interested in selling stocks short, the opposite form of the three questions posed above must be answered: Is the business doing poorly or deteriorating? Are valuations too high? Are supply/demand trends negative?

[3] Trade-offs between growth and valuation often come into play. High-growth companies often sport extremely high valuations and might be unattractive. Low-growth companies, on the other hand, if attractively valued, can sometimes make excellent investments.

remain strong, or is it possible that demand is peaking, the market is maturing, or that competition will accelerate? In addition, the investor might evaluate the strength and trustworthiness of company management. This is harder to do, and more subjective. One place to start is by looking at the company's track record. Has the present management grown the business successfully? Have stated goals been achieved? Another is to try to form a judgment by listening to what management has to say, on earnings conference calls and in news interviews, for example. If a company is not performing well on one or more of these factors—there is no such thing as a perfect investment—the investor must try to determine if poor performance is temporary or if the impairment is likely to be long term in nature.

Valuation can also be approached successfully from a rather simple point of view. A well-managed but mature company with only moderate growth prospects might become quite attractive at the right valuation level. For example, General Electric posted revenues of about $170 billion in 2007, making it unlikely that the company will grow rapidly going forward. However, its dividend yield as of this writing (August 2008) stood at over 4%, a yield not seen on GE since the early 1980s, and its price/earnings (P/E) ratio was at a multiyear low. GE's management training program serves as the model for corporate America, and its current management team appears quite able. Thus, although GE's growth potential may be limited, its shares may prove to have been a good investment at current prices. On the other hand, as of March 2008, analysts expected that online search and advertising company Google would be able to grow earnings per share by an average of 30% over each of the next three to five years. However, with an enterprise value (EV)-to-sales ratio of 10×, a value that would fall squarely in the bottom quintile of our EV-to-sales test, shares appear to have fully reflected much of this potential growth.

Valuing a stock should be approached in a similar manner to that in which an astute investor values real estate: by doing a lot of comparisons between the price of one property and the prices of similar properties. By doing comparisons between price and fundamentals, both from a historical perspective and relative to other current investment opportunities, the investor can gain an idea as to the relative value offered by a particular investment.[4]

Finally, we have the question of timing. Understanding supply/demand trends in the overall stock market and in individual stocks can save the investor a lot of money. In a bear market, good businesses go down with bad. In a bull market, an investor can make a lot of mistakes and still come out ahead. Therefore, the investor should seek to determine the primary trend of the stock market before committing money to "long" positions (purchases), particularly if such positions are expected to work out over the

---

[4] For these purposes, the simple valuation metrics presented in Chapter 4 should work quite nicely.

next six months to a year and a half. Understanding how to analyze the primary trends in the stock market is beyond the scope of this book. However, with a basic understanding of economics and technical analysis, the investor can develop the ability to determine the current trend—bull or bear—and the current "position" within the trend—early, midcycle, or late.

Equally important is the determination of supply/demand factors for an individual stock (and its industry). A business that is doing well purchased at reasonable valuations may make a sound investment, but a business that is doing well, purchased at reasonable valuations, and with positive supply/demand factors is more likely to work out in the desired time frame. Some of these supply/demand indicators, including relative strength and 52-week price range, have been discussed in this book. Other important indicators of supply/demand balance for a stock are support and resistance levels, moving averages, and trend reversal and continuation patterns.[5]

The art of investment—qualitative analysis—differs from quantitative analysis in two primary ways. While quantitative analysis uses the computer to analyze data,[6] qualitative analysis uses the human brain, a much more sophisticated machine. Also, while quantitative analysis relies solely on the historical record in determining fundamental trends, qualitative analysis uses the historical record primarily as a jumping off point to project probable future trends. Despite these differences, the important investment principles elucidated quantitatively in our investment mosaic—our empirically drawn map of the stock market—differ little from those principles used in qualitative analysis and described above. The quantitative analyst, using only historical data, seeks to answer the same three basic questions about any potential investment: Is the business doing well? Is the valuation attractive? and Are the supply/demand trends for the stock favorable?

MOSAICS: TOWARD A QUANTITATIVE VIEW OF INVESTING

A typical mosaic covers a planar surface (it is flat). Think of our investment mosaic as multidimensional. Profitability, valuation, cash flow, growth, capital allocation, and price momentum comprise the six sides or facets of our mosaic. Profitability measures how much value a company creates for shareholders. Growth, when combined with profitability, measures how quickly the ability to create value is increasing. Cash flow

---

[5] Investors seeking to develop their ability to analyze stock charts might start with John J. Murphy's excellent and easy-to-read book, *Technical Analysis of the Financial Markets*.

[6] One might rightly argue that quantitative analysis also relies heavily on the human mind in creating imaginative and sophisticated investment models. However, once those models are created, human judgment is usually intentionally kept out of the picture.

tells us that value is being realized in negotiable currency, and is not just ink printed quarterly on paper. Valuation ensures that the investor does not pay too much for profitability, growth, and cash flow. The results of capital allocation tell us whether or not management has shareholder interests in mind. And price momentum indicates that stock market participants share our favorable (or unfavorable) view of an investment. Our seventh factor, red flags, is more of a catch-all, but we'll consider it a seventh investment facet. Red flags can serve as warning signs that something is wrong at the company, financially, operationally, or competitively: debt is too high relative to profitability; capital intensity is increasing; working capital efficiency is decreasing; accounting policy is too aggressive. I'll cover the lessons contained in each of these seven investment facets below.

Profitability

Profitability tests provide an indicator of the quality of a company's management and assets. Companies that generate high levels of profitability, in terms of returns on capital invested, are likely to be able to generate similarly high returns on capital reinvested, as some portion of profits is put back into the company to fund growth. Thus, investors in profitable companies gain as income is reinvested and returns on investment are compounded. This compounding effect on reinvested capital explains the results of some of the greatest growth stocks in history, such as Pepsico, Intel, Cisco, and Wal-Mart. The lessons from our profitability tests include the following:

- Profitability factors work in general, generating strong excess returns, with good consistency and low volatility. They also work well across economic sectors.
- Profitability and valuation factors make a strong combination, since profitability determines the quality of company resources, and valuation determines the price the investor must pay for those resources.
- Income statement–based profitability combined with cash flow–based profitability provides a more complete picture of a company's ability to generate value.
- Investors should prefer highly profitable companies that use at least some excess cash to repurchase shares, reduce debt, and pay dividends. On the other hand, investors should avoid or sell short unprofitable companies that seek to expand their capital base by issuing large numbers of shares or large amounts of debt.
- Return on equity (ROE) works well as a measure of profitability. Return on assets does not work well quantitatively, perhaps because total assets are a poor measure of resources contributed by investors.

- Return on invested capital (ROIC), which takes into account total capital contributed (debt as well as equity), is a slightly better measure, quantitatively, than ROE.
- A simpler profitability test that is more effective than ROIC is EBITDA (earnings before interest, taxes, depreciation, and amortization) minus capex to invested capital. Since EBITDA excludes depreciation, capital expenditures are subtracted to account for the cost of maintaining and replacing plant and equipment.[7]
- Our strongest profitability test is economic profits, which uses ROIC to calculate profitability, then subtracts a capital charge, to account for the real or implied cost of contributed capital.
- The economic profits test can be improved substantially by using cash ROIC in place of income statement–based ROIC and by using price to sales in place of Beta when calculating the cost of capital (see Chapter 4 for the cost of capital calculation). In my view, a valuation factor such as price to sales more accurately represents risk than a volatility factor, such as Beta.

Valuation

Valuation is the *sine qua non* of quantitative models—it is the strongest of quantitative factors. We constructed valuation tests rather crudely, comparing the valuation of one company to that of all other companies, regardless of industry, and we ignored changing historical valuation levels. Nevertheless, these crude tests worked well, attesting to the strength of valuation factors.

- Valuation strategies work in general: they generate strong excess returns, are consistent over time, and work well across economic sectors.
- Of all the primary valuation strategies we tested, only two didn't work well: P/E to earnings growth (there is no good way to estimate future growth quantitatively) and dividend yield (companies with the highest dividend yields are often subject to dividend cuts).
- Growth and valuation strategies make a good combination, since the market rewards growth, but valuation keeps investors from overpaying for growth.
- Price momentum and valuation strategies also work particularly well together, since low valuation stocks can remain cheap, but momentum indicates that investors believe that something may be changing for the better at a company.

---

[7] However, using EBITDA alone works almost as well quantitatively, as does EBIT (earnings before interest and taxes).

- FCF to price and EV to EBITDA are by far the strongest and most consistent of the valuation strategies we tested. Both combine well with almost every quantitative factor presented in this book.
- P/E ratio, although a widely used valuation metric, isn't as strong quantitatively as the two preceding strategies. However, it works. Our testing shows that current year earnings per share (EPS) estimates work best with the P/E ratio strategy, perhaps because actual EPS figures don't provide an idea of future trends, and next-year EPS estimates look too far into the future to be of value.
- EV-to-sales and price-to-book ratios also work moderately well and are particularly useful for companies that have no earnings. However, by the same token, they have the drawback of giving the investor no insight into profitability. Combining them with a profitability factor helps eliminate this deficiency.

Cash Flow

Cash flow refers specifically to cash flow from operating activities (as opposed to cash flow from financing or investing activities). Operating cash flow generation is so important because unless accrual accounting–based earnings (earnings as reported on the income statement) are realized in cash, the business is not truly profitable. Like valuation and profitability, cash flow–based strategies are among the strongest and most consistent strategies we tested, demonstrating the importance of cash flow to investors.

- FCF, or operating cash flow less capital expenditures, works consistently better than operating cash flow alone in quantitative tests. The reason: although capital expenditures are not classified as an operating expense, capex is most often a nondiscretionary expense, so excluding it does not accurately represent the available, or discretionary, cash generated by a company.
- The one defect of cash flow–based strategies is that, while they worked very well for the first 13 or 14 years following the adoption of the cash flow statement (1989), they haven't worked well recently. This may be due to increased investor focus on FCF generation.
- However, this defect can be overcome by combining a cash flow–based factor with a valuation factor.
- The FCF-to-operating income ratio is an important measure of the quality of a company's income statement–based earnings. Generally speaking, the lower the FCF-to-income ratio, the more suspect are the income statement–based earnings.
- However, FCF levels vary according to the size and growth opportunities of the company. Smaller companies with significant growth opportunities

generally have lower FCF, whereas large, mature companies in slow-growth industries generally produce high levels of cash.

- Cash profitability strategies, such as cash ROIC and cash ROE,[8] also have strong and consistent returns.
- Companies with negative cash flows that have high levels of capital expenditures significantly underperform and should be avoided or sold short. Companies with negative cash flows that are unable to make sufficient capital expenditures also underperform and are unlikely to remain competitive.
- Companies with negative cash flows that are issuing significant amounts of shares and/or debt show very large negative excess returns and generally make good short-sale candidates. Companies with negative cash flows making large business acquisitions also underperform significantly.
- A combination of FCF generation, valuation, and sound capital allocation—the top quintile of the FCF plus net share repurchase plus dividend to price strategy—works well, indicating that these factors work together to drive stock market returns. When a profitability factor is added (ROE), excess returns are not only very strong but very consistent.

Growth

As we saw in Chapter 3, earnings growth is *the* most important factor that drives day-to-day stock returns. However, from a quantitative point of view, most growth strategies don't work as predictive factors. The reasons for this are that high growth is hard to sustain, and high growth companies usually carry high valuation multiples, which are knocked down when growth slows or fails to increase as expected. However, some degree of growth is an important factor in investment strategies. The growth scores we presented in Chapter 6 combine a FCF or earnings growth factor with a measure of the consistency (linearity) of that growth.

- Both the level of growth and the *consistency* of growth matter. Companies with high but volatile earnings or cash flow growth are less likely to outperform than companies with more moderate but consistent growth.
- FCF growth is a stronger driver of excess returns than EPS growth, perhaps because EPS growth is such a widely reported and closely followed metric.

---

[8] Cash return on equity is not shown as a single-factor strategy in this book. However, it is used in Chapter 5 in the price to book value and operating cash flow to equity strategy.

- FCF growth factors work well across economic sectors, while EPS growth factors do not.
- An investment strategy that combines high EPS or FCF growth with strong price momentum (a widely used strategy) results in not only high excess returns but also high volatility and increased risk. Such "momentum" stocks can go down as fast as they go up.
- The strongest two-factor growth combination is growth and valuation. Almost all combinations of growth and valuation factors work together. Such a combination can be called a "growth at a reasonable price" (GARP) strategy. GARP ensures that the investor does not overpay for growth, a key pitfall of many growth strategies.
- Companies that show high growth in capital expenditures should be avoided. The primary reason for this is that companies often invest the most in business expansion at the wrong time, for example, at the top of a business cycle.

Capital Allocation

Sound capital allocation practices are of paramount importance for any business that generates significant cash flow. All too often, however, business managers know little about capital allocation principles. Capital allocation involves the deployment of excess cash in ways that maximize the potential returns on that cash. Excess cash means cash above what a business needs to run and maintain its existing operations and to provide a margin of safety against bad times. For a business that has significant profitable growth opportunities,[9] excess cash should be reinvested, either through internal growth initiatives or through attractively priced business acquisitions. When opportunities for growth are more limited or not sufficiently profitable, excess cash should be paid out, if possible,[10] through cash dividends, shares repurchases, and debt reductions.

- Companies that significantly reduce shares outstanding consistently outperform, while companies that issue large amounts of shares consistently underperform. Companies that reduce shares increase the ownership position of existing shareholders, while those that issue large amounts of shares significantly dilute the positions of existing owners.
- The share reduction/increase strategy works well across economic sectors.

---

[9] That is, growth opportunities likely to return a significant profit, above some reasonable hurdle rate, where the hurdle rate represents the return investors might easily achieve elsewhere on money returned through dividends, share repurchases, and so on.

[10] Business realities, such as legal obligations to creditors or suppliers, often restrict the use of cash.

- Share reduction strategies can be significantly improved by adding a valuation factor. Companies that repurchase shares at low valuations outperform strongly. Share repurchases at higher valuations are less effective.
- Companies that reduce shares outstanding *and* have positive price momentum show strong outperformance, while companies issuing large numbers of shares that have negative price momentum strongly underperform.
- Companies that reduce debt moderately outperform, while companies that significantly increase debt underperform. Debt reduction reduces interest expense, decreasing financial risk and increasing the portion of earnings available to stockholders.
- The debt reduction strategy also works well across economic sectors.
- Debt reductions combined with share reductions make a strong investment strategy. Companies that significantly reduce shares and debt outperform, while those that significantly increase shares and debt underperform. The strategy shows that investors should prefer companies with large excess cash flows that use that cash in shareholder "friendly" ways.
- The external financing strategy combines share and debt repurchase/issuance into a single factor. In general, stocks of companies that make large and frequent trips to the capital markets—the bottom quintile of the external financing strategy—are punished. Investors should avoid or sell short such companies.
- The external financing strategy works particularly well in combination with a valuation strategy: companies that are issuing large amounts of shares and/or debt and are selling at high valuations see sharp declines in their shares.
- While some companies grow successfully through business acquisitions, a strategy of buying companies that make large cash business acquisitions significantly underperforms (meaning that generally it does *not* work). This is likely because companies often overpay for acquisitions, and acquisitions often do not work out as well as anticipated by management.
- Companies must make necessary capital expenditures in order to remain competitive and to expand their businesses. Companies that have excess cash and use that cash to fund high or moderately high levels of capital expenditures outperform. Companies that are short of cash and are funding capital expenditures at minimal levels significantly underperform.

Price Momentum

In Chapter 3, I presented a three-part model that explains stock price movements. Its constituents are *fundamentals, investor sentiment,* and *valuation.* Investor sentiment forms the all-important link between a company's fundamentals and its stock market valuation. Price momentum tells us something about investor sentiment. If price momentum for a stock is positive—demand is outpacing supply—investor sentiment for the shares has, at least temporarily, also turned positive. The result is often an increase in valuation multiples. If price momentum is negative—supply has the upper hand over demand—investor sentiment has turned bearish, and multiples are likely to contract. Thus, technical analysis in general and price momentum in specific provide the investor with important tools for gauging investor sentiment and for timing investment decisions.

- Relative strength measures the price momentum of one stock relative to that of another stock or group of stocks. Price momentum can be defined as the speed with which a stock moves up or down over a specified period of time. Relative strength is a basic price momentum factor that is widely used.

- Stocks with high short-term relative strength continue to outperform, while those with low short-term relative strength continue to underperform.

- Our testing shows that a relative strength calculation period of seven months produces optimal results in terms of consistency and excess returns. However, 12-month relative strength can also be used effectively. We calculate relative strength simply by comparing the seven-month price change of one stock to the seven-month price change of every other stock in our Universe.

- Over longer periods of time the action of relative strength reverses. For example, stocks with the highest 36-month relative strength go on to underperform significantly, on average, while stocks with the lowest 88-month relative strength go on to outperform significantly.

- The 52-week price range strategy produces stronger excess returns and is more consistent than the relative strength strategy. It can be stated simply: stocks close to their 52-week highs tend to outperform, while those at or near 52-week lows tend to continue to underperform.

- As previously mentioned, price momentum strategies work very well with valuation strategies. This may be because positive price momentum indicates that some investors see the presence of a fundamental (or other) "catalyst" that is likely to propel the stock higher.

- Price momentum also works well with profitability strategies. The combination of high ROIC and strong price momentum, for example, indicates that a stock is a strong potential investment.

Red Flags

Red flags include a miscellany of investment strategies that can be used to evaluate efficiency, conservatism, and risk. Strategies covered include debt payback, capital intensity, capital expense coverage, working capital efficiency, and accounting conservatism.

- Financial leverage strategies do not work to reduce risk. Why? Over the short term, the market rewards companies that take financial risk and punishes those that it deems too financially conservative. So companies with high debt ratios and low cash balances outperform, while those with low debt and high cash balances underperform.
- Debt payback strategies, on the other hand, work well as quantitative factors to reduce risk. Payback strategies measure debt against profitability. We use two in this book: total debt to EBITDA and operating cash flow to long-term debt. The latter works well as a single-factor strategy and works well across economic sectors.
- While companies must make necessary investments in capital expenditures to remain competitive, sharp increases in capital intensity may indicate an industry is becoming more competitive. The capex to property, plant, and equipment strategy measures capital intensity by comparing a single year's capital expenditures to the company's existing capital asset base.
- Increases in capital intensity reduce returns on invested capital by significantly increasing a company's capital base. They also reduce free cash flow.
- Companies that have both high capital intensity and low cash profitability are unlikely to remain competitive and underperform significantly. On the other hand, companies with low capital intensity and high cash profitability significantly outperform.
- Capital investment coverage measures the number of times operating cash flow covers capital expenditures. Operating cash flow to capex is our strongest negative single-factor strategy and also performs well as a positive strategy. Companies with high levels of cash relative to capital expenditures can pay dividends, repurchase shares, reduce debt, or increase business investments.
- The operating cash flow to capital expenditures strategy works well across economic sectors.

- The one-year increase in inventory plus receivables turnover strategy measures working capital efficiency. An increase in working capital efficiency adds to cash flow, while a decrease detracts from cash flow. The strategy works well when combined with a valuation factor.
- The depreciation-to-invested capital strategy measures accounting conservatism. Changes in depreciation policy can significantly affect a company's reported income. Since depreciation policy is subject to accounting estimates and to a choice of depreciation methods, the amount of depreciation expense a company records relative to capital can serve as a barometer of how aggressive or conservative a company is in its overall accounting.
- Companies that take ample depreciation charges outperform, while those that record minimal depreciation underperform.

CHAPTER 12

Combining the Factors

What's past is prologue; what to come, in yours and my discharge.

William Shakespeare, *The Tempest*

The research that forms the basis of this book was organized around the concept of building blocks. I define a *building block* as a quantitative factor that has investment value: its use results in portfolios that generate consistent positive or negative excess returns over time. Each building block tells us something about investment strategies that work (those that generate positive excess returns, represented by the top quintile of a strategy) and those that don't work (those that generate negative excess returns/the bottom quintile). The concept of building blocks is important because it implies that once a factor with investment value is identified, it can be combined with other such factors to create complex models that generate even stronger and more consistent excess returns.

Sometimes a building block generates much stronger results for the top quintile than for the bottom: it tells us what to purchase. At other times the bottom quintile of a building block underperforms a lot more than the top quintile outperforms: it tells us what to avoid and/or what to sell short. Some factors are too closely related and end up selecting the same or similar types of companies. Using such factors together in a model adds to complexity without increasing excess returns, and in some cases actually decreases returns. Other factors look at different facets of an investment strategy, identifying similar but separate investment characteristics. By looking at various two-factor tests, one develops a sense of which factors are too closely related and which are independent and add value to each other. We can then combine these factors into a more robust multifactor model—one that considers a variety of more or less independent investment factors—that can increase the strength and consistency of excess returns.

This chapter looks at the strongest of the building blocks, in terms of generating both positive and negative excess returns; shows how they interact with each other and provides suggestions for effectively combining them; and demonstrates how to construct more robust multifactor models. The ideas and tests presented in this book are indeed prologue; they provide a starting point. It is up to you, the reader, to take these ideas and build upon them, develop your own winning investment strategies, and successfully apply the strategies thus created to the ever-changing field of common stock investing.

THE STRONGEST BUILDING BLOCKS

A complete list of building blocks—the single-factor strategies presented in this book—can be found in Appendix A. We present over 40 single-factor strategies in this book, grouped under the seven *basic* investment categories that form the main chapters: profitability, valuation, cash flow, growth, capital allocation, price momentum, and red flags. Some of these strategies are strong in and of themselves. Others generate weaker and less consistent excess returns and are best used as combining factors. At the outset of this chapter, it may be worthwhile to look at the strongest single-factor strategies, both by excess returns alone and in terms of each strategy's Sharpe ratio, which also takes into account the volatility of returns.

Top 10 Single-Factor Strategies: Top Quintile By Excess Return

First, we'll look at the top 10 single-factor strategies by excess returns for the top quintile (see Table 12.1). Of the top 10, 3 relate to valuation, 2 to price momentum, 2 to profitability, 2 to cash flow, and 1 to valuation/capital allocation combined.[1] If we are looking for strong excess returns only, these strategies show us where to go. Momentum is the single-strongest factor by excess returns, followed by valuation, profitability, and cash flow, in more or less equal parts. So our primary four factors look at what kind of return a company's assets can generate (profitability), how much cash those assets generate, how much we must pay for those earnings or cash flows, and what the supply/demand balance for the stock is.

---

[1] I'm classifying cash return on invested capital (ROIC) under profitability and operating cash flow to capex under cash flow, even though these ratios are covered in Chapters 6 (Cash Flow) and 10 (Red Flags), respectively. Free cash flow plus share repurchase plus dividend to price is classified as a combined valuation/capital allocation strategy, even though it is covered in Chapter 6.

T A B L E   12.1

Top 10 Single-Factor Strategies by Excess Return for the Top Quintile

Strategy	Excess Returns by Quintile					Outperf.	Undperf.	Sharpe Ratio	
	Q1	Q2	Q3	Q4	Q5	Q1	Q5	Q1	Q5
28/16-Week Relative Strength Index	6.2%	1.8%	−0.6%	−1.3%	−3.2%	70%	77%	0.70	0.26
Free Cash Flow to Price	5.6%	2.7%	0.3%	−3.7%	−4.5%	78%	81%	0.78	0.14
Enterprise Value to EBITDA	5.3%	1.9%	0.3%	−2.3%	−4.9%	75%	71%	0.84	0.10
Free Cash Flow + Shr. Repur. + Div. to Price	5.1%	2.1%	0.4%	−2.0%	−5.2%	76%	83%	0.79	0.10
Economic Profits (cash ROIC & Price/Sales)	5.1%	2.3%	1.0%	−1.1%	−5.5%	76%	75%	0.87	0.10
Cash Return on Invested Capital	5.0%	2.4%	0.3%	−1.4%	−5.9%	79%	76%	0.83	0.07
Free Cash Flow to Operating Income	5.0%	2.6%	0.1%	−2.9%	−3.8%	75%	78%	0.68	0.17
Price to Earnings (Current FY EPS Est.)	4.7%	1.2%	0.0%	−1.9%	−2.2%	66%	58%	0.67	0.17
52-Week Price Range	4.3%	2.1%	0.0%	−2.2%	−3.9%	75%	75%	0.69	0.20
Oper. Cash Flow to Capex	4.2%	2.4%	0.9%	−0.4%	−7.2%	74%	79%	0.71	0.02

Top 10 Single-Factor Strategies: Top Quintile By Sharpe Ratio

When we look at the top 10 strategies for the top quintile by Sharpe ratio (see Table 12.2), the picture changes somewhat. Recall that the Sharpe ratio is calculated by subtracting the return for Treasury bills (the so-called risk-free rate) from the return for the strategy, then dividing that excess return by the standard deviation of returns for the strategy. This provides us with a risk-adjusted measure of return, with the standard deviation of a strategy's return representing risk. While the volatility of returns probably doesn't have much to do with risk for a long-term investment holding, for our 12-month holding period, it may give us some clue as to riskiness.

T A B L E   12.2

Top 10 Single-Factor Strategies by Sharpe Ratio for the Top Quintile

Strategy	Excess Returns by Quintile					Outperf.	Undperf.	Sharpe Ratio	
	Q1	Q2	Q3	Q4	Q5	Q1	Q5	Q1	Q5
Economic Profits (Cash ROIC & Price/Sales)	5.1%	2.3%	1.0%	−1.1%	−5.5%	76%	75%	0.87	0.10
Enterprise Value to EBITDA	5.3%	1.9%	0.3%	−2.3%	−4.9%	75%	71%	0.84	0.10
Cash Return on Invested Capital	5.0%	2.4%	0.3%	−1.4%	−5.9%	79%	76%	0.83	0.07
1-Year Reduction in Shares	3.1%	1.1%	1.7%	1.5%	−5.2%	69%	79%	0.81	0.14
Free Cash Flow Per Share Score	3.5%	1.9%	1.0%	−0.6%	−2.7%	80%	68%	0.81	0.33
Free Cash Flow + Shr. Repur. + Div. to Price	5.1%	2.1%	0.4%	−2.0%	−5.2%	76%	83%	0.79	0.10
Economic Profits (ROIC & Beta)	2.7%	1.3%	1.4%	0.3%	−0.9%	65%	65%	0.78	0.32
Free Cash Flow to Price	5.6%	2.7%	0.3%	−3.7%	−4.5%	78%	81%	0.78	0.14
Net Share Repurchase to Invested Capital	2.5%	1.7%	0.6%	−0.5%	−4.9%	68%	73%	0.78	0.12
External Financing to Assets	3.1%	2.3%	1.8%	−0.9%	−6.7%	68%	79%	0.77	0.06

The top 10 strategies by Sharpe ratio include 3 profitability factors, 3 capital allocation factors, 2 valuation factors, a growth factor, and a combined valuation/capital allocation factor. The growth factor is free cash flow (FCF) per share score, and two of the profitability factors are also cash flow based, so cash flows also make our top 10 list by Sharpe ratio. One conclusion here is that when we're looking to reduce volatility, we should favor companies that allocate capital in shareholder-friendly ways, which include share repurchases, debt reductions, and dividend payments. Share repurchases and dividends can reduce stock price volatility by helping to establish a "floor" under the stock price, for example, by providing a healthy dividend yield. In addition, companies that pay substantial dividends, reduce shares, and reduce debt are often larger companies that are generating high operating cash flows, and larger companies tend to be more stable. Another conclusion that shouldn't be too surprising is that both strong cash flows and a high return on capital (profitability) are important to the stability of excess returns. So, an investor seeking to reduce share price volatility in a portfolio should favor capital allocation, cash flow, and profitability factors, in addition to valuation.

Top 10 Single-Factor Strategies: Bottom Quintile By Excess Returns

Table 12.3 shows the top 10 single-factor strategies by excess returns (underperformance) for the bottom quintile. These are strategies that show us stocks to avoid or stocks we can use to construct lists of short-sale candidates. The top 10 list includes 3 cash flow factors, 3 profitability factors, 2 capital allocation factors, a valuation factor, and a combined valuation/capital allocation factor.[2] This tells us that short-sale strategies should include unprofitable companies that are generating negative cash flows, increasing their capital bases through share and debt issuance, and selling at high valuation multiples. In addition, note that the strategies presented in Table 12.3 all have relatively high Sharpe ratios for the top quintile. There is a strong overlap between this list and Table 12.2, and the strategies that work well for short portfolios also work well, when used in the opposite manner, to reduce volatility and increase excess returns, for long portfolios.

The list of top 10 single-factor strategies for the bottom quintile by Sharpe ratio differs by only a single strategy from Table 12.3, so I won't present it here[3] (enterprise

---

[2] Here, again, cash ROIC is classified as profitability, and free cash flow (FCF) plus net share repurchase plus dividend to price is classified as a combined valuation/capital allocation strategy. Also, I've classified FCF to long-term debt, operating cash flow to capex, and operating cash flow to capex plus interest as cash flow strategies, even though they are presented in Chapter 10 (Red Flags).

[3] The full list of single-factor strategies sorted by excess returns and by Sharpe ratio for the top and bottom quintiles can be found in Appendix A.

TABLE 12.3

Top 10 Single-Factor Strategies by Excess Return for the Bottom Quintile

Strategy	Excess Returns by Quintile					Outperf.	Underf.	Sharpe Ratio	
	Q1	Q2	Q3	Q4	Q5	Q1	Q5	Q1	Q5
Oper. Cash Flow to Capex	4.2%	2.4%	0.9%	−0.4%	−7.2%	74%	79%	0.71	0.02
External Financing to Assets	3.1%	2.3%	1.8%	−0.9%	−6.7%	68%	79%	0.77	0.06
Cash Return on Invested Capital	5.0%	2.4%	0.3%	−1.4%	−5.9%	79%	76%	0.83	0.07
Free Cash Flow to Long-Term Debt	3.5%	2.5%	1.2%	−0.7%	−5.9%	65%	75%	0.71	0.07
Economic Profits (Cash ROIC & Price/Sales)	5.1%	2.3%	1.0%	−1.1%	−5.5%	76%	75%	0.87	0.10
Oper. Cash Flow to Capex + Interest	3.1%	2.1%	0.4%	1.3%	−5.5%	67%	78%	0.74	0.09
EBITDA to Invested Capital	2.3%	2.0%	0.9%	0.3%	−5.2%	69%	79%	0.73	0.10
1-Year Reduction in Shares	3.1%	1.1%	1.7%	1.5%	−5.2%	69%	79%	0.81	0.14
Free Cash Flow + Repurch. + Div. to Price	5.1%	2.1%	0.4%	−2.0%	−5.2%	76%	83%	0.79	0.10
Enterprise Value to EBITDA	5.3%	1.9%	0.3%	−2.3%	−4.9%	75%	71%	0.84	0.10

value to sales makes the top 10 list by Sharpe ratio, and one-year reduction in shares does not). It seems that the strongest short-sale factors by excess return are also the most volatile. As mentioned many times in this book, this is partly because the downtrodden among companies and stocks tend to outperform significantly coming out of bear markets and at speculative tops in bull markets.

THE STRONGEST TWO-FACTOR COMBINATIONS

Since this book contains nearly twice as many two-factor strategies as it does single-factor strategies, I'll present a top 15 two-factor list, instead of a top 10. The full list of two-factor strategies, also sorted by excess returns and by Sharpe ratio, can be found in Appendix B. A lot can be learned from these lists.

Top 15 Two-Factor Strategies: Top Quintile By Excess Returns

Table 12.4 contains the top 15 two-factor strategies sorted by excess return for the top quintile. A true variety of investment factors are represented here, including valuation, price momentum, growth, profitability, and cash flow. The first point to notice is that 12 out of the 15 strategies include a valuation factor. Valuation is one of the strongest quantitative factors, and because it incorporates price, it is to some extent independent of other fundamental factors, so it combines well in a fundamental test.

Profitability appears in 5 of the top 15 strategies, in 4 of which it is combined with valuation. Profitability and valuation make a good combination, since such a combination ensures that the investor is buying a company capable of generating strong

TABLE 12.4

Top 15 Two-Factor Strategies by Excess Return for the Top Quintile

Strategy	Excess Returns by Quintile					Outperf. Q1	Undperf. Q5	Sharpe Ratio	
	Q1	Q2	Q3	Q4	Q5			Q1	Q5
28/16 Week RSI & 52-Week Price Range	10.7%	3.9%	−1.0%	−4.5%	−9.6%	80%	84%	0.78	−0.04
FCF to Price & 7-Month Relative Strength	9.5%	2.4%	−2.1%	−5.3%	−8.6%	76%	79%	0.97	−0.03
FCF PS 1-Year Growth & 28/16-Week RSI	9.0%	4.3%	−0.6%	−1.8%	−4.4%	73%	73%	0.79	0.15
ROIC & Cash ROIC	8.4%	3.2%	0.8%	0.2%	−10.9%	78%	79%	0.92	−0.09
FCF to Price & EPS Score	8.4%	4.0%	0.8%	−3.5%	−3.0%	82%	75%	0.90	0.16
7-Month RS & FCF + Shr. Repur. + Div. to Price	8.3%	1.7%	−0.8%	−2.8%	−10.0%	81%	94%	0.76	−0.07
FCF to Price & Cash ROIC	8.3%	2.8%	−1.1%	−4.0%	−10.9%	79%	81%	0.95	−0.11
Price to Book & Economic Profits (ROIC, Beta)	8.1%	2.0%	−1.1%	−3.1%	−9.9%	74%	74%	0.74	−0.06
FCF Per Share Score & EV to EBITDA	8.1%	3.1%	0.8%	−2.7%	−6.7%	76%	73%	1.03	0.07
Economic Profits (Cash ROIC) & EV to EBITDA	8.1%	1.9%	−1.7%	−2.5%	−6.0%	76%	76%	0.98	0.04
2 Yr Capex Growth & Free Cash Flow to Price	8.0%	3.5%	0.6%	−2.6%	−6.6%	79%	80%	0.79	0.05
EV to EBITDA & Free Cash Flow to Oper. Inc.	7.9%	2.4%	−0.8%	−3.9%	−7.9%	75%	74%	0.87	0.00
FCF to Operating Income & Price to Sales	7.9%	2.4%	−0.4%	−5.3%	−8.4%	72%	76%	0.82	−0.02
EBITDA-Capx to Inv. Cap. & FCF to Price	7.8%	2.4%	0.3%	−1.7%	−5.3%	74%	75%	0.89	0.09
88/36-Month Rel. Str. & EV to EBITDA	7.7%	2.3%	0.1%	−0.2%	−3.5%	69%	62%	0.83	0.12

earnings at a reasonable price. Momentum, which is purely price based, is also independent of fundamental factors. Momentum appears in 5 of these strategies and combines particularly well with valuation. Growth factors also appear 3 times in the top 15 strategies by excess return, 2 in concert with valuation and 1 with a momentum factor. Growth and valuation make a natural "growth at a reasonable price" (GARP) combination. Cash flow–based strategies also appear a few times in this list, again combining well with valuation.

Top 15 Two-Factor Strategies: Top Quintile By Sharpe Ratio

Table 12.5 lists the top 15 strategies for the top quintile by Sharpe ratio. The list of the top 15 strategies by Sharpe ratio differs significantly from the top 15 by excess returns (Table 12.4). A total of 9 out of the 15 strategies in the Sharpe ratio list were not in the excess returns list. Valuation continues to be a strong factor, appearing 12 times in the list. However, profitability becomes much more prominent, appearing 8 times (vs. 5 in Table 12.4). Momentum factors occur less, and growth occurs slightly less. One other major difference between the two lists is that factors that signal conservatism or shareholder friendliness by company management begin to appear significantly in Table 12.5. These factors include depreciation to invested capital (a measure of accounting conservatism that appears twice here), one-year reduction in shares outstanding, and external financing to invested capital.

TABLE 12.5

Top 15 Two-Factor Strategies by Sharpe Ratio for the Top Quintile

Strategy	Excess Returns by Quintile					Outperf.	Undperf.	Sharpe Ratio	
	Q1	Q2	Q3	Q4	Q5	Q1	Q5	Q1	Q5
FCF Per Share Score & EV to EBITDA	8.1%	3.1%	0.8%	−2.7%	−6.7%	76%	73%	1.03	0.07
Economic Profits (Cash ROIC) & EV to EBITDA	8.1%	1.9%	−1.7%	−2.5%	−6.0%	76%	76%	0.98	0.04
FCF to Price & 7-Month Relative Strength	9.5%	2.4%	−2.1%	−5.3%	−8.6%	76%	79%	0.97	−0.03
28/16-Week RSI & Economic Profits	7.4%	0.6%	−1.8%	−2.5%	−9.8%	70%	78%	0.97	−0.03
3-Yr Capex to Inv. Cap. & FCF to Price	5.7%	3.6%	1.1%	−4.5%	−7.1%	68%	79%	0.96	0.03
FCF to Price & Cash ROIC	8.3%	2.8%	−1.1%	−4.0%	−10.9%	79%	81%	0.95	−0.11
ROIC & Cash ROIC	8.4%	3.2%	0.8%	0.2%	−10.9%	78%	79%	0.92	−0.09
EV to EBITDA & Total Debt to EBITDA	6.0%	1.0%	−0.3%	−3.0%	−5.6%	75%	71%	0.91	0.10
Deprec. to Inv. Cap. & FCF+Shr. Repur.+Div. to Prc	6.4%	2.5%	1.0%	−4.2%	−9.7%	75%	83%	0.91	−0.08
FCF to Price & EPS Score	8.4%	4.0%	0.8%	−3.5%	−3.0%	82%	75%	0.90	0.16
Deprec. to Inv. Cap. & Extern. Finan. to Inv. Cap.	4.7%	2.7%	1.8%	−1.8%	−9.7%	74%	82%	0.90	−0.05
1-Yr Reduction in Shares & EV to EBITDA	6.0%	1.9%	1.3%	−1.7%	−9.7%	73%	73%	0.90	−0.04
EV to EBITDA & Return on Invested Capital	6.8%	2.2%	−0.1%	−2.2%	−7.4%	78%	77%	0.90	0.02
FCF + Dividend Yield & Return on Equity	6.7%	2.8%	0.7%	−3.1%	−9.7%	78%	78%	0.89	−0.05
EBITDA-Capx to Inv. Cap. & FCF to Price	7.8%	2.4%	0.3%	−1.7%	−5.3%	74%	75%	0.89	0.09

In addition, the three-year average capex to invested capital factor appears high on this list, in conjunction with FCF to price. This strategy selects attractively valued companies with excess cash that are investing strongly for future growth. So, the themes we see reflected in these strategies are valuation, profitability, cash flow, conservatism, investment for growth, and momentum.

Top 15 Two-Factor Strategies: Bottom Quintile By Excess Returns

The list of top 15 two-factor strategies by excess returns for the bottom quintile (see Table 12.6) looks completely different from the top-quintile lists (Tables 12.4 and 12.5). Capital allocation strategies dominate this list, including companies that are issuing large numbers of shares and large amounts of debt and making big cash business acquisitions. The capital expenditures to property, plant, and equipment (PP&E) strategy shows up four times on this list. Companies selected by this strategy are making very large investments in capital assets (PP&E) relative to their existing capital asset base, indicating that they are likely becoming more capital intensive and that their markets may be becoming more competitive. Also dominating the list are companies with negative cash flows, while companies with high valuations and poor profitability round out the list. Growth factors do not make the list. So, in constructing short-sale strategies, the investor should favor capital allocation, capital intensity, cash flow, profitability, and

T A B L E   12.6

Top 15 Two-Factor Strategies by Excess Return for the Bottom Quintile

Strategy	Excess Returns by Quintile					Outperf.	Undperf.	Sharpe Ratio	
	Q1	Q2	Q3	Q4	Q5	Q1	Q5	Q1	Q5
FCF to Price & External Financing to Assets	7.1%	2.8%	2.5%	−5.9%	−15.3%	72%	86%	0.86	−0.24
FCF to Operating Income & Extern. Finan. to Assets	7.0%	3.0%	1.8%	−6.3%	−14.4%	73%	82%	0.81	−0.20
Oper. Cash Flow to Capex & Capex to PP&E	4.4%	1.5%	−0.7%	−0.8%	−13.5%	71%	81%	0.76	−0.16
Price to Book & Operating Cash Flow to Equity	6.6%	4.3%	−0.5%	−3.6%	−13.2%	74%	79%	0.72	−0.16
Extern. Finan. to Assets & 52-Week Price Range	5.7%	3.4%	1.4%	−3.3%	−13.1%	71%	82%	0.84	−0.18
FCF to Long-Term Debt & Economic Profits	7.5%	5.1%	2.5%	−1.3%	−13.0%	74%	78%	0.88	−0.18
EV to Sales & 7-Month Relative Strength	6.1%	0.7%	1.3%	−0.5%	−12.9%	78%	86%	0.86	−0.18
Cash ROIC & Capex to PP&E	4.7%	1.9%	0.5%	−1.1%	−12.9%	74%	78%	0.82	−0.15
ROIC & 1-Yr Reduction in Shares OS	4.6%	1.2%	2.6%	−0.6%	−12.8%	62%	78%	0.86	−0.15
Economic Profits (Cash ROIC) & Capex to PP&E	5.3%	1.2%	0.0%	−0.5%	−12.4%	78%	76%	0.73	−0.14
FCF+Shr. Repur.+Div. to Price & 1-Year Red. in Shrs.	5.6%	1.7%	0.3%	−2.2%	−12.1%	72%	81%	0.88	−0.16
Acquisitions to Inv. Cap. & Capex to PP&E	5.5%	2.2%	−0.2%	−1.3%	−11.8%	70%	87%	0.81	−0.17
Oper. Cash Flow to Capex & Price to Capex	6.8%	4.4%	0.3%	−1.3%	−11.8%	72%	79%	0.76	−0.12
1-Yr. Chg. Invt.+Rcvbls. Turn. & Extern. Fin. to Assets	4.7%	2.2%	3.0%	−0.5%	−11.6%	66%	86%	0.82	−0.13
FCF to Price & Price to Sales	6.4%	2.0%	−1.0%	−5.6%	−11.3%	68%	76%	0.65	−0.10

valuation factors. The list of two-factor strategies by Sharpe ratio for the bottom quintile will not be shown here, as it is very similar to the excess returns list.

FACTORS THAT WORK TOGETHER—AND WHY

The two-factor strategies presented in this book are almost uniformly strong. However, they don't all combine equally well with each other. This section will give you an idea of the different types of two-factor strategies that make effective quantitative models, as well as the underlying fundamental and market-based reasons why they work. In Chapter 13, I'll show you how to take the factors and strategies presented in this book and turn them into effective stock screens that can serve as a starting point for individual stock selection or for generating quantitatively based stock portfolios. In creating these screens, you may want to use two, three, or even more quantitative factors to build a model that considers a variety of fundamental and market-based data in selecting companies and stocks. Such a multifactor model will likely provide greater reliability and consistency of returns and can also provide higher excess returns. However, the basic types of factors that combine well, and the reasons that they work, hold true whether you're constructing a two-factor, three-factor, or larger multifactor model. The list of strong two-factor combinations and example strategies that follows should give you a good idea of how to select factors to include in such a model.

Note: Each two-factor combination given below is followed by a list of examples (using section and figure titles). The chapter number that the example appears in is given in parentheses following the example, for your reference (e.g., Return on Equity and Price to Book Value (4)). Tests that have not been presented in this book are labeled *not shown*; however, they have been tested and they work.

The Primary Combinations

The strategies that follow are the strongest and most consistent two-factor combinations. They should be used as the basis for most quantitative tests.

Profitability and Valuation

Profitability and valuation are two of the strongest factors we tested. They are also somewhat independent of each other, since one measures a fundamental factor only, and one combines a market-based factor (price) with a fundamental factor. The pair works in either order, with the emphasis on profitability (by selecting it first) or with the emphasis on valuation. The rationale for this combination is simple: it selects companies that are able to generate significant returns on existing resources and ensures that the investor does not pay too much for these resources. Note that profitability can include both income statement–based profitability and cash flow–based profitability.

Examples: Free Cash Flow to Price and Cash Return on Invested Capital (*not shown*); Enterprise Value to EBITDA and Return on Invested Capital (5); Price to Book Value and Economic Profits (5); Return on Equity and Price to Book Value (4); Return on Invested Capital and Price to Sales (4); Cash Return on Invested Capital and Price to Invested Capital (6); Free Cash Flow Plus Dividend Yield and Return on Equity (6); Price to Book Value and Operating Cash Flow to Equity (5).

Growth and Value

Growth and valuation factors work very well together, even though growth factors on their own tend to be weak. Growth indicates that the company's income or cash flow–generating ability is increasing, while value ensures that the investor does not overpay for growth, thus resulting in a "growth at a reasonable price" strategy.

Examples: Free Cash Flow Per Share Score and Enterprise Value to EBITDA[4] (7); Free Cash Flow to Price and EPS Score (*not shown*);[5] Price to Earnings and EPS Score (5).

Valuation and Momentum

Momentum provides us with a factor that is independent from both valuation and fundamental factors, as well as one that is strong in its own right. Valuation and momentum work particularly well together. The problem with using valuation alone is that, while value factors tell us that a given stock is "cheap," they don't tell us if anything is occurring at the company that will cause it to become less cheap. Momentum provides such an indicator. Strong momentum tells us that the supply/demand balance for a company's stock is improving and that investors may believe something is changing for the better at the company.

Examples: Free Cash Flow to Price and Seven-Month Relative Strength (5); Enterprise Value to Sales and Seven-Month Relative Strength (*not shown*); 52-Week Price Range and Free Cash Flow to Price (9); 52-Week Price Range and Price to Book Value (9).

Cash Flow and Valuation

Cash flow–based strategies represent one of the strongest *basics* tested. However, most cash flow strategies share one common fault: they haven't worked well over the past few years. Adding a valuation factor to a cash flow–based factor corrects this fault. Cash flow factors identify companies that generate significant amounts of "excess" cash (a characteristic the market values highly), while a valuation factor ensures that the investor does not overpay for cash generation capabilities.

Examples: Enterprise Value to EBITDA and Free Cash Flow to Operating Income (5); Free Cash Flow to Operating Income and Price to Sales (6); Price to Book Value and Operating Cash Flow to Equity (5).

Secondary Combinations

The following strategies are also strong, but I view them as complementary to the combinations presented above. The strategies that follow can be used to successfully expand a multifactor quantitative screen or model.

---

[4] Note that one-year FCF growth can be used in place of the FCF score, and two-year EPS growth can be used in place of the EPS score.

[5] For a similar strategy, see earnings per share score and free cash flow plus dividend to price in Chapter 7.

Valuation and Valuation

Since valuation is our strongest quantitative factor, adding multiple valuation tests can improve a strategy's results. A good practice in using different valuation factors is to combine factors that look at price relative to different fundamental elements, such as price to earnings and price to cash flow.

Examples: Free Cash Flow to Price and Price to Sales (*not shown*); Free Cash Flow to Price and Enterprise Value to EBITDA (*not shown*); Price to Earnings and Enterprise Value to EBITDA (5).

Profitability and Profitability

As with valuation, profitability is such a strong factor that combining different profitability factors in a single quantitative screen makes sense. In particular, accrual accounting–based profitability tests (e.g., return on equity) combine well with cash-based profitability tests.

Examples: Return on Invested Capital and Cash Return on Invested Capital (4); Return on Equity and Return on Invested Capital (*not shown*); EBITDA Minus Capital Expenditures to Invested Capital and Operating Cash Flow to Capital Expenditures (4).[6]

Profitability and Momentum

The concept behind this combination is simple, and it works: purchase companies with high profitability when demand for their stock, as indicated by price momentum, is strong. However, adding a valuation factor to this strategy reduces volatility and risk.

Examples: 28/16 Week Relative Strength and Economic Profits (9); 52-Week Price Range and Return on Invested Capital (*not shown*); 52-Week Price Range and Return on Equity (9).

Valuation and Capital Allocation

This combination selects undervalued companies that have excess cash and are using that cash to grow their businesses or reward shareholders. Profitable capital allocation strategies from a quantitative point of view include moderate capital expenditures, share repurchases, debt reduction, and dividend payments. Note that valuation and share repurchases work together very well, since our testing shows that there is a direct relationship between the valuation at which shares are repurchased and subsequent excess returns (low valuations increase excess returns).

---

[6] While this last factor is not strictly profitability related, it does "get at" cash profitability.

Examples: Three-Year Average Capital Expenditures to Invested Capital and Free Cash Flow to Price (8); One-Year Reduction in Shares Outstanding and Enterprise Value to EBITDA (8); Free Cash Flow to Price and External Financing to Assets (5); Free Cash Flow Plus Share Repurchase Plus Dividend to Price and One-Year Reduction in Shares Outstanding (6).

Valuation and Red Flags

Red flag strategies, as presented in this book, tell us something about a company's financial conservatism, its capital intensity, or changes in its operating efficiency. The top quintile of red flag strategies contains companies that are doing something right, and the valuation factor tells us that these companies are priced attractively. Since red flags give us a limited view into company fundamentals, you might combine a two-factor model like this with a profitability factor.

Examples: Depreciation to Invested Capital and Free Cash Flow to Price (*not shown*);[7] Two-Year Average Capex Per Share Growth and Free Cash Flow to Price (7);[8] Operating Cash Flow to Capital Expenditures Plus Interest and Price to Capital Expenditures (10); One-Year Change in Inventory Plus Receivables Turnover and Free Cash Flow to Price (10).

Profitability and Capital Allocation

This combination identifies companies that are highly profitable, on either an income statement or cash flow basis, and are using excess cash to repurchase shares, reduce debt, and/or invest for growth. Essentially, these are companies that have the ability to generate a lot of capital and are allocating that capital wisely.

Examples: Return on Invested Capital and One-Year Reduction in Shares Outstanding (4); Cash Return on Invested Capital and Capex to Invested Capital (6); One-Year Reduction in Long-Term Debt and Economic Profits (8).

Growth and Profitability

Since it is possible for a company to have growth without profitability and profitability without growth, this combination ensures that companies in the top quintile have both. A growing business that is highly profitable can often make a good investment.

---

[7] But see Chapter 10 for the depreciation to invested capital and free cash flow plus share repurchase plus dividend to price strategy.

[8] Although two-year average capex growth is presented in Chapter 7 (Growth), it is really a risk-oriented factor, as companies with the lowest capex growth are placed in the top quintile and those with the highest growth in the bottom.

It should make an even better investment if purchased at an attractive price, so I favor combining growth, profitability, and valuation.

Examples: Free Cash Flow Per Share Score and Return on Equity (7); Earnings Per Share Score and Operating Cash Flow Per Share to Current Year EPS Estimate (7).[9]

Capital Allocation and Momentum

This combination selects companies that generate excess cash, are using at least some of that cash to repurchase shares and reduce debt, and whose stocks have a favorable supply/demand balance. Like other capital allocation combinations, this one works very well as a short-sale strategy.

Examples: External Financing to Assets and 52-Week Price Range (8); One-Year Reduction in Shares Outstanding and Seven-Month Relative Strength (8).

Profitability and Red Flags

The top quintile of this combination basically selects companies whose businesses are being run well. The profitability factor ensures that business resources are being used productively, and the red flags strategy makes sure that the business is conservatively financed or that its capital intensity is low. The bottom quintile—companies whose businesses are going badly—can be expected to underperform strongly.

Examples: Free Cash Flow to Long-Term Debt and Economic Profits (10); Free Cash Flow to Long-Term Debt and Return on Equity (10); Cash Return on Invested Capital and Capex to PP&E (6).

Capital Allocation and Red Flags

Capital allocation, as used here, indicates that the companies selected generate positive FCF (excess cash), use some of that cash to repurchase shares or reduce debt, and/or avoid cash business acquisitions. The red flags strategy adds to the strategy companies with conservative accounting policies, improving operating efficiency, and/or declining capital intensity. This combination represents a mix of approaches, but the common denominators are sound use of capital, conservatism, and efficiency.

Examples: Acquisitions to Invested Capital and Capital Expenditures to Property, Plant, and Equipment (8); One-Year Change in Inventory Plus Receivables Turnover and External Financing to Assets (*not shown*); One-Year Reduction in Shares Outstanding and

---

[9] Although operating cash flow per share to EPS is a cash quality of earnings measure, it also tells us something about profitability.

Depreciation to Invested Capital (8); Depreciation to Invested Capital and External Financing to Invested Capital (10).

SUGGESTIONS FOR COMBINING THE STRATEGIES

Beyond having an idea of which types of investment strategies to combine, the following list will give you some idea of how to create effective two-, three-, and multifactor screens and models.

- For the most effective two-factor quantitative models and screens, stick with the four primary combinations presented above: profitability and valuation, growth and value, valuation and momentum, and cash flow and valuation. Use the specific profitability, valuation, growth, cash flow, and momentum factors presented in this book, because they can be relied upon. Our research shows that the primary combinations presented above work well in most investment environments, generate strong excess returns, and do so with relatively low volatility.

- Note that each of the four primary combinations involves a valuation strategy. Valuation is the strongest of the *basics* and should be used liberally when constructing models and screens. A quantitative factor that works only moderately well can be strengthened significantly when used with a valuation factor.

- For a more comprehensive three-factor model or screen, combine a valuation factor with two of the factors listed above: profitability, growth, cash flow, and/or momentum.

- A successful three-factor screen/model can also be constructed by combining one of the factors listed above, under primary combinations, with one of the secondary combinations: profitability and momentum, valuation and capital allocation, valuation and red flags, profitability and capital allocation, growth and profitability, and so on. For example, combine valuation with profitability and momentum, or growth with valuation and red flags.

- Capital allocation factors can serve two purposes: (1) to add consistency and reduce risk in a long (top quintile) strategy, and (2) to create a strong short-sale or a long/short strategy.[10] Companies that issue large amounts of shares or

---

[10] Long/short strategies involve simultaneously buying stocks that are expected to outperform (e.g., stocks in the top quintiles of our quantitative strategies) and selling stocks expected to underperform (e.g., stocks in the bottom quintiles), with the idea of minimizing the investor's exposure to stock market swings.

debt or make large business acquisitions underperform significantly, as do companies that show sharp increases in capital spending. Note that capital allocation factors combine well with cash flow factors, since firms that have a lot of excess cash and return some of it to shareholders generally outperform.

- Red flags should also be used to reduce risk, increase consistency, and/or for short-sale or long/short strategies.

- Combine complementary investment factors. For example, combine a good long factor—one in which the top quintile outperforms strongly and consistently—with a good short factor—one in which the bottom quintile underperforms strongly and consistently. Also, combine income statement–based factors with cash flow–based factors, for example, an income statement profitability measure (return on invested capital) with a cash flow–based valuation measure (FCF to price).

- Combine factors that outperform during bull markets, such as growth and relative strength, with factors that outperform during bear markets, such as capital allocation and valuation.

- Combine strategies that have common denominators. Such strategies look at the same balance sheet, income statement, or cash flow items in different ways. Examples include ROE and price to book value, FCF to price and cash ROIC, and operating cash flow to capex and price to capex.

- Don't combine factors that measure very similar things. Not only do they not add to each other, but one similar factor often weakens the other. For example, price to sales and price to earnings do not work well together.

- Sometimes a factor that doesn't work well on its own will combine well, particularly when used with a strong factor with which it has a strong relationship. For example, in Chapter 8, we used the one-year reduction in long-term debt factor, which had 0% excess returns in the top quintile, in combination with the economic profits strategy, which had 5.1% excess returns, and ended up with a strategy that had 7.3% excess returns. In this case, the combination of high cash profitability and a shareholder-friendly use of that cash (to reduce debt) proved to be a good one. So, if you find a single-factor strategy that makes sense but doesn't test well, try combining it with a stronger factor that might reinforce it.

- When using debt ratios in quantitative tests to reduce risk, prefer debt payback ratios to financial leverage ratios. Debt payback ratios measure the level of debt relative to profitability. Companies with high profitability relative to debt outperform those with low profitability to debt. In contrast, financial leverage ratios measure only the degree of financial conservatism or aggressiveness at a firm (without reference to profitability). Over the short term, the market does not reward companies that are financially conservative, and companies with low leverage ratios tend to underperform. Total debt to EBITDA (earnings before interest, taxes, depreciation, and amortization) and FCF to long-term debt are two debt payback ratios that can be used to reduce risk.

THREE-FACTOR TESTS

The two-factor quantitative tests presented throughout this book use a simple stock selection method: we first screen our Universe of companies for the first factor in the test; we then screen from the remaining companies for the second factor. For example, if we're constructing the top quintile of a return on invested capital (ROIC) and price to sales test, we'd first take the top 20% of companies in our Universe by ROIC. From the top 20% by ROIC group, we'd then select the bottom 20% by price to sales (we want the companies with the lowest valuations). The result is that if our Universe contained 2,000 companies, we'd end up with approximately 400 companies for the top 20% by ROIC, and this would be whittled down to 80 companies by taking the lowest 20% by price to sales.

We follow the same approach for three-factor tests: we screen first on factor 1, from the remaining companies on factor 2, and from the remainder from the preceding step we screen on factor 3. The result, as you might guess, is a very small set size. Average portfolio sizes for the three-factor tests presented below range from 11 to 13. A small set size can be both a benefit and a detriment. Concentrated portfolios benefit the investor because, being less diversified, they offer the best opportunity for excess returns above the market. At the same time, concentrated portfolios can be a detriment primarily because returns from one or two companies can significantly influence results, creating a volatile strategy. However, I believe the three-factor tests presented here show how strong combinations of factors coupled with small portfolio sizes can enhance returns.[11]

Enterprise Value to EBITDA, Cash Return on Invested Capital, and Seven-Month Relative Strength

This test combines valuation, profitability, and price momentum—three strong *basics*—into a single strategy. The profitability factor tells us that we are purchasing high-quality assets, the valuation factor tells us that those assets are attractively priced, and the momentum factor tells us that investors may see a catalyst likely to propel the stock

---

[11] In Chapter 13, I'll show you how to get around the limitation of very small set sizes in three-factor tests by creating investment screens that use minimum values for each factor. I believe the screens presented in Chapter 13 will provide you with a very practical way to apply the data contained in this book.

higher. Also, by using EV to EBITDA in combination with cash ROIC, the test combines an income statement–based valuation metric with a cash flow-based profitability metric, providing a broader perspective on company fundamentals than just an income statement– or cash flow–based view alone. Note that excess returns are quite linear, indicating a high correlation between the factors tested and excess returns.

The top quintile outperforms by 13.3%, on average, higher than any of the two-factor strategies we tested (see Figure 12.1). It is relatively consistent and has a moderate maximum loss of 26%. However, the standard deviation of returns is high (0.23 vs. 0.15 for the S&P 500), resulting in a Sharpe ratio of 0.93—a high ratio, but not the highest we've seen. Alpha is also high, at 0.15, versus 0.04 for the S&P 500. The average portfolio size is 12, and the strategy selects mid- to large-cap stocks.

The bottom quintile underperforms by almost 14%, on average, and is very consistent. Alpha is a very low −0.25. On average 9 stocks underperform versus 3 that outperform, making the strategy very reliable as a short-sale strategy. The bottom quintile significantly outperforms only in 1990–1991, 1999–2000, and 2003–2004. So, short sellers primarily have to be concerned during the early stages of bull markets and highly speculative market tops like 1999.

Free Cash Flow to Price, Earnings Per Share Score, and Return on Invested Capital

This strategy brings together valuation, growth, and profitability, another strong combination. Growth and profitability look at two important aspects of the quality of a company's assets, while valuation helps ensure a reasonable price for those assets. Like the preceding strategy, this one combines a cash-based measure (FCF to price) with two accrual accounting–based measures (earnings per share score and ROIC).

The top quintile outperforms by 13.7%, on average, and is quite consistent (see Figure 12.2). The top quintile underperforms in only two periods: 1999–2000 and 2003–2004. However, returns are volatile, with a standard deviation of 0.26 (vs. 0.15 for the S&P 500) and a Beta of 1.08 vs. the Universe. The result is a moderate Sharpe ratio of 0.81. The bottom quintile underperforms by 7.6%, on average, and is also relatively consistent. An average of 8 out of 12 companies in the bottom quintile underperforms.

Enterprise Value to EBITDA, 52-Week Price Range, and Free Cash Flow Per Share Score

This strategy combines valuation, price momentum, and growth, another very strong grouping. The growth factor indicates that the business's cash flow generation capabilities are expanding, valuation prevents the investor from overpaying for that growth, and momentum indicates that supply/demand for the stock is positive. Again, note the strong combination of income statement–based and cash flow–based factors. Also, 52-week price range is the strongest and most consistent of our momentum factors.

1990–2007	1st Quintile	2nd Quintile	3rd Quintile	4th Quintile	5th Quintile	Universe	S&P 500*
CAGR – Annual Rebalance	26.3%	13.8%	8.6%	9.2%	−10.5%	10.3%	12.0%
Average Excess Return vs. Universe**	13.3%	3.6%	−0.9%	−4.2%	−13.8%	NA	1.5%
Value of $10,000 Invested (18 Years)	$664,145	$102,665	$43,893	$49,144	$1,368	$58,670	$76,297
% of 1-Year Periods Strategy Outperforms the Universe	70.4%	57.7%	46.5%	26.8%	21.1%	NA	56.3%
% Rolling 3-Year Periods Strategy Outperforms	85.7%	73.0%	39.7%	17.5%	11.1%	NA	68.3%
Maximum Gain	75.7%	120.3%	44.6%	64.6%	150.4%	59.2%	54.1%
Maximum Loss	−25.9%	−31.5%	−28.1%	−34.5%	−94.3%	−24.9%	−25.9%
Sharpe Ratio	0.93	0.52	0.45	0.18	−0.13	0.46	0.64
Standard Deviation of Returns	0.23	0.22	0.15	0.20	0.48	0.17	0.15
Beta (vs. Universe)	0.82	0.84	0.57	0.94	1.94	NA	0.78
Alpha (vs. Universe)	0.15	0.06	0.04	−0.03	−0.25	NA	0.04
Average Portfolio Size	12	12	12	12	13	NA	NA
Average Number of Companies *Outperforming*	6	7	6	5	3	NA	NA
Average Number of Companies *Underperforming*	5	5	6	7	9	NA	NA
Median Portfolio Value – EV to EBITDA	3.5	7.9	10.5	14.0	−11.4	10.2	9.1
Median Portfolio Value – Cash ROIC	32.3%	11.5%	7.1%	−0.8%	−43.6%	4.3%	8.4%
Median Portfolio Value – 7-Month Relative Strength	41%	16%	9%	1%	−27%	21%	6%
Average Market Capitalization	$5,188	$3,568	$6,503	$9,715	$1,059	NA	NA

* Equal-weighted average of S&P 500 returns. ** Annual holding period run quarterly for a larger sample size; arithmetic average excess returns.
Source: Standard & Poor's Compustat Point in Time Database; Charter Oak Investment Systems, Inc., Venues® Data Engine

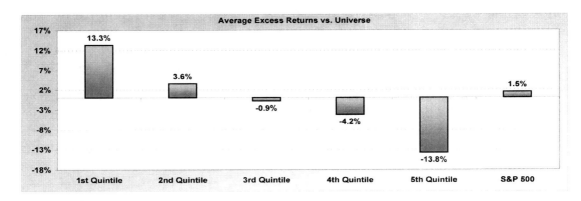

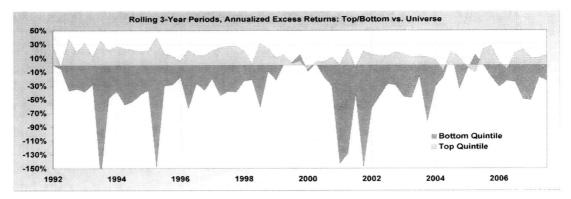

Figure 12.1 Enterprise Value to EBITDA, Cash Return on Invested Capital, and Seven-Month Relative Strength

1990–2007	1st Quintile	2nd Quintile	3rd Quintile	4th Quintile	5th Quintile	Universe	S&P 500*
CAGR – Annual Rebalance	18.3%	14.7%	6.6%	9.6%	−3.6%	10.3%	12.0%
Average Excess Return vs. Universe**	13.7%	5.8%	−1.1%	−2.0%	−7.6%	NA	1.5%
Value of $10,000 Invested (18 Years)	$207,427	$117,501	$31,829	$51,989	$5,204	$58,670	$76,297
% of 1-Year Periods Strategy Outperforms the Universe	71.8%	53.5%	45.1%	40.8%	28.2%	NA	56.3%
% Rolling 3-Year Periods Strategy Outperforms	87.3%	73.0%	30.2%	47.6%	12.7%	NA	68.3%
Maximum Gain	101.6%	62.0%	76.9%	88.9%	185.6%	59.2%	54.1%
Maximum Loss	−26.3%	−36.6%	−38.9%	−61.7%	−77.0%	−24.9%	−25.9%
Sharpe Ratio	0.81	0.69	0.36	0.24	0.00	0.46	0.64
Standard Deviation of Returns	0.26	0.20	0.19	0.24	0.49	0.17	0.15
Beta (vs. Universe)	1.08	0.83	0.86	1.16	1.97	NA	0.78
Alpha (vs. Universe)	0.13	0.08	0.01	−0.04	−0.19	NA	0.04
Average Portfolio Size	11	12	11	12	12	NA	NA
Average Number of Companies *Outperforming*	6	6	4	5	4	NA	NA
Average Number of Companies *Underperforming*	5	6	7	6	8	NA	NA
Median Portfolio Value – FCF to Price	15.2%	5.6%	2.8%	−0.4%	−12.8%	2.1%	3.3%
Median Portfolio Value – EPS score	68	57	48	29	6	41	40
Median Portfolio Value – Return on Invested Capital	32.3%	18.2%	13.3%	6.2%	−47.3%	8.8%	11.6%
Average Market Capitalization	$2,789	$8,238	$8,593	$4,890	$1,023	NA	NA

* Equal-weighted average of S&P 500 returns. ** Annual holding period run quarterly for a larger sample size; arithmetic average excess returns.
Source: Standard & Poor's Compustat Point in Time Database; Charter Oak Investment Systems, Inc., Venues® Data Engine

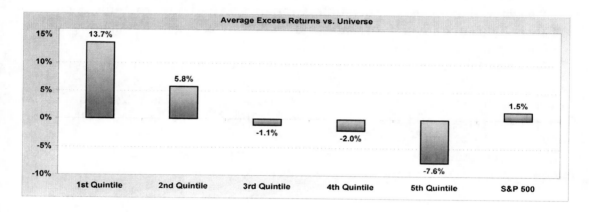

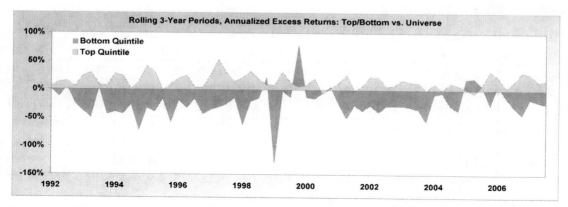

Figure 12.2 Free Cash Flow to Price, Earnings Per Share Score, and Return on Invested Captial

The result is a strategy that is very linear, with the top quintile outperforming by 12%, on average, and the bottom quintile underperforming by 12% (see Figure 12.3). Consistency is strong for both quintiles. Again, the standard deviation for the top quintile is relatively high (0.24 vs. 0.14 for the S&P 500), resulting in a high but not superlative Sharpe ratio of 0.87. An average of 6 out of 10 stocks in the top portfolio outperforms, and an average of 8 out of 11 stocks in the bottom portfolio underperforms, making this the most consistent strategy we've seen in this regard. Note that the top quintile is a true large-cap strategy, with an average market cap of $9 billion.

Free Cash Flow to Price, Cash Return on Invested Capital, and External Financing to Assets

The final three-factor strategy I'll present adds a new element to valuation and profitability: capital allocation (external financing to assets). However, the strategy contains one flaw in that it considers only cash flow–based factors and does not look at the income statement. I believe that this is what accounts for the weakness of the top quintile, especially in recent years. This strategy captures, in the bottom quintile, companies that are issuing large amounts of shares and/or debt, have negative cash flows, and are expensive. This is a *very* bad combination.

The result is a strong short-sale strategy. The bottom quintile underperforms by an average of 18% (see Figure 12.4). Note that $10,000 invested in this strategy over an 18-year period would have ended up as just $600. Alpha is a very low −0.25. Consistency is strong, and an average of 10 out of the 14 companies in the bottom quintile underperforms, with only 3 outperforming—a very favorable ratio. The bottom quintile selects small caps, with an average market capitalization of $800 million, one of the smallest we've seen in any strategy in this book.

A MULTIFACTOR MODEL

Multifactor models are more difficult to put together. Programs put out by companies such as FactSet and ClariFI offer multifactor optimization tools that allow the analyst to determine the best combination and weighting of investment factors to achieve desired results in terms of risk, return, and other investment parameters. The multifactor model presented here is intended just to provide an example of the kind of results one can expect from combining multiple building blocks in a quantitative test. Investors and portfolio managers interested in building complex quantitative models based on the factors presented in this book, as well as others of their own discovery, may wish to pursue this investigation further. A good place to start is by investigating products such as ClariFI's ModelStation and FactSet's Quantitative Analysis tools.

1991–2007	1st Quintile	2nd Quintile	3rd Quintile	4th Quintile	5th Quintile	Universe	S&P 500*
CAGR – Annual Rebalance	25.4%	12.7%	13.0%	4.5%	−6.3%	12.1%	13.5%
Average Excess Return vs. Universe**	12.3%	2.5%	1.0%	−4.8%	−12.2%	NA	1.4%
Value of $10,000 Invested (17 Years)	$466,435	$76,495	$79,305	$21,183	$3,322	$69,381	$86,051
% of 1-Year Periods Strategy Outperforms the Universe	73.8%	52.3%	58.5%	27.7%	30.8%	NA	56.9%
% Rolling 3-Year Periods Strategy Outperforms	84.2%	64.9%	64.9%	26.3%	8.8%	NA	68.4%
Maximum Gain	77.9%	52.7%	66.2%	123.3%	137.7%	59.2%	54.1%
Maximum Loss	−22.5%	−21.3%	−20.0%	−49.2%	−70.7%	−24.9%	−25.9%
Sharpe Ratio	0.87	0.65	0.58	0.15	−0.09	0.53	0.73
Standard Deviation of Returns	0.24	0.17	0.17	0.26	0.40	0.16	0.14
Beta (vs. Universe)	0.72	0.53	0.77	1.11	1.89	NA	0.75
Alpha (vs. Universe)	0.16	0.09	0.04	−0.06	−0.24	NA	0.05
Average Portfolio Size	10	11	11	11	11	NA	NA
Average Number of Companies *Outperforming*	6	5	5	4	3	NA	NA
Average Number of Companies *Underperforming*	4	5	5	6	8	NA	NA
Median Portfolio Value – EV to EBITDA	5.2	7.8	10.4	13.8	−91.3	10.2	9.2
Median Portfolio Value – 52-Week Price range	92%	82%	71%	57%	20%	60%	60%
Median Portfolio Value – FCF Score	51	43	39	24	9	32	33
Average Market Capitalization	$8,996	$4,557	$4,854	$5,361	$2,593	NA	NA

* Equal-weighted average of S&P 500 returns. ** Annual holding period run quarterly for a larger sample size; arithmetic average excess returns.
Source: Standard & Poor's Compustat Point in Time Database; Charter Oak Investment Systems, Inc., Venues® Data Engine

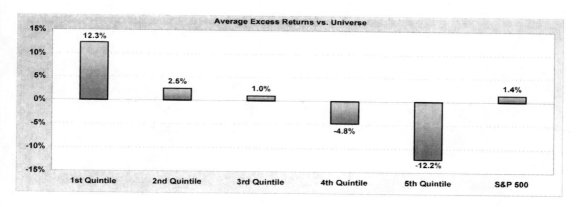

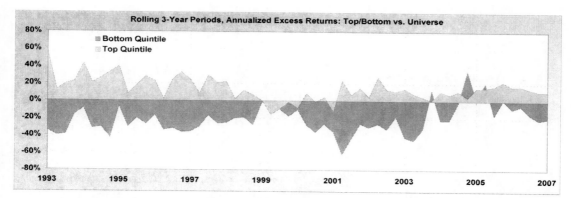

Figure 12.3 Enterprise Value to EBITDA, 52-Week Price Range, and Free Cash Flow Per Share Score

1990–2007	1st Quintile	2nd Quintile	3rd Quintile	4th Quintile	5th Quintile	Universe	S&P 500*
CAGR – Annual Rebalance	15.3%	15.7%	11.0%	–3.5%	–14.4%	10.3%	12.0%
Average Excess Return vs. Universe**	5.6%	3.4%	1.6%	–9.7%	–18.0%	NA	1.5%
Value of $10,000 Invested (18 Years)	$128,796	$138,807	$65,286	$5,232	$612	$58,670	$76,297
% of 1-Year Periods Strategy Outperforms the Universe	56.3%	57.7%	47.9%	26.8%	16.9%	NA	56.3%
% Rolling 3-Year Periods Strategy Outperforms	66.7%	57.1%	47.6%	9.5%	4.8%	NA	68.3%
Maximum Gain	77.8%	59.0%	63.8%	51.0%	105.4%	59.2%	54.1%
Maximum Loss	–31.0%	–17.3%	–32.4%	–74.5%	–76.1%	–24.9%	–25.9%
Sharpe Ratio	0.64	0.72	0.44	–0.08	–0.27	0.46	0.64
Standard Deviation of Returns	0.21	0.15	0.22	0.25	0.37	0.17	0.15
Beta (vs. Universe)	0.63	0.56	1.07	1.13	1.62	NA	0.78
Alpha (vs. Universe)	0.10	0.09	0.01	–0.11	–0.25	NA	0.04
Average Portfolio Size	13	13	13	13	14	NA	NA
Average Number of Companies *Outperforming*	6	7	6	5	3	NA	NA
Average Number of Companies *Underperforming*	6	6	7	8	10	NA	NA
Median Portfolio Value – FCF to Price	20.4%	5.8%	2.4%	–1.4%	–14.3%	2.1%	3.3%
Median Portfolio Value – Cash ROIC	49.4%	16.3%	7.2%	–3.2%	–59.9%	4.3%	8.4%
Median Portfolio Value – External Financing to Assets	–20.9%	–5.4%	0.1%	7.4%	86.1%	5.4%	0.3%
Average Market Capitalization	$2,733	$8,514	$5,320	$4,549	$778	NA	NA

* Equal-weighted average of S&P 500 returns. ** Annual holding period run quarterly for a larger sample size; arithmetic average excess returns.
Source: Standard & Poor's Compustat Point in Time Database; Charter Oak Investment Systems, Inc., Venues® Data Engine

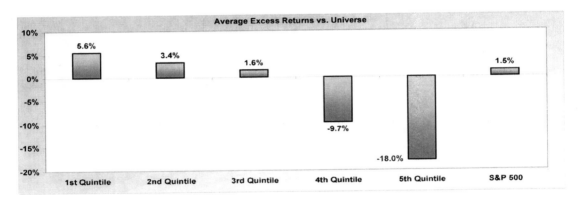

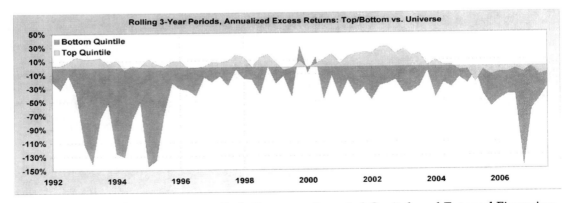

Figure 12.4 Free Cash Flow to Price, Cash Return on Invested Capital, and External Financing to Assets

Our approach to creating this model is somewhat simple, although it involves the use of statistical software. We first chose the strongest factors from each of five basic categories: valuation, profitability, price momentum, growth, and capital allocation. (We left out cash flow because it is redundant: cash flow measures are included in profitability, valuation, and growth.) We then created a score for each factor and each company over time. This means that, using the Charter Oak *Venues* Data Engine, we created a data item ("score") for each factor that consists of a company's percentile rank (from 1 to 100) on that factor for each period of time that the test is run. We created scores for each factor chosen: EV to EBITDA, FCF to price, ROIC, cash ROIC, EPS score, FCF per share score,[12] external financing to assets, one-year reduction in shares, seven-month relative strength, and 52-week price range. For example, each company in our database received a percentile score for each quarter tested on EV to EBITDA and, separately, on FCF to price.

We then used statistical software to run simulations to determine the best possible weighting of the individual factors in order to maximize the returns of the companies in the top quintile. A simulation "plugs in" multiple values for each variable (the weightings of our investment factors) in order to determine the combination of variables that maximizes a desired outcome—in this case, excess returns. Specialized software was used that can run hundreds or thousands of iterations on the variables (our investment factor weightings), in order to pinpoint the combinations of weightings that provide the highest excess returns. Simulations were run for both the top quintile (to maximize positive excess returns) and the bottom quintile (to maximize negative excess returns).[13] Table 12.7 presents the results of our simulation tests, in terms of the optimal weightings for both top and bottom deciles.[14]

The results of our multifactor model are shown in Figure 12.5. Note that the table shows the top two and bottom two deciles. The 10% of companies with the highest total score on the 10 weighted factors shown in Table 12.7 are put in the first decile, the next highest 10% of companies are put in the second decile, and so on.

The top decile outperforms by 7.5%, on average, and is quite consistent, outperforming for 75% of one-year and 93% of rolling three-year periods. It significantly underperforms only in 1999–2000 and 2003–2004. It has a Sharpe ratio of 1.13, the highest we've seen so far. The maximum loss is low and linear, rising from 17% for the top

---

[12] For this model, we use the same EPS and FCF scores that are presented in Chapter 7.

[13] We used a program that employs an algorithm called Monte Carlo simulation. There are a number of simulation software packages available. Also, Microsoft Office Excel has a Regression tool that can be used instead of simulation. To access this tool, check the Analysis ToolPak add-in (under Tools/Add-Ins), then choose Tools/Data Analysis/Regression.

[14] Note that we use deciles instead of quintiles to better illustrate the results of a multifactor test.

TABLE 12.7

Multifactor Model: Investment Factor Weightings (Weightings Add to 100%)[15]

Model Factors	Top 5 Deciles	Bottom 5 Deciles
Valuation		
EV to EBITDA	34.1%	30.4%
Free Cash Flow to Price	17.4%	6.4%
Profitability		
ROIC	12.5%	4.6%
Cash ROIC	11.3%	3.4%
Price Momentum		
52-Week Price Range	0.1%	12.2%
7-Month Relative Strength	1.5%	10.3%
Capital Allocation		
External Financing	2.7%	20.1%
1-Yr Reduction in Shares	1.8%	1.2%
Growth		
EPS Score	7.4%	0.4%
FCF Per Share Score	11.2%	10.8%

decile to 64% for the bottom decile. The bottom decile underperforms by over 9%, on average, and is also very consistent, underperforming for 85% of one-year and 88% of rolling three-year periods. It outperforms only in 1999–2000 and 2003–2004. Notice the decile results are relatively linear (although not perfectly linear), and the rolling three-year excess returns graph is much smoother than most of the other such graphs we've seen. In short, the strategy is stronger and more robust than all of the single-factor strategies we've presented, and provides a better risk/return balance than almost all of the two-factor strategies.[16]

Multifactor Model by Economic Sector

Results from our multifactor model are shown in Figure 12.6 by sector. You will notice that the results shown here are significantly different from all other sector tests presented in this book. Basically, the model works across every economic sector. The two

---

[15] The factor weightings for the bottom five deciles add to 99.8%, due to rounding errors.

[16] Results for quantitative tests generally improve as portfolio sizes diminish. So, results from a two-factor test with a portfolio size of 70 cannot be compared to results from a single-factor test with a portfolio size of 350. The portfolio size for the deciles used in this test is 130.

1991–2007	1st Decile	2nd Decile	9th Decile	10th Decile	Universe	S&P 500*
CAGR – Annual Rebalance	19.9%	18.2%	6.8%	0.7%	12.1%	13.5%
Average Excess Return vs. Universe**	7.5%	5.0%	−4.9%	−9.2%	NA	1.1%
Value of $10,000 Invested (17 Years)	$217,811	$171,560	$30,760	$11,184	$69,380	$86,051
% of 1-Year Periods Strategy Outperforms the Universe	75.4%	73.8%	23.1%	15.4%	NA	56.9%
% Rolling 3-Year Periods Strategy Outperforms	93.0%	89.5%	3.5%	12.3%	NA	70.2%
Maximum Gain	56.5%	62.7%	65.0%	86.9%	59.2%	52.4%
Maximum Loss	−17.4%	−19.9%	−50.6%	−64.1%	−24.9%	−25.9%
Sharpe Ratio	1.13	0.88	0.17	−0.02	0.53	0.72
Standard Deviation of Returns	0.14	0.16	0.23	0.32	0.16	0.14
Beta (vs. Universe)	0.59	0.72	1.32	1.64	NA	0.74
Alpha (vs. Universe)	0.13	0.09	−0.09	−0.18	NA	0.04
Average Portfolio Size	129	130	130	130	NA	NA
Average Number of Companies *Outperforming*	66	66	47	43	NA	NA
Average Number of Companies *Underperforming*	57	58	75	82	NA	NA
Median Portfolio Value – Multifactor Score (Simulation)	65	58	27	17	44	45
Average Market Capitalization	$4,617	$4,793	$4,556	$2,537	NA	NA

* Equal-weighted average of S&P 500 returns. ** Annual holding period run quarterly for a larger sample size; arithmetic average excess returns.
Source: Standard & Poor's Compustat Point in Time Database; Charter Oak Investment Systems, Inc., Venues® Data Engine

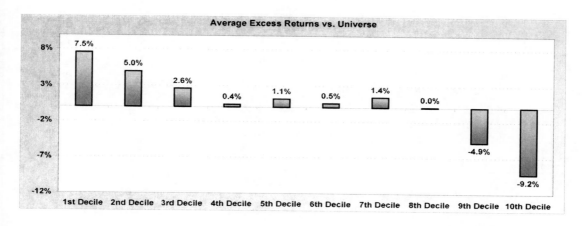

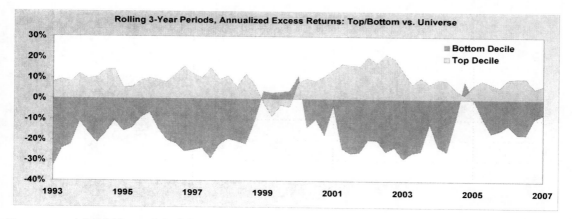

Figure 12.5 A Multifactor Model

Top Quintile

1988–2007	Energy	Materials	Industrials	Consumer Discretionary	Consumer Staples	Health Care	Financials	Information Technology	Telecom Services	Utilities	Universe	S&P 500*
CAGR – Quintile	21.6%	16.5%	15.7%	13.5%	14.0%	18.5%	20.1%	18.1%	13.0%	24.7%	12.1%	13.5%
CAGR – Sector	13.8%	11.6%	12.5%	9.6%	11.8%	12.2%	17.1%	9.1%	7.4%	12.9%	NA	NA
Excess Return vs. Sector	7.8%	4.9%	3.2%	3.8%	2.3%	6.3%	3.0%	9.0%	5.6%	11.8%	NA	NA
Value of $10,000	$279,018	$134,013	$118,670	$85,824	$92,920	$179,538	$223,778	$168,164	$80,044	$425,455	$69,380	$86,051
% 1-Year Outperformance	70.6%	76.5%	70.6%	58.8%	52.9%	58.8%	64.7%	64.7%	64.7%	76.5%	NA	NA
% 3-Year Outperformance	86.7%	93.3%	86.7%	86.7%	86.7%	93.3%	80.0%	86.7%	80.0%	86.7%	NA	NA
Maximum Gain	66.4%	57.7%	42.9%	44.0%	71.1%	79.5%	60.1%	58.1%	49.9%	105.0%	44.0%	41.4%
Maximum Loss	−12.1%	−10.0%	−4.6%	−18.7%	−19.9%	−13.1%	−12.8%	−32.8%	−21.4%	−17.5%	−19.1%	−18.1%
Standard Deviation	0.21	0.17	0.13	0.16	0.23	0.22	0.24	0.24	0.20	0.27	0.16	0.14
Beta (vs. Sector)	0.71	1.00	0.80	0.80	1.09	0.68	0.97	0.48	0.28	1.28	NA	NA
Alpha (vs. Sector)	0.11	0.05	0.06	0.06	0.02	0.10	0.04	0.13	0.11	0.09	NA	NA
Portfolio Size	16	22	43	51	15	30	24	41	6	2	NA	NA

Bottom Quintile

1988–2007	Energy	Materials	Industrials	Consumer Discretionary	Consumer Staples	Health Care	Financials	Information Technology	Telecom Services	Utilities	Universe	S&P 500*
CAGR – Quintile	4.9%	8.5%	6.0%	5.2%	8.7%	2.8%	8.7%	3.3%	−10.3%	1.2%	12.1%	13.5%
CAGR – Sector	13.8%	11.6%	12.5%	9.6%	11.8%	12.2%	17.1%	9.1%	7.4%	12.9%	NA	NA
Excess Return vs. Sector	−8.9%	−3.1%	−6.5%	−4.5%	−3.1%	−9.4%	−8.4%	−5.8%	−17.7%	−11.7%	NA	NA
Value of $10,000	$22,712	$40,038	$27,053	$23,499	$41,185	$16,011	$41,168	$17,292	$1,578	$12,188	$69,380	$86,051
% 1-Year Outperformance	23.5%	41.2%	17.6%	17.6%	47.1%	17.6%	23.5%	29.4%	29.4%	52.9%	NA	NA
% 3-Year Outperformance	0.0%	33.3%	6.7%	13.3%	46.7%	6.7%	13.3%	26.7%	33.3%	53.3%	NA	NA
Maximum Gain	61.2%	64.7%	48.5%	46.7%	39.9%	71.0%	46.1%	192.0%	348.0%	161.0%	44.0%	41.4%
Maximum Loss	−51.1%	−14.4%	−29.4%	−21.9%	−17.5%	−45.4%	−25.7%	−61.6%	−88.7%	−84.7%	−19.1%	−18.1%
Standard Deviation	0.31	0.19	0.17	0.19	0.14	0.31	0.19	0.54	0.96	0.53	0.16	0.14
Beta (vs. Sector)	1.20	1.13	1.12	0.99	0.82	1.05	0.67	1.29	2.43	2.19	NA	NA
Alpha (vs. Sector)	−0.10	0.02	−0.05	−0.06	0.06	−0.13	0.00	−0.13	−0.22	−0.15	NA	NA
Portfolio Size	17	23	46	55	18	32	27	44	6	3	NA	NA

* Equal-weighted average of S&P 500 returns.
Source: Standard & Poor's Compustat Point in Time Database; Charter Oak Investment Systems, Inc., Venues® Data Engine

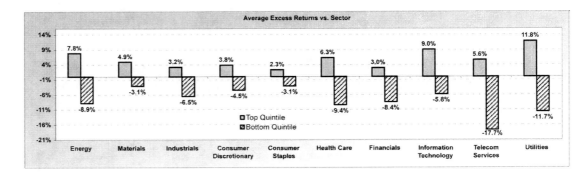

Figure 12.6 Multifactor Model by Economic Sector

exceptions seem to be the bottom quintiles of consumer staples and utilities, which have negative excess returns but are inconsistent. Notice also that maximum losses for the top quintiles of each sector are very low, with materials recording a 10% maximum loss and industrials a 5% loss. By combining a variety of investment factors, factors that examine a number of fundamental and market-based characteristics of a company and its stock, we create a robust single-factor strategy that works very well across economic sectors.

CHAPTER 13

Integrating the Strategies into Your Investment Approach

The "wisdom" of the ages implies *acting* on knowledge. The wise person learns the secret, acts on it and acquires wealth. The imprudent person learns the secret, but does *not* act on it.

Welles Wilder, *The Wisdom of the Ages in Acquiring Wealth*

Opportunity is missed by most people because it is dressed in overalls and looks like work.

Thomas Edison

Son, if you really want something in this life, you have to work for it. Now quiet! They're about to announce the lottery numbers.

Homer Simpson

The various strategies, screens, and models presented in this book provide the investor with fertile ground for developing his or her own quantitative investment techniques. But knowledge in itself is useless unless applied. This chapter focuses on application, and specifically on how a quantitative approach can be successfully employed in one's day-to-day investment process. Investment decision making usually revolves around generating investment ideas, determining through research which of those ideas to act on, and managing risk. This chapter shows how a quantitative approach can be used to help the investor—quantitative or qualitative—in each of these areas: idea generation, qualitatively vetting investment ideas, and risk management. In addition, it provides suggestions for the investor wishing to adopt a more purely quantitative investment process.

QUANTITATIVE SCREENS TO GENERATE INVESTING IDEAS

Any investment, from money spent on a shoeshine kit to a venture capital stake in a biotechnology firm, must start with an *idea*. For most stock investors, investment ideas occur somewhat at random. At best, the investor pores over financial periodicals, discovers what public company makes a popular product, or hears respected money managers discussing their stock picks on television. At worst, the investor buys shares of a company at which a relative works or follows a tip overheard at a dinner party. With regard to ideas, however, investors often overlook an investment maxim they would do well to heed: *a stock does not become attractive simply because it has come to your attention.*

The problem faced by investors, then, is how to find actionable investment ideas. There are a few ways to do this. One is to select and follow a group of businesses over time—a basic stock pool—and get to know them well, so as to spot attractive entry points.[1] Another is to do a lot of reading and listen to what professional investors have to say, *but to do one's own research*. More on this later. A third is to generate a list of potentially attractive stock investments, from a large universe of companies, by using a stock screening tool.

A well-constructed stock screen can provide an excellent starting point for selecting actionable investment ideas. I've seen a number of investment books that provide suggestions for stock screening. Although a lot of effort went into writing them, the problem I see with these books is twofold: in most cases, none of the screens presented have actually been tested; and many widely used screens, such as earnings growth and dividend yield, simply don't work. The investment screens presented in this chapter *do* work. Each screen is based on the individual building blocks and two-factor strategies presented in this book. In addition, we've tested each of the actual screens that follow to prove that, as written, they actually provide an investment portfolio that outperforms over time. You can use these screens, or screens like them, with the confidence that they will provide a promising list of potential investment ideas. Of course, not all of the stocks returned in a given screen will work—recall that a little more than half of the stocks in the top quintiles of our best two-factor investment strategies outperform each year. But with some investment research of your own, you should be able to develop a list of stocks with strong appreciation potential. (I'll provide suggestions on using the investment strategies presented in this book to do individual company research in the next section of this chapter.)

---

[1] Although this still begs the question of how to choose attractive companies for one's stock pool, from the point of view of both business strength and stock appreciation potential.

Since I don't know what screening program you'll be using,[2] the screens described here are written in general terms. Also, the ratio values used in each of these screens can be found in Appendix C, which provides the average portfolio values over time for each of the financial ratios used in our single-factor tests, by quintile. Finally, the results of a backtest done on each screen are presented below the screen description. You'll note that backtest results are often stronger than the results you saw for the corresponding quantitative tests presented in Chapters 4 through 10. The reason is that we've intentionally kept the output of these screens small, with portfolio sizes ranging from an average of 20 to 50. Also, for all of these screens, we've used the intersection of the values being tested, whereas the quantitative tests presented earlier use the top 20% for each quintile, no matter what the actual ratio values are. Therefore, the screens you'll see in this chapter present only those companies that rank highest on each investment factor.

Note that each screen includes only stocks with a current market capitalization greater than $500 million and a share price greater than $2. This is simply because stocks that do not meet these two criteria tend to be unduly volatile.

Two-Factor Screens

Screen Description
  1 Market Capitalization > 500
  2 Stock Price > 2
  3 EBIT/Invested Capital > 35%
  4 Free Cash Flow/Market Capitalization > 7%

Backtest Results

CAGR Strategy	CAGR Universe	Excess Return	% 1-Yr Outperf.	Max Gain	Max Loss	Sharpe Ratio	Beta	Alpha
21.3%	10.3%	10.9%	88.9%	68.2%	-2.5%	0.97	0.85	0.13

Figure 13.1 EBIT to Invested Capital and Free Cash Flow to Price

EBIT (earnings before interest and taxes) equals 12-month income from continuing operations plus interest expense plus income tax expense (see Figure 13.1). Operating

---

[2] The good news is that a variety of software-based and Internet browser-based screening tools are available to the individual and professional investor. Free Internet screening sites, as of this writing, are available from Yahoo!, Morningstar, and MSN Money, as well as a number of other sites. In particular, Yahoo! and MSN Money offer free downloadable screening software that provides both a number of screening criteria and flexibility in structuring the screens. Online brokerage firms often provide stock screening tools with a brokerage account membership. More complex screening applications are available for a fee from companies such as Standard & Poor's (Research Insight), Thomson Reuters, and Value Line.

income or net income can be substituted for EBIT, but in the latter case, the minimum value for the EBIT-to-invested capital ratio should be adjusted downward (i.e., to something below 35%). Invested capital is calculated as shareholders' equity plus long-term debt plus preferred stock plus minority interest. This calculation can be simplified by leaving out preferred stock and minority interest. Free cash flow (FCF) equals 12-month cash from operating activities minus 12-month capital expenditures. Market capitalization always refers to the market value of common equity (market price multiplied by common shares outstanding).

Notice the high Sharpe ratio (0.97) for this screen, as well as the very low maximum loss (2.5%). This shows us that the simple combination of strong income statement-based profitability, positive FCF, and a low valuation relative to cash provides a sound basis for stock selection.

Screen Description

1 Market Capitalization > 500
2 Stock Price > 2
3 Common Equity > 0
4 Enterprise Value > 0
5 Return on Equity >= 21%
6 Enterprise Value to EBITDA <= 7

Backtest Results

CAGR Strategy	CAGR Universe	Excess Return	% 1-Yr Outperf.	Max Gain	Max Loss	Sharpe Ratio	Beta	Alpha
17.6%	11.2%	6.4%	75.0%	49.3%	-14.7%	0.93	0.78	0.09

Figure 13.2 Return on Equity and Enterprise Value to EBITDA

We require that common equity and enterprise value (EV) be greater than zero (see Figure 13.2), because negative values could cause double negatives for return on equity (ROE) and EV to EBITDA (earnings before interest, taxes, depreciation, and amortization) ratios. ROE is calculated as 12-month income from continuing operations divided by total shareholders' equity. EV equals the market capitalization of common stock plus long-term debt minus cash and short-term investments. EBITDA equals income from continuing operations plus interest expense plus income tax expense plus depreciation and amortization. As with EBIT, above, operating income can be substituted for EBITDA (if this is done, the minimum value for the EV to EBITDA ratio might need to be increased slightly).

Screen Description
    1 Market Capitalization > 500
    2 Stock Price > 2
    3 Common Equity > 0
    4 Operating Cash Flow to Equity >= 38%
    5 Price to Sales <= 1

Backtest Results

CAGR Strategy	CAGR Universe	Excess Return	% 1-Yr Outperf.	Max Gain	Max Loss	Sharpe Ratio	Beta	Alpha
15.9%	10.3%	5.6%	83.3%	40.8%	-15.1%	0.81	0.75	0.08

Figure 13.3 Cash Return on Equity and Price to Sales

Operating cash flow to equity uses 12-month cash flow from operating activities divided by total stockholders' equity (see Figure 13.3). Price to sales is calculated as the market capitalization of common stock divided by 12-month sales.

Screen Description
    1 Market Capitalization > 500 mil
    2 Stock Price > $2
    3 2-Year Average EPS Growth >= 100%
    4 Price to Earnings(TTM) < 13
    5 Price to Earnings(TTM) >= 0

Backtest Results

CAGR Strategy	CAGR Universe	Excess Return	% 1-Yr Outperf.	Max Gain	Max Loss	Sharpe Ratio	Beta	Alpha
15.6%	11.2%	4.4%	70.0%	57.5%	-19.1%	0.72	0.95	0.05

Figure 13.4 Two-Year Average EPS Growth and Price to Earnings

This screen (see Figure 13.4) uses trailing 12-month (TTM) earnings per share (EPS) to calculate the price/earnings (P/E) ratio. The average analysts' estimate for the current year could also be used (and might slightly improve results). A constraint that the P/E ratio must be above zero is added to prevent companies with negative EPS from being included in the screen. This constraint could also be written as

$$EPS(TTM) > 0.$$

Screen Description
      1 Market Capitalization > 500
      2 Stock Price > 2
      3 Free Cash Flow to Market Cap < 27%
      4 Free Cash Flow to Market Cap >= 10%
      5 Price to Sales < 2
      6 Price to Sales >= 1

Backtest Results

CAGR Strategy	CAGR Universe	Excess Return	% 1-Yr Outperf.	Max Gain	Max Loss	Sharpe Ratio	Beta	Alpha
18.2%	10.3%	7.9%	77.8%	44.2%	-11.5%	0.89	0.59	0.13

Figure 13.5 Free Cash Flow to Price and Price to Sales

FCF equals 12-month cash flow from operations minus 12-month capital expenditures (see Figure 13.5). Price to sales is calculated as market capitalization divided by 12-month sales. Upper limits and lower limits are placed on valuation ratios to avoid outliers (unusual values that might indicate something other than an attractive valuation). Appendix C provides values for each single-factor strategy that can be used for both the upper and lower limits of a stock screen.

Screen Description
      1 Market Capitalization > 500
      2 Stock Price > 2
      3 Operating Income > 0
      4 Free Cash Flow to Operating Income > 80%
      5 Price to Sales < 0.8

Backtest Results

CAGR Strategy	CAGR Universe	Excess Return	% 1-Yr Outperf.	Max Gain	Max Loss	Sharpe Ratio	Beta	Alpha
19.0%	10.3%	8.7%	88.9%	49.3%	-17.7%	0.87	0.72	0.12

Figure 13.6 Free Cash Flow to Operating Income and Price to Sales

Net income or pretax income could be used in place of operating income in the FCF-to-operating income ratio (see Figure 13.6). The minimum value for the ratio value might have to be lowered in each of these cases, depending on resulting portfolio sizes.

Screen Description
1 Market Capitalization > 500
2 Stock Price > 2
3 Invested Capital > 0
4 Free Cash Flow to Invested Capital >= 16%
5 Price to Sales <= 0.9

Backtest Results

CAGR Strategy	CAGR Universe	Excess Return	% 1-Yr Outperf.	Max Gain	Max Loss	Sharpe Ratio	Beta	Alpha
18.6%	10.3%	8.3%	83.3%	43.7%	-6.3%	0.93	0.66	0.12

Figure 13.7 Cash Return on Invested Capital and Price to Sales

Cash return on invested capital (ROIC) is calculated as FCF (12-month operating cash flow less 12-month capital expenditures) divided by invested capital (common equity plus long-term debt plus preferred stock plus minority interest) (see Figure 13.7).

Screen Description
1 Market Capitalization > 500
2 Stock Price > 2
3 Common Shares Outstanding > 1 million
4 Enterprise Value > 0
5 1-Year Reduction in Common Shares > 3%
6 Enterprise Value to EBITDA < 8
7 Enterprise Value to EBITDA >= 4.5

Backtest Results

CAGR Strategy	CAGR Universe	Excess Return	% 1-Yr Outperf.	Max Gain	Max Loss	Sharpe Ratio	Beta	Alpha
15.6%	11.2%	4.4%	70.0%	49.5%	-11.6%	0.79	0.68	0.08

Figure 13.8 One-Year Reduction in Shares and Enterprise Value to EBITDA

One-year reduction in shares equals the latest number of common shares outstanding divided by common shares outstanding one year ago minus 1 (see Figure 13.8). The lower constraint for EV to EBITDA is used to screen out outliers.

Screen Description
   1 Market Capitalization > 500
   2 Stock Price > 2
   3 12-Month Price Change > 30%
   4 Enterprise Value to EBITDA < 8.3

Backtest Results

CAGR Strategy	CAGR Universe	Excess Return	% 1-Yr Outperf.	Max Gain	Max Loss	Sharpe Ratio	Beta	Alpha
16.3%	11.2%	5.1%	90.0%	51.7%	-13.2%	0.76	0.90	0.07

Figure 13.9 12-Month Price Change and Enterprise Value to EBITDA

Twelve-month price change is used as a proxy for seven-month relative strength (see Figure 13.9). Note that the 12-month price change value will vary depending on the market environment (in bull markets, use a higher percent change; coming out of bear markets or in sideways markets, use a lower percent change).

Screen Description
   1 Market Capitalization > 500
   2 Stock Price > 2
   3 Invested Capital > 0
   4 EBIT to Invested Capital < 40%
   5 EBIT to Invested Capital >= 23%
   6 Free Cash Flow to Invested Capital < 38%
   7 Free Cash Flow to Invested Capital >= 20%

Backtest Results

CAGR Strategy	CAGR Universe	Excess Return	% 1-Yr Outperf.	Max Gain	Max Loss	Sharpe Ratio	Beta	Alpha
16.9%	10.3%	6.6%	94.4%	49.1%	-8.5%	0.92	0.81	0.08

Figure 13.10 EBIT to Invested Capital and Cash Return on Invested Capital

This test looks at both income statement–based and cash flow statement-based profitability (see Figure 13.10). Results could be improved significantly by creating a three-factor test that adds a valuation factor (see Figure 13.15). Upper constraints are used to avoid outliers.

We require that capital expenditures be greater than zero (see Figure 13.11) to avoid double negatives that would arise from negative values for capital expenditures (which

Screen Description
    1 Market Capitalization > 500
    2 Stock Price > 2
    3 Capital Expenditures > 0
    4 Operating Cash Flow to Capex < 10.8
    5 Operating Cash Flow to Capex >= 3.5
    6 Price to Capex < 33.3

Backtest Results

CAGR Strategy	CAGR Universe	Excess Return	% 1-Yr Outperf.	Max Gain	Max Loss	Sharpe Ratio	Beta	Alpha
19.1%	10.3%	8.8%	77.8%	46.8%	-10.7%	0.97	0.68	0.12

Figure 13.11 Operating Cash Flow to Capex and Price to Capex

occur in rare cases when a company reports capex net of asset sales, etc.). Note the strong excess returns, low maximum loss, and high Sharpe ratio generated by this simple screen.

Three-Factor Screens

Screen Description
    1 Market Capitalization > 500
    2 Stock Price > 2
    3 Enterprise Value > 0
    4 EBIT to Invested Capital >= 26%
    5 Enterprise Value to EBITDA <= 7
    6 (Current Price - 52-Week Low) / (52-Week High - 52 Week Low) > 80%

Backtest Results

CAGR Strategy	CAGR Universe	Excess Return	% 1-Yr Outperf.	Max Gain	Max Loss	Sharpe Ratio	Beta	Alpha
21.1%	10.8%	10.3%	89.5%	78.1%	-15.0%	0.81	1.22	0.08

Figure 13.12 EBIT to Invested Capital, Enterprise Value to EBITDA, and 52-Week Price Range

See two-factor screens, (Figures 13.1–13.11), for definitions of financial items and ratios. Stocks within 10% of their 52-week highs could be substituted for the formula for 52-week price change (see Figure 13.12). This screen generates very strong and consistent excess returns, but is volatile, resulting in a moderate Sharpe ratio, a high Beta, and moderate Alpha.

Screen Description

1 Market Capitalization > 500
2 Stock Price > 2
3 Invested Capital > 0
4 Common Equity > 0
5 Free Cash Flow to Invested Capital >= 16%
6 Operating Cash Flow to Common Equity >= 38%
7 Price to Sales <= 1

Backtest Results

CAGR Strategy	CAGR Universe	Excess Return	% 1-Yr Outperf.	Max Gain	Max Loss	Sharpe Ratio	Beta	Alpha
20.0%	10.3%	9.6%	77.8%	40.7%	-5.4%	1.16	0.62	0.14

Figure 13.13 Cash Return on Invested Capital, Operating Cash Flow to Equity, and Price to Sales

This test combines two slightly different cash profitability measures (see Figure 13.13). While excess returns and the Sharpe ratio are very strong, the test's one weakness is that, like most cash flow strategies, it underperformed slightly recently (in 2006 and 2007).

Screen Description

1 Market Capitalization > 500
2 Stock Price > 2
3 Invested Capital > 0
4 Number of Common Shares Outstanding > 1 million
5 Free Cash Flow to Invested Capital >= 16%
6 1-Year Reduction in Shares >= 0.5%
7 Price to Sales <= 1

Backtest Results

CAGR Strategy	CAGR Universe	Excess Return	% 1-Yr Outperf.	Max Gain	Max Loss	Sharpe Ratio	Beta	Alpha
20.5%	10.3%	10.2%	77.8%	45.0%	-15.8%	1.01	0.74	0.13

Figure 13.14 Cash Return on Invested Capital, One-Year Reduction in Shares, and Price to Sales

Note that the one-year reduction in shares value is set to ⩾ 0.5% (see Figure 13.14), whereas > 3% is used in some of the two-factor screens. The more factors that are included in a screen, the looser the constraints must be in order to generate a sufficient number of companies that pass the screen. This is why I prefer more focused (two- or three-factor) screens to more complex screens.

Screen Description
    1 Market Capitalization > 500
    2 Stock Price > 2
    3 Invested Capital > 0
    4 EBIT to Invested Capital >= 23%
    5 Free Cash Flow to Invested Capital >= 20%
    6 Price to Sales <= 1

Backtest Results

CAGR Strategy	CAGR Universe	Excess Return	% 1-Yr Outperf.	Max Gain	Max Loss	Sharpe Ratio	Beta	Alpha
20.9%	10.3%	10.6%	83.3%	44.5%	-6.9%	1.13	0.66	0.14

Figure 13.15 EBIT to Invested Capital, Cash Return on Invested Capital, and Price to Sales

This screen (see Figure 13.15) shows the result of taking the two-factor income statement/cash profitability strategy, shown in Figure 13.10, and adding a valuation factor. Results are significantly stronger, as well as less volatile, producing a very high Sharpe ratio (1.13 for this strategy vs. 0.92 for the two-factor strategy shown in Figure 13.10) and Alpha (0.14 vs. 0.08).

Screen Description
    1 Market Capitalization > 500
    2 Stock Price > 2
    3 Common Equity > 0
    4 Enterprise Value > 0
    5 Return on Equity >= 21%
    6 Enterprise Value to EBITDA <= 7
    7 Capital Expenditures to Property, Plant & Equipment <= 13%

Backtest Results

CAGR Strategy	CAGR Universe	Excess Return	% 1-Yr Outperf.	Max Gain	Max Loss	Sharpe Ratio	Beta	Alpha
20.0%	11.2%	8.8%	75.0%	53.1%	-23.2%	0.87	0.78	0.12

Figure 13.16 Return on Equity, Enterprise Value to EBITDA, and Capex to Property Plant & Equipment

The capital expenditures to property, plant, and equipment (PP&E) ratio is calculated by dividing 12-month capital expenditures by the current value (or 12-month average value) for PP&E (see Figure 13.16).

Screen Description
    1 Market Capitalization > 500
    2 Stock Price > 2
    3 Common Equity > 0
    4 Long Term Debt (1 Year Ago) > 0
    5 Return on Equity >= 18%
    6 1-Year Reduction in Long Term Debt >= 13%
    7 Price to Book Value <= 2

Backtest Results

CAGR Strategy	CAGR Universe	Excess Return	% 1-Yr Outperf.	Max Gain	Max Loss	Sharpe Ratio	Beta	Alpha
23.3%	11.2%	12.1%	75.0%	65.6%	-13.2%	0.95	0.85	0.15

Figure 13.17 Return on Equity, One-Year Debt Reduction, and Price to Book Value

This is a simple screen (see Figure 13.17) that can be performed on most screening software and that generates high excess returns (an average of over 12%) and low volatility.

Screen Description
    1 Market Capitalization > 500
    2 Stock Price > 2
    3 Invested Capital > 0
    4 Common Equity > 0
    5 Free Cash Flow to Invested Capital >= 16%
    6 Return on Equity >= 20%
    7 Price to Sales <= 1

Backtest Results

CAGR Strategy	CAGR Universe	Excess Return	% 1-Yr Outperf.	Max Gain	Max Loss	Sharpe Ratio	Beta	Alpha
19.0%	10.3%	8.7%	83.3%	46.1%	-7.3%	1.00	0.68	0.12

Figure 13.18 Cash Return on Invested Capital, Return on Equity, and Price to Sales

This screen (see Figure 13.18) is a variation of Figure 13.13. It substitutes ROE for operating cash flow to equity. By using a combination of cash and income statement-based profitability, instead of two cash flow-based measures (as in Figure 13.13), excess returns decrease slightly, but consistency increases, and the major flaw of Figure 13.13—that it hasn't worked recently—is eliminated.

Screen Description
    1 Market Capitalization > 500
    2 Stock Price > 2
    3 Common Equity > 0
    4 Capital Expenditures > 0
    5 Operating Cash Flow to Capital Expenditures >= 3.5
    6 Price to Sales <= 1
    7 Return on Equity > 20%

Backtest Results

CAGR Strategy	CAGR Universe	Excess Return	% 1-Yr Outperf.	Max Gain	Max Loss	Sharpe Ratio	Beta	Alpha
21.8%	10.3%	11.5%	88.9%	67.9%	-19.4%	0.93	0.77	0.15

Figure 13.19 Operating Cash Flow to Capex, Price to Sales, and Return on Equity

This is a simple but strong cash flow, profitability, and valuation combination (see Figure 13.19). Note that this test is very similar to Figure 13.18. However, by using operating cash flow to capex here, instead of free cash flow to invested capital (in Figure 13.18), we significantly increase both excess returns and Alpha.

Screen Description
    1 Market Capitalization > 500
    2 Stock Price > 2
    3 Enterprise Value > 0
    4 Acquisitions = 0
    5 Capital Expenditures to Property, Plant & Equipment <= 15%
    6 Enterprise Value to EBITDA < 7

Backtest Results

CAGR Strategy	CAGR Universe	Excess Return	% 1-Yr Outperf.	Max Gain	Max Loss	Sharpe Ratio	Beta	Alpha
19.3%	11.2%	8.2%	80.0%	46.4%	-16.1%	1.02	0.79	0.11

Figure 13.20 Acquisitions, Capex to Property, Plant & Equipment, and Enterprise Value to EBITDA

The acquisitions data item in the Compustat database represents 12-month cash spent on business acquisitions (see Figure 13.20). It may seem surprising but is true that a simple strategy of avoiding companies that make business acquisitions improves excess returns. If this data item is not available, you can substitute a value from the one-year share reduction strategy, for example, one-year reduction in shares > 0.5%.

Screen Description
       1 Market Capitalization > 500
       2 Stock Price > 2
       3 Invested Capital > 0
       4 Capital Expenditures to Property, Plant & Equipment <= 15%
       5 Free Cash Flow to Invested Capital >= 16%
       6 Price to Sales <= 1

Backtest Results

CAGR Strategy	CAGR Universe	Excess Return	% 1-Yr Outperf.	Max Gain	Max Loss	Sharpe Ratio	Beta	Alpha
20.0%	10.3%	9.6%	77.8%	49.2%	-13.7%	0.88	0.77	0.13

Figure 13.21 Capex to Property, Plant & Equipment, Cash Return on Invested Capital, and Price to Sales

By changing the ratio values for this screen (see Figure 13.21), using the bottom quintile values for each financial ratio found in Appendix C, the investor could create a strong short-sale strategy.

VETTING INVESTMENT IDEAS

Once you have generated a list of potential investment ideas, you can use the strategies presented in this book to help narrow the list further. A concentrated portfolio of stocks that have been individually analyzed is likely to outperform the results of a larger quantitative screen that hasn't been looked at qualitatively. The following case study illustrates how the investment principles described in the preceding chapters can be applied in real life. In addition, I provide two templates in this section—one for company fundamental analysis and one for stock valuation analysis—that can be used to qualitatively evaluate the results of an investment screen (or any other potential stock investment).

Honeywell: A Case Study

In April 2008, Honeywell International, a $35 billion aerospace-industrial conglomerate, reported first quarter 2008 financial results. Honeywell's results provide an excellent case study of how the investment principles outlined in this book in the form of quantitative tests can be applied to qualitative investment research.

    First we'll take a look at Honeywell's statement of income. Figure 13.22 shows results for the March 2008 quarter versus the March 2007 quarter and also for the

(in millions, except per share)	Quarters			Years		
	Mar. '08	Mar. '07	% Chng.	2007	2006	% Chng.
Net sales	8,895	8,041	10.6%	34,589	31,367	10.3%
Costs of goods sold	6,672	6,150	8.5%	26,300	24,096	9.1%
Selling, gen., & admin. exp.	1,255	1,089	15.2%	4,565	4,210	8.4%
Operating profit	968	802	20.7%	3,724	3,061	21.7%
Operating profit margin	10.9%	10.0%		10.8%	9.8%	
Interest expense	115	97		456	374	
Other (income) expense	(22)	(11)		(53)	(111)	
Pretax income	875	716	22.2%	3,321	2,798	18.7%
Income taxes	232	190		877	720	
Tax rate %	26.5%	26.5%		26.4%	25.7%	
Net income	643	526	22.2%	2,444	2,078	17.6%
Earnings per share, diluted	$ 0.85	$ 0.66	30.2%	$ 3.16	$ 2.51	25.6%
Diluted shares outstanding	753	802	-6.1%	774	826	-6.3%

Source: company reports, Standard & Poor's Compustat

Figure 13.22 Honeywell International: Income Statement

preceding two full years (2007 and 2006). The first factor we can assess from the income statement is growth—not one of our strongest quantitative factors, but a widely followed measure of a company's success. Net sales grew 11% in the March quarter and 10% in all of 2007. More importantly, operating profit grew 21% in March (22% in 2007), net income grew 22% (18%), and earnings per share grew 30% (26%)—a strong showing by any account. EPS grew significantly faster than net income due to large share count reductions—this *is* one of our strong investment factors. Shares declined 6.3% in 2007 versus 2006 and 6.1% in the first quarter of 2008. If you look in Appendix C, you'll see that the maximum average value for the top quintile of the one-year reduction in shares strategy is 8.5%, and the minimum average value is 0%, so Honeywell would be classified well within the top quintile of this strategy. Also note that profitability is relatively strong, with operating margins at 11% for the March 2008 quarter, up from 10% for the March 2007 quarter. However, we'd also like to calculate another strong quantitative factor—return on invested capital—and to do this we have to turn to the balance sheet.

Figure 13.23 shows only those balance sheet items necessary to calculate profitability. Since Honeywell has no preferred stock or minority interest, invested capital

(in millions of dollars)	Mar. 31, 2008	Mar. 31, 2007	% Chng.	Dec. 31, 2007	Dec. 31, 2006	% Chng.
Long-term debt	6,576	4,704	39.8%	5,419	3,909	38.6%
+ Shareholders' equity	9,636	9,163	5.2%	9,222	9,720	-5.1%
= Invested capital	16,212	13,867		14,641	13,629	
	Quarters			Years		
	Mar. '08	Mar. '07		2007	2006	
Net income	643	526		2,444	2,078	
+ Interest expense	115	97		456	374	
+ Income taxes	232	190		877	720	
= Earns. before int. & taxes	990	813		3,777	3,172	
Return on invested capital	24.4%	23.5%		25.8%	23.3%	
Return on equity	26.7%	23.0%		26.5%	21.4%	

Source: company reports, Standard & Poor's Compustat

Figure 13.23 Honeywell International: Invested Capital and Profitability

consists entirely of long-term debt plus shareholders' equity. To calculate ROE, we simply take net income (from the income statement, Figure 13.22) and divide that into total stockholders' equity.[3] ROE for the most current periods (the quarter ended March 2008 and the year ended December 2007) is over 26%. In Appendix C, you'll find that average values for the top quintile of the ROE strategy range from about 18% (the minimum average portfolio value) to 44% (the maximum), so Honeywell falls squarely into the top quintile on ROE.[4] ROIC is calculated here as income before interest and taxes (EBIT) divided by total invested capital (long-term debt plus equity). EBIT to invested capital is over 24% for the quarter ended March 2008 and almost 26% for the year ended December 2007. Based on the EBIT-to-invested capital values found in Appendix C, this puts Honeywell in the bottom of the second quintile of this strategy. So, profitability, a strong quantitative factor, as measured by either ROE or ROIC, is another strong point for Honeywell. Next, we'll examine cash flows and capital expenditures.

Figure 13.24 looks at cash flow adequacy in a variety of ways. One-year FCF growth is one of our moderately strong building blocks. Honeywell grew FCF (operating cash flow after capital expenditures) by 25% for the first quarter of 2008 and 27% in

---

[3] Because ROE is traditionally calculated on a 12-month basis, to get the March 2008 and March 2007 ROE, I multiplied the quarterly net income values by 4 and divided this value by stockholders' equity.

[4] Of course, average ratios will vary by industry. Appendix C values for financial ratios will generally work well for industrial-type companies, but they will likely not work so well for financial companies and utilities.

(in millions of dollars)	Quarters			Years		
	Mar. '08	Mar. '07	% Chng.	2007	2006	% Chng.
Cash from operating activities	721	578	24.7%	3,911	3,211	21.8%
- Capital expenditures	150	120	25.0%	767	733	4.6%
= Free cash flow	571	458	24.7%	3,144	2,478	26.9%
Invested capital	16,212	13,867		14,641	13,629	
Cash ROIC	n/a	n/a		21.5%	18.2%	
Operating income	968	802		3,724	3,061	
Free cash flow to oper. inc.	59%	57%		84%	81%	
Property, plant & equip. (net)	5,012	4,710		4,985	4,797	
Capex to PP&E	n/a	n/a		15.4%	15.3%	
Operating cash flow to capex	4.8	4.8		5.1	4.4	

Source: company reports, Standard & Poor's Compustat

Figure 13.24 Honeywell International: Operating Cash Flows and Capex

all of 2007. Based on the values for one-year FCF growth in Appendix C, this puts Honeywell in the third quintile. Annual FCF divided by invested capital equals cash return on invested capital, one of our strongest building blocks. Cash ROIC for 2007 was 22%, up from 18% in 2006,[5] putting Honeywell in the top quintile of our cash ROIC strategy, based on average historical values.

Capital expenditures are another important investment factor. In general, companies that see their capital intensity (the level of capital expenditures required to stay competitive) increase tend to underperform, while companies that have low or declining capital intensity tend to outperform. Capex to PP&E—our barometer of changes in capital intensity—was 15% for Honeywell in both 2006 and 2007. This puts Honeywell in the second quintile of this investment strategy (Appendix C), indicating that capital intensity is unlikely to be increasing and may be decreasing. Operating cash flow to capex was nearly 5× in both 2007 and the first quarter of 2008, putting Honeywell in the bottom of the *first* quintile of this strategy and indicating that the ability to fund capital maintenance and expansion needs is strong.

On the whole, Honeywell has passed our fundamental analysis with flying colors, and from a fundamental viewpoint alone, would likely make a good investment. The qualitative investor would, of course, do additional research to determine business trends in Honeywell's major markets, its market share position in those markets,

---

[5] Because cash flows vary substantially from quarter to quarter, I don't annualize the March-quarter free cash flow numbers to calculate cash ROIC. Quarterly capex figures are also not annualized.

economic trends likely to effect the company, and so on. However, my goal here was simply to show how knowledge gained from the quantitative tests presented in this book could provide a sound basis for qualitative analysis.

A Company Evaluation Template

The investor using quantitatively based screens to identify potential investment ideas might use the techniques shown above to narrow the list of stocks that pass each screen. Just because a stock appears in a screen doesn't automatically make it a good investment idea. Keep in mind that quantitative analysis is a mechanical process that is usually quite limited in scope, so factors outside the scope of the screen often affect investment results. For example, a company might pass a profitability screen primarily because large asset write-offs have significantly reduced the value of stockholders' equity. Unless there is a good reason not to do so, these companies should be eliminated

Company Evaluation Template
HONEYWELL INTERNATIONAL INC (HON)   Fiscal Year End: December
(in millions of dollars, except ratios and per share amounts)

Fundamentals	2001	2002	2003	2004	2005	2006	2007
Income from Continuing Operations	−99	−220	1,344	1,281	1,581	2,078	2,444
+ Interest Expense	422	365	350	349	373	374	456
+ Income Taxes	−323	−725	296	399	742	720	877
= Earns. Bef. Interest & Taxes (EBIT)	0	−580	1,990	2,029	2,696	3,172	3,777
Stockholders' Equity	9,170	8,925	10,729	11,252	11,254	9,720	9,222
+ Long-Term Debt	4,731	4,719	4,961	4,069	3,082	3,909	5,419
+ Minority Interest	–	–	–	–	–	–	–
= Invested Capital	13,901	13,644	15,690	15,321	14,336	13,629	14,641
ROIC (EBIT / Invested Capital)	0.0%	−4.3%	12.7%	13.2%	18.8%	23.3%	25.8%
ROE (Inc. from Cont. Ops. / Stkhldrs' Equity)	−1.1%	−2.5%	12.5%	11.4%	14.0%	21.4%	26.5%
Operating Cash Flow	1,996	2,380	2,199	2,253	2,442	3,211	3,911
Capital Expenditures	876	671	655	629	684	733	767
= Free Cash Flow	1,120	1,709	1,544	1,624	1,758	2,478	3,144
Free Cash Flow Growth	–	52.6%	−9.7%	5.2%	8.3%	41.0%	26.9%
Free Cash Flow to EBIT	NM	395%	78%	80%	65%	78%	83%
Cash Return on Invested Capital	8.1%	12.5%	9.8%	10.6%	12.3%	18.2%	21.5%
Common Shares Outstanding (Diluted)	812	820	862	862	852	826	774
1-Year Increase/(Decrease) in Shares	–	1.0%	5.1%	0.0%	−1.2%	−3.1%	−6.3%
Long-Term Debt Outstanding	4,731	4,719	4,961	4,069	3,082	3,909	5,419
1-Year Increase/(Decrease) in LT Debt	–	−0.3%	5.1%	−18.0%	−24.3%	26.8%	38.6%
Property, Plant, & Equipment (PP&E)	4,933	4,055	4,295	4,331	4,658	4,797	4,985
Capital Expenditures to PP&E	17.8%	16.5%	15.3%	14.5%	14.7%	15.3%	15.4%
Operating Cash Flow to Capex	2.3	3.5	3.4	3.6	3.6	4.4	5.1
Earnings Per Share (Diluted)	−0.12	−0.27	1.56	1.49	1.86	2.51	3.16
EPS Growth	–	−125.0%	677.8%	−4.5%	24.8%	34.9%	25.9%

Source: Standard & Poor's Compustat, company reports

Figure 13.25 Company Evaluation Template: Fundamentals

from consideration. Also, while a company might look good on one investment factor, such as accrual accounting–based profitability, other investment factors, such as cash flow, might look terrible. Although there is no such thing as a perfect investment, a careful overall evaluation of companies that pass an investment screens should help to separate the winners from the losers.

The fundamental analysis template shown in Figure 13.25 summarizes all of the financial ratios used in our evaluation of Honeywell. While this template is simple compared to many of the sophisticated analysis techniques used on Wall Street, it covers the investment basics very well and can serve as a useful tool for the individual investor in vetting individual stocks. My experience is that simple but well understood approaches to investment analysis are often the best approaches.

The template uses seven years of annual data. A period of one or two years isn't enough to show the investor trends in fundamental data. For investors with an approximate 12-month investment horizon, 7 years provides a broad historical perspective without being academic. The investor may also want to add a column that shows the last 12-month values for each data item, to bring the template up to the present. The template can be easily constructed using Microsoft Excel or other spreadsheet software. Data items can be found in Securities and Exchange Commission Form 10-K filings and in company annual reports.

A Stock Evaluation Template

Equally important to fundamentals in evaluating any stock is a determination of the cheapness or dearness of its price. Valuation can be assessed in a number of ways. One widely used method, not well suited to quantitative analysis, is to calculate the discounted present value of projected future cash flows. Although this model is widely used in the investment world, we'll ignore it here. Instead, we'll prefer the much simpler valuation tests presented in the preceding chapters, which simply compared the valuation of one stock to that of all other stocks in our Universe. On average, low valuation stocks outperform, and high valuation stocks underperform.

However, valuation tests can be refined in a couple of ways. One is to compare a company's valuation to the average valuation for a group of peers. I didn't include peer valuations in the template in Figure 13.26 simply because it is difficult for the average investor to collect all this data. However, rows for peer comparisons could easily be added. Another valuation method is to compare a company's current valuation to its historical record. Ideally, one would do this using 10 years or more of data, to capture valuations at different points in the business cycle. However, the seven-year format used in Figure 13.26 should be sufficient for most purposes.

Stock Evaluation Template

HONEYWELL INTERNATIONAL INC (HON)

Price (March 31, '08): $56.42

Fiscal Year End: December

(in millions of dollars, except ratios and per share amounts)

Valuation	2001	2002	2003	2004	2005	2006	2007	Current
Market Value of Common Shares	44,112	42,832	41,807	44,047	44,210	37,284	37,847	42,001
+ Long-Term Debt	4,731	4,719	4,961	4,069	3,082	3,909	5,419	5,419
−Cash & Short-Term Investments	1,393	2,021	2,950	3,586	1,234	1,224	1,829	1,829
= Enterprise Value	47,450	45,530	43,818	44,530	46,058	39,969	41,437	45,591
Income from Continuing Operations	−99	−220	1,344	1,281	1,581	2,078	2,444	
+ Interest Expenses	422	365	350	349	373	374	456	
+ Income Taxes	−323	−725	296	399	742	720	877	
+ Depreciation & Amortization	723	730	661	650	697	794	837	
= EBITDA	723	150	2,651	2,679	3,393	3,966	4,614	
Enterprise Value to EBITDA	65.6	303.5	16.5	16.6	13.6	10.1	9.0	9.9
Free Cash Flow (from Fundamentals sheet)	1,120	1,709	1,544	1,624	1,758	2,478	3,144	
Free Cash Flow to Price	2.5%	4.0%	3.7%	3.7%	4.0%	6.6%	8.3%	7.5%
Earnings Per Share (Diluted)*	−0.12	−0.27	1.56	1.49	1.86	2.51	3.16	3.76
Price to Earnings	−451.1	−185.6	31.1	34.8	28.7	18.6	16.0	13.5
Sales	23,652	22,274	23,103	25,601	27,653	31,367	34,589	
Enterprise Value to Sales	2.0	2.0	1.9	1.7	1.7	1.3	1.2	1.3
Stockholders' Equity	9,170	8,925	10,729	11,252	11,254	9,720	9,222	
Price to Book Value	4.8	4.8	3.9	3.9	3.9	3.8	4.1	4.6

* The "Current" column for EPS contains the Wall Street analysts average EPS estimate for the current fiscal year.

Source: Standard & Poor's Compustat, company reports

Figure 13.26 Stock Evaluation Template: Valuation

Recall that our two strongest valuation metrics, which work for most industries, are enterprise value (EV) to EBITDA and free cash flow to price. These are presented in the template for Honeywell, along with price to earnings, EV to sales, and price to book value. A more sophisticated but easy to construct version of this template would be to calculate annual high and low values for each valuation metric, using the 52-week high and 52-week low stock prices for each year.[6] The investor could then compare the current valuation to the average 52-week high-low range, preferring to buy near low valuations and sell near high valuations.

Figure 13.26 shows that, as of the end of March 2008, Honeywell was selling at a discount to its historical average EV to EBITDA range, with an EV-to-EBITDA value of 10× versus historical values ranging from 9× to 17×.[7] Looking up the EV-to-EBITDA values in Appendix C, we see that average values for the third quintile range from 6.9× to 13.1×, so Honeywell would likely fall within this quintile. Honeywell fares much

---

[6] A 10-year format showing split-adjusted 52-week high and low historical prices can be found on the back of the Standard & Poor's Stock Report for a company, which can be found at many libraries and is also available online through a number of discount brokerage firms.

[7] I ignore the values of 66× in 2001 and 319× in 2002, because these were periods of unusually low earnings, and Honeywell was obviously *not* being valued on an EV-to-EBITDA basis.

better on FCF to price. Its current value is 7.5%, the next-to-highest value recorded over its seven-year history. Based on Appendix C results for FCF to price, Honeywell would fall within the second quintile. Without going further in our valuation exercise, we can see that while Honeywell is not priced like the cheapest stocks in our Universe, it seems to be priced attractively. Since Honeywell's fundamental performance over the past few years has been very strong, this is not surprising. My conclusion on Honeywell, based just on the fundamental and valuation data presented here, is that Honeywell would make a reasonably attractive purchase as of March–April 2008.

Quantitatively Based Risk Management

Quantitative risk management is a subject that usually involves modeling financial derivatives and other very complex tasks that have no relationship to the subject of this book. However, there are some simple applications of the quantitative techniques presented here that could be very useful for an equity research department or a group of portfolio managers seeking to manage risk. One application would be to use a multifactor model to maintain quantitative rankings on a group of stocks. Rankings from this list could be used in conjunction with qualitative recommendations from analysts or portfolio managers to ensure there is an appropriate balance between risk and expected return for a given security.

For example, let's say that we develop a quantitative model, based on the factors presented in this book, that ranks the largest 2,000 publicly traded U.S. companies. The model assigns each company in this universe a score from 1 to 100 based on its combined score on the individual investment factors evaluated. A company with a score of 99, for example, has a quantitative score that is greater than or equal to 99% of companies tested; a company with a score of 25 ranks higher than or equal to 25% of the companies tested. These scores could be used in conjunction with projected target prices from analysts/portfolio managers to limit risk. For example, companies with scores of 75 or higher might require only 20% potential upside to be put on a buy list. However, companies with scores from 50 to 74 might require 35% potential upside, and companies with scores from 25 to 49 might require 50%. Thus, companies with low quantitative rankings can be ranked as buys, but the analyst/portfolio manager must believe the opportunity is exceptional. Such a situation might well occur at the end of a bear market, such as occurred in 1991 or 2003, when stocks of low-profitability companies were severely beaten down. Although quantitative rankings for such stocks may be very low at this point, the analyst may see potential gains of 40%, 50%, or greater, thus justifying an "override" of the quantitative system.

Another method of proceeding is to create a quantitative model specifically aimed at selecting losing stocks. Several quantitative factors are particularly strong in this regard (i.e., they provide strong underperformance for the bottom quintile). These include operating cash flow to capex, external financing to assets, FCF to long-term debt, cash return on invested capital, EBITDA to invested capital, EV to EBITDA, economic profits, FCF to price, EV to sales, and capex to PP&E. These capital allocation, cash flow, valuation, profitability, and red flag strategies could be combined into a model that selects stocks of companies that are "at risk." This at risk list might be used as a "do not buy" list. Or perhaps, more appropriately, analysts and portfolio managers wishing to purchase (or recommend purchase of) stocks from this list would have to particularly justify such purchases.

CREATING QUANTITATIVE PORTFOLIOS

Investors may also take a more purely quantitative-driven approach to investing. Over time, various quantitative strategies have consistently outperformed. Using the quantitative strategies presented in this book, an investor could develop one or more quantitative models and invest funds on a quantitative basis only. I'll use a two-factor strategy as an example, although the quantitative model chosen might be much more sophisticated.

The economic profits and EV-to-EBITDA model presented in Chapter 4 generated excess returns for the top quintile of over 8%, over our 18-year test period, and was very consistent, underperforming significantly only in 1999–2000 and (modestly) in 2003–2004. The top quintile consists of 52 companies on average. The investor using this strategy might seek to narrow it slightly, taking the top 30 companies ranked by economic profits and EV to EBITDA. I would suggest investing in each of these companies in equal amounts. For example, once a year, the investor could invest $1,000 in each of 30 companies for a total of $30,000 invested. The portfolio would then be rebalanced or replaced the following year.[8]

Alternatively, the investor might purchase the top 10 stocks from this strategy (or the top 10 stocks not already owned) every quarter and hold each quarterly portfolio for a year. There are two major drawbacks to this approach: transaction costs are high, which could certainly eat away a portion of the expected excess return,[9] and portfolio stocks are not examined using any other quantitative or qualitative criteria. This latter fact means that the strategy might contain a predominance of companies from a certain industry, exposing the investor to undesired industry risk, or contain companies with strong historical results that are facing a deteriorating current environment. (For example, home

---

[8] In other words, the quantitative model would be rerun, and stocks not on the new list would be sold, while stocks on the new list but not already owned would be purchased.

[9] A brokerage such as FOLIOfn, which allows investors to buy and manage a basket of stocks at one time, might be used to minimize transaction fees. FOLIOfn also allows the investor to purchase and sell fractional shares.

builders came up repeatedly on quantitative screens in 2007, but continued to under-perform as industry fundamentals deteriorated.) On the other hand, the major advantage of a purely quantitative strategy is that it is mechanical, meaning that if the discipline is strictly followed, it will not be sabotaged by the investor's emotions.

Another approach an investor might take is to individually vet the stocks to be included in the quantitative portfolio. So, for example, the investor might run the top quintile of the economic profits and EV-to-EBITDA strategy each quarter, resulting in a list of about 50 stocks (depending on the universe used). The investor would then look at a variety of fundamental and valuation factors for each stock (the company and stock evaluation templates presented above would make a good starting point for this) in order to qualitatively select those stocks to be included in the portfolio and those stocks to be excluded. The investor might select five new stocks each quarter or each month and invest equal amounts in each. Again, the holding period for each quarterly or monthly portfolio would be 12 months. This approach can reduce transaction fees and has the potential to improve the performance of the overall strategy, depending on the individual's stock-picking skills. However, it has the major drawback of introducing emotion back into the investing process, meaning that the investor-selected stocks might significantly underperform the quantitative portfolio alone.

A FINAL THOUGHT

The strategies and screens presented in this book show that a quantitative approach to investing can aid the investor in his or her search for Alpha—above market investment performance—and that certain essential characteristics (the *basics*) that change little over time drive future stock market results. I believe that a combined quantitative/qualitative approach to investing is capable of yielding strong investment results, perhaps superior to those easily obtained by either approach alone. I also believe that a thorough understanding of "what works in the stock market," from a quantitative point of view, can help inform the investment decisions of any investor. I hope that the strategies and tests presented in this book will help the beginning investor to invest "based on the facts that matter," and not on tips and emotion, and inspire the professional investor to seek a more integrated investment approach that further expands and develops the quantitative principles presented here. Finally, while buying lottery tickets is certainly the easiest way to *try* to make money (as our friend Homer Simpson attested to at the beginning of the chapter), I hope that your investing approach is much more profitable and at least as much fun.

THE BUILDING BLOCKS

TABLE A.1

Building Blocks in Chapter Sequence

Strategy	Excess Returns by Quintile					Outperf.	Underper.	Sharpe Ratio	
	Q1	Q2	Q3	Q4	Q5	Q1	Q5	Q1	Q5
Profitability									
Return on Invested Capital	2.3%	1.5%	0.6%	0.1%	−4.3%	69%	74%	0.69	0.13
EBITDA-Capex to Invested Capital	2.6%	0.9%	0.6%	0.2%	−4.5%	71%	75%	0.76	0.13
EBITDA to Invested Capital	2.3%	2.0%	0.9%	0.3%	−5.2%	69%	79%	0.73	0.10
EBIT to Invested Capital	2.2%	1.2%	1.3%	0.2%	−4.7%	68%	77%	0.71	0.12
Return on Equity	2.2%	1.4%	0.8%	−0.1%	−3.6%	68%	73%	0.67	0.17
Return on Assets	1.4%	0.4%	0.4%	1.9%	−3.0%	52%	64%	0.56	0.18
Economic Profits	2.7%	1.3%	1.4%	0.3%	−0.9%	65%	65%	0.78	0.32
Economic Profits (No Beta)	2.7%	1.0%	1.1%	0.5%	−1.4%	66%	64%	0.74	0.30
Economic Profits (P/S instead of Beta)	3.2%	1.9%	1.7%	0.3%	−3.2%	65%	64%	0.73	0.21
Economic Profits (Cash ROIC & P/S)	5.1%	2.3%	1.0%	−1.1%	−5.5%	76%	75%	0.87	0.10
Valuation									
Free Cash Flow to Price	5.6%	2.7%	0.3%	−3.7%	−4.5%	78%	81%	0.78	0.14
Enterprise Value to EBITDA	5.3%	1.9%	0.3%	−2.3%	−4.9%	75%	71%	0.84	0.10
Price to Earnings (Curr. FY EPS Est.)	4.7%	1.2%	0.0%	−1.9%	−2.2%	66%	58%	0.67	0.17
Price to Earnings plus Dividends	3.8%	1.6%	0.3%	−1.9%	−2.0%	62%	57%	0.68	0.18
Enterprise Value to Sales	3.6%	1.3%	0.3%	0.0%	−4.7%	64%	69%	0.68	0.12
Dividend plus Share Repurchase Yield	2.4%	1.4%	0.0%	−0.1%	−4.3%	52%	74%	0.75	0.15
Price to Book Value	3.6%	1.5%	−0.3%	−2.4%	−1.9%	62%	60%	0.61	0.24
Cash Flow									
Free Cash Flow to Oper. Income	5.0%	2.6%	0.1%	−2.9%	−3.8%	75%	78%	0.68	0.17
Cash Return on Invested Capital	5.0%	2.4%	0.3%	−1.4%	−5.9%	79%	76%	0.83	0.07
FCF + Share Repurch. + Div. to Price	5.1%	2.1%	0.4%	−2.0%	−5.2%	76%	83%	0.79	0.10
Growth									
Free Cash Flow Per Share Score	3.5%	1.9%	1.0%	−0.6%	−2.7%	80%	68%	0.81	0.33
Earnings Per Share Score	1.9%	0.7%	0.6%	−0.3%	−0.3%	56%	57%	0.58	0.39
2 Year Capex Growth (Low to High)	2.1%	2.0%	0.8%	0.6%	−3.1%	64%	73%	0.58	0.26
Capital Allocation									
Net Share Repurch. to Inv. Cap.	2.5%	1.7%	0.6%	−0.5%	−4.9%	68%	73%	0.78	0.12
1 Year Reduction in Shares	3.1%	1.1%	1.7%	1.5%	−5.2%	69%	79%	0.81	0.14
1 Year Reduct. in LT Debt	0.0%	2.7%	2.1%	0.5%	−2.8%	68%	88%	0.46	0.33
Net Debt Reduction to Inv. Cap.	1.5%	2.1%	−1.1%	0.1%	−3.0%	65%	75%	0.61	0.28
Extern. Fin. to Assets (Low to High)	3.1%	2.3%	1.8%	−0.9%	−6.7%	68%	79%	0.77	0.06
3 Year Capex to Invested Capital	1.0%	1.9%	1.3%	−0.4%	−1.3%	66%	66%	0.59	0.38
Acquisitions to Inv. Cap. (Low to High)	2.9%	1.3%	−0.5%	−1.5%	−3.0%	75%	75%	0.69	0.32
Price Momentum									
7 Month Relative Strength	3.3%	0.7%	0.5%	−0.1%	−3.4%	60%	74%	0.44	0.22
88/36 Month Relative Strength	2.6%	1.1%	0.9%	1.0%	−1.5%	55%	61%	0.55	0.30
52 Week Price Range	4.3%	2.1%	0.0%	−2.2%	−3.9%	75%	75%	0.69	0.20
28/16 Week Relative Strength Index	6.2%	1.8%	−0.6%	−1.3%	−3.2%	70%	77%	0.70	0.26
Red Flags									
Total Debt to Inv. Cap. (Low to High)	2.3%	0.6%	0.2%	−1.5%	−1.3%	65%	60%	0.57	0.27
Free Cash Flow to Long-Term Debt	3.5%	2.5%	1.2%	−0.7%	−5.9%	65%	75%	0.71	0.07
Capex to PP&E (Low to High)	2.1%	1.0%	0.5%	−0.2%	−3.8%	62%	69%	0.67	0.15
Oper. Cash Flow to Capex	4.2%	2.4%	0.9%	−0.4%	−7.2%	74%	79%	0.71	0.02
Oper. Cash Flow to Capex + Interest	3.1%	2.1%	0.4%	1.3%	−5.5%	67%	78%	0.74	0.09
1 Year Chg. in Inventory Turnover	1.6%	1.3%	1.6%	0.2%	−3.0%	61%	81%	0.54	0.29
1 Yr. Chg. in Invent. + Rcvbls. Turn.	1.3%	1.8%	1.9%	0.2%	−3.7%	52%	75%	0.51	0.25
Depreciation to Invested Capital	1.7%	1.8%	0.5%	−0.8%	−2.2%	68%	74%	0.59	0.33

T A B L E   A.2

Building Blocks: Top Quintile by Excess Returns

Strategy	Excess Returns by Quintile					Outperf.	Underper.	Sharpe Ratio	
	Q1	Q2	Q3	Q4	Q5	Q1	Q5	Q1	Q5
28/16 Week Relative Strength Index	6.2%	1.8%	−0.6%	−1.3%	−3.2%	70%	77%	0.70	0.26
Free Cash Flow to Price	5.6%	2.7%	0.3%	−3.7%	−4.5%	78%	81%	0.78	0.14
Enterprise Value to EBITDA	5.3%	1.9%	0.3%	−2.3%	−4.9%	75%	71%	0.84	0.10
FCF + Shr. Repur. + Div. to Price	5.1%	2.1%	0.4%	−2.0%	−5.2%	76%	83%	0.79	0.10
Economic Profits (Cash ROIC & P/S)	5.1%	2.3%	1.0%	−1.1%	−5.5%	76%	75%	0.87	0.10
Cash Return on Invested Capital	5.0%	2.4%	0.3%	−1.4%	−5.9%	79%	76%	0.83	0.07
Free Cash Flow to Operating Income	5.0%	2.6%	0.1%	−2.9%	−3.8%	75%	78%	0.68	0.17
Price to Earnings (Current FY EPS Est.)	4.7%	1.2%	0.0%	−1.9%	−2.2%	66%	58%	0.67	0.17
52 Week Price Range	4.3%	2.1%	0.0%	−2.2%	−3.9%	75%	75%	0.69	0.20
Oper. Cash Flow to Capex	4.2%	2.4%	0.9%	−0.4%	−7.2%	74%	79%	0.71	0.02
Price to Earnings plus Dividends	3.8%	1.6%	0.3%	−1.9%	−2.0%	62%	57%	0.68	0.18
Enterprise Value to Sales	3.6%	1.3%	0.3%	0.0%	−4.7%	64%	69%	0.68	0.12
Price to Book Value	3.6%	1.5%	−0.3%	−2.4%	−1.9%	62%	60%	0.61	0.24
Free Cash Flow to Long-Term Debt	3.5%	2.5%	1.2%	−0.7%	−5.9%	65%	75%	0.71	0.07
Free Cash Flow Per Share Score	3.5%	1.9%	1.0%	−0.6%	−2.7%	80%	68%	0.81	0.33
7 Month Relative Strength	3.3%	0.7%	0.5%	−0.1%	−3.4%	60%	74%	0.44	0.22
Economic Profits (P/S instead of Beta)	3.2%	1.9%	1.7%	0.3%	−3.2%	65%	64%	0.73	0.21
1 Year Reduction in Shares	3.1%	1.1%	1.7%	1.5%	−5.2%	69%	79%	0.81	0.14
Oper. Cash Flow to Capex + Interest	3.1%	2.1%	0.4%	1.3%	−5.5%	67%	78%	0.74	0.09
Extern. Fin. to Assets (Low to High)	3.1%	2.3%	1.8%	−0.9%	−6.7%	68%	79%	0.77	0.06
Acquisitions to Inv. Cap. (Low to High)	2.9%	1.3%	−0.5%	−1.5%	−3.0%	75%	75%	0.69	0.32
Economic Profits	2.7%	1.3%	1.4%	0.3%	−0.9%	65%	65%	0.78	0.32
Economic Profits (No Beta)	2.7%	1.0%	1.1%	0.5%	−1.4%	66%	64%	0.74	0.30
88/36 Month Relative Strength	2.6%	1.1%	0.9%	1.0%	−1.5%	55%	61%	0.55	0.30
EBITDA-Capex to Invested Capital	2.6%	0.9%	0.6%	0.2%	−4.5%	71%	75%	0.76	0.13
Net Shr. Repurchase to Inv. Cap.	2.5%	1.7%	0.6%	−0.5%	−4.9%	68%	73%	0.78	0.12
Dividend plus Share Repurchase Yield	2.4%	1.4%	0.0%	−0.1%	−4.3%	52%	74%	0.75	0.15
Return on Invested Capital	2.3%	1.5%	0.6%	0.1%	−4.3%	69%	74%	0.69	0.13
Total Debt to Invested Capital	2.3%	0.6%	0.2%	−1.5%	−1.3%	65%	60%	0.57	0.27
EBITDA to Invested Capital	2.3%	2.0%	0.9%	0.3%	−5.2%	69%	79%	0.73	0.10
Return on Equity	2.2%	1.4%	0.8%	−0.1%	−3.6%	68%	73%	0.67	0.17
EBIT to Invested Capital	2.2%	1.2%	1.3%	0.2%	−4.7%	68%	77%	0.71	0.12
2 Year Capex Growth	2.1%	2.0%	0.8%	0.6%	−3.1%	64%	73%	0.58	0.26
Capex to PP&E (Low to High)	2.1%	1.0%	0.5%	−0.2%	−3.8%	62%	69%	0.67	0.15
Earnings Per Share Score	1.9%	0.7%	0.6%	−0.3%	−0.3%	56%	57%	0.58	0.39
Depreciation to Invested Capital	1.7%	1.8%	0.5%	−0.8%	−2.2%	68%	74%	0.59	0.33
1 Year Change in Inventory Turnover	1.6%	1.3%	1.6%	0.2%	−3.0%	61%	81%	0.54	0.29
Net Debt Reduction to Invested Capital	1.5%	2.1%	−1.1%	0.1%	−3.0%	65%	75%	0.61	0.28
Return on Assets	1.4%	0.4%	0.4%	1.9%	−3.0%	52%	64%	0.56	0.18
1 Yr. Chg. in Invent. + Rcvbls. Turn.	1.3%	1.8%	1.9%	0.2%	−3.7%	52%	75%	0.51	0.25
3 Year Capex to Invested Capital	1.0%	1.9%	1.3%	−0.4%	−1.3%	66%	66%	0.59	0.38
1 Year Reduction in Long-Term Debt	0.0%	2.7%	2.1%	0.5%	−2.8%	68%	88%	0.46	0.33

TABLE A.3

Building Blocks: Top Quintile by Sharpe Ratio

Strategy	Excess Returns by Quintile					Outperf.	Underper.	Sharpe Ratio	
	Q1	Q2	Q3	Q4	Q5	Q1	Q5	Q1	Q5
Economic Profits (Cash ROIC & P/S)	5.1%	2.3%	1.0%	−1.1%	−5.5%	76%	75%	0.87	0.10
Enterprise Value to EBITDA	5.3%	1.9%	0.3%	−2.3%	−4.9%	75%	71%	0.84	0.10
Cash Return on Invested Capital	5.0%	2.4%	0.3%	−1.4%	−5.9%	79%	76%	0.83	0.07
1 Year Reduction in Shares	3.1%	1.1%	1.7%	1.5%	−5.2%	69%	79%	0.81	0.14
Free Cash Flow Per Share Score	3.5%	1.9%	1.0%	−0.6%	−2.7%	80%	68%	0.81	0.33
FCF + Shr. Repur. + Div. to Price	5.1%	2.1%	0.4%	−2.0%	−5.2%	76%	83%	0.79	0.10
Economic Profits	2.7%	1.3%	1.4%	0.3%	−0.9%	65%	65%	0.78	0.32
Free Cash Flow to Price	5.6%	2.7%	0.3%	−3.7%	−4.5%	78%	81%	0.78	0.14
Net Share Repurchase to Inv. Cap.	2.5%	1.7%	0.6%	−0.5%	−4.9%	68%	73%	0.78	0.12
Extern. Fin. to Assets (Low to High)	3.1%	2.3%	1.8%	−0.9%	−6.7%	68%	79%	0.77	0.06
EBITDA-Capex to Invested Capital	2.6%	0.9%	0.6%	0.2%	−4.5%	71%	75%	0.76	0.13
Dividend plus Share Repurchase Yield	2.4%	1.4%	0.0%	−0.1%	−4.3%	52%	74%	0.75	0.15
Oper. Cash Flow to Capex + Interest	3.1%	2.1%	0.4%	1.3%	−5.5%	67%	78%	0.74	0.09
Economic Profits (No Beta)	2.7%	1.0%	1.1%	0.5%	−1.4%	66%	64%	0.74	0.30
EBITDA to Invested Capital	2.3%	2.0%	0.9%	0.3%	−5.2%	69%	79%	0.73	0.10
Economic Profits (P/S instead of Beta)	3.2%	1.9%	1.7%	0.3%	−3.2%	65%	64%	0.73	0.21
Free Cash Flow to Long-Term Debt	3.5%	2.5%	1.2%	−0.7%	−5.9%	65%	75%	0.71	0.07
Oper. Cash Flow to Capex	4.2%	2.4%	0.9%	−0.4%	−7.2%	74%	79%	0.71	0.02
EBIT to Invested Capital	2.2%	1.2%	1.3%	0.2%	−4.7%	68%	77%	0.71	0.12
28/16 Week Relative Strength Index	6.2%	1.8%	−0.6%	−1.3%	−3.2%	70%	77%	0.70	0.26
Return on Invested Capital	2.3%	1.5%	0.6%	0.1%	−4.3%	69%	74%	0.69	0.13
52 Week Price Range	4.3%	2.1%	0.0%	−2.2%	−3.9%	75%	75%	0.69	0.20
Acquisitions to Inv. Cap. (Low to High)	2.9%	1.3%	−0.5%	−1.5%	−3.0%	75%	75%	0.69	0.32
Free Cash Flow to Operating Income	5.0%	2.6%	0.1%	−2.9%	−3.8%	75%	78%	0.68	0.17
Enterprise Value to Sales	3.6%	1.3%	0.3%	0.0%	−4.7%	64%	69%	0.68	0.12
Price to Earnings plus Dividends	3.8%	1.6%	0.3%	−1.9%	−2.0%	62%	57%	0.68	0.18
Price to Earnings (Current FY EPS Est.)	4.7%	1.2%	0.0%	−1.9%	−2.2%	66%	58%	0.67	0.17
Return on Equity	2.2%	1.4%	0.8%	−0.1%	−3.6%	68%	73%	0.67	0.17
Capex to PP&E (Low to High)	2.1%	1.0%	0.5%	−0.2%	−3.8%	62%	69%	0.67	0.15
Net Debt Reduction to Invested Capital	1.5%	2.1%	−1.1%	0.1%	−3.0%	65%	75%	0.61	0.28
Price to Book Value	3.6%	1.5%	−0.3%	−2.4%	−1.9%	62%	60%	0.61	0.24
3 Year Capex to Invested Capital	1.0%	1.9%	1.3%	−0.4%	−1.3%	66%	66%	0.59	0.38
Depreciation to Invested Capital	1.7%	1.8%	0.5%	−0.8%	−2.2%	68%	74%	0.59	0.33
2 Year Capex Growth	2.1%	2.0%	0.8%	0.6%	−3.1%	64%	73%	0.58	0.26
Earnings Per Share Score	1.9%	0.7%	0.6%	−0.3%	−0.3%	56%	57%	0.58	0.39
Total Debt to Invested Capital	2.3%	0.6%	0.2%	−1.5%	−1.3%	65%	60%	0.57	0.27
Return on Assets	1.4%	0.4%	0.4%	1.9%	−3.0%	52%	64%	0.56	0.18
88/36-Month Relative Strength	2.6%	1.1%	0.9%	1.0%	−1.5%	55%	61%	0.55	0.30
1 Year Chg. in Invent. Turnover	1.6%	1.3%	1.6%	0.2%	−3.0%	61%	81%	0.54	0.29
1 Yr. Chg. in Invent. + Rcvbls. Turn.	1.3%	1.8%	1.9%	0.2%	−3.7%	52%	75%	0.51	0.25
1 Year Reduction in Long-Term Debt	0.0%	2.7%	2.1%	0.5%	−2.8%	68%	88%	0.46	0.33
7 Month Relative Strength	3.3%	0.7%	0.5%	−0.1%	−3.4%	60%	74%	0.44	0.22

TABLE A.4

Building Blocks: Bottom Quintile by Excess Returns

Strategy	Excess Returns by Quintile					Outperf.	Underper.	Sharpe Ratio	
	Q1	Q2	Q3	Q4	Q5	Q1	Q5	Q1	Q5
Oper. Cash Flow to Capex	4.2%	2.4%	0.9%	−0.4%	−7.2%	74%	79%	0.71	0.02
Extern. Fin. to Assets (Low to High)	3.1%	2.3%	1.8%	−0.9%	−6.7%	68%	79%	0.77	0.06
Cash Return on Invested Capital	5.0%	2.4%	0.3%	−1.4%	−5.9%	79%	76%	0.83	0.07
Free Cash Flow to Long-Term Debt	3.5%	2.5%	1.2%	−0.7%	−5.9%	65%	75%	0.71	0.07
Economic Profits (Cash ROIC & P/S)	5.1%	2.3%	1.0%	−1.1%	−5.5%	76%	75%	0.87	0.10
Oper. Cash Flow to Capex + Interest	3.1%	2.1%	0.4%	1.3%	−5.5%	67%	78%	0.74	0.09
EBITDA to Invested Capital	2.3%	2.0%	0.9%	0.3%	−5.2%	69%	79%	0.73	0.10
1 Year Reduction in Shares	3.1%	1.1%	1.7%	1.5%	−5.2%	69%	79%	0.81	0.14
FCF + Shr. Repur. + Div. to Price	5.1%	2.1%	0.4%	−2.0%	−5.2%	76%	83%	0.79	0.10
Enterprise Value to EBITDA	5.3%	1.9%	0.3%	−2.3%	−4.9%	75%	71%	0.84	0.10
Net Share Repurchase to Inv. Cap.	2.5%	1.7%	0.6%	−0.5%	−4.9%	68%	73%	0.78	0.12
EBIT to Invested Capital	2.2%	1.2%	1.3%	0.2%	−4.7%	68%	77%	0.71	0.12
Enterprise Value to Sales	3.6%	1.3%	0.3%	0.0%	−4.7%	64%	69%	0.68	0.12
EBITDA-Capex to Invested Capital	2.6%	0.9%	0.6%	0.2%	−4.5%	71%	75%	0.76	0.13
Free Cash Flow to Price	5.6%	2.7%	0.3%	−3.7%	−4.5%	78%	81%	0.78	0.14
Return on Invested Capital	2.3%	1.5%	0.6%	0.1%	−4.3%	69%	74%	0.69	0.13
Dividend plus Share Repurchase Yield	2.4%	1.4%	0.0%	−0.1%	−4.3%	52%	74%	0.75	0.15
52 Week Price Range	4.3%	2.1%	0.0%	−2.2%	−3.9%	75%	75%	0.69	0.20
Free Cash Flow to Operating Income	5.0%	2.6%	0.1%	−2.9%	−3.8%	75%	78%	0.68	0.17
Capex to PP&E (Low to High)	2.1%	1.0%	0.5%	−0.2%	−3.8%	62%	69%	0.67	0.15
1 Yr. Chg. in Invt. + Rcvbls. Turn.	1.3%	1.8%	1.9%	0.2%	−3.7%	52%	75%	0.51	0.25
Return on Equity	2.2%	1.4%	0.8%	−0.1%	−3.6%	68%	73%	0.67	0.17
7 Month Relative Strength	3.3%	0.7%	0.5%	−0.1%	−3.4%	60%	74%	0.44	0.22
28/16 Week Relative Strength Index	6.2%	1.8%	−0.6%	−1.3%	−3.2%	70%	77%	0.70	0.26
Economic Profits (P/S instead of Beta)	3.2%	1.9%	1.7%	0.3%	−3.2%	65%	64%	0.73	0.21
2 Year Capex Growth	2.1%	2.0%	0.8%	0.6%	−3.1%	64%	73%	0.58	0.26
Return on Assets	1.4%	0.4%	0.4%	1.9%	−3.0%	52%	64%	0.56	0.18
Net Debt Reduction to Invested Capital	1.5%	2.1%	−1.1%	0.1%	−3.0%	65%	75%	0.61	0.28
Acquisitions to Inv. Cap. (Low to High)	2.9%	1.3%	−0.5%	−1.5%	−3.0%	75%	75%	0.69	0.32
1 Yr. Chg. in Inventory Turnover	1.6%	1.3%	1.6%	0.2%	−3.0%	61%	81%	0.54	0.29
1 Year Reduction in Long-Term Debt	0.0%	2.7%	2.1%	0.5%	−2.8%	68%	88%	0.46	0.33
Free Cash Flow Per Share Score	3.5%	1.9%	1.0%	−0.6%	−2.7%	80%	68%	0.81	0.33
Price to Earnings (Current FY EPS Est.)	4.7%	1.2%	0.0%	−1.9%	−2.2%	66%	58%	0.67	0.17
Depreciation to Invested Capital	1.7%	1.8%	0.5%	−0.8%	−2.2%	68%	74%	0.59	0.33
Price to Earnings plus Dividends	3.8%	1.6%	0.3%	−1.9%	−2.0%	62%	57%	0.68	0.18
Price to Book Value	3.6%	1.5%	−0.3%	−2.4%	−1.9%	62%	60%	0.61	0.24
88/36 Month Relative Strength	2.6%	1.1%	0.9%	1.0%	−1.5%	55%	61%	0.55	0.30
Economic Profits (No Beta)	2.7%	1.0%	1.1%	0.5%	−1.4%	66%	64%	0.74	0.30
Total Debt to Invested Capital	2.3%	0.6%	0.2%	−1.5%	−1.3%	65%	60%	0.57	0.27
3 Year Capex to Invested Capital	1.0%	1.9%	1.3%	−0.4%	−1.3%	66%	66%	0.59	0.38
Economic Profits	2.7%	1.3%	1.4%	0.3%	−0.9%	65%	65%	0.78	0.32
Earnings Per Share Score	1.9%	0.7%	0.6%	−0.3%	−0.3%	56%	57%	0.58	0.39

TABLE A.5

Building Blocks: Bottom Quintile by Sharpe Ratio

Strategy	Excess Returns by Quintile					Outperf.	Underper.	Sharpe Ratio	
	Q1	Q2	Q3	Q4	Q5	Q1	Q5	Q1	Q5
Oper. Cash Flow to Capex	4.2%	2.4%	0.9%	−0.4%	−7.2%	74%	79%	0.71	0.02
Extern. Fin. to Assets (Low to High)	3.1%	2.3%	1.8%	−0.9%	−6.7%	68%	79%	0.77	0.06
Free Cash Flow to Long-Term Debt	3.5%	2.5%	1.2%	−0.7%	−5.9%	65%	75%	0.71	0.07
Cash Return on Invested Capital	5.0%	2.4%	0.3%	−1.4%	−5.9%	79%	76%	0.83	0.07
Oper. Cash Flow to Capex + Interest	3.1%	2.1%	0.4%	1.3%	−5.5%	67%	78%	0.74	0.09
EBITDA to Invested Capital	2.3%	2.0%	0.9%	0.3%	−5.2%	69%	79%	0.73	0.10
Enterprise Value to EBITDA	5.3%	1.9%	0.3%	−2.3%	−4.9%	75%	71%	0.84	0.10
Economic Profits (Cash ROIC & P/S)	5.1%	2.3%	1.0%	−1.1%	−5.5%	76%	75%	0.87	0.10
FCF + Shr. Repur. + Div. to Price	5.1%	2.1%	0.4%	−2.0%	−5.2%	76%	83%	0.79	0.10
Enterprise Value to Sales	3.6%	1.3%	0.3%	0.0%	−4.7%	64%	69%	0.68	0.12
Net Share Repurchase to Inv. Cap.	2.5%	1.7%	0.6%	−0.5%	−4.9%	68%	73%	0.78	0.12
EBIT to Invested Capital	2.2%	1.2%	1.3%	0.2%	−4.7%	68%	77%	0.71	0.12
Return on Invested Capital	2.3%	1.5%	0.6%	0.1%	−4.3%	69%	74%	0.69	0.13
EBITDA-Capex to Invested Capital	2.6%	0.9%	0.6%	0.2%	−4.5%	71%	75%	0.76	0.13
1 Year Reduction in Shares	3.1%	1.1%	1.7%	1.5%	−5.2%	69%	79%	0.81	0.14
Free Cash Flow to Price	5.6%	2.7%	0.3%	−3.7%	−4.5%	78%	81%	0.78	0.14
Dividend plus Share Repurchase Yield	2.4%	1.4%	0.0%	−0.1%	−4.3%	52%	74%	0.75	0.15
Capex to PP&E (Low to High)	2.1%	1.0%	0.5%	−0.2%	−3.8%	62%	69%	0.67	0.15
Free Cash Flow to Operating Income	5.0%	2.6%	0.1%	−2.9%	−3.8%	75%	78%	0.68	0.17
Price to Earnings (Current FY EPS Est.)	4.7%	1.2%	0.0%	−1.9%	−2.2%	66%	58%	0.67	0.17
Return on Equity	2.2%	1.4%	0.8%	−0.1%	−3.6%	68%	73%	0.67	0.17
Return on Assets	1.4%	0.4%	0.4%	1.9%	−3.0%	52%	64%	0.56	0.18
Price to Earnings plus Dividends	3.8%	1.6%	0.3%	−1.9%	−2.0%	62%	57%	0.68	0.18
52 Week Price Range	4.3%	2.1%	0.0%	−2.2%	−3.9%	75%	75%	0.69	0.20
Economic Profits (P/S instead of Beta)	3.2%	1.9%	1.7%	0.3%	−3.2%	65%	64%	0.73	0.21
7 Month Relative Strength	3.3%	0.7%	0.5%	−0.1%	−3.4%	60%	74%	0.44	0.22
Price to Book Value	3.6%	1.5%	−0.3%	−2.4%	−1.9%	62%	60%	0.61	0.24
1 Yr. Chg. in Invnt. + Rcvbls. Turn.	1.3%	1.8%	1.9%	0.2%	−3.7%	52%	75%	0.51	0.25
2 Year Capex Growth	2.1%	2.0%	0.8%	0.6%	−3.1%	64%	73%	0.58	0.26
28/16 Week Relative Strength Index	6.2%	1.8%	−0.6%	−1.3%	−3.2%	70%	77%	0.70	0.26
Total Debt to Invested Capital	2.3%	0.6%	0.2%	−1.5%	−1.3%	65%	60%	0.57	0.27
Net Debt Reduction to Invested Capital	1.5%	2.1%	−1.1%	0.1%	−3.0%	65%	75%	0.61	0.28
1 Yr. Chg. in Inventory Turnover	1.6%	1.3%	1.6%	0.2%	−3.0%	61%	81%	0.54	0.29
88/36 Month Relative Strength	2.6%	1.1%	0.9%	1.0%	−1.5%	55%	61%	0.55	0.30
Economic Profits (No Beta)	2.7%	1.0%	1.1%	0.5%	−1.4%	66%	64%	0.74	0.30
Economic Profits	2.7%	1.3%	1.4%	0.3%	−0.9%	65%	65%	0.78	0.32
Acquisitions to Inv. Cap. (Low to High)	2.9%	1.3%	−0.5%	−1.5%	−3.0%	75%	75%	0.69	0.32
1 Year Reduction in Long-Term Debt	0.0%	2.7%	2.1%	0.5%	−2.8%	68%	88%	0.46	0.33
Free Cash Flow Per Share Score	3.5%	1.9%	1.0%	−0.6%	−2.7%	80%	68%	0.81	0.33
Depreciation to Invested Capital	1.7%	1.8%	0.5%	−0.8%	−2.2%	68%	74%	0.59	0.33
3 Year Capex to Invested Capital	1.0%	1.9%	1.3%	−0.4%	−1.3%	66%	66%	0.59	0.38
Earnings Per Share Score	1.9%	0.7%	0.6%	−0.3%	−0.3%	56%	57%	0.58	0.39

TWO-FACTOR STRATEGIES

TABLE B.1

Two-Factor Strategies in Chapter Sequence

	Excess Returns by Quintile					Outperf.	Underper.	Sharpe Ratio	
Strategy	Q1	Q2	Q3	Q4	Q5	Q1	Q5	Q1	Q5
Profitability									
ROIC & Price to Sales	5.9%	2.4%	1.8%	−1.8%	−8.2%	70%	73%	0.78	0.00
ROIC & Cash ROIC	8.4%	3.2%	0.8%	0.2%	−10.9%	78%	79%	0.92	−0.09
ROIC & 1 Yr. Reduction in Shrs. OS	4.6%	1.2%	2.6%	−0.6%	−12.8%	62%	78%	0.86	−0.15
EBITDA-Capx to Inv. Cap. & FCF to Price	7.8%	2.4%	0.3%	−1.7%	−5.3%	74%	75%	0.89	0.09
EBITDA-Capex to Inv. Cap. & Oper. C.F. to Capex	6.2%	2.6%	0.8%	2.2%	−9.6%	76%	75%	0.79	−0.05
Return on Equity & Return on Assets	3.4%	0.1%	0.9%	0.9%	−8.3%	53%	75%	0.52	−0.01
Return on Equity & Price to Book Value	4.6%	2.3%	0.5%	−1.4%	−7.4%	65%	73%	0.66	0.02
Economic Profits (cash ROIC) & EV to EBITDA	8.1%	1.9%	−1.7%	−2.5%	−6.0%	76%	76%	0.98	0.04
Economic Profits (cash ROIC) & Capex to PP&E	5.3%	1.2%	0.0%	−0.5%	−12.4%	78%	76%	0.73	−0.14
Valuation									
FCF to Price & External Financing to Assets	7.1%	2.8%	2.5%	−5.9%	−15.3%	72%	86%	0.86	−0.24
FCF to Price & 7 Month Relative Strength	9.5%	2.4%	−2.1%	−5.3%	−8.6%	76%	79%	0.97	−0.03
EV to EBITDA & Return on Invested Capital	6.8%	2.2%	−0.1%	−2.2%	−7.4%	78%	77%	0.90	0.02
EV to EBITDA & FCF to Operating Income	7.9%	2.4%	−0.8%	−3.9%	−7.9%	75%	74%	0.87	0.00
EV to EBITDA & Total Debt to EBITDA	6.0%	1.0%	−0.3%	−3.0%	−5.6%	75%	71%	0.91	0.10
Price to Earnings & EV to EBITDA	7.1%	1.2%	0.5%	−3.2%	−5.0%	73%	73%	0.82	0.07
Price to Earnings & EPS Score	5.5%	1.5%	0.1%	−0.8%	0.0%	68%	55%	0.66	0.25
Prc to Earnings + Divs. & 52 Week Price Range	6.0%	2.7%	1.4%	−3.9%	−6.5%	69%	65%	0.79	0.04
EV to Sales & Free Cash Flow to Price	7.6%	3.6%	−0.8%	−2.2%	−8.9%	73%	76%	0.77	−0.03
EV to Sales & 7 Month Relative Strength	6.1%	0.7%	1.3%	−0.5%	−12.9%	78%	86%	0.86	−0.18
Price to Book Value & Economic Profits	8.1%	2.0%	−1.1%	−3.1%	−9.9%	74%	74%	0.74	−0.06
Price to Book & Operating Cash Flow to Equity	6.6%	4.3%	−0.5%	−3.6%	−13.2%	74%	79%	0.72	−0.16
Cash Flow									
FCF to Oper. Inc. & Acquisitions to Inv. Cap.	5.9%	3.1%	−0.6%	−5.6%	−8.8%	70%	86%	0.79	−0.04
FCF to Oper. Inc. & Extern. Fin. to Assets	7.0%	3.0%	1.8%	−6.3%	−14.4%	73%	82%	0.81	−0.20
FCF to Operating Income & Price to Sales	7.9%	2.4%	−0.4%	−5.3%	−8.4%	72%	76%	0.82	−0.02
Cash ROIC & Capex to PP&E	4.7%	1.9%	0.5%	−1.1%	−12.9%	74%	78%	0.82	−0.15
Cash ROIC & Capex to Invested Capital	6.6%	2.8%	0.7%	−2.4%	−10.4%	79%	82%	0.88	−0.10
Cash ROIC & Price to Invested Capital	6.7%	3.1%	0.1%	−3.0%	−9.2%	72%	74%	0.71	−0.04
FCF+Repur+Div to Prc & 1 Yr. Reduct. in Shrs.	5.6%	1.7%	0.3%	−2.2%	−12.1%	72%	81%	0.88	−0.16
FCF + Dividend Yield & Return on Equity	6.7%	2.8%	0.7%	−3.1%	−9.7%	78%	78%	0.89	−0.05
Growth									
FCF Per Share Score & EV to EBITDA	8.1%	3.1%	0.8%	−2.7%	−6.7%	76%	73%	1.03	0.07
FCF Per Share 1 Year Growth & 28/16 Week RSI	9.0%	4.3%	−0.6%	−1.8%	−4.4%	73%	73%	0.79	0.15
FCF Per Share Score & Return on Equity	7.0%	1.2%	2.1%	1.5%	−4.8%	71%	66%	0.85	0.13
EPS Score & Free Cash Flow + Dividend to Price	7.0%	2.6%	1.5%	−1.9%	−3.4%	79%	75%	0.80	0.15
EPS Score & Oper. Cash Flow PS to EPS Est.	6.1%	2.1%	2.5%	−0.3%	−6.0%	78%	75%	0.76	0.06
EPS Score & 1 Yr. FCF Gr. to 1 Yr. Inv. Cap. Gr.	5.3%	2.1%	−0.2%	−1.1%	−1.9%	60%	53%	0.81	0.33
2 Yr. Capex Growth & Free Cash Flow to Price	8.0%	3.5%	0.6%	−2.6%	−6.6%	79%	80%	0.79	0.05
2 Yr. Capex Gr. & Oper. Cash Flow to Inv. Cap.	6.7%	3.0%	1.8%	1.3%	−9.5%	78%	81%	0.80	−0.06

Capital Allocation

1 Yr. Reduction in Shares & EV to EBITDA	6.0%	1.9%	1.3%	−1.7%	−9.7%	73%	73%	0.90	−0.04
1 Yr. Reduction in Shares & 7 Month Rel. Str.	5.8%	0.0%	1.8%	−0.7%	−10.7%	70%	86%	0.81	−0.09
1 Yr. Reduction in Shares & Deprec. to Inv. Cap.	3.8%	1.6%	2.7%	−1.3%	−7.2%	66%	73%	0.86	0.03
Debt Red. to Inv. Cap. & Shr Repur. to Inv. Cap.	4.2%	3.7%	−2.5%	−0.1%	−8.4%	65%	81%	0.83	−0.01
1 Yr. Reduction in L.T. Debt & Economic Profits	7.3%	3.8%	3.6%	−0.3%	−9.4%	75%	74%	0.84	−0.06
Extern. Fin. to Assets & Acquisitions to Inv. Cap.	4.3%	2.9%	1.4%	−3.4%	−4.9%	68%	71%	0.82	0.00
Extern. Fin. to Assets & Price to Book Value	6.0%	2.4%	1.6%	−3.0%	−6.3%	69%	77%	0.75	0.04
Extern. Fin. to Assets & FCF + Dividend to Yield	7.3%	2.4%	1.3%	−3.5%	−8.5%	76%	78%	0.85	−0.02
External Fin. to Assets & 52 Week Price Range	5.7%	3.4%	1.4%	−3.3%	−13.1%	71%	82%	0.84	−0.18
3 Yr. Capex to Inv. Cap. & FCF to Price	5.7%	3.6%	1.1%	−4.5%	−7.1%	68%	79%	0.96	0.03
Acquisitions to Inv. Cap. & Capex to PP&E	5.5%	2.2%	−0.2%	−1.3%	−11.8%	70%	87%	0.81	−0.17

Price Momentum

7 Mo. Rel. Str. & FCF+Div.+Shr. Repur. to Price	8.3%	1.7%	−0.8%	−2.8%	−10.0%	81%	94%	0.76	−0.07
88/36-Month Rel. Str. & EV to EBITDA	7.7%	2.3%	0.1%	−0.2%	−3.5%	69%	62%	0.83	0.12
7 Mo. Rel. Str. & Price to Earnings plus Dividends	4.8%	1.3%	1.0%	−0.5%	−4.7%	69%	68%	0.65	0.10
52 Week Price Range & Free Cash Flow to Price	6.9%	2.5%	−1.2%	−7.8%	−9.5%	75%	72%	0.84	−0.06
52 Week Price Range & Return on Equity	6.3%	1.7%	0.2%	−2.0%	−9.1%	78%	77%	0.76	−0.03
52 Week Price Range & Price to Book Value	4.5%	2.7%	0.0%	−4.9%	−9.3%	64%	83%	0.81	−0.05
28/16 Week RSI & 52 Week Price Range	10.7%	3.9%	−1.0%	−4.5%	−9.6%	80%	84%	0.78	−0.04
28/16 Week RSI & Economic Profits	7.4%	0.6%	−1.8%	−2.5%	−9.8%	70%	78%	0.97	−0.03

Red Flags

FCF to Long-Term Debt & Economic Profits	7.5%	5.1%	2.5%	−1.3%	−13.0%	74%	78%	0.88	−0.18
FCF to Long-Term Debt & Return on Equity	6.0%	2.0%	1.1%	−1.8%	−10.1%	65%	81%	0.81	−0.06
Capex to PP&E & ROIC	4.4%	2.1%	1.2%	−1.3%	−7.3%	64%	68%	0.88	0.02
Capex to PP&E & 52 Week Price Range	4.9%	2.1%	1.5%	−3.3%	−9.0%	75%	79%	0.85	−0.03
Oper. Cash Fl. to Capex + Int. & Price to Capex	6.8%	4.4%	0.3%	−1.3%	−11.8%	72%	79%	0.76	−0.12
Oper. C.F. to Capex & Depreciation to Inv. Cap.	7.5%	5.1%	0.4%	−0.5%	−7.4%	78%	78%	0.84	0.01
1 Yr Chg. in Invt. + Rcvbls. Turn. & FCF to Price	7.3%	3.0%	1.5%	−4.0%	−8.0%	74%	83%	0.83	−0.01
Deprec. to Inv. Cap. & FCF+Repur.+Div. to Price	6.4%	2.5%	1.0%	−4.2%	−9.7%	75%	83%	0.91	−0.08
Deprec. to Inv. Cap. & Extern. Finan. to Inv. Cap.	4.7%	2.7%	1.8%	−1.8%	−9.7%	74%	82%	0.90	−0.05

TABLE B.2

Two-Factor Strategies: Top Quintile by Excess Returns

	Excess Returns by Quintile					Outperf.	Underper.	Sharpe Ratio	
Strategy	Q1	Q2	Q3	Q4	Q5	Q1	Q5	Q1	Q5
28/16 Week RSI & 52 Week Price Range	10.7%	3.9%	−1.0%	−4.5%	−9.6%	80%	84%	0.78	−0.04
FCF to Price & 7 Month Relative Strength	9.5%	2.4%	−2.1%	−5.3%	−8.6%	76%	79%	0.97	−0.03
FCF Per Shr. 1 Yr. Growth & 28/16-Week RSI	9.0%	4.3%	−0.6%	−1.8%	−4.4%	73%	73%	0.79	0.15
ROIC & Cash ROIC	8.4%	3.2%	0.8%	0.2%	−10.9%	78%	79%	0.92	−0.09
7 Mo. Rel. Str. & FCF+Div.+Shr. Repur. to Price	8.3%	1.7%	−0.8%	−2.8%	−10.0%	81%	94%	0.76	−0.07
Price to Book & Economic Profits	8.1%	2.0%	−1.1%	−3.1%	−9.9%	74%	74%	0.74	−0.06
FCF Per Share Score & EV to EBITDA	8.1%	3.1%	0.8%	−2.7%	−6.7%	76%	73%	1.03	0.07
Economic Profits (cash ROIC) & EV to EBITDA	8.1%	1.9%	−1.7%	−2.5%	−6.0%	76%	76%	0.98	0.04
2 Yr Capex Growth & Free Cash Flow to Price	8.0%	3.5%	0.6%	−2.6%	−6.6%	79%	80%	0.79	0.05
EV to EBITDA & FCF to Operating Income	7.9%	2.4%	−0.8%	−3.9%	−7.9%	75%	74%	0.87	0.00
FCF to Operating Income & Price to Sales	7.9%	2.4%	−0.4%	−5.3%	−8.4%	72%	76%	0.82	−0.02
EBITDA-Capx to Inv. Cap. & FCF to Price	7.8%	2.4%	0.3%	−1.7%	−5.3%	74%	75%	0.89	0.09
88/36 Month RS & EV to EBITDA	7.7%	2.3%	0.1%	−0.2%	−3.5%	69%	62%	0.83	0.12
EV to Sales & Free Cash Flow to Price	7.6%	3.6%	−0.8%	−2.2%	−8.9%	73%	76%	0.77	−0.03
Oper. Cash Fl. to Capex & Deprec. to Inv. Cap.	7.5%	5.1%	0.4%	−0.5%	−7.4%	78%	78%	0.84	0.01
FCF to Long-Term Debt & Economic Profits	7.5%	5.1%	2.5%	−1.3%	−13.0%	74%	78%	0.88	−0.18
28/16 Week RSI & Economic Profits	7.4%	0.6%	−1.8%	−2.5%	−9.8%	70%	78%	0.97	−0.03
Extern. Fin. to Assets & FCF + Dividend to Price	7.3%	2.4%	1.3%	−3.5%	−8.5%	76%	78%	0.85	−0.02
1 Yr. Reduction in L.T. Debt & Economic Profits	7.3%	3.8%	3.6%	−0.3%	−9.4%	75%	74%	0.84	−0.06
1 Yr Chg. in Invt. + Rcvbls. Turn. & FCF to Price	7.3%	3.0%	1.5%	−4.0%	−8.0%	74%	83%	0.83	−0.01
FCF to Price & External Financing to Assets	7.1%	2.8%	2.5%	−5.9%	−15.3%	72%	86%	0.86	−0.24
Price to Earnings & EV to EBITDA	7.1%	1.2%	0.5%	−3.2%	−5.0%	73%	73%	0.82	0.07
FCF Per Share Score & Return on Equity	7.0%	1.2%	2.1%	1.5%	−4.8%	71%	66%	0.85	0.13
FCF to Oper. Inc. & Extern. Fin. to Assets	7.0%	3.0%	1.8%	−6.3%	−14.4%	73%	82%	0.81	−0.20
EPS Score & Free Cash Flow + Dividend to Price	7.0%	2.6%	1.5%	−1.9%	−3.4%	79%	75%	0.80	0.15
52 Week Price Range & Free Cash Flow to Price	6.9%	2.5%	−1.2%	−7.8%	−9.5%	75%	72%	0.84	−0.06
EV to EBITDA & Return on Invested Capital	6.8%	2.2%	−0.1%	−2.2%	−7.4%	78%	77%	0.90	0.02
Oper. Cash Fl. to Capex + Int. & Price to Capex	6.8%	4.4%	0.3%	−1.3%	−11.8%	72%	79%	0.76	−0.12
FCF + Dividend Yield & Return on Equity	6.7%	2.8%	0.7%	−3.1%	−9.7%	78%	78%	0.89	−0.05
2 Yr Capex Gr. & Oper. Cash Flow to Inv. Cap.	6.7%	3.0%	1.8%	1.3%	−9.5%	78%	81%	0.80	−0.06
Cash ROIC & Price to Invested Capital	6.7%	3.1%	0.1%	−3.0%	−9.2%	72%	74%	0.71	−0.04
Cash ROIC & Capex to Invested Capital	6.6%	2.8%	0.7%	−2.4%	−10.4%	79%	82%	0.88	−0.10
Price to Book & Operating Cash Flow to Equity	6.6%	4.3%	−0.5%	−3.6%	−13.2%	74%	79%	0.72	−0.16
Deprec. to Inv. Cap. & FCF+Repur.+Div. to Price	6.4%	2.5%	1.0%	−4.2%	−9.7%	75%	83%	0.91	−0.08
52 Week Price Range & Return on Equity	6.3%	1.7%	0.2%	−2.0%	−9.1%	78%	77%	0.76	−0.03
EBITDA-Capex to Inv. Cap. & Oper. C.F. to Capex	6.2%	2.6%	0.8%	2.2%	−9.6%	76%	75%	0.79	−0.05
EPS Score & Oper. Cash Flow PS to EPS Est.	6.1%	2.1%	2.5%	−0.3%	−6.0%	78%	75%	0.76	0.06
EV to Sales & 7 Month Relative Strength	6.1%	0.7%	1.3%	−0.5%	−12.9%	78%	86%	0.86	−0.18
Prc to Earnings + Divs. & 52 Week Price Range	6.0%	2.7%	1.4%	−3.9%	−6.5%	69%	65%	0.79	0.04
FCF to Long-Term Debt & Return on Equity	6.0%	2.0%	1.1%	−1.8%	−10.1%	65%	81%	0.81	−0.06
Extern. Fin. to Assets & Price to Book Value	6.0%	2.4%	1.6%	−3.0%	−6.3%	69%	77%	0.75	0.04

1 Yr. Reduction in Shares & EV to EBITDA	6.0%	1.9%	1.3%	−1.7%	−9.7%	73%	73%	0.90	−0.04
EV to EBITDA & Total Debt to EBITDA	6.0%	1.0%	−0.3%	−3.0%	−5.6%	75%	71%	0.91	0.10
ROIC & Price to Sales	5.9%	2.4%	1.8%	−1.8%	−8.2%	70%	73%	0.78	0.00
FCF to Oper. Inc. & Acquisitions to Inv. Cap.	5.9%	3.1%	−0.6%	−5.6%	−8.8%	70%	86%	0.79	−0.04
1 Yr. Reduction in Shares & 7 Mo. Rel. Str.	5.8%	0.0%	1.8%	−0.7%	−10.7%	70%	86%	0.81	−0.09
3 Yr Capex to Inv. Cap. & FCF to Price	5.7%	3.6%	1.1%	−4.5%	−7.1%	68%	79%	0.96	0.03
External Fin. to Assets & 52 Week Price Range	5.7%	3.4%	1.4%	−3.3%	−13.1%	71%	82%	0.84	−0.18
FCF+Repur+Div to Price & 1 Yr. Reduct. in Shrs.	5.6%	1.7%	0.3%	−2.2%	−12.1%	72%	81%	0.88	−0.16
Price to Earnings & EPS Score	5.5%	1.5%	0.1%	−0.8%	0.0%	68%	55%	0.66	0.25
Acquisitions to Inv. Cap. & Capex to PP&E	5.5%	2.2%	−0.2%	−1.3%	−11.8%	70%	87%	0.81	−0.17
Economic Profits (cash ROIC) & Capex to PP&E	5.3%	1.2%	0.0%	−0.5%	−12.4%	78%	76%	0.73	−0.14
EPS Score & 1 Yr. FCF Gr. to 1 Yr. Inv. Cap. Gr.	5.3%	2.1%	−0.2%	−1.1%	−1.9%	60%	53%	0.81	0.33
Capex to PP&E & 52 Week Price Range	4.9%	2.1%	1.5%	−3.3%	−9.0%	75%	79%	0.85	−0.03
7 Month RS & Price to Earnings plus Dividends	4.8%	1.3%	1.0%	−0.5%	−4.7%	69%	68%	0.65	0.10
Deprec. to Inv. Cap. & Exter. Finan. to Inv. Cap.	4.7%	2.7%	1.8%	−1.8%	−9.7%	74%	82%	0.90	−0.05
Cash ROIC & Capex to PP&E	4.7%	1.9%	0.5%	−1.1%	−12.9%	74%	78%	0.82	−0.15
Return on Equity & Price to Book Value	4.6%	2.3%	0.5%	−1.4%	−7.4%	65%	73%	0.66	0.02
ROIC & 1Yr Reduction in Shrs OS	4.6%	1.2%	2.6%	−0.6%	−12.8%	62%	78%	0.86	−0.15
52 Week Price Range & Price to Book Value	4.5%	2.7%	0.0%	−4.9%	−9.3%	64%	83%	0.81	−0.05
Capex to PP&E & ROIC	4.4%	2.1%	1.2%	−1.3%	−7.3%	64%	68%	0.88	0.02
Extern. Fin. to Assets & Acquisitions to Inv. Cap.	4.3%	2.9%	1.4%	−3.4%	−4.9%	68%	71%	0.82	0.00
Debt Red. to Inv. Cap. & Shr. Repur. to Inv. Cap.	4.2%	3.7%	−2.5%	−0.1%	−8.4%	65%	81%	0.83	−0.01
1 Yr. Reduction in Shares & Deprec. to Inv. Cap.	3.8%	1.6%	2.7%	−1.3%	−7.2%	66%	73%	0.86	0.03
Return on Equity & Return on Assets	3.4%	0.1%	0.9%	0.9%	−8.3%	53%	75%	0.52	−0.01

T A B L E B.3

Two-Factor Strategies: Top Quintile by Sharpe Ratio

Strategy	Excess Returns by Quintile					Outperf.	Underper.	Sharpe Ratio	
	Q1	Q2	Q3	Q4	Q5	Q1	Q5	Q1	Q5
FCF Per Share Score & EV to EBITDA	8.1%	3.1%	0.8%	−2.7%	−6.7%	76%	73%	1.03	0.07
Economic Profits (Cash ROIC) & EV to EBITDA	8.1%	1.9%	−1.7%	−2.5%	−6.0%	76%	76%	0.98	0.04
FCF to Price & 7 Month Relative Strength	9.5%	2.4%	−2.1%	−5.3%	−8.6%	76%	79%	0.97	−0.03
28/16 Week RSI & Economic Profits	7.4%	0.6%	−1.8%	−2.5%	−9.8%	70%	78%	0.97	−0.03
3 Yr. Capex to Inv. Cap. & FCF to Price	5.7%	3.6%	1.1%	−4.5%	−7.1%	68%	79%	0.96	0.03
ROIC & Cash ROIC	8.4%	3.2%	0.8%	0.2%	−10.9%	78%	79%	0.92	−0.09
EV to EBITDA & Total Debt to EBITDA	6.0%	1.0%	−0.3%	−3.0%	−5.6%	75%	71%	0.91	0.10
Deprec. to Inv. Cap. & FCF+Repur.+Div. to Price	6.4%	2.5%	1.0%	−4.2%	−9.7%	75%	83%	0.91	−0.08
Deprec. to Inv. Cap. & Exter. Finan. to Inv. Cap.	4.7%	2.7%	1.8%	−1.8%	−9.7%	74%	82%	0.90	−0.05
1 Yr. Reduction in Shares & EV to EBITDA	6.0%	1.9%	1.3%	−1.7%	−9.7%	73%	73%	0.90	−0.04
EV to EBITDA & Return on Invested Capital	6.8%	2.2%	−0.1%	−2.2%	−7.4%	78%	77%	0.90	0.02
FCF + Dividend Yield & Return on Equity	6.7%	2.8%	0.7%	−3.1%	−9.7%	78%	78%	0.89	−0.05
EBITDA-Capx to Inv. Cap. & FCF to Price	7.8%	2.4%	0.3%	−1.7%	−5.3%	74%	75%	0.89	0.09
FCF+Repur+ Div to Price & 1 Yr. Reduct. in Shrs.	5.6%	1.7%	0.3%	−2.2%	−12.1%	72%	81%	0.88	−0.16
Cash ROIC & Capex to Invested Capital	6.6%	2.8%	0.7%	−2.4%	−10.4%	79%	82%	0.88	−0.10
FCF to Long-Term Debt & Economic Profits	7.5%	5.1%	2.5%	−1.3%	−13.0%	74%	78%	0.88	−0.18
Capex to PP&E & ROIC	4.4%	2.1%	1.2%	−1.3%	−7.3%	64%	68%	0.88	0.02
EV to EBITDA & FCF to Operating Income	7.9%	2.4%	−0.8%	−3.9%	−7.9%	75%	74%	0.87	0.00
ROIC & 1 Yr. Reduction in Shrs. OS	4.6%	1.2%	2.6%	−0.6%	−12.8%	62%	78%	0.86	−0.15
1 Yr. Reduct. in Shrs. & Deprec. to Inv. Cap.	3.8%	1.6%	2.7%	−1.3%	−7.2%	66%	73%	0.86	0.03
FCF to Price & External Financing to Assets	7.1%	2.8%	2.5%	−5.9%	−15.3%	72%	86%	0.86	−0.24
EV to Sales & 7 Month Relative Strength	6.1%	0.7%	1.3%	−0.5%	−12.9%	78%	86%	0.86	−0.18
Extern. Fin. to Assets & FCF + Divividend to Price	7.3%	2.4%	1.3%	−3.5%	−8.5%	76%	78%	0.85	−0.02
FCF Per Share Score & Return on Equity	7.0%	1.2%	2.1%	1.5%	−4.8%	71%	66%	0.85	0.13
Capex to PP&E & 52 Week Price Range	4.9%	2.1%	1.5%	−3.3%	−9.0%	75%	79%	0.85	−0.03
Oper. C.F. to Capex & Deprec. to Inv. Cap.	7.5%	5.1%	0.4%	−0.5%	−7.4%	78%	78%	0.84	0.01
1 Yr. Reduction in L.T. Debt & Economic Profits	7.3%	3.8%	3.6%	−0.3%	−9.4%	75%	74%	0.84	−0.06
52 Week Price Range & Free Cash Flow to Price	6.9%	2.5%	−1.2%	−7.8%	−9.5%	75%	72%	0.84	−0.06
Extern. Fin. to Assets & 52-Week Price Range	5.7%	3.4%	1.4%	−3.3%	−13.1%	71%	82%	0.84	−0.18
88/36 Month RS & EV to EBITDA	7.7%	2.3%	0.1%	−0.2%	−3.5%	69%	62%	0.83	0.12
Debt Red. to Inv. Cap. & Shr. Repur. to Inv. Cap.	4.2%	3.7%	−2.5%	−0.1%	−8.4%	65%	81%	0.83	−0.01
1 Yr. Chg. in Invt. + Rcvbls. Turn. & FCF to Price	7.3%	3.0%	1.5%	−4.0%	−8.0%	74%	83%	0.83	−0.01
FCF to Operating Income & Price to Sales	7.9%	2.4%	−0.4%	−5.3%	−8.4%	72%	76%	0.82	−0.02
Cash ROIC & Capex to PP&E	4.7%	1.9%	0.5%	−1.1%	−12.9%	74%	78%	0.82	−0.15
Extern. Fin. to Assets & Acquisitions to Inv. Cap.	4.3%	2.9%	1.4%	−3.4%	−4.9%	68%	71%	0.82	0.00
Price to Earnings & EV to EBITDA	7.1%	1.2%	0.5%	−3.2%	−5.0%	73%	73%	0.82	0.07
EPS Score & 1 Yr. FCF Gr. to 1 Yr. Inv. Cap. Gr.	5.3%	2.1%	−0.2%	−1.1%	−1.9%	60%	53%	0.81	0.33
FCF to Oper. Inc. & Extern. Fin. to Assets	7.0%	3.0%	1.8%	−6.3%	−14.4%	73%	82%	0.81	−0.20
FCF to Long-Term Debt & Return on Equity	6.0%	2.0%	1.1%	−1.8%	−10.1%	65%	81%	0.81	−0.06
1 Yr. Reduct. in Shrs. & 7 Mo. Relative Strength	5.8%	0.0%	1.8%	−0.7%	−10.7%	70%	86%	0.81	−0.09
Acquisitions to Inv. Cap. & Capex to PP&E	5.5%	2.2%	−0.2%	−1.3%	−11.8%	70%	87%	0.81	−0.17

52 Week Price Range & Price to Book Value	4.5%	2.7%	0.0%	−4.9%	−9.3%	64%	83%	0.81	−0.05
2 Yr. Capex Gr. & Oper. Cash Flow to Inv. Cap.	6.7%	3.0%	1.8%	1.3%	−9.5%	78%	81%	0.80	−0.06
EPS Score & Free Cash Flow + Dividend to Price	7.0%	2.6%	1.5%	−1.9%	−3.4%	79%	75%	0.80	0.15
Prc to Earnings + Divs. & 52 Week Price Range	6.0%	2.7%	1.4%	−3.9%	−6.5%	69%	65%	0.79	0.04
FCF Per Share 1 Year Growth & 28/16 Week RSI	9.0%	4.3%	−0.6%	−1.8%	−4.4%	73%	73%	0.79	0.15
EBITDA-Capex to Inv. Cap. & Oper. C.F. to Capex	6.2%	2.6%	0.8%	2.2%	−9.6%	76%	75%	0.79	−0.05
FCF to Oper. Inc. & Acquisitions to Inv. Cap.	5.9%	3.1%	−0.6%	−5.6%	−8.8%	70%	86%	0.79	−0.04
2 Yr. Capex Growth & FCF to Price	8.0%	3.5%	0.6%	−2.6%	−6.6%	79%	80%	0.79	0.05
28/16 Week RSI & 52 Week Price Range	10.7%	3.9%	−1.0%	−4.5%	−9.6%	80%	84%	0.78	−0.04
ROIC & Price to Sales	5.9%	2.4%	1.8%	−1.8%	−8.2%	70%	73%	0.78	0.00
EV to Sales & Free Cash Flow to Price	7.6%	3.6%	−0.8%	−2.2%	−8.9%	73%	76%	0.77	−0.03
7 Mo. Rel. Str. & FCF+Div.+Shr. Repur. to Price	8.3%	1.7%	−0.8%	−2.8%	−10.0%	81%	94%	0.76	−0.07
EPS Score & Oper. Cash Flow PS to EPS Est.	6.1%	2.1%	2.5%	−0.3%	−6.0%	78%	75%	0.76	0.06
Oper. Cash Fl. to Capex + Int. & Price to Capex	6.8%	4.4%	0.3%	−1.3%	−11.8%	72%	79%	0.76	−0.12
52 Week Price Range & Return on Equity	6.3%	1.7%	0.2%	−2.0%	−9.1%	78%	77%	0.76	−0.03
Extern. Fin. to Assets & Price to Book Value	6.0%	2.4%	1.6%	−3.0%	−6.3%	69%	77%	0.75	0.04
Price to Book & Economic Profits	8.1%	2.0%	−1.1%	−3.1%	−9.9%	74%	74%	0.74	−0.06
Economic Profits (Cash ROIC) & Capex to PP&E	5.3%	1.2%	0.0%	−0.5%	−12.4%	78%	76%	0.73	−0.14
Price to Book & Operating Cash Flow to Equity	6.6%	4.3%	−0.5%	−3.6%	−13.2%	74%	79%	0.72	−0.16
Cash ROIC & Price to Invested Capital	6.7%	3.1%	0.1%	−3.0%	−9.2%	72%	74%	0.71	−0.04
Return on Equity & Price to Book Value	4.6%	2.3%	0.5%	−1.4%	−7.4%	65%	73%	0.66	0.02
Price to Earnings & EPS Score	5.5%	1.5%	0.1%	−0.8%	0.0%	68%	55%	0.66	0.25
7 Mo. Rel. Str. & Price to Earnings plus Dividends	4.8%	1.3%	1.0%	−0.5%	−4.7%	69%	68%	0.65	0.10
Return on Equity & Return on Assets	3.4%	0.1%	0.9%	0.9%	−8.3%	53%	75%	0.52	−0.01

TABLE B.4

Two-Factor Strategies: Bottom Quintile by Excess Returns

Strategy	Excess Returns by Quintile					Outperf.	Underper.	Sharpe Ratio	
	Q1	Q2	Q3	Q4	Q5	Q1	Q5	Q1	Q5
FCF to Price & External Financing to Assets	7.1%	2.8%	2.5%	−5.9%	−15.3%	72%	86%	0.86	−0.24
FCF to Oper. Income & Extern. Fin. to Assets	7.0%	3.0%	1.8%	−6.3%	−14.4%	73%	82%	0.81	−0.20
Price to Book & Operating Cash Flow to Equity	6.6%	4.3%	−0.5%	−3.6%	−13.2%	74%	79%	0.72	−0.16
External Fin. to Assets & 52 Week Price Range	5.7%	3.4%	1.4%	−3.3%	−13.1%	71%	82%	0.84	−0.18
FCF to Long-Term Debt & Economic Profits	7.5%	5.1%	2.5%	−1.3%	−13.0%	74%	78%	0.88	−0.18
EV to Sales & 7 Month Relative Strength	6.1%	0.7%	1.3%	−0.5%	−12.9%	78%	86%	0.86	−0.18
Cash ROIC & Capex to PP&E	4.7%	1.9%	0.5%	−1.1%	−12.9%	74%	78%	0.82	−0.15
ROIC & 1 Yr. Reduction in Shrs. OS	4.6%	1.2%	2.6%	−0.6%	−12.8%	62%	78%	0.86	−0.15
Economic Profits (Cash ROIC) & Capex to PP&E	5.3%	1.2%	0.0%	−0.5%	−12.4%	78%	76%	0.73	−0.14
FCF+Repur.+Div. to Price & 1 Yr. Reduct. in Shrs.	5.6%	1.7%	0.3%	−2.2%	−12.1%	72%	81%	0.88	−0.16
Acquisitions to Inv. Cap. & Capex to PP&E	5.5%	2.2%	−0.2%	−1.3%	−11.8%	70%	87%	0.81	−0.17
Oper. Cash Fl. to Capex + Int. & Price to Capex	6.8%	4.4%	0.3%	−1.3%	−11.8%	72%	79%	0.76	−0.12
ROIC & Cash ROIC	8.4%	3.2%	0.8%	0.2%	−10.9%	78%	79%	0.92	−0.09
1 Yr. Reduct. in Shrs. & 7 Mo. Relative Strength	5.8%	0.0%	1.8%	−0.7%	−10.7%	70%	86%	0.81	−0.09
Cash ROIC & Capex to Invested Capital	6.6%	2.8%	0.7%	−2.4%	−10.4%	79%	82%	0.88	−0.10
FCF to Long-Term Debt & Return on Equity	6.0%	2.0%	1.1%	−1.8%	−10.1%	65%	81%	0.81	−0.06
7 Mo. Rel. Str. & FCF+Div.+Shr. Repur. to Price	8.3%	1.7%	−0.8%	−2.8%	−10.0%	81%	94%	0.76	−0.07
Price to Book & Economic Profits	8.1%	2.0%	−1.1%	−3.1%	−9.9%	74%	74%	0.74	−0.06
28/16 Week RSI & Economic Profits	7.4%	0.6%	−1.8%	−2.5%	−9.8%	70%	78%	0.97	−0.03
Deprec. to Inv. Cap. & Extern. Fin. to Inv. Cap.	4.7%	2.7%	1.8%	−1.8%	−9.7%	74%	82%	0.90	−0.05
1 Yr. Reduction in Shares & EV to EBITDA	6.0%	1.9%	1.3%	−1.7%	−9.7%	73%	73%	0.90	−0.04
Deprec. to Inv. Cap. & FCF+ Repur.+Div. to Price	6.4%	2.5%	1.0%	−4.2%	−9.7%	75%	83%	0.91	−0.08
FCF + Dividend Yield & Return on Equity	6.7%	2.8%	0.7%	−3.1%	−9.7%	78%	78%	0.89	−0.05
EBITDA-Capex to Inv. Cap. & Oper. C.F. to Capex	6.2%	2.6%	0.8%	2.2%	−9.6%	76%	75%	0.79	−0.05
28/16 Week RSI & 52 Week Price Range	10.7%	3.9%	−1.0%	−4.5%	−9.6%	80%	84%	0.78	−0.04
2 Yr. Capex Gr. & Oper. Cash Fl. to Inv. Cap.	6.7%	3.0%	1.8%	1.3%	−9.5%	78%	81%	0.80	−0.06
52-Week Price Range & Free Cash Flow to Price	6.9%	2.5%	−1.2%	−7.8%	−9.5%	75%	72%	0.84	−0.06
1 Yr. Reduction in L.T. Debt & Economic Profits	7.3%	3.8%	3.6%	−0.3%	−9.4%	75%	74%	0.84	−0.06
52 Week Price Range & Price to Book Value	4.5%	2.7%	0.0%	−4.9%	−9.3%	64%	83%	0.81	−0.05
Cash ROIC & Price to Invested Capital	6.7%	3.1%	0.1%	−3.0%	−9.2%	72%	74%	0.71	−0.04
52 Week Price Range & Return on Equity	6.3%	1.7%	0.2%	−2.0%	−9.1%	78%	77%	0.76	−0.03
Capex to PP&E & 52 Week Price Range	4.9%	2.1%	1.5%	−3.3%	−9.0%	75%	79%	0.85	−0.03
EV to Sales & Free Cash Flow to Price	7.6%	3.6%	−0.8%	−2.2%	−8.9%	73%	76%	0.77	−0.03
FCF to Oper. Inc. & Acquisitions to Inv. Cap.	5.9%	3.1%	−0.6%	−5.6%	−8.8%	70%	86%	0.79	−0.04
FCF to Price & 7 Month Relative Strength	9.5%	2.4%	−2.1%	−5.3%	−8.6%	76%	79%	0.97	−0.03
Extern. Fin. to Assets & FCF + Dividend to Price	7.3%	2.4%	1.3%	−3.5%	−8.5%	76%	78%	0.85	−0.02
FCF to Operating Income & Price to Sales	7.9%	2.4%	−0.4%	−5.3%	−8.4%	72%	76%	0.82	−0.02
Debt Red. to Inv. Cap. & Shr. Repur. to Inv. Cap.	4.2%	3.7%	−2.5%	−0.1%	−8.4%	65%	81%	0.83	−0.01
Return on Equity & Return on Assets	3.4%	0.1%	0.9%	0.9%	−8.3%	53%	75%	0.52	−0.01
ROIC & Price to Sales	5.9%	2.4%	1.8%	−1.8%	−8.2%	70%	73%	0.78	0.00
1 Yr. Chg. in Invt.+Rcvbls. Turn. & FCF to Price	7.3%	3.0%	1.5%	−4.0%	−8.0%	74%	83%	0.83	−0.01

EV to EBITDA & FCF to Operating Income	7.9%	2.4%	−0.8%	−3.9%	−7.9%	75%	74%	0.87	0.00
EV to EBITDA & Return on Invested Capital	6.8%	2.2%	−0.1%	−2.2%	−7.4%	78%	77%	0.90	0.02
Oper. Cash Fl. to Capex & Deprec. to Inv. Cap.	7.5%	5.1%	0.4%	−0.5%	−7.4%	78%	78%	0.84	0.01
Return on Equity & Price to Book Value	4.6%	2.3%	0.5%	−1.4%	−7.4%	65%	73%	0.66	0.02
Capex to PP&E & ROIC	4.4%	2.1%	1.2%	−1.3%	−7.3%	64%	68%	0.88	0.02
1 Yr. Reduction in Shares & Deprec. to Inv. Cap.	3.8%	1.6%	2.7%	−1.3%	−7.2%	66%	73%	0.86	0.03
3 Yr. Capex to Inv. Cap. & FCF to Price	5.7%	3.6%	1.1%	−4.5%	−7.1%	68%	79%	0.96	0.03
FCF Per Share Score & EV to EBITDA	8.1%	3.1%	0.8%	−2.7%	−6.7%	76%	73%	1.03	0.07
2 Yr. Capex Growth & Free Cash Flow to Price	8.0%	3.5%	0.6%	−2.6%	−6.6%	79%	80%	0.79	0.05
Prc. to Earns. + Div. & 52 Week Price Range	6.0%	2.7%	1.4%	−3.9%	−6.5%	69%	65%	0.79	0.04
Extern. Fin. to Assets & Price to Book Value	6.0%	2.4%	1.6%	−3.0%	−6.3%	69%	77%	0.75	0.04
Economic Profits (Cash ROIC) & EV to EBITDA	8.1%	1.9%	−1.7%	−2.5%	−6.0%	76%	76%	0.98	0.04
EPS Score & Oper. Cash Flow PS to EPS Est.	6.1%	2.1%	2.5%	−0.3%	−6.0%	78%	75%	0.76	0.06
EV to EBITDA & Total Debt to EBITDA	6.0%	1.0%	−0.3%	−3.0%	−5.6%	75%	71%	0.91	0.10
EBITDA-Capx to Inv. Cap. & FCF to Price	7.8%	2.4%	0.3%	−1.7%	−5.3%	74%	75%	0.89	0.09
Price to Earnings & EV to EBITDA	7.1%	1.2%	0.5%	−3.2%	−5.0%	73%	73%	0.82	0.07
Extern. Fin. to Assets & Acquisitions to Inv. Cap.	4.3%	2.9%	1.4%	−3.4%	−4.9%	68%	71%	0.82	0.00
FCF Per Share Score & Return on Equity	7.0%	1.2%	2.1%	1.5%	−4.8%	71%	66%	0.85	0.13
7 Mo. Rel. Str. & Price to Earnings plus Dividends	4.8%	1.3%	1.0%	−0.5%	−4.7%	69%	68%	0.65	0.10
FCF Per Share 1 Yr. Growth & 28/16 Week RSI	9.0%	4.3%	−0.6%	−1.8%	−4.4%	73%	73%	0.79	0.15
88/36 Mo. Relative Strength & EV to EBITDA	7.7%	2.3%	0.1%	−0.2%	−3.5%	69%	62%	0.83	0.12
EPS Score & Free Cash Flow + Dividend to Price	7.0%	2.6%	1.5%	−1.9%	−3.4%	79%	75%	0.80	0.15
EPS Score & 1 Yr. FCF Gr. to 1 Yr. Inv. Cap. Gr.	5.3%	2.1%	−0.2%	−1.1%	−1.9%	60%	53%	0.81	0.33
Price to Earnings & EPS Score	5.5%	1.5%	0.1%	−0.8%	0.0%	68%	55%	0.66	0.25

T A B L E   B.5

Two-Factor Strategies: Bottom Quintile by Sharpe Ratio

	Excess Returns by Quintile					Outperf.	Underper.	Sharpe Ratio	
Strategy	Q1	Q2	Q3	Q4	Q5	Q1	Q5	Q1	Q5
FCF to Price & Extern. Fin. to Assets	7.1%	2.8%	2.5%	−5.9%	−15.3%	72%	86%	0.86	−0.24
FCF to Operating Income & Extern. Fin. to Assets	7.0%	3.0%	1.8%	−6.3%	−14.4%	73%	82%	0.81	−0.20
FCF to Long-Term Debt & Economic Profits	7.5%	5.1%	2.5%	−1.3%	−13.0%	74%	78%	0.88	−0.18
EV to Sales & 7 Month Relative Strength	6.1%	0.7%	1.3%	−0.5%	−12.9%	78%	86%	0.86	−0.18
Extern. Fin. to Assets & 52 Week Price Range	5.7%	3.4%	1.4%	−3.3%	−13.1%	71%	82%	0.84	−0.18
Acquisitions to Inv. Cap. & Capex to PP&E	5.5%	2.2%	−0.2%	−1.3%	−11.8%	70%	87%	0.81	−0.17
Price to Book & Operating Cash Flow to Equity	6.6%	4.3%	−0.5%	−3.6%	−13.2%	74%	79%	0.72	−0.16
FCF + Repur. + Div. to Price & 1 Yr. Red. in Shrs.	5.6%	1.7%	0.3%	−2.2%	−12.1%	72%	81%	0.88	−0.16
ROIC & 1 Yr. Reduction in Shrs OS	4.6%	1.2%	2.6%	−0.6%	−12.8%	62%	78%	0.86	−0.15
Cash ROIC & Capex to PP&E	4.7%	1.9%	0.5%	−1.1%	−12.9%	74%	78%	0.82	−0.15
Economic Profits (Cash ROIC) & Capex to PP&E	5.3%	1.2%	0.0%	−0.5%	−12.4%	78%	76%	0.73	−0.14
Oper. Cash Fl. to Capex + Int. & Price to Capex	6.8%	4.4%	0.3%	−1.3%	−11.8%	72%	79%	0.76	−0.12
Cash ROIC & Capex to Invested Capital	6.6%	2.8%	0.7%	−2.4%	−10.4%	79%	82%	0.88	−0.10
ROIC & Cash ROIC	8.4%	3.2%	0.8%	0.2%	−10.9%	78%	79%	0.92	−0.09
1 Yr. Reduct. in Shrs. & 7 Mo. Relative Strength	5.8%	0.0%	1.8%	−0.7%	−10.7%	70%	86%	0.81	−0.09
Deprec. to Inv. Cap. & FCF+Repur.+Div. to Price	6.4%	2.5%	1.0%	−4.2%	−9.7%	75%	83%	0.91	−0.08
7 Mo. Rel. Str. & FCF + Div. + Shr. Repur. to Price	8.3%	1.7%	−0.8%	−2.8%	−10.0%	81%	94%	0.76	−0.07
Price to Book & Economic Profits	8.1%	2.0%	−1.1%	−3.1%	−9.9%	74%	74%	0.74	−0.06
1 Yr. Reduction in L.T. Debt & Economic Profits	7.3%	3.8%	3.6%	−0.3%	−9.4%	75%	74%	0.84	−0.06
2 Yr. Capex Growth & Oper. C.F. to Inv. Cap.	6.7%	3.0%	1.8%	1.3%	−9.5%	78%	81%	0.80	−0.06
FCF to Long-Term Debt & Return on Equity	6.0%	2.0%	1.1%	−1.8%	−10.1%	65%	81%	0.81	−0.06
52 Week Price Range & Free Cash Flow to Price	6.9%	2.5%	−1.2%	−7.8%	−9.5%	75%	72%	0.84	−0.06
FCF + Dividend Yield & Return on Equity	6.7%	2.8%	0.7%	−3.1%	−9.7%	78%	78%	0.89	−0.05
EBITDA-Capex to Inv. Cap. & Oper. C.F. to Capex	6.2%	2.6%	0.8%	2.2%	−9.6%	76%	75%	0.79	−0.05
52 Week Price Range & Price to Book Value	4.5%	2.7%	0.0%	−4.9%	−9.3%	64%	83%	0.81	−0.05
Deprec. to Inv. Cap. & Extern. Finan. to Inv. Cap.	4.7%	2.7%	1.8%	−1.8%	−9.7%	74%	82%	0.90	−0.05
Cash ROIC & Price to Invested Capital	6.7%	3.1%	0.1%	−3.0%	−9.2%	72%	74%	0.71	−0.04
28/16 Week RSI & 52 Week Price Range	10.7%	3.9%	−1.0%	−4.5%	−9.6%	80%	84%	0.78	−0.04
FCF to Oper. Income & Acquisitions to Inv. Cap.	5.9%	3.1%	−0.6%	−5.6%	−8.8%	70%	86%	0.79	−0.04
1 Yr. Reduction in Shares & EV to EBITDA	6.0%	1.9%	1.3%	−1.7%	−9.7%	73%	73%	0.90	−0.04
FCF to Price & 7 Month Relative Strength	9.5%	2.4%	−2.1%	−5.3%	−8.6%	76%	79%	0.97	−0.03
28/16 Week RSI & Economic Profits	7.4%	0.6%	−1.8%	−2.5%	−9.8%	70%	78%	0.97	−0.03
Capex to PP&E & 52 Week Price Range	4.9%	2.1%	1.5%	−3.3%	−9.0%	75%	79%	0.85	−0.03
52 Week Price Range & Return on Equity	6.3%	1.7%	0.2%	−2.0%	−9.1%	78%	77%	0.76	−0.03
EV to Sales & Free Cash Flow to Price	7.6%	3.6%	−0.8%	−2.2%	−8.9%	73%	76%	0.77	−0.03
FCF to Operating Income & Price to Sales	7.9%	2.4%	−0.4%	−5.3%	−8.4%	72%	76%	0.82	−0.02
Extern. Fin. to Assets & FCF + Dividend to Price	7.3%	2.4%	1.3%	−3.5%	−8.5%	76%	78%	0.85	−0.02
Debt Red. to Inv. Cap. & Shr. Repur. to Inv. Cap.	4.2%	3.7%	−2.5%	−0.1%	−8.4%	65%	81%	0.83	−0.01
Return on Equity & Return on Assets	3.4%	0.1%	0.9%	0.9%	−8.3%	53%	75%	0.52	−0.01
1 Yr. Chg. in Invt. + Rcvbls. Turn. & FCF to Price	7.3%	3.0%	1.5%	−4.0%	−8.0%	74%	83%	0.83	−0.01
EV to EBITDA & Free Cash Flow to Oper. Inc.	7.9%	2.4%	−0.8%	−3.9%	−7.9%	75%	74%	0.87	0.00

ROIC & Price to Sales	5.9%	2.4%	1.8%	−1.8%	−8.2%	70%	73%	0.78	0.00
Extern. Fin. to Assets & Acquisitions to Inv. Cap.	4.3%	2.9%	1.4%	−3.4%	−4.9%	68%	71%	0.82	0.00
Oper. Cash Fl. to Capex & Deprec. to Inv. Cap.	7.5%	5.1%	0.4%	−0.5%	−7.4%	78%	78%	0.84	0.01
Return on Equity & Price to Book Value	4.6%	2.3%	0.5%	−1.4%	−7.4%	65%	73%	0.66	0.02
Capex to PP&E & Return on Invested Capital	4.4%	2.1%	1.2%	−1.3%	−7.3%	64%	68%	0.88	0.02
EV to EBITDA & Return on Invested Capital	6.8%	2.2%	−0.1%	−2.2%	−7.4%	78%	77%	0.90	0.02
1 Yr. Reduction in Shrs. & Deprec. to Inv. Cap.	3.8%	1.6%	2.7%	−1.3%	−7.2%	66%	73%	0.86	0.03
3 Yr. Capex to Inv. Cap. & FCF to Price	5.7%	3.6%	1.1%	−4.5%	−7.1%	68%	79%	0.96	0.03
Economic Profits (Cash ROIC) & EV to EBITDA	8.1%	1.9%	−1.7%	−2.5%	−6.0%	76%	76%	0.98	0.04
Price to Earnings + Divs. & 52 Week Price Range	6.0%	2.7%	1.4%	−3.9%	−6.5%	69%	65%	0.79	0.04
Extern. Fin. to Assets & Price to Book Value	6.0%	2.4%	1.6%	−3.0%	−6.3%	69%	77%	0.75	0.04
2 Yr Capex Growth & Free Cash Flow to Price	8.0%	3.5%	0.6%	−2.6%	−6.6%	79%	80%	0.79	0.05
EPS Score & Oper. Cash Flow PS to EPS Est.	6.1%	2.1%	2.5%	−0.3%	−6.0%	78%	75%	0.76	0.06
FCF Per Share Score & EV to EBITDA	8.1%	3.1%	0.8%	−2.7%	−6.7%	76%	73%	1.03	0.07
Price to Earnings & EV to EBITDA	7.1%	1.2%	0.5%	−3.2%	−5.0%	73%	73%	0.82	0.07
EBITDA-Capx to Inv. Cap. & FCF to Price	7.8%	2.4%	0.3%	−1.7%	−5.3%	74%	75%	0.89	0.09
7 Mo. Rel. Str. & Price to Earnings plus Dividends	4.8%	1.3%	1.0%	−0.5%	−4.7%	69%	68%	0.65	0.10
EV to EBITDA & Total Debt to EBITDA	6.0%	1.0%	−0.3%	−3.0%	−5.6%	75%	71%	0.91	0.10
88/36 Mo. Relative Strength & EV to EBITDA	7.7%	2.3%	0.1%	−0.2%	−3.5%	69%	62%	0.83	0.12
FCF Per Share Score & Return on Equity	7.0%	1.2%	2.1%	1.5%	−4.8%	71%	66%	0.85	0.13
FCF Per Share 1 Year Growth & 28/16 Week RSI	9.0%	4.3%	−0.6%	−1.8%	−4.4%	73%	73%	0.79	0.15
EPS Score & Free Cash Flow + Dividend to Price	7.0%	2.6%	1.5%	−1.9%	−3.4%	79%	75%	0.80	0.15
Price to Earnings & EPS Score	5.5%	1.5%	0.1%	−0.8%	0.0%	68%	55%	0.66	0.25
EPS Score & 1 Yr. FCF Gr. to 1 Yr. Inv. Cap. Gr.	5.3%	2.1%	−0.2%	−1.1%	−1.9%	60%	53%	0.81	0.33

AVERAGE PORTFOLIO VALUES BY QUINTILE

The tables that follow provide average portfolio values over our test period by quintile for each single-factor strategy presented in this book.[1] The purpose of these tables is to provide financial ratio values for each factor that can be used by the reader in constructing stock screens. For the top and bottom quintiles, we provide high and low values. For the second, third, and fourth quintiles, we provide just the average values. In presenting the highest values for the top quintile and the lowest values for the bottom quintile, we exclude the highest/lowest 5% of values, since these likely represent statistical anomalies ("outliers"). For valuation ratios, and other ratios where the lowest values occur in the top quintile and the highest in the bottom, we exclude the lowest 5% of values from the top quintile and the highest 5% of values from the bottom quintile. My suggestion in using this data is that the reader begin a screen using the median "low" value for the top quintile (or "high" value, if a valuation ratio is being used), then modify the value according to how many results the screen returns. See Chapter 12 for examples of how these values can be used effectively in screens.

---

[1] With two exceptions: we provide values for two-year average earnings per share (EPS) growth instead of the EPS score and for one-year free cash flow (FCF) growth instead of the FCF score (both from Chapter 7), since the actual scores would be difficult or impossible to duplicate with most screening software. Note that we also include values for the operating-cash-flow to equity strategy (cash return on equity), as this factor is used, but not formally presented in Chapters 7 and 13.

T A B L E   C.1

Return on Invested Capital

Year	Q1* High	Q1* Low	Q2 Avg	Q3 Avg	Q4 Avg	Q5* High	Q5* Low
1987	26%	15%	13%	10%	7%	5%	−6%
1988	27%	16%	14%	11%	7%	6%	−5%
1989	29%	17%	15%	11%	8%	6%	−3%
1990	26%	16%	14%	10%	7%	6%	−3%
1991	29%	16%	13%	9%	6%	4%	−13%
1992	27%	16%	13%	9%	5%	3%	−13%
1993	27%	16%	14%	10%	6%	4%	−18%
1994	27%	17%	15%	10%	7%	5%	−7%
1995	28%	18%	15%	11%	7%	5%	−16%
1996	27%	17%	14%	10%	7%	5%	−15%
1997	29%	17%	14%	10%	7%	5%	−13%
1998	28%	17%	15%	10%	6%	4%	−16%
1999	30%	17%	14%	9%	3%	0%	−43%
2000	33%	18%	15%	10%	5%	2%	−28%
2001	27%	15%	13%	8%	2%	−1%	−37%
2002	26%	15%	12%	8%	3%	1%	−22%
2003	27%	15%	12%	8%	4%	1%	−25%
2004	30%	16%	14%	10%	6%	4%	−10%
2005	31%	18%	15%	10%	6%	4%	−12%
2006	31%	18%	15%	10%	7%	5%	−7%
2007	31%	18%	15%	10%	6%	4%	−11%
Minimum	26%	15%	12%	8%	2%	−1%	−43%
Median	28%	17%	14%	10%	6%	4%	−13%
Maxium	33%	18%	15%	11%	8%	6%	−3%

* Note: High values for Q1 exclude top 5% of portfolio values as outliers.
Low values for Q5 exclude bottom 5% of portfolio values as outliers.

TABLE C.2

EBITDA Minus Capex to Invested Capital

Year	Q1* High	Q1* Low	Q2 Avg	Q3 Avg	Q4 Avg	Q5* High	Q5* Low
1987	39%	21%	18%	11%	4%	0%	−18%
1988	37%	22%	18%	12%	6%	2%	−16%
1989	39%	23%	19%	12%	6%	3%	−14%
1990	40%	22%	18%	12%	5%	1%	−12%
1991	37%	21%	18%	12%	5%	1%	−20%
1992	38%	23%	19%	12%	6%	2%	−18%
1993	39%	23%	19%	13%	6%	1%	−23%
1994	39%	24%	20%	13%	7%	3%	−18%
1995	41%	25%	21%	15%	7%	2%	−26%
1996	38%	24%	20%	13%	6%	1%	−28%
1997	41%	24%	21%	14%	7%	3%	−26%
1998	44%	25%	21%	14%	7%	3%	−21%
1999	45%	26%	21%	13%	5%	0%	−28%
2000	43%	26%	21%	14%	6%	1%	−24%
2001	37%	22%	18%	11%	4%	−1%	−27%
2002	38%	22%	18%	12%	6%	2%	−16%
2003	40%	22%	18%	12%	6%	3%	−16%
2004	40%	23%	20%	14%	8%	6%	−11%
2005	41%	24%	20%	14%	8%	5%	−16%
2006	44%	25%	21%	14%	8%	5%	−16%
2007	42%	24%	21%	14%	7%	3%	−24%
Minimum	37%	21%	18%	11%	4%	−1%	−28%
Median	40%	23%	20%	13%	6%	2%	−18%
Maxium	45%	26%	21%	15%	8%	6%	−11%

* Note: High values for Q1 exclude top 5% of portfolio values as outliers.
Low values for Q5 exclude bottom 5% of portfolio values as outliers.

T A B L E   C.3

EBITDA to Invested Capital

Year	Q1* High	Q1* Low	Q2 Avg	Q3 Avg	Q4 Avg	Q5* High	Q5* Low
1987	51%	32%	28%	21%	16%	13%	2%
1988	48%	33%	29%	22%	16%	13%	3%
1989	51%	34%	30%	23%	17%	14%	5%
1990	51%	32%	28%	22%	17%	14%	5%
1991	50%	31%	27%	21%	15%	13%	−3%
1992	50%	32%	28%	21%	15%	12%	−3%
1993	50%	33%	29%	22%	16%	13%	−4%
1994	51%	34%	30%	23%	17%	14%	3%
1995	52%	35%	31%	24%	17%	14%	−4%
1996	50%	34%	30%	22%	17%	14%	−4%
1997	53%	35%	30%	23%	17%	14%	1%
1998	54%	35%	30%	23%	17%	14%	1%
1999	53%	34%	29%	21%	13%	9%	−31%
2000	55%	35%	30%	22%	14%	9%	−17%
2001	49%	32%	27%	19%	12%	8%	−15%
2002	48%	30%	25%	18%	12%	9%	−5%
2003	48%	30%	25%	18%	12%	9%	−6%
2004	50%	32%	27%	20%	14%	11%	0%
2005	52%	33%	28%	21%	14%	12%	−1%
2006	54%	34%	29%	21%	15%	13%	1%
2007	52%	33%	28%	21%	15%	12%	−3%
Minimum	48%	30%	25%	18%	12%	8%	−31%
Median	51%	33%	29%	21%	15%	13%	−3%
Maxium	55%	35%	31%	24%	17%	14%	5%

* Note: High values for Q1 exclude top 5% of portfolio values as outliers.
Low values for Q5 exclude bottom 5% of portfolio values as outliers.

T A B L E C.4

EBIT to Invested Capital

Year	Q1* High	Q1* Low	Q2 Avg	Q3 Avg	Q4 Avg	Q5* High	Q5* Low
1987	44%	26%	22%	16%	11%	8%	−5%
1988	41%	25%	22%	16%	11%	9%	−2%
1989	43%	26%	22%	16%	11%	9%	−2%
1990	42%	25%	21%	15%	11%	9%	−2%
1991	42%	24%	20%	14%	9%	7%	−10%
1992	41%	25%	21%	15%	10%	7%	−7%
1993	42%	25%	21%	15%	10%	7%	−9%
1994	43%	27%	23%	17%	11%	9%	−5%
1995	44%	28%	24%	17%	12%	9%	−13%
1996	41%	27%	23%	16%	11%	9%	−9%
1997	45%	27%	23%	17%	12%	10%	−7%
1998	46%	28%	24%	17%	11%	9%	−7%
1999	44%	26%	22%	15%	7%	3%	−20%
2000	46%	28%	23%	16%	9%	6%	−19%
2001	40%	25%	20%	13%	7%	2%	−28%
2002	40%	23%	19%	13%	7%	4%	−15%
2003	40%	23%	19%	13%	7%	4%	−15%
2004	42%	24%	21%	15%	10%	7%	−6%
2005	43%	26%	22%	15%	10%	7%	−7%
2006	46%	27%	23%	16%	11%	8%	−4%
2007	43%	26%	22%	15%	10%	7%	−7%
Minimum	40%	23%	19%	13%	7%	2%	−28%
Median	43%	26%	22%	15%	10%	7%	−7%
Maxium	46%	28%	24%	17%	12%	10%	−2%

* Note: High values for Q1 exclude top 5% of portfolio values as outliers.
Low values for Q5 exclude bottom 5% of portfolio values as outliers.

T A B L E   C.5

Return on Equity

Year	Q1* High	Q1* Low	Q2 Avg	Q3 Avg	Q4 Avg	Q5* High	Q5* Low
1987	32%	19%	17%	13%	8%	5%	−17%
1988	33%	21%	18%	14%	10%	7%	−11%
1989	34%	21%	18%	14%	10%	7%	−13%
1990	32%	20%	17%	13%	9%	6%	−12%
1991	33%	19%	16%	12%	6%	3%	−29%
1992	32%	19%	16%	12%	6%	3%	−22%
1993	34%	20%	17%	13%	8%	4%	−25%
1994	33%	20%	17%	13%	9%	6%	−18%
1995	34%	21%	19%	14%	9%	6%	−27%
1996	35%	21%	18%	13%	8%	5%	−23%
1997	35%	21%	19%	14%	9%	6%	−21%
1998	36%	22%	19%	13%	8%	5%	−22%
1999	40%	21%	18%	12%	4%	−1%	−71%
2000	43%	23%	20%	14%	7%	3%	−33%
2001	34%	19%	16%	11%	2%	−4%	−45%
2002	34%	18%	16%	10%	4%	1%	−29%
2003	35%	19%	16%	11%	5%	1%	−39%
2004	40%	21%	18%	13%	8%	5%	−18%
2005	41%	22%	19%	13%	8%	5%	−20%
2006	44%	23%	19%	14%	9%	6%	−14%
2007	43%	23%	19%	13%	8%	6%	−18%
Minimum	32%	18%	16%	10%	2%	−4%	−71%
Median	34%	21%	18%	13%	8%	5%	−22%
Maxium	44%	23%	20%	14%	10%	7%	−11%

* Note: High values for Q1 exclude top 5% of portfolio values as outliers.
Low values for Q5 exclude bottom 5% of portfolio values as outliers.

TABLE C.6

Return on Assets

Year	Q1* High	Q1* Low	Q2 Avg	Q3 Avg	Q4 Avg	Q5* High	Q5* Low
1987	16%	9%	8%	5%	2%	1%	−5%
1988	17%	10%	8%	5%	3%	1%	−4%
1989	18%	10%	8%	5%	3%	1%	−4%
1990	18%	10%	8%	5%	3%	1%	−3%
1991	18%	10%	7%	4%	2%	1%	−11%
1992	17%	10%	8%	4%	2%	1%	−9%
1993	17%	10%	8%	4%	2%	1%	−11%
1994	18%	10%	8%	5%	2%	1%	−6%
1995	19%	11%	9%	5%	2%	1%	−12%
1996	18%	10%	8%	5%	2%	1%	−11%
1997	18%	11%	8%	5%	2%	1%	−10%
1998	18%	10%	8%	5%	2%	1%	−13%
1999	19%	10%	8%	4%	1%	−1%	−36%
2000	20%	11%	9%	5%	2%	1%	−21%
2001	17%	9%	7%	3%	0%	−2%	−28%
2002	16%	9%	7%	3%	1%	0%	−16%
2003	16%	9%	7%	3%	1%	0%	−19%
2004	18%	10%	8%	5%	2%	1%	−8%
2005	19%	11%	9%	5%	2%	1%	−10%
2006	20%	11%	9%	5%	3%	1%	−6%
2007	19%	11%	9%	5%	3%	1%	−8%
Minimum	16%	9%	7%	3%	0%	−2%	−36%
Median	18%	10%	8%	5%	2%	1%	−10%
Maxium	20%	11%	9%	5%	3%	1%	−3%

* Note: High values for Q1 exclude top 5% of portfolio values as outliers.
Low values for Q5 exclude bottom 5% of portfolio values as outliers.

TABLE C.7

Economic Profits

Year	Q1* High	Q1* Low	Q2 Avg	Q3 Avg	Q4 Avg	Q5* High	Q5* Low
1987	7%	1%	0%	−3%	−6%	−8%	−19%
1988	8%	2%	1%	−2%	−5%	−7%	−20%
1989	10%	2%	1%	−2%	−5%	−7%	−18%
1990	10%	2%	1%	−2%	−5%	−7%	−16%
1991	9%	1%	0%	−3%	−7%	−10%	−26%
1992	9%	1%	0%	−3%	−7%	−10%	−20%
1993	9%	2%	1%	−2%	−6%	−9%	−22%
1994	9%	2%	1%	−2%	−5%	−8%	−21%
1995	11%	4%	2%	−1%	−5%	−7%	−24%
1996	12%	3%	2%	−1%	−5%	−8%	−22%
1997	12%	4%	2%	−1%	−4%	−6%	−20%
1998	13%	4%	2%	−1%	−5%	−7%	−23%
1999	15%	4%	2%	−1%	−6%	−9%	−26%
2000	19%	6%	4%	0%	−3%	−6%	−22%
2001	12%	5%	2%	−2%	−7%	−11%	−35%
2002	13%	3%	2%	−2%	−7%	−10%	−29%
2003	13%	3%	1%	−2%	−7%	−11%	−33%
2004	14%	4%	2%	−2%	−6%	−8%	−25%
2005	15%	5%	2%	−2%	−6%	−8%	−23%
2006	15%	5%	3%	−1%	−5%	−8%	−21%
2007	15%	5%	3%	−1%	−5%	−8%	−20%
Minimum	7%	1%	0%	−3%	−7%	−11%	−35%
Median	12%	3%	2%	−2%	−5%	−8%	−22%
Maxium	19%	6%	4%	0%	−3%	−6%	−16%

* Note: High values for Q1 exclude top 5% of portfolio values as outliers.
Low values for Q5 exclude bottom 5% of portfolio values as outliers.

TABLE C.8

Economic Profits (No Beta)

Year	Q1* High	Q1* Low	Q2 Avg	Q3 Avg	Q4 Avg	Q5* High	Q5* Low
1987	10%	2%	0%	−3%	−6%	−8%	−21%
1988	11%	3%	1%	−2%	−5%	−7%	−18%
1989	12%	3%	1%	−2%	−5%	−7%	−17%
1990	10%	2%	0%	−2%	−5%	−7%	−17%
1991	11%	1%	0%	−3%	−7%	−9%	−26%
1992	11%	1%	0%	−3%	−7%	−9%	−25%
1993	11%	2%	0%	−3%	−6%	−9%	−27%
1994	10%	3%	1%	−2%	−5%	−7%	−20%
1995	12%	4%	2%	−2%	−5%	−7%	−26%
1996	12%	3%	1%	−2%	−6%	−8%	−24%
1997	13%	4%	2%	−2%	−5%	−7%	−24%
1998	13%	4%	2%	−2%	−5%	−7%	−23%
1999	16%	4%	2%	−2%	−7%	−10%	−43%
2000	17%	5%	3%	−1%	−6%	−9%	−37%
2001	11%	3%	1%	−4%	−9%	−13%	−44%
2002	12%	2%	0%	−4%	−9%	−12%	−32%
2003	12%	2%	0%	−4%	−8%	−11%	−35%
2004	14%	3%	1%	−3%	−6%	−8%	−23%
2005	15%	4%	2%	−2%	−6%	−8%	−23%
2006	16%	4%	2%	−2%	−5%	−8%	−19%
2007	16%	4%	2%	−2%	−5%	−8%	−21%
Minimum	10%	1%	0%	−4%	−9%	−13%	−44%
Median	12%	3%	1%	−2%	−6%	−8%	−24%
Maxium	17%	5%	3%	−1%	−5%	−7%	−17%

* Note: High values for Q1 exclude top 5% of portfolio values as outliers.
Low values for Q5 exclude bottom 5% of portfolio values as outliers.

T A B L E C.9

Economic Profits (with Price to Sales Instead of Beta)

Year	Q1* High	Q1* Low	Q2 Avg	Q3 Avg	Q4 Avg	Q5* High	Q5* Low
1987	10%	2%	1%	−2%	−6%	−9%	−23%
1988	9%	4%	2%	−1%	−5%	−8%	−21%
1989	9%	3%	2%	−2%	−6%	−9%	−22%
1990	9%	3%	1%	−2%	−6%	−8%	−20%
1991	7%	1%	−1%	−4%	−9%	−12%	−30%
1992	8%	1%	−1%	−4%	−9%	−12%	−32%
1993	9%	1%	−1%	−4%	−9%	−12%	−33%
1994	8%	2%	0%	−3%	−7%	−11%	−25%
1995	9%	2%	0%	−3%	−8%	−12%	−30%
1996	8%	1%	0%	−4%	−10%	−13%	−33%
1997	9%	1%	−1%	−4%	−9%	−13%	−30%
1998	10%	2%	0%	−4%	−9%	−13%	−29%
1999	11%	2%	0%	−5%	−12%	−17%	−55%
2000	13%	3%	1%	−4%	−11%	−15%	−47%
2001	9%	1%	−1%	−6%	−13%	−19%	−52%
2002	9%	1%	−1%	−5%	−11%	−15%	−38%
2003	8%	0%	−2%	−6%	−13%	−17%	−44%
2004	10%	1%	−1%	−5%	−11%	−14%	−30%
2005	12%	2%	0%	−5%	−10%	−13%	−29%
2006	13%	2%	0%	−5%	−10%	−13%	−26%
2007	13%	2%	0%	−5%	−10%	−13%	−28%
Minimum	7%	0%	−2%	−6%	−13%	−19%	−55%
Median	9%	2%	0%	−4%	−9%	−13%	−30%
Maxium	13%	4%	2%	−1%	−5%	−8%	−20%

* Note: High values for Q1 exclude top 5% of portfolio values as outliers.
Low values for Q5 exclude bottom 5% of portfolio values as outliers.

TABLE C.10

Economic Profits (with Cash ROIC and Price to Sales)

Year	Q1* High	Q1* Low	Q2 Avg	Q3 Avg	Q4 Avg	Q5* High	Q5* Low
1990	14%	1%	−3%	−8%	−16%	−20%	−39%
1991	14%	0%	−3%	−9%	−17%	−22%	−44%
1992	12%	−1%	−4%	−9%	−17%	−21%	−46%
1993	12%	−1%	−5%	−11%	−19%	−23%	−50%
1994	13%	−1%	−4%	−10%	−18%	−22%	−48%
1995	13%	−1%	−4%	−11%	−20%	−25%	−50%
1996	12%	0%	−4%	−11%	−21%	−27%	−52%
1997	11%	−1%	−5%	−11%	−20%	−25%	−54%
1998	13%	−1%	−4%	−10%	−18%	−23%	−42%
1999	14%	0%	−3%	−9%	−18%	−23%	−45%
2000	12%	0%	−3%	−9%	−19%	−25%	−45%
2001	15%	1%	−2%	−9%	−18%	−23%	−45%
2002	20%	5%	2%	−5%	−12%	−17%	−33%
2003	18%	2%	−1%	−7%	−14%	−19%	−39%
2004	16%	2%	−1%	−7%	−14%	−18%	−35%
2005	16%	2%	−1%	−7%	−14%	−18%	−36%
2006	13%	1%	−2%	−8%	−14%	−18%	−36%
2007	17%	1%	−2%	−7%	−15%	−20%	−45%
Minimum	0%	−1%	−5%	−11%	−21%	−27%	−54%
Median	13%	0%	−3%	−9%	−17%	−22%	−45%
Maxium	20%	5%	2%	−5%	−12%	−17%	−33%

* Note: High values for Q1 exclude top 5% of portfolio values as outliers.
Low values for Q5 exclude bottom 5% of portfolio values as outliers.

T A B L E   C.11

Free Cash Flow to Price

Year	Q1* High	Q1* Low	Q2 Avg	Q3 Avg	Q4 Avg	Q5* High	Q5* Low
1990	27%	11%	8%	3%	−2%	−5%	−25%
1991	22%	9%	7%	3%	−1%	−3%	−14%
1992	18%	8%	6%	3%	−1%	−3%	−15%
1993	18%	7%	5%	2%	−2%	−4%	−16%
1994	20%	7%	6%	2%	−2%	−4%	−18%
1995	18%	7%	5%	2%	−2%	−3%	−14%
1996	16%	7%	5%	2%	−2%	−4%	−16%
1997	12%	6%	4%	2%	−1%	−3%	−17%
1998	13%	6%	5%	2%	−1%	−2%	−18%
1999	15%	6%	5%	2%	0%	−1%	−11%
2000	15%	7%	5%	2%	0%	−2%	−11%
2001	18%	8%	6%	3%	−1%	−3%	−15%
2002	25%	12%	9%	6%	2%	0%	−14%
2003	19%	8%	6%	4%	1%	0%	−9%
2004	18%	8%	6%	4%	1%	0%	−8%
2005	17%	8%	6%	4%	1%	0%	−10%
2006	15%	7%	6%	4%	1%	−1%	−10%
2007	19%	8%	7%	4%	1%	−1%	−16%
Minimum	12%	6%	4%	2%	−2%	−5%	−25%
Median	18%	7%	6%	3%	−1%	−2%	−15%
Maxium	27%	12%	9%	6%	2%	0%	−8%

* Note: High values for Q1 exclude top 5% of portfolio values as outliers.
Low values for Q5 exclude bottom 5% of portfolio values as outliers.

TABLE C.12

Enterprise Value to EBITDA

Year	Q1* Low	Q1* High	Q2 Avg	Q3 Avg	Q4 Avg	Q5* Low	Q5* High
1987	3.7	5.1	5.6	7.1	9.5	11.7	101.5
1988	3.9	5.4	5.9	7.3	9.6	11.6	50.3
1989	3.8	5.7	6.3	7.8	10.3	12.6	41.3
1990	3.4	5.0	5.6	6.9	9.0	10.6	28.7
1991	4.3	6.4	7.0	8.8	12.7	17.0	−152.3
1992	4.9	6.7	7.5	9.5	13.0	16.4	−80.6
1993	5.1	6.9	7.7	9.8	13.7	17.5	−98.3
1994	4.4	6.1	6.8	8.5	11.5	14.3	72.6
1995	4.5	6.5	7.4	9.6	13.8	18.0	−145.9
1996	5.0	7.0	7.9	10.3	15.3	20.9	−128.5
1997	5.4	7.6	8.5	11.0	15.7	20.2	314.9
1998	5.1	7.3	8.3	11.1	16.3	21.4	349.5
1999	4.9	7.3	8.6	13.1	27.4	65.9	−50.5
2000	4.4	6.9	7.9	11.2	20.2	35.9	−25.2
2001	4.6	7.2	8.3	11.5	18.5	27.4	−18.6
2002	4.1	6.7	7.5	9.8	13.7	17.3	−33.1
2003	5.2	7.9	8.9	11.8	17.2	22.9	−42.8
2004	5.2	7.8	8.8	11.4	15.5	19.0	1171.0
2005	5.1	7.7	8.6	10.9	15.2	19.3	−736.2
2006	4.9	7.6	8.5	10.8	14.2	17.3	273.3
2007	4.6	7.0	8.0	10.6	15.2	19.5	−186.8
Minimum	3.4	5.0	5.6	6.9	9.0	10.6	−736.2
Median	4.6	6.9	7.9	10.3	14.2	18.0	−25.2
Maxium	5.4	7.9	8.9	13.1	27.4	65.9	1171.0

* Note: Low values for Q1 exclude top 5% of portfolio values as outliers.
High values for Q5 exclude bottom 5% of portfolio values as outliers.

TABLE C.13

Price to Earnings (Current Year EPS Estimate)

Year	Q1* Low	Q1* High	Q2 Avg	Q3 Avg	Q4 Avg	Q5* Low	Q5* High
1987	6.1	8.6	9.6	12.2	16.5	20.4	−166.7
1988	6.0	8.8	9.8	12.0	15.3	17.5	142.9
1989	7.0	9.8	10.9	13.7	18.2	21.7	−100.0
1990	6.0	8.6	9.7	12.6	17.1	20.8	−40.0
1991	8.9	12.2	13.6	17.5	25.3	33.3	−29.4
1992	9.8	13.0	14.4	18.0	24.7	31.3	−32.3
1993	9.5	13.0	14.5	18.3	25.6	33.3	−38.5
1994	8.0	10.9	12.2	15.5	21.1	26.3	500.0
1995	9.3	12.3	13.8	17.5	25.0	33.3	−55.6
1996	10.5	13.5	15.0	19.0	27.8	38.5	−45.5
1997	11.8	15.4	16.8	20.6	28.2	35.7	−100.0
1998	10.3	14.5	16.1	21.3	31.7	41.7	−50.0
1999	8.8	12.8	15.5	25.6	69.0	500.0	−21.3
2000	8.6	12.5	14.5	20.8	39.2	76.9	−21.3
2001	10.4	14.9	17.4	24.7	50.0	142.9	−14.1
2002	8.4	12.5	13.8	17.7	27.0	38.5	−17.5
2003	11.1	15.4	17.2	22.5	35.1	52.6	−23.3
2004	10.8	15.6	17.2	21.3	28.6	35.7	−58.8
2005	9.8	14.7	16.1	19.8	26.7	33.3	−55.6
2006	9.5	14.9	16.3	19.4	25.3	31.3	−200.0
2007	9.2	13.2	14.7	18.7	25.6	32.3	−47.6
Minimum	6.0	8.6	9.6	12.0	15.3	17.5	−200.0
Median	9.3	13.0	14.5	18.7	25.6	33.3	−40.0
Maximum	11.8	15.6	17.4	25.6	69.0	500.0	500.0

* Note: Low values for Q1 exclude top 5% of portfolio values as outliers.
High values for Q5 exclude bottom 5% of portfolio values as outliers.

T A B L E C.14

Price to Earnings Plus Dividends (Current Year EPS Estimate)

Year	Q1* Low	Q1* High	Q2 Avg	Q3 Avg	Q4 Avg	Q5* Low	Q5* High
1987	5.3	7.5	8.2	10.2	13.8	17.5	−250.0
1988	5.2	7.5	8.3	10.1	13.1	15.6	76.9
1989	5.8	8.2	9.2	11.6	15.4	19.2	−142.9
1990	5.0	7.0	8.0	10.4	14.0	17.2	−166.7
1991	7.4	10.2	11.4	14.5	21.1	28.6	−28.6
1992	7.9	10.9	12.1	15.4	21.5	27.8	−41.7
1993	8.0	10.9	12.2	15.6	22.2	29.4	−45.5
1994	6.8	9.2	10.3	13.2	18.2	23.3	200.0
1995	7.5	10.6	11.8	15.2	22.2	30.3	−100.0
1996	8.5	11.6	12.9	16.7	25.3	35.7	−52.6
1997	9.8	13.2	14.7	18.5	25.3	32.3	−125.0
1998	8.6	12.5	14.1	18.9	29.0	40.0	−71.4
1999	7.6	11.4	13.5	22.0	58.8	333.3	−23.3
2000	7.2	11.2	12.9	18.5	35.7	71.4	−23.3
2001	9.1	13.5	15.3	21.7	44.4	100.0	−14.5
2002	7.5	11.0	12.3	16.0	24.1	34.5	−18.9
2003	9.5	13.9	15.4	20.0	31.7	47.6	−22.2
2004	8.8	13.5	15.2	19.2	26.0	32.3	−58.8
2005	8.0	12.7	14.1	17.9	24.7	31.3	−52.6
2006	7.6	12.3	13.9	17.4	23.1	28.7	−4126.2
2007	7.4	11.0	12.5	16.5	23.5	30.3	−58.8
Minimum	5.0	7.0	8.0	10.1	13.1	15.6	−4126.2
Median	7.6	11.0	12.5	16.5	23.5	30.3	−52.6
Maxium	9.8	13.9	15.4	22.0	58.8	333.3	200.0

* Note: Low values for Q1 exclude top 5% of portfolio values as outliers.
High values for Q5 exclude bottom 5% of portfolio values as outliers.

T A B L E   C.15

Enterprise Value to Sales

| Year | Q1* | | Q2 | Q3 | Q4 | Q5* | |
	Low	High	Avg	Avg	Avg	Low	High
1987	0.3	0.5	0.7	1.0	1.6	2.2	5.8
1988	0.3	0.6	0.7	1.0	1.6	2.2	5.0
1989	0.3	0.6	0.8	1.2	1.9	2.6	6.5
1990	0.3	0.5	0.7	1.1	1.8	2.4	5.6
1991	0.3	0.6	0.8	1.4	2.3	3.1	14.3
1992	0.4	0.7	0.9	1.5	2.3	3.1	10.3
1993	0.4	0.8	1.0	1.6	2.5	3.4	11.4
1994	0.4	0.7	0.9	1.4	2.3	3.1	7.8
1995	0.4	0.8	1.1	1.8	3.0	4.3	14.9
1996	0.5	0.9	1.1	1.9	3.3	4.8	14.5
1997	0.5	1.0	1.3	2.1	3.5	4.8	11.9
1998	0.5	1.0	1.3	2.1	3.5	5.0	13.0
1999	0.5	1.1	1.5	2.8	6.0	11.4	125.0
2000	0.5	1.0	1.3	2.4	4.8	7.4	35.7
2001	0.4	0.9	1.2	2.0	3.5	5.0	14.5
2002	0.4	0.8	1.0	1.7	2.8	3.9	8.4
2003	0.4	1.0	1.2	2.1	3.6	5.0	12.2
2004	0.5	1.0	1.3	2.1	3.6	5.2	13.0
2005	0.5	1.0	1.2	2.0	3.5	5.0	12.3
2006	0.5	1.0	1.2	2.0	3.4	4.8	10.9
2007	0.4	1.0	1.2	2.1	3.6	4.9	13.5
Minimum	0.3	0.5	0.7	1.0	1.6	2.2	5.0
Median	0.4	0.9	1.1	1.9	3.3	4.8	12.2
Maxium	0.5	1.1	1.5	2.8	6.0	11.4	125.0

* Note: Low values for Q1 exclude top 5% of portfolio values as outliers.
High values for Q5 exclude bottom 5% of portfolio values as outliers.

TABLE C.16

Dividend Plus Share Repurchase Yield

Year	Q1* High	Q1* Low	Q2 Avg	Q3 Avg	Q4 Avg	Q5* High	Q5* Low
1987	12%	5%	3%	1%	−1%	−2%	−24%
1988	14%	6%	5%	2%	1%	0%	−11%
1989	13%	5%	4%	2%	0%	0%	−10%
1990	16%	7%	5%	2%	0%	0%	−12%
1991	8%	4%	3%	1%	0%	−1%	−12%
1992	7%	3%	2%	1%	−2%	−3%	−19%
1993	6%	3%	2%	1%	−1%	−3%	−16%
1994	7%	3%	2%	1%	−1%	−2%	−18%
1995	7%	3%	2%	1%	0%	−1%	−14%
1996	7%	3%	2%	0%	−1%	−3%	−17%
1997	7%	3%	2%	0%	−1%	−1%	−13%
1998	11%	4%	3%	1%	0%	−1%	−12%
1999	10%	4%	2%	1%	−1%	−1%	−10%
2000	11%	4%	3%	1%	−1%	−2%	−21%
2001	6%	3%	2%	0%	−1%	−1%	−12%
2002	7%	3%	2%	0%	−1%	−1%	−15%
2003	6%	2%	1%	0%	0%	−1%	−8%
2004	7%	3%	2%	0%	−1%	−1%	−11%
2005	9%	4%	3%	1%	−1%	−1%	−10%
2006	11%	5%	4%	1%	0%	−1%	−11%
2007	16%	6%	4%	1%	0%	−1%	−11%
Minimum	6%	2%	1%	0%	−2%	−3%	−24%
Median	8%	4%	2%	1%	−1%	−1%	−12%
Maxium	16%	7%	5%	2%	1%	0%	−8%

* Note: Low values for Q1 exclude top 5% of portfolio values as outliers.
High values for Q5 exclude bottom 5% of portfolio values as outliers.

TABLE C.17

Price to Book Value

Year	Q1* Low	Q1* High	Q2 Avg	Q3 Avg	Q4 Avg	Q5* Low	Q5* High
1987	0.6	1.0	1.2	1.6	2.4	3.1	7.2
1988	0.7	1.1	1.3	1.7	2.5	3.1	6.8
1989	0.8	1.2	1.4	2.0	3.0	3.9	8.7
1990	0.5	0.9	1.1	1.6	2.5	3.4	8.4
1991	0.7	1.3	1.5	2.1	3.6	5.5	20.7
1992	0.9	1.4	1.6	2.3	3.6	4.8	13.1
1993	1.0	1.5	1.8	2.6	4.1	5.5	16.1
1994	0.9	1.3	1.6	2.2	3.3	4.4	12.4
1995	1.1	1.6	1.9	2.7	4.4	6.4	23.0
1996	1.1	1.7	2.0	2.9	4.8	6.7	20.3
1997	1.3	2.0	2.3	3.3	5.0	6.6	18.1
1998	1.0	1.8	2.1	3.1	5.2	7.7	25.0
1999	1.0	1.7	2.1	3.8	8.2	15.5	115.4
2000	0.9	1.7	2.1	3.1	5.4	8.2	26.1
2001	0.9	1.5	1.8	2.6	4.0	5.6	16.6
2002	0.7	1.3	1.5	2.0	3.0	3.8	10.3
2003	1.1	1.7	2.0	2.7	4.0	5.4	16.2
2004	1.2	1.8	2.1	2.9	4.1	5.3	15.6
2005	1.1	1.7	2.0	2.8	4.1	5.4	14.7
2006	1.2	1.8	2.1	2.9	4.2	5.4	15.7
2007	0.9	1.6	1.9	2.8	4.5	6.1	22.3
Minimum	0.5	0.9	1.1	1.6	2.4	3.1	6.8
Median	0.9	1.6	1.9	2.7	4.1	5.4	16.1
Maxium	1.3	2.0	2.3	3.8	8.2	15.5	115.4

* Note: Low values for Q1 exclude top 5% of portfolio values as outliers.
High values for Q5 exclude bottom 5% of portfolio values as outliers.

TABLE C.18

Free Cash Flow to Operating Income

Year	Q1* High	Q1* Low	Q2 Avg	Q3 Avg	Q4 Avg	Q5* High	Q5* Low
1990	177%	75%	59%	28%	−61%	−134%	−246%
1991	215%	86%	70%	39%	−44%	−114%	−254%
1992	192%	82%	66%	37%	−49%	−122%	−252%
1993	166%	75%	61%	32%	−60%	−137%	−280%
1994	158%	74%	60%	30%	−58%	−132%	−306%
1995	146%	70%	56%	28%	−60%	−133%	−268%
1996	153%	74%	60%	31%	−60%	−136%	−292%
1997	129%	70%	57%	29%	−58%	−132%	−283%
1998	136%	75%	60%	32%	−51%	−122%	−301%
1999	150%	77%	64%	41%	−37%	−104%	−230%
2000	153%	76%	63%	39%	−40%	−107%	−249%
2001	225%	98%	82%	52%	20%	0%	−228%
2002	338%	125%	103%	70%	41%	22%	−199%
2003	301%	113%	94%	65%	40%	25%	−174%
2004	207%	102%	87%	61%	33%	16%	−197%
2005	202%	100%	85%	59%	34%	18%	−195%
2006	174%	97%	81%	54%	23%	4%	−206%
2007	189%	97%	82%	56%	24%	5%	−250%
Minimum	129%	70%	56%	28%	−61%	−137%	−306%
Median	175%	80%	65%	39%	−42%	−110%	−250%
Maxium	338%	125%	103%	70%	41%	25%	−174%

* Note: High values for Q1 exclude top 5% of portfolio values as outliers.
Low values for Q5 exclude bottom 5% of portfolio values as outliers.

TABLE C.19

Cash Return on Invested Capital

Year	Q1* High	Q1* Low	Q2 Avg	Q3 Avg	Q4 Avg	Q5* High	Q5* Low
1990	31%	14%	10%	4%	−2%	−6%	−22%
1991	31%	15%	11%	5%	−1%	−5%	−26%
1992	29%	15%	11%	5%	−2%	−5%	−25%
1993	30%	15%	11%	4%	−3%	−7%	−30%
1994	31%	15%	11%	4%	−3%	−7%	−28%
1995	31%	15%	11%	4%	−4%	−9%	−30%
1996	30%	16%	12%	4%	−4%	−8%	−32%
1997	30%	14%	11%	4%	−3%	−7%	−32%
1998	31%	15%	12%	5%	−1%	−5%	−28%
1999	36%	16%	12%	5%	−1%	−5%	−29%
2000	32%	16%	12%	5%	−1%	−5%	−25%
2001	32%	17%	13%	6%	−1%	−5%	−23%
2002	38%	20%	16%	9%	3%	0%	−15%
2003	36%	18%	14%	8%	3%	−1%	−19%
2004	34%	18%	15%	8%	3%	0%	−18%
2005	34%	19%	15%	9%	3%	0%	−21%
2006	34%	19%	15%	8%	2%	−1%	−21%
2007	35%	19%	15%	8%	2%	−2%	−27%
Minimum	29%	14%	10%	4%	−4%	−9%	−32%
Median	32%	16%	12%	5%	−1%	−5%	−25%
Maxium	38%	20%	16%	9%	3%	0%	−15%

* Note: High values for Q1 exclude top 5% of portfolio values as outliers.
Low values for Q5 exclude bottom 5% of portfolio values as outliers.

T A B L E C.20

Operating Cash Flow to Equity

Year	Q1* High	Q1* Low	Q2 Avg	Q3 Avg	Q4 Avg	Q5* High	Q5* Low
1990	64%	38%	33%	23%	15%	11%	−12%
1991	68%	39%	32%	22%	14%	10%	−15%
1992	61%	35%	30%	21%	13%	8%	−17%
1993	62%	36%	30%	20%	11%	6%	−25%
1994	63%	37%	31%	21%	12%	8%	−16%
1995	63%	37%	31%	21%	12%	7%	−22%
1996	67%	37%	32%	22%	12%	7%	−22%
1997	69%	38%	32%	22%	12%	7%	−17%
1998	71%	39%	33%	22%	14%	9%	−14%
1999	76%	39%	33%	23%	13%	7%	−23%
2000	71%	39%	32%	21%	11%	5%	−17%
2001	76%	39%	32%	21%	11%	6%	−17%
2002	79%	40%	34%	24%	15%	10%	−9%
2003	78%	39%	32%	22%	13%	9%	−16%
2004	71%	39%	32%	22%	14%	9%	−15%
2005	69%	38%	32%	23%	15%	11%	−10%
2006	67%	38%	32%	23%	15%	10%	−6%
2007	73%	38%	32%	24%	16%	11%	−8%
Minimum	61%	35%	30%	20%	11%	5%	−25%
Median	69%	38%	32%	22%	13%	8%	−16%
Maxium	79%	40%	34%	24%	16%	11%	−6%

* Note: High values for Q1 exclude top 5% of portfolio values as outliers.
Low values for Q5 exclude bottom 5% of portfolio values as outliers.

T A B L E   C.21

Free Cash Flow Plus Dividend Plus Share Repurchase to Price

Year	Q1* High	Q1* Low	Q2 Avg	Q3 Avg	Q4 Avg	Q5* High	Q5* Low
1990	41%	16%	12%	5%	−2%	−6%	−29%
1991	28%	12%	9%	4%	−2%	−5%	−20%
1992	22%	10%	7%	3%	−3%	−7%	−31%
1993	21%	9%	7%	2%	−4%	−8%	−24%
1994	25%	10%	8%	3%	−3%	−8%	−28%
1995	22%	10%	7%	2%	−3%	−6%	−21%
1996	21%	10%	7%	2%	−4%	−7%	−27%
1997	16%	8%	6%	2%	−3%	−6%	−25%
1998	22%	9%	7%	3%	−2%	−4%	−24%
1999	23%	10%	7%	2%	−1%	−3%	−19%
2000	24%	11%	8%	3%	−3%	−6%	−31%
2001	23%	10%	7%	3%	−2%	−5%	−23%
2002	28%	14%	11%	6%	1%	−3%	−23%
2003	21%	10%	8%	4%	1%	−1%	−13%
2004	20%	10%	8%	4%	1%	−1%	−15%
2005	22%	11%	9%	5%	1%	−1%	−16%
2006	21%	12%	10%	5%	1%	−1%	−18%
2007	30%	14%	11%	6%	1%	−2%	−21%
Minimum	16%	8%	6%	2%	−4%	−8%	−31%
Median	22%	10%	8%	3%	−2%	−5%	−23%
Maxium	41%	16%	12%	6%	1%	−1%	−13%

* Note: High values for Q1 exclude top 5% of portfolio values as outliers.
Low values for Q5 exclude bottom 5% of portfolio values as outliers.

TABLE C.22

One-Year Free Cash Flow Growth (provided in place of the FCF score)

Year	Q1* High	Q1* Low	Q2 Avg	Q3 Avg	Q4 Avg	Q5* High	Q5* Low
1989	459%	173%	115%	19%	−67%	−114%	−665%
1990	761%	145%	89%	6%	−66%	−110%	−582%
1991	661%	152%	99%	17%	−43%	−74%	−355%
1992	598%	123%	76%	4%	−57%	−94%	−455%
1993	472%	117%	68%	−4%	−63%	−98%	−453%
1994	657%	128%	82%	10%	−56%	−97%	−417%
1995	639%	124%	76%	3%	−62%	−102%	−543%
1996	584%	138%	87%	11%	−53%	−93%	−447%
1997	449%	112%	70%	4%	−57%	−92%	−364%
1998	549%	127%	77%	5%	−53%	−88%	−438%
1999	578%	148%	100%	25%	−32%	−62%	−321%
2000	692%	142%	90%	13%	−50%	−87%	−388%
2001	622%	165%	107%	20%	−42%	−76%	−340%
2002	801%	168%	117%	36%	−21%	−48%	−196%
2003	600%	120%	77%	14%	−28%	−50%	−182%
2004	503%	116%	75%	17%	−25%	−49%	−231%
2005	597%	107%	66%	9%	−28%	−49%	−254%
2006	475%	99%	61%	5%	−38%	−64%	−248%
2007	505%	106%	69%	15%	−30%	−56%	−258%
Minimum	449%	99%	61%	−4%	−67%	−114%	−665%
Median	597%	127%	77%	11%	−50%	−87%	−364%
Maxium	801%	173%	117%	36%	−21%	−48%	−182%

* Note: High values for Q1 exclude top 5% of portfolio values as outliers.
Low values for Q5 exclude bottom 5% of portfolio values as outliers.

T A B L E C.23

Two-Year Average EPS Growth (provided in place of the EPS score)

	Q1*		Q2	Q3	Q4	Q5*	
Year	High	Low	Avg	Avg	Avg	High	Low
1987	167%	41%	29%	11%	−6%	−17%	−177%
1988	235%	61%	43%	18%	3%	−5%	−108%
1989	266%	53%	38%	18%	4%	−4%	−87%
1990	148%	34%	25%	9%	−4%	−12%	−82%
1991	169%	34%	23%	6%	−14%	−27%	−142%
1992	193%	44%	29%	8%	−11%	−24%	−196%
1993	266%	62%	42%	15%	−4%	−15%	−167%
1994	342%	69%	47%	18%	1%	−8%	−142%
1995	349%	75%	51%	20%	2%	−7%	−111%
1996	278%	65%	46%	20%	3%	−6%	−117%
1997	254%	59%	42%	19%	3%	−6%	−122%
1998	225%	55%	39%	16%	−1%	−12%	−117%
1999	289%	55%	38%	14%	−8%	−23%	−212%
2000	416%	87%	59%	22%	3%	−8%	−143%
2001	370%	60%	40%	11%	−16%	−34%	−251%
2002	284%	48%	32%	7%	−21%	−40%	−231%
2003	335%	82%	56%	21%	−3%	−17%	−197%
2004	399%	105%	73%	29%	9%	0%	−114%
2005	427%	95%	65%	26%	7%	−1%	−84%
2006	357%	76%	53%	22%	6%	−1%	−84%
2007	258%	65%	46%	19%	4%	−4%	−77%
Minimum	148%	34%	23%	6%	−21%	−40%	−251%
Median	278%	61%	42%	18%	1%	−8%	−122%
Maxium	427%	105%	73%	29%	9%	0%	−77%

* Note: High values for Q1 exclude top 5% of portfolio values as outliers.
Low values for Q5 exclude bottom 5% of portfolio values as outliers.

TABLE C.24

Two-Year Average Capex Growth

Year	Q1* Low	Q1* High	Q2 Avg	Q3 Avg	Q4 Avg	Q5* Low	Q5* High
1987	−38%	−14%	−5%	12%	34%	48%	127%
1988	−31%	−7%	1%	17%	40%	55%	138%
1989	−30%	−4%	5%	22%	46%	61%	180%
1990	−30%	−4%	3%	18%	39%	52%	152%
1991	−39%	−14%	−5%	11%	30%	43%	128%
1992	−41%	−18%	−11%	5%	26%	40%	111%
1993	−40%	−15%	−7%	10%	35%	52%	141%
1994	−34%	−9%	0%	17%	43%	60%	173%
1995	−30%	−3%	4%	21%	46%	61%	158%
1996	−28%	−3%	6%	22%	49%	67%	154%
1997	−27%	−5%	3%	19%	44%	60%	171%
1998	−25%	−4%	4%	20%	41%	54%	145%
1999	−34%	−9%	−1%	15%	37%	51%	125%
2000	−34%	−12%	−3%	14%	38%	54%	145%
2001	−33%	−12%	−4%	13%	38%	54%	141%
2002	−46%	−25%	−17%	0%	20%	32%	110%
2003	−53%	−27%	−19%	−3%	16%	27%	89%
2004	−38%	−13%	−5%	10%	30%	42%	121%
2005	−27%	−3%	4%	20%	42%	57%	142%
2006	−23%	0%	8%	23%	45%	60%	136%
2007	−22%	−1%	6%	21%	41%	55%	134%
Minimum	−53%	−27%	−19%	−3%	16%	27%	89%
Median	−33%	−9%	0%	17%	39%	54%	141%
Maxium	−22%	0%	8%	23%	49%	67%	180%

* Note: Low values for Q1 exclude top 5% of portfolio values as outliers.
High values for Q5 exclude bottom 5% of portfolio values as outliers

T A B L E C.25

Net Share Repurchase to Invested Capital

| Year | Q1* | | Q2 | Q3 | Q4 | Q5* | |
	Low	High	Avg	Avg	Avg	Low	High
1987	−9.0%	−0.9%	−0.5%	0.3%	2.3%	4.1%	31.6%
1988	−13.0%	−3.3%	−1.9%	−0.2%	0.4%	0.8%	15.5%
1989	−10.4%	−1.7%	−0.8%	0.1%	0.7%	1.2%	15.9%
1990	−9.9%	−2.3%	−1.2%	0.0%	0.7%	1.2%	20.7%
1991	−5.1%	−0.6%	−0.3%	0.2%	1.9%	3.5%	47.5%
1992	−5.7%	−0.1%	0.0%	0.4%	3.6%	6.5%	51.4%
1993	−6.6%	−0.1%	0.0%	0.4%	3.6%	6.3%	48.5%
1994	−7.2%	−0.5%	−0.2%	0.3%	2.8%	5.0%	41.3%
1995	−9.7%	−1.1%	−0.5%	0.3%	2.4%	4.1%	47.2%
1996	−9.9%	−1.4%	−0.7%	0.5%	5.2%	9.4%	69.5%
1997	−12.5%	−2.5%	−1.2%	0.4%	3.0%	5.3%	48.1%
1998	−18.5%	−4.9%	−2.6%	0.1%	2.2%	3.8%	35.5%
1999	−17.3%	−4.6%	−2.3%	0.3%	3.7%	6.5%	47.8%
2000	−17.3%	−4.9%	−2.6%	0.3%	4.9%	8.7%	77.0%
2001	−11.6%	−2.0%	−1.0%	0.4%	2.1%	3.4%	35.3%
2002	−13.5%	−2.1%	−1.1%	0.4%	1.7%	2.8%	25.2%
2003	−12.5%	−1.9%	−1.0%	0.3%	1.5%	2.5%	17.4%
2004	−14.9%	−2.8%	−1.4%	0.5%	2.2%	3.4%	26.4%
2005	−19.5%	−5.0%	−2.5%	0.4%	2.0%	3.1%	23.1%
2006	−25.0%	−8.0%	−4.4%	−0.2%	1.6%	2.7%	29.4%
2007	−32.9%	−8.9%	−4.9%	−0.2%	1.4%	2.4%	38.2%
Minimum	−32.9%	−8.9%	−4.9%	−0.2%	0.4%	0.8%	15.5%
Median	−12.5%	−2.1%	−1.1%	0.3%	2.2%	3.5%	35.5%
Maxium	−5.1%	−0.1%	0.0%	0.5%	5.2%	9.4%	77.0%

* Note: Low values for Q1 exclude top 5% of portfolio values as outliers.
High values for Q5 exclude bottom 5% of portfolio values as outliers

TABLE C.26

One-Year Reduction in Shares Outstanding

Year	Q1* High	Q1* Low	Q2 Avg	Q3 Avg	Q4 Avg	Q5* High	Q5* Low
1987	4.7%	0.0%	−0.1%	−0.7%	−3.2%	−5.3%	−31.9%
1988	8.4%	1.8%	0.9%	−0.2%	−1.2%	−2.1%	−20.5%
1989	6.3%	0.4%	0.2%	−0.4%	−1.8%	−2.9%	−24.9%
1990	6.4%	1.2%	0.6%	−0.3%	−1.8%	−2.9%	−21.1%
1991	3.3%	0.1%	−0.1%	−0.7%	−4.2%	−7.2%	−32.7%
1992	2.5%	0.0%	−0.2%	−1.1%	−5.5%	−9.4%	−43.2%
1993	2.4%	0.0%	−0.3%	−1.3%	−6.0%	−10.0%	−39.6%
1994	3.6%	0.0%	−0.2%	−1.0%	−4.3%	−7.0%	−37.3%
1995	4.2%	0.2%	−0.1%	−0.9%	−4.8%	−8.1%	−38.3%
1996	4.7%	0.3%	−0.1%	−1.2%	−6.2%	−10.3%	−45.7%
1997	4.7%	0.5%	0.0%	−1.2%	−6.2%	−10.4%	−45.9%
1998	6.6%	1.5%	0.6%	−1.0%	−5.7%	−9.7%	−56.7%
1999	7.0%	1.7%	0.8%	−1.0%	−5.6%	−9.3%	−47.5%
2000	8.3%	2.5%	1.2%	−1.2%	−7.3%	−12.3%	−46.9%
2001	4.1%	0.5%	0.0%	−1.2%	−4.6%	−7.2%	−34.4%
2002	4.5%	0.7%	0.1%	−0.9%	−3.4%	−5.5%	−29.0%
2003	4.9%	0.7%	0.1%	−0.9%	−2.8%	−4.2%	−21.1%
2004	4.3%	0.3%	−0.2%	−1.4%	−4.0%	−6.0%	−29.8%
2005	6.2%	1.2%	0.3%	−1.1%	−3.3%	−5.0%	−29.0%
2006	7.3%	2.4%	1.1%	−0.7%	−2.9%	−4.5%	−26.9%
2007	8.5%	3.0%	1.4%	−0.7%	−2.5%	−3.9%	−30.0%
Minimum	2.4%	0.0%	−0.3%	−1.4%	−7.3%	−12.3%	−56.7%
Median	4.7%	0.5%	0.1%	−1.0%	−4.2%	−7.0%	−32.7%
Maxium	8.5%	3.0%	1.4%	−0.2%	−1.2%	−2.1%	−20.5%

* Note: High values for Q1 exclude top 5% of portfolio values as outliers.
Low values for Q5 exclude bottom 5% of portfolio values as outliers.

TABLE C.27

One-Year Reduction in Long-Term Debt

Year	Q1* High	Q1* Low	Q2 Avg	Q3 Avg	Q4 Avg	Q5* High	Q5* Low
1987	56.2%	16.9%	9.8%	−3.1%	−32.5%	−56.3%	−411.6%
1988	46.9%	14.0%	8.0%	−2.4%	−23.6%	−40.4%	−228.2%
1989	49.6%	13.8%	7.9%	−4.1%	−28.1%	−46.0%	−286.7%
1990	54.8%	14.3%	8.1%	−1.8%	−18.5%	−31.4%	−151.2%
1991	79.7%	20.8%	13.1%	1.3%	−14.5%	−26.3%	−176.5%
1992	78.4%	24.4%	15.5%	2.1%	−14.8%	−27.3%	−167.5%
1993	80.4%	23.6%	15.0%	1.7%	−18.3%	−33.6%	−275.0%
1994	69.9%	20.0%	11.8%	−0.5%	−21.3%	−38.2%	−247.2%
1995	76.5%	19.9%	11.3%	−2.1%	−26.6%	−46.2%	−274.4%
1996	80.0%	19.6%	11.4%	−3.5%	−32.3%	−54.4%	−285.9%
1997	78.4%	17.3%	8.7%	−9.0%	−51.0%	−84.0%	−463.4%
1998	71.9%	14.2%	7.1%	−10.7%	−52.8%	−84.2%	−449.2%
1999	72.0%	15.2%	7.9%	−6.7%	−37.3%	−60.6%	−285.7%
2000	86.5%	19.9%	11.1%	−3.3%	−27.5%	−46.1%	−260.1%
2001	96.0%	24.4%	14.5%	−1.0%	−24.3%	−41.9%	−207.0%
2002	86.8%	23.1%	14.1%	0.6%	−18.6%	−33.3%	−193.7%
2003	88.1%	18.9%	11.1%	−0.3%	−17.9%	−31.8%	−173.3%
2004	84.6%	21.4%	13.2%	1.8%	−16.1%	−30.9%	−168.3%
2005	88.7%	21.7%	13.2%	2.3%	−13.0%	−26.0%	−153.8%
2006	83.6%	19.5%	11.0%	−0.8%	−21.2%	−38.4%	−250.0%
2007	82.6%	17.3%	8.9%	−5.0%	−30.9%	−51.2%	−261.8%
Minimum	46.9%	13.8%	7.1%	−10.7%	−52.8%	−84.2%	−463.4%
Median	79.7%	19.6%	11.1%	−1.8%	−23.6%	−40.4%	−250.0%
Maxium	96.0%	24.4%	15.5%	2.3%	−13.0%	−26.0%	−151.2%

* Note: High values for Q1 exclude top 5% of portfolio values as outliers.
Low values for Q5 exclude bottom 5% of portfolio values as outliers.

TABLE C.28

Net Debt Reduction to Invested Capital

Year	Q1* Low	Q1* High	Q2 Avg	Q3 Avg	Q4 Avg	Q5* Low	Q5* High
1987	−20.7%	−4.8%	−2.6%	1.3%	9.1%	15.3%	48.3%
1988	−19.3%	−4.4%	−2.4%	1.2%	7.9%	12.9%	37.0%
1989	−19.2%	−4.0%	−2.1%	1.8%	8.8%	13.9%	40.1%
1990	−18.2%	−3.7%	−1.9%	1.3%	6.1%	9.4%	25.8%
1991	−20.6%	−6.4%	−3.7%	−0.5%	3.2%	6.5%	20.7%
1992	−22.4%	−6.9%	−4.2%	−0.8%	2.7%	5.4%	21.9%
1993	−21.7%	−5.6%	−3.2%	−0.4%	4.3%	8.5%	28.3%
1994	−17.8%	−5.0%	−2.8%	0.0%	5.0%	9.3%	30.4%
1995	−16.3%	−3.9%	−2.1%	0.5%	5.8%	10.4%	33.4%
1996	−18.3%	−4.7%	−2.5%	0.8%	6.5%	11.3%	36.7%
1997	−18.8%	−3.9%	−2.0%	1.4%	8.6%	14.4%	43.5%
1998	−13.6%	−2.3%	−1.2%	2.4%	10.4%	16.0%	43.5%
1999	−16.3%	−3.0%	−1.5%	1.4%	8.0%	13.2%	39.4%
2000	−13.6%	−3.1%	−1.6%	0.8%	6.7%	11.6%	39.3%
2001	−17.7%	−5.6%	−3.1%	−0.3%	3.6%	7.3%	29.5%
2002	−19.2%	−7.7%	−4.8%	−1.0%	2.4%	4.8%	23.1%
2003	−16.2%	−5.6%	−3.3%	−0.4%	2.9%	5.7%	27.5%
2004	−15.3%	−5.3%	−3.0%	−0.4%	2.9%	5.7%	25.1%
2005	−16.0%	−4.3%	−2.3%	−0.2%	3.0%	5.9%	28.8%
2006	−13.9%	−3.4%	−1.7%	0.0%	4.5%	9.0%	30.2%
2007	−13.4%	−3.3%	−1.7%	0.8%	7.0%	12.4%	43.4%
Minimum	−22.4%	−7.7%	−4.8%	−1.0%	2.4%	4.8%	20.7%
Median	−17.8%	−4.4%	−2.4%	0.5%	5.8%	9.4%	30.4%
Maxium	−13.4%	−2.3%	−1.2%	2.4%	10.4%	16.0%	48.3%

* Note: Low values for Q1 exclude top 5% of portfolio values as outliers.
High values for Q5 exclude bottom 5% of portfolio values as outliers.

T A B L E   C.29

External Financing to Assets

Year	Q1* Low	Q1* High	Q2 Avg	Q3 Avg	Q4 Avg	Q5* Low	Q5* High
1987	−13.2%	−3.2%	−1.7%	1.6%	8.7%	14.0%	45.6%
1988	−14.5%	−4.9%	−2.9%	0.3%	5.3%	9.0%	28.3%
1989	−13.5%	−3.6%	−1.9%	1.3%	6.5%	10.2%	31.8%
1990	−11.8%	−3.5%	−1.9%	1.0%	5.0%	7.7%	25.9%
1991	−9.6%	−3.4%	−1.9%	0.8%	4.9%	7.8%	35.8%
1992	−9.9%	−3.6%	−2.0%	0.8%	5.1%	8.3%	37.4%
1993	−9.3%	−3.1%	−1.5%	1.4%	6.4%	10.1%	37.4%
1994	−9.6%	−3.0%	−1.5%	1.2%	6.7%	10.9%	38.7%
1995	−10.0%	−2.9%	−1.4%	1.5%	7.7%	12.5%	48.0%
1996	−10.2%	−2.9%	−1.4%	2.3%	11.0%	17.6%	62.4%
1997	−11.0%	−3.1%	−1.4%	2.3%	10.6%	16.9%	52.6%
1998	−13.3%	−3.5%	−1.6%	2.1%	9.4%	15.0%	44.3%
1999	−12.8%	−4.1%	−2.0%	2.0%	8.8%	13.7%	53.8%
2000	−11.8%	−4.2%	−2.1%	2.0%	10.4%	16.7%	76.7%
2001	−13.2%	−4.9%	−2.8%	0.5%	5.2%	8.7%	38.2%
2002	−14.5%	−5.6%	−3.8%	−0.7%	3.1%	5.6%	27.7%
2003	−12.2%	−4.9%	−3.0%	−0.2%	2.9%	5.0%	27.4%
2004	−12.5%	−4.7%	−2.9%	0.0%	3.7%	6.2%	31.2%
2005	−15.1%	−5.8%	−3.5%	−0.1%	3.7%	6.4%	31.1%
2006	−16.4%	−6.1%	−3.7%	−0.1%	4.0%	6.9%	33.6%
2007	−17.0%	−6.3%	−3.8%	−0.1%	5.3%	9.3%	45.2%
Minimum	−17.0%	−6.3%	−3.8%	−0.7%	2.9%	5.0%	25.9%
Median	−12.5%	−3.6%	−2.0%	1.0%	5.3%	9.3%	37.4%
Maxium	−9.3%	−2.9%	−1.4%	2.3%	11.0%	17.6%	76.7%

* Note: Low values for Q1 exclude top 5% of portfolio values as outliers.
High values for Q5 exclude bottom 5% of portfolio values as outliers.

T A B L E C.30

Three-Year Average Capital Expenditures to Invested Capital

Year	Q1* High	Q1* Low	Q2 Avg	Q3 Avg	Q4 Avg	Q5* High	Q5* Low
1987	24.2%	16.3%	13.9%	9.7%	6.6%	5.2%	1.9%
1988	24.7%	15.0%	12.8%	9.1%	6.2%	4.8%	1.6%
1989	24.5%	15.8%	13.4%	9.4%	6.1%	4.5%	1.4%
1990	23.6%	16.0%	13.7%	9.6%	6.2%	4.7%	1.4%
1991	23.7%	15.5%	13.2%	9.1%	5.9%	4.4%	1.0%
1992	22.4%	14.4%	12.2%	8.5%	5.5%	4.1%	1.0%
1993	22.6%	14.0%	11.8%	8.1%	5.1%	3.6%	0.7%
1994	22.8%	13.9%	11.8%	8.2%	5.3%	3.9%	0.8%
1995	24.3%	14.3%	12.0%	8.2%	5.3%	4.0%	1.0%
1996	25.3%	15.0%	12.5%	8.4%	5.3%	3.9%	0.6%
1997	26.2%	15.2%	12.5%	8.3%	5.4%	3.9%	0.5%
1998	24.8%	14.7%	12.2%	8.1%	5.0%	3.6%	0.5%
1999	24.5%	14.3%	11.8%	8.0%	5.1%	3.7%	0.8%
2000	25.3%	13.8%	11.3%	7.3%	4.5%	3.2%	0.7%
2001	24.1%	12.9%	10.6%	6.8%	4.1%	3.0%	0.7%
2002	22.5%	11.9%	9.8%	6.2%	3.7%	2.6%	0.7%
2003	22.0%	11.3%	9.0%	5.6%	3.4%	2.4%	0.7%
2004	18.9%	9.8%	7.8%	4.8%	2.8%	1.9%	0.5%
2005	20.6%	10.1%	8.0%	4.7%	2.7%	1.8%	0.5%
2006	22.2%	10.9%	8.5%	4.9%	2.8%	1.9%	0.4%
2007	24.8%	11.7%	9.2%	5.3%	3.0%	2.1%	0.5%
Minimum	18.9%	9.8%	7.8%	4.7%	2.7%	1.8%	0.4%
Median	24.1%	14.3%	11.8%	8.1%	5.1%	3.7%	0.7%
Maxium	26.2%	16.3%	13.9%	9.7%	6.6%	5.2%	1.9%

* Note: High values for Q1 exclude top 5% of portfolio values as outliers.
Low values for Q5 exclude bottom 5% of portfolio values as outliers.

TABLE C.31

Cash Acquisitions to Invested Capital

Year	Q1* Low	Q1* High	Q2 Avg	Q3 Avg	Q4 Avg	Q5* Low	Q5* High
1987	0.0%	0.0%	0.0%	0.0%	3.1%	6.1%	35.3%
1988	0.0%	0.0%	0.0%	0.0%	2.2%	4.3%	24.4%
1989	−0.2%	0.0%	0.0%	0.0%	2.3%	4.6%	24.9%
1990	0.0%	0.0%	0.0%	0.0%	1.5%	3.1%	20.6%
1991	0.0%	0.0%	0.0%	0.0%	1.1%	2.2%	13.6%
1992	0.0%	0.0%	0.0%	0.0%	0.9%	1.9%	16.1%
1993	0.0%	0.0%	0.0%	0.0%	1.5%	2.9%	19.3%
1994	0.0%	0.0%	0.0%	0.0%	2.1%	4.2%	26.1%
1995	0.0%	0.0%	0.0%	0.1%	2.8%	5.5%	29.5%
1996	0.0%	0.0%	0.0%	0.2%	4.0%	7.5%	32.5%
1997	0.0%	0.0%	0.0%	0.6%	5.2%	9.2%	37.9%
1998	0.0%	0.0%	0.0%	1.5%	7.4%	11.9%	39.4%
1999	0.0%	0.0%	0.0%	0.8%	5.9%	10.2%	32.3%
2000	0.0%	0.0%	0.0%	0.6%	4.1%	7.0%	27.8%
2001	0.0%	0.0%	0.0%	0.4%	3.5%	6.2%	24.0%
2002	0.0%	0.0%	0.0%	0.4%	3.0%	5.2%	23.3%
2003	0.0%	0.0%	0.0%	0.2%	2.5%	4.7%	21.5%
2004	0.0%	0.0%	0.0%	0.4%	3.7%	6.7%	27.8%
2005	0.0%	0.0%	0.0%	0.4%	3.4%	6.1%	28.2%
2006	0.0%	0.0%	0.0%	0.4%	3.6%	6.3%	27.8%
2007	0.0%	0.0%	0.0%	0.6%	4.1%	7.0%	31.8%
Minimum	0%	0%	0%	0%	1%	2%	14%
Median	0%	0%	0%	0%	3%	6%	28%
Maxium	0%	0%	0%	1%	7%	12%	39%

* Note: Low values for Q1 exclude top 5% of portfolio values as outliers.
High values for Q5 exclude bottom 5% of portfolio values as outliers.

TABLE C.32

Seven-Month Price Change

Year	Q1* High	Q1* Low	Q2 Avg	Q3 Avg	Q4 Avg	Q5* High	Q5* Low
1987	17%	−3%	−8%	−17%	−28%	−33%	−48%
1988	49%	21%	14%	5%	−4%	−8%	−23%
1989	49%	24%	17%	5%	−6%	−13%	−31%
1990	23%	5%	−1%	−12%	−24%	−30%	−49%
1991	86%	37%	26%	10%	−4%	−11%	−30%
1992	81%	35%	26%	11%	1%	−5%	−23%
1993	74%	33%	23%	8%	−3%	−8%	−24%
1994	60%	20%	13%	1%	−9%	−14%	−29%
1995	105%	44%	34%	17%	5%	−2%	−22%
1996	55%	28%	20%	7%	−6%	−14%	−39%
1997	81%	45%	36%	20%	5%	−4%	−27%
1998	80%	29%	18%	−1%	−15%	−23%	−46%
1999	285%	82%	50%	7%	−12%	−20%	−36%
2000	105%	48%	35%	13%	−9%	−22%	−56%
2001	57%	22%	14%	1%	−11%	−18%	−42%
2002	19%	0%	−5%	−14%	−25%	−31%	−54%
2003	106%	50%	40%	24%	13%	7%	−7%
2004	69%	35%	28%	16%	5%	0%	−21%
2005	71%	32%	24%	10%	−1%	−6%	−20%
2006	49%	25%	19%	9%	0%	−6%	−21%
2007	50%	17%	9%	−6%	−19%	−26%	−45%
Minimum	17%	−3%	−8%	−17%	−28%	−33%	−56%
Median	69%	29%	20%	7%	−6%	−13%	−30%
Maxium	285%	82%	50%	24%	13%	7%	−7%

* Note: High values for Q1 exclude top 5% of portfolio values as outliers.
Low values for Q5 exclude bottom 5% of portfolio values as outliers.

T A B L E   C.33

88/36-Month Price Change

Year	Q1* Low	Q1* High	Q2 Avg	Q3 Avg	Q4 Avg	Q5* Low	Q5* High
1987	−53.4%	−10.1%	7.8%	40.8%	76.2%	99.0%	223.8%
1988	−43.5%	−6.3%	6.9%	32.8%	47.9%	65.5%	155.4%
1989	−48.9%	−16.6%	−4.7%	22.7%	70.2%	92.2%	222.8%
1990	−70.0%	−42.1%	−30.7%	−7.6%	59.8%	84.3%	243.0%
1991	−42.2%	−8.3%	9.6%	46.0%	92.3%	128.2%	420.3%
1992	−48.8%	−18.2%	−1.7%	30.4%	80.1%	110.3%	341.7%
1993	−32.3%	12.5%	33.0%	75.0%	157.2%	212.5%	611.2%
1994	−44.5%	−9.7%	4.1%	32.2%	70.7%	100.0%	307.9%
1995	−27.6%	7.9%	23.6%	58.7%	91.6%	127.0%	349.3%
1996	−35.3%	0.0%	15.8%	50.6%	99.7%	131.3%	351.7%
1997	−28.6%	21.3%	42.5%	91.1%	174.7%	220.9%	458.5%
1998	−44.4%	8.2%	26.5%	68.4%	120.1%	157.5%	376.2%
1999	−44.8%	−6.0%	13.8%	60.2%	126.0%	184.8%	724.6%
2000	−53.4%	−21.4%	−5.2%	30.1%	86.2%	130.6%	518.1%
2001	−41.4%	−0.1%	15.1%	54.4%	75.9%	111.8%	342.2%
2002	−73.7%	−37.4%	−22.3%	7.8%	48.6%	72.8%	207.8%
2003	−79.7%	−33.3%	−11.4%	32.0%	81.5%	116.2%	383.6%
2004	−48.0%	−4.7%	13.6%	50.1%	91.2%	122.3%	356.6%
2005	−20.4%	17.6%	34.5%	75.9%	154.7%	204.3%	550.8%
2006	−30.2%	13.5%	28.3%	60.5%	88.9%	117.4%	304.0%
2007	−40.7%	−3.5%	12.1%	49.4%	75.7%	106.9%	287.6%
Minimum	−79.7%	−42.1%	−30.7%	−7.6%	47.9%	65.5%	155.4%
Median	−44.4%	−6.0%	12.1%	49.4%	86.2%	117.4%	349.3%
Maxium	−20.4%	21.3%	42.5%	91.1%	174.7%	220.9%	724.6%

* Note: Low values for Q1 exclude top 5% of portfolio values as outliers.
High values for Q5 exclude bottom 5% of portfolio values as outliers.
Quintiles 1 through 3 contain values for 88-month price change and quintiles 4 and 5 contain values for 36-month price change.

TABLE C.34

52-Week Price Range

Year	Q1* High	Q1* Low	Q2 Avg	Q3 Avg	Q4 Avg	Q5* High	Q5* Low
1987	68%	46%	39%	28%	18%	14%	6%
1988	98%	86%	78%	60%	39%	29%	11%
1989	100%	91%	82%	62%	37%	23%	8%
1990	94%	72%	60%	39%	25%	18%	6%
1991	100%	96%	92%	79%	55%	41%	16%
1992	100%	94%	89%	75%	52%	38%	15%
1993	99%	90%	82%	63%	42%	31%	12%
1994	97%	81%	68%	44%	25%	17%	6%
1995	100%	94%	90%	76%	54%	40%	13%
1996	99%	91%	85%	70%	46%	32%	9%
1997	99%	93%	87%	72%	48%	35%	10%
1998	99%	92%	83%	62%	41%	30%	11%
1999	98%	90%	81%	59%	33%	20%	6%
2000	98%	92%	83%	60%	31%	16%	4%
2001	96%	86%	79%	61%	41%	33%	15%
2002	88%	65%	56%	39%	25%	19%	8%
2003	99%	96%	93%	87%	77%	70%	44%
2004	98%	95%	91%	81%	62%	50%	22%
2005	95%	87%	80%	65%	44%	31%	11%
2006	96%	90%	85%	71%	49%	37%	16%
2007	93%	79%	67%	43%	21%	12%	3%
Minimum	68%	46%	39%	28%	18%	12%	3%
Median	98%	90%	82%	62%	41%	31%	11%
Maxium	100%	96%	93%	87%	77%	70%	44%

* Note: High values for Q1 exclude top 5% of portfolio values as outliers.
Low values for Q5 exclude bottom 5% of portfolio values as outliers.

T A B L E   C.35

28/16-Week Relative Strength Index

Year	Q1* High	Q1* Low	Q2 Avg	Q3 Avg	Q4 Avg	Q5* High	Q5* Low
1992	76	68	64	57	43	38	26
1992	77	69	66	59	50	45	33
1993	73	65	61	55	52	48	34
1994	69	60	57	50	44	40	29
1995	77	68	65	59	39	34	23
1996	73	65	62	55	44	38	25
1997	75	65	62	56	50	45	32
1998	69	60	56	49	41	36	24
1999	78	67	61	52	54	50	40
2000	72	63	59	52	42	37	25
2001	73	65	61	55	38	33	21
2002	59	52	49	45	57	53	42
2003	76	68	65	60	43	40	30
2004	76	67	65	59	53	49	38
2005	75	66	63	57	58	54	44
2006	73	64	61	55	49	44	31
Minimum	59	52	49	45	38	33	21
Median	74	65	62	55	49	42	31
Maxium	78	69	66	60	58	54	44

* Note: High values for Q1 exclude top 5% of portfolio values as outliers.
Low values for Q5 exclude bottom 5% of portfolio values as outliers.
Quintiles 1 through 3 contain values for 28-week RSI and quintiles 4 and 5 contain values for 16-week RSI.

TABLE C.36

Total Debt to Invested Capital

Year	Q1* High	Q1* Low	Q2 Avg	Q3 Avg	Q4 Avg	Q5* High	Q5* Low
1987	139%	64%	56%	40%	24%	15%	1%
1988	140%	65%	56%	41%	25%	16%	1%
1989	151%	68%	59%	42%	25%	15%	1%
1990	142%	67%	58%	42%	24%	14%	0%
1991	127%	66%	57%	39%	21%	11%	0%
1992	119%	64%	55%	37%	18%	8%	0%
1993	116%	63%	55%	37%	17%	7%	0%
1994	122%	63%	54%	36%	17%	7%	0%
1995	119%	61%	52%	34%	15%	6%	0%
1996	117%	61%	52%	35%	16%	5%	0%
1997	112%	62%	53%	36%	17%	7%	0%
1998	123%	64%	55%	38%	19%	8%	0%
1999	126%	67%	57%	37%	16%	5%	0%
2000	121%	65%	55%	35%	15%	4%	0%
2001	112%	65%	54%	35%	15%	4%	0%
2002	109%	65%	54%	35%	16%	5%	0%
2003	107%	62%	52%	33%	15%	4%	0%
2004	98%	59%	49%	32%	14%	4%	0%
2005	99%	57%	48%	31%	13%	3%	0%
2006	101%	58%	48%	31%	13%	4%	0%
2007	103%	60%	50%	32%	15%	5%	0%
Minimum	98%	57%	48%	31%	13%	3%	0%
Median	119%	64%	54%	36%	16%	6%	0%
Maxium	151%	68%	59%	42%	25%	16%	1%

* Note: High values for Q1 exclude top 5% of portfolio values as outliers.
Low values for Q5 exclude bottom 5% of portfolio values as outliers.

TABLE C.37

Free Cash Flow to Long-Term Debt

Year	Q1* High	Q1* Low	Q2 Avg	Q3 Avg	Q4 Avg	Q5* High	Q5* Low
1990	6.7	0.7	0.4	0.1	−0.1	−0.2	−1.5
1991	7.3	0.8	0.5	0.1	0.0	−0.1	−1.7
1992	8.1	0.9	0.6	0.1	−0.1	−0.2	−3.5
1993	8.3	0.8	0.5	0.1	−0.1	−0.2	−3.1
1994	8.6	0.8	0.5	0.1	−0.1	−0.2	−2.8
1995	6.6	0.8	0.5	0.1	−0.1	−0.3	−4.5
1996	8.9	0.8	0.5	0.1	−0.1	−0.3	−3.7
1997	9.9	0.8	0.5	0.1	−0.1	−0.2	−2.7
1998	11.8	0.8	0.5	0.1	−0.1	−0.2	−1.7
1999	10.5	0.7	0.4	0.1	−0.1	−0.2	−4.6
2000	12.2	0.7	0.5	0.1	−0.1	−0.2	−5.5
2001	6.9	0.8	0.5	0.2	0.0	−0.2	−7.2
2002	16.5	1.1	0.7	0.3	0.1	0.0	−0.9
2003	16.8	1.0	0.7	0.2	0.1	0.0	−0.9
2004	16.0	1.0	0.7	0.2	0.1	0.0	−0.8
2005	20.0	1.1	0.7	0.3	0.1	0.0	−0.7
2006	25.5	1.2	0.8	0.3	0.1	0.0	−0.7
2007	16.6	1.0	0.7	0.2	0.0	−0.1	−1.1
Minimum	6.6	0.7	0.4	0.1	−0.1	−0.3	−7.2
Median	10.2	0.8	0.5	0.1	−0.1	−0.2	−2.2
Maxium	25.5	1.2	0.8	0.3	0.1	0.0	−0.7

* Note: High values for Q1 exclude top 5% of portfolio values as outliers.
Low values for Q5 exclude bottom 5% of portfolio values as outliers.

T A B L E   C.38

Capital Expenditures to Property, Plant, and Equipment

Year	Q1*		Q2	Q3	Q4	Q5*	
	Low	High	Avg	Avg	Avg	Low	High
1987	5.7%	12.2%	15.4%	21.9%	31.5%	37.9%	73.3%
1988	6.4%	13.2%	16.1%	22.3%	31.1%	36.6%	71.7%
1989	5.7%	13.4%	16.2%	22.2%	30.8%	36.2%	62.3%
1990	7.5%	14.3%	16.9%	22.5%	30.4%	35.3%	68.2%
1991	5.7%	12.1%	14.8%	20.3%	29.2%	35.4%	66.5%
1992	5.4%	11.3%	14.1%	20.3%	30.5%	37.2%	70.3%
1993	4.8%	12.0%	15.0%	21.7%	33.7%	41.8%	79.3%
1994	6.4%	12.7%	15.9%	23.1%	35.6%	43.9%	84.5%
1995	6.3%	13.5%	16.8%	24.8%	38.6%	47.7%	85.4%
1996	7.0%	14.4%	17.8%	26.0%	41.1%	51.5%	96.7%
1997	7.7%	14.7%	18.4%	26.6%	40.3%	49.5%	90.9%
1998	8.1%	15.4%	18.9%	27.5%	41.4%	50.2%	80.9%
1999	7.5%	15.0%	18.6%	26.9%	39.7%	47.7%	88.9%
2000	6.9%	14.0%	17.9%	27.4%	44.7%	56.4%	106.2%
2001	6.9%	13.7%	17.4%	26.4%	39.7%	47.8%	82.6%
2002	5.3%	10.4%	13.4%	19.7%	28.9%	34.8%	66.3%
2003	4.9%	10.1%	12.9%	19.1%	27.7%	32.9%	63.8%
2004	5.0%	10.6%	13.4%	20.1%	30.6%	37.1%	69.6%
2005	6.3%	12.3%	15.3%	22.3%	33.9%	41.5%	74.5%
2006	7.0%	13.5%	16.8%	24.1%	35.5%	42.9%	72.6%
2007	7.9%	13.9%	17.3%	24.8%	36.5%	44.1%	73.7%
Minimum	4.8%	10.1%	12.9%	19.1%	27.7%	32.9%	62.3%
Median	6.4%	13.4%	16.2%	22.5%	33.9%	41.8%	73.7%
Maxium	8.1%	15.4%	18.9%	27.5%	44.7%	56.4%	106.2%

* Note: Low values for Q1 exclude top 5% of portfolio values as outliers.
High values for Q5 exclude bottom 5% of portfolio values as outliers.

T A B L E C.39

Operating Cash Flow to Capital Expenditures

Year	Q1* High	Q1* Low	Q2 Avg	Q3 Avg	Q4 Avg	Q5* High	Q5* Low
1990	7.8	2.9	2.3	1.3	0.8	0.5	−1.0
1991	10.6	3.4	2.6	1.5	0.9	0.6	−1.8
1992	10.4	3.4	2.6	1.5	0.8	0.5	−3.2
1993	10.9	3.2	2.5	1.4	0.7	0.4	−3.5
1994	10.7	3.3	2.6	1.4	0.8	0.5	−1.5
1995	12.0	3.1	2.4	1.4	0.7	0.4	−2.6
1996	10.1	3.2	2.5	1.4	0.7	0.4	−3.1
1997	8.7	3.1	2.4	1.4	0.8	0.4	−2.2
1998	9.4	3.3	2.6	1.6	0.9	0.6	−1.5
1999	9.1	3.6	2.8	1.6	0.9	0.5	−2.8
2000	8.5	3.7	2.9	1.6	0.8	0.5	−2.9
2001	12.1	4.3	3.3	1.8	0.9	0.5	−2.8
2002	18.4	6.4	4.9	2.7	1.4	0.9	−1.9
2003	18.4	6.0	4.6	2.5	1.4	0.8	−3.7
2004	19.5	6.4	4.9	2.6	1.4	1.0	−3.4
2005	19.9	6.3	4.8	2.6	1.4	1.0	−2.7
2006	17.3	6.1	4.6	2.5	1.3	0.8	−0.8
2007	17.4	6.2	4.7	2.4	1.3	0.8	−1.1
Minimum	7.8	2.9	2.3	1.3	0.7	0.4	−3.7
Median	10.8	3.5	2.7	1.6	0.9	0.5	−2.7
Maxium	19.9	6.4	4.9	2.7	1.4	1.0	−0.8

* Note: High values for Q1 exclude top 5% of portfolio values as outliers.
Low values for Q5 exclude bottom 5% of portfolio values as outliers.

TABLE C.40

Operating Cash Flow to Capex Plus Interest Expense

Year	Q1* High	Q1* Low	Q2 Avg	Q3 Avg	Q4 Avg	Q5* High	Q5* Low
1990	5.5	2.1	1.6	1.0	0.6	0.4	−0.6
1991	6.4	2.4	1.8	1.1	0.6	0.4	−0.9
1992	7.7	2.4	1.9	1.1	0.6	0.4	−1.9
1993	6.9	2.4	1.9	1.1	0.6	0.3	−2.8
1994	7.1	2.5	2.0	1.1	0.6	0.4	−1.1
1995	8.5	2.4	1.9	1.1	0.6	0.3	−1.8
1996	7.3	2.5	1.9	1.1	0.6	0.3	−1.9
1997	7.2	2.4	1.9	1.1	0.6	0.4	−1.4
1998	7.3	2.6	2.0	1.2	0.7	0.4	−0.8
1999	6.9	2.7	2.1	1.2	0.7	0.4	−2.0
2000	7.0	2.6	2.1	1.2	0.6	0.3	−2.2
2001	8.5	2.9	2.3	1.3	0.7	0.4	−2.2
2002	13.4	4.3	3.3	1.9	1.0	0.7	−0.9
2003	13.1	4.4	3.3	1.8	1.0	0.6	−2.2
2004	13.6	4.7	3.5	1.9	1.1	0.7	−1.7
2005	14.2	4.7	3.5	1.9	1.1	0.7	−1.3
2006	11.8	4.3	3.3	1.8	1.0	0.7	−0.5
2007	11.1	4.5	3.4	1.8	1.0	0.6	−0.7
Minimum	5.5	2.1	1.6	1.0	0.6	0.3	−2.8
Median	7.5	2.6	2.1	1.2	0.7	0.4	−1.5
Maxium	14.2	4.7	3.5	1.9	1.1	0.7	−0.5

* Note: High values for Q1 exclude top 5% of portfolio values as outliers.
Low values for Q5 exclude bottom 5% of portfolio values as outliers.

TABLE C.41

One-Year Change in Inventory Turnover

Year	Q1* High	Q1* Low	Q2 Avg	Q3 Avg	Q4 Avg	Q5* High	Q5* Low
1987	48.4%	15.0%	10.5%	2.4%	−5.4%	−9.5%	−26.1%
1988	38.6%	13.2%	8.6%	1.2%	−5.5%	−9.5%	−26.1%
1989	39.9%	13.1%	8.4%	0.5%	−6.2%	−9.6%	−26.5%
1990	40.5%	13.9%	9.1%	1.2%	−5.6%	−9.5%	−24.1%
1991	44.7%	13.2%	8.3%	0.5%	−6.1%	−9.8%	−25.5%
1992	45.3%	15.2%	10.3%	2.4%	−4.5%	−8.3%	−23.3%
1993	48.7%	16.1%	11.1%	2.7%	−4.3%	−8.1%	−26.4%
1994	67.7%	19.3%	13.0%	3.4%	−3.7%	−7.5%	−29.0%
1995	82.9%	17.5%	11.2%	1.2%	−6.5%	−10.7%	−27.6%
1996	67.1%	18.4%	12.0%	2.0%	−7.1%	−12.4%	−36.4%
1997	83.3%	20.8%	13.9%	3.1%	−5.2%	−9.5%	−29.0%
1998	67.4%	15.9%	10.0%	0.1%	−9.3%	−14.7%	−44.8%
1999	99.8%	22.3%	14.3%	2.4%	−6.5%	−11.4%	−34.4%
2000	117.2%	32.3%	20.6%	4.4%	−4.8%	−9.5%	−32.0%
2001	87.7%	15.5%	9.1%	−1.5%	−12.5%	−19.2%	−50.2%
2002	66.3%	18.8%	12.1%	1.7%	−10.0%	−18.1%	−46.3%
2003	81.8%	23.4%	15.2%	3.5%	−5.0%	−9.8%	−43.3%
2004	122.5%	27.8%	19.2%	6.4%	−2.4%	−6.9%	−27.9%
2005	72.8%	16.3%	10.1%	0.9%	−6.4%	−10.6%	−34.4%
2006	69.8%	16.2%	10.4%	1.2%	−6.3%	−10.3%	−34.1%
2007	52.0%	11.7%	6.9%	−0.9%	−8.1%	−12.5%	−33.6%
Minimum	38.6%	11.7%	6.9%	−1.5%	−12.5%	−19.2%	−50.2%
Median	67.4%	16.2%	10.5%	1.7%	−6.1%	−9.8%	−29.0%
Maxium	122.5%	32.3%	20.6%	6.4%	−2.4%	−6.9%	−23.3%

* Note: High values for Q1 exclude top 5% of portfolio values as outliers.
Low values for Q5 exclude bottom 5% of portfolio values as outliers.

TABLE C.42

One-Year Change in Inventory Plus Receivables Turnover

Year	Q1* High	Q1* Low	Q2 Avg	Q3 Avg	Q4 Avg	Q5* High	Q5* Low
1987	32.3%	9.8%	6.4%	0.7%	−4.8%	−8.0%	−23.7%
1988	32.4%	10.0%	6.5%	0.8%	−4.4%	−7.4%	−20.3%
1989	34.3%	8.1%	5.0%	−0.2%	−5.1%	−7.9%	−24.7%
1990	31.0%	8.6%	5.1%	−0.5%	−5.0%	−7.4%	−21.1%
1991	29.4%	9.7%	6.2%	0.5%	−4.7%	−7.5%	−20.3%
1992	28.9%	10.5%	7.0%	1.2%	−4.2%	−7.2%	−19.9%
1993	31.9%	9.9%	6.6%	1.0%	−4.6%	−7.9%	−25.5%
1994	27.4%	8.1%	4.9%	−0.6%	−6.0%	−9.1%	−24.3%
1995	31.1%	9.6%	6.0%	0.1%	−5.6%	−8.9%	−23.1%
1996	31.2%	8.4%	4.9%	−1.0%	−6.5%	−9.8%	−27.4%
1997	30.6%	10.0%	6.2%	0.1%	−5.7%	−9.2%	−25.7%
1998	32.7%	8.8%	5.2%	−0.9%	−7.4%	−11.5%	−29.9%
1999	36.6%	10.4%	5.8%	−1.5%	−8.0%	−11.9%	−31.4%
2000	43.9%	14.1%	8.9%	1.1%	−4.8%	−8.2%	−27.7%
2001	41.3%	9.7%	5.7%	−0.9%	−7.5%	−11.4%	−30.3%
2002	41.6%	14.0%	9.3%	1.8%	−5.7%	−10.4%	−26.0%
2003	48.2%	15.7%	10.8%	3.0%	−3.1%	−6.3%	−17.0%
2004	38.0%	14.1%	9.8%	2.7%	−3.7%	−7.3%	−19.2%
2005	31.5%	9.4%	6.1%	0.8%	−4.2%	−7.0%	−21.0%
2006	31.4%	10.5%	7.0%	1.2%	−4.0%	−6.9%	−19.3%
2007	27.1%	7.8%	4.7%	−0.5%	−5.4%	−8.3%	−24.3%
Minimum	27.1%	7.8%	4.7%	−1.5%	−8.0%	−11.9%	−31.4%
Median	31.9%	9.8%	6.2%	0.5%	−5.0%	−8.0%	−24.3%
Maxium	48.2%	15.7%	10.8%	3.0%	−3.1%	−6.3%	−17.0%

* Note: High values for Q1 exclude top 5% of portfolio values as outliers.
Low values for Q5 exclude bottom 5% of portfolio values as outliers.

T A B L E   C.43

Depreciation to Invested Capital

Year	Q1* High	Q1* Low	Q2 Avg	Q3 Avg	Q4 Avg	Q5* High	Q5* Low
1987	15.4%	9.5%	8.3%	6.3%	4.6%	3.8%	1.5%
1988	14.8%	9.7%	8.4%	6.4%	4.7%	3.8%	1.6%
1989	15.4%	10.0%	8.8%	6.7%	5.0%	4.2%	1.9%
1990	15.2%	10.1%	8.8%	6.7%	5.0%	4.2%	1.9%
1991	15.7%	10.1%	8.8%	6.6%	4.8%	4.0%	1.5%
1992	15.8%	9.9%	8.7%	6.5%	4.7%	3.8%	1.3%
1993	15.8%	10.4%	9.0%	6.6%	4.7%	3.8%	1.2%
1994	16.6%	10.2%	8.8%	6.4%	4.5%	3.6%	1.2%
1995	16.1%	10.1%	8.8%	6.5%	4.6%	3.6%	1.3%
1996	16.2%	9.7%	8.4%	6.3%	4.4%	3.3%	1.1%
1997	16.8%	10.0%	8.6%	6.3%	4.5%	3.5%	1.3%
1998	16.4%	9.9%	8.6%	6.4%	4.5%	3.6%	1.2%
1999	17.9%	10.4%	8.9%	6.6%	4.8%	3.8%	1.4%
2000	16.8%	9.9%	8.5%	6.3%	4.4%	3.3%	1.0%
2001	18.5%	10.1%	8.7%	6.5%	4.6%	3.6%	1.2%
2002	16.7%	9.4%	8.1%	5.8%	4.0%	3.0%	1.1%
2003	16.5%	9.4%	8.0%	5.6%	3.8%	3.0%	1.0%
2004	14.7%	8.8%	7.5%	5.3%	3.6%	2.7%	1.0%
2005	15.1%	8.8%	7.4%	5.2%	3.5%	2.6%	0.8%
2006	14.3%	8.7%	7.3%	5.1%	3.5%	2.7%	0.8%
2007	14.2%	8.5%	7.2%	5.0%	3.4%	2.7%	0.7%
Minimum	14.2%	8.5%	7.2%	5.0%	3.4%	2.6%	0.7%
Median	15.8%	9.9%	8.6%	6.4%	4.5%	3.6%	1.2%
Maxium	18.5%	10.4%	9.0%	6.7%	5.0%	4.2%	1.9%

* Note: High values for Q1 exclude top 5% of portfolio values as outliers.
Low values for Q5 exclude bottom 5% of portfolio values as outliers.

INDEX

461

CPSIA information can be obtained at www.ICGtesting.com
Printed in the USA
LVOW09*1214120515

438146LV00015BA/96/P